Frommer's

South Africa

3rd Edition

by Pippa de Bruyn

D0068345

Here's what the critics say about Frommer's:

"Amazingly easy to use. Very portable, very complete."
—*Booklist*

"Detailed, accurate, and easy-to-read information for all price ranges."
—*Glamour Magazine*

"Hotel information is close to encyclopedic."
—*Des Moines Sunday Register*

"Frommer's Guides have a way of giving you a real feel for a place."
—*Knight Ridder Newspapers*

WILEY

Wiley Publishing, Inc.

About the Author

Pippa de Bruyn was born in Durban, raised in Johannesburg, and has now settled in Cape Town. In 2003 she won the first-place gold Mondi Award (South Africa's most prestigious magazine award) for feature writing. She is also the coauthor (with Dr. Keith Bain) of Frommer's first complete guide to India.

Published by:

Wiley Publishing, Inc.

111 River St.
Hoboken, NJ 07030

ISBN 0-7645-3890-X
ISSN 1520-9822

Editor: Alexis Lipsitz Flippin
Production Editor: Ian Skinnari
Cartographer: Elizabeth Puhl
Photo Editor: Richard Fox
Production by Wiley Indianapolis Composition Services

Front cover photo: Mother and baby elephant in the bush
Back cover photo: Leopard in a tree

For information on our other products and services or to obtain technical support, please contact our Customer Care Department within the U.S. at 800-762-2974, outside the U.S. at 317-572-3993 or fax 317-572-4002.

Wiley also publishes its books in a variety of electronic formats. Some content that appears in print may not be available in electronic formats.

Manufactured in the United States of America

5 4 3 2

Contents

4 The Whale Coast & Garden Route: The Western Cape   135

5 Settler & Xhosa Country: The Eastern Cape   195

6 Place of Gold: Gauteng & North-West Province   213

7 Big-Game Country: Mpumalanga & Limpopo Province   258

List of Maps

An Invitation to the Reader

In researching this book, we discovered many wonderful places—hotels, restaurants, shops, and more. We're sure you'll find others. Please tell us about them, so we can share the information with your fellow travelers in upcoming editions. If you were disappointed with a recommendation, we'd love to know that, too. Please write to:

Frommer's South Africa, 3rd Edition
Wiley Publishing, Inc. • 111 River St. • Hoboken, NJ 07030

An Additional Note

Please be advised that travel information is subject to change at any time—and this is especially true of prices. We therefore suggest that you write or call ahead for confirmation when making your travel plans. The authors, editors, and publisher cannot be held responsible for the experiences of readers while traveling. Your safety is important to us, however, so we encourage you to stay alert and be aware of your surroundings. Keep a close eye on cameras, purses, and wallets, all favorite targets of thieves and pickpockets.

Frommer's Star Ratings, Icons & Abbreviations

Every hotel, restaurant, and attraction listing in this guide has been ranked for quality, value, service, amenities, and special features using a **star-rating system.** In country, state, and regional guides, we also rate towns and regions to help you narrow down your choices and budget your time accordingly. Hotels and restaurants are rated on a scale of zero (recommended) to three stars (exceptional). Attractions, shopping, nightlife, towns, and regions are rated according to the following scale: zero stars (recommended), one star (highly recommended), two stars (very highly recommended), and three stars (must-see).

In addition to the star-rating system, we also use **seven feature icons** that point you to the great deals, in-the-know advice, and unique experiences that separate travelers from tourists. Throughout the book, look for:

Finds	Special finds—those places only insiders know about
Fun Fact	Fun facts—details that make travelers more informed and their trips more fun
Kids	Best bets for kids, and advice for the whole family
Moments	Special moments—those experiences that memories are made of
Overrated	Places or experiences not worth your time or money
Tips	Insider tips—great ways to save time and money
Value	Great values—where to get the best deals

The following **abbreviations** are used for credit cards:

AE	American Express	DISC	Discover	V	Visa
DC	Diners Club	MC	MasterCard		

Frommers.com

Now that you have the guidebook to a great trip, visit our website at **www.frommers.com** for travel information on more than 3,000 destinations. With features updated regularly, we give you instant access to the most current trip-planning information available. At Frommers.com, you'll also find the best prices on airfares, accommodations, and car rentals—and you can even book travel online through our travel booking partners. At Frommers.com, you'll also find the following:

- Online updates to our most popular guidebooks
- Vacation sweepstakes and contest giveaways
- Newsletter highlighting the hottest travel trends
- Online travel message boards with featured travel discussions

What's New in South Africa

The most significant change that has taken place since 2001, when the 2nd edition of *Frommer's South Africa* was published, is the overwhelming sense of confidence that has somehow permeated even that most jaded of cities, the much maligned but newly regenerated Johannesburg, or Jozi, as she is now affectionately referred to. Not only has the country emerged as the fastest-growing tourism destination in the world, but its robust economic outlook (for the first time in 40 years the South African economy grew more than the global average!) is touted by many as the country's second miracle, following the peaceful dismantling of apartheid at the close of the millennium. Less pleasant—for locals as well as those planning to holiday here with limited funds—has been the rand's rollercoaster ride since 2001, when it was the world's worst-performing currency, to late 2002, when it was the world's best. Ironically, it has settled pretty much were it started when the ride began—at around R8 to the dollar—but its recent volatility means you need to check its status before perusing the dollar translations in this book. And if you're waiting for the rand to fall (as many expect it to) before paying for accommodations bookings or purchasing traveler's checks, it's worth noting that the rand, even at R8:$1, remains undervalued by some 35%, at least according to *The Economist*'s popular Big Mac index.

The rand's recent instability, coupled with the region's increased popularity, has, sadly, led to an increase in prices, particularly in the top-end accommodations, with the most opportunistic operators literally *doubling* their rates over the past 2 years. That said, luxury accommodation options and restaurants still offer comparative value for the sophisticated globetrotter, and this edition has expanded on its coverage of moderately priced establishments that still provide that luxurious sense of being on holiday—thankfully, South African B&Bs and guesthouses are generally considered to be of an unparalleled standard. Thankfully, too, the national and provincial parks have increased their fees only incrementally, so a self-drive safari is still very much in reach. It is a great deal more difficult to find a private game reserve on limited funds, but the best are summarized in chapter 2 under "Planning Your Safari."

CAPE TOWN & THE WINE-LANDS **Cape Town** is not only South Africa's prime leisure destination, but it's one of the top five in the world, according to the U.K.'s BBC viewers, who voted it the world's best city for a holiday. In addition, a report by CBS MarketWatch listed the city as the fourth-hottest international destination for U.S. travelers. To this end, the new international departures terminal in Johannesburg was opened with much acclaim in February 2003, and it's also worth noting that you can now fly directly to Maun, gateway to the Okavango Delta, from here.

The downside to the city's increased popularity is the phenomenal increase in accommodations rates, particularly in the top-end category, and if you're traveling here between November and

March you'd be well-advised to pre-book your accommodations some months in advance and a table at any of the top restaurants at least 2 weeks in advance. (Incidentally, Cape Town and the Winelands again swept the table in the 2002 national "Top 10" Eat Out restaurant awards, with Cape Town's **Blue Danube, Cape Colony,** and **La Colombe** wowing foodies' taste buds, and the Winelands featured strongly with **Bosman's, Haute Cabriere,** and **Le Quartier Francais**.) Of the many newcomers on the accommodations scene, **Hemingway House** gets my vote as the classiest guesthouse, while the gorgeous **An African Villa** represents the best value in the city. National Parks gave the international hotel group, Halcyon, a concession to upgrade the two national monuments in the Glen, Camps Bay: **The Round-house** and **Stan's Halt Youth Hostel.** Locals opposed to any commercialization of the Glen are slowing the process down, but once it is completed this is likely to be the best accommodations option in Cape Town, so watch the press for details.

Unlike so many city centers that deteriorate as business decentralizes to the suburbs, Cape Town has radically reduced "grime and crime," and many of the city center's heritage buildings are being transformed into new accommodations and retail hubs, kicking off with the transformation of the Old Mutual building, a fabulous example of the Art Deco period, into luxury-end flats—no doubt many of these will be up for holiday rentals upon completion, so check with the tourism bureau. The **International Convention Centre**—whose location on the foreshore makes for easy access to the **Waterfront**—was successfully completed mid-2003, and is already booked well into 2004; the attached five-star Arabella Sheraton is expected to be operating by August.

But perhaps the best news by far is that **Chapman's Peak Drive**—one of the world's most awesome coastal routes, which closed after a rock fall claimed a driver's life—reopened as a toll road in December 2003.

See chapter 3 for complete details.

WESTERN & EASTERN CAPE

With the rapid growth in **ecotourism,** areas where livestock farming has been less than successful are being restocked with game and turned into reserves, most of which are in the Eastern Cape (though Sanbona, a new 54,000-hectare/133,380-acre wildlife reserve situated 3 hours from Cape Town between Montagu and Barrydale on scenic Route 62 is the Western Cape reserve to look into). The popularity and proximity to Cape Town make these **malaria-free reserves** a good option for those with limited time, but do note that most of these are not Big 5 reserves. Those that are charge prices similar to the best in and near the Kruger, where the vegetation is a great deal more attractive.

Closer to Cape Town, **whale-watching** is still as popular as tracking the Big 5, with as many international visitors visiting South Africa to watch whales as go on game-viewing tours. The best place for land-based whale-watching is still **Hermanus,** and the new boutique hotel, **Birkenhead House,** owned by the same couple who brought us the sumptuous Royal Malewane lodge in Thornybush (adjacent to Kruger), is the place to do it from. Farther along the Garden Route the town of **Knysna** was again voted by local travelers as the best in the country. Its annual **gay festival** is now a permanent fixture on the calendar, much to the horror of the town's small but virulent population of fundamentalist Christians.

See chapters 4 and 5 for complete details.

GAUTENG, NORTH-WEST & THE NORTHERN CAPE **Johannesburg** has undergone quite a transformation since it was infamously known as the murder capital of the world, and it's grooving to a new-found confidence as it celebrates its self-proclaimed status as the sexiest city in Africa. The revitalized "Newtown Cultural Precinct" on the outskirts of the city center is a must on any visit here, as is the impressive new **Apartheid Museum** (adjacent to Gold Reef City). And the embodiment of this confidence is to be found in its newest designer hotel, the **Melrose Arch.** Styled along the Ian Shrager–Philippe Starck hotel-as-stage-set concept, it's a stroll away from the city's hippest club, Kilimanjaro, and the city's best (albeit touristy) African-themed restaurant, Moyo.

The **Saxon,** voted the World's Best Boutique Hotel at the 2001 World Travel Awards, continues to attract the elite, with Oprah and Charlize Theron recent entries in the guest register. The boho suburb of **Melville** is still a welcome diversion from the soulless mall culture of the northern suburbs, but is now more of a nightlife spot, with the best restaurants concentrated in Greenside (book a table at Yum before you leave!) and Parkhurst.

One of Soweto's top attractions, the **Hector Pieterson Memorial,** previously comprising makeshift steel shipping containers erected in 1996 in memory of the 1976 student protest in which police opened fire on hundreds of Sowetan schoolchildren, opened as a museum in 2002. The **Cradle of Humankind** (about an hour's drive from Johannesburg) again made headlines in 2003, when a new dating technique (called "burial cosmogenic dating") revealed that the Little Foot Skeleton, found in 1997, is 4.17 million years old—almost a million years older than initially thought and by far the oldest ever found in southern Africa.

In the Northern Cape, the vast **Kgalagadi Transfrontier National Park** has three new tented camps that offer true respite from the 21st-century rat race; of these, **Kalahari Tented Camp** is the most accessible, while the four en-suite reed cabins at **Bitterpan** are only accessible via four-wheel-drive vehicles.

See chapter 6 for complete details.

MPUMALANGA & THE LIMPOPO PROVINCE Arguably the continent's most exciting development in ecotourism has been the merging of South Africa's Kruger Park with Zimbabwe's Gonarezhou National Park and a huge big-game reserve in Mozambique's Gaza. Of more relevance perhaps are the new concessions allowed inside Kruger Park, where experienced operators are opening exclusive camps aimed at the top-end market. Of these, **Singita Lebombo** will no doubt feature in every top design magazine in the world; its raised glass boxes break the architectural mold of most camps (not a thatched roof in sight!), while its *Wallpaper*-inspired interiors are wonderfully modern. Hardly surprising considering that the original Singita, located in the adjacent Sabi Sand reserve, was again voted in 2002 by *Condé Nast Traveler* as the Best Travel Destination in the World.

West of the Kruger, and only a 3-hour drive north of Johannesburg, is **Welgevonden.** A vast, magnificent malaria-free wilderness that has been managed and restocked by a consortium of wealthy concession holders, Welgevonden continues to see the opening of new lodges and camps, providing an intimate and far more laid-back introduction to the bush than any options you'll find flanking the Kruger.

See chapter 7 for complete details.

KWAZULU-NATAL If ever there was a reason to visit Kwazulu-Natal,

Zululand tour guide **Graham Chennells** is it. Located in Eshowe, Zululand, Graham, aided by Walter Cele or Victor Mdluli, offers the most authentic and exhilarating opportunities to see real contemporary Zulu life in Africa—*National Geographic* commissioned no less than three film shoots of Graham's tours in 2002—anything from attendance at a Zulu wedding or coming-of-age celebration to *sangoma* (healer) rituals. The perfect place to base yourself is at one of the newly opened **lodges** situated in secluded areas of the **Hluhluwe-Umfolozi Game Reserve**. Run by KZN Wildlife as part of its "Red Ivory Collection," these lodges (which sleep 6–8) are only available for single bookings, which make them just right for a group or family or a couple prepared to pay a little extra for total privacy. The alternative is to overnight on the shores of the **Greater St Lucia Wetland Park,** proclaimed a World Heritage Site at the turn of the millennium. Pick of the bunch are still **Makakatana Bay Lodge** and **Hluhluwe River Lodge** (both also within easy driving distance of Hluhluwe), but you may also want to investigate the budget-priced **Charters Creek,** the lakeside camp that KZN Wildlife upgraded extensively in 2002. Nearby **Mkuze Falls** is still the best-value Big 5 private game reserve in the country.

The most interesting development in the Drakensberg region has been the opening of **Didima Camp** by KZN Wildlife in the Cathedral Peak Valley in 2002. It offers exceptional value-for-money accommodations at the base of the most magnificent mountain range in the country.

See chapter 8 for complete details.

VICTORIA FALLS & SURROUNDS Zimbabwe is going through hell. Inflation has soared to 270%, there are crippling shortages of fuel, medicines, and essential imports, and more than half the population is facing starvation. For the past 3 years, Robert Mugabe's desperate attempts to stay in power have pushed the country to the brink of civil war. Naturally, all this turmoil has resulted in a dearth of tourists, with even Victoria Falls feeling the pinch. That said, bear in mind that the falls are far from the action, located as they are in the southwestern tip, right on the border with Zambia and Botswana. While you are unlikely to encounter anything more disturbing than the desperation of vendors selling traditional crafts (and aggressive security forces, so stay calm and polite at Customs), this has curtailed some of the activities at the falls, like walking alone along the banks of the Zambezi, where a 27-year old Australian tourist was stabbed in January 2003. On the positive side, this is probably the one time you can get to view the jaw-dropping grandeur of Vic Falls in relative solitude, as well as negotiate bargain discounts in everything from luxury reserves to locally made crafts. Visitors can also bypass Zimbabwe by flying directly from Johannesburg to Livingstone and opting to stay on the Zambian side of the falls.

See chapter 9 for complete details.

BOTSWANA Little has changed here, and hurrah for that! Best news is that **Air Botswana** now flies directly from Cape Town to Maun, which connects two of the world's most phenomenal destinations in a matter of hours. **Chief's Camp, Mombo,** and **Jao** are still widely regarded as the top camps in the Okavango. Visitors to the delta can now also immerse themselves in Bushman culture and folklore by spending a night at **Gudigwa,** a 100% Bushman-owned camp that opened here in April 2003. Moving south, **Jack's Camp,** the most elegant desert camp in Africa, remains a top choice, not least because the en-suite bathrooms now have hot and cold running water.

See chapter 10 for complete details.

1

The Best of South Africa, Zimbabwe & Botswana

People come to southern Africa for its natural beauty, wildlife, and sunshine, and few leave disappointed. This immensely varied terrain supports a rich diversity of animals, birds, and plants, and offers a correspondingly diverse range of experiences. Whether you're here on safari or to enjoy the beaches, breathtaking drives, or unspoiled wilderness, this chapter will help you experience the very best southern Africa has to offer.

1 Unique Southern African Moments

- **Jiving with Jo'burg Jollers to the Sounds of Kwaito** (Gauteng): The best place to experience the melting pot of Rainbow Nation culture, and to celebrate the emergence of a cohesive national identity, is on the dance floors grooving to *kwaito*, South Africa's own homegrown version of house. Look out for performances by TKZee, Arthur, Bongo Maffin, and Boom Shaka. See chapter 6.

- **Freezing Your Butt Off on an Early-Morning Game Drive** (Limpopo Province, North-West, Mpumalanga, and Botswana): In winter (May–Aug), considered to be the best time of the year to go on safari (when animals are the most visible), rangers set off in their open-topped vehicles before dawn. See chapters 6, 7, and 10.

- **Getting Caught Up in the Cape Minstrels Carnival** (Cape Town): Every New Year, brightly dressed troupes of "coloured" men dance through the streets of Cape Town, singing to the quick-paced strum of banjos and the thump of drums. This tradition was inspired by American minstrels who came to

the Cape in the late 1800s, but the celebration actually dates back to 1834 when slaves took to the streets to celebrate their liberation. See chapter 2.

- **Spotting Zebra from the Highway** (Cape Town): Zebra, wildebeest, and various antelope graze on Table Mountain's slopes literally minutes from the city center. Look out for them from the highway as you drive in from the airport. See chapter 3.

- **Enjoying the Sunset from Table Mountain** (Cape Town): From this great vantage point, you can watch the sun sink into the Atlantic Ocean, turning the Twelve Apostles a deep pink; then walk across the tabletop to the lip and watch the city lights start to twinkle and the dusky outline of the hinterland mountains under a moonlit sky. See chapter 3.

- **Feeling Humbled at Mandela's Prison Cell** (Cape Town): Tours of Robben Island are pretty restrictive, but looking into the tiny cell where Nelson Mandela spent the majority of his time in prison leaves few unmoved.

Further insight into the years spent here is provided by guides who were incarcerated at the same time as Mandela, in what came to be known as the "University of Robben Island." See chapter 3.

- **Watching Whales from White Dunes** (Western Cape): At De Hoop Nature Reserve's Koppie Alleen, the white dunes stretch deep beneath the sea, turning its blue hue into a hypnotic turquoise. This is the perfect place to watch the Southern Right Whales who come to breed off the Overberg Coast—said to offer the best land-based whale-watching in the world. See chapter 4.

- **Walking Through Carpets of Flowers** (Northern Cape): In this annual miracle of spiritual proportions, the semi-arid and seemingly barren West Coast bursts into life after the first spring rains. More than 2,600 species of flowers literally carpet the Namaqualand plains for a few weeks before subsiding back into the soil for another year-long wait. See chapter 4.

- **Visiting the World's Largest Open-Air Gallery** (Western Cape, Eastern Cape, and KwaZulu-Natal): Created by the San hunter-gatherers, an ancient civilization all but destroyed by the migrating Nguni and white settlers, these rock-art paintings date back between 100 and 20,000 years, and document the history and spiritual beliefs of these gentle people. More than 15,000 sites are scattered throughout the country. See chapters 4, 5, and 8.

- **Seeing the Zulu Kings Reed Dance** (Kwazulu-Natal): Experience a scene that has been enacted for hundreds of years as you join some 15,000 Zulus, many dressed in tribal gear, to watch the virgin maidens dance for the Zulu Prince Gideon, who would traditionally pick a wife here. See chapter 8.

- **Soaking Up Victoria Falls** (Zimbabwe): The sight of more than 500 million liters of water a minute thundering into the Batoka Gorge, creating soaring rainbows and a mist of drenching spray, will never leave you. Enjoy the view with a champagne breakfast on Livingstone Island. See chapter 9.

- **Rafting the Churning Waters of the Zambezi** (Victoria Falls, Zimbabwe): There is absolutely nothing like hearing this mighty river pound past, drowning the guides' last-minute instructions as you plunge into such vividly named white waters as "the Muncher." See chapter 9.

- **Drinking the Waters of the Delta** (Okavango Delta, Botswana): As you're poled along in your *mokoro* (dugout canoe), past palm-fringed islands and aquatic game, sample the life-giving waters of the delta. Simply scoop up a handful (keeping an eye out for crocs!) and sip. See chapter 10.

2 The Wildest Animal Encounters

- **Staring Down a Roaring Lion** (private game reserves in Mpumalanga, Limpopo Province, North-West, and Botswana): Tourists are notoriously hungry for shots of big cats, and if you spend 2 nights at one of the top private game reserves you will certainly get close to lions and leopards, often on the first drive. If you're lucky enough to get close enough to have your vehicle shuddering from the powerful noise that erupts from the king of the jungle's gut, you are talking a truly wild animal encounter. See chapters 3, 4, and 10.

- **Waiting for a Leopard to Finish Its Dinner** (private game reserves, North-West, Mpumalanga, KwaZulu-Natal): Holing up in your room while a leopard gnaws its dinner outside your door might happen at any of the private game reserve lodges that are set in the bush. Animals roam freely in this environment, and if dinner happens to be on your patio, celebrate the fact that you're not it and plunder the minibar. See chapters 4, 7, and 8.
- **Taking a Bush Bath with Elephants** (Limpopo Province): You will find outdoor showers in most of the reserves and some coastal resorts, but very few alfresco baths, and only one where you could be disturbed by elephants. Garonga's bush bath, which is elevated on a hill, is best experienced at night, with candles, oils, champagne, and a guard walking the broad perimeter below. See chapter 7.
- **Stalking a Rhino on Foot** (Kruger National Park, Hluhluwe-Umfolozi Reserve): You will almost definitely track white rhino on the Bushman, Wolhuter, and Napi trails run by Kruger National Park, as well as on the Umfolozi trails run by the KwaZulu-Natal Nature Conservation Service (KN NCS) in Hluhluwe-Umfolozi, the Zululand reserve that boasts the highest concentration of rhino in the world. Despite their prehistoric appearance, white rhino are relatively shy, docile animals; it is the black rhino that is dangerous. See chapters 7 and 8.
- **Swimming with Penguins** (Boulders Beach, Cape Town): This is a beautiful place to swim; large boulders create natural swimming pools shared by the only land-breeding colony of jackass penguins. Watch them waddle and dive through the crystal-clear waters, which are slightly warmer than the Atlantic seaboard side—cold comfort considering how icy that is. See chapter 3.
- **Baiting Great White Sharks** (Hermanus & Mossel Bay, Western Cape): Descend in a steel cage to meet Jaws up close and personal. Specialist tour operators offer controversial cage diving off Dyer Island in "Shark Alley," where Great Whites hunt the resident seal population. Sharks swim within spitting distance of cages—not that there's much to spit when your mouth is dry with fear. See chapter 4.
- **Watching Rare Turtles Nest** (Zululand, KwaZulu-Natal): In November and December the female leatherback and loggerhead turtles leave the safety of the sea at night to lay their eggs above the high-tide mark on the northern beaches of KwaZulu-Natal. Two months later, hatchlings scramble out of their nests and make a run for the ocean. Only one or two out of every thousand make it to maturity; those that do, return to the same beach to produce the next generation. See chapter 8.
- **Avoiding a Territorial Hippo** (Victoria Falls, Okavango Delta): The upper reaches of the Zambezi and the Okavango Delta's watery channels are best explored by gliding along in a canoe, or *mokoro,* but you're also more than likely to meet a hippo this way. Always treat them with respect—despite a relatively docile appearance they are one of Africa's most dangerous mammals, and responsible for more deaths than the crocodile. See chapter 10.

3 The Best Private Game Lodges & Camps

- **Singita** (Sabi Sands Reserve, Mpumalanga): This is quite simply the best game lodge in South Africa. Modern design, organic materials, wraparound views of the Sand River, private timber decks and pools, a roving masseuse, exquisite food, and a choice of more than 12,000 bottles of wine (hand-picked by the well-known vintner Vaughn Johnson) ensure a fantastic stay—and top rangers and a traversing area second only to MalaMala ensure excellent sightings. See chapter 7.

- **Londolozi Bateleur & Tree Camps** (Sabi Sands Reserve, Mpumalanga): Londolozi is the flagship lodge of safari operator CCAfrica, known for setting the standard in luxury bush accommodations (they also established Singita, Makalali, and Phinda). Facilities are similar to Singita, though not as grand, or as exclusive. Londolozi is famed for its leopard, the most elusive of the Big 5. See chapter 7.

- **Honeyguide Tented Safari Camp** (Manyeleti Reserve, Mpumalanga): If the thought of a luxury hotel in the bush leaves you cold, Honeyguide's tented camp delivers a more authentically *Out of Africa* experience—right down to the tin baths and cheeky local elephants. The lack of commercial activity in the Manyeleti Reserve and the relatively low rate are also extra pluses. See chapter 7.

- **Royal Malewane** (Thornybush Reserve, Limpopo Province): With only 12 guests accommodated in privately situated suites that offer every luxury, this relative newcomer is set to become the name to bandy about in knowing circles. If you can bear to leave your private rim-flow pool and large viewing deck (or fireplace if it's winter), the game viewing is good, with an abundance of lion and elephant. See chapter 7.

- **Phinda Lodges** (Phinda Reserve, Zululand, KwaZulu-Natal): This is Africa's most diverse wilderness experience: You can dive with tropical fish or go big-game fishing in the morning, visit a Zulu village in the afternoon, and follow a pride of lions in the evening. Phinda has four distinctly different camps, of which the ultra-luxurious **Phinda Vlei** offers the most glorious setting. See chapter 8.

- **Ndumo Wilderness Camp** (Ndumo Reserve, KwaZulu-Natal): Not only is this one of the top birding destinations in Africa (others are Mkhuze, Okavango, and Kruger), it is also an incredibly beautiful reserve. More than 420 bird species are attracted to its diverse and lush vegetation—almost as many species as in Kruger, which is 190 times its size. The 6km (almost 4-mile) long Nyamithi Pan is considered by many to be one of the finest game drives in Africa. See chapter 8.

- **Jao Camp** (Okavango Delta, Botswana): Not only is this camp located in one of the finest concessions in the delta, but it is also one of the most gorgeous camps in Africa, with only eight privately located suites, each the epitome of understated elegance. See chapter 10.

- **Mombo Camp** (Moremi, Okavango, Botswana): At the confluence of two river systems, Mombo has long been regarded as one of the best game-viewing spots in Africa, attracting large numbers of plains game and their attendant predators—leopard, wild dog, and lion are frequently sighted here. See chapter 10.

- **Jack's & San Camp** (Makgadik-gadi Pans, Botswana): Situated under palm trees on the fringe of the pans, and beautifully decorated to resemble a classic 1940s safari camp, this is one of the most unusual experiences in Africa. See chapter 10.

4 The Best National Parks & Provincial Nature Reserves

- **Kgalagadi (Kalahari) Transfrontier Park** (Northern Cape): This is one of the largest conservation areas in Africa—twice the size of Kruger—yet because of the long distances you need to travel to reach it, this desert reserve is seldom included in the first visitor's itinerary. It is starkly beautiful, with red dunes, blonde grasses, and sculptural camelthorn trees contrasting with cobalt-blue skies. Despite its aridity, the reserve supports a number of predators, including the famed black-maned "Kalahari" lion, hyena, wild dog, and cheetah. See chapter 6.

- **Pilanesberg National Park** (North-West): This reserve is southern Africa's most accessible (it's just 2 hr. from Johannesburg), which is both a blessing and a drawback, depending on whether you have serious time constraints or a need for solitude. Lying on the eroded remains of a 1.4-billion-year-old extinct volcanic crater—one of only three in the world—the 58,000-hectare (143,260-acre) reserve supports more than 35 large mammal species. See chapter 6.

- **Madikwe Game Reserve** (North-West): A relative newcomer, this 75,000-hectare (185,250-acre) reserve has been transformed by Operation Phoenix, the largest game-translocation exercise ever undertaken. Its highly diverse eco-zones (including Kalahari sandveld) allow it to support an unusual range of species—which is why it's been dubbed the "Magnificent 7" reserve (cheetah and wild dog being added to the lineup). Best of all, it's malaria-free. See chapter 6.

- **Kruger National Park** (Mpumalanga and Limpopo Province): One of Africa's greatest game parks, with probably the best developed infrastructure, Kruger is the most cost-effective, do-it-yourself way to go on safari. Accommodations are pretty basic, but clean, functional, and affordable; and the park teems with wildlife. It has more than 147 mammals, 114 reptiles, and 500 bird species to spot. See chapter 7.

- **De Hoop Nature Reserve** (Whale Coast, Western Cape): A magnificent coastal reserve featuring deserted beaches, interesting rock pools, beautiful *fynbos* (uniquely diverse shrublands), a wetland with more than 200 bird species, and a number of small game. Limited accommodations ensure that the reserve is never crowded. See chapter 4.

- **Tsitsikamma National Park** (Garden Route, Western Cape): Stretching from Storms River Mouth to Nature's Valley, this coastline is best explored on foot, via the 5-day Otter Trail. If you're pressed for time, or if the trail is full, take the 1km (just over a half-mile) walk to the mouth, or complete the first day of the Otter Trail, which terminates at a beautiful waterfall. See chapter 4.

- **Goegap Nature Reserve** (Namaqualand, Northern Cape): This is one of the best places in Namaqualand to witness the floral transformation after the first spring rains. A recommended way to explore the reserve is to hire a bike and complete the two trails that traverse the reserve. Grazing among the flowers are zebra, springbok, and the stately gemsbok, or oryx. See chapter 4.

- **Greater St Lucia Wetland Park** (Zululand, KwaZulu-Natal): This World Heritage Site encompasses five distinct ecosystems, including the croc-rich estuary, the Mkhuze savanna, and offshore coral reefs. It is also close to Hluhluwe-Umfolozi, the province's largest Big 5 reserve, which supports the densest rhino population in Africa. See chapter 8.

- **The Kosi Bay Nature Reserve** (Maputaland, KwaZulu-Natal): This chain of four lakes fringed by lush and varied vegetation (marsh forests, mangroves, giant swamp figs, dune forests, raffia palm forest) is home to rare birds (Pels fishing owl and the palm nut vulture) and tropical fish. Kosi Bay is a delight for hikers, birders, and canoeists alike, though it takes some commitment to get to this northeastern corner of South Africa. See chapter 8.

- **The uKhahlamba-Drakensberg Park** (KwaZulu-Natal): The Drakensberg in its entirety is spectacular, but if you have time to visit only one region, head north for the Amphitheatre. One of the most magnificent rock formations in Africa, it is also the source of South Africa's major rivers, the Vaal, the Orange, and the Tugela.

Rolling grasslands, breathtaking views, and crystal-clear streams can only be explored on foot or horseback. See chapter 8.

- **The Victoria Falls National Park** (Victoria Falls, Zimbabwe): This World Heritage Site offers the most stupendous views of the 1,000m (3,280-foot) wide falls, and the constant spray, crowned by a permanent rainbow, sustains a lush and verdant rain forest. See chapter 9.

- **Moremi Game Reserve** (Botswana): No visit to Botswana would be complete without a trip to Moremi, which makes up much of the eastern shores of the delta and offers arguably the best game viewing in southern Africa. Covering an area of 487,200 hectares (1,203,384 acres), including woodlands, wetlands, waterways, islands, and pans, this reserve is home to lion, elephant, cheetah, wild dog, leopard, buffalo, and more than 500 species of birds. See chapter 10.

- **Chobe National Park** (Botswana): This park includes the fabulous game areas of Savuti and Linyanti—river systems that provide life for abundant game including lion, leopard, wild dog, and elephant; the Chobe River is in fact the best place to see elephants in Africa, and from the boats that operate along its shores it's possible to see dozens of them swimming across the rivers between Botswana and Namibia. See chapter 10.

5 The Best Beaches

- **Long Beach** (Cape Town): This 4km (2½-mile) long stretch of sand—almost as wide as it is long—is both the city's best walking beach and the best place to go horseback riding. Even if you don't have time to sample the

waves, at least stop to admire it during your Chapman's Peak Drive. See chapter 3.

- **Clifton** (Cape Town): A beautiful beach just minutes from the city center, this is where Cape Town's beautiful people like to parade. It's also the most wind-free area in Cape Town—handy when the southeaster, known locally as the Cape Doctor, is driving you mad. Divided by large boulders into First, Second, Third, and Fourth beaches, it is accessible only via steep steps. Other great Cape Town beaches include Camps Bay and Llandudno. See chapter 3.

- **De Hoop Nature Reserve** (Whale Coast, Western Cape): Tall white dunes sliding into the sea, coves, evocative limestone outcrops, an aquamarine sea, and picture-perfect rock pools make this reserve's beaches the most glorious in the Overberg, if not the entire Cape. See chapter 4.
- **Noetzie** (Garden Route, Western Cape): One of the closest beaches to Knysna is also the most charming, not least because of the mini-castles overlooking it. If the sea is too wild, take a dip in the lagoon. See chapter 4.
- **Plettenberg Bay** (Garden Route, Western Cape): It's a toss up between Lookout and Robberg Beach, but safe to say that "Plet," as the locals call it, has the best

beaches on the Garden Route. Pity about the monstrous houses that overlook them. Head for Lookout for a view of the distant Outeniqua Mountains, and Robberg for whale-watching. See chapter 4.

- **Port St Johns** (Wild Coast, Eastern Cape): The entire Wild Coast is renowned for its magnificent, deserted coastline; but since Port St Johns is one of the more accessible points, you may wish to head straight here and laze away the sultry days on Second Beach, a perfect crescent fringed with tropical vegetation. For total seclusion, head for Umngazi, a few miles south. See chapter 5.
- **Rocktail Bay** (Maputaland, KwaZulu-Natal): With the "Holiday Coast" surrounding Durban largely ruined by an uninterrupted ribbon of development, and the Greater St Lucia Wetland Park's beaches marred by four-wheel-drive tracks, the province's best beaches lie in northern Maputaland. Rocktail Bay offers total seclusion for a maximum of 22 guests. See chapter 8.

6 The Best Outdoor Adventures

- **Tracking Big Game on Horseback** (Limpopo Province and Okavango Delta, Botswana): Experience Africa as the pioneers did. Equus Wilderness Horse Safaris offers relatively luxurious facilities and the chance to track rhino, giraffe, zebra, and many species of antelope in the Waterberg Conservancy; while Okavango Horse Safaris offers an alternative form of transport to the popular *mokoro* (dugout canoe). See chapters 7 and 10.
- **Throwing Yourself Off Table Mountain** (Cape Town): Attached to a rope, of course. At 100m (328

ft.), this is the highest commercially run abseil in the world, and the most exhilarating way to see the city and the Atlantic seaboard. See chapter 3.

- **Paragliding Off Lion's Head to Camps Bay Beach** (Cape Town): It's a breathtaking ride hovering over the slopes of Table Mountain. As you slowly glide toward the white sands of Camps Bay, lapped by an endless expanse of ocean, you'll have time to admire the craggy cliffs of the Twelve Apostles. See chapter 3.
- **Kayaking to Cape Point** (Cape Town): Kayaking is the most

impressive way to view this towering outcrop, the southwestern-most point of Africa. It's also the ideal opportunity to explore the rugged cliffs that line the coastline, with numerous crevices and private coves to beach yourself on. See chapter 3.

- **Mountain Biking Through the Knysna Forests** (Garden Route, Western Cape): Starting at the Garden of Eden, the 22km (14-mile) Harkerville Red Route is considered the most challenging in the country. Its steep, single-track slip paths take you past indigenous forests, silent plantations, and magnificent coastal fynbos. See chapter 4.

- **Bungee Jumping Off Bloukrans River Bridge** (Garden Route, Western Cape): The real daredevils do the highest bungee jump in the world in just their birthday suits, leaping 216m (708 ft.) and free-falling (not to mention screaming) for close to 7 seconds. See chapter 4.

- **Surfing "Bruce's Beauties"** (Cape St Francis, Eastern Cape): Bruce's Beauties, the waves featured in the 1960s cult classic *Endless Summer,* form an awesome right-point break. They need a massive swell, however, and don't work very often; the same goes for Super-tubes, hailed the "perfect wave," in nearby Jeffrey's Bay. See chapter 5.

- **Surfing the Mighty Zambezi River** (Victoria Falls, Zimbabwe): Not content with merely rafting down the Zambezi, the latest adrenaline rush offered by river operators is plunging into the churning waters attached to nothing more than a boogie board, and riding the 2m to 3m (6-ft.–10-ft.) high waves. See chapter 9.

- **Riding an Elephant Through the African Wilderness** (Victoria Falls and Okavango Delta, Botswana): This is a great way to explore the delta, not only because of the elevated view and the proximity with which you can approach animals, but because you can't feel safer—no one in the jungle messes with an elephant. See chapters 9 and 10.

7 The Best Places to Discover South African Culture & History

- **Diagonal Street** (Johannesburg, Gauteng): On one side of the street, *sangomas* (healers) enter a pungent *muti* (folk medicine) shop to purchase jars of crushed baboon skull, lizards' feet, and crocodile fat, while on the other, accountants flashing cellphones exit the glass walls of "Diamond House," the gleaming high-rise designed by Chicago architect Helmut Jahn. It is this kind of contrast that can make visiting Johannesburg such an electrifying experience. See chapter 6.

- **The Hector Pieterson Memorial** (Soweto, Gauteng): When schoolchildren took to the streets on June 16, 1976, in a peaceful protest against the decision to use Afrikaans as the sole means of instruction in schools, police opened fire, killing, among others, young Hector Pieterson. This was a turning point in the battle against apartheid. Widespread riots and international condemnation followed, and nothing would ever be the same. The best way to see it is with a township tour. See chapter 6.

- **Cradle of Humankind** (Gauteng): Having shot to fame in 1947 with the discovery of a 2½-million-year-old hominid skull, the region continues to produce fascinating finds about the origins of mankind. Tours with paleontologists introduce you to many intriguing aspects of human evolution, in an area that has remained unchanged for millions of years. See chapter 6.

- **Voortrekker Monument** (Pretoria, Gauteng): This massive granite structure commemorates the Great Trek, in particular the Battle of Blood River (fought between Trekkers and Zulus on December 16, 1838), and remains hallowed ground for Afrikaner nationalists. See chapter 6.

- **Robben Island** (Cape Town): A prison for political activists since the 17th century, including its most famous prisoner, Nelson Mandela, the island was commonly known as the "Alcatraz of Africa." Today the island is a museum and a nature reserve, and a tangible symbol of South Africa's transformation. See chapter 3.

- **Bo-Kaap** (Cape Town): This Cape Malay area, replete with cobbled streets and quaint historical homes, was one of the few "nonwhite" areas to escape destruction during the apartheid era, despite its proximity to the city. A walk or drive through the streets should be combined with a visit to the **District Six Museum** (© 021/ 424-3846), which commemorates a less fortunate community. Visible today only as cleared land on the southern outskirts of town (opposite the Bo-Kaap), this once vibrant suburb was razed to the ground in the 1960s. See chapter 3.

- **Wuppertal Moravian Mission Station** (Cederberg, Western Cape): Located at the end of a long, dusty road in the Cederberg Mountains, Wuppertal remains unchanged to this day, and is both architecturally and culturally a living legacy of the early missionaries. Other mission stations worth visiting are Elim and Genandendal, both in the Overberg. See chapter 4.

- **The Nelson Mandela Museum** (Umtata, Eastern Cape): A wonderful tribute to Africa's greatest statesman with posters, photographs, and videos documenting his life and work. Among the interesting memorabilia are the many gifts from respectful statesmen, adoring children, boxers, and other admirers. See chapter 5.

- **Rorke's Drift** and **Isandlwana** (Battlefields, KwaZulu-Natal): These two Anglo-Zulu War battlefield sites, within walking distance of each other, encompass both the British Empire's most humiliating defeat, and its most heroic victory in the colonies. At the Battle of Isandlwana, more than 1,300 armed men were wiped out by a "bunch of savages armed with sticks," as the mighty Zulu nation was then referred to. Hours later, 139 British soldiers (of which 35 were ill) warded off a force of 4,000 Zulus for 12 hours, for which an unprecedented 11 Victorian Crosses were awarded. See chapter 8.

- **Kwa Muhle Museum** (Durban, KwaZulu-Natal): Excellent user-friendly displays explain how the "Durban System" not only exploited the indigenous peoples but made them pay for its administration. It's a good introduction to the discriminatory laws that preceded apartheid. See chapter 8.

- **The Vukani Collection Museum** (Eshowe, KwaZulu-Natal): While most Westerners head for the cultural villages to gain some insight into Zulu tribal customs and culture, Vukani is where Zulu parents take their children. With the largest collection of Zulu artifacts in the world, and an informative curator/guide, this is a highly recommended excursion, particularly for those interested in crafts. Note that if you aren't venturing this far afield, the **Campbell Collections** in Durban is an alternative. See chapter 8.

- **Victoria "Street" Market** (Durban, KwaZulu-Natal): The most culturally diverse city in southern Africa is Durban, and the best place to see this diversity is in the streets surrounding the Victoria "Street" Market. The number of shops selling anything from saris to spices is not surprising (Durban has the greatest Indian population outside of India); but woven into this dense and fragrant fabric are Zulu *sangomas* (healers) selling traditional medicines *(muti)* made of barks and animal parts, and street hawkers pawning everything from fresh fruit to haircuts. See chapter 8.

8 The Most Authentic Culinary Experiences

- **Ordering a Cape Malay Dish** (Cape Town): Typified by mild, sweet curries and stews, this cuisine is easy on the uninitiated palate. The most authentic restaurant is Biesmiellah, located in the Bo-Kaap in Cape Town, but one of the loveliest environments is at Paddagang, in Tulbagh—the *waterblommetjie bredie* (waterlily stew) is arguably the best in the Cape. See chapter 3.

- **Lunching in the Vineyards** (Winelands): Set aside at least one afternoon to lunch in the Winelands overlooking vine-carpeted valleys. If you're based in Cape Town, try **Constantia Uitsig** (© 021/794-4480), on the Constantia Wine Route. A great Winelands choice is a window table at **La Petite Ferme** (© 021/876-3016), which overlooks the lush Franschhoek Valley. See chapter 3.

- **Braaing Crayfish on the Beach** (West Coast, Western Cape): The West Coast open-air all-you-can-eat beach *braais* (barbecues) are legendary, giving you an opportunity to try a variety of local fish as well as sample local preparation styles. It's virtually impossible, but try not to fill up on the bread (baked on the beach) and the farm-fresh butter. Your best bet is Muisbosskerm, near Lamberts Bay, and ideal if you want to combine a trip to the Cederberg. See chapter 4.

- **Eating with Your Fingers:** You'll find that the African staple *pap* (maize-meal prepared as a stiff porridge that resembles polenta) is best sampled by balling a bit in one hand and dipping the edge into a sauce or stew—try *umngqusho,* a stew made from maize kernels, sugar beans, chiles, and potatoes, and said to be one of Mandela's favorites. A number of restaurants in Gauteng serve traditional food.

- **Dining Under the Stars to the Sounds of the Bush** (private game reserves throughout South Africa, Victoria Falls, and Botswana): There's nothing like fresh air to work up an appetite, unless it's the smell of sizzling food cooked over an open fire. Happily, dinners at private game reserves combine both more often than not. Weather permitting, meals are served in a *boma* (a reeded enclosure), or in the bush on tables placed in riverbeds or under large trees. Armed rangers and massive fires keep predators at bay. See chapters 7, 9, and 10.

- **Chewing Biltong on a Road Trip:** *Biltong,* strips of game, beef, or ostrich cured with spices and dried, are sold at farm stalls and butcher shops throughout the country. This popular local tradition that dates back to the Voortrekkers is something of an acquired taste, but it's almost addictive once you've started.

2

Planning Your Trip to Southern Africa

Most first-time visitors to South Africa are amazed at how sophisticated the infrastructure is here, but it's still a developing country—the high levels of poverty and fear of crime are obviously common complaints, and service standards can be patchy. Although generally smaller than those in Europe and the United States, South Africa's major cities offer all the same facilities, and it's a good idea to start your southern African trip here. Unless you're heading into really remote areas (which Botswana camps constitute), don't worry about finding what you need: anything you've forgotten can be bought here, credit cards are an accepted form of payment, and you're as likely to be affected by water- or food-borne illnesses as you would be back home. You'll also find a reasonably efficient tourism infrastructure, with plenty of services and facilities designed to help you make the most of your trip. Start by browsing the Web and contacting your local travel agent. Or simply read this chapter.

1 The Regions in Brief

SOUTH AFRICA

South Africa once consisted of four large provinces with borders created during the country's colonial past. These were where, by law, the white population resided. The black "tribes" were crammed into a number of shamefully small, quasi-independent homelands peppered throughout the country. After the 1994 elections (which finally saw Nelson Mandela the rightful leader of the New South Africa), the country was redivided into nine new provinces.

For the first-time visitor, there are usually three crucial stops: a trip to **Big-Game Country,** most of which is located in Mpumalanga and the Limpopo Province, a visit to **Cape Town** and its **Winelands,** and, time allowing, a self-drive tour of the **Garden Route** in the Western Cape.

GAUTENG & FREE STATE Situated on the inner plateau, or highveld, the Free State and Gauteng were originally covered with grasslands. In the Free State this made way for farming, while the discovery of gold in the late 19th century was to change the Gauteng landscape irreparably. Today Johannesburg International Airport is the biggest and busiest in sub-Saharan Africa; and **Johannesburg** (or Jo'burg, as it is also known to locals) its busiest city. Here in the "Place of Gold" you can visit some of the country's best museums and galleries, explore the **Cradle of Humankind,** recently declared a World Heritage Site, where paleontologists are probing the origins of mankind, and the famous gold mines of the **Witwatersrand** ("ridge of white waters"). Here miners dig deeper than anywhere else in the world; and although gold resources are starting to dwindle, all the country's major industries are based in Gauteng. The resulting urban sprawl covers most of the province and houses an estimated population of 5 to 7 million. Downtown Johannesburg is notoriously dangerous, but in the northern suburbs of **Sandton, Rosebank,** and **Hyde Park,** you'll find luxurious hotels and elegant shopping centers. Johannesburg's northern suburbs blend almost seamlessly into **Pretoria,** the country's administrative capital. Jo'burg is where you'll see the growing black middle class flexing its financial muscle and where Africans from all over the continent congregate to shop, party, and get down to business.

THE NORTH-WEST & THE NORTHERN CAPE

This is *Thelma and Louise* territory, perfect for people who like taking road trips past endless horizons with very little sign of human habitation. The North-West is not as arid as the neighboring Northern Cape and is much more accessible; its most famous attraction—**Sun City** and its centerpiece, the **Palace of the Lost City**—can be visited as a day-trip from Johannesburg or Pretoria. The region also has two excellent, malaria-free Big 5 game reserves. The Northern Cape is the least accessible and the least populated province in South Africa, and—perhaps as a consequence—has some of the most beautiful scenery in the world, though the starkness of the desert reserves won't strike a chord in everyone. But no one can remain unmoved in the spring when the first rains transform the vast arid plains into horizon-filled fields of flowers of Namaqualand.

MPUMALANGA AND THE LIMPOPO PROVINCE

To the east of Gauteng and the Free State lies the **Escarpment**—the end of the Drakensberg mountain range that rises in the Eastern Cape, running up the western border of KwaZulu-Natal before dividing Mpumalanga and the Limpopo Province into the high- and lowveld. Traveling through the Escarpment to reach Kruger and the lowveld's Big-Game Country, you will find some of the country's most gorgeous views, the world's third largest canyon; the largest man-made forests in the world, and the country's first gold-rush towns, one of which has been declared a living monument. Traveling east on scenic mountain passes, you will drop thousands of feet to the lowveld plains before reaching Big-Game Country. If you want to see Africa's wild animals on a budget, **Kruger National Park** offers the best deal on the continent—a high density of game combined with spotlessly clean, albeit spartan, accommodations. Along its western flank, with no fences between, lie the **private game lodges** in the **Sabi Sand, Manyeleti,** and **Timbavati reserves,** offering a variety of experiences—from over-the-top decadent luxury chalets to East-African safari tents or rough huts.

THE WESTERN & EASTERN CAPE

The least African of all the provinces, the Western Cape is also the most popular, primarily due to the legendary beauty of its capital city, **Cape Town,** the **Winelands,** and the scenic coastal belt called the **Garden Route,** which winds through South Africa's well-traveled Lakes District. It also offers some of the best beach-based whale-watching in the world on the **Overberg coast;** the world's most spectacular spring flowers display on the West Coast, north of Cape Town; and in the **Karoo,** the quaint *dorps* (small towns) that typify rural Afrikaans culture. The mountains and hills that trail the coastline are a botanist's and hiker's dream, with the Cape floral kingdom—an awesome array of more than 8,000 species—a treat year-round. The Eastern Cape is where you'll find the Big 5 reserve closest to Cape Town, as well as two of the country's top trails: the **Otter Trail**

Southern Africa

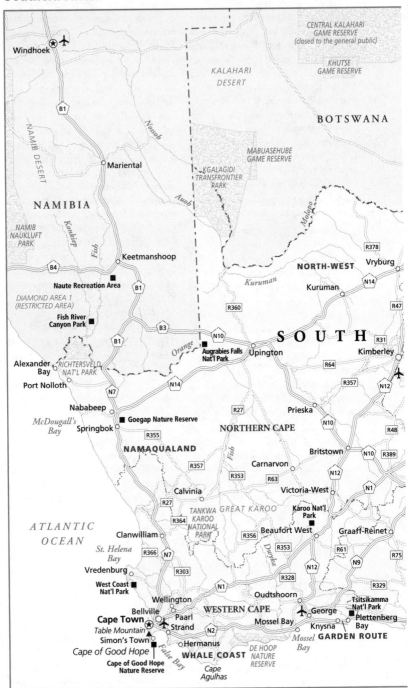

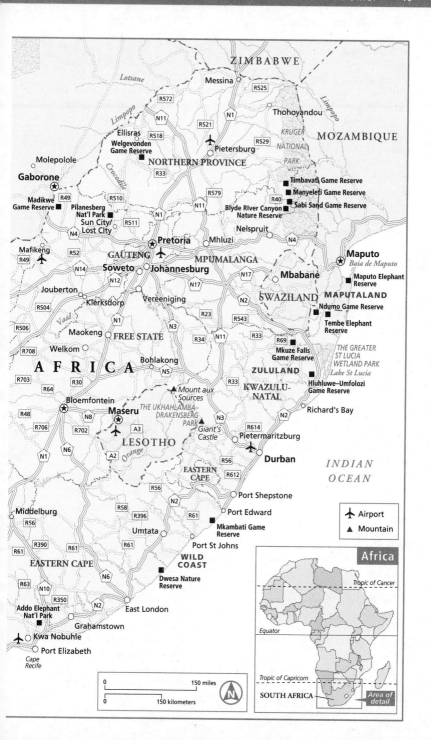

in the Tsitsikamma National Park, the exit point of the Garden Route, and the **Wild Coast,** bordering KwaZulu-Natal.

Established as a port in 1652, Cape Town was the first gateway to southern Africa from Europe, and subsequently retains a more colonial feel than any other major city. It is cut off from the rest of the country by the Hex River and by the mountains of the Cederberg and Swartberg, and has its own distinctive climate—cool, wet winters and hot, windy summers—ideal for the wine and deciduous fruits that further cocoon the Cape's inhabitants from the harsh realties of the hinterland. Insularity has bred its own problems, however. Gang warfare in the Cape Flats, homelessness, and drug trafficking are all serious problems. In a city this size, such problems are hardly unusual, but what is surprising is how cut off from them you'll feel as a visitor.

KWAZULU-NATAL   Hot and humid in summer, warm and balmy in winter, the KwaZulu-Natal coast offers excellent beach holidays, with temperatures never dropping below 61°F (16°C), and the Indian Ocean kept warm by the Mozambique Current that washes past its subtropical shores. Unfortunately, this is no well-kept secret, and development along most of its south and much of its north coast (Durban being the center) has resulted in another paradise lost, and an endless string of ugly, indifferent holiday and timeshare resorts. There are exceptions, the best of which lie north, like **St Lucia Wetland Park,** Africa's biggest estuary and home to large populations of Nile crocodile and hippo, and within easy striking distance of Hluhluwe-Umfolozi, the province's largest Big 5 resort.

After Cape Town, **Durban** is the most enjoyable city to visit, with great museums, arts and crafts, restaurants, the busiest port in Africa, and an interesting blend of cultures—besides the Zulu, the largest group in South Africa, the biggest population of Indians outside of India resides here. It is also well situated should you be interested in combining a visit to a Big 5 game reserve with diving or snorkeling, taking one of the historic battlefields tours, or hiking through the majestic Drakensberg.

ZIMBABWE

A country of great natural beauty, Zimbabwe has a wide variety of habitats: In the west lie the expanses of the Kalahari sand; traveling east, you pass through woodland savanna and open grassland, until, in the east, you come up against the lush montane forests of the Eastern Highlands. However, with president Robert Mugabe's relentless pursuit of a land "redistribution" policy, as well as serious food shortages, press oppression, and victimization of the opposition party leader, the Zimbabwean dollar remains in free fall. Although this means there are bargains to be had, traveling can be difficult, with periodic fuel and food shortages, and an almost nonexistent phone exchange. Thankfully, the country's primary attraction, **Victoria Falls,** remains relatively untouched, and is still easy to reach and safe to visit. Chapter 9 deals with the best way to experience what has justifiably been described as one of the wonders of the world, from both the Zimbabwean and Zambian side.

BOTSWANA

Straddling the Tropic of Capricorn in southern Africa, Botswana is truly one of the last pristine wilderness areas on the continent. Roughly the size of France, it is bordered by Namibia to the west and north, Zimbabwe to the east, and South Africa to the south.

A sparsely populated country of just over 1 million inhabitants, Botswana offers a varied wilderness experience, from forest to salt pan, bushveld to rolling savanna, ancient lake beds to palm-fringed islands. The waterless Kalahari covers two-thirds of its surface, so it is nothing short of incredible that it is also home to one of the world's largest inland delta systems—the **Okavango Delta,** highlight of Botswana. This 15,000-sq.-km (5,790-sq.-mile) inland flood plain fans out in the northwestern corner of the country, creating a paradise of palms, papyrus, and crystal-clear channels and backwaters. The life-giving waters provide a much-needed oasis for birds and animals, and consequently unparalleled opportunities for humans to view them.

In addition to the delta, Botswana has **Chobe National Park** to the northeast, a 12,000-sq.-km (7,450-sq.-mile) park that is famed for its huge elephant herds (it's home to some 35,000 elephants); while to the southeast are the spectacular wide-open spaces of **Makgadikgadi** and **Nxai Pans.** Time (and money) allowing, a visit to these should be included in your itinerary.

2 Visitor Information

SOUTH AFRICA Contact **South African Tourism** (www.southafrica.net; info@southafrica.net).

In the United States 500 5th Ave., Suite 2040, New York, NY 10110 (© **212/730-2929**); For brochures call © **800/782-9772.**

In Canada 4117 Lawrence Ave. E., Suite 2, Ontario M1E 2S2 (© **0416/966-4059**).

In the United Kingdom Nos. 5–6 Alt Grove, Wimbledon SW 19 4DZ (© **08701/550044**).

In Australia Level 9, 5 Elizabeth Street, Sydney 2000, N.S.W. Australia (© **02/9231-4444**). New Zealand has no office.

ZIMBABWE Contact the Zimbabwean Tourism Authority (www.zimbabwetourism.co.zw; info@ztazim.co.zw).

In the United States 1270 Ave. of the Americas, Suite 2315, New York, NY 10020 (© **212/486-3444**).

In Canada Zimbabwe High Commission, 332 Somerset St., West Ottawa, Ontario K2P OJ9 (© **613/237-4388**).

In the United Kingdom 429 Strand, London WC2R 05A (© **0207/240-6169**).

In Australia The High Commission, 11 Culogoa Circuit, O'Malley,

---

⌒Tips Websites to Surf for the Latest Happenings

The official South African tourism website **www.southafricatourism.com** offers a comprehensive listing of events taking place throughout the country and links you to **www.africaexperts.com**, the division of Goway Travel that specializes in safaris and vacations to suit all budgets.

For the latest news and tips and overviews on countries throughout Africa, go to **www.getawaytoafrica.co.za**, the site of Africa's best-selling travel magazine; also take a look at **www.africanexplorer.co.za**, a virtual magazine that features some of the country's top local journalists. To find out what's happening in South Africa, from politics to art exhibitions, visit **www.mg.co.za**, the home page for the *Mail & Guardian,* South Africa's best national newspaper. To get a live, close-up view of the action in Big-Game country, click onto **www.africam.co.za**.

Canberra ACT 2606 (© 02/6286-2700). There is no representation in New Zealand.

BOTSWANA   For more information visit www.gov.bw.

In the United States   The Embassy of the Republic of Botswana, 1531–3 New Hampshire Ave. NW, Washington, D.C. 20036 (© 202/244-4990).

In the United Kingdom   6 Stratford Place, London W1N 9AE (© 0207/499-0031).

3 Entry Requirements & Customs

Citizens of the United States, Canada, Australia, and New Zealand need only a valid passport for a 90-day stay in South Africa and Botswana. European nationals can stay up to 6 months in South Africa, 90 days in Botswana. To enter Zimbabwe, U.S., Canadian, Australian, and New Zealand citizens are issued visas on arrival for US$30/US$45 (single/multiple entry); U.K. citizens are charged £34/£44 (single/multiple entry). A Zambian visa costs US$35 (£40 if you are U.K. citizen). Day visitors to the Zambian side of Victoria Falls can purchase a US$10 day visa at the bridge. If you plan to stay on the Zambian side, but are transferring from Victoria Falls airport in Zimbabwe, your lodge—given warning—can arrange a visa waiver for Zambia; you will then only need a multiple entry visa for Zimbabwe.

For longer stays in southern Africa, visit the Aliens Control Section at the Department of Home Affairs at 56 Barrack St., Cape Town (© 27/21/462-4970); or 77 Harrison St., Johannesburg (© 27/11/836-3228). For visits to all southern African countries, visitors need a return ticket and may have to prove that they'll have sufficient funds during their stay.

For additional information on entry requirements, travelers may contact the embassies listed under "Visitor Information," above.

PASSPORT INFORMATION

Safeguard your passport in an inconspicuous, inaccessible place like a money belt. If you lose it, visit the nearest consulate of your native country as soon as possible for a replacement. Passport applications are downloadable from the Internet sites listed below.

FOR RESIDENTS OF THE UNITED STATES

If you're applying for a first-time passport, you need to do it in person at 1 of 13 passport offices throughout the United States; a federal, state, or probate court; or a major post office (though not all post offices accept applications; call the number below to find the ones that do). You need to present a certified birth certificate as proof of citizenship, and it is wise to bring along your driver's license, state or military ID, and social security card. You also need two identical passport-size photos (2 in. × 2 in.), taken at any corner photo shop (not one of the strip photos, however, from a photo-vending machine).

For people over 15, a passport is valid for 10 years and costs $60 ($45 plus a $15 handling fee); for those 15 and under, it's valid for 5 years and costs $40. If you're over 15 and have a valid passport that was issued within the past 12 years, you can renew it by mail and bypass the $15 handling fee. Allow plenty of time before your trip to apply; processing normally takes 3 weeks but can take longer during busy periods (especially spring). For general information, call the **National Passport Agency** (© 202/647-0518). To find your regional passport office,

> ### (Tips Phone Home: Calling to and from South Africa
>
> **To call southern Africa from another country:** Dial international access code (United States or Canada 011, United Kingdom or New Zealand 00, Australia 0011), plus country code (the country code for South Africa is 27; for Zimbabwe it is 263; for Botswana it is 267), plus the local number minus the 0.
>
> **To make an international call from South Africa:** Dial 09, then the country code (United States or Canada 1, UK 44, Australia 61, New Zealand 64), the area code, and the local number.
>
> **To charge international calls from South Africa:** Dial AT&T Direct (℗ 0-800-99-0123); Sprint (℗ 0800-99-0001); or MCI (℗ 0800-99-0011).
>
> At press time, AT&T Direct, Sprint, and MCI did not have international toll-free access numbers from Zimbabwe or Botswana.
>
> **To make a local call:** Drop the country code and add a zero (0) to the city code (except in Botswana, which has no city codes). At press time you did not have to dial the city code when calling from within the city limits, but this is set to change sometime in 2003; ask your host or dial ℗ 1023. Note that if you are using a mobile phone, you always need to enter the city code before the telephone number.
>
> **Mobile/cell numbers:** Be aware that numbers that start with the code 082, 083, 084, 072, 073 are mobile or cell numbers, and these codes must not be dropped.
>
> **Looking for a number: In South Africa:** Call directory assistance at ℗ 1023 for numbers in South Africa, and ℗ 0903 for international numbers. To track down a service call ℗ 10118.

call the **National Passport Information Center** (℗ 900/225-5674; travel.state.gov).

FOR RESIDENTS OF CANADA

You can pick up a passport application at one of 28 regional passport offices or most travel agencies. The passport is valid for 5 years and costs C$60. Children under 16 may be included on a parent's passport but need their own to travel unaccompanied by the parent. Applications, which must be accompanied by two identical passport-size photographs and proof of Canadian citizenship, are available at travel agencies throughout Canada or from the central **Passport Office, Department of Foreign Affairs and International Trade,** Ottawa K1A 0G3 (℗ **800/567-6868;** www.dfait-maeci.gc.ca/passport). Processing takes 5 to 10 days if you apply in person, or about 3 weeks by mail.

FOR RESIDENTS OF THE UNITED KINGDOM

To pick up an application for a standard 10-year passport (5-year passport for children under 16), visit the nearest Passport Office, major post office, or travel agency. You can also contact the **United Kingdom Passport Service** at ℗ **0870/571-0410** or visit its website at www.passport.gov.uk. Passports are £33 for adults and £19 for children under 16, with an additional £30 fee if you apply in person at a Passport Office. Processing takes about 2 weeks (1 week if you apply at the Passport Office).

FOR RESIDENTS OF IRELAND

You can apply for a 10-year passport, costing €57, at the **Passport Office,** Setanta Centre, Molesworth Street, Dublin 2 (ℂ **01/671-1633;** www.irl gov.ie/iveagh). Those under age 18 and over 65 must apply for a €12 3-year passport. You can also apply at 1A South Mall, Cork (ℂ **021/272-525**) or over the counter at most main post offices.

FOR RESIDENTS OF AUSTRALIA

Apply at your local post office or passport office or search the government website at www.dfat.gov.au/passports/. Passports for adults are A$126, and for those under 18, A$63.

FOR RESIDENTS OF NEW ZEALAND

You can pick up a passport application at any travel agency or Link Centre. For more information, contact the **Passport Office,** P.O. Box 805, Wellington (ℂ **0800/225-050**). Passports for adults are NZ$80, and for those under 16, NZ$40.

CUSTOMS

When entering South Africa, items for personal use are duty-free.Goods intended as gifts or trade are duty-free up to the value of R3,000 ($375) and thereafter taxed at 20%. You're allowed to bring in up to 2 liters of wine, 1 liter of spirits, 50 milliliters of perfume, 250 milliliters of eau de toilette, and 200 cigarettes or 50 cigars or 250g grams of tobacco.

The above restrictions on alcohol, perfume, and tobacco also apply to Zimbabwe and Botswana.

Before leaving your home country, register your foreign-made electronic equipment with customs.

IMPORT RESTRICTIONS

Returning U.S. citizens who have been away for 48 hours or more are allowed to bring back, once every 30 days, $400 worth of merchandise duty-free, as well as 1 liter of alcohol, 200 cigarettes, 100 non-Cuban cigars, and original works of art. You'll be charged a flat rate of 10% duty on the next $1,000 worth of purchases. Be sure to have your receipts handy. On gifts, the duty-free limit is $100; consider mailing items home—you can send certain packages valued at $200 (marked "personal use") home duty-free. You cannot bring fresh foodstuffs into the United States; tinned foods, however, are allowed. For more information, contact the **U.S. Customs Service** (1301 Constitution Ave., P.O. Box 7407, Washington, D.C. 20044 (ℂ **202/927-6724**), and request the free pamphlet "Know Before You Go" or read it at www.customs.ustreas.gov/travel/kbygo.htm.

U.K. citizens returning from a non-EC country have a customs allowance of 200 cigarettes, 50 cigars, or 250 grams of smoking tobacco; 2 liters of still table wine; 1 liter of spirits or strong liqueurs (over 22% volume); 2 liters of fortified wine, sparkling wine, or other liqueurs; 60 milliliters perfume; 250 milliliters of toilet water; and £145 worth of all other goods, including gifts and souvenirs. People under 17 cannot have the tobacco or alcohol allowance. For more information, contact **HM Customs & Excise,** Passenger Enquiry Point, 2nd Floor, Wayfarer House, Great South West Road, Feltham, Middlesex TW14 8NP (ℂ **0181/910-3744,** or **44/181-910-3744** from outside the United Kingdom), or consult their website at www.open.gov.uk.

Canadian citizens returning are allowed a C$500 exemption (note that this can only be used once a year and only after an absence of 7 days), as well as 200 cigarettes, 1 kilogram (2.2 lb.) of tobacco, 40 imperial ounces of wine or liquor, and 50 cigars. In addition, you're allowed to mail gifts to Canada from abroad at the rate of C$60 a day, provided they're unsolicited and don't contain alcohol or tobacco (write on the package "Unsolicited gift, under $60 value"). All valuables should be declared on the Y-38 form before departure from Canada, including serial numbers of valuables you already own, such as expensive foreign cameras. For a clear summary of Canadian rules, write for the booklet "I Declare," issued by **Revenue Canada,** 2265 St. Laurent Blvd., Ottawa K1G 4KE (℡ **613/993-0534**).

The duty-free allowance in Australia is A$400 or, for those under 18, A$200. Personal property mailed back should be marked "Australian goods returned" to avoid payment of duty. Upon returning to Australia, citizens can bring in 250 cigarettes or 250 grams of loose tobacco, and 1,125 milliliters of alcohol. If you're returning with valuable goods you already own, such as foreign-made cameras, you should file form B263. A helpful brochure, available from Australian consulates or Customs offices, is

"Know Before You Go." For more information, contact **Australian Customs Services,** GPO Box 8, Sydney, NSW 2001 (℡ **02/9213-2000**).

The duty-free allowance for **New Zealand** is NZ$700. Citizens over 17 can bring in 200 cigarettes, 50 cigars, or 250 grams of tobacco (or a mixture of all three if their combined weight doesn't exceed 250g); plus 4.5 liters of wine and beer, or 1.125 liters of liquor. New Zealand currency does not carry import or export restrictions. Fill out a certificate of export, listing the valuables you are taking out of the country; that way, you can bring them back without paying duty. Most questions are answered in a free pamphlet available at New Zealand consulates and Customs offices: *New Zealand Customs Guide for Travellers, Notice no. 4.* For more information, contact **New Zealand Customs,** The Customhouse, 17–21 Whitmore St., Box 2218, Wellington (℡ **04/473-6099** or 0800/428-786; www.customs.govt. nz).

4 Money

CASH

For the most favorable rates, change money at banks (the exception to this is Zimbabwe where the bank exchange rate is far from favorable; because of the huge differences in exchange rates, the best currency in Vic Falls is foreign or traveler's checks).

The **South African currency unit** is the **rand** (R), with 100 cents making up R1. Notes come in R10, R20, R50, R100, and R200. Minted coins come in 1, 2, and 5 rand denominations, and 1, 2, 5, 10, 20, and 50 cents—small change doesn't buy much; use it for tips. At press time, the rand was gaining strength and exchange rates were just under R8 to the US$1 and R12 to the £1. The rand has strengthened considerably in the past two years, gaining 41% on the dollar in

2002 and about 18% in the first half of 2003. But according to the Big Mac index, the rand is still undervalued by some 32%, so there's little point in delaying your vacation to await a drop in the rand's value.

In **Zimbabwe** the monetary unit is the **Zimbabwe dollar,** abbreviated as Z$ and comprising 100 cents. Notes come in denominations of Z$2, Z$5, Z$10, Z$20, Z$50, and Z$100. Coins come in 1, 5, 10, and 50 cents, and Z$1 and Z$2. The conversion rate at the time of going to press was US$1 = Z$810, or £1 = Z$1,304. Note that travelers to Zimbabwe are usually required to pay for all lodging with credit cards or internationally convertible currency such as U.S. dollars or British pounds.

The **pula** (which incidentally means "rain") is the official currency of **Botswana.** One pula (P) is divided into 100 thebe. Bills come in P1, P2, P5, P10, P20, and P50 and coins in 1t, 2t, 5t, 10t, 25t, 50t, and P1. This is the most expensive region in southern Africa; at press time, the exchange rates were P4.85 to US$1, or P7.80 to £1.

For up-to-the-minute currency conversions go to www.xe.com/ucc.

TRAVELER'S CHECKS

Note that credit cards are generally accepted throughout southern Africa, particularly MasterCard and Visa, and you can use them to draw cash at ATMs which you'll find throughout South Africa, making traveler's checks are somewhat redundant.

You can get traveler's checks at almost any bank. American Express offers denominations of $10, $20, $50, $100, $500, and $1,000; you can also purchase them in South African rands. You'll pay a service charge ranging from 1% to 4%. You can also get American Express traveler's checks over the phone by calling ⓒ **800/221-7282;** by using this number, Amex gold and platinum cardholders are exempt from the 1% fee. AAA members can obtain checks without a fee at most AAA offices.

Visa offers traveler's checks at Citibank locations nationwide, as well as several other banks. The service charge ranges between 1.5% and 2%; checks come in denominations of $20, $50, $100, $500, and $1,000. MasterCard also offers traveler's checks. Call ⓒ **800/223-9920** for a location near you.

ATMS

ATMs offering 24-hour service are located throughout South Africa. ATMs are linked to a national network that most likely includes your bank at home. **Cirrus** (ⓒ **800/424-7787;** www.mastercard.com) and **PLUS** (ⓒ **800/843-7587;** www.visa.com) are the two most popular networks; check the back of your ATM card to see which network your bank belongs to. Be sure to check the daily withdrawal limit before you depart, and make sure your PIN is valid.

CREDIT CARDS

American Express, Diners Club, MasterCard, and Visa are accepted at most hotels, restaurants, and stores in South Africa, though the latter two are the most popular here. Many lodges in Botswana do not accept credit cards (though in all likelihood you will be booking and paying for these ahead of time as part of a safari). For the most part, however, you'll find credit cards to be invaluable when you travel. They are a safe way to carry money and provide a convenient record of all your expenses. You can also withdraw cash advances from any bank. At most banks, you don't even need to go to a teller; you can get a cash advance at the ATM if you know your PIN. If you've forgotten your PIN or didn't even know you had one, call the phone number on the back of your credit card and ask. It usually takes 5 to 7 business days, though some banks will provide the number over the phone if you pass security clearance.

5 When to Go

Because southern Africa is such a large area, with each region offering different seasonal benefits, the time you go should only help determine where you go.

SOUTH AFRICA

The summer months (Nov–Feb) tend to attract the majority of visitors (particularly from Europe). Fortunately, the country is big enough to absorb these increased numbers without causing the discomfort most people associate with busy seasons. Be aware, however, that accommodation prices do increase in summer, some by as much as 80%; and if you dislike crowds you should try to avoid South Africa's busiest school holidays, which take place over December and the Easter long weekend. Spring (Sept and Oct) and autumn (Mar and Apr) are considered by many to be the best times to visit, when temperatures are not quite so high (the balmy to baking days of Feb and Mar are particularly popular in Cape Town). Winter (June–Aug) brings substantial benefits too: from July to November are the months when the Southern Right whales migrate to the Cape's southern

coast, providing guaranteed sightings. From May to August are considered the best months for sighting big game: the foliage is less dense, malaria areas offer a lower risk, and many of the private game reserves drop their prices substantially. This is also a good time to visit Botswana and Zimbabwe, though Victoria Falls will not be in full flood (Zimbabwe is a summer rainfall area), and malaria remains a high risk year-round in both these areas. Cape Town gets winter rainfall during what it calls its Green Season (May–Aug), though there are always sunny breaks. Thanks to the year-round sunshine that the Garden Route and Karoo enjoy, any time is a good time to tour this region.

Average Temperatures & Rainfall in Southern Africa
Minimum/Maximum Temperatures & Monthly Rainfall in Inches

		Jan	Feb	Mar	Apr	May	June	July	Aug	Sept	Oct	Nov	Dec
Cape Town,	Temp °F	61/79	59/79	57/77	54/73	50/68	46/64	45/63	45/64	46/66	50/70	55/75	59/77
South Africa	Temp °C	16/26	15/26	14/25	12/23	10/20	8/18	7/17	7/18	8/19	10/21	13/24	15/25
	Rain (in.)	0.6	0.7	0.7	2.0	3.5	3.3	3.5	3.1	2.0	1.4	.5	.6
Johannesburg,	Temp °F	59/79	57/77	55/75	52/72	46/66	41/61	41/61	45/66	48/72	54/75	55/77	57/77
South Africa	Temp °C	15/26	14/25	13/24	11/22	8/19	5/16	5/16	7/19	9/22	12/24	13/25	14/25
	Rain (in.)	4.5	3.8	2.9	2.5	0.9	0.3	0.3	0.2	0.1	2.7	4.6	4.3
Victoria Falls,	Temp °F	65/85	64/85	62/85	57/84	49/81	43/76	42/77	47/82	55/89	62/91	64/90	64/86
Zimbabwe	Temp °C	18/30	18/30	17.30	14/29	9/27	6/24	6/24	8/28	13/32	17/33	18/32	18/30
	Rain (in.)	6.6	5	2.8	1.0	0.1	0	0	0	0.7	1.1	2.5	6.8
Maun	Temp °F	66/90	66/88	64/88	57/88	48/82	43/77	43/77	48/82	55/91	64/95	66/93	66/90
Botswana	Temp °C	19/32	19/31	18/31	14/31	9/28	6/25	6/25	9/29	13/33	18/35	19/34	19/23
	Rain (in.)	4.3	3.2	2.8	1.0	0.3	0.1	0	0	0	1.2	2.0	3.8

THE CLIMATE

Depending on where you are, average maximum temperatures can vary from 80°F/27°C (Cape Town) to 90°F/32°C (Kruger National Park) in the summer, and from an average 69°F/21°C (Cape Town) to 77°F/25°C (Durban) in winter. While summer is the most popular time, high humidity in KwaZulu-Natal can make for muggy days, and gale-force winds often occur in Cape Town and Port Elizabeth. Winter visitors would be well advised

to pack warm clothes—despite higher average temperatures than in the United States or Europe, South Africa is simply not geared for the cold, and insulation and central heating are low on the priority list. Temperatures in the interior fluctuate wildly in winter; you're best off layering.

RAINFALL

South Africa is generally considered an arid region, with two-thirds of the country receiving less than 500 millimeters (20 inches) of rain a year. In the interior, rain usually falls in the summer, and spectacular thunderstorms and the smell of damp earth bring great relief from the searing heat. The Garden Route enjoys rain year-round; and in Cape Town and surrounds, the rain falls mostly in the winter, when the gray skies are a perfect foil for the burnt orange strelitzias, pink proteas, and fields of white arum lilies, not to mention the perfect accompaniment to crackling fires and fine red wines.

HOLIDAYS

If you are traveling during the South African school holidays (check exact dates with South African Tourism), make sure you book your accommodation well in advance. Flights can also be impossible, particularly over the Christmas holidays (usually early Dec to mid-Jan). Easter holidays (usually the end of Mar to mid-Apr) can also be busy, while the Kruger is almost always packed during the winter vacation (mid-June to mid-July). There's another short school break in spring, from late September to October 7.

Public holidays in South Africa include New Year's Day; March 21 (Human Rights Day); Good Friday, Easter Sunday and Monday; April 27 (Founders/Freedom Day); May 1 (Workers Day); June 16 (Soweto/Youth Day); August 9 (Women's Day); September 24 (Heritage Day); December 16 (Day of Reconciliation); Christmas Day; and December 26 (Boxing Day).

ZIMBABWE

Zimbabwe's climate is similar to that in South Africa's northern provinces, with a summer rainy season and most of the rainfall occurring between December and mid-March. Summers are warm to hot (late Oct, Nov, and Dec can be uncomfortable), and winters are mild. Malaria is still a danger

in many areas; there are tsetse flies in parts of the Zambezi Valley and in the southeast; and be aware that certain rivers, lakes, and dams are infected with bilharzia. Victoria Falls are often at their fullest from January to mid-April, at the end of the rainy season, though this is also when the mist created by the falling water may obscure the view, and malaria-carrying mosquitoes are at their most prolific. Temperatures are pleasantly reduced from May to October (81°F/27°C). Many think the best time to see the falls is from August to December, when the view is clearer (though the flow of the water is at its lowest). From June to December is high season for many of the upmarket lodges, which raise their prices during these months.

Holidays in Zimbabwe are New Year's Day, January 1; Good Friday through Easter Monday; Independence Day, April 18; Workers Day, May 1; Africa Day, April 25; Heroes Day, August 11; Defense Forces Day, August 12; Christmas Day; and Boxing Day, December 26.

BOTSWANA

Botswana has a pleasant subtropical climate with low humidity. Rain falls during the summer months, from November to March—this is a great time to visit the delta if you're interested in birds and plants, but it can get very hot. From April to September, the days are mild to warm, but temperatures drop sharply at night and early in the morning, particularly around June and July. Most consider these 2 months the best time to visit the delta, when the rain that falls on the Angolan bushveld plains seeps down to create what is referred to as the "flood." At this time, waterlilies bloom, countless aquatic creatures frolic in the water, and a huge diversity of game from the surrounding dry areas moves into the delta.

Holidays in Botswana are New Year's Day, January 2 (public holiday);

July 1 (Sir Seretse Khama Day); third Monday and Tuesday in July (President's Day); September 30 (Independence Day); Christmas; Boxing Day; Good Friday, Easter Monday; May 1, Labour Day; and Ascension Day (40 days after Easter).

CALENDAR OF EVENTS

A comprehensive list of events with dates for the current year can be found on www. southafrica.net; alternatively check with the regional tourism branch—see relevant chapters for contact details.

January

Cape Minstrels Carnival, Cape Town. Festive Cape Malay or "coloured" groups compete and parade, dressed in colorful outfits, through the city's streets, singing and jiving to banjo beats. Several days in January.

Spier Arts Festival, Spier Estate, Stellenbosch, Winelands. The Western Cape's premier arts festival features local and international opera, classical music, comedy, jazz and drama at the Spier Amphitheatre. January to March.

Shakespeare Open Air Festival, Maynardville, Wynberg, Cape Town. Pack a picnic to enjoy this annual Shakespeare play performed in the Maynardville Gardens. Mid-January.

Appletiser Summer Sunset Concerts (Kirstenbosch Gardens, Cape Town). Catch a new act every Sunday at 5:30pm in one of the world's most beautiful gardens on the slopes of Table Mountain. December to March.

Duzi Canoe Race, Pietermaritzburg, KwaZulu-Natal. The country's most prestigious canoeing event covers the 115km (71 miles) between Pietermaritzburg and Durban. Late January.

J&B Metropolitan Horse Race, Kenilworth Race Course, Cape Town. The Western Cape's premier horse-racing event is Cape Town's excuse to party, and attracts many of the city's socialites. Last Saturday in January or first in February.

South Africa Open, new venue every year. South Africa's golfing greats battle it out on one of the country's premier courses. Mid- or late January.

February

Sangoma Khekheke's Annual Snake Dance, Zululand, Kwazulu-Natal. Some 6,000 to 8,000 Zulus gather to slaughter cattle and dance under the auspices of Sangoma Khekheke. Late February.

FNB Vita Dance Umbrella, Wits Theatre, Johannesburg. A platform for the best contemporary choreography and dance in South Africa. February 20 to March 20, 2004.

March

Cape Argus Cycle Tour, Cape Town. The largest of its kind in the world, this race attracts some 30,000 cyclists and covers 105km (65 miles) of Cape Town's most scenic routes. Second Sunday of every March.

North Sea Jazz Festival, Cape Town. The best local jazz talent joined by international greats (including great line-up from all over Africa) perform for enthusiastic audiences for 2 days. Late March.

Klein Karoo National Arts Festival, Oudtshoorn, Western Cape. Showcases the country's best, with many productions (often in Afrikaans) premiering here. Predominantly drama, as well as excellent dance and music acts. End of March.

April

Two Oceans Marathon, Cape Town. This 56km (35-mile) scenic route attracts some 12,000 athletes. Easter Saturday.

May

MasterCard Cape Gourmet Festival, Cape Town. The Cape's top restaurants participate in the gourmet capital's most exciting sampling exercise; for 2003 it was R85 ($10) for a two-course meal at all participating restaurants, including a glass of wine. Mid- to late May.

June

Comrades Marathon, Pietermaritzburg, KwaZulu-Natal. More than 13,000 runners participate in this 89km (55-mile) race, which started in 1921. Mid-June.

Standard Bank National Arts Festival, Grahamstown, Eastern Cape. The largest arts festival in the southern hemisphere features performances from cutting-edge to classical. Pack warm woolies. Late June to early July.

July

Knysna Oyster Festival, Knysna, Garden Route, Western Cape. The festival encompasses the Forest Marathon, a mountain-bike cycling tour, a regatta, a golf championship, and flea markets. First Friday to second Saturday of every July.

Rothmans July Handicap, Greyville Racecourse, Durban. This horseracing event has a stakes of 1 million rand ($125,000). First Saturday of every July.

Ocean Action, Durban beachfront. This world-class water sports and beach-related tournament includes what is still referred to as the Gunston 500, one of the world's premier surfing events. Mid- or late July.

August

Namaqualand Wild Flower Season, Western and Northern Cape. From mid-August (could be later depending on rain), the semi-arid West Coast is transformed into a floral paradise with more than 2,600 species in bloom. August to October.

Jomba Dance Festival, Elizabeth Sneddon Theatre, Durban. A 10-day contemporary dance festival featuring the best of KwaZulu-Natal's considerable dance and choreography talent. Late August to early September.

September

Haenertsburg and Magoebaskloof Spring Festival, Limpopo Province. Flowering azaleas, cherry blossoms, and crabapples are celebrated with a crafts market, carnival, exhibitions, and evening events. Call for dates.

Arts Alive International Festival, Johannesburg. This urban arts festival features local talent and international stars. Includes the Jazz on the Lake Concert held at Zoo Lake. Call for dates.

Whale Festival, Hermanus, Western Cape. The Whale Festival includes drama performances, an arts ramble, a crafts market, and whale-route lectures and tours. Late September to early October.

Darling Wildflower and Orchid Show and Hello Darling Arts Festival, Arcadia Street, Darling, West Coast. Combine a trip to see the flowers with a show at Evita se Perron hosted by Pieter Dirk Uys, South Africa's most famous female impersonator. End of September.

International Eisteddfod of South Africa, Roodepoort, Gauteng. This competitive international music and dance festival features entrants from some 30 countries—gospel choirs are the S.A. highlight. Late September to early October

King Shaka Day Celebrations and the **Zulu Kings Reed Dance,** Zululand, Kwazulu-Natal. King Shaka Day sees all the Zulu heads, from Chief Buthelezi (leader of the IFP party) to Prince Gideon, dressed in full traditional gear, addressing their minions in a moving day celebrating Zulu traditions. Later in the month some 15,000 Zulu maidens participate in the colorful Reed Dance, in which the king would traditionally choose a new wife but the moralist Prince Gideon, mindful of the AIDS crisis, uses the opportunity to address some of the issues affecting the nation today by abstaining. Both events are highly recommended. September 22.

October

Shembe Celebrations, Zululand, Kwazulu-Natal. The prophet Shembe, the fourth successor of the first prophet, presides over a congregation of some 30,000 who gather to hear his words; Sundays, when Shembe leads the crowds into prayer-dancing, are the highlight. Last three weeks of October.

December

Mother City Queer Project, Cape Town. This masked costume ball features some 10 dance zones and costumed teams celebrating Cape Town's vibrant and creative queer culture. The best party of the year. Early December.

Million Dollar Golf Challenge, Sun City, North-West Province. This high-stakes tournament attracts the world's best golfers. Call for dates.

Appletiser Summer Sunset Concerts (Kirstenbosch Gardens, Cape Town). Start of the new season; pack a picnic and get there by 4:30pm to grab a choice spot on the lawn before concert starts at 5:30pm. Program runs to March.

Vortex New Year's Eve Rave Party (Grabouw, Cape Town surrounds). An almost week-long non-stop camp-out party where Cape Town's hippest hippies pay homage to the beat from dusk to dawn.

6 Planning Your Safari

What are the safari options available?

Wildlife viewing is the reason most set their sights on southern Africa. As a result, a number of ways to experience the bush have been developed. You can opt for a **self-drive safari** in a national park, fly straight to a luxurious lodge in a **private game reserve,** or—best of all—combine the two. The more adventurous take their chances on a specialist safari and go on **foot, horseback, bike, canoe,** or even on the back of an **elephant.** If you're keen to walk the wilderness accompanied by an experienced, armed game ranger, the trails in **Umfolozi,** 30,000 hectares (74,100 acres) of pristine bush and savanna (with no roads or paths other than those created by animals), are rated by experienced hikers as South Africa's best, particularly the 4-day **Traditional Trail** (see chapter 8). Alternatively, the walking safaris in **Kruger National Park,** which offers a choice of seven separate wilderness trails, are also highly recommended (see chapter 7). For game spotting on horseback, book a safari with Equus Safaris in the the Waterberg Mountains (see chapter 7), or take a day ride in a reserve in the **Victoria Falls** vicinity (see chapter 9). Botswana highlights (see chapter 10) include cycling safaris offered in **Tuli,** quad-bike safaris at **Jack's Camp** in the Makgadikgadi Pans, and *mokoro* (dugout canoe) safaris in the **Okovango delta**—one of the best ways to get around the waterways. If you've always had a soft spot for the pachyderm, you can mount your very own elephant in Mpumalanga, Botswana or Victoria

Falls—one of the benefits is that they can get remarkably close to game.

Which country should I focus on?

South Africa has the best-managed national parks in Africa, as well as some of the most luxurious private reserves; but if you're looking for the original untamed Eden, nothing beats Botswana, particularly the Okovango delta. This is largely due to a government policy aimed at low-density, high-cost tourism. So be warned: Little here comes cheap. Until the landgrab and economic crisis is resolved in Zimbabwe, visiting here should be restricted to Victoria Falls, which is close to the Botswana and Zambian border.

How do I get around between reserves?

In South Africa, the **major reserves** are concentrated in **Mpumalanga and the Limpopo Province** (chapter 7), and you can reach them by flying directly to Johannesburg or Cape Town, then catching a connecting flight to an airport in or near the reserves; from here you can hire a car or arrange a transfer with your lodge. Or you can opt for the 4- to 5-hour (or more if you include the Blyde River Canyon) drive from Johannesburg; the scenery is pleasant, and there are fabulous lodging options along the way.

To reach **KwaZulu-Natal's** reserves, most of which are in Zululand, fly from Johannesburg or Cape Town to Durban or Richard's Bay airport. The biggest reserve, Hluhluwe-Umfolozi, is a 3-hour drive from Durban, and 2 hours from Richard's Bay.

Port Elizabeth airport is less than an hour from the **Eastern Cape reserves;** this is often the start or exit point of the 7-hour driving trip along the Garden Route to or from Cape Town.

From South Africa you'll have to fly via Johannesburg airport to get to **Botswana's reserves,** most of which are reached by charter flight from Maun or Kasane.

For recommended safari operators that include the cost of flights to and around southern Africa, see "Package Tours" in "Getting There," later in this chapter.

What should I do if I'm on a budget?

By far the best budget option is to rent a car and drive yourself around the reserves, concentrating on the national parks (like Kruger) and/or the provincial reserves (like Hluhluwe-Umfolozi). The roads in these reserves are in good condition, so you won't need a four-wheel-drive. There are a number of advantages besides cost: You can set your own pace, take in more than one environment (many visitors, for instance, combine a trip to Kruger with a KwaZulu-Natal reserve trip), and bring the kids (many private game reserves don't accept children). Kruger accommodation is usually in semi-serviced *rondawels* (pronounced ron-*da*-villes, these are round, thatch-roofed cottages with kitchens and en-suite bathrooms) that offer excellent value for money (around R380/$48 a night). Cheaper units won't have their own kitchen, but all feature a fridge, tea-making facilities, and a barbecue area. Linens and towels are also provided. Most rest camps have a shop selling supplies, including basics like dishwashing liquid, wood, fire-lighters, tinned foods, frozen meat, toiletries, and aspirin; you can also purchase field guides here. Most also have a restaurant serving breakfast, lunch, and dinner. Try and combine this with at least 2 nights in a private reserve (for reasons below)–the best Big 5 budget options close to Kruger are **Honeyguide** and **Umlani.** These range from R3,400 to R3,960 ($425–$496) a night for two, including game drives and all meals. The best Big 5 budget option close to Hluhluwe is

Mkuze Falls (from R2,200–R5,000/ $270–$625 double including game drives and all meals).

Do I need to visit a private reserve?

The best reason to visit a private reserve is that you are guaranteed to see more animals, and you will learn more about the intricacies of the bush. Visitors are taken for game drives in an open-topped vehicle by an armed and knowledgeable ranger, usually helped by a tracker, and in radio communication with other vehicles. Sightings are excellent on game drives (at least two of the Big 5 in one drive), and it's great to have your questions answered without having to flip through a book. In certain reserves like **Sabi Sand, Timbavati, Thornybush,** and **Phinda,** rangers are allowed to drive off-road, taking you almost within touching distance of animals. A typical day starts with a 3-hour, early-morning game drive, where eight (or fewer, at the more expensive lodges) guests are accompanied by a game ranger and tracker—followed by a large cooked breakfast, possibly in the bush. A guided walk is generally offered before lunch, and afternoons are spent relaxing at the pool or on a viewing deck. Night drives take place during the sunset/early-evening hours, with drinks (sundowners) served in the bush, and the last hour or so is spent driving with a spotlight. Night drives can be incredibly dull (it's pitch black), or totally exhilarating, with nocturnal predators stalking—and killing—prey, a rare but privileged sighting. Dinners are large, often buffet, and usually served under the stars by firelight.

What's the difference between the private reserves? Should I visit more than one?

It's definitely worth combining reserves, moving to new landscapes that support different species. If this is

your first time, it's worth choosing a Big 5 reserve—the presence of lion, leopard, rhino, elephant, and buffalo usually mean a great concentration of other species as well. The Big 5 reserves flanking Kruger (**Sabi Sands, Manyeleti, Timbavati**) are your best bet in South Africa, as there are no fences between them and Kruger, creating a massive wilderness area. Sabi Sands is the private reserve that has the highest concentration of both game and luxury lodges. Big 5 reserves that have the additional bonus of being malaria-free are **Welgevonden** (a pretty reserve very close to Johannesburg) **Makweti** in the North-West, and **Shamwari** in Eastern Cape.

Although the reserves surrounding Kruger are typical of the African bush and savanna, the **Okavango Delta** offers a lush landscape that attracts an incredible variety of bird life (not to mention a dense concentration of game)—and is a must on any safari itinerary. Then there are the desert reserves like **Tswalu, Kgaligadi Transfrontier Park,** and **Makgadigadi Pans**—with huge horizons and stark landscapes, these support species that have adapted to harsh conditions, like cheetah and gemsbok (oryx). By contrast, KwaZulu-Natal's semitropical climate creates a more junglelike environment—beautiful, but spotting animals is a little more difficult in dense foliage—and a safari can be combined with diving and snorkeling excursions. The relatively uncluttered landscape of the Eastern Cape is great for game viewing, but it doesn't have the drama of the reserves in the north, and is primarily used as a tack-on to the Garden Route.

I've decided on the private reserve . . . how should I choose my lodge?

It's worth mentioning that some of the larger lodges simply feel like plush hotels. Select a private lodge that takes no more than 8 to 12 guests per camp—this means you are given very personal service and the peace to absorb your surroundings, and privacy is paramount—units are usually set far apart, often with luxuries like private plunge pools. If, however, you want to get a real feel for the bush, consider tented bush camps, where essentials like hot water and en-suite bathrooms are standard features, but canvas walls allow the sounds of the bush to connect you with the outdoors. If you don't mind living out of a suitcase, moving from camp to camp is the ideal way to see different environments as well as plentiful game; and nowhere does it get as good as Botswana—see chapter 10 for a listing of safari operators who specialize in this area, as well as for a detailed description of the type of accommodations available.

If I'm visiting a private reserve, do I still need to include a National Park or provincial reserve in my itinerary?

Not necessarily. In a national park or provincial reserve you are, after all, in a closed vehicle, you can't leave the road, and you're not trained to spot animals in the bush. On the other hand, you may appreciate the relative privacy: There's nothing like spotting a cheetah on the side of the road, with no other soul in sight—a privilege you'll never have in a private reserve, where other guests are onboard, and another vehicle is on the way as soon as an animal is spotted.

When's the best time to go on safari?

The dry winter months (June–Oct, particularly Oct) are considered best. That's when the vegetation has died back and animals are easier to see and concentrated around the diminishing sources of water. Unless it was a particularly wet summer, the malaria risk is also considerably lower. But spring and summer bring their own benefits: Many animals have young (there's nothing quite as delightful as a baby giraffe), the vegetation is lush and often flowering, and colorful migrant birds adorn the trees. It is more difficult to spot animals in spring and summer, however, and you'll almost definitely need to spend time in a private reserve if you want to be assured of seeing big game.

How long do I need to spend on safari?

To honestly say you've experienced the bush, you'll need a minimum of 3 nights and 2 full days.

How safe am I on safari?

You are undertaking a journey through a landscape where wild animals abound, and irresponsible behavior

Where & When to See Game

	Jan	Feb	Mar	Apr	May	June	July	Aug	Sept	Oct	Nov	Dec
Kruger National Park	P	P	P	F	F	G	E	E	E	E	G	F
Private Game Reserves	G	G	G	G	G	E	E	E	E	E	E	G
Moremi & Okavango Delta	G	G	G	G	E	E	E	E	E	E	E	G
Chobe	F	F	F	G	G	E	E	E	E	E	E	G
Makgadikgadi & Nxai Pan	E	E	E	E	G	F	F	P	P	P	F	G

E = Excellent, G = Good, F = Fair, P = Poor

Tips Wilderness Etiquette

Because southern Africa is constantly afflicted by drought and tap water is not recycled, try to use as little water as possible, even in cities. Don't stray from paths—this leads to erosion. If you're in a four-wheel-drive vehicle, do not thunder along unspoiled dunes or bush. If you smoke, be sure to extinguish matches and cigarettes and carry the butts with you— they take more than 20 years to biodegrade. Never touch, scratch, or wet rock art. Never approach wildlife if they appear in any way disturbed by your presence—rules regarding marine animals are particularly strict.

could result in death. Malaria is also a serious threat—potentially fatal. See "Staying Healthy," below, for tips on how to ensure you survive your safari.

I've heard that walking safaris are the best way to experience the bush. Is this true?

In a sense, yes. Guided by an armed ranger, you will see many things that people in cars blindly cruise by, and the experience of spotting rhino just yards away on foot is unforgettable. The emphasis, however, is not on tracking game (no ranger would take you within striking distance of a big cat) as much as it is on understanding the intricacies of the relationships in the bush, and communing with nature. The ranger is armed, so there is no real danger, and the wilderness trails in Kruger and Hluhluwe reserves enjoy an unblemished safety record.

What should I pack?

Pack light, particularly if you are taking a charter plane to Botswana, which only allows one soft-sided bag weighing 10 kilograms (22 lb.).

Choose colors that blend in with the bush: gray, brown/beige, and khaki are best. Loose cotton clothing tends to be the most comfortable and protects your limbs from mosquitoes. If you intend to walk, you'll need long pants to protect you from prickly vegetation and ticks, as well as comfortable hiking boots. A warm sweater, coat, long pants, scarf, and gloves are recommended during evening game drives in winter (May–Aug); you'll also need warm sleepwear. A fitted broad-brimmed hat, swimwear, good sunglasses, and sunscreen are essential in summer. Though many lodges supply insect repellent, pack your own, as well as every other malaria precaution (see "Health, Safety & Insurance," below). And, of course, don't forget binoculars and a camera (a telephoto lens is ideal) and plenty of film, though you can usually purchase more at the camp. If you bring a video camera, pack a 12-volt adapter for charging the batteries (keep in mind, however, that electricity isn't always supplied on safaris).

7 Other Active Vacations

Surrounded by oceans and with a diverse landscape that includes forests, rivers, mountains, and large tracts of pristine wilderness, southern Africa is the ideal destination for outdoor adventure. For more details on any of the activities mentioned below, see the "Staying Active" sections in specific chapters. For a complete list of operators specializing in adventure pursuits, purchase the **Getaway Adventure Guide** or go to its website for details: www.getawaytoafrica.com.

The Western Cape (which includes Cape Town) and Victoria Falls are the two adventure centers of southern

Africa. Both are well-serviced by one-stop shops where staff will advise and make bookings for every adventure activity available. In Cape Town visit Long Street where a number of one-stop adventure shops are located– **Adventure Village** (© **27/21/424-1580;** www.adventure-village.co.za), is recommended. The most helpful outfit in Vic Falls Village is **Backpackers Bazaar** (© **263/13/45828;** backpack@africaonline.co.zw).

ABSEILING With numerous mountainsides to drop off, and a number of rivers to drop into, the Western Cape offers the most scenic abseiling (rappelling) options in South Africa; see chapters 3 and 4 for details.

BALLOONING For the best hot-air balloon views, head for the Pilanesberg game reserves in the North-West and drift over the savanna looking for big game. A close second is to sample a glass of wine while soaring over its source in the Winelands of the Western Cape. For information on ballooning operators, see chapters 3 and 4.

BIRD-WATCHING Situated on one of the world's biggest continents, with a range of totally different environments, the southern African region offers hours of rewarding bird-watching, and many species occur nowhere else but here. The best areas are Ndumo and Mkhuze in KwaZulu-Natal, the bush savanna of Mpumalanga and the Limpopo Province, and the Okavango delta in Botswana. For the best bird-watching safaris in southern Africa, contact **Peter Lawson** (© **27/13/741-2458**).

BOARDSAILING (WINDSURFING) The most exhilarating windsurfing spots are in the Scarborough and Kommetjie area on Cape Town's western seaboard, off the Cape Point coast, and at Langebaan on the West Coast, where the wind comes up almost every afternoon (see chapters 3 and 4).

BUNGEE/BRIDGE-JUMPING You can take the highest bungee jump in the world at Bloukrans River Bridge—216m (708 ft.), which rather makes the 65m (213 ft.) from the Gouritz River Bridge seem like child's play. Both these jumps are on the Garden Route, Western Cape (see chapter 4). At 104m (341 ft.), the world's second-highest bungee jump is off the Victoria Falls Bridge (see chapter 9).

CANOEING & KAYAKING Canoes can usually be rented wherever there's water—check the regional chapters or with the local tourism bureaus. This is certainly a great way to explore the upper reaches of the Zambezi River (see chapter 9) and South Africa's "Lakes District" in the Garden Route (see chapter 4). Kayaking is offered along the coast as well as on certain rivers, but takes considerably more practice. Gliding through the waters in a dugout canoe (called a *mokoro*) in the delta is one of the highlights of a trip to Botswana (see chapter 10).

DIVING You'll need to take a recognized dive course before plunging down in the deep to meet some of the 2,000 species that live off the African shores. If you're doing it here (and this is one of the cheapest places in the world to do so), make sure the organization is part of the **South African Underwater Union (SAUU),** which is affiliated with agencies worldwide. Sodwana Bay in northern KwaZulu-Natal is the most popular dive destination (see chapter 8). The Cape coast is good for wreck-diving. For more information, contact **SAUU** (© **27/21/930-6549**).

FISHING With more than 2,500km (1,550 miles) of coastline, rock, and surf, anglers are spoilt for choice here. The confluence of the warm Indian Ocean and the cold Atlantic is responsible for one of the highest concentrations of game fish in the world, including marlin. June through November are particularly popular months on the KwaZulu-Natal coast, for which you need no license (see chapter 8). Spear fishermen won't leave disappointed either; for more information, contact SAUU (see "Diving," above). Trout fishing is also extremely popular, particularly in the Dullstroom area (Mpumalanga), the Drakensberg (KwaZulu-Natal), and the mountains of the Western Cape. For more information, call the **Federation of SA Flyfishers** (© 27/ 11/462-6687). For organized fly-fishing holidays, contact **Ultimate Angling** (© 27/21/686-6877).

GOLFING   Courses in KwaZulu-Natal and the Western Cape are usually very beautiful and incorporate the natural environment. Unique to Africa are the courses where you may bump into wild animals (in Mpumalanga and the Limpopo Province, in particular). Many of the best courses have been designed by world champion and Johannesburg native Gary Player.

HANG- & PARAGLIDING   To combine flights with beautiful scenery, head for Wilderness in the Western Cape, considered the best area for coastal flying, or dive off Lion's Head for a bird's-eye view of Cape Town. To fly alone, you'll need to complete a course here, or ensure that your license is recognized. If you've never flown before, simply do a tandem flight with an instructor. See relevant chapters for schools or clubs in the various regions.

HIKING   South Africa has the most comprehensive trails network in Africa, from short rambles to tough 2-week hikes covering everything from fragrant botanical gardens, indigenous forests, savanna, and fynbos-clad mountains to uninhabited coastlines. Unique to Africa are trails in game reserves where you may encounter big game on foot, the best of which are

the Umfolozi trails in KwaZulu-Natal. Also keep an eye out for **"kloofing"** trails, on which you follow a river through a mountain gorge (kloof), swimming and clambering your way out. Most of the best hiking trails are in the Western Cape and KwaZulu-Natal, as well as in Mpumalanga and the Limpopo Province (see chapters 3, 4, 7, and 8). Hikers may wish to contact the **National Hiking Board of South Africa** (© 012/336-7500) or consider purchasing *The Complete Guide to Walks and Trails in Southern Africa* by Jaynee Levy (Struik).

MOUNTAIN BIKING   For pure scenic splendor, the best trails are in the Western Cape. Explore the Cape's Winelands, Table Mountain, Cape Point, or the indigenous forests and superb coastline of the Garden Route. Bikes can be rented wherever there are trails. For more information, read *Guide to Mountain Bike Trails in the Western Cape* by Paul Leger (Red Mill Publications) or contact Suzie Mills (© 27/11/837-8205; suzie@clip-in. co.za), a passionate biker and fount of knowledge on trails throughout South Africa.

MOUNTAINEERING   The most challenging and popular mountains are in KwaZulu-Natal (Drakensberg) and the Western Cape (Table Mountain, Cederberg). Table Mountain alone offers more than 500 routes. Some of the best mountains are privately owned, but local climbing clubs can provide permits. For more information, contact the **Mountain Club of South Africa** (© 27/21/465-3412).

PARACHUTING   (SKYDIVING) You need no previous experience to do a same-day jump—simply complete an accelerated free-fall course or try a tandem jump. For the best views, leap into the skies above Stellenbosch in the Cape's Winelands (see chapter 3), then reward yourself with some serious wine tasting after the event.

RIDING   There are horse trails throughout southern Africa, ranging from 2-hour excursions around town surrounds (Noordhoek Beach in Cape Town is particularly recommended) to week-long expeditions. One of the best wilderness experiences is found in the Waterberg, Limpopo Province (see chapter 7). If horses aren't your bag, you can mount an ostrich in Oudtshoorn (chapter 4), a camel in Cape Town (chapter 3), or an elephant in Botswana or Victoria Falls (chapters 9 and 10).

SAILING   You'll find the yacht facilities in South Africa excellent, with winds averaging 15 to 25 knots. Offshore sailing requires that you belong to a recognized yacht club; to find out more about local harbor regulations, contact the **South African Sailing** (© **27/21/439-1147;** www.sailing. org.za)

SHARK-CAGE DIVING   Unlike scuba diving, this requires no experience. Great White sharks are baited by operators who lower cages (usually containing two persons) into the water to view this protected species feeding close up. This activity is offered in the Western Cape—off Dyer Island, near Hermanus; and in Mossel Bay, Garden Route. See chapter 4.

SURFING   For many, Jeffrey's Bay in the Eastern Cape (chapter 5) represents the surf mecca of Africa; but KwaZulu-Natal's Durban, with its year-round warm weather and water and consistently good waves, is South Africa's real surfing center.

WHITE-WATER RAFTING   Commercial river running is a well-developed industry, and no experience is necessary if you're escorted by a reputable outfit (that is, registered with **South African Rafting Association [SARA]**). The Zambezi below Victoria Falls offers one of the greatest adrenaline trips on water, and is not to be missed even if you've never rafted before. The biggest wildwater after this is the Tugela River in KwaZulu-Natal (runnable only in summer). Other rivers worth rafting are the Blyde in Mpumalanga, an 8km (5-mile) descent with grade 3 to 5 rapids; the Doring (late Aug to Sept) and the Palmiet in the Western Cape; and the Orange in the Northern Cape; the latter offers the most relaxing rafting trip. Ask what you should wear or bring when making a booking. For details, see the "Staying Active" sections in chapters 4, 7, and 9.

8 Health, Safety & Insurance

STAYING HEALTHY

Visiting southern Africa should pose no serious threat to your health: Hospitals are efficient (though in an emergency you'd be better off going to a private hospital—facilities are better and you'll avoid a lengthy wait), hygiene is rarely a problem, tap water is safe, stomach upsets from food are rare, there are no weird tropical viruses, and medical aid is generally always within a 2-hour drive. Procedures, particularly dental and plastic surgery, are in fact so highly rated (and relatively inexpensive) that there is now a roaring trade in safari-surgery holidays. That said, there are a few things to watch out for. Malaria in certain areas is problematic; AIDS is rampant; bilharzia and tick-bite fever can be unpleasant; and precautions against the summer sun are essential. Plus, if you're used to civilized, law-abiding drivers, you'll find South African road manners leave a lot to be desired, and drunk driving can be a problem.

Unless you're already covered by a health plan while you're abroad, it's a good idea to take out medical travel insurance, particularly if you're going to participate in adventure activities (see the section on travel insurance below). Be sure to carry your identification card in your wallet.

Pack prescription medications in your carry-on luggage. Carry written prescriptions in generic, not brand-name form, and dispense all prescription medications from their original labeled vials. Also bring along copies of your prescriptions in case you lose your pills or run out. If you wear glasses or contact lenses, pack an extra pair.

Contact the **International Association for Medical Assistance to Travelers (IAMAT) (✆ 716/754-4883** or 416/652-0137; www.iamat.org) for tips on travel and health concerns in the countries you'll be visiting. The United States **Centers for Disease Control and Prevention (✆ 404/332-4559;** www.cdc.gov) provides up-to-date information on necessary vaccines and health hazards by region or country.

For up-to-date travel advisories, log on to the **State Department website** (http://travel.state.gov/travel_warnings.html) or www.fco.gov.uk/travel (in the U.K.); www.voyage.gc.ca (in Canada); or www.dfat.gov.au/consular/advice (in Australia).

OF SPECIAL CONCERN

AIDS   South Africa has more people living with AIDS than any other country in the world—if you're entering into sexual relations, use a condom. There's no real risk that you'll contract the virus from medical treatment.

BILHARZIA   Do not swim in dams, ponds, or rivers unless they are recommended as bilharzia free. Symptoms are at first difficult to detect—tiredness followed by abdominal pain and blood in the urine or stools—but are effectively treated with praziquantel.

CREEPY CRAWLIES   You are unlikely to encounter snakes—they are shy, and, with the exception of puff adders, they tend to move off when they sense humans approaching. If you get bitten, stay calm—very few are fatal—and get to a hospital. Scorpions and spiders are similarly timid and most are totally harmless. To avoid them, shake out clothing that's been lying on the ground, and be careful when gathering firewood. If you're hiking through the bush, beware of ticks; tick-bite fever is very unpleasant, though you should recover in 4 days—to remove ticks, smear Vaseline over them until they let go.

INOCULATIONS   No shots are necessary, unless you're from a country where yellow fever is endemic, in which case you'll need a vaccination certificate. As a general precaution, you might want to make sure your polio and tetanus shots are up to date, and ask your doctor or a travel-health specialist about vaccinations for hepatitis.

MALARIA   Parts of northern KwaZulu-Natal, the Kruger National Park and surrounding reserves, Zimbabwe, and Botswana are all high-risk malaria zones, though some become low-risk areas in the dry winter months (see **www.travelclinic.co.za** for a map). Both Hluhluwe-Umfolozi (KwaZulu-Natal) and the Kruger are usually low-risk areas from May to September (generally this means no medication is necessary, though other protective measures are advisable; see below), but please note that this depends on the rainfall during the previous summer. Always check with a travel clinic or contact malaria@mweb.co.za. Another useful website is www.meditravel.co.za.

Do I need to take drugs?

If you are entering a high-risk zone for the first time, a course of anti-malarial tablets (prophylactic), for which you will need a prescription, is essential. What is prescribed is dependent on your health profile, but the latest anti-malarial drug, Malarone, is the most effective (98%), has the least side effects, and you only have to take it one day before entering a malarial area and continue the course for only 7 days after you leave the area. The downside is at R35 ($4.50) a tablet, taken daily, it's quite expensive, and available in South Africa only at travel clinics (see websites above). Larium is 91% effective but has strong potential side effects so should be started 2 weeks prior to entering the area to allow you to switch if necessary (this should happen within 3 days). Side effects may include depression, anxiety, disorientation, dizziness, insomnia, strange dreams, nausea, or headaches; the principal contraindications are a history of anxiety, psychiatric problems, or epilepsy. If you've taken Larium before, and suffered no side effects, you can start the course 1 week before. If you do suffer side effects, the medication is usually changed to an antibiotic containing Doxycycline—a daily tablet taken 1 day before. Both Larium and Doxycycline need to be taken 28 days after leaving the area—and make sure to take your full course of tablets.

Are tablets enough?
Keep in mind that as no prophylactic is totally effective your best protection is to avoid being bitten. Sleep under a mosquito net if possible, burn mosquito coils or plug in mosquito destroyers if you have electricity; wear loose, full-length clothing, and cover exposed skin with insect repellent.

How do I know if I've got it?
The flulike symptoms—fever, diarrhea, headaches, and joint pains—can take up to 6 months to develop. Consult a doctor immediately—a delay in treatment can be fatal.

What if I'm traveling with kids or I'm pregnant?
Taking medication is not advisable for children under the age of 5 and pregnant women. Your best bet is to choose a malaria-free reserve—the best Big 5 reserves are Pilanesberg and Madikwe in the North-West, Welgevonden in the Limpopo Province, and Shamwari in the Eastern Cape. In the dry winter months, the Kruger and the Hluhluwe-Umfolozi reserve in Zululand (3 hr. from Durban) have a very low risk.

SUN   Remember that the sun doesn't have to be shining for you to burn—wear a broad-brimmed hat at all times, and apply a high-factor sunscreen or total block—at least initially. Wear sunglasses that reduce both UVA and UVB rays substantially, and stay out of the sun between 11am and 3pm. Children should be kept well covered at the beach; it can take as little as 15 minutes for an infant's skin to develop third-degree burns.

STAYING SAFE
IN THE CITIES   The rules are the same as all over the world, though the high incidence of crime warrants extra caution in southern African cities. Always be aware of the people around you, whether you're walking down a busy city street or driving through a deserted suburb—if you sense danger, act on your instincts. Don't flash expensive jewelry or fancy cameras; wear handbag straps across the neck, and keep a good grip on items. Don't walk any of the major city center streets after dark, especially if you're alone. Keep your car doors locked at all times, particularly in Johannesburg (it's a good idea to also lock your room, even in hotels, and don't open the door unless you're expecting someone). Avoid no-go areas like Hillbrow and Berea, the inner-city suburbs of Johannesburg, and find out from your

hotel how to get where you're going and what's been happening on the streets recently. Finally, if confronted by an assailant, keep calm, and don't resist in any way.

With such widespread poverty, you will inevitably have to deal with beggars, some of them children. Money is often spent on alcohol or drugs, and many argue that donating to a relevant charity, such as a street shelter, is a more effective way to combat the problem; if you'd like to donate to a shelter, you can make a deposit into (account name) **Yizani Centre,** ABSA Bank (branch code) 312109, (account number) 4052941173. Some beggars offer services, such as watching or cleaning your car. There is no need to feel intimidated, and how much you decide to tip is entirely personal, though with unemployment running at some 40%, this is the best way to help the many who need the dignity of some semblance of employment as much as your small change.

TOURING THE COUNTRYSIDE
Do not pick up hitchhikers, and if you're on a self-drive holiday, keep a cellphone with you to call the **Automobile Association of South Africa (AA) (℮ 0800/03-3007)** should you break down or the police should you feel under threat. If you are at a remote site or beach, be aware of who is there when you approach the spot, and don't leave your car until you feel safe. Also be aware of anyone approaching a remote site; remain close to your vehicle until you feel safe.

IN THE GAME RESERVES Visitors to the National Parks and reserves should bear in mind at all times that they are in a wilderness area: Even those animals that look cute are wild and should not be approached. If you're on a self-drive safari, make sure you only get out of your vehicle at designated sites. While most rest camps in the national parks are fenced for your protection, this is not the case with lodges and camps situated in private reserves: animals, including dangerous ones like hippos, lions, and elephants, roam right through them. After dark it's essential that you are accompanied to and from your room by a guide. Even when you're in a safari vehicle on a game drive, your ranger will caution you not to stand up, make sudden or loud noises, or otherwise draw attention to yourself. Occasionally, the ranger may leave the vehicle to track game on foot; always remain seated in the vehicle. It is probably not necessary to point out that lions and crocodiles are dangerous; however, you will hear more than once that hippos kill more humans in Africa than any other animal, and you should take this seriously. Hippos may look harmlessly ponderous, but they can move amazingly fast and are absolutely lethal when provoked. Even some of the smaller animals should be treated with a great deal of respect: The honey badger is the most tenacious of adversaries, and even lions keep their distance.

INSURANCE

Check your existing insurance policies before you buy travel insurance to cover trip cancellation, lost luggage, or medical expenses. You're likely to have partial or complete coverage already. The cost of travel insurance varies widely, depending on the cost and length of your trip, your age, health, and the type of trip you're taking. For information on **car-rental insurance,** go to the "By Car" section of "Getting Around," later in this chapter.

TRIP-CANCELLATION INSURANCE Trip-cancellation insurance helps you get your money back if you have to back out of a trip, if you have to go home early, or if your travel supplier goes bankrupt. Allowed reasons for cancellation can range from sickness to natural disasters to the State

Department declaring your destination unsafe for travel. For information, contact one of the following insurers: **Access America** (© 866/807-3982; www.accessamerica.com); **Travel Guard International** (© 800/826-4919; www.travelguard.com); **Travel Insured International** (© 800/243-3174; www.travelinsured.com); and **Travelex Insurance Services** (© 888/457-4602; www.travelexinsurance.com).

MEDICAL INSURANCE Most health insurance policies cover you if you get sick away from home—but check, particularly if you're insured by an HMO. With the exception of certain HMOs and Medicare/Medicaid, your medical insurance should cover medical treatment—even hospital care—overseas. However, most out-of-country hospitals make you pay your bills up front, and send you a refund after you've returned home and filed the necessary paperwork. If you require additional medical insurance,

try **MEDEX International** (© 888/MEDEX-00 or 410/453-6300; www.medexassist.com) or **Travel Assistance International** (© 800/821-2828; www.travelassistance.com; for general information on services, call the company's Worldwide Assistance Services, Inc., at © 800/777-8710).

LOST-LUGGAGE INSURANCE On domestic flights, checked baggage is covered up to $2,500 per ticketed passenger. On international flights (including U.S. portions of international trips), baggage is limited to approximately $9.07 per pound, up to approximately $635 per checked bag. If you plan to check items more valuable than the standard liability, you may purchase "excess valuation" coverage from the airline, up to $5,000. Be sure to take any valuables or irreplaceable items with you in your carry-on luggage. Lost luggage may also be covered by your homeowner's or renter's policy.

9 Tips for Travelers with Special Needs

TIPS FOR TRAVELERS WITH DISABILITIES

While not as sophisticated as those in first-world countries, facilities are generally satisfactory, with a growing number of tourist attractions designed to be disability-friendly. All major airlines can provide assistance, and Avis and Budget offer cars with automatic transmissions and hand controls. Note that many of the national parks, including the Kruger, as well as the KwaZulu-Natal Nature Conservation Service (KN NCS) camps, have specially adapted huts. **Titch Tours** (© 27/21/686-5501; titcheve@iafrica.com) plots tailor-made trips, from car hire to arranging guides, for the physically and visually challenged throughout southern Africa. Other companies specializing in tours throughout the country for travelers

with disabilities are **Flamingo Adventure Tours** (© 021/557-4496; www.flamingotours.co.za), and **Wheelchair Travel Club** (© 011/725-5648/50; wheeltra@mweb.co.za). **Eco-Access** (© 27/11/477-3676) will provide information for self-drive safaris and travel. The **National Council for the Physically Disabled** (© 27/11/726-8040; ncppdsa@cis.co.za) will advise on equipment rental in all the major cities.

You can join the **Society for Accessible Travel and Hospitality** (www.sath.org) for $45 annually, $30 for seniors and students, to gain access to their vast network of connections in the travel industry.

FOR GAY & LESBIAN TRAVELERS

South Africa's constitution outlaws any discrimination on the basis of sexual orientation, making it the most progressive gay policy in the world. Cities are gay-friendly, with Cape Town often called "the gay capital of Africa." (See "The Great Gay EsCape" in chapter 3 for details on gay-friendly accommodations and nightlife, written by Cape Town's most celebrated queen.) More information about gay-friendly or gay-only places and events can be found in the *Pink Map*, a free pocket-size guide available at Cape Town tourism desks or the more comprehensive *Cape Gay Guide*. Or simply contact the official gay info center **Atlantic Tourist Information** (© 27/21/434-2382; www.cape-town.org).

Wanderwomen is a personalized women's-only travel agent; visit www.wanderwomen.co.za or call © 021/683 9215.

Remote rural areas may be less accepting, with both blacks and whites tending to be very conservative, so take care when venturing off the beaten tourist track. Zimbabwean president Robert Mugabe is a virulent homophobic, but establishments at Victoria Falls are safe to visit as a couple.

In the United States, contact the **International Gay & Lesbian Travel Association (IGLTA)** (© 800/448-8550 or 954/776-2626; www.iglta.org), which links travelers with the appropriate gay-friendly service organizations or tour specialists.

TIPS FOR SENIORS
South Africa is not a difficult destination for seniors to navigate, with driving on the "wrong" side of the road probably the most intimidating aspect you'll have to face. Admission prices to attractions are often reduced for seniors (known as "pensioners" in South Africa), so don't be shy about asking for discounts, and always carry some kind of identification, such as a driver's license, that shows your date of birth. Accommodations discounts are unusual; national parks, for instance,

offer special rates, but these tend to be for South African nationals only.

In the United States, members of **AARP** (601 E St. NW, Washington, D.C. 20049; © **800/424-3410** or 202/434-2277; www.aarp.org) offers members a wide range of special benefits, including *AARP The Magazine* and a monthly newsletter and can offers tours through international affiliates like Collette Vacations and Globus.

TIPS FOR FAMILIES
South Africa is regarded as the most child-friendly country in Africa, with plenty of family accommodations options, well-stocked shops, sunshine, safe beaches, high hygiene standards, animals, and babysitters and burgers on tap. Hotels usually provide discounts for children under age 12, and children under age 2 sharing with parents are usually allowed to stay for free. Ages and discounts vary considerably, however, so it's best to check beforehand. South Africa also has a large number of excellent self-catering cottages, hotels, and guest lodges. Bear in mind that most private game reserves will not accept children under age 12, and since prophylactics are not recommended for those under age 5, choose a malaria-free area, or visit during a dry winter (see "Malaria," above).

TIPS FOR STUDENTS
South Africa has a large number of lodges and activities catering to the growing backpacker market—once here, you can contact **Africa Travel Centre** at © **27/21/423-5555** in Cape Town (www.backpackers.co.za; backpack@backpackers.co.za).

Alternatively, become a member of Hostelling International before you leave; contact the South African branch for local bookings (© 27/21/424-2511; www.hisa.org.za; info@hisa.org.za).

10 Getting There

BY PLANE
TO SOUTH AFRICA

You can fly directly to Johannesburg and Cape Town, the major airport hubs in South Africa. From both of these airports you can fly into airports adjoining the Kruger National Park or the surrounding private game reserves in Mpumalanga and the Limpopo Province (many have their own airstrips), and to Durban in KwaZulu-Natal (a 3-hr. drive from the Zululand reserves). Port Elizabeth, the exit or start of a Garden Route trip, is a short flight from Cape Town or Johannesburg. To add Botswana to a trip to South Africa you will have to fly via Johannesburg, then fly to Maun, gateway to the Okavango, or Kasane. Vic Falls can be reached from Kasane, or you can fly to Livingstone or Victoria Falls airport. For details on getting to each province, go to the "Arriving" sections in each chapter.

From the U.S., the only direct flight to South Africa is with **South African Airways (SAA)** (① 800/722-9675; www.flysaa.com) and **Delta Air Lines** (① 800/221-1212; www.delta.com). Both fly directly from New York (JFK) to Johannesburg (at 17 hr., this is the longest nonstop commercial flight in the world), and nonstop from Atlanta to Johannesburg and Cape Town; alternatively you can fly from Washington, D.C., L.A., Miami, or San Francisco via a European capital with a European carrier like Air France or Virgin. This is also how you will fly from Montreal or Toronto.

From the United Kingdom, **SAA** (① 0171/312-5005; www.flysaa.com) and **British Airways** (① 0181/897-4000; www.british-airways.com) offer the most direct flights. **British Airways** (① 800/AIRWAYS; www.british-airways.com) also operates a number of flights from New York to South Africa via London. Connection time is usually no longer than an hour, and flights continue on to Johannesburg, Cape Town, and Durban. **Virgin Atlantic Airways** (① 800/862-8621 in the United States, or 0293/747-747 in Britain; www.virgin-atlantic.com) also flies daily from New York to Johannesburg via London, and offers a few direct flights from London to Cape Town. Alternatively, check out any of the European carriers like **KLM** (① 800/447-4747 in the United States, 08705/074074 in the United Kingdom, or 800/505-747 in Australia; www.klm.com), which flies via Amsterdam and **Air France** (www.airfrance.fr), which flies via Paris.

From Australia and New Zealand, contact **SAA** (① 02/9223-4448) or **Qantas** (① 13-13-13; www.qantas.com.au/).

TO ZIMBABWE

The easiest way to get to **Victoria Falls International Airport** (① 263/13/4250) is to fly via Johannesburg; contact the following airlines: **SAA** (① 27/11/978-1763; www.flysaa.com) or **British Airways Comair** (① 27/11/921-0222), both fly daily; **Air Zimbabwe** (① 27/11/970-1647; www.airzim.co.zw) is due to resume this flight but you're probably safer booking with the former. Nationwide Air (① 011/327-3000; www.flynationwide.co.za) flies daily directly from Johannesburg to Livingstone, the closest town on the Zambian side of the falls.

Air Botswana (see below) flies from Kasane (gateway to Chobe) to Victoria Falls; alternatively it will fly you from Gaborone and Maun to the capital, **Harare International Airport** (① 263/14/57-5111 or 263/14/57-5188), from where you can fly to Victoria Falls, though with the current political and economic situation this is a rather long-winded way of getting to the falls, and worth dropping from your itinerary if this is the only way to connect.

TO BOTSWANA

No matter where you're coming from, you'll probably have to make a connection in Johannesburg. If the delta is your destination, you'll need to fly to Maun, the airport just south of the Okavango Delta: **Air Botswana** is the only international carrier that flies here directly from Johannesburg—and as of 2003, directly from Cape Town (© **267/686-0391;** fax 267/686-0598 in Botswana; © 27/11/975-3614, fax 27/11/970-4305 in Johannesburg. The toll-free number in the U.S. and Canada is © **800/518-7781,** where it's marketed through Air World Incorporated. In the U.K., call **BA Travel Shops** (© **0207/707-4575**). Air Botswana also flies from Johannesburg to Kasane (ideal to reach the Chobe reserve), and from Kasane to Victoria Falls.

In the unlikely event that you will want to visit Gaborone, the capital, **Air Botswana** also flies from Johannesburg to **Sir Seretse Khama International** (© **267/395-1921**), as do SAA and **British Airways.**

To charter a light aircraft, contact an air-charter company that operates small planes from Maun to all the delta camps. Note that strict luggage restrictions apply: 10 to 12 kilograms (22–25 lb.), preferably packed in soft bags. Charter prices vary, so be sure to compare the following companies' prices for the best deal: **Sefofane** (© **267/686-0778**) is recommended; alternatively **Mac Air** (© **267/686-0635**); **Swamp Air** (© **267/686-0569**); or **Delta Air** (© **267/686-0044**).

FINDING THE BEST AIRFARE

Keep in mind that high season for the Okavango is in winter (June/July–Sept/Oct), and for South Africa in summer (Sept/Oct–Apr)—during peak season (Dec–Feb) it can be difficult to get a flight at the last minute. A great way to see the country is to travel overland from, say, Johannesburg or Hoedspruit/Nelspruit (in Big-Game Country) to Cape Town via Durban; or to drive the Garden Route, then fly back from Port Elizabeth to Cape Town. Purchasing an "open-jaw" ticket will allow you to arrive in one city and depart from another.

The benefits of researching and booking your trip online can be well worth the effort in terms of savings and choice. These days, Internet users can tap into the same travel-planning databases that were once accessible only to travel agents. Sites such as **Travelocity, Expedia,** and **Orbitz** allow consumers to comparison shop for airfares, access special bargains, book flights, and reserve hotel rooms and rental cars.

BY BOAT

Safmarine, a container-ship operator, offers berths for up to 12 fare-paying passengers on its Tilbury, United Kingdom, to Cape Town, Port Elizabeth, and Durban routes. Book through © **01/703/33-4415,** fax 01/703/33-4416, in the United Kingdom; or © **27/21/425-2470,** fax 27/21/421-7868 in South Africa.

PACKAGE & ESCORTED TOURS

Before you start your search for the lowest airfare, you may want to consider booking your flight as part of a travel package such as an escorted tour or a package tour.

Escorted tours are structured group tours, with a leader. The price usually includes everything from airfare to hotels, meals, tours, admission costs, and local transportation. *Note:* Since escorted tour prices are based on double occupancy, the single traveler is usually penalized.

Package tours are simply a way to buy airfare and lodging, or book a safari, at the same time. For far-off destinations like South Africa or Botswana, they can be a smart way to go; by using a reputable operator, you put your trip in the hands of someone who knows the area well enough to help you plan the best vacation for your interests. Note that you will pay for the operator's expertise, however, and this book is designed to help you create your own great itinerary.

Packages vary widely. Keep in mind that though we recommend companies based in Africa, it is usually easiest to book their services through a representative in your home country. Most of the U.S.- and U.K.-based operators listed below and elsewhere in the book represent several reputable African-based companies. For more safari and tour operators, also see individual chapters, particularly the Botswana chapter, which covers the best in the business.

Companies specializing in top-end safaris and southern Africa trips include **Abercrombie & Kent** (www.abercrombiekent.com), **Ker & Downey** (www.kerdowney.com), **Uncharted Outposts** (www.uncharted outposts.com), and **Orient-Express Safaris** (www.orient-express.com). For tours covering southern and eastern Africa, the following U.S.-based companies are highly recommended:

South African–born Julian Harrison is the extremely knowledgeable proprietor of the excellent **Premier Tours** (© **800/545-1910;** www.premier tours.com; info@premiertours.com)—he was named one of *Condé Nast Traveler*'s Top Travel Agents in the U.S. in 2003—and offers safaris that range from the do-it-yourself, eco-conscious, participation type to high-end luxury, and combines these with general sightseeing trips to suit the individual. Premier also acts as an air

consolidator and offers some of the lowest airfares to Africa.

For safari-specific trips, particularly to Botswana, the highly recommended **Wilderness Safaris** (© **27/ 11/883-0747;** www.wilderness-safaris. com) specializes in putting together excellent value-for-money itineraries that cover visits to a variety of Botswana camps and/or Zimbabwe and/or great beach and birding destinations in KwaZulu-Natal. They are recommended for the quality of their guides (and staff in general) and—with a maximum of eight guests on any safari—the quality of the experience.

Another good local company is **Pulse Africa** (© **27/11/327-0468;** www.africansafari.co.za), specialist tour planners to eastern and southern Africa as well as the Indian Ocean Islands—the staff has an excellent eye for quality accommodations and will put together anything from gastronomic and horticultural tours to fishing and horseback safaris.

Born Free Safaris is another good operator with trips from the Cape to northern safari locales, though their moderate/budget options are not as good as those suggested in this book (12504 Riverside Dr., North Hollywood, CA 91607; © **800/372-3274;** fax 818/753-1460; www.bornfree safaris.com).

Alternatively, take a look at **"South African Stories"** on www.southafrica tourism.com; this connects you to www.goway.com, which offers itineraries like the affordably priced "Cape & Kruger" (in mid-2003 this 11-day itinerary cost only $1,899, including airfare from New York), as well as a large cross section of the most interesting ways to travel in South Africa.

For those travelers who prefer the freedom of independently customizing and booking their trip online, e-gnu offers soup-to-nuts trip implementation to exotic locales. Among their offerings are luxury bush lodges and wilderness camps in South Africa, Botswana, and Zimbabwe (www.e-gnu.com).

11 Getting Around

With a well-maintained and well-organized road system, a good range of car-rental companies, and the best internal flight network on the continent, a combination of flight and road travel is recommended in South Africa—that is, you overland to a certain point and then fly out. If you have time on your hands, nothing beats the romance of rail—if you can afford it, steam into Johannesburg or Cape Town on the Blue Train (see below). At the other end of the scale, those with a tight budget can opt to travel by bus: The major intercity bus companies are reliable for long-distance hauls, and some are fairly flexible; for this, the Baz Bus, which offers a hop-on, hop-off service on interesting routes throughout the country, is unbeatable.

Traveling in Zimbabwe and Botswana is not as straightforward—public transport is unreliable, roads can be bad, fuel in Zimbabwe can be scarce, and help can take a long time coming in the event of a road emergency. Safest, particularly with limited time, is to fly directly to your intended destination with transfers prearranged.

BY PLANE

If you have limited time to cover Africa's large distances, flying is your best bet, though internal flights can be very expensive. The good news for anyone planning to fly around the country: As a result of pressure created by the budget airline **Kulula.com** (www.kulula.com), South African Airways (SAA) is now slashing many of its fares (some as much as 40%) on established routes. These seats book up fast; the easiest way to book is online at www.flysaa.com.

Domestic airlines servicing all of the major cities in South Africa are SA Express and SA Airlink (both domestic subsidiaries of SAA; © **27/11/978-1111;** www.flysaa.com); Nationwide (© **27/11/390-1660;** www.flynationwide.co.za); BAComair (© **27/11/921-0222;** www.ba.co.za), and relative newcomer Kulula (© 086-158-5852; www.kulula.com)—the latter specializes in discounted fares and is well worth looking into, though the cheaper seats on busy routes book up fast.

BY CAR

Given enough time, this is by far the best way to enjoy South Africa—you wind along relatively empty roads through some of the most spectacular scenery in the world. Certainly in urban centers you'll need a car (or taxi) to get around, because public transport in the cities is generally not geared toward tourists and can be unsafe (though Cape Town is slowly getting its act together). All the major car-rental companies have agencies here, and there are a host of local companies as well. All offer much the same deals, but cars are in big demand and short supply during the busiest period (Nov–Jan), so book well in advance.

Prefer a home on wheels? **Britz Africa** (© **27/11/396-1860;** fax 27/11/3961937; www.britz.co.za) offers fully-equipped camper vans and four-wheel-drive vehicles, and will pick you up in your vehicle from the airport. Britz currently charges R1,015 ($125) a day for a double-cab four-wheel-drive pickup for between 5 and 20 days.

CAR RENTALS You'll need a driver's license to rent a car—your home driving license is good for 6 months—and most companies in South Africa stipulate that drivers should be a minimum of 21 years (in Botswana you must be 25 or older). Armed with a letter of authority from the rental agency, vehicles rented in South Africa may be taken into Botswana and Zimbabwe, though this requires 72 hours' notice, and additional insurance charges are applicable. You can leave the vehicle in these countries for a fee; in South Africa, you can hire a one-way rental car to any of the major cities. It's best to pre-book your vehicle. The following major companies have branches in South Africa:

Avis (© **800/331-1212** in the United States; © **800/TRY-AVIS** in Canada; © **0990/900-500** in the United Kingdom; © **1800/22-5533** in Australia; © **09/526-2847** in New Zealand; © **0800/021-111** in South Africa; www.avis.com).

Budget (© **800/527-0700** in the United States; © **0800/181-181** in the United Kingdom; © **1300/36-2848** in Australia; © **09/375-2222** in New Zealand; © **0861/01/6635** in South Africa; www.budget.com).

Hertz (© **800/654-3131** in the United States; © **0990/996-699** in the United Kingdom; © **13-30-39** in Australia; © **09/309-0989** in New Zealand; © **27/21/386-1560** in South Africa; www.hertz.com).

CAR-RENTAL INSURANCE

Before you drive off in a rental car, be sure you're insured. Hasty assumptions about your personal auto insurance or a rental agency's additional coverage could end up costing you tens of thousands of dollars—even if you are involved in an accident that was clearly the fault of another driver.

Even if you already hold a private auto insurance policy, coverage probably doesn't extend outside the United States. Before you leave, find out whether you are covered in the area you are visiting, whether your policy extends to all persons who will be driving the rental car, how much liability is covered in case an outside party is injured in an accident, and whether the type of vehicle you are renting is included under your contract.

Most major credit cards provide some degree of coverage as well—provided they were used to pay for the rental. Terms vary widely, however, so be sure to call your credit-card company directly before you rent.

ON THE ROAD IN SOUTHERN AFRICA

GASOLINE   Fuel is referred to as "petrol" and is available 24 hours a day in major centers. At press time, one liter cost approximately R3.86 (45¢) (4 liters is approximately 1 gal.). Gas stations are full serve, and you are expected to tip the attendant R2 to R5 (25¢–65¢). *Note:* Credit cards are not accepted as payment.

ROAD   CONDITIONS   AND RULES   In South Africa, you'll find an excellent network of tarred roads, with emergency services available along the major highways; you cannot rely on this sort of backup on road conditions in Zimbabwe or Botswana. Driving in all three countries is on the left side of the road—repeat the mantra "drive left, look right," and wear your seatbelt at all times; it's mandatory, and in any case, driving skills on the road vary considerably. A broken line means that you may pass/overtake; a solid line means you may not. Generally the speed limit on national highways is 120kmph (75 mph), 100kmph (62 mph) on secondary rural roads, and 60kmph (37 mph) in urban areas.

BREAKDOWNS   The **Automobile Association of South Africa (AA)** extends privileges to members of AAA in the United States and the Automobile Association in Britain. The local emergency toll-free number is © **0800/03-3007.**

BY TRAIN

Spoornet (© **086-000-8888**) runs most of the intercity rail services; ticket

We Only Have One Week: Where to Go?

The 7- to 9-night itineraries below hit the highlights of the various parts of the country for first-time visitors. If you plan to stay longer than a week, combine or extend any of the below itineraries.

- **The Best of the Cape Coast** Spend 3 nights in **Cape Town** or the **Winelands** (all within 45 min. from Cape Town airport), and spend one day driving the mountainous coastline (see "Peninsula Driving Tour" in chapter 3) and another exploring the lush vineyards and sampling the terrific wines. On the fourth day, drive to **Swellendam** traveling via the coastal route to the whale-watching haven of **Hermanus** (see chapter 4) where you could lunch before traveling to historic Swellendam for the night. From Swellendam or Montagu you travel to **Oudtshoorn.** Spend the night here and traverse the Swartberg pass to **Prince Albert** in the morning; but first prize is to spend the night in this tiny hamlet. Cross back into the **Klein Karoo** via Meyeringspoort, possibly stopping for lunch at Jemima's (Oudtshoorn) and then continue on to **Wilderness** or **Knysna.** Spend 2 nights here, taking in the indigenous forests, lagoons, and deserted beaches. Catch a flight from Plettenberg Bay or George back to Cape Town or Johannesburg to fly home (or to go on safari). Alternatively, take the 3-hour drive to see the Big 5 at **Shamwari Game Reserve,** or book into the luxurious **Hacklewood Hill** (Port Elizabeth) and do a day trip to **Addo Elephant Park.** *Note:* You may want to delete the Winelands from this trip during the winter months (May–Aug), when the region experiences its highest rainfall.
- **The Wonders of the World** Spend 2 nights in **Cape Town,** then overnight on the **Blue Train** (or **Rovos Rail**) and trundle up to **Johannesburg/Pretoria.** Fly to a private game reserve drive adjoining **Kruger National Park** for 2 nights (preferably Singita or Royal Malewane), then transfer via Maun to an **Okavango Delta camp** in Botswana. Stay here a minimum 2 nights (if you can stretch it to 4 you should consider transferring to another camp in the delta), then fly to **Vic Falls** (possibly via Kasane) before returning to Jo'burg to fly home.
- **The Best of Southern African Wildlife and the Coast** Fly to Maun and spend 4 nights in Botswana's **Okavango Delta** on safari, moving between 2 camps offering "dry" and "wet" activities. From here, fly to Richards Bay in KwaZulu-Natal, and transfer to **Rocktail Bay** for 2 days of beach walks and snorkeling. (If you're a keen bird-watcher, transfer to **Ndumo** private game reserve instead.) Transfer to spend 1 night in **Durban** and discover the delights of South Africa's most multicultural city, or to **Cape Town,** arguably the most beautiful city in the world. If this is the first time you've ever been here, you will need to extend your stay by at least 2 more nights.

prices for first class are comparable to a bus ticket to the same destination. Second class costs considerably less, but is inadvisable from a comfort and safety point of view. Coupes in first class take only two people, making them ideal for couples. Note that the journey from Johannesburg to Cape Town takes 27 hours—longer than the bus.

If the journey is as important as the destination, splurge on what was voted the World's Leading Luxury Train at the 2001 World Travel Awards: The famous **Blue Train** (© 27/12/334-8459; www.bluetrain.co.za) is a luxury hotel on wheels, and currently runs between Pretoria/Johannesburg and Cape Town, as well as making a few trips along the Garden Route. Travel through beautiful scenery, dining on fine food in plush surroundings (marble en-suite bathrooms, fabric-lined wardrobes, a personal butler to take care of your every need). Another luxury option is the beautifully restored Edwardian carriages of **Rovos Rail** (© 27/12/421-4020; www.rovos.co.za). Rovos covers the same routes as the Blue Train, as well as a number of exciting options, like the 13-day journey to Tanzania or the 9-day journey to the Kruger, Durban, Garden Route, and Cape Town.

If you like the romance of rail, but can't face the steep fares, book the new Premier Class coupe from Cape Town on **Shozolozo,** South Africa's main line passenger services (© **086-000-8888**). The train arrives from Cape Town every Wednesday (and departs for Cape Town from Pretoria/Johannesburg every Thurs), and costs R1,485 ($185) per person one-way (all inclusive).

BY BUS

The three established intercity bus companies are **Greyhound, Intercape,** and **Translux.** There's not much to choose between them, though Greyhound offers a pass to frequent users. Johannesburg to Cape Town takes approximately 19 hours. An alternative to these is the **Baz Bus,** which offers a flexible hop-on, hop-off scheme for backpackers and covers relatively inaccessible areas—definitely the best way to explore the Garden Route, Eastern Cape (including the Wild Coast), Drakensberg, St Lucia, and the Mpumalanga reserves if you can't afford a rental car or guided tour. The two most popular routes are Cape Town to Port Elizabeth (the Garden Route) at a cost of R720 ($88) one-way; and Cape Town to Johannesburg via Drakensberg or Big-Game Country at a cost of R1,650 ($205) or R2,020 ($250) respectively. Prices are one-way, and there's no time limit on this hop-on hop-off ticket.

- **Baz Bus National** (www.bazbus. com) In Cape Town, © **27/21/439-2323;** fax 27/21/439-2343.
- **Greyhound** (www.greyhound.co. za) In Johannesburg, © **27/11/276-8500;** in Cape Town, © **27/21/505-6363;** in Port Elizabeth, © **27/41/363-4555;** in Durban, © **27/31/309-7830.**
- **Intercape** (www.intercape.co.za) In Pretoria, © **27/12/654-4114;** in Cape Town, © **27/21/380-4400.**
- **Translux** In Johannesburg, © **27/11/774-3333;** in Pretoria, © **27/12/315-2333;** in Cape Town, © **27/21/449-3333;** in Port Elizabeth, © **27/41/507-1333;** in Durban, © **27/31/361-8333.**

12 Tips on Accommodations

The choice of accommodations can make or break a holiday, and with South Africa's current popularity this is one area worth tying up before you leave. The selection in this book covers a wide variety of budgets, but all share the common ability to delight, be it because of a fabulous location, special decor, or beautiful views. If, however, you have trouble deciding without a photograph, the following is highly recommended: **Portfolio** (www.portfolio collection.com) brings out an attractive range of free booklets profiling the full spectrum of options across the country. The "B&B Collection" offers fair to excellent budget options, some in quite luxurious surroundings. In the "Retreats Collection" the focus is upmarket guesthouses; top of the range is the "Country Places Collection," which includes some of the best game lodges in the country. Each review comes with at least one photograph. You can order these booklets or utilize Portfolio's reservations service by calling ✆ **27/11/880-3414** or e-mailing collection@iafrica.com. Other companies worth checking out are **Superior Choices** (www.superior choices.com) and **Exclusive Getaways**

(www.getaways.co.za), both of which profile upmarket properties (including game lodges).

Portfolio, Superior Choices, and Exclusive Getaways all have game lodges in their collections, but if a safari is the primary reason you're heading south, you'd be well advised to take a look at the excellent selection in **Classic Safari Camps of Africa** (www.classicsafaricamps.com).

Note: South Africa has a great selection of self-catering options—good for families or for those wishing to prolong their stay—and thanks to restaurant delivery services in most urban centers, you won't even have to cook. See individual chapters for suggestions or go to **www.farmstay.co.za** for more off-the-beaten-track options.

FAST FACTS: South Africa

For "Fast Facts" for Zimbabwe and Botswana, see chapters 9 and 10, respectively.

American Express **In South Africa**   Report card loss to the Johannesburg branch at ✆ **27/11/359-0200.** Other branches are located in Cape Town, Durban, Port Elizabeth, Pretoria, and Richard's Bay.

Banks & ATM Networks See "Money," earlier in this chapter.

Business Hours Shops are generally open from Monday to Friday, from 8:30 or 9am to 4:30 or 5pm, and Saturday from 8:30am to 1pm. In smaller towns, they often close between 1 and 2pm. Many of the larger shopping malls (like the V&A Waterfront) are open from 9am to 9pm daily. South African "cafes" (local mini-marts) are usually open from 7am to 8pm daily; some stay open until 10pm. Public offices open at 8am and close at 3:30pm, from Monday to Friday. Bank hours are usually from Monday to Friday from 9am to 3:30pm, and Saturday from 8:30am to 11am. Banks often closed from 12:45 to 2pm in rural areas.

Currency See "Money," earlier in this chapter.

Drugstores Drugstores are called "chemists," or pharmacies; ask the local tourism bureau for directions, see city listings, or look under "pharmacies" in the Yellow Pages.

Electricity Electricity in southern Africa runs on 220/230V,50Hz AC, and sockets take round- or flat-pinned plugs. Most hotel rooms have sockets for 110V electric razors. Bring an adapter/converter combination, but also be aware that many bush camps do not have electricity at all.

Embassies & Consulates The U.S. embassy in Pretoria is located at 877 Pretorius St., Arcadia, Pretoria, ✆ **27/12/342-1048**. Other offices are in Johannesburg, ✆ 27/11/644-8000; Cape Town, ✆ 27/21/421-4280; and Durban, ✆ 27/31/305-7600.

Emergencies Ambulance: ✆ **10177** or 999. Police: ✆ **10111**. Fire: Consult the front pages of the local telephone directory for brigade numbers.

Holidays See "When to Go," earlier in this chapter.

Information See "Visitor Information," earlier in this chapter.

Language There are 11 official languages in South Africa, but English dominates as the lingua franca here, as well as in Botswana and Zimbabwe. It's often a second language, though, so be patient, speak slowly, and keep a sense of humor.

Liquor Laws Most liquor stores (called "bottle stores" in South Africa) are closed on Saturday afternoons and Sundays.

Maps See "Getting Around," earlier in this chapter.

Newspapers The weekly *Mail & Guardian* (www.mg.co.za) is one of the most intelligent papers and comes out every Friday with a comprehensive entertainment section. Local papers include the *Star* or the *Sowetan* in Johannesburg, the *Cape Argus* in Cape Town, the *Natal Mercury* in Durban, and the *Eastern Province Herald* in Port Elizabeth. *Business Day* is South Africa's version of the *Wall Street Journal* or *Financial Times*.

Magazines **Getaway** (www.getawaytoafrica.com) is an excellent monthly magazine that covers destinations throughout Africa and is well worth purchasing for cheap accommodations listings and up-to-date information. *SA City Life* carries entertainment listings for all three major cities as well as features of local interest. *Eat Out* (www.eat-out.co.za), *Wine Magazine Top 100 Restaurants Guide* (www.winetoday.co.za), and *Style Restaurant Guide* (www.stylemagazine.co.za) cover top restaurants in South Africa. The CNA and Exclusive chains sell these as well as international press and magazines.

Police Call ✆ **10111**.

Taxes A value-added tax (VAT) of 14% is levied on most goods and services; check that it's included in any quoted price. Foreign visitors can claim VAT back on goods over R250 ($30) by presenting the tax invoice (make sure it has a VAT registration number on it) together with their passport at a VAT refund office (airports, selected shopping centers, and visitor bureaus) before departing. Call ✆ **021/934-8675** to find out where and hours.

Telephone & Fax For telephone tips, see " Phone Home: Calling to and from South Africa," above. If you have problems getting through to anyone, or need a new number, use the directory assistance service by dialing ✆ **1023** for numbers in South Africa, and ✆ **0903** for international numbers. Be patient, speak slowly, and check spellings with your operator.

Pay phones require a minimum of 80¢ for a local call; because hotels often charge a massive markup, it's worth purchasing a telephone card (used in specific pay phones) for international calls—these card pay phones are also often the only ones working. Cards are available from post offices and most news agents, and come in units of R20 ($2.50), R50 ($6.25), R100 ($12.50), and R200 ($25).

Vodacom has 24-hour desks at all major international airports offering mobile phones for rent—a recommended option if you haven't pre-booked your entire holiday.

Time Zone   South Africa is 2 hours ahead of GMT (that is, 7 hr. ahead of Eastern Standard Time).

Tipping   Add 10% to 20% to your restaurant bill, 10% to your taxi. Porters get around R4 (50¢) per bag. There are no self-serve garages; when filling up with fuel, tip the person around R2 to R5 (35¢–60¢). It's not unusual to leave some money for the person cleaning your hotel room. Be generous if you feel the service warrants it—this is the best way to alleviate the poverty you may find distressing.

Useful Telephone Numbers   **Computicket** (*©* **27/11/340-8000** in Johannesburg; *©* 27/83/915-8000 in Cape Town and Durban) is a free national booking service that covers cinema and concert seats, as well as intercity bus tickets; payment can be made over the phone by credit card. In South Africa, call directory assistance at *©* **1023** for numbers in South Africa, and *©* **0903** for international numbers.

Water   Tap water is safe to drink in all city and most rural areas. Always ask in game reserves.

Weather   You can see what tomorrow's weather will be in every region at www.weathersa.co.za. Alternatively, call *©* **082 162**.

3

The Mother City:
Cape Town & the Winelands

Cape Town, the oldest port in southern Africa, is regularly heralded as one of the most beautiful cities on earth. The massive sandstone bulk of Table Mountain, often draped in a flowing "tablecloth" of clouds, forms an imposing backdrop to the city while pristine, uncrowded beaches line the cliff-hugging coast. Mountainous slopes sustaining the world's most varied botanic kingdom (some 9,000 species strong) overlook fertile valleys carpeted with vines, and minutes from the city center you can spot zebra and wildebeest grazing unperturbed by the hubbub below. A global hot spot (*Newsweek* rated it as one of the world's 8 new meccas, and in a recent BBC poll, the city ranked fifth in "50 Places to See Before You Die"), the city feels—and is—very different from the rest of Africa.

Situated in the far southwestern corner, Cape Town is physically separated from the rest of the continent by a barrier of mountains. The hot, dry summers and cool, wet winters are Mediterranean, while the Atlantic Ocean is as frigid here as it is off the coast of Maine.

Unique, too, is the Cape's architectural heritage—Cape Dutch homesteads, neo-Gothic churches, Muslim minarets, and English-inspired Georgian and Victorian buildings speak of the influences of a multifaceted colonial past.

Inevitably, colonialism has left its mark on the residents of Cape Town as well; the majority of the population is made up of the mixed-blood descendants of European settlers, Asian slaves, and indigenous people. This Afrikaans-speaking group is referred to as the "coloureds," a divisive designation conferred during the apartheid era, when they were relocated behind Table Mountain into the grim eastern interior plain known as the Cape Flats. Since the scrapping of influx control in 1986, this area has seen phenomenal growth, and today squatter towns form a seamless ribbon of cardboard-and-corrugated-iron housing that most visitors only glimpse on their way from or to the airport. Cape Town's newest residents come from the poverty-stricken Eastern Cape, others from as far afield as Somalia, Angola, and Mozambique, making it one of South Africa's fastest growing cities—and unfortunately, the gangster-ridden Cape Flats have made it the most violent, a situation that city manager Wallace Mgoqi is trying to address by investing R145 million in urban renewal projects. Although violent crime is mostly contained in these areas, visitors to Cape Town should take the same precautions they would in any large city.

Many who come to Cape Town choose to just whip straight out from the airport to the Winelands, where you can stay amid some of the best-preserved examples of Cape Dutch architecture in the area and sample award-winning wines. This is a great area in which to base yourself if you're looking for a relaxing, rural escape, with the bright lights of the city a mere 60-minute drive away; the coastal town of Hermanus, "capital" of the Whale Coast, a 70-minute drive away; and the lakes, lagoons, and forests of the Garden Route an easy 4- to 5-hour drive along the N2.

1 Orientation

ARRIVING

BY PLANE   Cape Town International Airport (② 021/934-0407) is comfortable and efficient, and is now served by 21 national and international airlines. The unprecedented popularity of the destination during the 2002/2003 season led to some delays; if anyone is picking you up ask them to call ② 021/937-1200 to check arrival times. (*Note:* If you've arrived early or are waiting for a connection, you can now relax in a Rennies Travel "Premier Club" lounge which offers the same facilities as a First Class lounge; entry costs R80/$10 in the international terminal and R42/$5 in the domestic terminal.) The airport is a 22km (13 ½-mile) drive from the center of town, so it should take no longer than 20 to 30 minutes to get into the city and surrounds (set aside twice that time during the evening rush hours of 4–6pm). The **Magic Bus Shuttle** (② 021/934-5455, mbuscpt@passenger.co.za) offers a door-to-door service; from the airport to the city center costs a minimum of R140 ($18); ideally, you should book this a day or two in advance. If you have any problems, contact Sean Casey (② 082-954-4867; seancasey12@hotmail.com), who offers the same service for similar rate. You'll find taxis directly outside the terminals; the same trip costs in the region of R160 ($20), but make sure you agree on a price upfront. Car-rental desks are located inside the arrival terminals, and a bureau de change stays open for international flights, though the rates aren't always the best, so use an ATM instead.

BY CAR   If you're traveling directly from Johannesburg, you will drive in on the N1, traveling past the Wineland's area of Paarl. From Port Elizabeth, via the Garden Route, you'll approach the city center on the N2, passing Stellenbosch in the Winelands. The N2 splits into the M3 (the highway that connects the southern suburbs to the City Bowl suburbs) and Eastern Boulevard, which joins the N1 as it enters the perimeter of town. The entrance to the Waterfront is clearly signposted off here.

BY BUS   The main intercity buses, **Greyhound, Intercape,** and **Translux,** all terminate at the junction of Strand and Adderley streets. Note that the **Baz Bus**—a minibus service aimed at backpackers—offers a more flexible hop-on, hop-off option throughout the country. (See chapter 2 for regional numbers.)

BY TRAIN   The luxurious **Blue Train** (② 021/449-2672) and **Rovos Rail** (② 021/421-4020) roll in to Cape Town station from Johannesburg/Pretoria and at certain times of the year from the Garden Route; see chapter 2 for details. If you love rail travel, a charming alternative (and certainly more affordable) is to book a Premier Class coupe from Johannesburg/Pretoria on **Shozoloza Mail** (② 086-000-8888), South Africa's main line passenger services. The train departs for Cape Town from Pretoria/Johannesburg every Thursday (and departs for Johannesburg/Pretoria every Tues) and costs R1,485 ($185) per person one way (all inclusive). It's worth noting that the bus is quicker, albeit not as comfortable (the Trans-Karoo to Jo'burg is 25 hr., and the bus takes 18 hr.).

VISITOR INFORMATION

You'll find a **Cape Town tourism desk** at the airport (✆ **021/937-1234;** International terminus open 7am–5pm daily; domestic 8am–midnight daily), but the best place to gather information is at **Cape Metropolitan Tourism** 🎯🎯🎯 (✆ **021/426-4260;** www.cape-town.org; Mon–Fri 8am–6pm, Sat 8:30am–2pm, Sun 9am–1pm). Located in the Pinnacle Building, at the corner of Burg and Castle streets, this is the best bureau in South Africa, with a great number of knowledgeable staff on hand to assist with anything from specialized tour bookings to transport queries and general information. Also present is a wine bar where you can do wine tastings and arrange for exports, a foreign exchange desk, a VAT desk (to claim back the VAT on your purchases; see planning chapter for details), and an excellent Internet cafe. There are literally hundreds of brochures, but look for the series of special interest maps—from "Arts & Crafts Map" to the "Pink Map," there's something to suit everyone. Shuttles to top attractions (see "Getting Around," below) as well as city walking tours depart regularly from here.

Note: The **SAA-Netcare Travel Clinic** (✆ **021/419-3172;** www.travel clinic.co.za), which offers expert advice and medical services (inoculations, malaria tablets) should you be traveling farther afield, has moved to Fountain Medical Centre on Adderley Street. **MTI Medi-Travel International** offers a similar service, and is perhaps more conveniently located in the Waterfront Clocktower (✆ **021/419-1888;** www.meditravel.co.za).

CITY LAYOUT

Cape Town lies on a narrow peninsula that curls southward into the Atlantic Ocean. Its western and eastern shores are divided by a spinal ridge of mountains, of which Table Mountain is the most dramatic landmark. The city center, located on the western shore, is known as the **City Bowl,** the "bowl" created by the table-topped massif as backdrop, flanked by Devil's Peak to the east, and the embracing arm of Signal Hill to the west. Suburbs on the slopes face north to overlook the city center and harbor, where you'll find the **Victoria & Alfred Waterfront,** situated at the icy waters of Table Bay. Within easy striking distance from both the City Bowl and the Waterfront are the dense built-up suburbs of **Green Point** and **Sea Point.** Moving farther south, the western slopes of the Cape Peninsula mountain range slide almost directly into the sea, and it is here, along the dramatic coastline referred to as the Atlantic seaboard, that you can watch the sun sinking from Africa's most expensive real estate. Of these, the beaches of **Camp's Bay** and **Clifton** 🎯 are the most conveniently located— reached from the City Bowl via Kloofnek, they are a mere 10- to 15-minute drive from the city center.

Traveling along the Atlantic seaboard is the most scenic route to Cape Point, but the quickest route is to travel south along the eastern flank of the mountain, via the M3, past the **southern suburbs** of Woodstock, Observatory, Rondebosch, Claremont, Wynberg, Kenilworth, Bishopscourt, and Constantia (the closest wine-producing area to the city, some 30 min. away), and then snake along the False Bay seaboard to the Point. These eastern slopes, which overlook False Bay (so called by early sailors who mistook it for Table Bay), are the first to see the sun rise, and have price tags still affordable for locals.

East of the peninsula are the **Cape Flats,** where the so-called "Cape coloureds" live (see "The Coloured Class: A New Race" in the "Appendix: South Africa In Depth"), and the **"black suburbs"** of Guguletu, Langa, Nyanga, and

Khayalitsha, reached via the N2. The N2 also provides access to the airport and the Winelands, which lie north of it. **Stellenbosch,** unofficial capital of the Winelands, is just over an hour's drive from the center of town, and from here the pretty valley of **Franschhoek,** some 85km (53 miles) northeast of Cape Town, is reached via the scenic Helshoogte Pass. A quicker route to Franschhoek is via the northern-bound N1, the highway that connects Cape Town to **Paarl,** a 40-minute drive from the center of town.

Pick up a free city map at the tourism office or consider investing in a detailed street atlas like **"Mapstudios A–Z Streetmap,"** sold at most newsagents.

Finally, if you get lost, don't despair—with Table Mountain as a visual guide, it's difficult to stay lost for long.

NEIGHBORHOODS IN BRIEF

City Bowl ✿✿ Within striking distance of the Waterfront, beaches, and Winelands, and in easy reach of most of the city's best restaurants, this is the most convenient place to stay. Opt to stay in the one of the elegant guesthouses on the mountain slopes of the upmarket suburbs of Oranjezicht, Higgovale, and Tamboerskloof, with excellent views of the city and harbor.

Victoria & Alfred Waterfront The Waterfront ✿✿ is considered one of the most successful in the world, and one of Cape Town's top attractions. Hotels have glorious sea and mountain views, and many shopping, dining, and entertainment options are right at your doorstep; but you'll pay for the privilege of staying here (the cheap options aren't worth it), and it's a little out of touch with the rest of the city.

Mouille Point, Green Point, Sea Point These border the Waterfront, and as such are also conveniently close to the city, with a number of value-for-money options. The beachfront has been largely ruined by the construction of dense high-rise apartments, and pockets along the Main Road are hangouts for hookers and drug dealers. This area used to be the heart of Cape Town's nightlife, and there are still a number of excellent restaurants on

Main Road, but exercise caution after dark.

Atlantic seaboard ✿✿✿ If you're looking for a beach holiday, there is only one place to be: the Atlantic seaboard, where Table Mountain drops steeply into the ocean, creating a magnificent backdrop to the seaside "villages" of Bantry Bay, Clifton, Camps Bay, Bakoven, and Llandudno. Besides offering the most beautiful beaches (of which Camps Bay is the most accessible), you'll find gorgeous people strutting their stuff on these pristine, fine white sands, and awesome sunsets.

Hout Bay Surrounded by mountains, this charming town has its own harbor, and marks the start of the breathtaking **Chapman's Peak Drive** ✿✿✿ (scheduled to reopen in early 2004), which snakes past Noordhoek, Kommetjie, and Scarborough before reaching the Cape Point Nature Reserve. These seaside towns have retained a quaint villagelike feel, but are a little far from the city's attractions and restaurants.

False Bay Distance from city attractions and the Winelands is also the drawback of these suburbs, which are (driving south to north) **Simon's Town** ✿, Fish Hoek, **Kalk Bay** ✿, St James, and Muizenberg. The sea is a few degrees warmer on this side of the mountain, however, and because this part of the coast faces east, dawn can be breathtaking, though at the expense of any sunsets.

Southern suburbs The two worth highlighting are Observatory and Constantia. **Observatory** (less than 10 min. from town), with its quaint Victorian buildings and narrow streets, offers a number of good restaurants and an interesting bohemian feel—its proximity to both the University of Cape Town and Groote Schuur hospital makes for a particularly eclectic mix of people. Considered less brash than the Atlantic seaboard, the oak-lined streets and old, established mansions of **Constantia** ✹✹ are arguably the city's most exclusive addresses, with the lush surrounds of the Cape's oldest wine-producing area attracting the rich and famous.

Cape Flats This is where the majority of "coloureds" (the apartheid name for people of mixed descent) live, many forcibly relocated from District Six (a now-razed suburb adjacent to the city) by apartheid policies. The residents of the Cape Flats suffer from high unemployment and a lack of cohesive identity and hope, and the area has become a fertile breeding ground for gangster-run urban terrorism, further complicated by the rise of Pagad (People Against Gangsterism and Drugs), though a number of recent arrests appear to have staunched the latter's ironically violent methods. Even farther east are the "black suburbs" (historically referred to as "townships") of Guguletu, Langa, and Nyanga, and the vast shantytowns of Khayalitsha (visible from the N2 as you drive into town from the airport). To get a balanced view of Cape Town, a visit to these areas is recommended; see "Getting Around," below, for township tours.

Winelands No trip to Cape Town would be complete without at least a day spent here; indeed, many prefer to stay here for the duration of their visit—Cape Town lies no more than an hour or so away, the airport 45 minutes. The university town of **Stellenbosch** ✹✹ is the cultural center of the Winelands, and its oak-lined streetscape offers the greatest sense of history. However, **Franschhoek** ✹✹✹—reached via either Stellenbosch or Paarl—is located in the prettiest of the wineland valleys, and is considered the Wineland's cuisine capital; if you visit only one wine-producing region, make sure it's Franschhoek. Deciding where to stay is ultimately a matter of availability; places situated on wine estates with views of the vineyards and mountains are most desirable. The town of **Paarl** is not as attractive, but the surroundings, on gracious wine farms and old estates, offer great accommodations options.

Northern suburbs With their kitsch postmodern palaces and endless "first-home" developments, these suburbs don't really warrant much attention. However, if you're heading north to see the West Coast you should consider stopping at Blouberg Beach for the postcard view of Table Mountain across the bay. To reach Blouberg Beach, take the R27 Marine Drive, off the N1.

2 Getting Around

Contained by the mountain, the city center is small enough to explore on foot. Public transport in Cape Town is marginally better than that in other South African cities—trains will take you to the southern suburbs and False Bay beaches, and buses to the Waterfront, Sea Point, Camps Bay, and Hout Bay.

However, to explore the Atlantic seaboard, Cape Point, or the Winelands, you're better off renting a car.

BY PUBLIC & PRIVATE TRANSPORTATION

BY TRAIN   If you're heading to the southern suburbs, Paarl, or Stellenbosch, contact **Cape Metropolitan transport information** (⦿ **0800-656-463**) for routes and fares. Trains however are not always reliable, clean, or safe; choose first-class cars with other occupants, and watch your bags. A recommended trip is the spectacular cliff-hugging route along the False Bay seaboard to Simon's Town aboard **Biggsy's Restaurant Carriage & Wine Bar** (⦿ **021/449-3870**), with breakfast, lunch, or snacks en route; the return from the city station takes 2 ½ hours; tickets are R24 ($3) per person, excluding drinks and meals. Breakfast is an extra   R28 ($3.50) ("champagne" breakfast R43/$5), lunch is R65 ($8), and snacks run at about R15 ($1.95)

BY BUS   The most useful way to get around the city is with **Cape Town Explorer,** a hop-on, hop-off bus that visits the city's top attractions, departing from the tourism offices from 10am to 3pm (see "Organized Cruises & Tours," below). Municipal buses depart from the center of town (principal terminals are around the Golden Acre shopping center on Adderley St.) to various points of interest including Sea Point and Hout Bay. Contact **Golden Arrow** (⦿ **080-121-2111** or 021/934-0540) for routes, times, and fares. A **V&A Waterfront bus** (⦿ **021/408-1000**) leaves from Adderley Street (in front of the station) every 15 minutes from 6am to 11pm daily; the trip costs R2.10 ($25¢); alternatively head for the tourist bureau where shuttles are regularly departing (maximum 10 min. wait) for the Waterfront (R15/$1.95), Kirstenbosch (R40/$5), Table Mountain cable car (R30/$3.75), and airport (R100/$13 for one; R130/$16 for two; can arrange pickup from hotel).

BY CAR   Cape Town is a relatively car-friendly city with a minimum of traffic jams and enough parking lots to warrant driving into town—try the **Picbel Arcade** (entrance off Strand St.), **Golden Acre Parking Garage** (entrance off Parliament St.), the **Pay & Display** on the Grand Parade (entrance off Buitenkant St.), or the **lot** opposite **Heritage Square** (entrance off Shortmarket St.). It can be difficult to find parking on the street, but if you do you'll need to purchase an Addo parking card; look for the city police (dressed in black and white uniforms), who will assist. Self-appointed "parking attendants" will offer to watch your car; although you are under no obligation to reward these irritants, it is customary to tip those who are clearly hired by local businesses (they will have some form of uniform or hand over a card) in the area on your return; R2–R5 (25¢–60¢) is adequate.

There are numerous car-rental companies in Cape Town. For a cheaper deal, try **Easy Rent-A-Car** (⦿ **021/424-3951**), **Value** (⦿ **021/696-2298**), or **Swan** (⦿ **021/465-4729**). For a one-way rental to another province you'll have to use a company with nationwide offices, such as **Avis** (⦿ **021/424-1177**); **Budget** (⦿ **021/418-5232**); **Hertz** (⦿ **021/400-9630**); or **Imperial** (⦿ **021/421-5190**). **Felix Unite** (⦿ **021/670-1300**) acts as a rental broker and gives good-value fixed-rate deals. To feel the wind in your hair, rent a beach buggie ⦿ **084-428-4443** or a classic Cadillac convertible ⦿ **021/423-1800;** www.motostars.com) and tool stylishly along the coast.

BY TAXI   Much cheaper than a metered taxi are **Rikkis,** which keep prices down to R9–R15 ($1–$1.95) by continuously picking up and dropping off

---

Fun Fact **Bumper Cars**

The accident-prone minibus taxis, which transport the majority of South Africans, are known as **Zola Buds**, after the barefoot runner who careened into Mary Decker in the 1984 Olympics. It's worth noting that those servicing the City Bowl and Camps Bay areas are usually in much better shape and offer a cheap and convenient way to get around. To hail one, simply step into the road and stick your finger in the air.

---

passengers en route. These open-sided, three-wheeled vehicles will drop you off anywhere in the City Bowl, the Waterfront, or Camps Bay; call ✆ 021/423-4888 for a pickup anywhere in these areas (or hail one) from 7am to 7pm, weekdays, Saturday 8am to 4pm.

Metered taxis don't cruise the streets looking for fares; you'll have to phone. It's expensive, but it's also the best and safest form of transportation after dark. Contact **Sea Point Taxis** (✆ 021/434-4444; R8/$1/km) or **Marine Taxis** (✆ 021/434-0434; R9.50/$1.25/km).

BY BIKE   Hire a Harley (✆ 021/434-2603; www.harley-davidson-capetown.com; R1,000/$125/day) or get off the road and hire a mountain bike from the **Beach Club** (✆ 021/438-0066) in Camps Bay or from **Downhill Adventures** (✆ 021/422-0388) in town. **Rent 'n Ride** (✆ 082-881-1588) supplies bicycles as well as rollerblades and jet skis.

ORGANIZED CRUISES & TOURS

Note that these tours concentrate on the city and immediate surroundings; for tours farther afield, like four-wheel-drive journeys up the West Coast, or whale and dolphin safaris on the Whale Coast and Garden Route, see chapter 4.

BY BOAT   One of the best vantages of Cape Town is undoubtedly from the sea. Tours cost from R30 ($3.75) per person depending on the duration and destination, with a sunset cruise from the harbor to Clifton highly recommended (R150/$19). The **Boat Owner and Charter Association** (call Ms. Pollet: ✆ 021/418-0134) offers a large range of vessels to cater to all interests, but it's worth highlighting the following enterprises: the **Waterfront Boat Company** (✆ 021/418-5806) has a 58-foot gaff-rigged schooner called *Spirit of Victoria* that cruises the Table Bay and Blouberg area, and a luxury motorboat, *Condor,* that cruises to Clifton Bay. Or you can set sail for Clifton on *Tigresse* (✆ 021/424-1465), a luxury catamaran. For personalized yachting charters, contact Jan (✆ 082-830-3501). Or get your pulse racing and strap up with **Atlantic Adventures** (✆ 021/712-5497) who set off at 120km/h across Table Bay in a rubber duck. **Drum Beat Charters** (✆ 021/791-4441) and **Circe** (✆ 021/790-1040) both offer 40-minute trips from Hout Bay Harbour to see the Cape fur seals on Duiker Island.

BY BUS   A large number of operators offer driving tours of the city and its surrounds—recommended companies that offer tours in minibuses include **African Eagle** (✆ 021/464-4266), **Legend Tours** (✆ 021/697-4056), and **Mother City Tours** (✆ 021/448-3817).

Topless Tours (✆ 021/511-1784) offers tours aboard an open double-decker bus—its **Cape Town Explorer** (R80/$10) is a great way to orient yourself; catch it from 9:30am at Cape Town Tourism, and hop on and off at any of the designated points along the 2-hour city tour, which includes the cable car, Signal Hill, and Camps Bay. Last round is at 5:15pm December through February; 3pm March through November. **Hylton Ross** (✆ 021/511-1784) and **Atlas** (✆ 021/460-4700) are long-standing operators offering a variety of half-day, full-day, and four-day tours. To choose, check the selection at www.hylton ross.co.za.

BY AIR   For an aerial tour of the city or peninsula, contact **Court Helicopters** (✆ 021/934-0560) or **Civair Helicopters** (✆ 021/419-5182). **Cloud 9 Air Charter** (✆ 021/434-9994) offers shark-viewing flights along the Whale Coast; **Federal Air** (✆ 021/934-1383) offers scenic flights as far afield as Bushmanskloof game reserve in the Cederberg (see chapter 4); **Aquilla** (✆ 021/712-1913) takes to the sky in microlights; and **ThunderCity** (✆ 021/934-8007) caters to adrenaline junkies with expensive tastes—an hour ride in one of their fighter planes costs from R28,000 ($3,500).

TOWNSHIP TOURS   For a more holistic view of the still essentially segregated Cape Town community, a township tour is essential. The tourism bureau will put you in contact with a "Trail of Two Cities" operator: A tour initiated for the 2002 World Summit on Sustainable Development, this introduces the visitor to some of the interesting entrepreneurs working in the poorer areas of the city, from the likes of Golden Nongawuza, who, after a vivid dream, started making flowers from discarded cans in his Khayalitsha shack, to Victoria Mxenge, who has a group of previously homeless women cultivating arum lilies. **Tana-Baru Tours** (✆ 021/4240719) and **Grassroute Tours** (✆ 021/706-1006) provide insight into the Cape Muslim culture of the Bo-Kaap and the forced removals from District Six, and also takes you through the predominantly black communities of Langa, Gugulethu, and/or Khayalitsha. **One City Tours** (✆ 021/ 387-5351) and **Thuthuka Tours** (✆ 082-979-5831) concentrate on interesting aspects of the black Cape Town community; the latter offers recommended Gospel Tours, Evening Jazz Tours, and Xhosa Folklore Tours, where you can witness ancestor rituals and *"umcimbi"* rites. For more on these, see "Cultural Sights: Cape Muslim to Khayalitsha," later in this chapter.

SPECIALIST TOURS   **Daytrippers** (✆ 021/511-4766) specializes in combining hiking, biking, and sea kayaking with sightseeing tours of the peninsula. For **wine tours,** see "Winelands," later in this chapter.

FAST FACTS: Cape Town

American Express Main local offices are in the city center at Thibault Square (✆ 021/419-3085) and at the Waterfront (Shop 11A in Alfred Mall; ✆ 021/419-3917). City center hours are from 8:30am to 4:30pm Monday through Friday, and from 9am to noon Saturday. Waterfront hours are from 9am to 7pm Monday through Friday, and from 10am to 5pm Saturday and Sunday.

Airport See "Arriving," earlier in the chapter.

Area Code The area code for Cape Town and surrounding Winelands is **021.**

Babysitters Contact **Supersitters** (✆ 021/439-4985; R25/$3.15/hour before midnight, thereafter R35/$4.35/hour).

Bookstores For books on Cape Town and South Africa, head for **Exclusive Books** (© 021/419-0905) in Victoria Wharf, Victoria & Alfred Waterfront, open Monday through Saturday from 9am to 10:30pm, Sunday from 10am to 9pm. **Traveller's Bookshop** (© 021/425-6880), also in Victoria Wharf, is also recommended.

Car Rentals See "Getting Around," earlier in the chapter.

Climate See "When to Go," in chapter 2.

Doctors & Dentists Call © 021/671-3634 or 021/671-2924 for a 24-hour referral service. SAA **Netcare Travel Clinic** is located in the Fountain Medical Centre, Adderley Street (© 021/419-3172). **MTI Medi-Travel International** is in the Clocktower, Waterfront (© 021/419-1888).

Driving Rules See "Getting Around," earlier in this chapter.

Drugstores See "Pharmacies," below.

Embassies & Consulates **U.S.:** 4th floor, Broadway Centre, Heerengracht Street (© 021/421-4280); **Canada:** 19th floor, Reserve Bank Building, corner St Georges Mall & Hout Street (© 021/405-2400); **U.K.:** 15th floor, Southern Life Centre, 8 Riebeeck St. (© 021/425-3670).

Emergencies For an ambulance, call © **10177**; for police call © **10111**; in case of fire, call © **021/535-1100**; for a sea rescue, call © **021/449-3500.**

Hospitals **Groote Schuur** (© 021/404-9111) in Observatory is the Cape's largest hospital; **Somerset Hospital** (© 021/402-6911) at the Waterfront may be more conveniently located; however, for immediate attention in more salubrious surrounds you're best off heading for a private clinic (this is why medical insurance is so advisable). **The Chris Barnard Memorial Hospital** (© 021/480-6111) is in the center of town, at 181 Longmarket St. **Claremont Hospital** (© 021/674-4050) is closest to Constantia. Contact **Mediclinic** (© 021/883-8571) if you're in Stellenbosch in the Winelands.

Hot Lines **Automobile Association** (for vehicle breakdown, © **0800/ 01-0101**); **Rape Crisis** (© 021/447-9762 or 083444-1394 after hours).

Internet Access There are numerous Internet cafes all over the city, but the Cape Metropolitan Tourism (see "Visitor Information," above) is probably the most convenient place to surf, given the volume of hard-copy information at your disposal. Alternatively, ask your host for the nearest Internet access.

Maps See "City Layout," earlier in this chapter.

Mobile-Phone Rental You can rent a phone in the International Arrivals terminal at the airport from **MTN Rentals** (© 021/934-3261) or from **Cellucity,** Kiosk 5, Victoria Wharf Centre, Waterfront (© 021/418-1306) for about R15 ($1.95) a day.

Newspapers & Magazines The morning paper, *Cape Times,* and the more sensationalist afternoon and evening paper, *Argus,* are sold at most street corners. You'll find international titles at the Waterfront (see "Bookstores," above.

Pharmacy **Lite-Kem** (© 021/461-8040), at 24 Darling St., opposite the city post office, is open Monday through Saturday from 7:30am to 11pm and Sunday from 9am to 11pm. **Sunset Pharmacy** (© 021/434-3333) in Sea Point Medical Centre, Kloof Road, is open daily from 8:30am to 9pm.

Post Office The central branch is located on the corner of Parliament and Darling streets (℃ **021/464-1700**), on the second floor. Hours are Monday through Friday from 8am to 4:30pm (Wed from 8:30am), and Saturday from 8am to 12pm.

Restrooms The city's large population of homeless people means that the hygiene of public restrooms can be of varying and dubious quality. You're best off going to a coffee shop or restaurant, or visiting a gas station.

Safety Under the banner BUSINESS AGAINST CRIME, the city has installed closed-circuit cameras in town, put a dedicated police force on the streets, and created 24-hour care centers for Cape Town's street children. As a result, crime in the city center has been drastically reduced. This is no reason to let down your guard, however. Muggings can be avoided by taking the same precautions you would in any large city. Be aware of street children, many of whom beg at large intersections. Visitors are requested to give them food or to make a donation to one of the childcare centers rather than provide them with cash, which is more often than not used to purchase drugs. It is inadvisable to pull over and stop on the N2 (the airport highway), and it's worth traveling with a cellphone in case your car breaks down. For detailed advice, pick up a brochure on safety from any tourism office.

Spa/salon treatments There are numerous wellness centers and hotel spas, but if you're in the city and just want a 1- or 2-hour pampering session, the most convenient option, with a wide range of therapies, is the highly-rated **S.K.I.N.** on the Waterfront (℃ **021/425-3551**).

Taxis See "Getting Around," earlier in this chapter.

Weather Call ℃ **082-231-1640**.

3 Where to Stay

As Cape Town's popularity grows, so do its accommodation options, though sadly the top-end options are now a great deal pricier, which may impact on the city's reputation as a great-value destination. The City Bowl suburbs on the slopes of Table Mountain and Camps Bay remain the most popular areas to stay, with most options listed providing great views and/or good access to restaurants, attractions, and beaches. If you're traveling between May and September, it's worth checking on low (or "green") season rates, but with the city's popularity spreading throughout the year, discounted rates may be harder to come by.

Note: The airport is no more than a 20- to 30-minute drive from most hotels, so it's not necessary to move to an airport hotel for early-morning or late-night flights; instead, try to arrange for an early or late check-in to coincide with your flight. All the places listed below will arrange airport transfers.

CITY BOWL

For easy access to sights, top restaurants, and beaches, you can't beat the **City Bowl.** The center itself has one option really worth considering: The elegant boutique-styled **Cape Heritage Hotel** (℃ **021/4244646**) on Heritage Square gives immediate access to some of the city's finest restaurants (see Heritage Square options in "Where to Dine," later in this chapter). Prices range from

Cape Town Accommodations

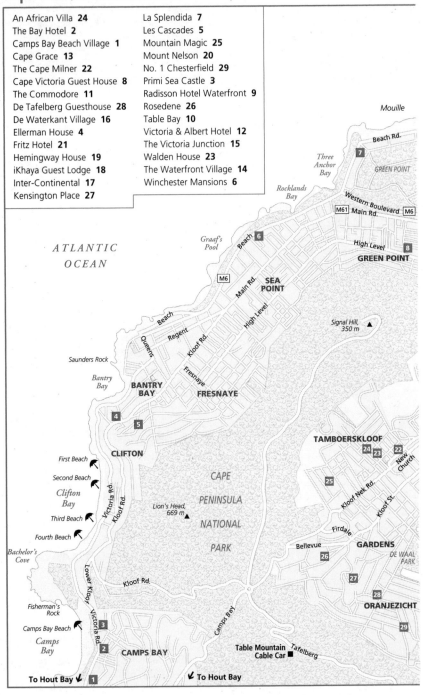

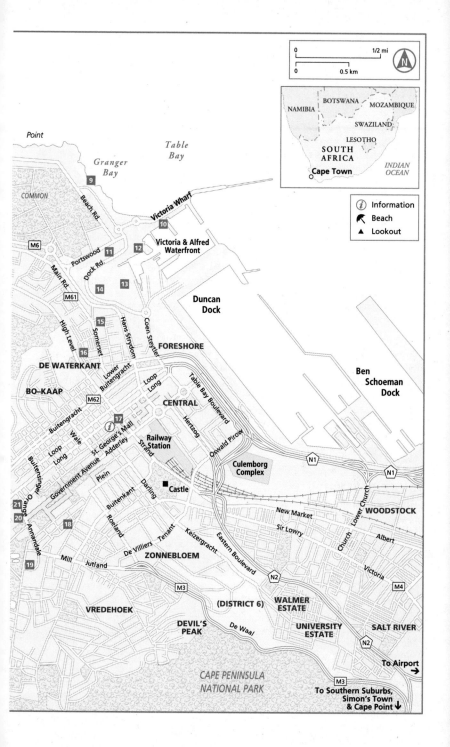

Point

*Granger
Bay*

*Table
Bay*

COMMON

9

Beach Rd.

Victoria Wharf

10

Victoria & Alfred
Waterfront

M6

Portswood

11

12

Dock Rd.

Main Rd.

M61

13

14

Duncan
Dock

Coen Steytler

15

Hans Strydom

High Level

Somerset

FORESHORE

16

Lower Buitengracht

DE WATERKANT

Loop

Long

BO-KAAP

M62

CENTRAL

Table Bay Boulevard

Ben
Schoeman
Dock

Buitengracht

17

Wale

Hertzog

Oswald Pirow

Loop

Long

St George's Mall

Adderley

Railway
Station

Strand

Culemborg
Complex

N1

N1

Government Avenue

Plein

Castle

Buitensingel

Orange

Buitenkant

Darling

New Market

Church

Lower Church

WOODSTOCK

21

Roeland

Keizergracht

Sir Lowry

Albert

20

18

Tennant

Eastern Boulevard

De Villiers

Victoria

Amandale

Mill

Jutland

ZONNEBLOEM

N2

M4

19

M3

(DISTRICT 6)

WALMER
ESTATE

SALT RIVER

VREDEHOEK

DEVIL'S
PEAK

De Waal

UNIVERSITY
ESTATE

N2

CAPE PENINSULA
NATIONAL PARK

M3

To Airport
→

To Southern Suburbs,
Simon's Town
& Cape Point ↓

0 · · · · · · 1/2 mi
0 · · · · · · 0.5 km

N

NAMIBIA

BOTSWANA

MOZAMBIQUE

SWAZILAND

LESOTHO

SOUTH
AFRICA

Cape Town

INDIAN
OCEAN

ⓘ Information

🏖 Beach

▲ Lookout

Tips **Great Self-Catering Options**

Renting an apartment or home can be a good value-for-money option for longer stays, particularly for families, and thanks to Mr. Delivery (see "Where to Dine," later in this chapter), you won't even have to cook. A good budget option is **Mountain Magic** (© 021/424-8577)—three suites with kitchenettes and great views of Table Mountain for a mere R225 ($28) per person. Slightly more expensive (at least in season) but way more hip, **Village & Life** (© 021/422-2721; www.villageandlife.com) runs a variety of accommodations options (almost all featured on their website), in three "villages": **De Waterkant** (City Bowl with harbor views), **Camps Bay,** and the **Waterfront.** All three are within walking distance of coffee shops and restaurants. Another website worth checking out is **www.cliftononsea.com**, which offers an excellent range of accommodations options sleeping from 2 to 10 people, most with pools and all with superb sea and sunset views of Africa's "Cote d'Azure." Prices range from R350 to R1,000 ($44–$125) per person per night. At the top end of the scale (we're talking butlers, chauffeurs, and chefs, should you so require), take a look at **www.capeportfolios.com**.

R1,070 to R1,310 ($130–$160) double; take a look at its tasteful colonial-styled interiors on www.capeheritage.co.za. The **Cape Sun Inter-Continental** (© 021/488-5100; www.interconti.com), a block from the tourist office, has been bought by Holiday Inn. Its brash '70s styling (tons of brass and glass) is amusingly retro; a mountain-facing standard room on the 30th floor offers good value at R899 ($110) double. But my money remains on one of the options located in the suburbs situated on the mountain slopes with fabulous views of the "Bowl"—of the accommodations listed below, **De Waterkant Village** is the vibiest choice, and **Mount Nelson, Hemingways,** and **Kensington Place** the classiest. **An African Villa** gets the vote for the best value.

VERY EXPENSIVE

Hemingway House ✦✦✦ This (along with Kensington Place) is the most fabulous, romantic boutique guesthouse in the Cape Town. Featuring four plush rooms built around a serene courtyard with pool, the house can accommodate a maximum of eight guests, all of whom have access to the entire house (including a classy English/Provençal country-style kitchen that would delight anyone who actually wants to cook, and an outdoor, undercover lounge adjacent to the pool, furnished with comfortable couches that invite hours of reading, and warmed in the evenings by a wood-burning fire). Despite having no design background, owner Josie has created the kind of environment you find in top interiors magazines, but the many personal touches mean the house has a wonderful lived-in ambience; it feels more like staying in the home of a friend who just happens to have impeccable taste than overnighting in some superchic hotel. If you can bear to tear yourself away from the courtyard, the hotel is within walking distance of the city center attractions. Drawbacks are the fact that it has no view, and it's not exactly cheap; opt for the Garden Suite or Courtyard Bedroom (R1,800/$225)—they're a tad smaller but just as gorgeous (four-poster beds, antiques). If you're traveling with a group, I can't think of a better place to host a house party.

Sno 1 Lodge Street, Cape Town 8001. ©/fax **021/461-1857.** www.hemingwayhouse.co.za. 4 units. R1,800–R2,200 ($$225–275) double, including breakfast. AE, DC, MC, V. **Amenities:** Dining room (chef on request); honor bar; pool; limited room service; laundry. *In room:* TV, video, hair dryer, heated towel rails.

Kensington Place ★★★   This modern boutique hotel, voted one of the top 10 guesthouses in the world by *Tatler*, is situated in a prestigious residential area, with beautiful views of the city, harbor, and mountain. A sense of opulence pervades; each bedroom is the size of a mini suite and has a balcony overlooking the city; ask for one (no. 1, 2, or 3) on the top floor for the best city views. Rooms feature expensive finishes and luxurious fabrics; beds are dressed in pale cotton linen, and bathrooms have underfloor heated marble and custom-made bathtubs. The plunge pool is surrounded with timber decking and has a comfortable outdoor lounge area replete with billowing curtains—a calm oasis from bustling Kloof Street, with its excellent restaurant choices, a short stroll away. Despite its small size, service is excellent. Dinners are provided on request. *Note:* The boutique-styled **Les Cascades** is the seaside alternative (see later in this chapter).

38 Kensington Crescent, Higgovale 8001. © 021/424-4744. Fax 021/424-1810. www.kensingtonplace.co. za. 8 units. High season: R1,700–R2,100 ($210–$260) double. Low season: R1100–R1,300 ($138–$162) double. Rates include breakfast. AE, DC, MC, V. Children 16 and over only. **Amenities:** Pool; 24-hr. room service; massage; laundry. *In room:* TV, DVD, minibar (one room only), hair dryer.

Mount Nelson ★★★   Since opening its doors in 1899 to provide luxury accommodation for the passengers of the Union and Castle lines, the "Nellie," as she's affectionately known, has been the undisputed grand dame of Cape Town's high society. Its enduring popularity and inclusion in numerous top hotel lists (the most recent by readers of *Condé Nast Traveler* as Best Leisure Hotel in Africa) is due to unparalleled service standards, beautifully appointed and large rooms, and 9 acres of mature gardens with all the tranquillity of the country (despite its location 15 min. from the city center). Over the years her image had become a little fusty, but with the acquisition of surrounding properties in the late '90s, some tasteful refurbishing, and the relaxation of dress codes, the likes of U2 and Gaultier mingle with the traditionally gray-haired clientele. A massive breakfast buffet and light meals are served in the **Oasis** restaurant, overlooking the large pool and gardens. The elegant **Cape Colony Restaurant** (see "Where to Dine," later in this chapter) offers more formal dining in a wonderful old-fashioned atmosphere. *Tip:* Do take a look at Ellerman House (later in the chapter) before booking here.

76 Orange St., Gardens 8001. © 021/483-1000. Fax 021/483-1782. www.mountnelsonhotel.orient-express.com. 201 units. R4,660–R5,360 ($575–$665) double; R6,990–R11,060 ($870–$1,400) suite. Dec 18–Jan 5, 7-night minimum stay. AE, DC, MC, V. **Amenities:** 2 restaurants; bar; 2 pools; 2 tennis courts; gym; salon; room service; laundry; squash. *In room:* A/C, TV, DVD, minibar, hair dryer.

EXPENSIVE

The Cape Milner ★★   Totally overhauled 2 years ago, this hotel, aimed primarily at upmarket businessman, film crews, and trendy young globetrotters, is modeled on the top boutique hotels in London and New York. Expect clean, modern lines in shades of gray and white, slick designer furniture, and finishes in dark wood offset by brushed aluminum. Ask for a Table Mountain room (suites aren't as good value) on the top floor if you want a good view of the mountain, but keep in mind that these are on a relatively busy road; the cheaper Signal Hill rooms (interlinked for families) are a little cut off from the hotel but are very peaceful. It's within walking distance of several restaurants and the city center.

2 Milner Rd., Tamboerskloof 8001. ℂ 021/426-1101. Fax 021/426-1109. www.capemilner.com. 57 units. High season (Oct–Mar): R1,050–R1,720 ($130–$210). Low season: R480–R560 ($60–$70). AE, DC, MC, V. **Amenities:** Restaurant; bar; pool; room service; massage; babysitting; laundry. *In room:* TV, A/C, hair dryer.

No. 1 Chesterfield 🌟　Of all the guesthouses situated on the slopes of Table Mountain, this provides the most beautiful setting—a gracious home surrounded by a large, mature garden with oak trees and a pool. The rooms are tastefully furnished and all relatively large; ask for one on the top floor for the city views—the best one comes with its own balcony. One of the first houses in the City Bowl to be converted into a guesthouse, it has recently been taken over by a London family who are in the process of upgrading many of the furnishings and fittings. Overall, it's still a very comfortable option, but if you prefer a more modern look, with a boutique-hotel–type atmosphere, you'd be better off at Rosedene or the Cape Milner (or, for sheer opulence, the similarly priced Cape Heritage Hotel in the center of town).

1 Chesterfield Rd., Ornajezicht 8001. ℂ 021/461-7383. Fax 021/461-4688. www.one-chesterfield.com. 8 units. High season: R1,300 ($160) double. Low season: R880 ($110) double. Rates include breakfast. AE, DC, MC, V. Children on request. **Amenities:** Bar; pool; room service; laundry. *In room:* TV, hair dryer, fans, underfloor heating.

Rosedene 🌟🌟　Perched high above Table Bay, where Table Mountain meets the slopes of Lion's Head, this classy Balinese-themed guesthouse offers good views of the city and mountain. There's also quick access to Camps Bay and Clifton beaches, and to the cableway; and the restaurants at the top end of Kloof Street are just a stroll away. (If you want to order in, the staff will set up a table for you.) Ask for room nos. 8 through 11—situated on the top floor of this two-story building, they have the best views. At R3,000 ($375), a new three-bedroom annex represents good value for a group or family. The small, top-floor patio features a Jacuzzi from which you can watch the cloud "cloth" tumbling down Table Mountain. Rosedene also trades in Bali furniture and artifacts—you may choose to ship home half your room! It's a small lodge, but 24-hour reception ensures that guests' needs are well tended. All in all, this is a good alternative to Kensington Place if you're watching your budget.

28 Upper Kloof St., Higgovale 8001. ℂ 021/424-3290. Fax 021/424-3481. www.rosedene.co.za. 15 units. High season: R1,080 ($135) double; house R3,000 ($375). Low season: up to 40% discount. Rates include breakfast. AE, DC, MC, V. Children by arrangement. **Amenities:** Bar; plunge pool; Jacuzzi; limited business services; laundry. *In room:* A/C (room nos. 8–11), TV, minibar, hair dryer.

MODERATE

Another guesthouse in this price category worth looking at is **De Tafelberg Guesthouse** (www.detafelberg.com; from R700–R1,500/$88–188 double). Situated high up on the slopes of Oranjezicht, the deep balcony (where breakfast is served), pool, and most of the elegantly furnished rooms offer superb views of the city and harbor.

De Waterkant Village 🌟🌟 *Value*　Situated in the oldest residential area of Cape Town, amid partly cobbled streets and quaint Cape Malay architecture, De Waterkant has an almost European feel, and offers some of the best-value options in town. You can choose from over 70 fully serviced self-catering apartments and cottages—either surf the website or specify when booking whether you want a plunge pool and/or a really good view (the luxury category) and whether you prefer modern furnishings or a Cape cottage style. If you don't care to self-cater, a good-value option is the elegantly furnished De Waterkant

House, which has a small plunge pool and lounge overlooking the harbor; book the large Harbour View suite (R820–R940/$100–$118 double, depending on season), which comprises the entire top floor and has stunning views. Staff will stock your cottage with food and other items given prior warning (but be warned that service standards are a little lax—laundry, for instance, can be a problem). The quaint **Village Café** is a pavement deli/coffee shop that serves breakfast and lunch, or you might take a wander to **Dutch,** another charming bistro-style cafe. A host of nightlife options await a stroll away, in Somerset Street.

Note: If the Village is full, contact **De Waterkant Lodge and Cottages** (© 419-1097; www.dewaterkant.co.za).

1 Loader St., De Waterkant 8001. © 021/422-2721 or 021/409-2500. Fax 021/418-6082. www.de waterkant.com. 74 units. Cottages (high season): R780 ($98) standard, R980 ($120) luxury, R2,000 ($250) superior; (low season) R680 ($85) standard, R880 ($110) luxury, R1,500 ($188) superior. De Waterkant House: high season R580–R940 ($72–$118) double; low season from R420 ($52). AE, DC, MC, V. **Amenities:** Pools (some cottages feature private plunge pools, also the De Waterkant House); babysitting; laundry; tourist information center. *In room:* A/C (some cottages), TV, hair dryer.

iKhaya Guest Lodge ⭐ iKhaya means "the home" in Xhosa, and this is exactly how the laid-back atmosphere feels at this Dunkley Square lodge, a 5-minute walk from the city center. A strong African theme pervades: Stone-clad pillars, hand-hewn doors, reed ceilings, ceremonial masks, and rough timber chairs create a look that's third-world chic (if you prefer first-world chic, you're better off at the Cape Milner). Accommodation choices include self-catering apartments and a luxury loft; but unless you need the space, the standard and executive rooms offer real value. The rooms are finished in earth tones, the hand-carved beds are made up with quality linens, and bathrooms have blue-gum floors and brass taps. Each room has its own enclosed patio with chairs; the most popular have a view of Table Mountain (R780/$98) and overlook the Square's bars and restaurants—the Greek restaurant **Maria's** is linked to the lodge.

Wandel Street, Gardens 8010. © 021/461-8880. Fax 021/461-8889. www.ikhayalodge.co.za. 20 units. R730–R7,800 ($90–$985) double; R990 ($112) apartments; R1,280 ($160) loft. Rates include breakfast. AE, DC, MC, V. Children by arrangement. **Amenities:** Restaurant; bar; business services; room service; laundry. *In room:* A/C, TV, hair dryer.

Walden House ⭐ This quiet, turn-of-the-20th-century guesthouse offers stylish rooms in one of the city's oldest residential areas. White features are pre-dominant—from the floorboards to the linen—with many wicker touches. The R850 ($106) rooms are slightly on the small side but comfortable (though men may find them a tad feminine), and with a choice of twin rooms or queen-size beds. The spacious garden suite (R920/$115) offers the best value and is a personal favorite, but the most popular room remains the upstairs **luxury suite,** with a door opening onto the first-floor veranda (which features a good view of Table Mountain). Kloof Street, with its large selection of restaurants, is just a short drive away. While this is a very pretty option, and well-managed, if you're looking for a little more action, De Waterkant House offers comparable accommodation, for less money, in a much more trendy, vibrant area, and the more modern An African Villa is much better value.

5 Burnside Rd., Tamboerskloof 8001. © 021/424-4256. Fax 021/424-0547. www.walden-house.com. 6 units. R850–R1,000 ($106–$125) double; R1,200 ($150) suite. Rates include breakfast. AE, DC, MC, V. Children age 12 and over only. **Amenities:** Limited room service; laundry. *In room:* TV, minibar, hair dryer, heated towel rails, complimentary bottle of wine.

INEXPENSIVE

Unless your taste runs to minimalist, **Parker Cottage** (www.parkercottage.co.za; from R550/$69 double) is another good option—the decor is a little more fussy than the guesthouses listed below, but it's pretty and extremely professionally run. If you're on a serious budget, consider booking a double room in one of the city's first-rate backpacker lodgings: the **Backpack** (© **021/23-4530;** www.back packers.co.za; R275/$34 double; R330/$38 en-suite) is highly recommended. It's clean, with a courtyard, cafe, bar, travel center, shuttle bus, and pool, and an easy stroll from the nightlife and restaurant options along Kloof and Long streets.

An African Villa ★★ *Value* This opened to no fanfare in the closing months of 2002 and is already proving near impossible to get in—the down side of combining superb value with exceptional style. A traditional double-story Victorian semi-detached house in Tamboerskloof, the "villa" has been fabulously transformed by owner Jimmy van Tonder into what he describes as a Zen-Africa look—muted tones and earthy textures offset with playful touches of vivid red. The rooms on the second floor are marginally preferable; some have picture-perfect windows (the bright green lemon trees a great contrast to the soothingly muted interiors), particularly the suite (R700/$88 double) opening onto a narrow balcony overlooking the street. Barring the fact that there is no pool or real view to speak of, the greatest drawback is its sheer popularity, but the good news is that Jimmy has a number of excellent-value accommodations options spread around Tamboerskloof—the **View Suites** ★★ are large self-catering studios and one-bedroom apartments with superb city or mountain views, decorated in Jimmy's inimitable (pre-Zen) playful style; ask for no. 11. Alternatively, his own home, the 1894 **Liberty Lodge,** has four charming B&B units; ask for one of the en-suite rooms on the first floor—they share a balcony with more lovely views of the city. All options are walking distance to restaurants.

Reception for all 3 options at 33 De Lorentz St., Tamboerskloof 8001. © 021/423-2264. Fax 021/423-2274. www.capetowncity.co.za. 12 units. High season: R550–R700 ($69–$88) double. Low season: Ask about discounts. Rates include breakfast. AE, DC, MC, V. **Amenities:** Laundry. *In room:* Some with A/C, TV, hair dryer.

Fritz Hotel ★ *Value* Situated off Kloof Street (the "restaurant strip") on the outskirts of the city (a 5-min. walk to the center), and furnished with Art Deco and '50s pieces, the Fritz Hotel is another bargain. Ask for room no. 6, 7, 12, or 14; these open onto the first-floor veranda, with room nos. 6 and 14 by far the biggest. Each of the patio suites on the ground floor each has a small garden area. Room no. 11 is small but has a great view of Table Mountain from the bed (not the choice for Imelda Marcos though—the cupboard is tiny). Breakfasts and drinks are served in the courtyard, which—like the whole hotel—has a lovely relaxed atmosphere.

1 Faure St., Gardens 8001. © 021/480-9000. Fax 021/480-9090. www.fritzhotel.co.za. 13 units. High season: R500–R650 ($69–$82) double. Low season: R375–R450 ($45–$56) double. Rates include breakfast. AE, DC, MC, V. **Amenities:** Bar; business services; laundry. *In room:* TV, fax, minibar, hair dryer on request.

WATERFRONT
VERY EXPENSIVE

Cape Grace ★★★ *Kids* The Cape Grace is the classiest option in the Waterfront area, and was the hotel of choice when the Clintons were in town (no, they didn't cart any of the furniture off). It was also named the best city hotel in Africa in 2001 and 2002. The difference between this hotel and the Mount Nelson is primarily one of location; the Cape Grace is in a marina, situated on its own promontory and surrounded by water on all three sides, while the Nellie is surrounded by gardens. It also doesn't have the graciousness of the century-old Mount Nelson, and—from an exclusivity point of view—cannot compete with the Ellerman. The luxury (standard) rooms truly are luxurious, both in size and furnishings, with French doors opening onto mountain or harbor views; superior rooms are slightly larger, with walkout balconies. The hotel has recently extended by another floor—here you'll find the highly recommended loft luxury rooms as well as the loft terrace rooms and a penthouse. The two- and three-bedroom suites, with fully equipped kitchens, are ideal for families. The Cape Grace is in fact the most family-oriented luxury hotel in the country: Kids are welcomed with their own cards and gift hampers, and are read stories and provided with milk before bed, and you can rent anything from a car seat to a pram.

The lively **Bascule** bar regularly hosts some great New World DJs, and the newly refurbished restaurant, **one.waterfront,** is regularly voted one of the top restaurants on the Waterfront.

West Quay, V&A Waterfront 8002. ⓒ **021/410-7100.** Fax 021/419-7622. www.grace.co.za. 102 units. High season: R3,700–R3,880 ($450–$485) double; R6,600 ($825) 1 bedroom; R8,650 ($1,080) 2 bedrooms; R8,650 ($1,080) 3 bedrooms and penthouse. Low season: R2,900–R3,680 ($360–$450) double; R5,600 ($700), 1 bedroom; R7,380 ($910) 2 bedrooms; R9,200 ($1,150) 3 bedrooms. All rates include breakfast. Children under age 12 stay free in parents' room. AE, DC, MC, V. **Amenities:** Restaurant; bar; pool; concierge; room service; babysitting; laundry; well-stocked library. *In room:* A/C, TV, minibar.

Table Bay ⭐⭐ Competing with the Mount Nelson, Ellerman, and Cape Grace as the preferred location for the rich and famous, this glitzy hotel is located in a prime position on the Prince Alfred Breakwater—views are standard features here. It doesn't have the sense of exclusivity or privacy of the aforementioned competitors (Michael Jackson is reputed to have stayed here because he wanted to hear his fans chanting in the parking lot), but the service standards are equally high; best of all, it's ideal for shopaholics: the hotel is directly connected to the Waterfront's Victoria Mall. The public spaces (designed by the Lost City team) are superb: The cavernous lobby, renowned for its large floral displays, is finished in marble and teak, and the comfortable lounge area frames Table Mountain with large triple-volume windows. Standard rooms are small and dull; opt for a luxury room or suite (or a room at the Cape Grace instead).

Quay 6, V&A Waterfront 8002. ⓒ **021/406-5000.** Fax 021/406-5767. www.suninternational.com. 329 units. High season: R3,115–R3,885 ($380) double; R5,280–R22,185 ($660–$2,770) suite. Low season: R2,345–R2,920 ($290–$360) double; R3,970–R16,645 ($495–$2,080) suite. AE, DC, MC, V. **Amenities:** 2 restaurants; bar; pool; gym; spa; business services; salon; room service; laundry. *In room:* A/C, TV, minibar, hair dryer.

EXPENSIVE

An alternative to the Victoria & Alfred (but not as well situated) is the **Commodore** (ⓒ **021/415-1000;** www.legacyhotels.co.za; high season: R1,800–R1,850/$225–$230 double; low season: R1,630–R1,850/$200–$230). Located 300m (984 ft.) from the Portswood entrance to the V&A Waterfront, the Commodore offers comfortable rooms at relatively low rates, making it very popular with tour groups. Business-class rooms cost a negligible R50 ($6.50) more than standard rooms in season but feature extras like minibars, are more spacious, and offer the best views.

Radisson Hotel Waterfront ⭐⭐ *Value* The Radisson (formerly the Villa Via) is located on the outskirts of the Waterfront (500m/1,600 ft. from the entrance), but enjoys an exceptional setting—right on the sea. It offers the best value for money on the Waterfront, particularly in winter, but be warned:

Although service is well meaning, standards can lag. That said, almost every room—furnished in dark blues and gold, with a nautical theme—has an excellent sea view. The infinity pool (irritatingly small) is right on the ocean's edge, and two catamarans, moored in the Waterfront, are available for guests' use. **Tobago's,** the hotel restaurant, has an excellent reputation, though new management may change this.

Beach Road, Granger Bay 8002. ℭ 021/418-5729. Fax 021/418-5717. www.radissonsas.com. 182 units. High season: R1,950–R2,150 ($244–$$265) double; R2,450 ($305) suite; R3,650 ($450) 2-bedroom. Ask about low season rates. Children sharing stay free. AE, DC, MC, V. **Amenities:** Restaurant; bar; pool; day membership to the adjacent golf club; complimentary access to a nearby health club; salon and spa; business and secretarial services; room service; laundry. In room: A/C, TV, minibar, coffee- and tea-making facilities, hair dryer.

Victoria & Alfred Hotel ⭐   Situated alongside the Alfred Basin's working dock, in the historic 1904 North Quay warehouse now called Alfred Mall, this hotel is the most centrally located Waterfront choice. (*Note:* Although the Radisson is not as conveniently located, it offers better views, a pool, and marginally better rates; see below.) Bedrooms, dressed in wrought iron and veneer, are disappointingly bland, and go some way toward explaining the favorable rate. They are spacious, though, each featuring a king-size bed. Rooms on the second floor, particularly nos. 225 through 234, have the best views. The **Waterfront Café** has a reasonably good reputation and is particularly popular for breakfast; you can dine alfresco while enjoying the excellent view of Table Mountain. The **Green Dolphin,** one of Cape Town's premier (but pricey) jazz venues, is in the same building, and **Den Anker,** one of the best Waterfront restaurants, is a short stroll away.

Pierhead, Waterfront 8002. ℭ 021/419-6677. Fax 021/419-8955. www.vahotel.co.za. 68 units. R1,760–R2,390 ($220–$295) double. Children age 2–12 years in parents' room R90 ($11). AE, DC, MC, V. **Amenities:** Restaurant; bar; access to nearby health club; regular shuttle bus to city center; room service; massage; babysitting; laundry. In room: A/C, TV, minibar, tea- and coffeemaking facilities, hair dryer, trouser press.

GREEN POINT & SEA POINT

These suburbs are close to town and the Waterfront, but ironically (considering their location at the beginning of the Atlantic seaboard), the lay of the mountain makes access to beaches a little more time-consuming than from the City Bowl. That said, the area offers views of the sea and good value, particularly when compared with accommodations in the adjacent Waterfront. If none of the below appeals, check out the delightful **Cape Victoria Guest House** (ℭ 021/ 439-7721; www.capevictoria.co.za; R595–R1,320/$73–$65), run by excellent hostess Lily (whose architect son converted the building); it has been featured in numerous design magazines.

EXPENSIVE

The Victoria Junction ⭐   Situated a few minutes from the city and the Waterfront, with a number of excellent restaurants and nightlife options in the immediate vicinity (including the best gay club in town), this hotel offers the feeling of being at the heart of Cape Town without being in the city center. A South African version of the New York loft apartment, the Junction features exposed brick walls, industrial steel decor, stylized furniture, and some large original artworks, and is popular with the film industry types who flock to Cape Town in the summer months. Choose between a standard room (ask for a harbor or mountain view on the 4th floor) or one of the lofts on the 5th floor. **The Set** is the hotel's theme restaurant, where fusion food is served under suspended steel frames, booms, and mounted cameras, but for one of the best dining experiences in town, cross the road to **The Restaurant** (see "Where to Dine," later in this chapter). *Note:* You're not close to the ocean, so there are no sea views.

Corner Somerset and Ebenezer roads, Cape Town 8001. © 021/418-1234. Fax 021/418-5678. www.protea hotels.com. 172 units. R1,040 ($130) double; R1,705 ($210) loft apartments (ask for low-season discounts). Children under 16 stay free. AE, DC, MC, V. Amenities: Restaurant; bar; lap pool; access to the nearby Health & Racquet Club; a dedicated shuttle service; salon; room service; laundry. In room: A/C, TV, minibar, hair dryer.

Winchester Mansions 🏛🏛   Built in the 1920s in the Cape Dutch style, this gracious low-slung hotel faces the sea, though a busy road and broad swath of park lie between it and the ocean. The hotel has recently converted its loft space into standard rooms and suites; these feature classy modern interiors, with earthy tones and dark wood. The original standard rooms are furnished in rich colors offset by cream walls, and exude an old-fashioned charm (a few antiques, floral artworks); the best options are the Winchester rooms, though you must specify a sea-facing room (no additional charge). The pool has also been enlarged and a wellness spa added. Incidentally, the Winchester bar and restaurant is very popular with locals, particularly on Sundays, when a jazz brunch is served to the strains of live music in the beautiful colonnaded central courtyard, built around a fountain and encircled with trees. Family accommodation is available.

221 Beach Rd., Sea Point 8001. © 021/434-2351. Fax 021/434-0215. www.winchester.co.za. 53 units. High-season: R1,250–R1,600 ($155–$200) double; R1,600–2,750 ($200–$340) suites. Rates include breakfast. AE, DC, MC, V. Amenities: Restaurant; bar; pool; room service; laundry. In room: A/C (on 3rd and 4th floors), TV, minibar, tea- and coffee-making facilities, hair dryer, undercarpet heating.

MODERATE

La Splendida 🌟 (*Value*)   If you can't afford the Waterfront or Atlantic seaboard, but want to be close to the ocean, this is a great option. Just minutes from the Waterfront and the city center, this small hotel is separated from the sea only by a road, and offers the best value-for-money views in town. The Art Deco exterior wouldn't look out of place in Miami, and the interiors are very chic and comfortable, though the seagrass carpets are to be replaced with tiles. You have your choice of mountain- and sea-view rooms—a sea-view room, is worth the extra R180 ($22); note that the penthouse can sleep four. Pack your in-line skates, as the promenade stretches all the way past Sea Point. Meals are served at the ground-floor restaurant, which opens onto a terrace that features a tiny plunge pool. A potential drawback in winter (June–Aug) is the noise from the foghorn—this is, after all, the closest that boats leaving the harbor come to shore before turning out to sea, and the foghorn makes sure it stays that way.

121 Beach Rd., Mouille Point 8001. © 021/439-5119. Fax 021/439-5112. www.lasplendida.co.za. 22 units. High season: R525–R705 ($65–$88) double; R840 ($105) suite; R960 ($120) penthouse. Low season: R485 ($60) double; R625 ($75) suite; R705 ($88) penthouse. AE, DC, MC, V. Children by arrangement. Amenities: Restaurant/bar; (tiny) pool; room service; massage; babysitting; laundry. In room: A/C, TV, minibar, hair dryer on request.

ATLANTIC SEABOARD

For most visitors to the Cape, waking up to a seascape and strolling down to the beach takes first prize, but you'll need to shell out for the privilege (and book early!). Camps Bay has by far the most options, and offers the city's most easily accessible beach, lined with dozens of sea-facing bars, coffee shops, and restaurants. It's also a mere 10- to 15-minute drive from the center of town. There are numerous B&Bs in the area (check out www.portfoliocollection.com), of which three really stand out: **Atlantic Suites** (www.atlanticsuites-campsbay.com; high season R1,500/$188 double) is the top choice, with two luxurious suites leading out onto a patio with infinity pool and beautiful sea views. **Atlantic View** (www.atlanticviewcapetown.com; R1,000–R2,000/$125–$250 double depending on room) has three sea-facing rooms and one facing the mountains, as well as a great patio featuring an infinity pool and stunning views. **Le Gouverneur** (www.legouverneur.co.za; high season R1,500/$188 double) has five rooms, two of which are sea-facing, and a gorgeous pool area overlooking the Atlantic. Equally gorgeous (we're talking *Wallpaper* shoot) but pricey is the new **Cape Retreat** (www.caperetreat.com; R2,000–R3,000/$250–$375 double), a classy five-roomed guesthouse with distant sea views. If you're on a budget, take a look at **Camps Bay Beach Village** (www.villageandlife.com)—its studio apartments, built around a heated pool, offer great value at R780/$95 double.

VERY EXPENSIVE

The Bay Hotel ⭐⭐   The Bay Hotel's shopping mall architecture is a bad reminder of the 1980s, but if you're a beach lover, the location, directly opposite Camps Bay's palm-lined beachfront, more than makes up for it. All rooms have had a much-needed refurbishment, with modern muted colors replacing the original pastel theme, and are spacious, featuring a small lobby (for unobtrusive room service) and a split-level bed and seating area. Rooms facing the sea are pricey, but because this is the hotel's raison d'être, you should probably shell out or consider one of the cheaper alternatives (like the elegant Atlantic Suites or chic Atlantic View; see above). Service is good (it is, after all, a member of the *Small Luxury Hotels of the World*) though not in the same class as, say, the Ellerman House (see below). A number of restaurant choices are within walking distance.

Victoria Road, Camps Bay 8005. ☎ 021/438-4444. Fax 021/438-4455. www.thebay.co.za. 78 units. High season: R2,150 ($260) non-sea-facing double; R3,240 ($400) sea-facing double; R5,920 ($735) suite; R9,650 ($1,200) penthouse. Low season: R1,290 ($160) non-sea-facing double; R1,940 ($240) sea-facing double; R2,960 ($365) suite; R4,820 ($600) penthouse. AE, DC, MC, V. Children age 12 and older only. **Amenities:** 2 restaurants (including Blues); 2 bars; pool; concierge; salon; room service; massage; laundry. *In room:* A/C, TV, minibar, hair dryer.

Ellerman House ⭐⭐⭐   Situated on a spectacularly elevated site overlooking the Atlantic Ocean and premier suburb of Bantry Bay, this gorgeous Relais & Chateaux member is in a class of its own, and—with only 11 rooms—the most exclusive address in Cape Town. Once the stately residence of Sir John and Lady Ellerman, the house has been meticulously restored to its original early-20th-century splendor, with renovations and additions blending seamlessly. The views, which evoke comparisons with the Riviera, are a feature of almost every window (of which there are many) and balcony, and the sheer grace and style of the place makes you feel like royalty. If you're staying in room no. 6 (no view) or room no. 3 (view, but no balcony), spend your days on the broad patio (where drinks and meals are served) or in the terraced garden with a large pool, from where you can see forever. For a view from your bathtub, book room no. 1. The chefs create each day's menus around fresh produce, and will honor any special requests. Personally, I think it's the best choice to be had in Cape Town.

180 Kloof Rd., Bantry Bay 8001. ☎ 021/430-3200. Fax 021/430-3215. www.ellerman.co.za. 11 units. R3,100–R5,100 ($385–$640) double; R7,250 ($900) suite. Rates include airport transfer, breakfast, laundry, tea/coffee, drinks (except wine and champagne), and ad hoc secretarial services. AE, DC, MC, V. Children age 14 and older. **Amenities:** Dining room; bar; pool; gym; sauna; concierge; business services; room service; massage; laundry; library; wine cellar. *In room:* A/C, TV, minibar, hair dryer.

EXPENSIVE

Les Cascades ★★ *Finds* Situated high on the Bantry Bay cliffs, this beautifully appointed boutique villa exudes the kind of class found at the Kensington in town. Every room is finished in warm, modern earth tones and offers fantastic views of what appears to be the edge of the world. The deluxe rooms are huge, but even the standard rooms are extremely spacious, each with king-size bed, full bathroom, and a private deck area with seating. The dining room-cum-lounge (featuring a classy mix of African, Indian, and Balinese furniture) opens onto a timber sun deck and infinity pool, inviting you to spend hours staring into the horizon. There is always someone on hand to assist guests with anything from tour bookings to arranging lunch and dinner. The biggest drawback is the fact that you have to drive to get to the beach or restaurants.

48 De Wet Rd., Bantry Bay 8005. (C) **021/434-5209.** Fax 021/439-4206. www.lescascades.co.za. 5 units. High season: R1,350–R1,650 ($168–$205) double. Low season up to 40% discount. AE, DC, MC, V. **Amenities:** Dining room/bar; 3 pools; business services; room service; laundry. *In room:* A/C, TV, minibar, hair dryer.

Primi Sea Castle ★ *Kids* Situated directly across the beach, these apartments (all with sea views) are the self-catering, child-friendly alternative to the Bay Hotel. The open-plan living areas, recently redecorated in shades of brown and beige, are pretty tasteless, but feature sleeper couches, and modern, fully equipped kitchens. The sidewalk cafes, restaurants, bars, and Camps Bay supermarket are all within strolling distance. *Note:* If you need to be surrounded with good taste in order to relax, the decor here could be a real drawback; I suggest you take a look at www.lionsview.co.za or www.balibay.co.za, or the many options carried by www.capeportfolios.com and www.villageandlife.com.

15 Victoria Rd., Camps Bay 8005. (C) **021/438-4010.** Fax 021/438-4015. www.castles.co.za. 8 units. High season: R1,725 ($214) studio; R2,150 ($264) 1 bedroom; R3,000–R3,250 ($373–$405) 2 bedrooms; R4,000 ($498) 3 bedrooms. Low season: R760 ($95) studio; R1,000 ($125) 1 bedroom; R1,125–R1,180 ($140) 2 bedrooms; R1,625 ($202) 3 bedrooms. Rates include a continental breakfast. Children under age 12 sharing stay free. AE, DC, MC, V. **Amenities:** Pool (some apts have plunge pools/Jacuzzis); concierge; laundry. *In room:* TV, underfloor heating.

SOUTHERN SUBURBS

If the beach isn't your scene, and you prefer your landscape filled with mountains and trees, you'll find blissful peace in **Constantia,** the wine-producing area closest to the city, some 20 to 30 minutes away (halfway between the city and Cape Point). Closer to town is **Bishops Court** and **Newlands,** home to landmark rugby stadiums and the world's largest rugby museum; it's ideal for sports fans, though much of it is bland middle-class suburbia (though it does have some large, gracious lodging properties that may suit the older traveler). This is not the case in bohemian **Observatory,** a mere 7 minutes from the center of town, and popular with artists, hippies, students, and backpackers.

To get a sense of the location of the following places, see the "Peninsula Driving Tour" map, later in the chapter.

VERY EXPENSIVE

Cellars-Hohenort Hotel ★★ With expansive views of the densely forested eastern slopes of Table Mountain behind, and the valley and mountains towering above False Bay in front, the Cellars-Hohenort is a genteel hotel that would suit the older traveler looking for an out-of-town, cheaper alternative to the Mount Nelson. Antique furnishings and original artworks adorn the original Hohenort manor house; this is also where the best rooms are located. All rooms are comfortably furnished with floral fabrics adorning the king-size or twin beds.

Finds **B&B** *Ubuntu*

To experience real *ubuntu,* the warm spirit of African hospitality, you can arrange to spend a night in one of the city's "townships," or black sub-urbs. Portfolio has approved four B&Bs (**Kopanong, Majoro's, Luyolo's, and Malebo's**), and recommends that you combine your transfer and overnight stay with a **Township Music Tour** (for bookings, call ℭ **021/790-8826** or 021/426-4260).

Considerable pluses are the beautiful 9-acre garden, and the dining; it's a Relais & Chateaux member, and well deserving of this distinction: **The Greenhouse** (where Prince Philip, incidentally, hosted his World Fellowship dinner) is one of the best restaurants in Cape Town (see "Where to Dine," below), and the **Cape Malay Kitchen** provides an excellent introduction to regional cuisine.

P.O. Box 270, Constantia 7848. ℭ **021/794-2137**. Fax 021/794-2149. www.cellars-hohenort.com. 53 units. High season: R2,050–R2,750 ($255–$335) double; R3,600–R4,200 ($445–$520) suite. Low season: R1,950–R2,350 ($244–$290) double; R3,530–R3,600 ($440–$450) suite. Rates include breakfast. AE, DC, MC, V. Children age 12 and over only. **Amenities:** 2 restaurants; 2 bars; 2 swimming pools; full-scale golf green (designed by Gary Player); tennis; salon; room service; laundry; croquet lawn. *In room:* TV.

Constantia Uitsig ★★   Part of the Constantia Wine Route, the aptly named Constantia Uitsig (*uitsig* means "view") has commanding vistas of the surround-ing vineyards and mountains, and there's a calm sense of rural peace on this working wine farm. Even so, it's the food that draws people here: The farm boasts three tip-top restaurants (see "Where to Dine," below), of which **Uitsig** and **La Colombe** are regularly ranked by food critics in their top 10 Cape restaurants. It's wonderful to simply roll back to one of the 16 well-appointed suites dotted in the butterfly- and bird-filled gardens, the Cape Dutch architec-ture echoing that of the 17th-century manor house. Uitsig's lawns extend onto a cricket oval—with its unhindered view of the mountains and distant sea, and attractive Victorian pavilion, it's a popular destination for players and enthusiasts from around the world. *Note:* If Uitsig is full, or if you're a keen golfer, check out the 18-hole championship golf course at **Steenberg Country Hotel** (ℭ **021/713-2222;** www.steenberghotel.com; from R2,150/$265 double), another beauti-fully restored 17th-century wine farm.

Spaansgemacht Road, P.O. Box 32, Constantia 7848. ℭ **021/794-6500**. Fax 021/794-7605. www.constantiauitsig.co.za. 16 units. High season: R2,100–R2,500 ($260–310) double; R3,000–R4,300 ($375–$540) suite. Low season: R1,400–R1,500 ($175–$188) double; R1,800–R2,400 ($225–$300) suite. AE, DC, MC, V. **Amenities:** 2 restaurants; bar; pool; room service; babysitting; laundry. *In room:* A/C, TV, minibar, tea- and coffee-making facilities, hair dryer.

FALSE BAY

This is a very laid-back choice, probably more suited to the older traveler or someone who's been to Cape Town before and loved the naval atmosphere and Victorian architecture of Simon's Town. Staying here, you are well positioned for major attractions like the penguins at Boulders (within walking distance) and Cape Point (some 10 min. away), but it's 40 minutes from the city center. Fam-ilies should definitely consider the **British Hotel Apartments** (www.british-hotel.co.za; R300/$37 per person)—lovely, large old-fashioned apartments in a Victorian-era hotel with sea views. **Simon's Town Quayside Lodge** (off Jubilee Sq., St Georges St.; ℭ **021/786-3838;** www.quayside.co.za; R695–R895/

$85–$110 double) is part of the Simon's Town Harbour development, with a number of shops and Bertha's Restaurant below, right on the water. Most of the rooms, decorated in a pleasant nautical theme, have French doors opening onto beautiful views of the False Bay coast and Simon's Town yacht basin.

4 Where to Dine

For centuries Cape Town has set the table for a varied and increasingly discerning audience, with world-class fare augmented by historical venues and great views. For harbor settings and mountain views, head for the Waterfront; for uninterrupted ocean views and great sunsets, the Atlantic seaboard is tops. Enjoy at least one lunch or dinner in the southern suburb of Constantia or the Winelands, where you can drink in views of the vineyards and mountains along with a selection of fine Cape wines. For people-watching, head for the pavement cafes on historic Greenmarket Square during the day, the nearby Heritage Square at night. If you prefer to browse the streets for dinner, take a stroll along Victoria Road in Camps Bay, the restaurant strip that lines the beachfront—a great place to dine in summer, when the sun sets around 8pm–or head for Kloof Street, which runs down the slope of Table Mountain into Long Street.

If you're setting off for Cape Point, a journey that will take you the better part of the day, try and time lunch at one of the recommended restaurants in the Constantia area, or overlooking the False Bay coast.

Finally, make sure to sample at least one dish inspired by the unique hybrid of Cape cultures. For traditional fare you can't get more authentic than Biesmillah in the Bo-Kaap, but there's more to Cape cuisine than *bobotie* and *denningvleis*. Cape Town's scenic setting and regular influx of cosmopolitan visitors has attracted some of the world's top chefs, many of whom are creating a new and exciting "modern Cape" cuisine, combining local ingredients with elements of the Portuguese, Dutch, French, German, English, Indian, and Malaysian influences that have made up the city's multicultural past. Bon appetit.

CITY BOWL

There is simply not enough space to cover the many superb restaurants concentrated in this area, so a mention will have to suffice in the following cases. Located at 102 New Church St. is the **Blue Danube,** where owner-chef Thomas Sinn is considered one of the top three chefs in Cape Town (he has featured in almost every foodie's top 10 selection since the early '90s), but personally I find his food a little too fussy. Book a table (© **021/423-3624**), and let me know what you think! Newcomer **Madame Zingara,** located on 192 Loop St. (© **426-2458**), is another name you'll encounter when looking for recommendations; owner-chef Richard Griffin has a reputation for originality (his filet with chocolate-chili sauce is legendary), but getting a table here can be difficult, even when you've booked. **Ginja** is another newcomer that keeps getting rave reviews, not

---

Tips Eating In

If you're staying in a B&B or self-catering, contact **Mr Delivery** (© **021/423-4177** in town; © **021/439-9916** in Sea Point; © **021/761-0040** in Constantia) and ask them to drop off a menu. Mr Delivery delivers meals from more than 20 restaurants and takeaway joints (some of which are described below), as well as groceries, directly to your door.

Cape Town Dining

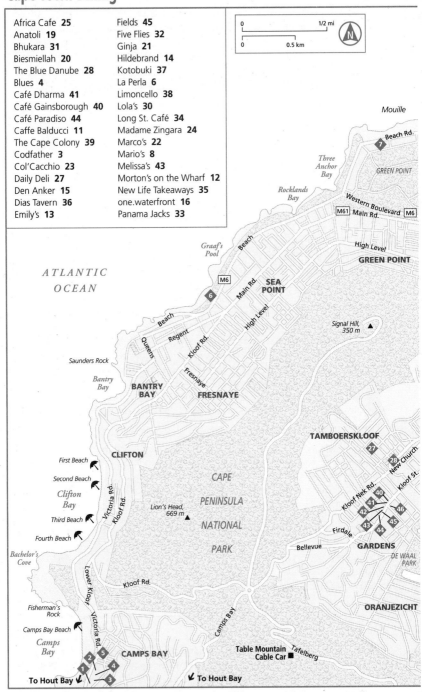

Africa Cafe **25**
Anatoli **19**
Bhukara **31**
Biesmiellah **20**
The Blue Danube **28**
Blues **4**
Café Dharma **41**
Café Gainsborough **40**
Café Paradiso **44**
Caffe Balducci **11**
The Cape Colony **39**
Codfather **3**
Col'Cacchio **23**
Daily Deli **27**
Den Anker **15**
Dias Tavern **36**
Emily's **13**

Fields **45**
Five Flies **32**
Ginja **21**
Hildebrand **14**
Kotobuki **37**
La Perla **6**
Limoncello **38**
Lola's **30**
Long St. Café **34**
Madame Zingara **24**
Marco's **22**
Mario's **8**
Melissa's **43**
Morton's on the Wharf **12**
New Life Takeaways **35**
one.waterfront **16**
Panama Jacks **33**

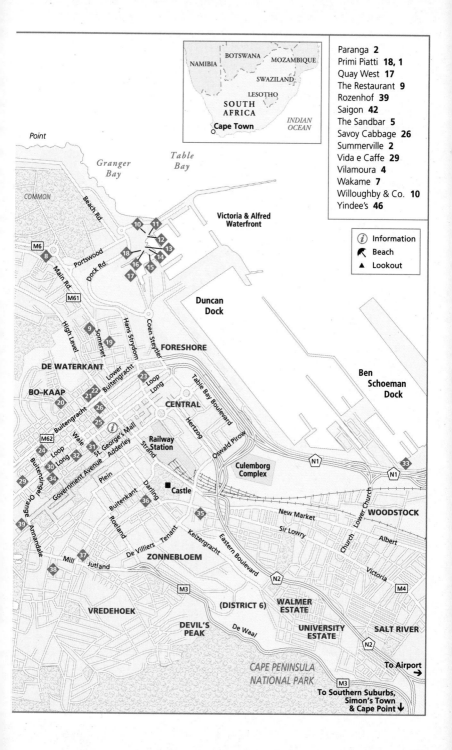

Paranga **2**
Primi Piatti **18, 1**
Quay West **17**
The Restaurant **9**
Rozenhof **39**
Saigon **42**
The Sandbar **5**
Savoy Cabbage **26**
Summerville **2**
Vida e Caffe **29**
Vilamoura **4**
Wakame **7**
Willoughby & Co. **10**
Yindee's **46**

i Information
↖ Beach
▲ Lookout

The Dining Mile

If you like looking at venues before deciding where to eat, take a stroll down Kloof Street. This is the road that runs parallel to Kloof Nek, which takes you up the saddle of the mountain and over into Camps Bay. Aside from the spots reviewed in full, the street has some lively and eclectic dining choices.

Starting at the top, stroll down the hill to **Cafe Paradiso** ✿✿ (110 Kloof St.; ✆ **021/423-8653**), a sprawling terra-cotta villa with Italian-style decor and Mediterranean-style food that will delight those bored with modern haute cuisine. This is an ideal late breakfast or luncheon (it's open all afternoon) or balmy evening venue: book a table under a tree or umbrella on the terrace outside—the interior is dull and you'll miss the view of the city—and peruse the no-nonsense menu; a personal favorite is the tender Greek lamb, served warm on a cold shredded spinach salad and topped with home-made mayo.

Next up, a block down from Melissa's (see review below) and the vegetarian-only Fields, is **Saigon** ✿✿ (corner Kloof and Camp; ✆ **021/424-7669**), an elevated venue with great views that specializes in Vietnamese cuisine (don't miss the crystal prawn spring rolls: steamed prawns, carrots, cucumber, noodles, basil, mint, and peanut sauce). **Cafe Dharma** (68 Kloof St.; ✆ **021/422-0909**), next door, doesn't look like much from the outside, but it's a great spot—an open-plan house around a central courtyard, dressed in heavy Balinese furniture—and highly recommended for a pre- or postdinner drink. The vibe, created by Cape Town's happening, young (mid-20s and up) crowd, is great, but you'll find better food across the road at **Yindee's** ✿✿✿ (✆ **021/422-1012**). According to its loyal following Yindee's is Cape Town's best Thai restaurant.

A little farther down is **Cafe Gainsborough** ✿✿ (64 Kloof St.; ✆ **021/422-1780**), a casual bistro-type restaurant built around an open-plan kitchen. Get there early (no bookings) to grab a table on the sidewalk and enjoy the view of table mountain. The small menu has Flemish overtones.

Numerous takeout joints and casual eateries follow, two of which are worth highlighting: **Café Bardeli** (on Darters Rd., just off Kloof St.; ✆ **021/423-4444**) is a trendy hangout attracting media types and models. Despite this, the atmosphere is relaxed, food is good, and prices low. Behind is **Cohibar** (✆ **021/423-4444**), a London-style cigar bar with leather horseshoe booths. **Vida e Caffe** (34 Kloof St.; ✆ **021/426-0627**) is the trendiest coffee shop in the city, while **Lola's** (228 Long St.; ✆ **021/423-0885**), within walking distance from here (Kloof merges with Long, the heart of backpacker territory), is where, in their own words, "faggy Afro-trash meet to slip sexy music." This stretch offers the city's most vibrant nightlife, particularly in summer (see "Cape Town After Dark," later in this chapter).

least because of its location in a wonderful dilapidated double-volume space on 121 Castle St. (© **021/426-2368**), but here again the fusion food strikes me as rather fussy. If you like pizza, the best topping ever is to be found at **Limoncello,** a tiny restaurant in Gardens frequented by locals rather than tourists; order the ultra-thin, crispy (tomato-free) pizza base, topped with smoked salmon, lemon juice, and fresh rocket (arugula), or opt for the tender squid, fried with chili and garlic (starter or main).

EXPENSIVE

Africa Café ✿✿ AFRICAN   Portia and Jason de Smidt have expanded the cafe to ever bigger premises, beautifully decorated by Portia, but still serve a great selection of traditional dishes from all over Africa. Meals are brought to your table in bowls—a "communal feast" shared in the African tradition—and you can eat as much as you want. Delicious dishes include the Malawi *mbatata* balls (sweet potato and cheese rolled in sesame seeds), West Coast mussels served in a Cape Malay coconut sauce, Tunisian *briouats* (potatoes and garlic in phyllo pastry), Ethiopian *sik sik wat* (lean, succulent lamb in a mild berbere and paprika sauce), Moroccan *zeilook* (aubergine, dhania, and garlic dip), Tanzanian mango chicken (strips of chicken filet, a little tough, in a tangy sauce), South African *ithanga* (pumpkin and cinnamon fritters)—all served with warm Xhosa potbread. Leave space for the Egyptian *basboussa* (semolina cake with almonds and yogurt) and Moroccan almond fritters. There's a great moment when the wooden floorboards start to shake as the ululating staff dance through the restaurant with real unrestrained joy. All in all, it's a rather touristy experience, but still well worth it.

Heritage Sq., 108 Shortmarket St., Cape Town. © **021/483-1000**. Reservations essential. Set-price menu: R125 ($15) per person. Mon–Sat 6:30–11pm. AE, DC, MC, V.

Finds Sampling South African Cuisine

Although recommended, Africa Café essentially caters to the well-heeled Western traveler. If you'd like to sample South African cuisine along with other Africans (for considerably less money), head for the balcony of the **Pan African Market,** Long Street (no phone), for lunch with the traders, or **Marco's Place,** 15 Rose St. (© **021/423-5412**. More touristy, but still authentic, is a meal arranged at **Masande Xhosa Restaurant** (© **021/371-5104**) in Crossroads, or **Lelapa** ("the home") (© **021/694-2681**) in Langa. Masande serves a buffet of *umngqusho nenyama* (samp, beans, and lamb stew), *isonka samanzi* (steamed bread), spinach and pap (porridge) balls, and grilled chicken; Lelapa offers more hard-core African dishes (tripe, for example) tempered with a range of vegetables to assuage Western tastes. Another venue worth considering is the new **Imvelo Xhosa Restaurant** in the Waterfront Clocktower (© **021/421-8666**), not least because almost every element, from the wine choices on offer to decor, is linked to an empowerment initiative. For instance, to boost skills in the industry, the staff was selected not for prior experience but on the basis of personality and passion—with the exception of the chef, Abel Bokwe, who's been fine-tuning his skills for three decades. Recommended choices are the *smoorsnoek* (a fish filet prepared with fresh tomato and onion sauce), followed by ostrich stew and samp.

The Cape Colony ✰✰✰ INTERNATIONAL/MODERN CAPE   Rated one of the top 10 hotel restaurants in the world by *Hotels Magazine USA*, this is by far the grandest of the restaurant options on the Kloof Street strip, and is highly recommended, even if you're only here for a few days, not least because of its location in the grand Mount Nelson. It has a wonderful atmosphere created by the discreet, pampering service, the talented jazz duo who never overwhelm, and the plush, old-fashioned decor—with banquette seating and individual table lamps to create soft pools of light on the impeccable table appointments. Food is flawless, both from a flavor and presentation point of view, thanks to the inspired Garth Stroebel, who creatively mixes traditional ingredients with international preparation styles; the menu changes regularly, but look for Colony classics like smoked crocodile served with spinach, red onion, and samosa wafer, or the ostrich stroganoff with forest mushrooms and fine pasta. The delicately spiced Cape Malay kingklip is served with pickled onion ragout, while soya-cured duck breast with Asian vegetables and barbecue dressing remains a perennial favorite.

Mount Nelson Hotel, Gardens (entrance off Kloof St.). ✆ **021/483-1198.** Main course R75–R120 ($9–$15) dinner. AE, DC, MC, V. Daily 7.30–10pm.

Five Flies ✰✰ FRENCH/INTERNATIONAL   Located in the old Netherlands Club and the adjacent Rembrandt House (which dates back to 1754), this is one of the classiest venues in the Cape. The chef who put it on the map, French-classic-trained Gerard Reidy, is now the consulting chef, but first reports indicate that standards are still high and the delicious combinations unfussy (it may be worth calling to see whether Chef Reidy is in the kitchen; also ask to be seated in a room far from the tour groups who occasionally turn raucous). The menu—which offers any combination of two, three, or four courses for a set price—changes every 3 months, but you can expect dishes like the slow-roasted duck with wok-fried vegetables and Oriental plum sauce; roast kingklip with a basil and pinenut crust and cumin sauce served on grilled red pepper and sweet potato mash; or medallions of beef filet, Wellington-style, with mushroom duxelles, spinach, and hollandaise.

16 Keerom St., Cape Town. ✆ **021/424-4442.** Reservations essential. 2 courses R95 ($12); 3 courses R125 ($15); 4 courses R145 ($18). AE, DC, MC, V. Mon–Sun 12–3pm; daily 7–10:30pm.

Rozenhof ✰✰✰ CONTINENTAL   Located in a house that dates back to 1852, Rozenhof has been delivering the same understated menu since 1984, unfazed by passing fads and the mushrooming of competition. The food is delicious, the service intelligent (waiters have usually served at Rozenhof for some time), and the ambience warm. Diners are seated in one of three rooms, ensuring an intimate experience even when the restaurant is full. Many of the dishes have remained unchanged since the restaurant opened; the cheese soufflé starter with herb-and-mustard cream is a must, as is one of the linefish preparations—almond-crusted on leeks braised in citrus butter is a favorite. The crispy roast

---

Tips **High Tea at the Nellie**

High tea at the **Mount Nelson** is a Cape Town institution: crustless cucumber and salmon sandwiches offset by a vast array of tarts and cakes, all the better to sink into the comfortable armchairs to the sounds of the tinkling piano. It's a wonderful way to experience the grande dame's gracious ambience (✆ **021/483-1198;** R85/$10; 2:30–5:30pm).

Finds Going Local

If you want to feel like a laid-back Capetonian, grab a pavement table at super-friendly **Daily Deli,** 13 Brownlow Rd., Tamboerskloof (© **021/426-0250**), and order the aubergine bake, followed by a piece of cheesecake. If you want to feel like a trendy Capetonian, only a pavement table at **Vida e Caffe,** 34 Kloof St. (© **021/426-0627**), will do. Order a cappuccino and a Quattro (four cheese) muffin or custard tartlet, and watch the city's producers, photographers, film crews, designers, and the like hard at (net)work. Both are open daily, but not at night.

---

duck is also an old favorite; try it glazed with mandarin and ginger and served with a warm orange vinaigrette. The restaurant also offers an extensive, well-chosen wine list.

18 Kloof St., Gardens. © **021/424-1968.** Reservations recommended. Main courses R55–R90 ($7–$11). AE, DC, MC, V. Mon–Fri 12:30–3:30pm; Mon–Sat 7–10:15pm.

Savoy Cabbage ★★ INTERNATIONAL   This stylish restaurant celebrates the European trend for "sophisticated peasant food," and if you like the more interesting cuts of meat, you'll find this one of the country's best. New owner Peter Pankhurst, who took over from Janet Telian in 2002, has changed very little, with the menu dependent on what Peter has picked up at the market. A few stalwarts he dared not remove are Telian's tomato tart; the pear, plum, pepper cheese, and walnut salad; the sweetbreads with lemon, chives, and mushrooms; and the lamb- and rice-filled cabbage rolls poached in broth. The venue—a narrow double-volume L-shape with old brick walls exposed and juxtaposed with glass and steel fittings—is as interesting as the food. The back entrance connects you to Heritage Square's central courtyard—consider an after-dinner drink upstairs at the Po-Na-Na Bar to mingle with Cape Town trendies.

101 Hout St., Heritage Sq. © **021/424-2626.** Reservations recommended. Main courses R65–R90 ($8–$11). AE, DC, MC, V. Mon–Fri 12–2:30pm; Mon–Sat 7–10:30pm.

MODERATE

Bhukara ★★★ NORTH INDIAN   Sabi Sabharwal met his Afrikaans wife in Italy and followed her home, an act of love for which Capetonians are truly grateful. Bhukara was recently voted the best Indian restaurant in the country; certainly it's the city's most stylish (though acoustics can be a bit of a problem when the place is full) and specializes in Mughal food and tandoori barbecues. Meats are tender and the flavors full and vibrant: Make sure you try the legendary butter chicken. Chefs leave no fat on meat and use only the freshest ingredients, including the spices. Their motto, "Only the best will do, whatever the cost," must be what kept Shakira and Michael Caine coming back for more.

33 Church St., Cape Town. © **021/424-0000.** Reservations recommended. Main courses R36–R70 ($4.50–$8.75$) (R130/$16 for prawns). AE, DC, MC, V. Mon–Sat 12–3pm; daily 6.30–11pm.

Biesmiellah ★ Value CAPE MALAY   A number of places offer Cape Malay fare, but none is as authentic as Biesmiellah. Run by two generations of the Osman family in the historic Malay quarter of Bo-Kaap, Biesmiellah has been serving the local Cape Muslim community, and increasingly, tourists, for 2 decades. The *denningvleis,* a sweet-sour lamb cutlet stew, served with saffron rice, almonds, raisins, and mashed potatoes, is recommended, as is the *pienang* curry, a beef cutlet stew prepared with bay leaves. In keeping with Muslim tradition, no alcohol is allowed on the premises. Biesmiellah also offers takeaways—try the *roti* (flatbread) stuffed with cubed mutton.

2 Upper Wale St., Cape Town. © 021/423-0850. Reservations recommended. Main courses R40–R52 ($5–$6.50). AE, DC, MC, V. Mon–Sat 12–10pm.

Kotobuki ★★ JAPANESE   Kotobuki is considered by most aficionados to be Cape Town's best sushi restaurant despite a venue that resembles an old school hall and harsh lighting (though it's worth noting that the options listed below are starting to oust this stalwart from its prized position–perhaps it's their sheer proximity to the ocean!). It's also often closed—if the chef doesn't like the look of the fish that day, he simply won't prepare it. Other top sushi options in the city are **Willoughby & Co.** (© **021/418-6116**) and **Cape Town's Fish Market** (© 021/418-5977) in the V&A Waterfront—although these are located in a mall, many Capetonians won't settle for sushi elsewhere.

Avalon House, Mill St., Gardens. © 021/462-3675. Reservations essential. Rolls (6) R15–R25 ($1.95–$3); two sushi pieces R15–R34 ($1.95–$4.25). Main courses R25–R67 ($3–$8.25). AE, DC, MC, V. Tues–Fri 12:30–2pm and 7–10:30pm; Sat–Sun 7–10pm.

INEXPENSIVE

Col'Cacchio ★★ *(Kids)* PIZZA   If you like your pizza base thin and crispy, Col'-Cacchio is the best in town (though Limoncello and Shoga's are recent contenders; see intro, above). Recommended choices include the Tre Colori (smoked salmon, sour cream, and caviar), and the Prostituto (avocado, bacon, feta, and spinach). Salads are large and fresh (try the smoked chicken and pepperdew), and service is fast. It's a large and laid-back venue (with a child-friendly staff; ask for a bit of dough to "shape and bake"). Col'Cacchio is served by Mr Delivery, so you won't even have to leave home to enjoy it—though the pizzas are definitely best fresh from the wood-burning oven. If you find yourself in the Claremont area, sister restaurant, **Morituri** (214 Main Rd.; © **021/683-6671**), serves exactly the same menu.

Seeff House, 42 Hans Stridom Ave. © 021/419-4848. Main courses R30–R54 ($3.75–$7). AE, DC, MC, V. Mon–Fri 12–2:30; daily 6–11pm.

Dias Tavern *(Value)* PORTUGUESE   This is a bit of a dive, with red plastic chairs alternating with plastic-covered booth seats, but Dias is famous for its delicious steak dishes. Try their *espetada* (chunks of marinated sirloin, skewered and carried, flaming-hot, to the table) or *trinchada* (cubes of sirloin in a garlic and wine sauce). Not the venue for vegetarians, Dias does not bother with vegetables; meals are served with a choice of bread or potatoes. Unless you enjoy eating to the live accompaniment of a wannabe Julio Iglesias, don't dine here on Friday or Saturday evenings. *Note:* If you're craving a meat fix in more salubrious surroundings, **The Famous Butcher's Grill** in the Day's Inn on Buitengracht Street (© **021/422-0880**) is regularly rated one of the top in the country.

27 Caledon St., Cape Town. © 021/465-7547. Main courses R25–R62 ($3–$7.50). AE, DC, MC, V. Mon–Sat 12pm–late.

Melissa's ★★ ITALIAN/DELI   A delicious buffet of eight great salads (roasted beetroot and feta, for example, or baby tomatoes soaked in balsamico with fresh basil and coriander), a selection of two to three quiches (try the roasted vegetables and cream cheese) and two pasta dishes (spinach and ricotta; beef chorizo and chili), as well as a selection of the best cakes and tarts in town, make this one of Kloof Street's most popular eateries. With limited table seating

---

Tips Vegetarian?

It's not easy being a vegetarian in a country so carnivorous that chicken is served as a side order to red meat. Thankfully, Capetonians are blessed with **Fields** (© 021/423-9587), a health-shop–cum-deli on 84 Kloof St. that serves strictly vegetarian- and vegan-only meals and freshly squeezed juices in a casual environment; unfortunately, it closes in the evenings between 7 and 8pm. In the city center, there's **Lola's,** a buzzing pavement cafe at 228 Long St. (© 021/423-0885), and the **Sunflower Health Café,** at 111 Long St. (© 021/424-6560).

---

and a window bar stacked full of magazines (ideal for solitary diners), you'd be well advised to get here early. Self-service only. Everything in the well-stocked continental deli is delicious, and it's ideal for picnics.

94 Kloof St., Cape Town. © 021/424-5540. Meals weighed by the plate, average R30–R40 ($3.75–$5). AE, MC, V. Mon–Fri 7:30am–8pm; Sat–Sun 8am–8pm. Also in Constantia (© 021/794-4696) and Newlands (© 021/683-6949).

WATERFRONT

If your idea of good eating is dining on fresh West Coast mussels, washed down with Belgian beer, in a casual atmosphere and with great harbor views, **Den Anker** ✹✹✹ (Pierhead; © 021/419-0249) should be your first stop (to get to Pierhead, ask for a map at one of the information desks in Victoria Wharf). Rabbit, simmered in Belgian beer and served with applesauce and potato croquettes, is another specialty, and the steaks are out of this world. Then there's **Hildebrand** ✹ (Pierhead; © 021/425-3385), the Waterfront's most elegant (and old-fashioned) Italian restaurant, also situated right on the water.

In the Victoria Wharf shopping center, **Willoughby & Co** ✹✹✹ (lower level; © 021/418-6116) is the best place for fresh, unpretentious seafood dishes (excellent sushi bar, too). If eating in a mall in the most beautiful city in the world depresses you, the terrace (with harbor views) of the newly opened **Baia Seafood Restaurant** ✹✹ (© 021/421-0935) is where to be seen; food's good too.

For standard pub fare, grab an outdoor table right on the water at **Quay Four Tavern** (Quay Four, Pierhead; © 021/419-2008), or head for **Ferryman's** on East Pier Road (© 021/419-7748), the perfect place to sample a fresh draught of Mitchell's beer (the brewery is adjacent). Back in the shopping center, **Morton's on the Wharf** (upper level; Victoria Wharf; © 021/418-3633), an imitation French Quarter restaurant specializing in Cajun and Creole cooking, is another popular restaurant with good views of the harbor. If you're simply looking for a break from shopping, grab a deep leather sofa at **Caffe Balducci** ✹✹ (Quay 6, Victoria Wharf; © 021/421-6002). With the exception of the carpaccio, the Italian/Californian–inspired food isn't that great, but the cappuccinos, cakes, and atmosphere make up for it—this is the most elegant cafe in the Waterfront, and great for people- (and fashion-) watching.

Another Victoria Wharf option that cooks all day is **Primi Piatti** ✹✹ (© 021/419-8750), but unlike Balducci it offers unbelievably good value and faster-than-lightning service. Try the delicious pasta dishes or the equally good thin-based pizzas.

For a more refined atmosphere, head for **one.waterfront** ✹✹ (© 021/410-7100) in the Cape Grace, considered the best hotel restaurant in the Waterfront.

Almost totally surrounded by water, with tranquil views across the marina, this newly revamped restaurant is an elegant choice, but not the place to come for plain cooking. Chef Bruce Robertson delights in complex flavors, hence such favorites as marinated beef in truffle oil, topped with duck liver paté, and served with pommes William and Madeira sauce.

Emily's 𝔸𝔸 (© 021/421-1133), where modern South African cuisine was pioneered, has now taken up residence in the Clocktower Precinct, and is your best fine dining option here. The menu changes daily, but the emphasis is on quality ingredients, combined in truly unique ways—fresh oysters are flown in from Namibia, and beef is specially bred and matured in Kimberley, Northern Cape. Renowned for its baked mussels and oysters, fine patés, and terrines, Emily's places a strong emphasis on African spices and local styles, with at least one traditional Malay-inspired spiced dish on the menu.

Finally, no review of Waterfront restaurants would be complete without a mention of **Panama Jacks** 𝔸𝔸 (Quay 500; © **021/447-3992**), the celebrated seafood restaurant that predates the Waterfront development. Located in the working harbor section—head for the Royal Cape Yacht Club, and take the second road left—it has no view or elegance, but serves superb, simple seafood dishes steamed, grilled, or flambéed; fresh crayfish (lobster) is the specialty.

SEA POINT & GREEN POINT

One more establishment in this area deserves a mention: Not much has changed at **La Perla** 𝔸𝔸 (Beach Rd.; © **021/434-2471**), the Italian restaurant that opened on the Sea Point promenade in the '60s, with well-matured waiters dishing up excellent pasta dishes (albeit old-fashioned toppings—no sign of Jamie Oliver here) and truly superb seafood.

Expensive

The Restaurant 𝔸𝔸𝔸 INTERNATIONAL/MODERN CAPE   Graeme Shapiro worked his way across the globe, from Ireland and London to Thailand and Australia, before returning home in 1996 to open a restaurant that would quickly shoot to the top of every food critic's hot list—and stay there. The grilled ostrich filet with sweet potato and *vygie* (sour fig) sauce is a signature dish; or look for grilled springbok (venison) loin with red cabbage, celeriac rosti, and honeybush/red currant sauce; grilled squid with pumpkin seed pesto and peppery greens; seared oysters and foie gras on brioche toast sauced with Cape-style brandy cream; or fresh Thai mussels with chili jam and coconut cream. End with a scoop of prickly pear sorbet and honey and Rooibos tea ice cream. Unlike many of the many creative chefs favored by foodies, Shapiro's taste combinations are simpler (or possibly just shorter), and they really work—highly recommended.

51A Somerset Rd., Green Point. © **021/419-2921**. Reservations essential. Main courses R65–R78 ($8–$9.75). AE, DC, MC, V. Mon–Sat 7–10pm.

Moderate

Anatoli 𝔸 *Finds* TURKISH   Housed in an old, gutted warehouse with exposed bricks and Persian carpets creating a spacious yet warm environment, Anatoli has been serving up Cape Town's best Turkish *mezze* (appetizer) platter since 1986. Served with loaves of bread so freshly baked they're too hot to touch, mezze choices are carried to the table on huge trays. There the waiters describe the dishes, which include hot potato rolls made with cheese, egg, chili, parsley, and baked in phyllo; cold taboulleh made with cracked wheat, mint, tomato, and cucumber; lamb meat balls with walnut; and seriously good *dolmades* (stuffed grape leaves). Choose a selection to share, and don't bother with mains. A great choice if you're looking for an informal, relaxed evening.

25 Napier St., Green Point. ✆ 021/419-2501. Mezze (appetizers) R18 ($2.25) each. Main courses R55 ($7). AE, DC, MC, V. Mon–Sat 6:30–11.30pm.

Mario's ★★ *Finds* ITALIAN   Don't let the unprepossessing decor fool you; the kitchen serves authentic Italian cuisine, and a long list of Capetonian regulars will attest to it. Mario passed away back in the early 1980s, but his widow, Pina, has single-handedly kept the family business growing, now ably assisted by her daughter Marlena and son Marco. The menu features everything you'd expect from an Italian restaurant (pasta is homemade and delicious), but the specials— almost as numerous as the menu items—are what's really likely to get your mouth watering. Pheasant, guinea fowl, quail, wild duck, rabbit—you name it, Pina cooks it.

89 Main Rd., Green Point. ✆ 021/439-6644. Main courses R38–R75 ($4.50–$9). (Prawns R125/$16). AE, DC, MC, V. Tues–Fri and Sun 10:30am–2.30pm; Tues–Sun 6:30–10:30pm.

Wakame ★★ SEAFOOD/SUSHI   Although some locals rue the day the old Harbour Tavern (a kitsch '70s relic) closed down, anyone who loves an ocean view while imbibing its fresh bounty, skillfully sliced, diced, wrapped, and/or cooked, will raise a glass of sake to the team who transformed it into the elegant Wakame. This is the best place to eat with a sea view. An airy interior where Japanese chefs display their skill steps down (to maximize the number of seats with a view), and ceiling-length glass doors fold back entirely to reveal a post-card-perfect view of the tankers and containerships sailing in and out of the nearby harbor. Sushi and sashimi are made to order, but here service can be too tardy; besides, Wakame has a great menu to choose from. Here seared tea-smoked tuna served on wasabi mash is flavorful, and the shrimp and butter sauce is simply delicious, but the top rating goes to the sesame-crusted tuna, served on bok choy and topped with slivers of deep-fried sweet potato. Unlike any of the Atlantic Seaboard options (see below)—all of which (with the exception of Blues) suffer from a certain brashness, their glorious views tainted by a low-level aggression on the part of the waitstaff—the atmosphere here is laid-back, and the food a great deal more innovative.

Corner of Beach Rd. and Surrey Place, Moulle Point. ✆ 021/433-2377. Reservations recommended for dinner in season. Main courses R58–R72 ($7.50–$8.90). AE, DC, MC, V. Daily noon–2:30pm and 7–9:30pm.

ATLANTIC SEABOARD: THE SUNSET STRIP

When the summer sun starts its slow descent into the ocean, you simply have to be on the Atlantic seaboard soaking up the last of its pink rays. Victoria Road, the street that hugs Camps Bay's palm-fringed beachfront, is where you'll find the most options, all with good-to-glorious views of the ocean and white-sand beach.

A general note of caution: In season the atmosphere can be a bit frenzied, and any genuine desire to service needs or produce noteworthy food takes a backseat to trying to turn over as many tables as possible (Blues being the exception); if you're looking for a more laid-back sunset alternative, head for Wakame in Moulle Point (see review above).

La Med (the Glen Country Club, clearly signposted off Victoria; ✆ 021/ 438-5600) is a rather tacky indoor/outdoor bar in a sublime location, with lawns that run into the ocean. The standard pub grub, beer garden, and sheer size (it seats over 500) can attract a rowdy crowd; for better-looking drinking partners, keep south down Victoria Road into Camps Bay proper. First up is the

Sandbar (© 021/438-8336), one of Camps Bay's oldest sidewalk bistros, and known to serve a mean strawberry and mango daiquiri.

Even better views are to be had from the newly extended Promenade Centre, which enjoys the choicest position on the Atlantic seaboard. **Paranga** (© 021/438-0404) is on the first floor with great banquette seating along the walls (book seats 35–38 for best views) and serves light lunches all afternoon and dinner from 7pm. Above is **Summerville,** for more great views and excellent fresh fish. But if it's the coolest cocktail bar in Cape Town you're looking for, you'll have to climb one more flight of steps to reach **Eclipse** (© 021/438-0883). Furnished only with couches (on which you'll find Pamela Anderson–lookalikes lounging about) and with a strict waitron policy (only the gorgeous need apply), it offers a surreally beautiful view to contend with all that flesh. Alongside these newer options is the stalwart **Blues** (© 021/438-2040), also with great views, and the most old-fashioned (read: grown-up) establishment on the Promenade. You often need to book a dinner table days before, proof that with a sublime location (and waiters with good teeth), you can get away with inconsistent cuisine standards. The newly opened **Blues Cafe,** below, which has DJs playing world music on Thursdays, is a great deal more trendy (as offspring usually are). Adjacent to Blues is **Baraza** (© 021/438-1758), finished in muted earth tones and furnished with comfortable sofas, with a counter that runs the length of the window to offer more elevated views of the sunset strip. Adjoining Baraza is **Vilamoura** (© 021/438-1850), which serves mainly Portuguese fare, even though the baroque interior with Miro-style murals is anything but. Below is **Café del Mar** (© 021/438-0156), which serves light meals all day and well into the night.

SOUTHERN SUBURBS

The Constantia wine estate, Uitsig, is fortunate enough to house three fabulous dining options: The first, Constantia Uitsig, is reviewed in full below because the venue—an old Cape Dutch farm that dinner guests have the run of—is simply the best, but most rate the food at **La Colombe** (© 021/794-2390) higher. Chef Frank Dangereux specializes in classic Provençal cuisine (even the French say you won't taste better anywhere in France), so if you have a soft spot for rich reduction sauces, book here, but bear in mind you'll have to forfeit the sublime view Constantia Uitsig offers. Best-case scenario: Sample both! If you're in the mood for more casual fare, at friendlier prices, Constantia's **Spaanschemat River Café** (© 021/794-3010) is where local legend Judy Badenhorst is again dishing up superb deli-style food (as well as more substantial items such as succulent linefish or Karoo-lamb burger with cucumber/mint relish) in a garden setting. Her smoked salmon and scrambled eggs crepe, topped with chives and hollandaise sauce, is one of the best breakfasts in town.

Another Constantia option worth considering, mostly for its lovely garden setting, is the **Greenhouse** (© 021/794-2137) at the Cellars-Hohenhort hotel. Chef Phil Alcock has worked with the likes of Marco Pierre and Raymond Blanc, and service is impeccable.

VERY EXPENSIVE

Buitenverwachting ★★★ INTERNATIONAL/MODERN CAPE Like Uitsig, Buitenverwachting (meaning "above expectation") is situated on one of the historic Constantia wine farms, with lovely views and an exceptional reputation. But Buitenverwachting is more formal and more expensive, and from a consistency point of view, the food is also better—it wows almost everyone who eats there and tends to make it into the top three of every food critic's Cape listing.

Austrian chef Edgar Osojnik combines local ingredients with international techniques and flavors, like preparing kingklip in the tandoor and serving it with gingered bisque and basmati-pea samosas, or creating a creamy polenta-spinach soup and topping it with osso-buco tartlets. Crayfish is pan-fried and served with a Buiten-Brut bisque and spaghettini-artichoke bake. End with the "chocolate variation"—it's a masterpiece. A less pricey option is **Café Petit** in the courtyard, which is open for lunch. You can also arrange for takeout picnic fare.

Klein Constantia Rd., Constantia. ✆ **021/794-3522.** www.buitenverwachting.co.za. Reservations essential. Main courses R89–R130 ($11–$16); crayfish R290 ($25). AE, DC, MC, V. Tues–Fri 12–1:30pm; Tues–Sat 7–8:30pm; Cafe Petit lunches from R27 ($3.25), Tues–Sat 11.30–3.30pm.

EXPENSIVE

Constantia Uitsig ✿✿✿ INTERNATIONAL/ITALIAN Situated on the Constantia wine route, Uitsig (literally, "views") combines perfect mountain and vineyard views with a predominantly Italian menu. Chef Frank Swainston tries to update his menu, but patron pressure has ensured you will have the following choices, all recommended: paper-thin fish carpaccio, served with avocado; *bouchée de moules* (mussels in puff pastry in a spinach and saffron veloute); jointed wild duck with porcini mushrooms; grilled springbok loin served with a caramelized honey and lemon sauce; and the legendary *trippa alla Florentina* (a tomato-based tripe with carrots, celery, and onions). Swainston's Marquise au Chocolat is the most sinful dessert ever made. Sadly, consistency has become a bit of a problem, with some dishes simply not up to par, but staff are superb at assisting with new choices, and it still rates tops as an overall experience.

Spaanschemat River Rd.. ✆ **021/794-4480.** www.constantiauitsig.co.za. Reservations essential. Main courses R40–R77 ($5–$11) (Prawns: R120/$15). AE, DC, MC, V. Daily 7:30–9:30pm; Tues–Sun 12:30–2:30pm. June–Sept closed Mon lunch.

(Kids) Family-Friendly Restaurants

Most city restaurants have limited space, but the outdoor seating and coloring books at **Cafe Paradiso** ✿ (✆ **021/423-8653**; 110 Kloof St.) makes this a popular, good-value venue (with delicious food) for parents in the know. If the kids are clamoring for pizzas, check out **Col'-Cacchio** (✆ **021/419-4848**; see above)—ask for a bit of dough to make 'n' bake in the pizza oven. The old stalwart **McDonald's** (✆ **021/419-3715**), in Green Point, has a kids' playground; for a better-quality burger, the best city option is **Colorado Spur Steakranch** (✆ **021/426-5321**) on Kloof Street; it has an indoor playground, and child-friendly staff hand out balloons, coloring paper, and crayons. The most child-friendly venue on the beach is at **Dunes Bar & Restaurant** (✆ **021/790-1876**) in Hout Bay: Relax at a table with your feet in the sand and watch junior check out the swings and climbing frame—don't forget the sunblock. **Wharfside Grill** (✆ **021/790-2130**), also in Hout Bay, has a great harborside location and offers kiddie portions. If you're on your way to or back from Cape Point, pop in at **Barnyard Farmstall** (✆ **021/712-6934**) in Tokai for great country fare amid bales of straw and strutting roosters.

Tips **Picnic Fare**

Table Mountain is one big garden, and its "tabletop" makes a great picnic venue, as does Kirstenbosch, particularly during the summer when sunset concerts are held every Sunday from December to March. You can order a picnic hamper from the **Picnic Company** to be delivered to your door (© **021/706-8470;** R75/9 per person plus R30/$3.75 delivery). But for a real feast, take your pick at **Melissa's** (94 Kloof St.; © **021/424-5540**) or order a picnic basket, replete with cutlery. **Giovanni's** (103 Main Rd., Sea Point; © **021/434-6893**) is a real Italian deli with mouthwatering prepared meals and sandwiches. If you're thinking of picnicking on one of Cape Point's deserted beaches, check out Kalk Bay's **Olympia Café.**

A great Winelands option is **Le Pique Nique** (© **021/870-4274**), at Boschendal, where you can buy a hamper filled with local delicacies and spread out on their oak-shaded lawns.

FALSE BAY

You'll find the best restaurants in the charming and increasingly trendy fishing village of Kalk Bay. The **Harbour House** ✪✪ (Main Road; © **021/788-4133**) is the best venue in False Bay, and one of the few on the entire coast where you can sit with the ocean crashing on the rocks just below. Linefish are listed in chalk on the board and scratched off as they disappear down the hungry mouths of patrons.

If you feel like eating something other than seafood, **Olympia Cafe & Deli** ✪✪ (Main Road; © **021/788-6396**), diagonally opposite the turnoff to Harbour House, is an excellent deli serving light meals. **Cape to Cuba** ✪✪ (Main Road; © **021/788-1566**), in a comfortable, eclectically dressed lounge-type venue right on the sea, offers lamb shank on the bone as a house specialty. Moving out of Kalk Bay, it's worth noting that **Bon Appetit** ✪ (© **021/786-2412**), a small but excellent French restaurant on the main coastal road running through Simonstown, is considered one of the best in the city. Leaving Simonstown to approach Cape Point you'll see the **Black Marlin** (Main Road; © **021/786-1621**). a venue that enjoys one of the best sea views in the Cape, making it a popular tourist spot; seafood is the specialty, so order the linefish—and ask for all three butters (lemon, garlic, and chile) on the side.

5 Exploring Cape Town

From ascending its famous flat-topped mountain to indulging in the sybaritic pleasures of the winelands, Cape Town has much to offer sightseers. You could cover the top attractions in three days, but to really get a sense of how much the city and surrounds have to offer, you'll need to stay at least a week.

THE CAPE PENINSULA NATIONAL PARK

Nowhere else in the world does a wilderness with such startling biodiversity survive within a dense metropolis; a city housing some 3 million people effectively surrounds a national park, clinging to a mountainous spine that stretches from the massif of Table Mountain to the jagged edges of Cape Point. Hardly surprising then, that the city's best attractions are encompassed by the Cape Peninsula National Park: world-famous **Table Mountain,** also known as Hoerikwaggo, "mountain of the sea"; **Cape Point,** the most southwesterly tip of Africa; **Kirstenbosch Botanical Gardens,** showcase for the region's ancient and incredibly varied floral kingdom; and **Boulders,** home to a colony of rare African penguins. Ascending Table Mountain warrants half a day, as does a visit to Kirstenbosch—though you could include it as part of a (rather rushed) day-long Peninsula Driving Tour, which encompasses Boulders and Cape Point; for details, see "Farther Afield: Discovering the Peninsula," below.

Table Mountain 𝘈𝘈𝘈   This huge, time-sculpted slab of shale, sandstone, and granite that rose from the ocean some 250 million years ago is Cape Town's most instantly recognizable feature. Recently incorporated into the Cape Peninsula National Park, thereby affording it the highest level of protection, the flat-topped mountain dominates the landscape, climate, and development of the city at its feet, and provides Cape Town with a 6,000-hectare (14,820-acre) wilderness at its center.

The best view of the mountain is from Table Bay (another good reason to take the Robben Island tour; see below), from where you can get some idea of the relative size of the mountain—while the city shrinks to nothing, the "mountain of the sea" can be seen from 150km (93 miles) at sea. Other views of the mountain are no less beautiful, particularly from the wooded eastern flanks of **Constantiaberg,** which greet the sun every morning, and the bare buttresses of a series of peaks named the **Twelve Apostles,** who are kissed by its last rays. The fact that the mountain alone has more plant varieties (some 1,470 species) than the entire British Isles is flaunted with pride, and it is thought to be the most climbed peak in the world, with some 350 paths to the summit.

You can ascend the mountain on foot or via cable car, and once there, spend a few hours or an entire day exploring. The narrow table is 3km (almost 2 miles) long, and 1,086m (3,562 ft.) high. **Maclear's Beacon** is its highest point. The upper cable station and restaurant are on the western edge, from where you can view the Twelve Apostles towering over Camps Bay. Walk eastward, and you'll have a view of the southern suburbs. The back table, with its forests, fynbos, and the reservoirs that supply Cape Town with its water, is a wonderful place to hike, but much of it is off limits.

⌒ *Fun Fact* **A Devil of a Wind**

Legend has it that the "tablecloth," the white cloud that tumbles over Table Mountain, is the work of retired pirate Van Hunks, who liked nothing more than to climb Devil's Peak and smoke his pipe while overlooking Cape Town. One day the devil, not happy that someone was puffing on his patch, challenged him to a smoking contest. Needless to say, the competition continues to rage unabated, particularly in the summer months. The downside of this magnificent spectacle is that hurricane-force winds will simultaneously whip around Devil's Peak and rip into the city at speeds of up to 150km (93 miles) an hour. The "Cape Doctor," as the southeaster is often called, is said to clear the city of pollution, germs, and litter; but most just wish Van Hunks would give it up and stop infuriating the devil. For sanity's sake, head for the Atlantic seaboard, where the most protected beach is Clifton. Alternatively, escape to the Winelands, or visit in March and April, when the wind usually dies away completely.

Cape Town Attractions

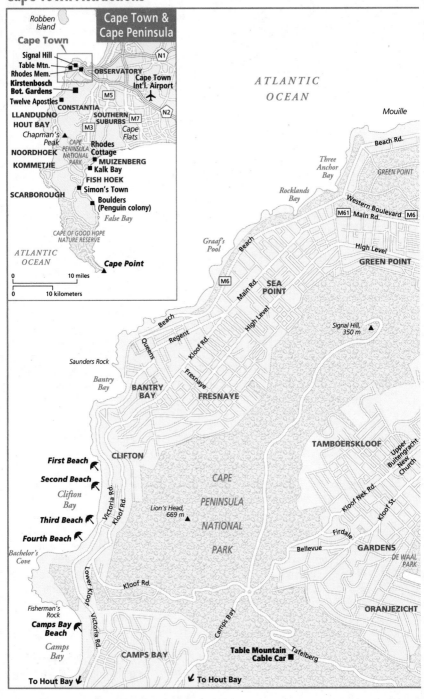

Cape Town & Cape Peninsula

Robben Island

Cape Town

- Signal Hill
- Table Mtn.
- Rhodes Mem.
- **Kirstenbosch Bot. Gardens**
- Twelve Apostles

OBSERVATORY

Cape Town Int'l. Airport

N1

M5

CONSTANTIA

LLANDUDNO

HOUT BAY

SOUTHERN SUBURBS

Cape Flats

M7

N2

M3

Chapman's Peak

CAPE PENINSULA NATIONAL PARK

Rhodes Cottage

NOORDHOEK

KOMMETJIE

MUIZENBERG

Kalk Bay

FISH HOEK

SCARBOROUGH

Simon's Town

Boulders (Penguin colony)

False Bay

CAPE OF GOOD HOPE NATURE RESERVE

ATLANTIC OCEAN

Cape Point ▲

0   10 miles

0   10 kilometers

ATLANTIC OCEAN

Mouille

Beach Rd.

Three Anchor Bay

GREEN POINT

Rocklands Bay

Western Boulevard

M61   Main Rd.

M6

High Level

GREEN POINT

Graaf's Pool

Beach

M6

Main Rd.

High Level

SEA POINT

Signal Hill, 350 m ▲

Beach

Queens

Regent

Kloof Rd.

Fresnaye

Saunders Rock

Bantry Bay

BANTRY BAY

FRESNAYE

TAMBOERSKLOOF

Upper Buitengracht New Church

First Beach 🏖

CLIFTON

Second Beach 🏖

Clifton Bay

Third Beach 🏖

Fourth Beach 🏖

Bachelor's Cove

CAPE PENINSULA NATIONAL PARK

Lion's Head, 669 m ▲

Victoria Rd.

Kloof Rd.

Kloof Nek Rd.

Kloof St.

Firdale

Bellevue

GARDENS

DE WAAL PARK

Fisherman's Rock

Lower Kloof

Kloof Rd.

Camps Bay Beach

Victoria Rd.

Camps Bay

Camps Bay

CAMPS BAY

ORANJEZICHT

Table Mountain Cable Car ■   Tafelberg

To Hout Bay ↙

To Hout Bay ↙

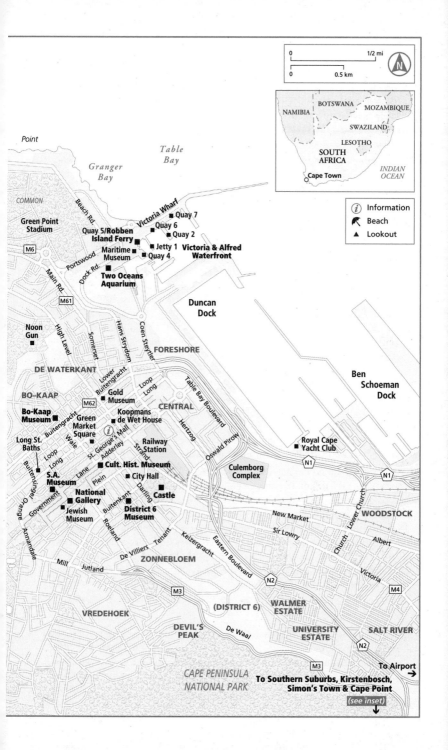

Tips   Beware the Giant Hamsters

On a visit to Table Mountain, you will certainly encounter the **dassie,** or rock hyrax, on the summit. These large, furry, rodentlike animals are (despite appearances) related to elephants; and although they are relatively tame, they do bite.

By cable car: Cars depart every 15 minutes from the lower station (Tafelberg Rd.; ✆ **021/424-5148**) daily (weather permitting) between 8 and 8:30am until between 6 and 9pm, depending on the season. A return ticket costs between R75 and R105 ($9 and $13) for adults and R40 and 55 ($5 and $7) for children, depending on the season (free for children under 3). Operating since 1929 but upgraded in 1997, the Swiss-designed cable car has a floor that rotates 360 degrees, giving everyone a chance to gape at the breathtaking views during the 4-minute journey up. The upgrade has meant that queues are now much shorter—even during the busiest months from November to April, the longest you'll wait is 30 minutes. Afternoons are generally less crowded.

On foot: The most commonly used route to the top is via **Platteklip Gorge**—the gap is visible from the front, or north face, of the mountain. The route starts just east of the lower cable station (see below) and will take 2 to 3 strenuous hours. Be sure to bring water. A more scenic route starts at the Kirstenbosch Botanical Gardens and climbs up the back via **Skeleton Gorge.** It's steep, requiring reasonable fitness, but should take approximately 2 hours to the summit. Rather than walk another hour to the upper cable station, most return by walking down via **Nursery Ravine.** Be aware that the mountain's mercurial weather can surprise even seasoned Capetonians—more people have died on Table Mountain than on Mount Everest. Don't climb alone, stick to the paths, and take water and warm clothes. For guided hikes, contact **Table Mountain Walks** (✆ **021/715-6136**). The **Mountain Rescue** number is ✆ **10177.**

Boulders ✶✶   A few minutes from the center of Simon's Town, on the way to Cape Point, is the turnoff to pretty Boulders, named after a cluster of large granite boulders that have created a number of small sheltered bays and provided sanctuary for a breeding colony of African penguins (formerly known as "jackass penguins" because of their braying). You can swim at the main beach, which the penguins visit, but the best place to view them is from the raised boardwalk overlooking Foxy Beach; they are a treat to watch, and almost human in their interactions. A monogamous species, the penguins mate in January and nest from February to August.

The Boulders (off M4), Simon's Town. ✆ **021/786-2329.** Admission R10 ($1.30) adults, R5 (65¢) children. 8am–6pm daily.

Cape of Good Hope Nature Reserve ✶✶✶   The Cape of Good Hope Nature Reserve is most famous for **Cape Point,** the farthest tip of the Cape Peninsula. There are a number of drives and picnic sites in the reserve, which is home to baboons, zebra, eland, red hartebeest, ostrich, and the pretty bontebok. (Be aware that the baboons, which have become habituated to humans, can be dangerous; don't approach them, keep your car windows closed, and never feed them.) The usually windswept reserve can be pretty bleak, but the coastal views are arresting, and the beaches—which are seldom visited—are almost always deserted. The walks from Gifkommetjie and Platboom Beach on the west coast (incidentally, a good place for windsurfing) are recommended, or follow the turnoff to Bordjiesdrif or Buffelsbaai Beach on the east coast, where you can swim in protected tidal pools or even *braai* (barbecue). At Buffelsbaai, you can see the remains of one of the more than 20 ships that have wrecked on this coast.

Most head straight for Cape Point, taking the funicular (R25/$3 round-trip; 8/10am–5/5:30pm, depending on season) to the viewing platforms surrounding the old lighthouse (built too high, it was often obscured by mists) and walking to the "new" lighthouse—built after yet another liner wrecked itself on the coast in 1911 and the most powerful on the South African coast. The spectacular view from these cliffs, towering more than 600 feet above the lashing ocean, is truly "bird's-eye"—hundreds of seagulls wheel below. ***Note:*** Despite the T-shirt slogans, and the name of the Cape Point restaurant, this is not the meeting place of two oceans; that would be Cape Agulhus, to the southeast of Cape Point.

Entrance off M4 and M65. © 021/780-9204. R25 ($3) adults, R10 ($1.30) ages 7–17. Oct–Mar daily 6am–6pm; Apr–Sept daily 8am–5pm.

Kirstenbosch Botanical Gardens ★★★   Situated on the eastern slopes of Table Mountain, Kirstenbosch is the third-most-visited attraction in Cape Town and is without a doubt one of the most beautiful gardens in the world, its shaded lawns and gurgling streams the perfect antidote to the searing summer heat. With the cultivated sections seamlessly blending into the adjoining nature reserve, some 8,000 of South Africa's 22,000 plant species (including a giant baobab tree) grow here. There are a number of themed walks and areas; as an introduction to the indigenous flora, the *fynbos* walk is recommended. Of historic interest are the remains of the wild almond hedge that Jan Van Riebeeck planted in 1660 to demarcate the colony from the indigenous Khoi. Easiest is to hire an audio guide or avail yourself of the free guided garden walks that take place on Wednesday, Tuesday and Saturday, or take a golf cart tour (R20/$2.60). **Summer sunset concerts** ★★★ are held every Sunday at 5:30pm from December to March and feature some of Africa's best acts (as well as a few mediocre options)–call to find out what's on. There are two restaurants (© **021/762-9585**): the self-service **Fynbos** (9am–5pm) and adjacent **Silver Tree,** serving a la carte lunches and dinners. Lovely venue and views, but the food is nothing to write home about, and increasingly pricey.

Rhodes Ave. (off the M5), Newlands. © 021/799-8899, or 021/761-4916 on weekends. www.nbi.ac.za. R18 ($2.35) adults, R5 (65¢) children 6–18. Concerts R30 ($3.75) adults, R10 ($1.30) children. Sept–Mar daily 8am–7pm; Apr–Aug daily 8am–6pm. Tours: Free guided garden walks every Tues at 9am and Sat at 11am; forest walk is Wed at 9am. Audio guides for self-guided tours (R30/$3.70). Specialized themed tours are offered monthly; call to see what's on. Golf-cart tours (R20/$2.60) depart every hour from 8am.

Rhodes Memorial   Rhodes Memorial was erected in honor of Cecil Rhodes, the man who, incidentally, donated the land for Kirstenbosch Gardens in 1902. Rhodes made his fortune in the Kimberley diamond mines and became prime minister of the Cape in 1890. A true British imperialist, he "owned" Zimbabwe (previously known as Rhodesia), and it was his lifelong dream to see a Cape-to-Cairo railway line built so that the "sun would never set on the British Empire." The memorial is an imposing granite staircase flanked by lions and overlooking the Cape Flats and Table Bay. In one of the Cape's most bizarre juxtapositions, herds of wildebeest and zebra graze on the slopes around the memorial, oblivious to rubberneckers driving the M3 below. An informal restaurant behind the memorial has outdoor tables with some of the best views in Cape Town—a great breakfast venue.

Fun Fact   **Every Breath You Take**

The air at Cape Point is believed to be particularly pure—hence the establishment of one of the World Meteorological Organization's 20 Global Atmosphere Watch stations here, which monitors long-term changes in the chemistry of the earth's atmosphere.

Off the M3 (De Waal Dr.), Groote Schuur Estate (signposted turnoff just after the University of Cape Town). ℭ **021/689-9151.** Free admission. 8am–7pm.

ATTRACTIONS IN THE CITY BOWL

Cape Town is South Africa's oldest and most pleasant city center, featuring a combination of Cape Dutch, Georgian, Victorian, and 20th-century architecture. The major axis, **Adderley Street,** runs past the railway station, cutting the city in half. East of Adderley is the **Castle of Good Hope, Grand Parade,** and **City Hall.** West are the more charming shopping areas, the best of which, **Long Street** and **St George's Mall** (a pedestrian street), run parallel to Adderley. **Greenmarket Square,** a lively flea market surrounded by coffee shops, lies between these two streets and Longmarket and Shortmarket streets. South of Adderley Street (where it takes a right turn at the Slave Lodge and melds with Wale St.) is the **Company Gardens,** where most of the museums are situated.

The city is small, so the best way to get to know it is on foot; you can take a guided walking tour (departing from the tourism office), or wander at your own pace: Start at the Castle, then head down Darling Street to Adderley Street. Either turn right to look at the brilliant blooms trading at Trafalgar flower market before continuing up Darling to browse the markets and shops at Greenmarket Square, Church Street, and Long Street, or turn left onto Adderley to complete a loop that takes in the Slave Lodge, the Company Gardens, the National Gallery, and/or South African museum, before returning down Queen Victoria Street or Long Street to Greenmarket Square.

Castle of Good Hope ★★   Built between 1666 and 1679, the castle—really a pentagonal fortress typical of the Dutch defense system adopted in the early 17th century—is the oldest surviving building in South Africa, and marks the original shoreline. Once the hub of civilian and administrative life, the long-serving castle is still the regional headquarters of the South African Defence Force, though the most invasive force it's ever dealt with are the tourists ambling through its ramparts (and more recently, some 5,000 camp brides and other gay revelers at "The Wedding," an annual masked ball that was hosted here in 2002). The fort combined local materials (note the slate paving stones, taken from Robben Island in the 17th c.) with European imports (the bell at the entrance was cast in Amsterdam in 1697) and looks much as it has for centuries.

Get here at 9am sharp or noon if you want to see the Key Ceremony, a kind of 'Changing of the Guard' (Mon–Fri only). There are 30-minute tours departing at 11am, noon, and 2pm (ask about the many ghosts that wander its ramparts), or you can explore on your own. Unless you're fascinated with colonial military might, you can give the **Military Museum** a miss, but do visit the **William Fehr Collection.** An arch-conservationist, Dr. Fehr (1892–1968) collected paintings and graphics that provide insight into the early colonists and how they were to change the face of the Cape completely. Thomas Baines's painting *The Greatest Hunt in Africa* depicts the slaughter of 30,000 animals in honor of the visiting Prince Alfred.

During the day, light meals and refreshments are served in the central courtyard at **Die Goewerneur Restaurant** (Mon–Sat 9am–4pm). For reservations, call © **021/461-4895.**

Corner of Buitenkant and Strand sts. © 021/469-1249. R15 ($1.95) adults, R6.50 (85¢) children. Mon–Sat 9am–4pm. William Fehr: Mon–Sat 9:30am–4pm.

The Slave Lodge 🕏   Built in 1679 to house the Dutch East India Company's slaves, this building currently houses the South African Cultural History Museum. Exhibits are drawn from the lives of the early Cape colonists (including the slaves), with various artifacts from the 17th, 18th, and 19th centuries on display, and drawings and photographs that give visitors an idea of what Cape Town looked like before the land reclamation project and development of the mountain's slopes. One of the most interesting collections is the inscribed "post office stones" under which passing ships would leave their mail; American visitors may be interested in the exhibits from the *Alabama,* a Confederate ship that used to restock in Cape Town. The museum is currently undergoing renovations as part of a 5-year overhaul, and once it has reopened, it aims to provide a greater focus on the colony's slave history as well as the story of Cape Town's other peoples.

49 Adderley St. © 021/460-8200. Free during renovations; check prices after completion. Daily 8:30am–4:30pm.

South African Museum and Planetarium 🕏   Founded in 1825, South Africa's oldest museum has in recent times come under fire for what many described as apartheid ideology: In March 2001 it finally closed its Khoi-San diorama, a hunter-gatherer exhibit dating back some 40 years; the display of life-size indigenous people in a natural-history museum was an embarrassing faux pas, suggesting as it did that they were part of the animal world. That said, the museum's ethnographic displays are excellent, with displays on traditional medicine, the use of wood (used to tell the time), and African mathematics and alphabetic symbols. The Lydenburg heads, which date back to around A.D. 500, are some of the earliest examples of African art. The natural-history side includes a few fascinating exhibits, particularly the fossil gallery, with evidence dating life back 300 million years providing valuable insight into the now-barren Karoo; and the four-story whale well, hung with two whale skeletons; others, like the stuffed *kwagga* (an extinct relative of the zebra) foal, are simply macabre.

(*Fun Fact* **All that Glitters . . .**

The **Gold of Africa Museum** is the newest addition to Cape Town's attractions, housing an African collection of gold artifacts purchased from the Barbier-Mueller Museum in Geneva for R11 million ($1.2 million). Created in Mali, Senegal, Ghana, and Cote d'Ivoire during the 19th and 20th centuries, the collection is a refreshing change from the mostly Eurocentric designs available commercially, and the intention is to foster an appreciation for and pride in African design. The museum is housed in the historic **Martin Melck House** (Strand St.; © **021/405-1540;** R20/$2.60 per person), constructed in 1781 as the parsonage for the pretty Lutheran Church, located next to the house.

Cultural Sights: Cape Muslim to Khayalitsha

On the slopes of Signal Hill—the arm that stretches out of Table Mountain to overlook the city and harbor—is the suburb of **Bo-Kaap.** Home to a section of the Cape's Muslim community (often referred to as the Cape Malays despite the fact that only 1 percent of their forefathers, skilled slaves imported by the Dutch, were born in Malaysia), this is one of the city's oldest and most interesting areas. Narrow cobbled streets lead past colorful 19th-century Dutch and Georgian terraces and quaint mosques; try to visit at sunrise and sunset when the air is filled with the song of the muezzins in their minarets, calling the community to prayer.

Start at the **Bo-Kaap Museum** ★, at 71 Wale St. (© 021/481-3939; Mon–Sat 9:30am–4:30pm; R5/65¢ adults, R2/25¢ children). The museum gives some idea of the furnishings of a relatively wealthy 19th-century Cape Muslim family. One block south, at Dorp Street, is **Auwal,** South Africa's oldest mosque, dating back to 1795, and said to be where Afrikaans was first taught.

The protected historic core of the Bo-Kaap ranges from Dorp to Strand streets, and between Buitengracht and Pentz streets—the best way to experience them is on foot, with a local guide, like **Tana-Baru Tours** ★★ (© 021/424-0719). A 2-hour tour ends with tea and traditional Malay cake at a private home (R100/$13 per person) or a five-course informal lunch (R125/$15). (Its 3-hr. "Route of Many Cultures" tours is also recommended as one of the most authentic ways of understanding how segregation tore communities apart, with guides providing personal accounts while visiting District Six and the Cape Flats.)

Alternatively, head up steep Longmarket on your own and stop for tea and traditional *melktert* (milk tart) at the **Noon Gun Tea Room and Restaurant** ★ (273 Longmarket St.; © 021/424-0529). The name "Noon Gun" derives from the Signal Hill cannon fired by the South African Navy daily at noon—a tradition that has informed Capetonians of their imminent lunch break since 1806. The tearoom features magnificent views of the city and mountain, and serves authentic Cape Malay fare.

The charm of the Bo-Kaap provides some measure of what was lost when **District Six** was razed; opposite the Bo-Kaap, and clearly visible from any raised point, this vacant land is located on the city's southern border. When bulldozers moved in to flatten the suburb in 1966, an estimated 60,000 Cape Muslims (referred to as coloureds) were living in what was condemned as a ghetto by the apartheid hardliners. Much like Sophiatown in Johannesburg, District Six housed people from every walk of life—musicians, traders, teachers, craftsmen, *skollies* (petty criminals), hookers, and pimps—and was one of South Africa's

Between Government Ave. and Queen Victoria St.. © 021/481-3800. Museum: R8 ($1) adults, free for children. Planetarium show: R10 ($1.30) adults, R5 (65¢) ages 3–16. Museum: Daily 10am–5pm. Planetarium show: Mon–Fri 2pm; Sat–Sun 12, 1, and 2:30pm (children's show at 12pm); Tues 8pm.

South African National Gallery ★★★   This small gallery, started with an initial donation by Victorian randlord Sir Abe Bailey, has room to exhibit only most inspired and creative communities, producing potent poets, jazz musicians, and writers. When the bulldozers finally moved out, all that was left were a few churches and mosques—in a weird attempt at morality, religious buildings were exempt from the demolition order. The community was relocated piecemeal to the Cape Flats—a name that accurately describes both the geography and psychology of the area. Many believe that Cape Town's current gangster problems, spawned in the fragmented, angered, and powerless Cape Flats communities, are a direct result of the demise of District Six.

Renamed Zonnebloem ("sunflower"), the so-called white area of District Six remained largely vacant, as even hardened capitalists spurned development in protest, and only the state-funded Cape Technicon was ever built on the land (purchased, incidentally, for 1 rand). Restitution is finally underway, with a "homecoming ceremony" held in November 2000 and construction of homes for some of the more than 1,700 wrongly evicted resumed in April 2003. Life will never be the same here again, but most hope that by returning the stolen land to the original families, the damage done to the national psyche can be reversed. Until then, the scar on the cityscape is a constant reminder.

Most organized tours of District Six include a trip to **Guguletu** and **Langa,** two of Cape Town's oldest "townships," as black suburbs are still referred to, and the shantytowns of **Khayelitsha.** While you can self-drive to craft centers like Sivuyile Tourism Centre in Guguletu (see "Shopping," below), to get an in-depth understanding of how "the other half" of Cape Town lives, a tour is definitely recommended. Other than Tana-Baru (see above), you could book a tour with **Grassroots** (© 021/706-1006) or **Legend Tours** (© 021/697-4056). Most kick off either from the Bo-Kaap or District Six museums, then head for a short visit to the townships to visit a crafts center, an "informal" home, *shebeen* (traditional drinking house), and housing project; both can extend the tour to include Robben Island, though you don't really need a tour guide to visit the latter. The highly recommended **One City Tours** ☆ (© 021/387-5351) concentrates on the experiences of the black Cape Town community: "Ekhaya" concentrates on history from a black perspective; "The Gospel Truth" takes you to different church services in the townships; and the "Shebeen Crawl and All That Jazz" is a nocturnal pub crawl through the townships. **Township Music Tours** ☆ (© 021/790-8826) specializes in introducing visitors to the sounds of Mbanqanga, Afro-jazz, and marimba and percussion; after eating at an informal township restaurant, guests are taken to a shebeen for a session of live music.

5% to 8% of its collection of more than 8,000 artworks. Despite this, and despite a lack of funding, it is considered by many to be the country's premier art museum, with many artworks reflecting South Africa's turbulent and painful history. Under the expert guidance of Marilyn Martin, the gallery has collected works neglected by other South African galleries, including rare examples of what used to be considered crafts, such as Ndebele beadwork and *knopkierries* (fighting sticks). The gallery also often hosts excellent traveling exhibitions, the most recent being a superb retrospective of one of South Africa's greatest living artists, William Kentridge, put together by MOMA.

Government Ave.. © 021/467-4660. R5 (65¢).Tues–Sun 10am–5pm.

ATTRACTIONS AT THE WATERFRONT

Redevelopment of this historic core started in the early 1990s, and within a few years the Victoria & Alfred Waterfront had been rated as the best of its kind, successfully integrating a top tourist attraction with southern Africa's principal passenger and freight harbor. Views of Table Mountain and the working harbor, as well as numerous restored national monuments and a wide array of entertainment options, attract an estimated 20 million visitors a year. The smells of diesel and fish mingle with the aromas wafting from pavement bistros, tugboats mingle with catamarans, and tourists mingle with, well, tourists. (If you're seeking tattooed sailors and ladies of dubious repute, you'd be better off taking a drive down to Duncan Dock, where the large working ships dock.)

A rather sanitized place, the Waterfront contains some **400 stores** that are open until 9pm daily, and there is a choice of more than **70 restaurants,** as well as **11 mainstream-movie screens** (© 021/419-9700), 7 art-movie screens (© 021/425-8222), and an **IMAX theater** that shows predominantly wildlife movies (© 021/419-7364). Don't limit your exploration to the Victoria Wharf shopping center, which feels like any other mall in a large city—take a stroll from Quay 5 to Pierhead Jetty. Beer lovers should make the detour to **Mitchell's Brewery** to sample the excellent handmade ales (© 021/419-5074; tours 3pm Mon-Fri). The Waterfront is host to the **SA Maritime Museum** (© 021/405-2880), a rather dry exhibition consisting mostly of model ships. Its floating exhibit, the **SAS *Somerset,*** the only surviving boom-defense vessel in the world, is moored on North Quay, but is currently under repair and closed until further notice.

If you do only two things in the Waterfront, you should book a **boat trip,** preferably to Robben Island, and visit the **Two Oceans Aquarium** (see below). Most cruises (see "Organized Cruises & Tours" earlier in the chapter) take off from Quay 5, including the Robben Island ferry. ***Steamboat Vicky*** (© 083-651-0186; R30/$3.75), which tools around the harbor, takes off from North Quay.

Robben Island ✮✮✮   To limit access to the delicate ecosystem of the island, only tour groups organized by the Department of Arts, which manages the Robben Island Museum (encompassing the entire island), are allowed to land on the island, declared a World Heritage Sight in 1999. Visitors are transported via the *Makana* or the *Autshumato,* luxury high-speed catamarans that take approximately 25 minutes. (The views of Table Mountain and Cape Town as you pull out of the harbor are fantastic—don't forget your camera.) The 45-minute bus tours of the island provide passing glimpses of the **lepers' church and graveyard;** PAC-leader **Robert Sobukwe's house,** where he was imprisoned; the **"warden's village,"** a charming collection of houses and a school; the **lighthouse; World War II fortifications;** Robben Island's **wildlife** (a variety of antelope, ostrich, and African penguins); and the **lime quarry,** worked by political prisoners (take sunglasses—the brightness ruined many inmates' and wardens' eyes). The tour's highlight is the prison where you can view the tiny cell in which

Island of Tears

The remarkably varied history of Robben Island goes back some 400 years. It has served variously as a post office, a fishing base, a whaling station, a hospital, a mental asylum, a military base, and—most infamously—as a penal colony, for which it was dubbed "South Africa's Alcatraz." The banished have included Angolan and West African slaves, princes from the East, South African chiefs, lepers, the mentally insane, French Vichy POWs, and, most recently, opponents of the apartheid regime. But all that changed on September 24, 1997, when the Robben Island Museum was officially opened by its most famous political prisoner.

The island, once the symbol of political oppression and enforced division, was to be transformed into a symbol of reconciliation. In Mandela's words, "Few occasions could illuminate so sharply the changes of recent years; fewer still could bring to sharp focus the challenges ahead." Rising to this challenge is an eclectic complement of staff—artists, historians, environmentalists, ex-political prisoners, and ex-wardens. It's hard to imagine how a group of people with such diverse backgrounds and ideologies could work together, but it seems anything is possible once you've established common ground; in this case, the 586 hectares (1, 447 acres) of Robben Island.

Patrick Matanjana, one of the prison tour guides, spent 20 years behind bars on the island. Now he spends time at Robben Island's bar, fraternizing with the very people who upheld the system he was trying to sabotage. "They know me; they respect me," he says when asked what it's like to sit and drink with former enemies. "We are trying to correct a great wrong. They also buy the drinks," he grins. The island's ironies don't end here. Even the bar, the Alpha 1 Officers' Club, has historic significance: This is where Patrick's latrine bucket would have been emptied in the 1960s and 1970s, before the prisoners had access to toilets (not to mention beds, hot water, or adequate nutrition).

Despite the radical changes, the remaining ex-wardens, now mostly in charge of island security, do not want to leave. "You cry twice on Robben Island," explains skipper Jan Moolman, who first stepped onto the island in 1963 as one of PAC-leader Robert Subukwe's personal wardens. "The day you arrive, and the day you have to leave."

For the many day-trippers, all it takes is the sight of Mandela's cell.

Mandela spent 18 of his 27 years of imprisonment. To make the experience even more poignant, an ex-political prisoner conducts this part of the tour, giving a firsthand account of what it was like to live here. Tours take 3½ hours (including boat trip) and can feel very restricted—to get a real feel for the village (not to mention the most spectacular sunset view of Table Mountain), it's worth trying to arrange a night in one of the old wardens' cottages: A fascinating counterpoint to the more publicized prison, the village seems stuck in time, its deserted streets and low fences conjuring up the nostalgic 1950s. You can make inquiries through **Zuki** at ℂ **021/409-5141;** preference is given to groups or people doing research or engaged in some artistic endeavour. Don't expect any luxuries, and take your own picnic hamper with bottled water.

Tickets and departure from the Clocktower terminal on Quay 5, close to Jetty 1. (C) **021/419-1300.** R150 ($10) adults, R75 ($9) ages 4–17. Ferries depart every hour from 8.30am–3pm. Tours may be increased to include sunset tours in summer, and decreased in winter or because of inclement weather—please call ahead.

Two Oceans Aquarium ★★★ (Kids) This is by far the most exciting attraction at the Waterfront itself. From the brightly hued fish found on coral reefs to exhilarating encounters with the Great White sharks, more than 3,000 live specimens are literally inches from your nose. Besides the Indian and Atlantic underwater tanks displaying the bizarre and beautiful, there are a number of well-simulated environments including tidal pools, a river ecosystem, and the magnificent Kelp Forest tank. The walk through the aquarium (30–90 min., depending on how long you linger) ends with an awesome display on deep-sea predators. There are child-height window benches throughout and a "touch pool" where kids can touch kelp, shells, and anemones. On weekends kids are entertained in the Alpha Activity center with face painting and puppet shows. Predators are fed at 3:30pm daily (the large sharks on Sun).

Between New Basin and Dock Road. (C) **021/418-3823.** R50 ($6.50) adults, R20 ($2.60) ages 4–17. Daily 9:30am–6pm.

6 Farther Afield: Discovering the Peninsula

THE CONSTANTIA WINE ROUTE

Groot Constantia is a good place to start your exploration of the Cape's oldest Winelands, an area that comprises **Groot Constantia, Klein Constantia, Buitenverwachting, Uitsig,** and **Steenberg.** All feature Cape Dutch homesteads, oaks, and acres of vineyards, and because they're about 30 minutes from town, spending time here is definitely recommended, particularly if you aren't venturing into the surrounding Winelands. If you're looking for an ideal luncheon venue, look no further than Buitenverwachting or Uitsig—both are located on the eastern slopes of the Constantiaberg, with views of vineyards and the distant sea, and both are renowned for their cuisine (see "Where to Dine," earlier in this chapter).

Groot Constantia ★★ Groot Constantia was established in 1685 by Simon van der Stel, the then governor of the Cape, who reputedly named it after his daughter Constancia, and planted the Cape's first vines. A century later, the Cloete family put Constantia on the international map with a dessert wine that became the favored tipple of the likes of Napoleon, Bismarck, King Louis Philippe of France, and Jane Austen (see "Vin de Constance," above). An outbreak of phylloxera in the 1860s bankrupted the family, however, and the land

---

(Finds **Vin de Constance**

Constantia's famous dessert wine, so treasured by the great names of 18th-century Europe (even Jane Austen was moved to describe its "healing powers on a disappointed heart"), is today made in much the same way by Klein Constantia (part of the Constantia estate until 1712). Visit Klein Constantia to sample this nectar—you can purchase it only from the estate—if you're lucky enough to find some in stock.

lay fallow until 1975, when substantial replanting began. Today Groot Constantia is known for its reds, particularly the Gouverneurs Reserve. In addition to tasting the wines in the modern cellars here, you can also visit a small museum showing the history of the manor, as well as the Cape Dutch house itself, furnished in beautiful late–18th-century Cape Dutch furniture. Behind the house are the old cellars, originally designed by French architect Louis Thibault; note the celebrated pediment sculpted by Anton Anreith in 1791. The cellars now contain an interesting museum of wine. The pleasant restaurant, **Jonkershuis** (© **021/794-6255**), serves traditional Cape Malay dishes.

M3, take the Constantia turnoff; follow the Groot Constantia signs. © 021/794-5149. R8 ($1) museum; R20 ($2.60) wine tasting; R25 ($3) wine tasting and cellar tour. Daily 10am–5pm winter; 9am–6pm summer.

DRIVING TOUR   A PENINSULA DRIVE

Start	Take the M3 out of town; this follows the eastern flank of the mountain, providing access to the southern suburbs.
Finish	Kloof Nek roundabout in town.
Time	The full tour will take at least 1 full day.

Not all the sites listed below are must-sees; personal interest should shape your itinerary. Because this is a circular route, it can also be done in reverse, but the idea is to find yourself on the Atlantic seaboard at sunset.

Note: Part of Chapman's Peak Drive—expected to reopen as a toll road by December 2003—is currently closed because of the danger of rockfalls. If the road has still not reopened, change the route as follows: After visiting Cape Point, head back to town via Ou Kaapse Weg and Silvermine Nature Reserve, rejoining the M4 north. If you haven't yet visited Kirstenbosch, you could do so now, time allowing. Alternatively, head through Constantia (past the Alphen Hotel), over Constantia Neck and descend into Hout Bay. You can drive the first section of Chapman's Peak before doubling back to follow the Atlantic seaboard, passing the coastal suburbs of Llundudno (a gorgeous little beach) and Camps Bay when the sun is setting. Finish the tour as below. Alternatively, travel along the M6 to Hout Bay, ascend part of Chapman's Peak, then wind your way over Constantia Nek to Kirstenbosch, then take the M3 to Kalk Bay and continue as below.

As you approach the Groote Schuur Hospital on your left, scene of the world's first heart transplant in 1967, keep an eye out for the wildebeest and mountain zebra grazing on the slopes of the mountain. Art lovers should consider taking the Mowbray turnoff to the:

1 Irma Stern Museum.

Drop in at the **Irma Stern Museum** (Cecil Rd.; © **021/685-5686;** Tues–Sat 10am–5pm; R7/90¢). A follower of the German Expressionist movement, and acknowledged as one of South Africa's best 20th-century artists, Stern was also an avid collector of Iberian, African, and Oriental artifacts, and the museum also exhibits new talents.

Back on the M3, still traveling south, you will pass Mostert's Mill on your left, another reminder of the Cape's Dutch past, and look out for a turning on your left to

2 Rhodes Memorial.

You can see the imposing memorial high up on the slopes on your right (see "The Cape Peninsula National Park", earlier in this chapter); the restaurant behind the memorial has awesome views so break for tea here if you have the time. Back on the M3 you will pass a series of imposing ivy-clad buildings—the **University of Cape Town,** built on land donated by Rhodes. If you're interested in colonial architecture, you can make an appointment to visit **Groote Schuur,** also donated by Rhodes and designed by Herbert Baker, "the architect of the Empire," and up until the end of Mandela's term, the official government residence; call Alta Kriel (② **021/686-9100**).

From here the suburbs become increasingly upmarket. Take the turnoff to:

❸ **Kirstenbosch Botanical Gardens.**
(See "The Cape Peninsula National Park," earlier in this chapter). Consider visiting Kirstenbosch (you'll need at least an hour, preferably more) before heading through the suburbs of Bishop's Court and Wynberg for Constantia.

If you've decided against Kirstenbosch you may have time along the way to visit the:

❹ **Groot Constantia Estate.**
You can visit the 17th century manor house and wine museum, and possibly try a wine tasting (see above). Alternatively, set aside a full afternoon to travel the full Constantia Wine Route, visiting at least three estates.

Keep traveling south on the M3 until it runs into a T-junction, then turn left to the next T-junction where you join the M4; turn right and look out for Boyes Dr. or the:

❺ **Natale Labia Museum.**
Note: For an elevated view with gorgeous coastal views, take **Boyes Drive** (clearly marked off the M4 before the Natale Labia Museum) to Kalk Bay. This short detour of the coastal route is often less congested than the narrow road that runs through the coastal suburbs of Muizenberg, St James, and Kalk Bay, though you'll miss much of the interesting architecture in what used to be the favored seaboard of the wealthy randlords. The Venetian-style **Natale Labia Museum** (Main Rd.; ② **021/788-4106;** Mon–Fri 10am–5pm; R3/40¢),

once the home of the Count and Countess Labia, is a fabulous example. A satellite of the South African National Gallery, it occasionally hosts some very good exhibitions upstairs, but is in danger of closing due to lack of funds.

Another attraction on Muizenberg's Main Rd. (also called the Historical Mile) is:

❻ **Cecil Rhodes's Cottage.**
This house (Main Rd.; ② **021/788-1816;** Mon–Fri 9:30am–4:30pm, Sat–Sun10am; donation welcome) is the place where Rhodes purportedly died—a remarkably humble abode for a man who shaped much of southern Africa's history. For more information about this area, visit **Peninsula Tourism** (52 Beach Rd.; ② **021/788-1898**).

Continue on Main Rd. to the quaint fishing village of Kalk Bay.

TAKE A BREAK
Whether you've taken Muizenberg's main road or Boyes Drive, stop in at quaint **Kalk Bay** to browse the antiques shops, galleries, junk shops, and retro-modern boutiques. You can lunch here; try the excellent **Olympia Deli** for light meals, or, for ocean views try **Cape to Cuba** or **Harbour House;** see "Where to Dine," earlier in this chapter.

The drive then resumes its way south along the M4 to Fish Hoek and the naval village of:

❼ **Simon's Town.**
This vies with Kalk Bay as the most charming of the False Bay towns, lined with double-story Victorian buildings, which is why many regular visitors to the Cape choose to stay here. If you feel like lingering visit the **Simon's Town Museum** (Court Rd., ② **021/786-3046;** Mon–Fri 9am–4pm, Sat 10am–4pm, Sun 11am–4pm) or take a 40-minute cruise around the bay (② **082-737-5263**). For more details on what the town has to offer, visit the

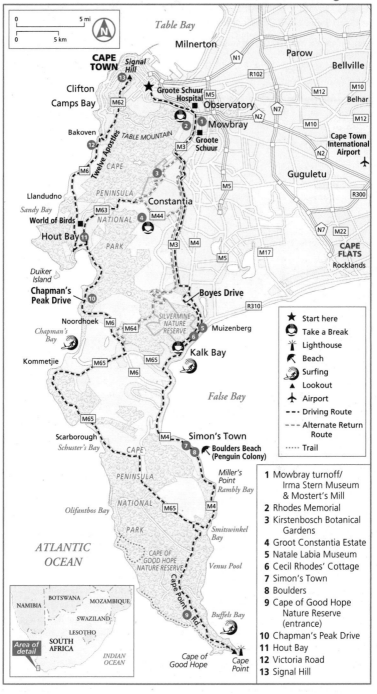

Peninsula Driving Tour

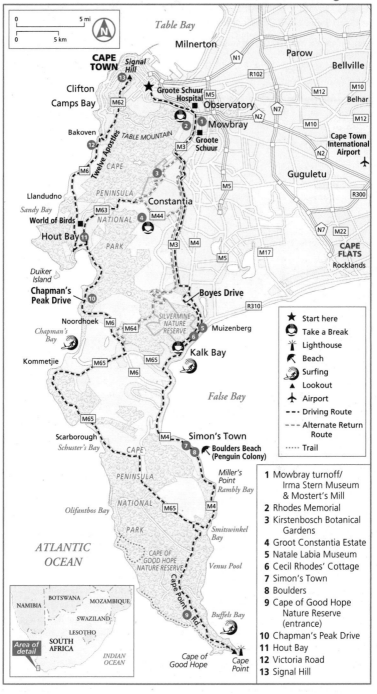

Table Bay

Milnerton

CAPE TOWN
Signal Hill

Parow

Bellville

Clifton

Camps Bay

Bakoven

Groote Schuur Hospital

Observatory

Mowbray

Groote Schuur

Cape Town International Airport

Guguletu

Llandudno

Sandy Bay

World of Birds

Hout Bay

Duiker Island

Chapman's Peak Drive

Noordhoek

Chapman's Bay

Kommetjie

TABLE MOUNTAIN

Twelve Apostles

CAPE

PENINSULA

NATIONAL

PARK

Constantia

Boyes Drive

SILVERMINE NATURE RESERVE

Muizenberg

Kalk Bay

False Bay

CAPE FLATS

Rocklands

Legend

★ Start here
Take a Break
Lighthouse
Beach
Surfing
▲ Lookout
✈ Airport
- - - Driving Route
- - - Alternate Return Route
..... Trail

Scarborough

Schuster's Bay

Simon's Town

Boulders Beach (Penguin Colony)

Miller's Point

Rambly Bay

CAPE

PENINSULA

NATIONAL

PARK

Olifantbos Bay

ATLANTIC OCEAN

CAPE OF GOOD HOPE NATURE RESERVE

Smitswinkel Bay

Venus Pool

Cape Point Rd.

Buffels Bay

Cape of Good Hope

Cape Point

NAMIBIA BOTSWANA MOZAMBIQUE

SWAZILAND

LESOTHO

SOUTH AFRICA

Area of detail

INDIAN OCEAN

1 Mowbray turnoff/ Irma Stern Museum & Mostert's Mill
2 Rhodes Memorial
3 Kirstenbosch Botanical Gardens
4 Groot Constantia Estate
5 Natale Labia Museum
6 Cecil Rhodes' Cottage
7 Simon's Town
8 Boulders
9 Cape of Good Hope Nature Reserve (entrance)
10 Chapman's Peak Drive
11 Hout Bay
12 Victoria Road
13 Signal Hill

0   5 mi

0   5 km

N

Chapman's Peak Drive

Boyes Drive

Simon's Town Tourism Bureau, also on Court Road (© **021/786-3046**).

Whatever you do, don't miss an opportunity to stop at nearby:

❽ Boulders Beach.

View the large breeding colony of jackass (African) penguins that settled here in the early 1980s, much to the horror of the residents who now have to deal with the attendant coachloads of tourists.

From Simon's Town it's 15 minutes to the entrance to the:

❾ Cape of Good Hope Nature Reserve.

Once inside, take the Circular Drive to spot game, or head for one of the usually deserted beaches; if you're pressed for time, head straight for Cape Point (see "Exploring the Cape Peninsula National Park," earlier in this chapter). From the nature reserve, it's a relatively straightforward—and spectacular—drive back to town (if Chapman's Peak is open; if not, see tip above). Take the M65 left out of the reserve past the **Cape Point Ostrich Farm** (© **021/780-9294;** daily 9:30am–5pm, tours R20/$2.60), and travel through the pretty coastal town of **Scarborough** (passing the aptly named **Misty Cliffs**) and **Kommetjie** (you can opt to bypass Kommetjie) to **Noordhoek.**

If Chapman's Peak is closed, take the M64, rejoin the M3 then head back to Hout Bay

via the M63. If it has opened, follow the signs for the M6 to Hout Bay, and ascend the exhilarating:

❿ Chapman's Peak Drive.

Built between 1915 and 1922, this winding 10km (6.2-mile) drive must rate as one of the top in the world, with cliffs plunging straight into the ocean, dwarfing the vehicles snaking along its side. Not surprisingly, hundreds of international car commercials have been shot here.

From Chapman's Peak you descend into:

⓫ Hout Bay.

Here you could head for the harbor and book a cruise to view the seal colony and seabird sanctuary on **Duiker Island** (see "Organized Cruises & Tours," earlier in this chapter) or visit the **World of Birds Sanctuary in Valley Road** (© **021/790-2730;** 9am–5pm daily; R35/$4.50), home to more than 330 species.

From Hout Bay you can now take the coast-hugging:

⓬ Victoria Road (or M6).

Take this road to town—with any luck this will coincide with sunset.

Follow the M6 through Camps Bay and turn right at the sign KLOOF NEK ROUND HOUSE to snake up the mountain to the Kloof Nek roundabout and take the turn-off to:

⓭ Signal Hill.

The views from the hill are breathtaking, particularly at night, when the twinkling city lies spread before you.

7 Surf & Sand

You'll find Cape Town's most beautiful beaches along the Atlantic seaboard, with Clifton, Camps Bay, and Llandudno the most popular. A combination of four beaches semi-separated by large granite boulders, **Clifton** is often the only place where the wind isn't blowing and is good for swimming (albeit freezing), but it's a long walk back through the cliff-hugging village to your car. **Camps Bay** offers easy access, and has numerous bars and cafes within strolling distance. You can also hire loungers and umbrellas on the beach (in season), even summon a personal masseuse; for the latter, call © **082-9407465.** Laid-back **Llandudno** is one of the city's prettiest beaches, though parking can be a real problem during high season. **Sandy Bay,** adjacent to Llandudno, is the Cape's only nudist beach. Reached via a narrow footpath, it is secluded and popular with gay men and wankers—this is not a great spot for women, unless you're in a group. The pristine, empty 8km (4¾-mile) stretch of **Long Beach** ✿, featured in a thousand television commercials, is best traversed on horseback. On the False Bay side, where the water is two to three degrees warmer, you could try for the safe waters of **Fish Hoek,** or swim with the penguins at **Boulders.**

8 Especially for Kids

Many of the Waterfront activities have been designed with children in mind, making it Cape Town's foremost family destination. The top attractions here are the five-story **IMAX cinema,** which shows predominantly wildlife shows, and the **Two Oceans Aquarium.** Face painting, drawing, and puzzles are on offer in the aquarium's Alpha Activity center, and staff often arrange sleepovers and excursions to interesting and educational locations for ages 8 to 12. Call ℰ **021/ 418-3823** to find out what special kids' entertainment will be available when you're in town. On the way, stop at the **Scratch Patch,** where kids literally scratch through mounds of semi-precious stones, selecting their own "jewels."

Catch the kiddies' **Blue Train** in Mouille Point (ℰ **021/434-8537;** Mon–Fri 3–5pm; Sat–Sun 11–5pm) or the 12pm **Planetarium** show every Saturday and Sunday, where they attempt to answer simple astronomy questions, like "Why is the sky blue?" and "Is the sun round?" To get there, take a stroll along Government Avenue (enter from Orange St., opposite Mount Nelson) armed with a bag of nuts to feed the almost-tame squirrels. Afterward, ascend **Table Mountain** in the rotating cable car. For an even bigger thrill, see the mountain upturned by riding the stomach-churning "Cobra" at **Ratanga Junction** (ℰ **0861/200-300;** Wed–Sat in summer 10am–5/6pm; closed winter), Cape Town's biggest amusement park, 8km (almost 5 miles) from town off the N1.

Chill out with a picnic next to a stream at **Kirstenbosch Gardens,** or head for the shady oaks at **Le Pique Nique,** Boschendal, near Franschhoek. Then visit **Butterfly World** (ℰ **021/875-5628**), where 22 different species of butterfly flit about a tropical garden, or **Drakenstein Lion Park** (ℰ **021/863-3290**), a sanctuary for captive-born lions—both are near Paarl. Other kid-friendly attractions in the Paarl area include **Le Bonheur Crocodile Farm** (ℰ **021/863-1142**) and the **Paarl Diamant Horse Riding Farm** (ℰ **021/863-8203**).

Walk through the **World of Birds Sanctuary** (Valley Rd.; ℰ **021/790-2730**), in Hout Bay, and then take one of the cruises to **Seal Island,** departing from Hout Bay Harbour. **Imhoff Farm** (ℰ **021/783-4545**) in Kommetjie offers country-style refreshments, camel rides, horseback riding, crafts shops for kids, and a snake and nature park to entertain.

When all else fails, there's always the beach. Try **Boulders,** where the temperature is slightly warmer, tidal pools are safe, and the penguins add unique entertainment value—visit the **Warrior Toy Museum** (ℰ **021/78-1395**) on Georges Street, Simon's Town, on your way.

9 Staying Active

For one-stop adrenaline shopping, head straight for **Adventure Village** (229 Long St.; ℰ **021/424-1580;** www.adventure-village.co.za), where the staff will organize bookings for almost every adventure activity under the sun (for numbers not available below, contact them directly). This is also where bookings to Victoria Falls can be made, as well as many specialized overland and safari trips throughout southern Africa.

ABSEILING   **Abseil Africa** (© 021/424-4760) will throw you 100m (328 ft.) off Table Mountain—attached to a rope, of course (R250/$30). But their best trip is **Kamikaze Kanyon** 🔆: a day's kloofing (scrambling down a river gorge) in a nature reserve, ending with a 65m (213-ft.) waterfall abseil (R450/$55).

BALLOONING   Board a balloon in the early morning and glide over the Paarl Winelands—the 1-hour flight (R1,550/$190 per person) takes off every morning from November to April, and includes a champagne breakfast at the Grande Roche. Contact **Wineland Ballooning** (© 021/863-3192).

BIRD-WATCHING   The peninsula attracts nearly 400 species of birds; Kirstenbosch, Cape Point, and Rondevlei Nature Reserve are some of the best areas for sightings. For guided tours of the area and further afield, contact **Birdwatch Cape** (© 021/762-5059; www.birdwatch.co.za).

BOARDSAILING & KITESURFING   Big Bay at Blouberg (take R27 Marine Dr. off the N1) provides consistent wind, good waves, and a classic picture-postcard view of Table Mountain. Another popular place is Platboom, off the Cape of Good Hope Nature Reserve, and Milnerton Lagoon. Contact the **Kite Shop** (© 021/421-6231). Or head north for Langebaan Lagoon (see chapter 4).

BOATING   The most exhilarating boating experience is called "oceanrafting," reaching speeds of up to 130kmph (80 mph) across Table Bay in a 12-seater inflatable (© 021/425-3785; R250/$30). For more options, see "Organized Cruises & Tours," earlier in this chapter.

CANOEING/KAYAKING   **Felix Unite** (© 021/670-1300) offers relaxing river trips on the tranquil Breede River—the closest is the Wine Route Adventure, which includes tasting wines of the area and costs R295 ($36) per person. **Real Cape Adventures** (© 082-556-2520) covers almost every sea kayaking route on the West and Southern coasts and caters to all levels of ability—request a trip to the rugged coastline of Cape Point.

DIVING   Wreck diving is popular here, and the coral-covered wrecks at Smitswinkel Bay are particularly worth exploring. Also Maori Bay, Oak Burn, and Bnos 400. Call **Dive Action** (© 021/511-0815). (For shark-cage diving at Hermanus, 1 hr. away, see chapter 4).

FISHING   **Big Game Fishing Safaris** (© 021/674-2203) operates out of Simon's Town on a 12m (40-ft.) catamaran and offers bottom/reef fishing (as well as crayfish lunches, sundowner cruises, on-board skeet shooting. and shark-cage diving). Trout fishing is popular in the crystal-clear streams found in the Du Toits Kloof Mountains near Paarl and in Franschhoek, where salmon trout is a specialty on every menu. For guided trips, call Tim at **Ultimate Angling** (© 021/686-6877); for general advice, tuition, and permits in Franschhoek, contact Mark at **Dewdale Fly Fishery** (© 021/876-2755).

GOLFING   The **Royal Cape** (© 021/761-6551) has hosted the South African Open many times. **Milnerton Golf Club** 🔆 (© 021/552-1047) is the only true links course in the Cape, with magnificent views of Table Mountain, but is best avoided when the wind is blowing. **Rondebosch** (© 021/689-4176) and **Mowbray** (© 021/685-3018)—both located off the N2—have lovely views of Devil's Peak (the latter course is the more demanding). **Clovelly** (© 021/782-1118) in Fish Hoek is a tight course requiring some precision. **Steenberg** (© 021/713-2233) is the course to play in Constantia.

In the Winelands, the Gary Player–designed **Erinvale** ⚹ (Lournesford Rd.; ✆ **021/847-1144**) in Somerset West is considered the best, but **Stellenbosch** (✆ **021/880-0103**), on Strand Road, is another worthwhile course, with a particularly challenging tree-lined fairway.

HIKING   Most hikers start by climbing Table Mountain, of which there are a number of options (see "Table Mountain," earlier in this chapter); call the **Mountain Club** (✆ **021/465-3412**). For hikes farther afield, contact **Cape Eco Trails** (✆ **021/785-5511**) or Ross at **High Adventure** (✆ **021/447-8036**)—as a trained climbing instructor, Ross can spice up your walk with some exhilarating ascents. If you're staying in Stellenbosch, the trails (5.3–18km/3–11 miles) in the mountainous **Jonkershoek Nature Reserve** are recommended. Recommended reading for hikers: *Day Walks in and Around Cape Town,* by Tim Anderson (Struik), and Mike Lundy's *Best Walks in the Peninsula* (Struik).

HORSEBACK RIDING   Take an early morning or sunset ride on spectacular Long Beach, Noordhoek, by contacting **Sleepy Hollow** (✆ **021/789-2341;** R130 to R170/$16 to $21 for 90 min; another R30/$3.75 gets you some bubbly on the beach). For beach rides closer to town, contact the **Riding Centre** (✆ **021/790-5286**), in Hout Bay (R100/$12 per hour). To ride through the vines on horseback or in a carriage, stopping for wine tastings, see "Getting Around" in Franschhoek and Stellenbosch, later in this chapter.

MOUNTAIN BIKING   There are a number of trails on Table Mountain, Cape Point, and the Winelands, but the Tokai Forest network and Constantiaberg trails are the best; contact **Day Trippers** (✆ **021/511-4766;** R195–R235/$24–$29) for guided rides on the Constantiaberg and Cape Point; **Downhill Adventures** (✆ **021/422-0388;** R350–R500/$44–$63) for guided rides on Table Mountain, Cape Point, and Winelands. Call Bobby ✆ **082-881-1588;** R400/$50 a day; delivery or collection R35/$4.50) for bike rentals only.

PARAGLIDING   Soar off Lion's Head for a jaw-dropping view of mountains and sea, and land at Camps Bay Beach or La Med bar for cocktails at sunset. This is an exhilarating trip; no prior experience is necessary (R750/$95). Contact Ian at **Paraglide Cape Town** (✆ **082/727-6584**).

SANDBOARDING   South Africa's answer to snowboarding takes place on the tallest dunes all around the Cape; contact **Downhill Adventures** (see above) for trips and tuition (✆ **021/422-0388**).

SKYDIVING   Freefall for up to 30 seconds, attached to an experienced instructor. Tandem dives are offered off the West Coast (contact **Adventure Village,** above) or 3,600m (12,000 ft.) over the Stellenbosch Winelands; contact **Cape Parachute Club** (✆ **082-800-6290; R700/$88**).

SURFING   The beaches off Kalk Bay reef and Noordhoek are considered hot spots. Muizenberg and Big Bay at Blouberg (take R27 Marine Dr. off the N1) are good for beginners. Call ✆ **082-234-6340** for the daily surf report; for equipment or advice, call **Charlie Moir** (✆ **083-444-9442**) in Cape Town.

WHALE-WATCHING   Hermanus, just over an hour's drive on the N2, is one of the world's best land-based spots (see chapter 4). Call the **Whale Hotline:** ✆ **083-910-1028.** For the best whale-watching in the city, drive along the False Bay coast, or contact Evan at **Atlantic Adventures** (✆ **083-680-2768**), which operates trips out of Simon's Town. Contact the **Waterfront Boat Club** (✆ **021/418-58065**) for trips in Table Bay, departing from the Waterfront.

10 Shopping

You'll find a large selection of shops and hundreds of street hawkers catering to the African arts-and-crafts market; because very little of it is produced locally, however, you pay a slight premium—and, of course, the better the gallery, the larger the premium. Beadwork is a local tradition; a wide variety of beaded items is for sale at the tourism bureau, also the place to pick up an "Arts & Crafts Map."

GREAT SHOPPING AREAS
IN TOWN
In the heart of the city center, the cobbled **Greenmarket Square** (Mon–Sat 9am–4pm) is brimful of traders selling clothing, crafts, and souvenir or gift items. Weather permitting, it's worth browsing here just for the atmosphere, though you'll find better-quality items at the shops on Church Street's cobbled walkway. To get to the Square, walk straight up Shortmarket Street and take your first left onto Long Street for the **Pan African Market,** probably the best place to pick up crafts in Cape Town (see "Best Buys," below). Follow the flow of the traffic to the pedestrianized section of **Church Street.** Street traders deal in antiques here, and there are a number of interesting shops. Check out **Peter Visser Gallery** (on the corner of Long and Church sts.; ✆ 021/423-7870), which specializes in contemporary South African art and ceramics; **Gilles de Moyencourt** (54 Church St.; ✆ 021/424-0344) deals in overpriced but interesting Africana and other quirky antiques; the **Collector** (52 Church St.; ✆ 021/423-1483) trades in the expensive end of what they term "tribal" artifacts and antiques. Don't miss **African Image,** on the corner of Church and Burg (see below). Art lovers should stop in at **Cape Gallery** (60 Church St.; ✆ 021/423-5309) and the **Association of Visual Arts** (35 Church St.; ✆ 021/424-7436).

Keep walking down Church Street to **St George's Mall**—a pedestrian street that runs the length of town. Buskers and street dancers perform here, and a small selection of street hawkers peddle masks and sculptures. For a larger selection, head 1 block down to Adderley Street, cross via the Golden Acre, and browse the station surroundings, where the streets are paved with wood and soapstone carvings. It's also paved with pickpockets, so don't carry valuables here. If you've had your fill of African crafts, head back up to **Long Street** and walk toward the mountain. This is the city's most interesting shopping street—lined with Victorian buildings, Long Street houses antiques shops, galleries, gun shops, porn outlets, hostels, and cafes/bars, as well as Turkish baths. Purchase your first piece of *droë wors* (like biltong, but sausage) at **Morris the Butcher** at 265 Long St. (✆ 021/423-1766).

ON THE WATERFRONT
Shopping here is a far less satisfying experience than in the bustling streets of town; at the end of the day Victoria Wharf is simply a glam shopping center with a nice location. There are, however, a few gems, like Out of Africa (next to Exclusive Bookshop) for a fantastic, albeit pricey, range of items from all over the continent. Art lovers shouldn't miss the **Everard Read Gallery** (see "Best Buys," below).

BEST BUYS
AFRICAN SOUVENIRS
African Image This store offers a slightly more expensive but well-chosen selection of authentic crafts and tribal art ranging from headrests and baskets to beadwork and cloth. Church Street. ✆ 021/423-8385.

Amulet Goldsmiths   Add value to the world's safest investment by commissioning Gerika and Elizabeth, the city's most talented duo, to make a contemporary jewelry item (or simply pick one up at their studio). 14 Kloofnek Rd., Tamboerskloof. ℂ 021-4261149.

A.R.T. Gallery   This gallery sells brightly hued African-motif tableware, created by popular ceramist Clementina van der Walt, as well as a selection of textiles, woodwork, baskets, and ceramics created by up-and-coming local artists. Main Road, Kalk Bay ℂ 021/788-8718.

Heartworks   It's more of a crafts showcase, but items here are chosen with a modern design slant; look for beautiful ceramics and bead- and wirework. Gardens Centre, Mill St. ℂ 021/465-3289.

Pan African Market   Three stories of rooms overflow with excellent quality goods from all over Africa, from tin picture frames to large, intricate carvings and beautiful pieces of beadwork. There's also a cozy cafe with traditional food on the first-floor balcony. 76 Long St. ℂ 021/426-4478.

Philani Flagship Printing Project   Vibrant hand-painted textiles created by a group of Xhosa women whose training was funded by the Department of Welfare. Choose among various designs, made into T-shirts, scatter pillows, wall-hangings, placemats, aprons, cards, and oven mitts. 5 Old Klipfontein Rd., Crossroads. ℂ 021/374-9160.

Uncedo Pottery Projects   Excellent ceramics—tiles, teapots, sushi plates, mugs—at unbelievably low prices, bought directly from those who are making them. There are two studios attached to the college; make sure you visit both (rather than just the crafts center) Sivuyile College, corner NY1 & NY4, Guguletu. ℂ 021/633-5461.

Vlisco   This shop has the widest range of vibrant traditional African fabrics, as well as clothing, like the shirts made popular by Mandela. (**Mnandi,** at 90 Station St., Observatory, stocks a similar selection.) 45 Castle St. (diagonally opposite Cape Town Tourism in town). ℂ 021/423-2461.

FINE ART
The Bell-Roberts Gallery   Host to regular, interesting exhibitions by up-and-coming artists. 199 Loop St. ℂ 021/422-1100.

Everard Read Gallery   For one of the best selections of South African art, particularly African landscapes and wildlife paintings, this is your best bet—be warned, though: you won't find a bargain here 3 Portswood Rd, Waterfront. ℂ 021/418-4527.

Joào Ferreira Gallery   Also a good bet for contemporary works by artists like William Kentridge—whose video work *History of the Main Complaint* has a room all to its own in the Tate Modern in London—which Joào both exhibits and sources. 80 Hout St. ℂ 021/423-5403.

FOOD
Atlas Trading Co.   Re-create the mild, slightly sweet curry flavors of Cape Malay dishes back home by purchasing a bag of mixed spices from the Ahmed family, proprietors of Atlas. 94 Wale St. ℂ 021/423-4361.

Joubert & Monty   This is one of the best places to sample good biltong; try a bit of kudu and beef—ask for the latter to be slightly moist, and sliced. Waterfront. ℂ 021/418-0640.

The Great Gay EsCape

Cape Town has become one of the great international gay destinations—like sister cities San Francisco, Sydney, and Miami, this is a sexy seaside spot, with a variety of queer things to do, and a trip down the Garden Route a good extension to your travels, particularly during May when the gay La Loerie Festival is held in Knysna. Promoted as "Africa's Queer Capital" (South Africa's constitution is the only one in the world to expressly protect the rights of homosexuals), Cape Town's queer tribes are rich and varied, with different events and venues catering to their needs. The international stereotypical GWM (gay white male) subculture exists here as elsewhere, with a mix of muscle men, fashion victims, straight-looking types, and a handful of drag queens. Local lesbian life is more low-key—more along the lines of ceramics classes and having meetings about making documentaries about women.

Most gay-friendly venues are situated in and around the City Bowl, particularly the "De Waterkant Queer Quarter" in Green Point, Sea Point's Main Road, and the mountain end of Long Street. The "De Waterkant Queer Quarter"—west of the city in Green Point, centered around Somerset Road and running up the slopes of Signal Hill to Loader Street—is where you'll find the best selection of clubs, bars, bathhouses, cafes, and guesthouses. Check the local press, *The Pink Map*, or visit www.cape-town.org for more information. **Wanderwomen** is a personalized women's only travel agent. Visit www.wanderwomen.co.za for info or call ② **021/683 9215.**

A GAY NIGHT OUT Traveling from town to Green Point, the first stop worth considering is the buzzy **Manhattans** (74 Waterkant, corner of Dixon; ② **021/421-6666**), a friendly low-volume chatty bar with a good-value restaurant, which gets busy after 9pm nightly. (Sun roast specials are also recommended.) Farther along is **Village Café** (corner of Napier and Waterkant sts.; ② **021/421-0632**), a charming little coffee shop/restaurant, good for a breakfast or daytime relax. You can walk from here to **On Broadway** (corner of Somerset and Dixon; ② **021/418-8338**), a great cabaret and theater restaurant, with excellent shows (in summer season, book early for "Mince," featuring some of South Africa's best female impersonators). Head down Somerset to **Bronx** (27 Somerset Rd., corner of Napier; ② **021/419-8547**), a very popular late-night bar with an entertaining dance floor; open from 9pm to 4am nightly, with different events (like karaoke on Mon). **Bar Code** (Hudson St., off Somerset; no phone) is a men's-only leather cruise bar—ask at the bar about the underwear parties and leather nights. Still in the same area,

Woolworths If you're planning to have a barbecue, purchase some Grabouw *boerewors* (literally, "farmers sausage") from any branch of Woolworths. Waterfront. ② **021/415-3411.**

WINE
Caroline's Fine Wine Cellar Caroline has an exceptional nose for finding those out-of-the way gems most Capetonians, let alone visitors, simply don't

but getting steamier, the **Hot House** (18 Jarvis St.; ✆ **021/418-3888**) is a European-style men's-only leisure club, with sauna, steam room, and outdoor sun deck with spectacular views over the city and the harbor.

Back in town you'll find **The Brunswick** at 17 Bree St. (✆ **021/421-2779**): Cape Town's oldest gay bar has drag, cabaret, and theater shows, as well as fabulous cocktails and dinners—reservations are crucial. Moving uptown, to Long Street, **Lola's** (corner of Long and Buiten; ✆ **021/423-0885**) is the queerest vegetarian joint in town, with an Afro-trash crowd and slip-sexy music. Just around the corner, up Buiten Street, is **Priscilla's** (✆ **021/422-2378**)—this cozy, sedate gay bar and restaurant attracts an older crowd and is most welcoming to new visitors.

BEST BEACHES Clifton's **Third Beach** is where you'll find international male models parading in garments so tight you can tell what religion they are. **Sandy Bay** is Cape Town's nudist beach, with discreet cruising at the far end of the main beach. But beware: The freezing ocean will bring you down to size.

GAY EVENTS Cape Town's biggest queer celebration and Africa's biggest gay circuit party, is the annual **MCQP Costume Party,** held during the MCQP Festival. It's a massive fancy dress costume ball held at great venues (2002 was at the Castle, the oldest building in Cape Town and still the regional HQ of the SA Defense Force!) and attended by thousands of queers of all ages and persuasions, with some 10 dance floors playing a rich variety of music. A new theme is explored each year. For details, call ✆ **083/309-1553** or go online at www.mcqp.co.za). The **La Loerie Festival,** held at the end of May, when some 5,000 camp revelers take to the streets of Knysna, on the Garden Route. Call ✆ **044/386-0011.**

RECOMMENDED GUESTHOUSES There are a variety of options to be had in **De Waterkant Village** (see "Where to Stay," earlier in this chapter), which is situated in the heart of the Queer Quarter, within easy walking distance of clubs and bars. **Amsterdam Guest House** (19 Forest Rd.; ✆ **021/461-8236**; www.amsterdam.co.za; from R595/$75 double) is an extremely popular men's-only guesthouse situated on the slopes of the city with a pool, Jacuzzi, sauna, and sling; early booking is essential. **Parker Cottage** (Carstens, Tamboerskloof; ✆ **021/424-6445**; R550/$69 double; www.parkercottage.co.za) is a neat, graciously decorated Victorian home away from home that will suit the older traveler.

—by Andre Vorster, Cape Town's most celeb queen and "mother" of MCQP (Mother City Queer Projects)

have the time or know-how to track down. Arguably the best wine shop in Cape Town. V&A Waterfront ✆ **021/425-5701** or 15 Long St. ✆ 021/419-8984.

Steven Rom This liquor merchant has a large selection in stock but will also track down and order anything you request (even once you're home) and arrange freighting. Galleria Centre, 76 Regent Rd., Sea Point. ✆ **021/439-6043**. www.winecellar.co.za.

.11 Cape Town After Dark

Pick up a copy of the monthly *Cape etc.* or *SA Citylife* magazines. Alternatively, the weekly *Mail & Guardian* covers all major events, as does the local daily *The Argus*—look in the "Tonight" section, or Friday's insert "Top of the Times" in the *Cape Times.* You can book tickets to theaters and movies and most major music/party events by calling **Computicket** (℃ **021/421-0777;** www. computicket.co.za) and supplying your credit-card details.

THE PERFORMING ARTS

Critics in the Mother City, as elsewhere, pull no punches, so watch the press. Anything directed or produced by Martinus Basson or Mark Fleischman is not to be missed. In summer, take in one of the outdoor concerts (see below). Take a look at what's on at the city's **ARTscape Theatre** (previously the Nico Malan Theatre; Foreshore; ℃ **021/421-7839**) or **Baxter Theatre** (Main Rd., Rondebosch; ℃ **021/685-7880**). If you like your entertainment light, the **Theatre on the Bay** (Camps Bay; ℃ **021/438-3301**) hosts a frothy mix of comedies and farces, while **On Broadway** (21 Somerset Rd., Green Point; ℃ **021/418-8338**) is one of the city's best cabaret venues (particularly if you like your cabaret camp). The **Independent Armchair Theatre** (Lower Main Rd., Observatory; ℃ **021/447-1540**) is a lounge-style theater that hosts an irregular, cult-variety selection of offbeat comedy shows, but for a guaranteed laugh, catch the steam train to Darling station, a small town an hour from town, for a performance by South Africa's most famous drag satirist, Tannie Evita, at "Evita se Perron" (see "West Coast" in chapter 4, or call ℃ **022/492-2831/51;** www.evita.co.za).

OUTDOOR CONCERTS

Summer brings a wealth of fantastic outdoor concerts; tops for venue are the Sunday **Kirstenbosch Summer Concerts** (℃ **021/799-8783**, or 021/761-4916 weekends): Bring a picnic and relax to great music, from jazz bands to Cape Minstrel troupes, popular acoustic groups to the Philharmonic Orchestra, while the sun sets behind the mountain. Concerts start at around 5pm, but get there early in order to secure your patch of lawn. **Maynardville Open Air Theatre** (Church and Wolf sts., Wynberg) hosts an annual Shakespeare play against a lush forested backdrop—performances vary from year to year but invariably put a contemporary spin on the Bard. Free concerts are held at the **V&A Waterfront amphitheatre** (℃ **021/408-7600**); acts range from winners of school talent contests to good jazz. It's worth taking the 30-minute drive to Stellenbosch, where you can choose between the lineup at **Oude Libertas Amphitheatre** (Adam Tas Rd.; ℃ **021/809-7473**) or the **Spier Summer Festival** (Spier Wine Estate; ℃ **021/809-1105**), which serves up local and international opera, theater, and music acts. Note that you can catch a steam train to Spier from the Waterfront, and eat there or picnic on the estate lawns.

THE CLUB, PUB & MUSIC SCENE

During the summer season, Cape Town becomes one big party venue. Get into the mood with sundowners at a trendy bar in Camps Bay (see "Where to Dine: Atlantic Seaboard," earlier in this chapter) or with a bottle of bubbly on a well-situated beach or the top of Table Mountain. You will, however, want to pace yourself—getting to *any* party before 11pm will see you counting barstools. Expect good nights out from Wednesday onwards, and head for one of the following three areas: **Long Street,** particularly the mountain end (near the Turkish

Baths), is the central city's hot party area. A selection of the best nightspots are listed below, but do pop into **Jo'burg,** frequented by a self-styled selection of hipster trendies, and owned by local character Bruce Gordon—he's the one with the barcode tattooed on his arm, done in 2003 when he was exhibited as an artwork at the National Gallery. Next door (well almost) is **Lola's** (✆ **021/423-0885**), a casual corner cafe which attracts an eclectic melange of gay, bohemian, and backpacker types; across the road, single-malt devotees frequent the plush leather settees of **Kennedy's Cigar Bar** (✆ **021/424-1212**).

Another big party strip near the city center is **Somerset Street** in Green Point, where Club 55 and The Bronx dominate. Known as Cape Town's Gay Quarter, it is nonetheless very straight friendly. **Lower Main Road** in Observatory, Cape Town's "bohemian" suburb, is another cool place to hang out. Check out quaint bars like **Café Ganesh** (✆ **021/448-3435**) and the over-the-top baroque **Touch of Madness** (✆ **021/448-2266**), or **Club Africa (Club de Danse et Musique Africaine)** ✪ (corner of Lower Main and Station roads; ✆ **021/686-3872**), a vibey little venue featuring a broad range of African dance music.

LIVE MUSIC

It's off the beaten tourist track, but you can catch regular Cape jazz sessions featuring hot artists like pianist Hotep Galeta, saxophonist Robbie Jansen, and guitarist Alvin Dyers at **West End** (College Rd., Athlone; ✆ **021/637-9132**). For a jazzy afternoon in the city center, hang out on the balcony of **Seasons Lounge** (120 Loop St., corner of Wale St.; ✆ **021/422-3913**) on Saturdays. The **Green Dolphin Restaurant** at the V&A Waterfront (✆ **021/421-7471**) caters to the discerning supper-club jazz enthusiast, attracting an excellent lineup of local and international performers (the food is pretty mediocre and pricey). Be on the lookout for African divas Judith Sephuma and Sylvia Mdunyelwa, as well as the Gavin Minter Quartet. **Manenberg's Jazz Café** at the Clock Tower Precinct, V&A Waterfront (✆ **021/421-5639**) serves up an African-soaked array of jazz flavors geared toward the tourist trade. **CD Wherehouse** (V&A Waterfront; ✆ **021/425-6300**), South Africa's finest specialist music store, showcases a variety of free in-store performances across all genres; call for times. Back in town, **Mercury Live** (previously The Jam) is hardly the most slick or sophisticated venue, but it's still the only place in the city where you'll find a regular lineup of original South African bands. While the emphasis is on modern rock, also look out for the city's premier drum 'n' bass party on the first Saturday of each month. Downstairs at the broom-cupboard–size **Mercury Lounge,** you can catch a cutting-edge selection of up-and-coming acts, with Tuesdays always a good opportunity to hook up with a "who's who" of Mother City musicians (43 de Villiers St., Zonnebloem. ✆ **021/465-2106**).

CLUBS

Afterlife ✪✪   The hippest dance club in the sleepy hollow of Stellenbosch, where regular "Entra Mi Casa" sessions are headed by deck wizard Ryan Dent (Platform Records) and some of the country's finest DJs playing funk, classic, and cutting-edge house are showcased all night long. 37 Andringa St., Stellenbosch. ✆ 072-380-8693.

Baseline ✪✪✪   This double-story club is where 20-something lookers get down to a variety of musical grooves from deep 'n' funky house to super-smooth R&B (Wed is always full). A restaurant by day, this über-trendy club offers a comfortable downstairs lounge area and a pretty steamy first-floor dance floor.

If you don't dance, you can always chill on the large balcony that provides a full view of Long Street. 74 Long St., Cape Town. ✆ 021/426-1506.

Club 55 ★★★ Situated in the heart of Green Point and surrounded by some of the best gay pride clubs in Cape Town. With two dance levels and a balcony overlooking the main downstairs dance floor, clubbers of all persuasions are guaranteed a great party, with the emphasis on retro-disco-driven sexy fun. 22 Somerset Rd., Green Point. ✆ 021/425-2739.

The Curve ★★ *Finds* One of the few clubs in the still largely segregated city where the rainbow nation gather to groove together—expect a heady sonic fusion of everything from jazz hop and hip-bop, Jamaican soul, and Chicano funk to an Afro-Caribbean fusion of salsa, cumbia, dance hall, Afrobeat, soukous, kwaito, rai, soul makossa, and a smattering of drum 'n' bass. 178 Lower Main Rd., Observatory. ✆ 021/448-0183.

Deluxe ★★★ A luxurious trend-setting experience in sound and vision, pioneering a new breed of "style funk" clubs. It's the truly hip and happening clubber's choice, where old-school soul meets disco for an always funky groove. Corner of Long & Longmarket sts., City Center. ✆ 021/422-4832.

Fuse ★★ With a small but potent pool of DJs playing styles ranging from the true retro genres of Motown, soul, funk, acid jazz, disco, and '80s synth-pop to the more contemporary deep house, electro, drum 'n' bass and hip-hop sounds, this intimate venue is recommended for the more eclectic clubber. Style is retro with a modern twist, elegant and sophisticated without being too, too serious. So dress accordingly. 21 Somerset Rd., Green Point. ✆ 021/421- 4019.

Ivory Room ★★ Super-stylish and super-exclusive. Expect a sexy, sophisticated interior, decor, music, and yes, people too! Fridays offer a mix of uplifting vocal house and retro sounds; on Saturdays, expect "a contemporary upbeat tempo." But unless you're a member (or match their sociographics), don't bother knocking. 196 Loop St., City Center. ✆ 021/422-3257.

Rhodes House ★★★ The place where beautiful people come to mingle with the truly gorgeous. Summertime is party time, with loads of Cuban/Latin-themed evenings, while winter is strictly reserved for private functions. Aimed at the 25-plus market, this upscale club in a double-story national monument remains Cape Town's best-dressed venue, with plenty of couches, two bars, and a small dance floor. Catering to the model and film crowd, it has a strict dress code (so phone beforehand to find out if it's themed) and usually a line to get in. 60 Queen Victoria Rd., City Center. ✆ 021/424-8844.

Snap ★★ Kwaito (home-grown South African house) meets R&B with a hip-hop flavor for a truly indigenous blend of sophisticated and urban street grooves. Dress for success. 6 Pepper St., off Long St., City Center. No phone.

Sutra Groove Bar ★★★ Sumptuous interiors evoke a self-indulgent level of sophisticated Eastern-retro chic. Ample bars, seating, and socializing areas downstairs let you succumb effortlessly to the state-of-the-art sound from a star-studded DJ lineup that keeps the groove flowing upstairs with a smooth mix of soul, slow-funk, and down-tempo house flavors. 86 Loop St., City Center. ✆ 021/422-4218/9.

BARS

Baraza ★ This funky bar with great elevated views of Camps Bay's palm-fringed beach always pulls a crowd who lounge around sipping cocktails and watching the sun go down. The Promenade, Victoria Rd., Camps Bay. ✆ 021/438-1758.

Bascule ⭐⭐⭐   This classy whiskey bar and wine cellar, situated on the edge of the yacht marina, hosts regular Sunday summer sunset sessions. Wednesdays and Fridays are when DJs spin the coolest world music. Cape Grace Hotel, V&A Waterfront. ℂ **021/410-7100.**

Bossa Nova ⭐   An upmarket Latino-lounge-cum-club with a wonderfully chilled atmosphere and funky decor, this is *the* place to salsa the night away. Somerset Rd., Green Point. ℂ **021/425-0295.**

Buena Vista Social Café ⭐⭐   This small Cuban themed cafe is the ideal spot to enjoy laid-back jazz flavors. Main Rd., Green Point. ℂ **021/433-0611.**

Dharma ⭐⭐⭐   A favorite with the inner-city "boho" set, this intimate Balinese-styled venue, complete with comfy seating in a courtyard centered around an old tree, is apparently steeped in feng shui. Whatever the reason, it attracts an interesting mix. Monday nights offer special live gigs with an acoustic duo who also team up with different artists every Wednesday and Saturday. DJs on Sundays create an engaging sonic fusion. 68 Kloof St. ℂ **021/422-0909.**

Po Na Na Souk ⭐⭐ End your day in an inner-city oasis where you can slowly sip a cocktail as you relax on a balcony overlooking the historic Heritage Square courtyard or cozy up with cushions in a fully winterized indoor area. A great place to people-watch. Heritage Sq., 100 Shortmarket St., City Center. ℂ **021/423-4889.**

EVENTS

MCQP ⭐⭐⭐ More than just an excuse to party in a funny frock, Cape Town's "Mother City Queer Party" has mushroomed from an annual gala costume party to a full-fledged weeklong celebration of all things "queer." Venue changes annually. ℂ **021/426-5709**. www.mcqp.co.za.

YDE Art Party ⭐⭐ This annual young, up-and-coming artist showcase has evolved into one of the biggest all-night party events on the Cape Town calendar with an innovative mix of local and international artists showcasing work alongside DJs and live acts. Venue changes annually. ℂ **021/797-8002.** www.yde.co.za.

North Sea Jazz Festival ⭐⭐⭐ South Africa's premier jazz gathering offers audiences a many-flavored musical feast with a 50/50 split between local and international artists, ranging from old school to avant-garde improvisation, straight ahead contemporary tones to smooth jazz, hip-hop, and live electro-acoustic jazzy house. ℂ **021/422-5651.** www.nsjfcapetown.com.

12 The Winelands

South Africa has 13 designated wine routes, of which the area called the Winelands—comprising the routes of Somerset West, Stellenbosch, Paarl, and Franschhoek—is by far the most popular. While the towns are all within easy driving distance from each other, there are well over 150 estates and farms to choose from, and first-time visitors are advised to concentrate on those that offer a combination of historic architecture, excellent wines, and/or views of the vineyard-clad mountains. True oenophiles should refer to the box "Collecting Cape Wines," below, and spend the day with an expert who can tailor-make your tour to suit your specific interests (see "Exploring the Winelands," below). You can treat the Winelands as an excursion from Cape Town or base yourself here—no more than 30 to 75 minutes from the bright lights of the city, this is a great area to immerse yourself in rural peace and fine wines. Accommodations options are also excellent, with most offering better value than their Cape Town counterparts.

If you have time to concentrate on only one area, make it Franschhoek, the prettiest (and most touristy) of the Winelands valleys, with the best selection of restaurants; or Stellenbosch, which has a charming historic center and the densest concentration of estates. Both are within easy driving distance of each other, via the scenic Helshoogte Pass.

EXPLORING THE WINELANDS

This is a large, mountainous area, and you're best off exploring it by car, so that you can choose your own estates and pace. Don't try to cover the entire Winelands in a day; tackle no more than four to six estates a day, and don't forget to book a luncheon table with a vineyard view. If you're serious about your wine, take a guided tour with a specialist. For tailor-made trips into selected and often lesser-known cellars, accompanied by a true wine-lover, you can't beat a tour with **Stephen Flesch.** Former chairman of the Wine Tasters Guild of S.A., Stephen personally knows many of the winemakers and proprietors of the top wine estates, and has a thorough knowledge of South African wines that spans four decades. He will take into account your particular interests or preferences and tailor a personalized itinerary, including a delightful lunch (he is, after all, secretary of Cape Town's Slow Food Convivium) at an estate or a great Winelands restaurant. Rates are R900/$112 per day (R650/$80 half day) for a single person; R300/$37 extra for each additional person. You can contact him at © 021-705-4317, but it's advisable to book well in advance by e-mailing him at sflesch@iafrica.com. If Stephen is unavailable, **Vineyard Ventures** (© 021/434-8888) also offers customized tours.

If you prefer the idea of a self-drive tour, then purchase a copy of John Platter's *South African Wine Guide*—updated annually and now in its 23rd printing, it's still the best in the business. The guide not only lists every estate and its wines, but provides star ratings, and though the author is careful not to say anything nasty, you very quickly learn to read between the lines.

Note: Even though the majority of wine estates accept credit cards for wine purchases, you should keep some cash on hand—most estates charge a fee (R5–R25/65¢–$3 per person) for a wine-tasting session.

STELLENBOSCH

46km (28½ miles) E of Cape Town

The charming town of Stellenbosch was founded in 1679 by Governor Simon van der Stel, who, among other achievements, built Groot Constantia and planted hundreds of oak trees throughout the Cape. Today Stellenbosch is, in fact, known informally as Eikestad, or "city of oaks." The beautifully restored and oak-lined streetscapes of **Dorp, Church,** and **Drosdty** make Stellenbosch the most historic of the Winelands towns (it has the largest number of Cape Dutch houses in the region), but outside of the historic center much is suburban sprawl. But this is also a university town, site of the country's most prestigious Afrikaans university, with attendant coffee shops and student bars, and it also promotes itself as the cultural center of the Cape, with a number of great theater options. Contact the Tourism Bureau to find out what's on at the open-air amphitheaters at **Oude Libertas** and **Spier,** or put on your dancing shoes and head for **Afterlife** (see "Cape Town After Dark," earlier in this chapter).

ESSENTIALS

VISITOR INFORMATION   **Stellenbosch Tourism Bureau** (© 021/883-3584; www.istellenbosch.org.za) is by far the most helpful in the Winelands,

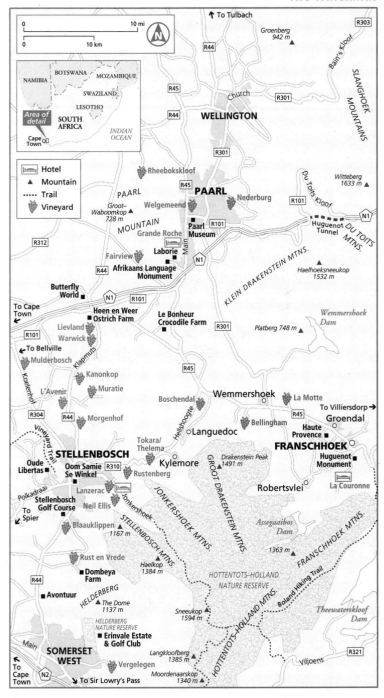

Three Dramatic Wineland Drives ★★★

Wines seem to thrive in the most beautiful environments. If you want to see as much of the landscape as possible, try one of these drives for a terrific—and breathtaking—overview of the region. Traversing four mountain ranges and encompassing both Franschhoek and Stellenbosch, the **Four Passes Route** will take a full day including a few stops for wine tastings and lunch. Head out of the city center on the N2, bypassing the turnoff for Stellenbosch (R310) and Somerset West (R44), and ascend the Hottentots Holland Mountains via **Sir Lowry's Pass,** with breathtaking views of the entire False Bay. Take the Franschhoek and Villiersdorp turnoff, traveling through the town of Grabouw, and traverse the Groenland Mountains via **Viljoen's Pass.** This takes you through fruit-producing valleys (exquisite in spring when bare brown branches are covered in pink and white blossoms) and past the Theewaterskloof Dam. Look for a right turn marked Franschhoek, and ascend the Franschhoek Mountains via the **Franschhoek Pass,** stopping at La Petite Ferme (see later in this chapter) for tea with a view. Drive to Stellenbosch via the equally scenic **Helshoogte Pass,** stopping at Boschendal to tour the historic Cape Dutch Manor House. Take the R310 back to the N2 or overnight in Stellenbosch.

The second drive takes in the Breede River Valley and the historic town of Tulbagh. Take the N1 out of town, past Paarl, then tackle the majestic **Du Toit's Kloof Pass** (if you've made a late start, take the tunnel). Once through the Du Toit's Kloof Mountains, you are approaching the Breede River Valley, a less publicized wine-producing region but no

and you'd be well advised to head to their office as soon as you arrive—besides giving expert advice on where to stay and what to do, they provide the excellent "Discover Stellenbosch on Foot" leaflet (R2/25¢), which indicates more than 60 historical sites with accompanying text. The Tourism Bureau is located at 36 Market St. (summer hours: Mon–Fri 8am–6pm, Sat 9am–5pm, Sun 9:30am–4:30pm; winter [May–Aug] hours: Mon–Fri 9am–5pm, Sat 9:30am–4:30pm, Sun 10am–4pm). Adjacent is the **Adventure Centre** (www.adventureshop.co.za), which lists a huge variety of activities in the region.

GETTING AROUND   TOWN   Guided walking tours (90 min.) leave the Tourist Bureau every day at 10am and 3pm. For historic and twilight walks in town at a time that's convenient for you, contact **Sandra Krige** (© 021/883-9633;** hkrige@iafrica.com). The town center is small enough to explore on foot, but you can rent a bicycle from **Piet se Fiets** (© 021/887-3042,** R15/$1.95/hour; R65/$8/day) or the slightly more expensive **Village Cycles** (© 021/887-0779).

WINE ESTATES   See "Exploring the Winelands," above, for specialist tours and self-drive tips. Note that if you don't want to drive, you can visit five wine Stellenbosch estates by using the hop-on, hop-off **Vinehopper bus** (© 084-875-5959;** R135/$16 per person) To explore the Spier estate on horseback, contact **Spier Little Creek Horse Trails** (© 021/881-3683).

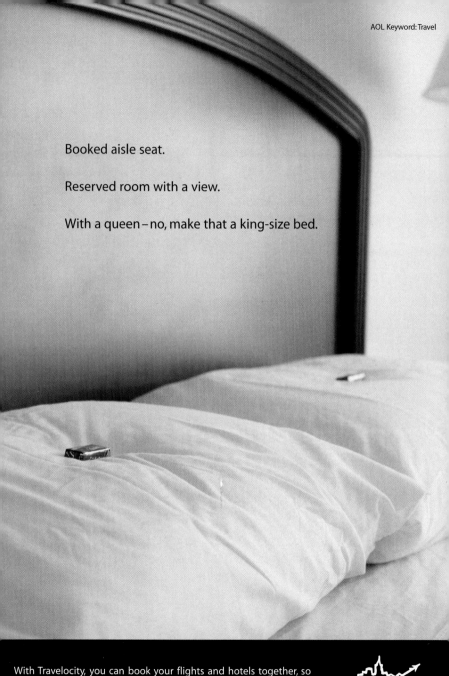

less attractive than the more famous Winelands areas, and producing wines with a distinctive berry flavor. Keep an eye out for the turnoff to the right marked Rawsonville, then follow the signs north (left) to Goudini Spa and **Slanghoek;** stop here to taste the award-winning Noble Late Harvest. This scenic back road meets the R43 in a T-junction—turn left and follow the signs to the small town of Wolseley before taking the R46 to Tulbagh. Once there, stroll down charming Church Street to admire the Cape Dutch and Victorian buildings, perfectly restored after an earthquake damaged them in 1969, and lunch at **Paddagang** (© 023/230-0242): Their *waterblommetjie bredie* (waterlily stew) is arguably the best in the Cape. After lunch you might want to sample one of the Tulbagh Estate's wines before overnighting **at Hunters** © 023/0582; R450/$56 double) or nearby **Bartholomeus Klip** (see "Paarl: Where To Stay," later in this chapter). Alternatively, head back to Wolseley, this time taking the R303 to Wellington via **Bain's Kloof Pass** ⚲, a spectacular pass created by the father of the celebrated master engineer responsible for the Swartberg Pass outside Oudtshoorn. From Wellington, follow the signs to Paarl or Franschhoek, where you could overnight, or head for the N1 and back to Cape Town.

The third drive, another full day, takes you along the dramatic Coastal Route to Hermanus, snaking along cliffs that plunge into the ocean, before turning off to sample the wines growing in the Hemel en Aarde (Heaven and Earth) valley. For more details on this drive, see "The Coastal Route: Gordon's Bay to Hermanus" in chapter 4.

EN ROUTE TO STELLENBOSCH FROM CAPE TOWN

Vergelegen ⚲⚲ (© 021/847-1334; daily 9:30am–4pm; call for tour times) is the only must-see estate on the Somerset West or "Helderberg" Wine Route, which lies a few miles from Stellenbosch. Vergelegen (or, "far location") was built by reprobate Willem Adriaan van der Stel, who took over from his father as governor of the Cape in 1699, only to abuse his power by building Vergelegen on land that did not actually belong to him and by using the Dutch East India Company slaves and resources to compete with local farmers. He was sacked in 1707 and the farm demolished and divided. Today this beautifully restored wine estate, surrounded by gorgeous gardens, is known to be Mandela's favorite, as well as the only one to host Queen Elizabeth II and the Clintons during their respective state visits. The restaurant, **The Lady Phillips** (© 021/847-1348), serves excellent light meals in a wonderful atmosphere.

To get here, take the N2, pass the R310 (the first road from Cape Town that leads to Stellenbosch) and take exit 43, which takes you onto the R44. Follow this into town, keeping an eye out for Lourensford Road. Vergelegen is some 3km (about 2 miles) farther on this road. There is a R10 ($1.25) entry fee; cellar tours are a further R10 ($1.25); wine tasting (Mon–Sat) R5 (65¢).

To get to Stellenbosch from here (some 20 min. away), head back to the R44 and turn right (at the Lord Charles Hotel). Red-wine lovers are advised to look out for the sign to **Rust en Vrede** ⚲⚲⚲ ("rest and peace") along the way—turn right onto Annandale Road to sample these raunchy reds (© 021/881-3881;

Mon–Fri 9am–5pm, Sat 9am–4pm in season). Families in search of a picnic should turn left and head for **Spier** (© 021/809-1100; daily 9am–5pm; picnic baskets packed if booked in advance). Among the many activities on offer at Spier are scenic horseback rides through the estate's vineyards. A little farther along the R44 is the turnoff for **Blaauwklippen** (© 021/880-0133; Mon–Fri 9am–4:45pm, Sat 9am–4pm), where from October 1 to April 30 you can take a coach ride through the vineyards.

WHAT TO SEE & DO IN TOWN

If you have time for only one historic stop in town, make it the **Village Museum** ⚘⚘⚘ (18 Ryneveld St.; © 021/887-2902; Mon–Sat 9:30am–5pm, Sun 2–5pm; admission R15/$1.95), which comprises the Schreuderhuis Cottage (1709), the Cape Dutch Blettermanhuis (1789), the Georgian Grosvenor House (1803), and the Victorian Murray House (1850). Each house has a guide done up in period dress, and the artful styling of the furniture, combined with the accessible explanations on the architecture and fashion of these eras, make these the best house museums in the country.

From here head south along Drosdty Street, turn right onto Dorp Street, and then stroll down the oak-dappled street to **Oom Samie Se Winkel** ⚘ (© 021/887-2612; 8:30am–5:30pm weekdays, 8:30am–5pm weekends, till 6pm in summer), a Victorian-style general dealer bursting at the seams with knick-knacks, and a great place to pick up souvenirs, such as step-by-step *bobotie* spice packs, dried-fruit rolls, and dirt-cheap enamel plates. It has a charming tearoom, complete with sunning cats and clucking chickens, behind the shop.

THE STELLENBOSCH WINE ROUTE

This is the oldest in the country, with more than 100 estates and farms to choose from, almost all of which are reached via the three major roads radiating from the town center. Note that it's worth double-checking opening times if you're traveling over the weekend. If you head southwest on the R306, you should consider visiting the 300-year-old **Neethlingshof** (© 021/883-8988; Mon–Fri 9am–5pm, Sat–Sun 10am–4pm; in high season [Aug–Jan] hours are extended) just for the pleasure of driving up its gracious pine-lined avenue—once there, however, you may find the experience relatively commercial, though it's worth it to taste their Noble Late Harvest. To reach **Zevenwacht** (© 021/903-5123; Mon–Fri 8am–5pm, Sat–Sun 9:30am–5pm)—one of the prettiest wine estates in the country, with a manor house on the edge of a tranquil lake and views all the way to the ocean—take the M12 to Kuilsriver.

Most of the wine estates are located off the R44, which runs north to Paarl. First stop should be the beautiful **Morgenhof** to sample the merlot and chardonnay (© 021/889-5510; Mon–Fri 9am–4:30pm, Sat–Sun 10am–3pm; in Nov–April hours extend to 6pm), followed by **L'Avenir** (© 021/889-5001; 9am–5pm daily) to try the Pinotage. The turnoff for tiny **Muratie,** still one of the most noncommercial estates, is next. This is a must if you like port (beware—the nonvintage is as easy to drink as grape juice!) and berry-rich red wines (© 021/865-2330; Mon–Fri 9am–5pm, Sat–Sun 10am–4pm). Muratie is followed by **Kanonkop** (© 021/884-4656) famous for its reds, the equally acclaimed **Warwick** (© 021/884-4410; see "Women Making Waves" box, below), and **Lievland** (© 021/875-5226).

Some of the best estates on the Stellenbosch wine route are located on the Helshoogte Pass, which links Stellenbosch with Franschhoek; see "Stellenbosch to Franschhoek," below, for recommendations.

Fun Fact **Women Making Waves**

In what has traditionally been a male-dominated world, a number of South African women are making headlines with a crop of respected wines. Proof of their prowess lies in the drinking, of course, so schedule a visit to the following Stellenbosch estates: **Warwick** (© 021/884-4410), where owner Norma Ratcliffe produces a fine Cape blend called Three Cape Ladies and a Bordeaux-style blend called Trilogy; **Morgenhof** (© 021/889-5510), where Rianie Stryjdom is producing a superb Cabernet Reserve; **Jordan** (© 021/881-3441), where Kathy Jordan produces a fine sauvignon blanc and a solid cabernet. Carmen Stevens is not only female but the first "coloured" (the South African term to denote mixed-blood descent) winemaker—her talents have been harnessed by **Welmoed** (© 021/881-3800); try the Shiraz. In Paarl stop at **Welgemeend** (© 021/875-5210), a family-run boutique winery, where daughter Louise Hofmeyer produces an excellent Estate Reserve.

Finally, if you're tired of tasting wine, take the 10km (6-mile) circular drive through the **Jonkershoek Nature Reserve,** stopping for lunch at **Lanzerac**—ask for a map from the Tourism Bureau. This is also where you'll find **Neil Ellis** (© **021/887-0649;** Mon–Fri 9:30am–4:30pm, Sat 10am–2pm), another estate producing superb wines.

WHERE TO STAY

It makes sense to stay within the historic center—attractions and a great selection of restaurants and coffee shops are only a short stroll along the oak-lined streets away. Given this, the best option is River Manor (see below), but you may also want to investigate the following. The recently opened **Roosenwijn Guest House** ✦ (© **021/883-3338;** www.stellenguest.co.za) offers comfortable rooms tastefully decorated in Afrikaans-Afro chic for between R500 and R700 ($62 and $88), depending on the season. Given its location (a 2 min. walk from the center) and the attractiveness of the decor, this is the best deal in town, but it doesn't have a great pool or any real garden to speak of. Opposite is **Bonne Esperance** (© 021/887-0225; www.bonneesperance.com; R570/$70 double), which you should consider only if you can get an upstairs room, specifically no. 5, 14, or 15. Even more central, but not as good value are **Eendracht** (© 021/883-8843; www.eendracht-hotel.com; R578–R1,238/$72–$155), which has bright but impersonal rooms and no real public spaces right in the center of historic Dorp Street; and **D'Ouwe Werf,** the oldest inn in South Africa, and popular for its old-fashioned hospitality (© **021/887-1608;** www.ouwewerf. com; R880–R1,190/$110–$148). If you don't mind having to drive everywhere, you should also take a look at **Summerwood** (© **021/887-4112;** www. summerwood.co.za; R1,300/$162 double), a top-caliber guesthouse situated on the Jonkershoek Road. Excellent hosts (Hilary and Malcolm Forbes), an intimate atmosphere (only nine rooms, of which I recommend no. 8 for best views), large rooms, and a great pool and garden are the main reasons to book here.

Lanzerac Manor & Winery ✦✦✦ *Kids*   The Lanzerac is by far the best accommodations option in Stellenbosch, and one of the top in the Winelands. Part of a working wine estate (which, incidentally, produced the Cape's first Pinotage, unique to the region, and still a first-rate example of the variety), the

Collecting Cape Wines

The flavor treasures of the Cape are sprinkled across the fan-shaped Cape vineyard region. They are usually found in one of many tiny cellar salesrooms at the end of a farm drive in the foothills of a granite- and sandstone-peaked mountain range. Using Cape Town and its Table Mountain as the handle of the fan, one can collect most of these gems on a circular sweep through the Cape Peninsula and Stellenbosch and Paarl valleys.

Looking for crisp, firm white wines and succulent sweeties, you should begin in Constantia, just a few minutes from the city center. **Buitenver-wachting** ("beyond expectation") regularly delivers the boldest and most spicy sauvignons, rich honeylike chardonnay, and a boldly structured, blended red called "Christine." Nearby, **Klein Constantia** competes with an equally dramatically fruited sauvignon blanc and one of the sweet wonders of the world, Vin de Constance. To find more of the Cape's great white wines, you should sweep southward around the scenic shores of False Bay to Somerset West and the Helderberg wineries.

Vergelegen, spectacularly mounted on the crest of an eroded mountain, produces a steely, racy sauvignon blanc, a multitextured chardonnay, and a lime-flavored semillon called Noble Late Harvest—a sweet wine with a good 20 years of pleasure in the bottle.

On the other side of the Helderberg mountain range, close to Stellenbosch, we meet some great reds: Crescendo from **Cordoba** with its earth-and-pepper richness and **Grangehurst's** twin red blockbusters, cabernet sauvignon–merlot and Pinotage. Even closer to Stellenbosch, you'll find another example of ripe-fruited Pinotage at **Vriesenhof.**

The Stellenbosch valley floor is bordered to the north by the Bottelary Hills, home to many of the area's best vineyards. The southern slopes, called "Polkadraai," shelter the luscious, sweet Noble Late Harvest wines of **Neethlingshof,** oozing with litchi, kiwi, and apricot fruit; the dense and creamy Pinotage reds from **Uiterwyk;** and two oak-aged white charmers from **Jordan** at the end of the cul-de-sac, where chardonnay and sauvignon blanc develop enhanced fruit flavors. Just over the hill (or by road around the R306), you'll encounter the vine-clad slopes of **Saxenburg,** facing the waves of False Bay, where the Private Collection labels of shiraz, cabernet sauvignon, and Pinotage require reservation and patience to acquire.

manor and its outlying rooms and suites sit sublimely amid rolling vineyards in the beautiful Jonkershoek Valley, with spectacular views of the Helderberg mountain range from every angle. The standard "classic" rooms, furnished in reproduction antiques and expensive fabrics, are comfortable, but for real privacy opt for one of the huge luxury rooms situated in separate chalets in the gardens. The Lanzerac's position as the Winelands' most upmarket hotel (this excludes the classy intimate guesthouses that appear to be gaining in popularity) is challenged only by Grande Roche, and though it's not as slick as its Paarl competitor, some

On the other side of Stellenbosch, in the valley called Jonkershoek, Etienne le Riche crafts a densely hued, chunky cabernet sauvignon on a tiny farm called **Leef op Hoop** ("Live on Hope"); and, near the end of the road, **Neil Ellis** practices his skills with one of the Cape's most respected cabernet sauvignons, a rich, complex chardonnay, and two cool-climate–origin sauvignon blancs, from the West Coast (Groenekloof) and South Coast (Elgin).

Nearby, high on the mountain slopes, the tiny **Thelema Vineyards** offers four Cape classic wines: an opulent, creamy chardonnay; a gooseberry-flavored sauvignon blanc; a minty merlot; and probably most revered of all Cape cabernets, Thelema Auction Reserve Cabernet Sauvignon. It's also worth stopping at **Tokara,** the most expensive winery ever built in the Western Cape, to marvel at the technology and the views. Downhill, to the west of these wineries, is **Rustenberg,** home of many of the Cape's great reds over the last 40 years; search out the labels of Rustenberg and Peter Barlow. Next door, the terraced vineyards of **Morgenhof** produce a merlot with a dark chocolate and coffee character, and a firm-fleshed chardonnay with maturation potential.

Two great Pinotages beckon the traveler toward Paarl, where you'll find Marc Wiehes **L'Avenir** Pinotage with its fragrant red-currant flavor, which contrasts dramatically with the massive structure and cherry-rich style of the lauded Pinotage from neighboring **Kanonkop.**

Crossing an invisible boundary line into Paarl, the first stop should be with **Villiera's** prized champagne-style bubbly, Tradition (try the Monro Brut "Millenium Cuvee"), followed by the farm's intensely spicy Bush Vine sauvignon blanc. Compare this with the nearby **Mulderbosch** sauvignon, another acclaimed white.

Fairview, with its goat-encrusted tower, produces some of the Cape's most finely modeled wines, with a powerful, peppery shiraz and plum-like Pinotage providing two standouts.

Two of Paarl's top vineyards specialize in cabernet sauvignon and merlot: The merlot produced at **Veenwouden** is dense and complex with gentle flavors; while **Plaisir de Merle** has a deliciously soft and round cabernet sauvignon. A finely structured shiraz from **La Motte** completes the lineup from Paarl and the Franschhoek Valley. Enjoy.

—by Graham Knox, wine connoisseur and author of
Cape Wines: Body & Soul

would appreciate the fact that the Lanzerac is a great deal more laid-back. It also welcomes children, with huge lawns for them to romp on.

Lanzerac Rd., Stellenbosch 7599. ☎ 021/887-1132. Fax 021/887-2310. www.lanzerac.co.za. 48 units. High season: R2,700–R3,900 ($335–$495) double; R5,350–R8,060 ($665–$1,005) suite. Low season (June–Sept): R1,520–R2,180 ($190–$270) double; R2,910–R4,350 ($360–$540) suite. Rates include breakfast. Children's rates on request. AE, DC, MC, V. **Amenities:** 3 restaurants; bar; 3 pools; room service; babysitting; laundry. *In room:* A/C, TV, minibar, coffee- and tea-making facilities, hair dryer, underfloor heating.

River Manor & Spa ★★ A few minutes' stroll from the historic attractions of Stellenbosch, this charming guesthouse, comprising two interlinked properties and a brand-new spa, is situated on an oak-lined road that follows the course of the Eerste River. Colonial-themed rooms are graciously outfitted (historical prints, turn-of-the-20th-century trunks, and plenty of wicker) and very comfortable, but the real reason this gets my vote are the great public spaces. Two pools are surrounded by table- and lounger-dotted lawns, and for those who want to escape the sun, there are deep verandas with comfortable chairs and striped awnings. The best-value rooms are no. 6 (R1,200/$150 double), which has a semi-private, comfortably furnished veranda attached, and, to a lesser extent, no. 14, which is also a little more private than most classic rooms; other than these you're better off booking a superior room. River Manor will provide picnic baskets and dinner on request, though there are restaurants within walking distance. *Note:* If you're watching your budget, Roosenwijn (see above) is an excellent alternative.

No 6 The Avenue, Stellenbosch 7600. © 021/887-9944. Fax 021/887-9940. www.rivermanor.co.za. 16 units. R1,200–R1,730 ($150–$215) double. Rates include breakfast. Children by request only. MC, V. **Amenities:** Two pools; room service; laundry. *In room:* A/C, TV, tea- and coffee-making facilities, hair dryer.

WHERE TO DINE

Stellenbosch does not have the caliber of restaurants Franschhoek is famed for, but there are a few stalwarts that seldom disappoint. Recommended restaurants within walking distance of the historic center are the **Greek Kitchen** (42 Ryneveld St.; © 021/887-7703), a small, laid-back place with outdoor seating and excellent slow-roasted lamb; the nearby **Fishmonger** (Ryneveld St; © 021/887-7835), with fresh, simple seafood; and, around the corner, **Decameron** (50 Plein St.; © 021/883-3331), the best Italian restaurant in town. Oenophiles should head for **Wijnhuis** (© 021/887-5844) in the Dorpsmeent Complex on Andringa Street, where you can dine on average Mediterranean-type fare with a tasting of the region's best wines (R25/$3 to sample six).

Moving out of town, **33 Stellenbosch,** on the Vlottenberg Road (© 021/881-3793), is, like 96 Winery Road, a highly rated country-style restaurant. There are also a few good options on the Helshoogte Pass (which leads to Franschhoek): **Tokara** (© 021/808-5959) is located in a state-of-the-art architectural gem and has superb views, but the food is overpriced and has received mixed reviews recently. The neighboring restaurant, **The Green Door** ⋆ (© 021/885-1149), is no architectural masterpiece, but views are sublime and the country-style food is a great deal less overdressed—steamed salmon trout, served with a caper and dill sauce, is the specialty.

96 Winery Road ⋆⋆ *Finds* This is one of the most unassuming and unpretentious restaurants in the Cape, yet it has a loyal following of locals who appreciate the informal atmosphere, unfussy, delicious food, great wine list, and excellent service (this is one place where waiters really know their wines). The menu changes every 6 months (with fresh and seasonal menu changes daily), but established favorites include Karoo shoulder of lamb; fresh Saldanha Bay mussels; pork belly strips served on sweet potato with homemade tomato chutney; crispy duck, roasted with ginger and sage and served on creamy potato bake; seared Norwegian salmon, served with a miso sauce on a vermicelli-noodle stir-fry; and the legendary dry-aged steaks. In season, bookings need to be made two weeks in advance.

Zandberg Farm, Winery Rd., Helderberg region. © 021/842-2020. Reservations recommended. Main courses R60–R82 ($7.50–$10). AE, DC, MC, V. Daily 12–5pm; Mon–Sat 7am–10pm.

FRANSCHHOEK

33km (20½ miles) E of Stellenbosch; 79km (49 miles) E of Cape Town via Stellenbosch; 85km (53 miles) SE of Cape Town via Paarl

If you only have time for one Winelands town, head for Franschhoek ("French corner"), the land Simon van der Stel gave the French Huguenots fleeing religious persecution in 1688. This small valley, surrounded by soaring mountains, is so lush a local once compared it to "living in a lettuce"; aside from its scenic advantages, it also boasts the highest concentration of top-quality restaurants, and a number of excellent accommodations options. It's very faux French, and some might find it a tad too touristy, but relative to the other Winelands options, it's easy to navigate and offers the most rural atmosphere.

ESSENTIALS

VISITOR INFORMATION   Make sure to pick up one of the helpful maps at the **Franschhoek Tourism Bureau** (on the main road going into town, at 85 Huguenot Rd.; © **021/876-3603;** Mon–Fri 9am–5pm, Sat–Sun 10am–5pm; hours are extended Oct–Apr).

GETTING AROUND   The town is small enough to traverse on foot, but to visit the wine farms you will need a car. For wine-tasting expeditions to two farms on purebred Arab horses, contact **Paradise Stables** (© **021/876-2160;** R260/$32; 9:30am–1pm and 2–6pm); pack a picnic and stop along the way. If you'd like to tour the region on a bike, hire one for R60/$7.50/day from **Bike Point** (© **083-235-3260**); for cycling tours, take a look at **Cycling Holidays** (http://cyclingholidaysouthafrica.com).

STELLENBOSCH TO FRANSCHHOEK: THE HELSHOOGTE PASS

From Stellenbosch the R310 heads over the scenic Helshoogte Pass, linking it with Franschhoek and Paarl, both of which lie some 30 minutes from the center of Stellenbosch. If you're heading to Franschhoek from Stellenbosch, follow the R310 for 2km (just more than 1 mile) before turning left into Ida's Valley and heading for **Rustenberg** ★★ (© **021/887-3153;** Mon–Fri 8:30am–4:30pm, Sat 9am–12:30pm). This gorgeous estate is renowned for its red wines, as well as its peaceful and beautiful setting, with a historic manor house contrasting with a brand new tasting center and state-of-the-art milking parlor. The estate has no restaurant, but visitors are welcome to picnic under the oaks. Or you can stop for lunch or tea at the **Green Door,** located at the top of the Helshoogte Pass, with lovely views, or push on to **Boschendal** ★★★ (© **021/870-4200;** 8:30/9:30am to 4:30/5pm, depending on what you wish to visit; wine tastings on Sun is only done in season [Nov–Apr]). Having traversed the pass, you will come to a T-junction where the R310 intersects with the R45—turn left for Paarl, right for Franschhoek and Boschendal. Together with Vergelegen and Constantia, Boschendal is one of the Winelands' most photographed estates, combining an excellent manor house museum with beautiful grounds and great wines. Boschendal also offers a number of dining options (see below).

THE FRANSCHHOEK WINE ROUTE

The following estates, all clearly signposted off Main Road and its extension, Huguenot Road, are recommended. **La Motte** ★ (© **021/876-3119;** Mon–Fri 9am–4:30pm, Sat 10am–3pm), which has been producing wines for 3 centuries, is worth seeing for its modern designer tasting room, not to mention its superb red wines. **Agusta Wines** (✆ **021/876-3195;** daily 9am–5pm) on Grande Provence Farm is worth visiting for its semi-sweet Angels Tears wine, and **Mont Rochelle Mountain Vineyards** (✆ **021/876-3000;** Mon–Sat 11am–4pm; Sept–Apr, Sun 11am–1pm), still owned by a descendant of the French Huguenots, for its glorious setting. If you're hungry, head for **Moreson Soleil de Matin** (✆ **021/876-3055;** Tues–Sun 11am–5pm; May–Nov until 4pm), where the sauvignon blanc is a good choice with lunch at the estate's delightfully relaxed **Bread & Wine Restaurant** ★ (Wed–Sun noon–4pm), worth visiting for its oven-fresh foccacia alone, served with Mediterranean-style dips.

A visit to the **Cabriere Estate** ★ (✆ **021/876-2630;** tastings and cellar tours Mon–Sat 11am and 3pm) is also recommended—and not just for the excellent bubbly. Every Saturday at 11am you can witness a demonstration by winemaker Achim von Arnim, who uncorks his bottles by slicing the neck off with a sabre, followed by an in-depth (2 hr.) tasting and tour.

The boutique-style **Boekenhoutskloof** ★★ (✆ **021/876-3320**) produces internationally acclaimed wines, particularly the reds—tastings, conducted by the winemaker himself, are by appointment only, one well worth making.

Huguenot Road intersects with Lambrecht Road at a T-junction at the base of the Franschhoek Mountains. Opposite is the **French Huguenot Monument,** erected in honor of the French Protestant refugees who settled here between 1688 and 1700. Its three arches symbolize the Holy Trinity. Turn left to drive the Franschhoek Pass for lunch at **La Petite Ferme**—a must, if you can get a table; see below).

WHERE TO STAY

Another accommodations option worth noting is **L'Auberge du Quartier Français** (✆ **021/876-2151;** www.lequartier.co.za; from R1,950–R2,350/$244–$290 double). This is the most expensive option in the valley, but the fact that it is "in" the valley (rather than overlooking it, like La Couronne or La Petite Ferme) is a drawback. That said, rooms are elegant, comfortable, and spacious and feature wood-burning fireplaces to ward off winter chills; book room no. 12 or 16, each with a leafy private seating area in the garden.

If you're on a budget, or looking for a romantic getaway, it's worth noting that a number of self-catering cottages are situated on wine farms, some with swimming pools and/or fireplaces and featuring lovely mountain and vineyard views. You don't even have to cook: With more than 25 restaurants to choose from, this is the way to go if you're serious about sampling a selection of the valley's finest fare. **Klein Dassenberg Cottages** (✆ **021/876-2107;** from R220/$28 double); **Blueberry Hill** (✆ **021/876-3362;** R450/$55 double); **Vineyard Cottages** (✆ **021/876-3194;** R145/$18 per person); or the idyllic **Bird Cottage** (✆ **021/876-2136;** R120/$15 per person) are all recommended. If you want to be in town, book the picture-postcard-cute **Lavender Cottage** (✆ **021/876-2666;** R200/$25 per person). Flyfishermen should book the cottage at **Three Streams** (✆ **021/876-2485;** R600/$75)—it's renowned for its smoked trout, and visitors have exclusive access to one of the farm's trout dams.

Auberge Clermont ★★   On a working wine farm in the old wine cellar, this auberge is inspired by the tastes and colors of Provence. Even the gardens, redolent with the scents of lavender and roses, are reminiscent of the South of France. Rooms are large and beautifully decorated; bathrooms are equally spacious, with double basins, separate showers, and heated towel racks. Breakfast is served in your room or under the 400-year-old oak trees. For families, there is a spacious three-bedroom, two-bathroom self-catering villa in a formal French garden. *Note:* The pool is on the small side.

Robertsvlei Rd., Franschhoek 7690. (C) 021/876-3700. Fax 021/876-3701. www.clermont.co.za. 6 units. R850–R950 ($105–$119) double; R1,050–R1,100 ($130–$138) suite; R1,100–R1,250 ($138–$155) villa. Rates include breakfast, except for villa. Ask about winter (May–Sept) discounts. AE, DC, MC, V. **Amenities:** Dining room/bar; pool; tennis court; limited room service; laundry. *In room:* TV (some), hair dryer, underfloor heating.

La Cabriere Country House ★★ (Value)

A good choice if you want exclusivity and affordability, La Cabriere Country House has only five guest rooms, but each is luxuriously and individually decorated with a surprisingly successful blend of African and Provençal fabrics, furniture, and *objets*. The well-traveled owners have incorporated all the best elements of guesthouses they've visited in various parts of the world, ensuring attention to detail not normally expected in this price range. Three of the rooms have fireplaces, and all have French doors that lead out into the garden with its Koi pond, inviting swimming pool, and valley and vineyard vistas. Breakfasts are lavish affairs enjoyed poolside or in the privacy of your room. *Note:* The winter rate offers exceptional value.

Middagkrans Rd., Franschhoek 7690. (C) 021/876-4780. Fax 021/876-3852. www.lacabriere.co.za. 4 units. R950 ($119) double; rates include breakfast. Ask about winter discounts. AE, DC, MC, V. Children over age 15 accepted. **Amenities:** Dining room; pool; laundry. *In room:* TV, minibar, hair dryer, fireplace (some).

La Couronne ★★★

Once the holiday home of the president of the Ivory Coast, La Couronne ("the crown") is on a hill overlooking the Franschhoek valley and mountains; the views from every window of this luxuriously appointed boutique hotel are challenged only by those at La Petite Ferme (see below). The rooms are spacious and comfortable with luxuries like underfloor heating, down pillows, and leather or skin armchairs and ottomans. Decor is either English-manor style in shades of gold and yellow (ask for no. 3, the unofficial honeymoon suite) or African themed. Most rooms have spacious bathrooms, though some are cheapened by the choice of fittings. Every two years a new wing with more luxurious suites is built; the next wing, due to open in December 2003, will again feature the latest luxuries. The large pool and comfortable and elegant public spaces (once again, with wraparound views) mean you could easily spend the entire day at the hotel. The restaurant, which has always had an excellent reputation, is under the direction of a new chef.

Robertsvlei Rd. (turn right at the monument), Franschhoek 7690. (C) 021/876-2770. Fax 021/876-3788. www.lacouronnehotel.co.za. 17 units. High season: R1,776–R2,880 ($222–$350)) double. Low season (May–Oct 15): R1,040–R2,030 ($130–$250) double. Rates include breakfast. AE, DC, MC, V. **Amenities:** Restaurant; cigar bar; pool; room service; babysitting; laundry; trout fishing. *In room:* A/C (some rooms), TV, hair dryer.

La Petite Ferme ★★★

These spacious B&B suites, located on the Franschhoek Pass, combine the most exquisite views of the valley with luxurious touches like private plunge pools and fireplaces—hence the top rating, despite the fact that it's not a hotel. Each morning a continental breakfast is served on your veranda from where you can appreciate a sweeping view of the valley; luncheons and dinners can be enjoyed at the adjacent restaurant or at Haute Cabriere across the road. Since these are two of the best dining options around (see "Where to Dine," below), you may find it unnecessary to descend into the valley at all.

Franschhoek Pass Rd., Franschhoek 7690. (C) 021/876-3016. Fax 021/876-3624. lapetite@iafrica.com. 3 units. R1,100 ($140) double, includes breakfast. AE, DC, MC, V. Children under age 16 not accepted. **Amenities:** Restaurant; room service (day only); laundry. *In room:* TV, minibar, tea- and coffee-making facilities, hair dryer, fireplace, plunge pool.

WHERE TO DINE

Franschhoek calls itself "the wine and food capital of the Cape," and although most Capetonians would disagree, it certainly can claim that title in the Winelands. In addition to those listed below, another fixture on the foodie map is **Monneaux** (© 021/876-3386), located in Franschhoek Country House on the main road into town. Relative newcomer **Klein Olifantshoek** (© 021/876-25666) is another worth considering—you can take a look at these and other menus at the tourism bureau in town. For a great informal lunch, head for **Bread & Wine** (© 021/876-3692) at the La Motte estate.

Boschendal 🐾🐾 TRADITIONAL S.A./COUNTRY CAFE/PICNIC This beautiful Cape Dutch estate offers three different dining experiences. The luncheon buffet—a great place to break a fast—is served in the original wine cellar, with a huge buffet table covered from end to end with tasty traditional Cape Malay and South African dishes (don't miss the malva pudding). It's not all heavy tradition though, with lighter treats like venison carpaccio with Satsuma preserve, watercress with local goat's cheese and walnuts, and Franschhoek specialties like smoked salmon trout. Still, it's tempting to overeat; if you're not that hungry, head for the wrought-iron tables under the oaks at Le Café and order one of the delicious quiches (the smoked salmon trout is recommended). From October to April you can purchase a picnic hamper to enjoy on the lawns shaded by more ancient oaks. (Ask about the full-moon picnics, held Dec–Mar.)

Pniel Rd., off R310 between Franschhoek and Paarl, Groot Drakenstein. © 021/874-1152. Buffet lunch daily noon–5pm (arrivals no later than 1:30pm; reservations essential), R180 ($22) per person. Le Café 10am–5pm daily, R30–R50 ($3.75–$6.50). Le Pique Nique, R88 ($11) per person, book in advance. AE, DC, MC, V.

Haute Cabriere Cellar Restaurant 🐾🐾🐾 INTERNATIONAL/MODERN CAPE The ideal dinner venue (in contrast with La Petite Ferme and Le Provençal, where views make them ideal for lunch), the rose-covered "Russian bunkhouse" is almost hidden from the road, and the vaulted ceiling gives it a modern medieval feel. Only the well-respected wines of this estate—handpicked to complement each of Matthew Gordon's dishes—are served, and there are no appetizers or main courses, just full or half portions or shared platters to mix and match. The menu is seasonal; start with oysters and a celebratory flute of Pierre Jourdan Brut Savage (summer), or the *tian* (casserole) of four types of Franschhoek salmon trout served with Belle Rose (winter); then try the roasted loin of springbok in a Cape Malay spice jus with corn tempura (summer), or grilled Scottish salmon with creamed spinach and potato galette and horseradish (winter). Finish with Belgian chocolates (handmade in the valley under the Huguenot label) with Fine de Jourdan potstill brandy (brandy distilled in a traditional copper pot) and coffee.

Pass Rd.. © 021/876-3688. Portions R40–R90 ($5–$11). AE, DC, MC, V. Daily 12–3pm; Fri–Mon 7–9pm.

La Petite Ferme 🐾🐾🐾 FRENCH COUNTRY If you are only spending one day in Franschhoek, make sure you lunch here: Book a table on the veranda, order the signature deboned smoked rainbow trout served with a creamy horseradish sauce, and allow plenty of time to drink in both the view and one of the farm's great wines. Even the locals can't resist dining here—situated on the Franschhoek Pass with a breathtaking view of the entire valley, this family-owned and -managed restaurant has arguably the best setting in South Africa. Though popular table 7 is considered the prime position and is booked for months in advance, on a recent visit I found that table 4 has just as good a view. Food is refreshingly simple—try the Portuguese-style calamari, marinated in red wine and grilled. End with La Petite Ferme's own plums, poached in red wine and served with meringues and ice cream.

Pass Rd. ⓒ 021/876-3016. Reservations essential. R38–R70 ($4.75–$8.75). AE, DC, MC, V. Daily 12–4pm.

Le Quartier Francais ⭐⭐ PROVENÇAL/MODERN CAPE It's considered by many to be the best in Franschhoek—and in this haute cuisine environment, that takes some doing. In my experience, I've found that standards can be inconsistent, and it may be worth calling to see if executive chef Margot Janse is in the house. That said, the venue, overlooking its own sheltered gardens in the center of town, is charming, and Margot is renowned for her innovative flavor combinations. The menu changes daily, but signature dishes include the double-baked beetroot and rocket (arugula) soufflé topped with apple and hazelnuts; olive oil–poached salmon trout with smoked salmon fritter, cucumber, and seaweed; grilled springbok loin in balsamic broth with curried gnocchi, roast onions, and mushrooms; and Margot's delicious caramelized lemon tart.

Corner of Berg & Wilhelmina sts. ⓒ 021/876-2151. Main courses R72–R86 ($8.75–$11). AE, DC, MC, V. Daily 7–9pm throughout year. Summer lunch (mid-Oct to mid-May) daily 12–2:30pm. Winter lunch (mid-May to mid-Oct) only on Sat–Sun noon–2:30pm.

Topsi & Company ⭐⭐⭐ INNOVATIVE COUNTRY/VEGETARIAN Featured in Robert Carrier's *Great Dishes of the World* (Smithmark Publishing), Topsi is often described as "the doyenne of Cape chefs"; and her honest home-style cooking is refreshing, her ebullient presence in the open-plan kitchen and dining room a delight. Located in an unassuming building off the main road, and furnished with portraits, rugs, mismatched wooden furniture, and a parrot, Topsi serves interesting cuts like calves' liver, baked and served on parsnip purée, or no-nonsense but delicious basics like her filet of trout baked on a bed of leeks and thyme, with baby potatoes and beetroot, or shredded duck and crunchy cabbage served in a crepe with nectarines and satay sauce. Topsi's vegetarian daughter ensures wonderful nonmeat options like the ricotta, spinach, and butternut crepe-cake with tapenade and caramelized apple stack. *Note:* Topsi's is unlicensed.

7 Reservoir St. West (next to the library). ⓒ 021/876-2952. Main courses R42–R68 ($5–$8.50). AE, DC, MC, V. Wed–Mon noon–2:30pm and 7–9pm.

PAARL

33km (20½ miles) NW of Franschhoek, 56km (35 miles) E of Cape Town

Paarl is named after the great granite rocks that loom above the town—the first European party to visit the area in 1657 watched the dawn sun reflecting off the glistening boulders after a night of rain, and named it Peerlbergh ("Pearl Mountain"). These 500-million-year-old domes are one of the world's largest granite outcrops, second only to Ayers Rock in Australia. The town's large size makes it a less attractive destination than the chi-chi village of Franschhoek and the oak-lined avenues of Stellenbosch, but there are a number of excellent wine estates to visit (get a map from the information bureau), and Main Street, with its 2km (just more than 1 mile) stretch of beautifully preserved buildings, is worth taking a leisurely drive along. Most visitors also find a visit to the **Taal Monument** (the large phallic sculpture clearly visible on the slopes of Paarl Mountain) worthwhile—the views of the valley and False Bay are excellent. To get here, drive down Main Street, passing the KWV headquarters on your left, and look for the signs to your right.

ESSENTIALS

GETTING THERE To get to Paarl from Franschhoek (some 30km/19 miles northwest), retrace your footsteps down Huguenot Road and take the R303 to Paarl (off the main road, after the turnoff to La Motte). Once in town, look for the first traffic circle and turn left onto Market; keep going until Market meets Main Street.

VISITOR INFORMATION The **Paarl Information Bureau** (© 021/872-3829; www.paarlonline.com; Mon–Fri 8:30am–5pm, Sat 9am–1pm, Sun 10am–1pm) is at 216 Main St.

WHERE TO STAY

Unlike Stellenbosch, it's not really ideal to stay in town—it's not as attractive a place. Just as well then that Paarl has perhaps the best selection of Cape Dutch homestead-cum-guesthouses, some on working wine farms, in the Winelands, the best of which are described below.

Bartholomeus Klip ★★★ This luxury country lodge is not in Paarl, but is located some 30 minutes' drive away, on a working wheat and sheep farm that has a 4,500-hectare (11,115-acre) nature reserve stocked with buffalo, zebra, wildebeest, gemsbok, eland, springbok, bontebok, and hartebeest, as well as the rare geometric tortoise, one of the world's most endangered reptiles. A wonderful base from where you can combine a bit of wildlife viewing (there are optional game drives in open-topped Land Rovers in the morning and evening) with wine tastings and a day trip to the city (a 75-min. drive away), or just really unwind. Accommodation is in a restored Victorian homestead, elegantly furnished in period style. There are only five bedrooms; the best option by far is the beautiful suite, which has its own entrance and a private veranda with great views. It's a peaceful place to truly unwind, with little to do but enjoy the exceptional food (included in the rate), laze around on loungers—the large, deep farm-style pool is wonderful—and walk, cycle, or drive through the reserve.

Elandskloof Mountains, Hermon. © 022/448-1820. Fax 022/448-1829. www.parksgroup.co.za. 5 units. R2,350 ($290) double; R2,600 ($325) suite. Low season (May–Aug) R1,600 ($200) double; R1,960 ($245) suite. Rates include brunch, high tea, 3-course dinner, and all game activities. AE, DC, MC, V. Children under age 18 not admitted. **Amenities:** Dining room; pool; laundry; game drives; game walks; canoeing; mountain biking. *In room:* Hair dryer.

Grande Roche ★★★ Located in a beautifully restored 18th-century Cape Dutch estate, surrounded by lush gardens and with the Drakenstein Mountains as dramatic backdrop, this—together with Lanzerac—is the most expensive accommodations option in the Winelands. It has all the amenities you'd expect from a classy hotel (not to mention a top-rated restaurant, **Bosman's**, see below), and even though it's only minutes from Paarl's town center, the mountain and vineyard views that embrace the homestead create a relaxing country atmosphere. The doubles have integrated lounges/bedrooms, and are extremely luxurious and roomy, so no need to book a suite. Most rooms also come with private terraces. Service is tip-top—a request for train information was doggedly researched by one of the managers. Many people come for the relaxing spa treatments; it's not unusual to see robe-clad guests blissfully wandering the grounds. *Note:* The hotel is closed from June to August.

P.O. Box 6038, Paarl 7622. © 021/863-2727. Fax 021/863-2220. www.granderoche.co.za. 35 units. High season (Oct–Mar): R2,300–R3,500 ($290–$435) double; R4,950 ($625) honeymoon suite. Dec 12–Jan 10 5-night minimum stay. Low season (Apr–May and Sept): R1,600–R2,500 ($200–$310) double; honeymoon suite R3,750 ($470). Rates include breakfast. AE, DC, MC, V. Children age 7 and older only. **Amenities:** Restaurant;

bar; 2 pools; spa; fitness center; salon; room service; massage; laundry. *In room:* A/C, TV, minibar, underfloor heating (some rooms).

Palmiet Valley ★★ Situated on a working wine farm in a historic homestead dating back to 1717, Palmiet Valley is arguably the most beautifully furnished guesthouse in the Winelands, with lovely antiques in every room (book one with a fireplace if you're traveling in winter). Once outdoors, you can enjoy beautiful views of the surrounding vineyards and craggy mountains from every angle, including the terrace and decent-size pool. Four-course dinners are served in the period-styled dining room at one table; you can request a more private option if you like. A chauffeur-driven limo is available for daily charter or airport transfers.

PO Box 9085, Klein Drakenstein 7628. ✆ **021/862-7741.** Fax 021/862-6891. www.palmiet.co.za. 10 units. R1,490 ($185) double; R1,800 ($225) honeymoon suite. Winter rates less 20%. Rates include breakfast. MC, V. **Amenities:** Dining room; wine tasting; bar; pool; room service; laundry; mountain bikes; horseback riding. *In room:* A/C, CD players, coffee- and tea-making facilities, hair dryers, fireplaces (some rooms).

Roggeland ★★ The visitors who book at Roggeland—another gracious Cape Dutch homestead in the Klein Drakenstein Valley—are a who's who of traveling writers and foodies, all of whom rave about this 300-year-old estate. World-famous chef Robert Carrier called it an inspiration, *Travel & Leisure* described it as one of the world's 20 best hotels, and the *New York Times* named it the preferred choice of hotels in the Winelands. Furnishings are more fusty than at Palmiet (food is the main reason to come here), but rooms are spacious and comfortable, the location is tranquil, and the service discreet and efficient. *Note:* Space allowing, nonguests are welcome to book for dinner, something I really recommend (R140/$18 per person).

P.O. Box 7210, Northern Paarl 7623. ✆ **021/868-2501.** Fax 021/868-2113. www.roggeland.co.za. 11 units. R520–R970 ($65–$120) double. Rates include breakfast and 4-course dinner with pre-dinner wine. AE, DC, MC, V. **Amenities:** Restaurant; pool; mountain bikes; horseback riding. *In room:* Tea- and coffee-making facilities, hair dryer.

WHERE TO DINE

Bosman's Restaurant ★★★ INTERNATIONAL/MODERN CAPE   The first and only hotel restaurant in Africa to achieve Relais Gourmand status, and listed one of the top 10 in the world by *New Straits Times,* Bosman's has been wowing local and international food critics alike for years. Menus change regularly, but there are always a number of set-menu choices (including a "Flavors of the Cape" sampler and a vegetarian-only menu), or you can opt for the a la carte. Current popular starters are the Cape peninsula seafood salad with lemon foam, or seared foie gras with baked apple soufflé and port wine and red pepper reduction. Karoo lamb with a Provençal jus and served with a gratinée ragout is another winner, and Amarula ice cream with mascarpone cheese and peach lasagna the perfect ending. Unfortunately, the fabulous cuisine is marred by

---

⌐ Fun Fact The Last Step to Freedom

Paarl made headlines when President Mandela, who spent his last years here under house arrest, took his final steps to freedom from the Victor Verster prison on the outskirts of town on February 11, 1990. This was the first time South Africans could see how 27 years of incarceration had changed Mandela. Many, in fact, had never seen his face—under the Prisons Act, not even old pictures were allowed to be published.

service that confuses sophistication with cloying formality—the grandiose lifting of cloches (done in unison) and fiddling with cutlery is irritating and a request for a glass of tap water is likely to be met with an upturned nose. You may be oblivious to these slight irritations, however, when you're dining on the restaurant veranda on a glorious star-filled night where the breeze is warm and rows of green vineyards stretch out before you.

Plantasie St. (in the Grande Roche Hotel). © 021/863-2727. Reservations essential. 3-course lunch menu R165 ($20). Dinner set menu R380–R520 ($45–$65); main courses average R110 ($14). AE, DC, MC, V. Sept-May daily 7–10:30am, noon–2pm, and 7:30–9:30pm. Closed June-Aug.

Rhebokskloof ★★ SOUTH AFRICAN/CONTINENTAL   Located in what is called "The Victorian Restaurant and Terrace," this is a great luncheon venue with a superb setting overlooking the estate's manicured lawns and lake—book a seat on the terrace for shady, alfresco dining in summer, or near the fireplace for warmth in winter. Chef Andreas Roscher changes his menu four times a year, and alternates between a light, value-for-money luncheon menu and a slightly more robust (and pricey) dinner menu. Recommended starters include the smoked ostrich or biltong and chicken salads—a good introduction to these S.A. delicacies; or the trio of rosti, topped with salmon tartare, onion and tomato salsa, and creamed mushrooms. Heavier but no less delicious house specialties are the springbok shanks braised in red wine, trio of game (kudu, ostrich, and springbok), and pan-roasted beef medallions served with a peppercorn sauce.

Rhebokskloof Estate, Agter Paarl. © 021/869-8386. www.rhebokskloof.co.za. Reservations essential in season. Main courses: R30–R60 ($4–$8) lunch, R60–R80 ($8–$10) dinner. AE, DC, MC, V. Thurs–Mon 9am–8pm; Tues–Wed 9:30am–5pm. (In season hours are extended).

4

The Whale Coast & Garden Route: The Western Cape

The Western Cape, Africa's southwesternmost tip, is the most popular tourist destination in South Africa, and with good reason. Aside from the sybaritic pleasures of Cape Town and its wine routes (see chapter 3), a vast Southern Right whale nursery stretches along the Cape's southern coast. Some of the best land-based whale-watching sites in the world are in the Overberg, with whales migrating to its shallow coastal basin to mate and calve from mid-July to November. The Whale Coast, of which the coastal town of Hermanus is the unofficial capital, is an easy (and beautiful) day trip from Cape Town, but there's plenty to do and see should you choose to spend a few days here.

East of the Overberg are the coastal lakes and forests of the Garden Route, fringed by the majestic mountains that separate it from the ostrich farms and vineyards of the Klein Karoo, and the distinctive architecture of the small settlements dotted in the vast arid plains of the Great Karoo. This is a wonderful part of the world to explore by car, and although you can drive the entire Garden Route from Cape Town in approximately 5 to 6 hours, you should spend at least 2 nights along the route—preferably more—to discover the beauty off the beaten N2 track. It's a great place to do nothing but unwind—but this scenic coastal belt, which encompasses South Africa's "Lakes District," also takes pride of place on the itinerary for adrenaline junkies, with a rush of activities ranging from the highest bungee jump in the world to cage-diving for Great White sharks.

Moving north from Cape Town, along what is simply known as the West Coast, you'll find numerous treasures, among them laid-back open-air beach restaurants, the bewitching Cederberg Mountains, and—after the first rains fall, usually in August—the annual miracle of spring, as the seemingly barren plains are abloom with spectacular flower displays. You can explore the West Coast on a day trip, but to find yourself alone, surrounded by a floral carpet as far as the eye can see, you'll need to take a side-trip to Namaqualand in the Northern Cape.

Fun Fact Africa's Floral Kingdom

The **Cape Floral Kingdom** covers .04% of the world's land surface, yet it contains 24,000 plant species, and is considered the most diverse of the world's six floral kingdoms—comparable only to the Boreal Kingdom, which comprises all of Northern America, Europe, and Asia. Popular indigenous species that have found their way into gardens across the world include the gardenia, red-hot poker, arum lily, strelitzia (bird of paradise), agapanthus, gladioli, and freesias.

1 Staying Active

Pick up a copy of "Garden Route—Outdoor Adventure," a listings guide published by the **Garden Route's Regional Tourism Office** (✆ **044/873-6314;** www.capegardenroute.org) and available at any of the region's tourism bureaus, or the comprehensive brochures on hiking and whale-watching.

ABSEILING   Take a 45m (148-ft.) abseil (rappel) in the Kaaimans River in Wilderness, then canoe out (R220/$27 per person). Call **Eden Adventures** (✆ **044/877-0179**). Even more exhilarating is canoeing over to Knysna's Western Head in the Featherbed Nature Reserve—not least because the drop here is 70m (224 ft.), and is followed by a 90-minute quad-bike ride. Contact **S.E.A.L.** (✆ **083-654-8755;** R380/$48).

BLACK-WATER TUBING   Not quite as exhilarating as whitewater rafting, but equally spectacular, is a half day spent floating on a tractor-tire inner tube down the Storms River. Once you enter the narrow gorge, you can look up to see nothing but the dramatic cliff face, dripping ferns, and a sliver of sky above. Trips cost R295 ($36) per person, including kit and lunch. **StormsRiver Adventures** (✆ **042/281-1836;** www.stormsriver.com) offers this and a host of other activities in the Tsitsikamma area.

BOATING   You can cruise the ocean all along the coast; recommendations can be found under each section.

BOARDSAILING & KITE-SURFING   If you get your rush from the combined power of water and air, Langebaan Lagoon on the West Coast is considered one of the best sites in South Africa, particularly in the early afternoon when the wind picks up. Book lessons and rent equipment from the **Cape Windsurf Centre** in Langebaan (✆ **022/772-1114;** www.capesport.co.za).

BUNGEE/BRIDGE-JUMPING   There are two sites: The original **Gourits River bridge-jump** (✆ **044/697-7001;** R150/$19 per person), between Albertinia and Mossel Bay on the N2, is a 65m (213-ft.) jump. The **Bloukrans River bridge-jump** (✆ **042/281-1458;** R550/$69 per person), 40km (25 miles) east of Plettenberg Bay, is the highest bridge-jump in the world, a stomach-churning 7-second, 216m (709-ft.) free fall. Both operate daily from 9am to 5pm.

CANOEING   Naturally one of the best ways to explore South Africa's "Lakes District" is via its many waterways. Canoes can be rented throughout the area—contact the local tourism bureau wherever you are. Recommended canoe trips are the 3-day guided **Wilderness Canoe Trail** (R340/$42 per person) starting at the Ebb & Flow rest camp at Wilderness National Park (✆ **044/877-1197**); and the 2-hour **Keurbooms River Canoe Trail** ★★★ near Plettenberg Bay (✆ **044/535-9648**). The latter is unguided and takes you 7km (4¼ miles) upstream through totally untouched vegetation, to an overnight hut where you're assured of total privacy. The luxury of solitude will cost you R400 to R520 ($50–$63) per person per night, depending on the day; all you have to supply is food. For various catered overnight canoe trips, contact **Blue Sky Adventures** (✆ **044/343-1757**). For kayaking tours on the ocean, contact **Dolphin Adventures** (✆ **044/384-1536**).

DIVING   There are two snorkeling and diving routes in the Tsitsikamma National Park: **StormsRiver Adventures** (✆ **042/281-1836;** www.stormsriver. com) provides guides, equipment, and dive courses. Gear and guides can also be rented from **Diving Adventures** (✆ **044/533-1158**) in Plettenberg Bay; ask about Jacob's Reef, another good spot off the Plett coast. **The Heads Adventure**

Centre (① **044/384-0831**) can assist with any diving queries or equipment rentals in the Knysna area, where there are a number of wrecks to explore. **The Mossel Bay Diving Academy** (① **044/693-1179** or 082-896-5649) specializes in dives west of Knysna.

GOLFING   You're really spoiled for choice on the Garden Route, which is becoming known as S.A.'s "Golf Coast," supplanting that of KwaZulu-Natal.

In George   The **George Golf Club** course ★★ (① **044/8736116**) will run you R230 ($28), while the **Fancourt** ★★★ links course and the brand new Bramble Hill course at Fancourt (① **044/804-0000**) will cost R650 to R850 ($82–$105) and R150 ($19), respectively; if you're not up to par, sign up with the Fancourt Golf Academy. Fancourt has two other Gary Player–designed championship courses, but you have to stay at Fancourt to play these.

In Knysna   A relatively new links course, designed by Ronald Fream and David Dale, is perched atop the Knysna East Head cliffs. It costs nonmembers R400 ($50) to play **Sparrebosch** ★★ (① **044/384-1222**).

In Plettenberg Bay   Choose between the challenging 18-hole course in ever-green surrounds at the **Plet Country Club** (① **044/533-2132**; R200/$25) or the Gary Player–designed **Goose Valley** ★ (① **044/533-0846**; R350/$44).

In Hermanus   Top course here is at the new **Arabella Country Estate,** 20 minutes from Hermanus, voted one of the country's top 10 courses in 2002; call ① **028/284-0000** (R350/$44).

HIKING   Garden Route   For serious hikers, the following four are worth not-ing: the 108km (67-mile) 7-day **Outeniqua Trail** ★ (① **044/382-5466**), which takes you through plantations and indigenous forests (shorter versions available); the 64km (40-mile) 5-day **Tsitsikamma Trail** ★★ (① **012/481-3615**), an inland version of the more famous Otter Trail, which includes long stretches of *fynbos* (hardy indigenous evergreen vegetation) as well as forests and rivers; the 26.6km (16½-mile) 2-day **Harkerville Trail** ★★ (also called the Mini Otter Trail, and a good alternative), which features forest and coastal scenery (① **044/382-5466**). Best of all is the 42km (26-mile) 5-day **Otter Trail** ★★★, South Africa's most popular trail. It's a tough coastal walk, taking you through the **Tsitsikamma National Park,** past rivers and through indigenous forests, with magnificent views of the coast; its popularity means it must be booked at least a year in advance (① **012/426-5111,** www.parks-sa.co.za). The 3-night **Dolphin Trail** is a new lux-ury trail, with all luggage portaged, comfortable fully catered accommodation, plenty of time for lolling in tidal pools, and trained field guides accompanying walkers (① **042/280-3561;** www.dolphintrail.co.za). If you don't have the time (or energy!) for overnight trails, the 10km (6-mile) **Pied Kingfisher Trail** in Wilderness National Park covers a variety of beautiful habitats; the 9.5km (almost 6-mile) **Kranshoek Walk** in the Harkerville Forest is a great forest environment; and the 9km (5½-mile) **Robberg Trail** in Plettenberg Bay is definitely worth exploring for its wild coastline and whale-watching opportunities. *Note:* Don't miss the 1km (just more than a half-mile) trail to the Storms River mouth.

West Coast   Avid hikers are advised to find out more about the **Cederberg Wilderness Area,** which lies some 3 hours north of Cape Town—with its strange twisted rock formations and tea-colored streams, this is a hiker and climber's paradise, plus it's off the beaten track (① **022/931-2088**).

HORSEBACK RIDING   In Hermanus   Contact **Klein Paradys Equestrian Centre** (① **028/284-9422**).

In Swellendam   Short or full-day excursions in the Langeberg Mountains are offered by **Two Feathers Horse Trails** (© **082-956-9452**).

In Knysna   **Cherie's Riding Centre** (© **044/343-1575**) offers scenic trails along the Swartvlei Lake and forests, as well as a beach ride that includes a light lunch. **Forest Horse Rides** (© **044/388-4764**) takes small groups through the Knysna forests.

In Plettenberg Bay   Contact **Equitrailing** (© **044/533-0599**) to explore fynbos and forests, or **Hogwarts** (© **044/535-9017**), on the Bitou River.

MOUNTAIN BIKING   **In and Around George**   To tour the foothills of the Outeniqua Mountains (close to George), contact **Eden** (© **044/877-0179**); the half- and full-day tours often combine other activities. Eden also cycles the Swartberg Pass—thankfully only down!

In Knysna   All three of the Diepwalle State Forest trails are ideal for mountain biking, particularly Harkerville, which has four color-coded routes: The Harkerville red route, which includes forest, fynbos, and the craggy coastline, is considered one of the best in South Africa—book early. For more information on trails in the **Knysna State Forests,** contact Mrs. van Rooyen (© **044/382-5466**) or Jacques at **Knysna Cycle Works** (© **044/382-5153,** www.knysna cycles.co.za). For guided bike tours, contact **Outeniqua Biking Trails** (© **044/532-7644**).

PARAGLIDING & GLIDING   Wilderness is considered South Africa's best site for coastal flying, particularly from August to May. Paragliding courses last 7, 10, and 14 days, or you can take a flight with a qualified instructor. Experienced pilots can rent equipment. Contact Bruce Watney from **Wings Over Wilderness** on his mobile phone (© **082-412-6858**) or at wow@atlantic.net. If you're based in Knysna and loathe to travel, contact **Smile High** (© **044/384-0308** or 082-652-1952), which operates at Brenton-on-Sea.

For a bird's-eye view of Plettenberg Bay, call **Stanley Island** (© **044/535-9442**); the two-seater glider flight is 30 minutes and costs R280 ($35) a person.

QUAD BIKING   Traverse a 20km (13-mile) trail in the Featherbed Nature Reserve. Call **S.E.A.L. Adventures** (© **044/382-5599** or 083-654-8755; R280/$35 per person).

SANDBOARDING   It's like snowboarding, only on sand. Contact **Downhill Adventures** (© **021/422-0388**) to surf the dunes at Betty's Bay, on the coastal road to Hermanus.

SHARK-CAGE DIVING   **In Hermanus**   Boats go out from Gansbaai (a coastal town some 30km [19 miles] east of Hermanus) to Dyer Island. This, and nearby Geyser Island, are favorites of the jackass penguin and seal breeding colonies, whose pups are an all-time favorite Great White shark snack—so much so that they call the channel between the islands "Shark Alley." The sharks are baited, and you stand a good chance of seeing one from the boat or from the cage—if you want to use the scuba gear provided you will need to present your diver's license. A number of operators offer a similar service for more or less the same price: **White Shark Adventures** (© **082-822-6290**) arranges pickups from Cape Town and provides a picnic breakfast and all equipment during the dive, lunch, and dropoff service for R950 ($119) (R1,000/$125 for credit cards)—if you don't see a shark, you are given a complimentary slip for another dive. **Ivanhoe Sea Safaris** (© **082-926-7977**) is a recommended local operator.

In Mossel Bay   Shark Africa ⭐⭐⭐ (℃ **082-455-2438** or 044/691-3796) is the only operator in Mossel Bay, so your close-up encounter with a Great White is likely to be less crowded and frenzied than in Gansbaai; cost is R900 ($112) for the shark-cage dive, R600 ($75) for viewing from boat only (closed Dec school holidays); you get a 50 percent reduction on the shark cage dive in the unlikely event that you don't see a Great White.

SKYDIVING/PARACHUTING   Try dropping from a height of 900m (2,953 ft.) with **Skydive Citrusdal** (℃ **021/462-5666**), based in the citrus-growing area 90 minutes north of Cape Town. With 1-day training for the novice costing R625 ($77), including the first jump, and additional jumps costing R150 ($19), this is one of the cheapest drops from a plane in South Africa.

SURFING   Top spots in the Western Cape include **Inner and Outer Pool and Ding Dangs** at Mossel Bay; **Vic Bay** (a good right-hand point break) and **Elands Bay** ⭐, the best spot on the West Coast. For more information, e-mail Paul at nirvan@ilink.nis.za. Call **Ocean Life Surf Shop** (℃ **044/533-3253**) for rentals in Plett; see chapter 3 for rentals in Cape Town.

WHALE-WATCHING   Some of the best land-based whale-watching in the world happens on the Overberg coast, particularly Hermanus (see "Exploring the Overberg & the Whale Coast," below), and the Garden Route from June to October/November. For boat-based encounters, note that only 13 to 20 boat-based whale-watching permits are issued for the entire South African coast—so make sure your operator has a permit. Boats are allowed to approach no closer than 50m (164 ft.), but the whales, curious, will often swim right up to the boat. See relevant sections below for recommended companies.

WHITE-WATER RAFTING   Felix Unite (℃ **021/670-1300**) runs rafting trips on the Breede River near Swellendam, but it's pretty tame when compared with the Doring River, considered the best in the Western Cape and running from mid-July to mid-September. **River Rafters** (℃ **021/712-5094**) organizes all-inclusive weekend trips that include an overnight under a cave overhang for R795 ($99) per person. Base camp is 4 hours from Cape Town, in the Cederberg area. River Rafters also runs 4-day year-round trips on the Orange River, on the border with Namibia.

2 Exploring the Overberg & Whale Coast

During the 17th century, the Dutch settlers saw the jagged Hottentots Holland mountain range as the Cape Colony's natural border, beyond which lay what they called Overberg: literally, "over the mountain." Today this coastal area—wedged between the Cape Peninsula and the Garden Route, with mountains lining its northern border and the ocean on its south—encompasses a vast patchwork of grain fields, fruit orchards, and fynbos-covered hills.

There are two main routes through it: the N2, which traverses its northern half and is the quickest way to reach the Garden Route; and the slightly more-circuitous and scenic Coastal Route, which is highly recommended, particularly during the whale-watching months.

Known as "the graveyard of ships," this rugged coastline is pounded by both the Atlantic and Indian oceans, which meet at L'Agulhas, Africa's most southerly point. East of this point is Arniston (Waenhuiskrans to locals), a bleak fishing village overlooking a magnificent turquoise bay; and De Hoop Nature Reserve, which vies with the Garden Route's Tsitsikamma as the most beautiful coastal

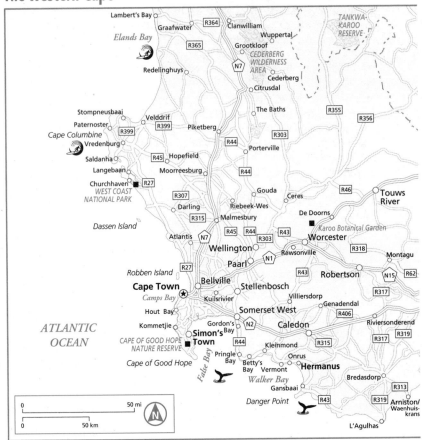

reserve in South Africa. The Overberg gives visitors the opportunity to view a wealth of rare fynbos (see "Africa's Floral Kingdom," earlier in the chapter), as well as sightings of South Africa's national bird, the endangered blue crane.

Another sanctuary-seeker is the Southern Right whale; these return in increasing numbers every spring to mate and nurse their young off the "Whale Coast." The towns of Hermanus and Die Kelders, which overlook Walker Bay, and Koppie Alleen in De Hoop Nature Reserve are considered the best locations for viewing these oddly elegant, 60-ton, callus-encrusted cetaceans.

THE COASTAL ROUTE: GORDON'S BAY TO HERMANUS

You can reach Hermanus in about 80 minutes via the N2, but the coastal route, which adds another 40 minutes to the journey, and snakes along the sheer cliffs of the Hottentots Holland Mountains as they plunge down to the oceans below, is the recommended route. To take it, head for **Gordon's Bay,** an easy 40-minute drive from Cape Town on the N2, and take the coastal route (R44) out of town. Keep an eye out for **whales** and **dolphins** in **False Bay** as you descend the cliffs and bypass the Steenbras River mouth and Koüelbaai (pronounced *cool*-buy), a beautiful beach and break favored by surfers. Between rocky outcrops along this

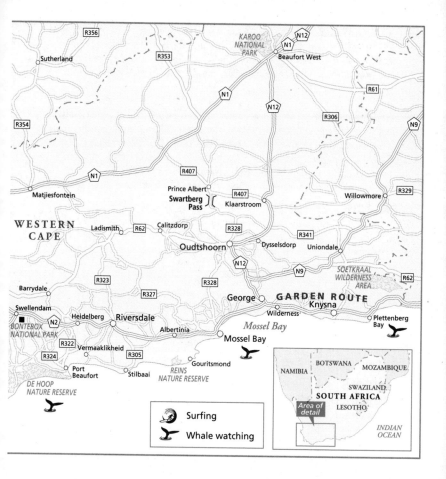

Map labels:

R356, R353, KAROO NATIONAL PARK, N1, N12, Beaufort West, Sutherland, R61, N1, N12, R306, R354, N9, N1, R407, Prince Albert, Swartberg Pass, R407, Klaarstroom, Willowmore, R329, Matjiesfontein, WESTERN CAPE, Ladismith, R62, Calitzdorp, R328, Dysselsdorp, Uniondale, Oudtshoorn, R341, N12, N9, SOETKRAAL WILDERNESS AREA, R62, Barrydale, R323, R328, George, GARDEN ROUTE, Swellendam, R327, Wilderness, Knysna, Heidelberg, Riversdale, Plettenberg Bay, BONTEBOK NATIONAL PARK, N2, Albertinia, Mossel Bay, R322, Vermaaklikheid, R305, Mossel Bay, R324, Port Beaufort, Stilbaai, Gouritsmond, REINS NATURE RESERVE, DE HOOP NATURE RESERVE

Inset map: NAMIBIA, BOTSWANA, MOZAMBIQUE, SWAZILAND, SOUTH AFRICA, LESOTHO, Area of detail, INDIAN OCEAN

Legend: Surfing; Whale watching

stretch of coast, you'll find small sandy coves shaded by ancient milkwood trees and grassy sunbathing areas.

Having crossed the Rooiels River (named after the red alder trees that grow in the riverine bush up the gorge, and twisting through a beautiful and usually deserted beach) and then the Buffels River, you enter the sprawling holiday village of **Pringle Bay.** Just past Pringle Bay, where the R44 cuts inland past the Grootvlei marshlands, is a less traveled detour to **Cape Hangklip** (pronounced *hung*-clip—literally, "hanging rock"). This 460m (1,509-ft.) high wedge of rock was often mistaken for Cape Point, which, incidentally, is how False Bay came by its name. After skirting three lagoon-type lakes—estuaries blocked by coastal dunes—you reach **Betty's Bay,** home to a remarkable number of ugly holiday cottages, one of only two land-based colonies of jackass penguins (the other is in Cape Town), and the beautiful **Harold Porter Botanical Gardens** (© 028/ 272-9311; open Mon–Fri 8am–4.30pm; Sat–Sun 8am–5pm; R7/90¢). Take one of the four trails up the mountain to the **Disa Kloof Waterfall** (duration 1–3 hr.) to appreciate the beauty of the Cape's coastal fynbos.

If you need to stop for lunch, or want a 5-star hotel experience attached to one of the country's best 18-hole golf courses (with the requisite spa for golf widows), stop at the **Sheraton's The Western Cape Hotel & Spa,** situated on the new Arabella Country Estate. The estate's lawns run into the Bot River lagoon, which provides lovely views, and the hotel offers every comfort known to man; call ℘ **028/284-0000** or visit www.arabellasheraton.co.za (from R1,400/$175 a room).

The R44 now heads northeastward in the direction of Caledon, while the road to Hermanus branches eastward from the inland side of the Palmiet Lagoon. This is called the R43; take it and keep an eye out for the R320 turnoff, which will take you past the vineyards of the **Hemel-en-Aarde** (literally, "Heaven and Earth") Valley. Here, you can go on wine tastings at the small but excellent selection of farms that make up the **Hermanus Wine Route** (see "What to See and Do," below), stopping for lunch along the way (see "Where to Dine," below).

HERMANUS

With a backdrop of mountains, a large lagoon and long white beach, deep rock pools, and a wealth of coastal fynbos, **Hermanus** was destined to develop into one of South Africa's premier holiday resorts. The best times to visit Hermanus are autumn and spring, when aficionados come from afar to view the whales in **Walker Bay.** Humpback, Brydes, and Minke whales make occasional appearances, but the bay is essentially frequented by Southern Right whales.

Whales aside, there are seven **wine farms** in the Hemel-en-Aarde Valley to visit, the opportunity to have a **close encounter with a Great White shark** (see "Staying Active," above), **long beaches** to walk, and a number of **good trails** in the Walker Bay and Fernkloof nature reserves. With Hermanus as your base, the **picturesque villages** of Arniston and Elim are only a day's excursion away.

ESSENTIALS

VISITOR INFORMATION The excellent **Hermanus Tourism Bureau** (The Old Station Building, corner of Mitchell and Lord Roberts St.; ℘ **028/ 312-2629;** www.hermanus.co.za) is open Monday through Saturday from 9am to 5pm, and from August to April on Sunday from 10am to 3pm.

GETTING THERE **By Car** To rent a car, see "Cape Town Essentials," chapter 3. Hermanus lies 112 km (69 miles) east of Cape Town via the N2 (just under an hour). The N2 route is a pretty drive, but the winding coastal route from Gordon's Bay, at times snaking along cliffs that plunge into the sea, is simply breathtaking (see "Coastal Route: Gordon's Bay to Hermanus," above).

By Bus Contact **Hylton Ross** (℘ **021/511-1784**) for scenic day trips to Hermanus via the coastal route on Wednesdays or Sundays.

GUIDED TOURS **Casa Blanca Tours** (℘ **028/316-3170**) offers a variety of day and overnight tours covering the Overberg, as well as flexible special-interest tours covering the wine, whales, history, or art of the region. Call **Fernkloof Nature Reserve** (℘ **028/312-1122**), or Lee Berman at the **Botanical Society** (℘ **028/313-8000**) to find out about specialized fynbos tours. **Whale & Dolphin Safari** (℘ **044/382-3815;** www.explore-southafrica.co.za) offers a 4-day marine tour from Cape Town to Port Elizabeth, via Hermanus. For an insight into the greater community, take a walking tour of the Hermanus township, Zwelihle, the first black township established in the Overberg, with Wilson Salukazana, a registered SATOUR guide and proprietor of **Ubuntu Tours** (℘ **073-214-6949**).

By Boat **Walker Bay Adventures** (℘ **028/314-0925**) runs 2-hour sundowner cruises on the lagoon for R70 ($8.75) per person, and also rents a variety of seaworthy vessels. See "Whale-Watching," below, for operators with permits for whale-watching.

On Foot   Whale Coast Tours (✆ **028/312-4063**) conducts a variety of coastal and mountain guided walks for those wanting a greater insight into the whales, fynbos, or birdlife of the region.

On Horseback   Contact **Klein Paradys Equestrian Centre** (✆ **028/284-9422**).

WHAT TO SEE & DO
SURF & SAND

The sweeping 30km (18½-mile) curve of **Grotto Beach** can be seen from most vantage points of Walker Bay. This is a great family beach, made for long walks and swimming. Closer to town, **Voëlklip** is a popular swimming beach where the hip youth hang out; and the closest beach, **Langbaai** (*lung*-buy), offers the best bodysurfing, though currents can render it hazardous.

WILDFLOWERS

The **Fernkloof Nature Reserve** (✆ **028/313-0300**), which overlooks the town, offers more than 50km (31 miles) of hiking trails to explore the coastal fynbos of the region as well as providing great views of Walker Bay.

WINE TASTING

The six wineries that comprise the **Hermanus Wine Route** are all located on the R320 (see "The Coastal Route: Gordon's Bay to Hermanus," above). The oldest and most respected are **Bouchard Finlayson** (✆ **028/312-3515**) and **Hamilton Russell** ★★★ (✆ **028/312-3595**). The latter has the dubious distinction of producing South Africa's most expensive wines—a chardonnay and a pinot noir—but admittedly they are absolutely delicious, with the chardonnay voted one of the top 20 in the world. You can sample them for free, but you will be hard-pressed to walk away without a purchase. Tastings are held in a beautiful setting, on weekdays from 9am to 5pm, Saturday from 9am to 1pm. Another worth seeking out, with glorious valley and lake views, is **Sumaridge** (✆ **028/312-1097**), the valley's newest winery. You can settle for just tasting (Mon–Fri 9am–5pm; Sat–Sun 10am–3pm), but picnics can also be arranged by calling ahead (✆ **083-636-1180**).

WHALE-WATCHING

The once-threatened Southern Right whale (a protected species since 1946) is enjoying a major comeback, with the population on the South African coastline nearly doubling over the past decade. In recent years, as many as 2,000 whales have followed the annual migration from Antarctica, to flirt, mate, and calve in the warmer waters off the southern Cape coast.

One can clearly view these playful, gentle giants—sometimes at a distance of only 10m (some 30 ft.)—from the craggy cliffs that run along the Hermanus shoreline. For the best sightings, take the 12km (7½-mile) cliff path from New Harbour east to Grotto Beach and the lagoon. Beware of the waves—a young visitor was swept off the rocks in 2000 and drowned. Also recommended are the terraces above the Old Harbour, where a telescope and a plaque provide basic information about the bay and its whales.

Hermanus is very proud of the fact that it is the only town in the world to have a "whale crier": During whaling season, Wilson Salukazana walks the town streets blowing a kelp horn in a sort of Morse code to alert the town's inhabitants to the presence and whereabouts of whales. If you don't understand the code, never mind; Salukazana also wears a sandwich board and carries a mobile phone (© **083-212-1074**). Contact him for reports of the latest whale sightings, or the museum (© **028/312-1475**).

For assured "up close" encounters, consider boarding a boat with a license to approach the whales (up to 50m/16 ft.). Bank on paying about R300/$37; some of the longest-running operators are **Ivanhoe Sea Safaris** (© **082-926-7977**), **Southern Right Charters** (© **082-353-0550**), and **HFC Boat–based Whale Cruisers** (© **082-369-8931**).

Note: The limestone cliffs of De Kelders, southeast along the R43, provide a superb view of Walker Bay and the whales, and are never as crowded as Hermanus in season.

WHERE TO STAY

If you prefer to self-cater, **Hermanus Accommodation Centre** (© **028/313-0004;** www.adept.co.za/hermanus) offers a range of options starting from about R100 ($12) per person.

Auberge Burgundy ⟨⭐⟩   A replica of a Provençal or Tuscan villa, the Auberge Burgundy has a wonderful location opposite the Old Harbour. Rooms are spacious, each with walk-in dressing room and opening onto a balcony with views of either the ocean or the garden, which in spring is redolent with the scent of roses and lavender. The **Burgundy** restaurant (where breakfasts are served) is just opposite (see "Where to Dine," below), but a number of other options are within easy walking distance. Ask for a room or suite with a view of the ocean, but don't be too disturbed if they're all taken—almost every room has something to recommend it (except for some unfortunate fabric choices), and the pool deck has an excellent view.

16 Harbour Rd., Hermanus 7200. © **028/313-1201**. Fax 028/313-1204. www.auberge.co.za. 18 units. R900 ($112) double; R1,000–R1,200 ($125–$150) suite; R2,200 ($265) 3-bedroom penthouse. Rates include breakfast. AE, DC, MC, V. Children over age 12 only. **Amenities:** Restaurant; pool; limited room service; laundry. *In room:* TV, minibar, tea- and coffee-making facilities, hair dryer, heated floors and towel rails.

Birkenhead House ⭐⭐⭐   A glam boutique hotel decorated in the Ian Shrager tradition, this exclusive guesthouse is aimed at a slightly younger market than the Marine, or at least those who like to mingle in a closed environment (no one but the maximum 22 hotel guests are allowed on the premises). Decor is eclectic—French Baroque meets 21st-century modern, with a few pieces of kitsch thrown in for good measure—with white and cream the predominant colors throughout. The public spaces (of which there are several) are wonderfully over-the-top (massive gilded mirrors, French antiques, Philippe Starck lights, chandeliers, large Disneyesque white couches . . .), but not all bedrooms are created equal. The top choice by far are nos. 1 and 2, built right at the front of the "house," with the only unobstructed views of the sea. Not even the honeymoon suite comes close. Officially opened in May 2003, at press time it still had a great many rough edges, but because it's owned by the same couple who brought us Royal Malewane (one of the most beautiful game lodges flanking the Kruger), these kinks will hopefully be smoothed out in time. Neither of the two pools are big enough for my liking, but Hermanus's best swimming beaches flank the rocky outcrop on which the hotel is built.

7th Ave., Voelklip, Hermanus 7200. © **028/314-8000**. Fax 028/314-1208. www.royalmalewane.com. 11 units. R3,500–R5,500 ($438–$688) double including all meals, local beverages (excellent wines), tea, coffee, laundry. AE, DC, MC, V. Call for winter and extended stay rates. No children under 10. **Amenities:** Gourmet dining; two pools; spa; gym; laundry; all excursions arranged. *In room:* TV, DVD player, minibar, hair dryer.

Grootbos Nature Reserve ★★★ *Kids*

Located just beyond Hermanus, this is the best place in the Western Cape to learn about the eccentricities of the smallest and most diverse floral kingdom in the world. There's a fynbos drive in the reserve every morning with one of the resident botanists, and evening walks or boat tours in Walker Bay with the resident marine biologist. Guests are also welcome to walk, ride, or bike through the 1,000-hectare (2,470-acre) reserve, which features the largest milkwood forest in the world and—among other rarities—porcupine, lynx, and bush buck. Guests are accommodated in luxurious privately situated stone and timber cottages—each a fully-equipped open-plan house with large fireplace, multilevel sun decks, and views of Walker Bay and the surrounding fynbos vegetation. Dinner is a three-course affair that centers on seafood from Walker Bay, game dishes in season, and homegrown vegetables.

Off the R43, 33km (20 miles) east of Hermanus. © **028/384-0381.** Fax 028/384-0552. www.grootbos.com. 13 units. R3,800 ($480), includes all meals and activities; minimum 2-night stay. AE, DC, MC, V. Children's rates on request. **Amenities:** Dining room; bar; pool; children's programs; babysitting; laundry; horseback riding; guided walks. *In room:* TV, minibar, hair dryer, fireplace.

Marine Hotel ★★★

Situated on the craggy cliffs close to the town center and Old Harbour, this grand dame of Hermanus (built in 1902) has wonderful views of Walker Bay and its whales. Rooms face either the sea or the courtyard (with pool); others have distant views of the mountain. Even if you're not here to see the whales, it's worth spending an additional R800 ($100) for a luxury room; the best-value category to feature gorgeous ocean views (note that one luxury has a mountain/pool view, so do specify). Rooms are all tastefully furnished and finished in soothing mute colors, and refreshingly, owner Liz Mcgrath prefers to renovate to create fewer rooms with more space. Guests can choose to relax in the comfortable wicker-furnished sea-facing bar or the pool terrace, or head for an invigorating swim in the large tidal pool below the cliffs. This Relais & Chateaux establishment also offers a choice of excellent restaurants: No prizes for guessing what **Seafood at the Marine** specializes in. The **Pavillion** has the view and serves a larger variety of meals. The hotel has recently introduced the by now de rigeur beauty spa.

Marine Dr., Hermanus 7200. © **028/313-1000.** Fax 028/313-0160. www.marine-hermanus.co.za or www.collectionmcgrath.com. 42 units. R2,050–R2,500 ($255–$310) double depending on season; R2,750–R3,300 ($335–$400) luxury double depending on season; R4,200–R5,050 ($348–$430) suite depending on type and season. AE, DC, MC, V. No children under age 12. **Amenities:** 2 restaurants; bar; pool; spa; concierge; room service; laundry. *In room:* A/C, TV, minibar, hair dryer, underfloor heating, heated towel rails.

Nelshof ★ *Value* *Kids*

This blue-and-white-themed B&B, located in an old 1921 family home, is charming, and owner Pamela Nel has decorated it in the comfortable Cape-cottage-cum-beach-house style with great flair. Best of all, it enjoys one of the best locations in Hermanus, with a pretty purple-themed garden spilling onto the fynbos and rocks upon which the sea crashes, and a wide veranda from which to enjoy whale-watching and the like. It also offers direct access to a swimming beach (there's no pool) and the Hermanus cliff path. The two sea-facing suites, both with entrances off the veranda, are the best and have attached single rooms, ideal if you're traveling with children or a friend. It's a totally unpretentious and good-value option.

37 Tenth St., Voelklip, Hermanus 7200. ©/fax **028/314-0201.** www.nelshof.co.za. 4 units. High season: (Sept-Apr) sea-facing: R840 ($105) double; mountain-facing: R760 ($95) double; garden flat R680 ($85) double. Low

season: sea-facing: R620 ($77); mountain-facing: R560 ($70); garden flat R520 ($64). All rates include break-fast. Ask about third-person/children rates. AE, DC, MC, V. **Amenities:** Sea-facing Jacuzzi; laundry. *In room:* TV, tea- and coffee-making facilities.

WHERE TO DINE

Hermanus and its surrounds offer a plethora of dining options; besides those reviewed below, the following are highly recommended. **Milkwood** ★★ (© 028/316-1516), a casual seafood restaurant located just above the Onrus beach, scores top rating for location; the food's not bad either—try a plate of oysters, followed by linefish, and wash it down with the region's delicious Birkenhead beer. **Mogg's Country Cookhouse** ★★ (© 028/312-4321), located at the end of a dirt track on a farm in the Hemel en Aarde Valley, is a rustic venue where mother and daughter team Julia and Jenny serve up value-for-money home-cooked cuisine—the small a la carte menu changes weekly, but expect delicious combinations like roasted tomato and pepper soup, calamari with caper mayonnaise or chicken medallions, rocket and cherry tomatoes on home-made tagliatelli. Carnivores will also find a good reason to head for the Hemel en Aarde Valley: Bruce Henderson's laid-back **B's Steakhouse** ★★ (© 028/316-3625) is regularly rated one of the top steakhouses in the country.

Back in town you may also want to try **The Rock** (© 028/312-2920), a casual seafood restaurant with a superb setting next to the New Harbour, or **Meditterea** (© 028/313-1685), also known for its lovely sea views, great seafood selection (try the pesto kingklip), and the house speciality, slow-roasted lamb. If you're stuffed to the gills with seafood, try **Rossi's** (© 028/312-2848), rated Hermanus's best Italian restaurant; Yannis Dzerefos's **The Greeks @ Trattoria** (© 028/312-3707) for—yes—Greek cuisine, or the **Cuckoo Tree** (© 028/312-3430) for French-style food; the crispy duck with orange and Van der Hum (a liqueur) sauce is recommended. Stanford, a quaint inland village a few miles east of Hermanus, has the following gems: **Mariana's** (© 028/341-0272; Fri–Sun only) for super-fresh country cooking; and **Paprika** (© 028/341-0662; Wed–Sun only) for predominantly Middle Eastern cuisine cooked by owner-chef Robin. *Note:* Neither sells wine, so BYOB.

Bientang's Cave ★ *Kids* SEAFOOD Few restaurants in the world can best this location—a cave in the rocks just above the sea, with a fabulous view of Walker Bay and the whales at play. Predictably, seafood is Bientang's specialty. Try one of two fresh linefish, grilled daily—the snoek with apricot, a traditional South African combination, is recommended. With the fresh sea breeze to build up an appetite, you might want to order one of the buffet options—option A (R180/$22) gives you a chance to sample almost every item on the menu; alternatively, opt for B: a choice of six salads, followed by bouillabaisse (tomato-based soup with calamari, prawns, mussels, linefish, and saffron), a choice of two linefish, and dessert—a steal at R150 ($19). A kids' menu is available for smaller appetites.

Off Marine Dr., next to Old Harbour, Hermanus 7200. © 028/312-3454. Reservations essential. Main courses R50–R130 ($6.50–$16). AE, DC, MC, V. Daily 11:30am–4pm; Fri–Sat 6:30–9:30pm.

The Burgundy ★★ FRENCH/AFRICAN Located in the oldest building in Hermanus (the stone-and-clay cottage was built by a Swedish boat builder in 1875), The Burgundy is another casual eatery serving simple but excellent meals. Try the Moroccan fish (grilled linefish in chili crust, served with *tzatziki,* a Greek cucumber sauce), or traditional *bobotie* (mild Malay curry) with pumpkin fritters. Vegetarians can enjoy quiche served with couscous or a variety of grilled vegetables. When booking, ask for a table on the veranda or lawn—both overlook Walker Bay. The Burgundy is also open for tea and scones.

Marine Dr. (opposite Old Harbour). ℂ 028/312-2800. Reservations essential in season. Main courses R30–R95 ($3.75–$12). AE, DC, MC, V. Daily (except Sun dinner) 10–12am tea; 12–2:15pm lunch; 3:15–4:15pm tea; 7–9:15pm dinner.

Seafood at the Marine ★★★ FUSION SEAFOOD   Generally considered the best seafood restaurant in the Overberg, with chef Louis van Reenen injecting Continental creativity into the natural local bounty drawn from the ocean and fertile valleys. Start with chilled cucumber and coconut soup, marinated *concasse* of tomatoes, or tempura prawns and vegetables, served with a lemon grass vinaigrette. Popular main courses include Rich Man's Fish and Chips, served in the *Financial Mail;* a ravioli of prawns and creamed leek; and pan-fried prawns with basil and lemon butter and shaved Parmesan, served on homemade angel-hair pasta. The muted modern decor, like the rest of the hotel, is wonderful, but the restaurant has no sea view.

The Marine Hotel. ℂ 028/313-1000. Reservations recommended. 3 courses R125 ($16); 2 courses R95 ($11). AE, DC, MC, V. Daily 12–2pm and 7–10pm.

MORE WHALE COAST DESTINATIONS

Two coastal destinations east of Hermanus worth visiting are the village of **Arniston** ★★ and the **De Hoop Nature Reserve** ★★★. To reach either, head east to Stanford on R43, then turn northeast on R326 for 27km (16½ miles) before turning right and heading south for Bredasdorp. Once there, you can either immediately go south on R316 toward Arniston, or north on R319 for De Hoop. If, however, you want to take a side trip to Africa's southernmost tip, where the Indian and Atlantic oceans meet, turn south on R319 for **L'Aghulus.** Bar the interesting facts of its location, the place itself has little to recommend a visit, unless you wish to view the wreck of the freighter *Meisho Maru 38* or visit the **Lighthouse Museum** (ℂ 028/435-6078), built in 1849 and now a satellite of the Shipwreck Museum in Bredasdorp (see below). The adjacent coffee shop and restaurant (open daily) is where Lydia Brown serves good home-style cooking. If you are taking the R319 south don't miss a turn through the tiny town of **Elim.** Established as a Moravian mission station in 1824, the town remains unchanged and is still inhabited by Moravian church members who make their living from harvesting fynbos.

Arniston, a small fishing village and popular getaway, lapped by a startling turquoise sea, lies only 24km (15 miles) south of Bredasdorp on R316. If you see signs for "Waenhuiskrans," don't panic—Arniston, named after a British ship that wrecked here in 1815, is also officially called Waenhuiskrans. For centuries, the local fishermen have been setting out at first light to cast their lines

---

⌒ *Moments* Fish Stew by Candlelight

One of the most authentic experiences in the Overberg has to be dining in the heart of the Kassiesbaai community—on a prearranged night you can delight in pan-fried yellowtail and green bean stew, prepared by the local fisherwomen, and served by candlelight in one of the century-old fishing cottages. The meal costs R80 ($10) per person; to book call Lillian Newman (ℂ 028/445-9000). Lillian, a resident of Kassiesbaai, can also arrange for a guided tour.

and returning at night to the quaint lime-washed, thatched cottages clustered on the dunes overlooking the sea—these dwellings, some of which date back 200 years, have collectively been declared a national monument and are picture-postcard pretty, though doubtless less romantic to live in. You can take a wander through the sandy streets of what is called the **Kassiesbaai community** 🏃 on your own, but it's more considerate to visit with the local community guide. Then take a stroll along the unspoiled coastline.

The **De Hoop Nature Reserve** 🏃🏃🏃 (© 028/425-5020; entry R15/$1.95 per person) has what many consider to be the best whale-watching spot on the entire coast, Koppie Alleen; but most visitors are here to explore one of the most beautiful coastal reserves in the world—50km (30 miles) of pristine white beach dunes, limestone cliffs, rock pools, wetlands, coastal fynbos, and no one to disturb the peace but zebra, several species of antelope, and more than 260 species of birds. Once in the reserve, there are limited routes (you can drive to the beach or accommodations), so the reserve is best explored on foot (ask about the Vlei Trail) or on a mountain bike (though you'll have to hire one in Hermanus or in Cape Town). Do note that the reserve hours (7am–6pm) are strictly enforced, and that visitors intending to overnight should report to the reserve office no later than 4pm on the day of arrival.

WHERE TO STAY & DINE

If the thought of self-catering at De Hoop sounds like too much work, **Buchu Bushcamp,** which adjoins the reserve, has a restaurant that services five comfortably equipped thatched chalets (R550/$69 per chalet), and proprietor Rory, a conservationist who used to head up the team at De Hoop, offers guided walks in the reserve. Contact the camp at © **028/542-1602** or visit www. buchu-bushcamp.com.

The Arniston Hotel 🏃   This is the best hotel in the region, with a great location directly opposite the exquisitely colored sea. It's a place to come for a real sense of getting away from the rat race, but not from some of its better by-products, like room service. The luxury sea-facing rooms are a vast improvement over the standard sea-facing rooms, and while the pool-facing rooms are less windy (yes, the wind often blows here), it's a shame to miss out on the surreal view. Dining is good, particularly the linefish, but if you're spending more than one night do try to book a meal in the Kassiesbaai fishing community (see "Fish Stew by Candlelight," above).

P.O. Box 126, Bredasdorp 7280. © 028/445-9000. Fax 021/4459633. www.arnistonhotel.com. 30 units. R900–R1,100 ($112–$138) double; R1,400 ($175) for recommended luxury sea-facing units. Rates include breakfast. AE, DC, MC, V. **Amenities:** 2 restaurants; bar; pool; room service; babysitting; laundry; boating; cycling. *In room:* A/C (some), TV, hair dryer, tea- and coffee-making facilities.

De Hoop Nature Reserve 🏃 *Kids*   This is one of the most peaceful places on earth, with only a handful of people to explore the 36,000-hectare (88,920-acre) reserve (see above) once the gates close for nonresidents at 6pm. The small self-catering cottages are basic—two bedrooms, one bathroom, and an open-plan kitchen and dining room—and there is no shop or restaurant. Pack an overnight picnic or barbecue; each cottage has its own *braai* (barbecue) site, and wood can be bought at the entrance. The nearest shop and gas station is at Ouplaas, 15km (9 miles) from De Hoop, so it's best to stock up at Bredasdorp or Swellendam. Only three cottages are equipped with bedding; opt for these slightly more luxurious units—they also enjoy a better location. De Hoop is ideal for young children—it has a game trail, a wetlands trail, and endless sand dunes and coves to romp in, but no TV. Check-in time is currently between 2 and 6pm; it's probably a good idea to call ahead to make sure this is still the case.

Wydgeleë, Private Bag X16, Bredasdorp 7280. Bookings and enquiries (ℭ 028/425-5020. Reserve: 028/542-1253. Fax 028/425-5030. www.capenature.org.za. 10 units, each with 4–6 beds. R285–R350 ($35–$44) basic cottage/4 people; R430–R535 ($54–$65) luxury cottage/4 people. R70–R135 ($9–$17) per extra person. (Campsites R85 ($10). AE MC V.

3 Swellendam & the Overberg Interior

Swellendam: 220km (136 miles) E of Cape Town

Most people who choose to drive through the Overberg interior (as opposed to the Whale Coast) are on their way to the Garden Route, and may rush through without realizing that there are a few excellent pit stops along the way. As you head east from Cape Town on the N2, here are some suggestions on what to stop and see as you travel to Swellendam.

After ascending **Sir Lowry's Pass** ★★, you'll reach the fruit-growing areas of Grabouw and Elgin (the area produces 65 percent of South Africa's apple export crop) and the first of many farm stalls dotted along the way. **Peregrine** ★★★ (opposite the Grabouw turnoff) is one of the oldest, and arguably the best—stop here for fresh farm produce and various traditional "road trip" treats (see the appendix). This is one of the best places in the Cape to sample *biltong* (air-dried meat strips) and *droë wors* (air-dried sausage). The adjacent bakery is also excellent—the pies (try the springbok), *melktert* (custard tart), and *koeksisters* (deep-fried dough soaked in syrup) are out of this world.

The first detour you might consider is the R406, which loops past the villages of **Genadendal** and **Greyton.** Genadendal is the oldest Moravian mission village in Africa, with buildings dating back to 1738. The **Genadendal Mission and Museum Complex** documents the activities of the missionaries and their flock. For guided tours, call (ℭ **028/251-8582** (open Mon–Thurs 8.30am–1pm and 2–5pm, Fri 8.30am–1pm and 2–3:30pm, Sat 9am–12pm).

Greyton, a few minutes farther east on the R406, was developed much later, and by a more affluent community. Set at the foot of the Riviersonderend Mountains, with many beautifully restored Victorian and Georgian buildings, it's a great deal more attractive than Genadendal, and a good place to stop for lunch—grab a table on the stoep (veranda) at the **Oak & Vigne** (ℭ **028/254-9037;** open daily, closed for dinner). If you feel like spending the night, your best bet is **Greyton Lodge** (ℭ **028/254-9876;** R175–R275/$21–$34 per person, depending on season), a cozy country inn that has a good reputation for its dining. Other than strolling the streets the main attraction here is the 14km (8½-mile) **Boesmanskloof Trail,** which traverses the mountains to the town of McGregor. A good alternative is the 9km (5½-mile) walk to **Oak Falls**—the highlight of the route—instead. For information, call (ℭ **028/254-9620.**

SWELLENDAM

Swellendam, a pretty town situated at the foot of the Langeberg Mountains and appropriately billed as "the historic heart of the Overberg," is the perfect halfway stop (for lunch or the night) for visitors driving from Cape Town to the Garden Route directly via the N2.

ESSENTIALS

VISITOR INFORMATION   The Swellendam Tourism Bureau is in the Oefeninghuis at 36 Voortrek St. (ℭ **028/514-2770;** Mon–Fri 8am–5pm, Sat 9am–1pm).

The Route Less Traveled

To reach the Garden Route from Cape Town, it's worth considering an alternative route, highly recommended for its empty roads, spectacular mountain scenery, vineyard valleys, small town architecture, and wide open plains. With no detours or stops, this scenic route will add only 45 minutes should you decide to rejoin the N2 at Swellendam (a 2-hr. journey via the N2 from Cape Town), but ideally you should turn off and overnight in Montagu, then continue on the **R62** through the Klein Karoo to Oudtshoorn—this should take 2½ hours. You will then need to overnight in Oudtshoorn or Prince Albert before heading south to George to enter the Garden Route.

Travel north from Cape Town on the N1, on the toll road that takes you through the **Du Toitskloof Tunnel.** Time allowing, bypass the tunnel and traverse the **Du Toitskloof Pass**—the soaring mountain and valley views from the 1:9 gradient road are well worth the extra 15 minutes.

At Worcester, capital of the Breede River region, the **Karoo National Botanical Gardens** (© 023/347-0785; open Mon–Fri 8am–1pm and 2-4.30pm; Aug–Oct also Sat–Sun 9am–4pm), off Roux Road, are definitely worth viewing, particularly in spring (admission R10/$1.25). The gardens showcase the weird and wonderful plants from S.A.'s semi-arid regions.

From here, head southeast on the R60 to Robertson, keeping an eye out for the ultramodern **Graham Beck cellar and tasting room** (© 023/626-1214; open Mon–Fri 9am–5pm, Sat 10am–3pm), worth a stop if you like sparkling wine—the award-winning nonvintage *brut* is used at presidential inaugurations, and many consider the vintage *brut* (made from 100% chardonnay grapes) the best *methode champenoise* in the country.

From Robertson it's another 20km (12½ miles) southeast on the R60 to Ashton (note that there is a truly exceptional restaurant here, **Fraai Uitzicht 1798,** located among the vineyards; it's no longer a well-kept

GETTING THERE **By Car** The quickest way to get to Swellendam is via the N2 as described above. Alternatively, you can travel the more attractive R62 mountain and semi-desert route (see "The Route Less Traveled," above).

By Bus **Intercape, Translux, Greyhound,** and **Baz Bus** pass through daily on their way to the Garden Route. See chapter 2 for contact details.

GETTING AROUND **On Foot** This is the best way to explore the small village and Drosdty Museum complex. Hiking trails in the nearby Marloth Nature Reserve lead into the Langeberg Mountains; for permits and maps of hikes, including the popular but tough 5-day Swellendam Trail, contact the reserve office (© 028/514-1410 or 072-601-4145).

On Wheels **Bontebok National Park** (© 028/514-2735; open daily 7am–7pm) lies 7km (4½ miles) out of town and is accessible by car or mountain bike. Rent bikes from **Swellendam Backpackers Lodge** (© 028/514-2648; R60–R114/$7.50–$14 per day).

On Horseback Short or full-day excursions in the Langeberg Mountains are offered by **Two Feathers Horse Trails** (© 082-956-9452 or 082-494-8279).

secret, so bookings are essential on weekends (✆ **023/626-6156**). The dramatic 10km (6-mile) **Cogmanskloof Pass** ⚘ leads off the R60, taking you to the pretty town of **Montagu** ⚘⚘, voted "village of the year"— with no stops, Montagu is about 2 hours from Cape Town. Overnight at one of the four garden cottages at Aasvöelkrans (✆ **023/614-1228**; www.aasvoelkrans.co.za), a delightful guesthouse located on a stud farm at the foot of the Langeberg Mountains, and the best-value option in town. Take an evening stroll and admire the town's Victorian architecture and soaring brick-red mountains, or enjoy a therapeutic dip in the nearby hot springs (though from an aesthetic point of view, these have been ruined by the resort that's sprung up around them). The **springs** (✆ **023/614-1050**) are a constant 109°F (43°C), and are open daily from 8am to 11pm, for R25 ($3) per person.

From Montagu you can either retrace your footsteps through the **Cogmanskloof Gorge** to rejoin the R60 south to Swellendam or take the road east to Barrydale (if you need to a pit stop, **Clarke of the Karoo** is the best restaurant here; (✆ **028/572-1017**). Along the way you'll pass signs for the new **Sanbona Wildlife Reserve**, situated in the Warmwaterberg. A beautiful 54,000-hectare (133,000-acre) reserve, accommodating only 12 guests in six open-plan luxury suites, Sanbona offers game drives (currently only antelope and rhino, with plans to introduce lion and buffalo), horseback riding, trout fishing, Bushman paintings, masseuse on tap, superb stargazing, and total tranquillity (www.sanbona.com). From Barrydale, travel to the small village of **Calitzdorp;** leave enough time for a short stop to taste some of the Cape's best fortified wines at **Boplaas** (✆ **044/213-3326**) and **Die Krans** (✆ **044/213-3314**). Make sure you arrive in Oudsthoorn before dark if you wish to tackle the Swartberg Pass to overnight at Prince Albert.

HISTORIC SWELLENDAM

Back in the early 1700s, the Dutch East India Company was most perturbed by the number of men deserting the Cape Colony to find freedom and fortune in the hinterland. Swellendam was consequently declared a magisterial district in 1743, making it the third-oldest white settlement in South Africa and bringing its reprobate tax evaders once again under the Company fold. In 1795 the burgers finally revolted against this unwanted interference and declared Swellendam a republic, but the Cape's occupation by British troops later that year made their independence rather short-lived. Swellendam continued to flourish under British rule, but a devastating fire in 1865 razed much of the town. Almost a century later, transport planners ruined the main road, Voortrek Street, by ripping out the oaks that lined it, ostensibly to widen it. Two important historical sites to have survived on this road are, at number 36, the **Oefeningshuis** (where the tourism bureau is located), built in 1838, and, at number 11, the over-the-top baroque **Dutch Reformed Church,** built in 1901.

The **Drostdy Museum complex** ⚘⚘ (✆ **028/514-1138**) comprises the Drostdy, the Old Goal and Ambagswerf (Trade's Yard), Mayville House, and

Zanddrift, now an excellent day-time restaurant (see below). The Drostdy was built by the Dutch East India Company in 1747 to serve as residence for the *landdrost* (magistrate), and features many of the building traditions of the time: yellowwood from the once abundant forests, cow-dung and peach-pit floors, elegant fireplaces, and, of course, Cape Dutch gables. The Drostdy also houses an excellent collection of late-18th-century and early-19th-century Cape furniture in the baroque, neoclassical, and Regency styles.

WHERE TO STAY & DINE

Swellendam's small-town rural ambience is starting to change as a number of young entrepreneurs, both local and foreign, have opted to drop out and live the rural life, opening quirky or modern alternatives to the more traditional options reviewed below. One in particular deserves a mention: **Bloomestate,** owned by Dutch couple Miranda and Niels, will suit younger travelers with a preference for contemporary design. Miranda and Niels designed most of the furniture and fittings, utilizing the skills of local craftsmen (or, if all else failed, importing Philippe Starck). The new rooms, spacious and pleasing to the eye (albeit slightly bland), have been built on a single raised platform (pity they're not totally separate suites), with doors opening onto landscaped gardens and a heated saltwater pool. Rates are R700 to R950 ($88–$119) double, including breakfast (© **028/514-2984;** www.bloomestate.com).

The best place to eat dinner is still **Herberg Roosje;** for a more fine-dining experience, try **Klippe Rivier** (see below for reviews on both), though **The Old Mill** (© **028/514-2790**), where Belgium owner Nikki serves up Flemish delicacies (like slow-stewed rabbit) and quirky takes on new ingredients (try the venison quiche), is also proving popular.

Herberg Roosje Van De Kaap ★★ *Value*   Conveniently located opposite the Drostdy Museum, this quaint country inn is the ideal place to stay over on your way to the Garden Route. Some of the rooms are a bit on the small side, but the tasteful furnishings and general welcoming ambience more than make up for this—if you want more space, book one of the garden suites or the honeymoon suite. The inn has no lounge, but guests tend to gather around the sparkling pool and the equally charming restaurant, **Roosje Van De Kaap,** which serves a la carte meals with a strong Italian slant in an informal atmosphere—definitely consider eating here even if you don't stay. Pizzas are popular, as is the Cape Duo (*bobotie,* curried lamb) and the filet Roosje, tender beef medallions prepared in garlic butter and herbs—an all-time favorite.

5 Drostdy St., Swellendam 6740. ©/fax **028/514-3001**. roosje@dorea.co.za. 9 units. R350–R460 ($44–$56) double, includes breakfast. MC, V (note that using your credit card carries a small surcharge here). **Amenities:** Restaurant; pool; laundry. *In room:* Hair dryer on request.

Klippe Rivier Country House ★★★   This Cape Dutch homestead, dating back to the 1820s, is by far the most luxurious address to overnight in Swellendam, though it's pretty pricey and service can be a tad snooty. Furnished with beautiful antiques and run like a small luxury hotel, Klippe Rivier lies on the outskirts of town, which means you'll have to drive to visit the Drostdy Museum. Choose between the spacious downstairs suites (each with its own fireplace and walled-in garden) and the more contemporary upstairs suites (each with a private balcony overlooking the mountains and gardens). For total privacy, request the honeymoon cottage, set well away from the main house. Klippe Rivier has its own vegetable gardens and orchards, and fresh milk is collected daily. The three-course dinners featuring country-style cooking (R140/$18) can last several hours, concluding in the library or lounge with coffee and chocolate truffles.

Box 483, Swellendam 6740. ☏ 028/514-3341. Fax 028/514-3337. www.klipperivier.com. 7 units. R1,500 ($188) double, including breakfast. Call for winter specials. AE, DC, MC, V. Children under age 8 not permitted. **Amenities:** Dining room; pool; limited room service; laundry. *In room:* A/C/fans, hair dryer, fireplace (downstairs rooms only)/heaters.

4 Exploring the Garden Route & Klein Karoo

The Garden Route has become the country's most popular tourist destination after Cape Town, drawing visitors year-round to its indigenous forests, freshwater lakes, wetlands, hidden coves, and long beaches. You can traverse mountains, explore caves, bike through forests, encounter a white shark, visit an ostrich farm, paraglide onto the beach, or boat down the many rivers and lakes of South Africa's most famous garden. The mountains that range along the Garden Route's northern border beckon with a series of spectacular passes that cut through to the Afrikaans hinterland of the Klein Karoo. Besides providing a stark contrast to the lush coast, the dusty *dorpies* (little towns) dotted throughout this arid area have developed a distinctive architectural style, the best-preserved examples being found in the tiny hamlet of **Prince Albert** ★★★. **Oudtshoorn** ★★ is the center of the Klein Karoo, and this is where you'll find the region's most famous attractions: ostrich farm tours, the Cango Caves, and the **Swartberg Pass** ★★★, a dramatic road trip connecting Oudtshoorn with Prince Alfred.

The narrow coastal strip that forms the Garden Route stretches from the rural town of Heidelberg in the west to Storms River Mouth in the east; and from the shore of the Indian Ocean to the peaks of the Outeniqua and Tsitsikamma coastal mountain ranges. This is the official boundary description, but for many, Mossel Bay marks the entry point in the west, and Port Elizabeth the eastern point of the route. (See chapter 5, "Eastern Cape," for transport details to and from Port Elizabeth.)

Highlights of this region include the Wilderness National Parks "Lakes District," with some of the Garden Route's loveliest coastline; Knysna's lagoon- and forest-based activities; and Plettenberg Bay, which combines some of South Africa's best swimming beaches with beautiful fynbos and forest surrounds in areas like the Crags. The real "garden" of the Garden Route, however, is the Tsitsikamma National Park, where dense indigenous forests interrupted only by streams and tumbling waterfalls drop off to a beautiful coastline.

OUDTSHOORN & THE KLEIN KAROO

The Klein ("little") Karoo—a sun-drenched area about 250km (155 miles) long and 70km (43½ miles) wide—is wedged between the coastal mountains that separate it from the Garden Route and the impressive Swartberg mountain range in the north. To reach it from any angle, you have to traverse precipitous mountain passes, the most spectacular of which is the Swartberg Pass, connecting the Klein Karoo with its big brother, the Great Karoo. Unlike this vast dry land that stretches well into the Northern Cape and Free State, the "little" Karoo is watered by a number of streams that flow down from the mountains to join the Olifants River. Grapes grow here (Calitzdorp produces some of the country's best port), as does lucerne (alfalfa), which is why farmers in the region were able to successfully introduce the ostrich—lucerne is a favorite food of the ostrich.

> ⸿ *Fun Fact* **Feather Barons and Ostrich Palaces**
>
> It was the ostrich that put the Klein Karoo on the map: During the late 19th and early 20th centuries, when the world decided that ostrich feathers were simply the hautest of haute, Oudtshoorn, where the first ostriches were farmed, found itself crowned the feather capital of the world. Local ostrich farmers, known then as "feather barons," became millionaires overnight, building themselves luxurious "ostrich palaces," clearly identifiable by their sandstone turrets and other baroque touches. Sadly, the boom went bang in 1914, with the sobering outbreak of WWI. The profitable trade in feathers never really recovered, with fickle Dame Fashion seeking her postwar inspiration elsewhere, but with the current health scares surrounding red meat, the ostrich is again enjoying a surge in popularity—it's a delicious and low-fat alternative to beef, and bears absolutely no resemblance to chicken.

Today the **ostrich farms,** together with the **Cango Caves**—a series of subterranean chambers some 30km (18½ miles) from Oudtshoorn—are the main draws of the region, but it is the **Swartberg Pass,** rated one of the most spectacular drives in Africa, the **unique sandstone architecture,** and the **small-town Afrikaans ambience** that makes no Garden Route itinerary complete without a sojourn in Oudtshoorn, center of the Klein Karoo.

ESSENTIALS

VISITOR INFORMATION   You'll find the **Oudtshoorn Tourism Information Bureau** (© 044/279-2532; www.oudtshoorn.com; open Mon–Fri 8am–5pm, Sat 9am–1pm) on Baron van Rheede Street.

GETTING THERE By Plane   There are no scheduled flights here.

By Car   Whichever way you approach it, you'll have to traverse a mountain pass to get to Oudtshoorn. Via the N1 from Jo'burg or Cape Town, you'll head south on the R407 to Prince Albert before tackling the majestic Swartberg Pass. Alternatively, you can come via Calitzdorp (see "The Route Less Traveled," above). The quickest way to get here is to travel along the N2 to Mossel Bay before heading north over the Robinson Pass (R328), or to George before heading north over the Outeniqua Pass (N12). Oudtshoorn is an hour (88km/55 miles) from Mossel Bay and 45 minutes (55km/34 miles) from George.

By Bus   **Intercape** and **Translux** travel from Johannesburg daily; Translux travels from Cape Town to Port Elizabeth. The **Baz Bus** operates a shuttle between Oudtshoorn and George. See chapter 2 for regional phone numbers.

By Train   The **Blue Train** stops at Oudtshoorn on its Garden Route Tour (see chapter 2 or chapter 3).

GETTING AROUND   Avis (© 044/272-4727) has an office on Voortrekker Street. If you need a taxi, contact **DD Transport** (© 044/279-2176).

SPECIAL EVENTS   Every April, Oudtshoorn hosts the **Klein Karoo National Arts Festival (KunsteFees)** ⭐⭐⭐, one of the biggest and considered the best cultural festival in South Africa. Contact the Tourism Bureau for more information.

The Klein Karoo & the Garden Route

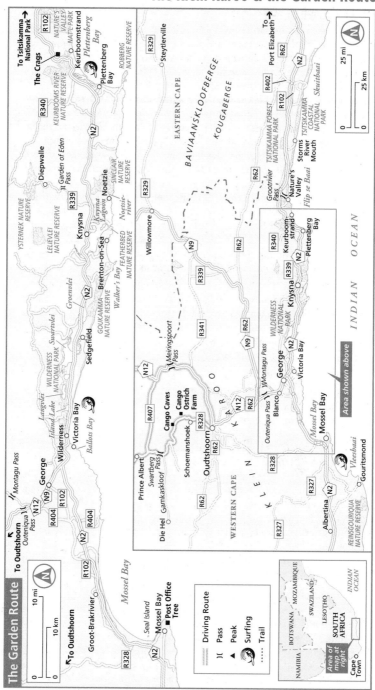

WHAT TO SEE & DO

With the introduction of wire fencing and sweet lucerne, the large-scale domestication of the ostrich first became possible in the 1800s. But it was only when Victorian fashion victims developed an insatiable appetite for ostrich feathers around 1880 that it became a reality, and land values in the Oudtshoorn area shot up overnight. At the height of the feather boom, the so-called feather barons built lavish town houses where they would occasionally overnight, before returning to their marble-floored farmhouses.

The best preserved of these "ostrich palaces" (albeit not the grandest) is the **Le Roux Town House,** a satellite of the CP Nel Museum, where you can peruse photographs of other houses that didn't survive the 20th century. Fortunately, more of these magnificent sandstone buildings survived than were knocked down; though most are closed to the public, they're worth taking a walk or drive past (you can pick up a map from the tourism office). Note particularly **Pinehurst** on Jan van Riebeeck Street, now part of a teachers' training college, and the elegant **Mimosa** on Baron van Reede Street. The latter street becomes the R328, which leads out of town to the ostrich farms (see below), the Rust-en-Vrede waterfall (a 74m [243-ft.] drop under which you can cool off in summer), and the Cango Caves, Oudtshoorn's biggest attraction after the ostrich.

Arbeidsgenot 🎯🎯   Arbeidsgenot (meaning "the pleasure of work") is not a feather palace, but the humble abode of C. J. Langenhoven, author of South Africa's first national anthem, and his family from 1901 to 1950. It's a delightfully authentic house museum, not least because everything has been left exactly as it was when the man penned his noteworthy novels and poems.

217 Jan van Riebeeck Rd. 📞 **044/272-2968.** Admission R8 ($1) adults, R4 (50¢) children. Mon–Fri 9:30am–1pm and 2–5pm; Sat 9:30am–1 pm.

CP Nel Museum 🎯   Located in a handsome sandstone building opposite the Tourist Information Bureau, this old-fashioned museum has many exhibits relating to Oudtshoorn's boom period, as well as photographs of some of the ostrich palaces that never made it past the 1950s. It also houses a synagogue and exhibits relating to Oudtshoorn's once-large Jewish community—in fact, Oudtshoorn was often derisively referred to as "Little Jerusalem" by those envious of the success of the feather merchants, most of whom were Jewish. Admission includes entry to the **Le Roux Town House,** a "mini" feather palace on High Street. Built in 1909, the interior features some original pieces dating back to the Le Roux family's heyday, but the majority of the furnishings—imported from Europe between 1900 and 1920—have been bought and placed *in situ* by the museum.

Corner of Baron van Rheede St. and Voortrekker Rd. 📞 **044/272-7306.** Admission R10 ($1.30) adults, R2 (25¢) children under age 13. Mon–Fri 8am–5pm; Sat 9am–4pm.

The Cango Caves 🎯🎯 *Kids* The **Cango Caves** were first explored in 1780 by a local farmer who was lowered into the dark, bat-filled chamber now named in his honor. The **Van Zyl Hall,** 107m (351 ft.) across and 16m (52 ft.) high, has some truly incredible million-year-old limestone formations, including the "Organ Pipes." A second chamber was discovered in 1792, and a century later the caves opened as a tourist attraction. Regrettably, they were damaged in the 1960s and 1970s, when the floors were evened out with concrete; ladders, colored lights, and music were installed; and a separate entrance was chipped away for "non-whites" (who had tours at different times).

Today the caves enjoy a slightly more respectful treatment, with wardens fighting an ongoing battle to keep the limestone formations from discoloring from exposure to lights and human breath (though their running commentary is a tad irritating). There are two tours to choose from: the hour-long "standard" tour, which departs every hour and visits six chambers; or the 90-minute "adventure" tour, which covers just more than 1km (a little over a half-mile), some of which must be crawled—under no circumstances tackle this if you're overweight, claustrophobic, have heart, knee, or breathing problems, or are not wearing sensible shoes and trousers.

Approximately 30km (19 miles) from town on the R328. © 044/272-7410. Standard tour R35 ($4.50); Adventure tour R50 ($6.50). The caves are open 9am–4pm daily.

VISITING AN OSTRICH FARM

The ostrich remains the primary source of income for Oudtshoorn, with thousands flocking to see, touch, eat, and (yes) even ride the giant birds. There are some 400 ostrich farms, of which Highgate (incidentally the biggest ostrich farm in the world), Safari, Oudtshoorn, and Cango all vie for the tourist buck—R28 to R35 ($3.50–$4.25) to be exact—offering more or less the same 45- to 80-minute tour. These include an explanation of ostrich farming (from incubation to tanning), guided tours of the farm, the opportunity to sit on an ostrich, and an ostrich "derby." All offer meals with ostrich on the menu (you usually need to pre-book).

Of the farms, **Cango Ostrich Farm** ★★ (© 044/272-4623) is the best, not least because of its location overlooking the beautiful Schoemanshoek Valley. The progressive and charming owner, Danie Lategan, is adamant that individuals should never be tagged onto large tour groups, and visitors take a brief walk from one process to the next, rather than being driven around a large farm. Finally, while you can sit on an ostrich, they are not raced here, saving you the embarrassment of this circus display. The 45-minute tours (R32/$4) take place daily from 9am to 4.30pm; lunch (or dinner) is served in restored laborer's cottages with great views overlooking the valley. You can also order a wine tasting with your meal and sample the distinctive flavors of the Klein Karoo.

A BREATHTAKING DRIVE

For many, the greatest highlight of visiting the Klein Karoo is traversing the Swartberg Mountains to Prince Albert, a charming 18th-century Groot Karoo town that lies 100km (62 miles) north.

To reach the **Swartberg Pass** ★★★, a 27km (17-mile) gravel road built more than 100 years ago by master engineer Thomas Bain, take the R328 (also known as Cango Valley Rd.) north from Oudtshoorn. About 1km (a little more than a half-mile) before the road terminates at the Cango Caves, you'll find a turnoff to the west, signposted Prince Albert. This marks the start of the pass, which soon begins its steep ascent. By the time you reach the summit, you will have enjoyed stupendous views of the Klein Karoo, which lies some 1,220m (4,002 ft.) below. Stop to gird your loins, for the journey has only just begun. The northern descent is hair-raising—10km (6 miles) of zigzags, serpentines, twists, and steep gradients on a narrow dirt road with nothing between you and the abyss but a good grip on the wheel. (You'll note a turnoff to the west that will take you to **Die Hell,** or **Gamkaskloof** ★★★. This is another magnificent drive, particularly popular with fynbos lovers, but unless you overnight in one of the rudimentary Cape Nature Conservation cottages you'll have to return the

---

Finds Olive, Anyone?

Prince Albert has a reputation for producing some of the country's finest olives—it even has an Olive Festival in April. Sample these at **Sampie se Plaasstal** (at the bottom end of Church St.; ✆ **023/541-1345**; daily 8am–6pm). Among the other *padkos* ("food for the road") items, all locally produced, are springbok or ostrich pies, dried fruit rolls, and biltong.

---

way you came—set aside most of the day for this detour. For guided hikes in Die Hell, contact **Saxe-Coburg Lodge** (✆ **023/541-1267**).

The road continues to twist and turn before finally winding its way out of the Swartberg. At this point, you can either go to Prince Albert or turn back into the mountains and return to Oudtshoorn via Meiringspoort. Opt for **Prince Albert** ✮✮✮; the town is an architectural gem, with almost all the buildings preserved and maintained in their original 19th-century form. If you're in need of real tranquillity, or wish to wander the streets at sunset to view the mix of architectural styles, consider spending the night—recommendations are listed below; alternatively, contact **Prince Albert's Tourism Information** (Church St., ✆ **023/541-1366;** open Mon–Fri 9am–5pm, Sat 9am–12pm).

To return to Oudtshoorn, take the road back to the Swartberg Pass, keeping an eye out for the R407, which takes you east through Meiringspoort. This is another spectacular drive, though this time the views are up.

In prehistoric times, the Great Karoo was a swamp that apparently broke through to the sea at Meiringspoort. The majestic **Meiringspoort Pass** ✮, a natural ravine created by the course of what came to be known as the Groot River, features soaring cliffs and spectacular rock formations. The 25km (16-mile) tarred road follows and crosses the river several times as it winds along the floor of the gorge.

WHERE TO STAY
IN AND AROUND OUDTSHOORN

De Opstal ✮   Stopping in Schoemanshoek Valley (just outside Oudtshoorn, on the way to the Cango Caves and close to the Cango Ostrich Farm) is an excellent opportunity to get a feel for the rural Klein Karoo. Certainly if you're interested in Afrikaans "boere" culture, De Opstal rates as one of the most authentic Afrikaans guesthouses in the country. Matilda de Bod is an eighth-generation Schoeman, still living on the original Schoemanshoek Valley farm, though she and her husband, Albertus, now share it with guests. The 1830 farmhouse, stables, and milking parlor have all been converted into en-suite bedrooms, and in 2002 four more rooms were added. These have the most modern amenities, but my personal favorite is still the huge honeymoon suite (no. 1), with its large bed and fireplace (essential in winter—windows close with shutters rather than glass). Meals are traditional and hearty (foodies would be better off eating at Jemima's, see below), and invariably feature ostrich.

P.O. Box 1425, Oudtshoorn 6620. Schoemanshoek Valley; 12km (7 miles) north from Oudtshoorn on R328. ✆ 044/279-2954. Fax 044/272-0736. 18 units. R700–R900 ($88–$112) double, including breakfast. AE, DC, MC, V. **Amenities:** Dining room/lounge/bar; pool; room service; laundry. *In room:* A/C, TV, minibar, tea- and coffee-making facilities, fireplaces (all but 2 rooms, specify in winter!).

Rosenhof Country House ✮✮   This is the most upscale place to stay in Oudtshoorn: a calm gracious oasis, beautifully furnished, with selected works by famous (white) South African artists, and in springtime, a rose-filled garden that saturates the senses. Rooms are built around a courtyard, each with its own entrance. Though each has a different theme, they share the most important characteristics: space, beautiful linens, well-sprung beds, and elegant, traditional taste. The courtyard contains a large pool—a necessity during the searing summer heat. The staff is very eager to please, and despite the hotel's relatively small size, there are such luxuries as room service. Meals are a five-course affair (R120/$15), served in the original homestead, which dates back to 1852. Ingredients are local, with herbs picked fresh from the garden.

264 Baron van Reede St., Oudtshoorn 6620. ℂ 044/272-2232. Fax 044/272-2260. 14 units. R1,380 ($170) double, including breakfast; R1,980 ($248) suite. AE, DC, MC, V. Children by prior arrangement only. **Amenities:** Dining room; bar, lounge; pool; room service; laundry. *In room:* A/C, TV, minibar, tea- and coffee-making facilities.

PRINCE ALBERT

Other B&B establishments worth noting are **Dennehof** ⚡ (ℂ **023/541-1227**), a tasteful, tranquil oasis on the outskirts of the village that offers excellent value at R390 to R600 ($49–$75) double—the self-catering cottage (R600/$75) is the one to book; **Collins House** (ℂ **023/541-1786;** R450–R600/$56–$75 double), a centrally located two-story Victorian with a pool; and the cottage at **Saxe-Coburg Lodge** (ℂ **023/541-1267;** R360/$45 double), also with pool.

De Bergkant Lodge and Cottages ⭐⭐   This guesthouse, recently upgraded, is the best place to stay in town, and was recently voted one of the top 10 places to stay in the country by a European publication; sadly, this has meant an almost 50% increase in rates. Situated in a national monument in the Cape Dutch style, with Victorian-style bathrooms, and beautifully furnished with antiques, the guesthouse now has an additional three rooms built in a Georgian-style building and a new 15m (48-ft.) saltwater swimming pool. Owner Charles offers attentive, intelligent service, with dinners on request. Children are welcome.

5 Church St., Prince Albert. ℂ/fax **023/541-1088.** www.debergkant.co.za. 8 en-suite rooms. R1,400 ($175) double, including breakfast. AE, DC, MC, V. Off-street parking. **Amenities:** Dining room; pool. *In room:* A/C.

WHERE TO DINE

Prince Albert finally has a restaurant to suit the rather sophisticated palates that are now moving through this Karoo dorp: the **Blue Fig** (61 Church St.; ℂ **023/541-1900**) offers a slightly more contemporary take on traditional Karoo items (the rolled loin of Karoo lamb is superb); don't miss the baked figs for dessert (dinner Wed–Mon; lunch Wed–Sun; no credit cards; BYOB). For the real thing, untainted by modern touches, book a table at the down-to-earth **Karoo Kombuis** (Droedrift St.; ℂ **023/5411110,** dinner Mon–Sat; no credit cards; BYOB); choose between traditional *bobotie* (lightly curried ground beef cooked in a savory egg custard and served with yellow rice), Karoo lamb pie, chicken pie, or Karoo leg of lamb, followed by sticky malva pudding or steamed lemon pudding.

(*Tips* **Putting the Karoo into Lamb**

Karoo lamb is on just about every menu in the Western Cape, and where better to sample it but here in the little Karoo? In this semi-arid region, farms are the size of small countries, and sheep range far and wide to nibble on wild herbs like *brakbos* and *gannabos* (the equivalent of wild rosemary). The result is tender, herb-infused meat.

Jemima's ★★★ *Value* SOUTH AFRICAN INNOVATIVE   This is not only the best restaurant in Oudtshoorn, but it was voted one of the top 10 in the country in the highly regarded "Eat Out" awards. Run with flair by sisters Celia and Annette le Roux (who, incidentally, have no formal restaurant training, and who used their parents' home to secure a bank loan), Jemima's typifies sincere Karoo hospitality and laid-back country style. Traditional South African fare is given innovative twists, such as snoek samosas with curried peach salad, ravioli (homemade) with spicy *boerewors* (a uniquely South African mince and pork sausage); Karoo lamb platter with a mint-flavored *frikkadel* (meatball) in mus-catel jus; and ostrich Wellington. This is also the only restaurant in the Klein Karoo where vegetarians are well cared for, with such offerings as fresh pasta (with lemon and Parmesan or chili and garlic) and mushrooms in phyllo pastry served with salsa verde; much of the fresh produce comes direct from the farm where the sisters grew up.

94 Baron van Reede St. ☎ **044/272-0808**. Main courses R18–R47 ($2.35–$6) lunch, R20–R75 ($2.60–$9) dinner. MC, V. Tues–Fri 11am–2pm; Tues–Sun 6:30–10pm.

ENTERING THE GARDEN ROUTE—MOSSEL BAY

Traveling east on the N2, the first sign of the fast-approaching town of Mossel Bay, unofficial entry point of the Garden Route, is the sci-fi spectacle of the MossGas oil plant on your left. The town does not really improve on closer inspection, but if you're traveling by at noon, it does have one of the best seafood restaurants on the coast (see "Where to Stay & Dine," below) and a few inter-esting attractions.

Mossel Bay is approximately 4 hours from Cape Town on the N2, and 20 minutes from George.

WHAT TO SEE & DO

Mossel Bay was the site of the first European landing on the South African coast, when Bartholomieu Dias, having battled a fearsome storm, tacked in for water and safety in 1488. **The Bartholomieu Dias Museum Complex** (☎ **044/691-1067**) comprises a collection of historic buildings, of which the **Maritime Museum** is excellent. It relates the early Portuguese, Dutch, and British seafaring history (which is a bit text-heavy), and houses a life-size replica of the caravel in which Dias set sail in 1487—it's hard to imagine going where no man has gone before in something that looks like a large toy. The ship on display was built in Portugal and sailed from Lisbon to Mossel Bay in 1987 to commemorate the 500th anniversary of Dias's arrival on southern Cape soil. The museum, located on Market Street, is open Monday through Friday from 8:15am to 5pm, and Saturday and Sunday from 9am to 4pm. Admission is R5 (65¢), R10 ($1.30) to access the ship.

Mossel Bay is also one of the best places along the coast to get up close and personal with a Great White shark (see "Staying Active," earlier in this chapter); if you'd prefer your ocean interlude with a little less adrenaline, contact **Seven Seas** (☎ **044/691-3371**) or **Romanza** (☎ **044/690-3101**) for pleasure cruises or trips to Seal Island; a 90-minute cruise costs approximately R40/$5.

(*Fun Fact* **Claim to Fame**

Mossel Bay features in the *Guinness Book of Records* as having one of the mildest all-year climates in the world—it's second only to Hawaii.

Fun Fact **The Original Snail Mail**

Outside the Maritime Museum is the **Post Office Tree,** South Africa's first post office. In 1501 the first of many sailors sent his mail by leaving a letter stuffed in an old boot and tied to what the city fathers claim is this particular milkwood tree. Soon this became an informal postal system, with letters picked up by passing ships and distributed accordingly. Today you can post a letter in a boot-shaped post box and it will be stamped with a special postmark.

For more information, contact the **Tourism Bureau** (*©* **044/691-2202;** www.gardenroute.net/mby; open Mon–Fri 8am–6pm, Sat–Sun 9am–4pm), located in the historical center, at the corner of Church and Market streets.

WHERE TO STAY

The official western point of the Garden Route is in fact Heidelberg, which has two accommodations options worth highlighting. The first is the **Garden Route Game Lodge** (*©* **028/735-1200;** from R1,470/$180) off the N2, 5km (3 miles) from Albertinia. It's touted as a "Big 5" reserve, and this claim is substantiated by a grand total of eight lions (all in a separate enclosure), two leopards, two rhinos, two buffalo, and two elephants. If you're looking for a true safari experience, see chapter 2 for more viable options. A little farther along you'll see a sign for **Rein's Coastal Nature Reserve** (*©* **028/745-3322;** www.reinsouthafrica.com; from R850/$105 double), which offers comfortable accommodation in a 3,550-hectare (8,768-acre) fynbos reserve—opt for one of the fisherman's cottages (R1,080/$135 double) if you're looking for tranquil solitude. It's a bit off the beaten track—35km (22 miles) from the N2, to be exact.

The Old Post Office Tree Manor *★*   This is one of the best places to stay in Mossel Bay, as much for the views as for its excellent restaurant (see The Gannet entry, below) and proximity to the Tourism Bureau and the Dias museum complex. "Manor," however, is a much-abused word in South Africa, and this place proves to be no exception—though rooms are clean and relatively spacious, they don't exactly make you feel like the landed gentry. The furniture doesn't look like it's changed much since the hotel opened; far more uplifting are the views of the ocean (ask for room no. 20, 30, or 31). If you don't manage to bag a room with a view, repair to the **Blue Oyster.** This cocktail bar enjoys exceptional views of Munro Bay and its great whale-watching opportunities.

Corner of Church and Market sts., Mossel Bay 6500. *©* **044/691-3738.** Fax 044/691-3104. www.oldpost tree.co.za. 30 units. R730–R800 ($90–$100) double, including breakfast. Call for specials. Children sharing room with parents pay 50%. AE, DC, MC, V. **Amenities:** Restaurant; bar; pool; room service; babysitting; laundry. *In room:* TV, tea- and coffee-making facilities, hair dryer, fans.

WHERE TO DINE

The Gannet *★★* *(Kids)* SEAFOOD   Conveniently located across the road from the main museums and a stone's throw from the Tourism Bureau, The Gannet is an excellent seafood restaurant, but with a small (rather unimaginative) range of pizzas and pastas (lunch), and meat dishes (dinner), even the nonseafood lover won't leave disappointed. The linefish, basted with lemon butter and herbs and grilled or fried to tender perfection, is so fresh that it's almost moving. The seafood casserole, baked in a clay pot with a creamy wine sauce, is another house specialty; or try the grilled marinated tuna *sosatie,* coated with a dill and ginger sauce. Beleaguered parents will be pleased to know the restaurant is also child-friendly, with a separate kids' menu. Weather permitting, you can dine alfresco in the garden overlooking the bay, keeping an eye out for whales and dolphins.

Market St., Bartholomieu Dias Museum Complex. ℂ **044/691-1885.** Main courses R49–R185 ($6.25–$23). AE, DC, MC, V. Mon–Fri 7am–10pm; Sat–Sun 8am–11pm.

GEORGE & WILDERNESS

Halfway between Cape Town and Port Elizabeth, the sprawling city of George won't win any beauty competitions, but it is the commercial heart of the Garden Route, with the most transport connections and a large choice of restaurants. It's not worth overnighting in this inland town, however, as its attractions are few and far from scintillating, and the coastal town of Wilderness, with a number of pleasant lodging options, is a 10-minute drive away. Knysna, lies 30 minutes east, while Plettenberg Bay is an hour away.

ESSENTIALS

VISITOR INFORMATION The George Tourism Bureau (ℂ **044/801-9295;** www.georgetourism.co.za; open Mon–Fri 9am–5:30pm, Sat 9am–1pm) is located at 124 York St. *Note:* It's not essential to stop here; Knysna has an excellent tourism bureau.

GETTING THERE **By Air** You can fly to **George Airport** (ℂ **044/876-9310**) from Cape Town, Johannesburg, or Durban with **SAA** (ℂ **044/801-8434**) or **Nationwide** (ℂ **044/801-8414**).

By Train Sadly, the intercity trains running between Cape Town and Port Elizabeth have been canceled. If you've got money to burn, board the Edwardian **Rovos Rail** (ℂ **012/315-8242;** www.rovos.co.za), which does the 24-hour run from Cape Town to George—a beautiful route, with a wine or brandy-tasting stop—during the summer months. Tickets are R6,585 ($820) per person, sharing. Alternatively, travel the Garden Route and Klein Karoo on the **Union Limited** (ℂ **021/449-4391;** fax 021/449-4395; www.transnetheritagefoundation.co.za) in elegantly restored en-suite carriages dating back to the 1930s and 1940s. The 5-day Golden Thread Tour sets off from Cape Town to Mossel Bay via the Breede River, then heads for George and Oudtshoorn before steaming to Knysna, returning to Cape Town via Paarl. The 6-day tour costs R7,500 ($935) per person, including all side tours and meals. The Blue Train also stops here on its Cape-Town-to-Port-Elizabeth Garden Route Tour (see chapter 2).

By Bus The intercity buses (**Intercape, Greyhound, Translux,** and **Baz Bus**) travel from Cape Town along the Garden Route to Port Elizabeth. See chapter 2 for regional numbers.

GETTING AROUND **By Car** There are six companies offering rental cars at the airport including **Avis** (ℂ **044/876-9314**), **Budget** (ℂ **044/876-9204**), or **Hertz** (ℂ **044/801-4700**).

GUIDED TOURS **By Bus** **Eco Afrika** (ℂ **082-472-9696**) offers the largest variety of tours, from township visits and golf tours to photographic safaris and adventure tours. For trips in a customized four-wheel-drive vehicle (take the great drive to Oudtshoorn via two mountain passes; or to Knysna via seven passes, with various activities included), contact **Pearl's Joy Adventures** (ℂ **072-433-0598**).

By Train You can travel between George and Knysna on the **Choo-Tjoe steam train,** one of the region's top attractions; for details, see the "Knysna" section, later in this chapter. Another fun option is to trundle to the top of the scenic

Montagu Pass in an **Outeniqua Power Van**—a little motorized trolley used for rail inspections; the trip (R60/$7.50) takes 3 hours (with a 45-minute stop on the mountain for a BYO picnic); contact (© **044/801-8239**).

By Air Swan (© **044/442-3532**) offers helicopter flights covering a range of attractions from the ostrich farms and Cango Caves of Oudtshoorn, to flights over the coast to Knysna, Noetzie, and Plettenberg Bay.

WHAT TO SEE & DO

The best reason to be in George itself is to board the **Choo-Tjoe steam train** that runs between George and Knysna (though you can board in Knysna and do the return journey by road with **Kontours,** © **082-569-8997**); see the Knysna section of this chapter for details. *Note:* Trainspotters and vintage-car lovers could probably spend the better part of the day examining the locomotives and cars in the **Outeniqua Railway Museum,** adjacent to the platform from where the Choo-Tjoe and Outeniqua Power Vans depart and arrive.

You are spoiled for choice when it comes to the number of **excellent drives** leading out of George. To do a circular route to Oudtshoorn, take the **Outeniqua Pass** (or R29) to Oudtshoorn, then return via the **Montagu Pass,** a gravel road dating back to 1843. If you're heading to Wilderness or Knysna, consider taking the **Seven Passes Road.** This, the original road linking George and Knysna, lacks the great sea views of the N2, but it takes you through dense indigenous forests, crosses streams via a number of quaint Edwardian bridges, and finally traverses the **Homtini Pass,** another engineering feat by the famous Thomas Baines. Alternatively, head down the N2 for the most direct route to the pretty town of Wilderness—8km (5 miles) away via the **Kaaimans River Pass.**

Wilderness is anything but, with a residential development creeping up the forested hills that overlook the Touw River estuary, and a string of ugly mansions lining the beach; yet it is effectively an island within the national park, and still the smallest and most tranquil of the coastal towns along the Garden Route— hence the proliferation of B&Bs over the years. Set around the mouth of the Touw River, it marks the western end of a chain of lakes that stretches some 40km (25 miles) east, most of which are under the control of the **Wilderness National Park.** Although the beaches along this stretch are magnificent, strong currents regularly claim unsuspecting and inexperienced swimmers. You're better off floating in the waters of the **Serpentine,** the waterway that links Island Lake, Langvlei, and Rondevlei to the Wilderness lagoon. Don't be put off by the tea-colored water or frothy bubbles; these are caused by plant oxides and oxygenation, and the water is perfectly clean.

You can explore the area on foot on a number of trails that take from 1 to 4 hours to walk, or cover some 15km (9 miles) of inland waterways in a canoe. **The Wilderness National Park** (reception: © **044/877-1197**) issues trail maps and rents canoes for R25 ($3) an hour. Ask about the 3-day canoe trail (see "Staying Active," earlier in this chapter). To reach the park, follow signs off the N2, 2km (1.2 mile) east of Wilderness; should you wish to overnight in the park, see review below. For details, contact the helpful **Wilderness Tourism Information Bureau** on Leila's Lane (© **044/877-0045;** www.wildernessinfo. co.za; open Mon–Fri 8am–6pm, Sat 8am–1pm, Sun 3–5pm).

WHERE TO STAY
In George

Fancourt Hotel and Country Club Estate ✪✪✪ *Kids* This is without a doubt the best address in George, and a destination in its own right for keen golfers. Host of the 2002 President's Cup, Fancourt boasts four excellent golf courses, of which two—designed by Gary Player and consistently rated among the top four in South Africa—are only open to guests. Besides the golf academy there is a fabulous health spa to ease aching shoulders (or nagging golf widows) and four pools to choose from. In fact, you don't have to be a golfer to appreciate the luxurious atmosphere, lovely setting, and helpful staff. Rooms are either in the original manor house or set in the beautifully landscaped gardens. Not much differentiates them, other than price; rooms are smaller in the manor house, but they are closer to all amenities. The luxe two-bedroom Garden Suites or "lodges" are ideal for families. *Note:* **Land's End Guest House** (for contact details, see "Where to Stay: In Victoria Bay," below) has purchased a 2-bedroom garden suite on the 18th fairway of the Montagu course, about 250m (800 ft.) from the hotel. The lodge costs R950 ($119) a night for two people, representing a great savings. Remember to request that the lodge be serviced on booking.

Montagu St., Blanco, George 6530. ✆ **044/804-0000.** Fax 044/804-0710. www.fancourt.co.za. 100 plus units. R1,540–R3,315 ($190–$400) double; R2,255–R3,660 ($280–$450) 1-bedroom suite; R4,010–R6,175 ($500–$765) 2-bedroom suite. Rates quoted depend on season; ask about discounted winter rates. AE, DC, MC, V. **Amenities:** 4 restaurants; 2 bars; 4 (2 heated) swimming pools; 4 golf courses; 4 tennis courts; health and beauty spa; children's programs; babysitting; room service; squash court; mountain bikes, and 6km (3³⁄₄-mile) trail. *In room:* A/C, TV, minibar, tea- and coffee-making facilities, hair dryer.

In Victoria Bay

Hilltop Country Lodge ★★   Located at the end of a private road on a 12-hectare (30-acre) private nature reserve, Hilltop is literally perched on the hill that separates the cove of Victoria Bay from the endless beach of Wilderness. Rooms are pretty (some may find them a little bland) and relatively spacious, each with a private entrance and outside area/balcony, but the real reasons to fork out (it's relatively pricey when compared to, say, Moontide) are the stupendous mountain and sea views that you enjoy from every vantage (including the pool), and the great hiking opportunities; you can walk all the way down to the Touws River estuary, though it's a tough hike, particularly if you can't arrange a pickup. Service is professional but a little uptight. Dinners aren't served here, but the restaurants of George and Wilderness lie just a 10-minute drive away.

Victoria Bay Heights. P.O. Box 10016, George 6530. ✆ **044/889-0142.** Fax 044/889-0151. www.hilltop countrylodge.co.za. 6 units. Seaview rooms R880–R1,200 ($110–$150) double, depending on season. Honeymoon suite R1,250–R1,700 ($155–$212). Mountain view room R750–R900 ($95–$112). Rates include breakfast. AE, DC, MC, V. Children by arrangement only. **Amenities:** Lounge; honesty bar; pool; mountain bikes; laundry. *In room:* TV, tea- and coffee-making facilities, hair dryer, underfloor heating.

Land's End Guest House ★ *Finds*   "The Closest B&B to the Sea in Africa," it trumpets, and at 6m (19 ft.) from the high-water mark, this is no doubt true. Land's End is the last house on the only residential road in Vic Bay; beyond lie the rocks and the ocean, and beside you is the safest swimming bay for miles around. The guesthouse is run in a very laid-back manner (the proprietor is a surfer) and furnished in a homey fashion, with lovely touches like complimentary sherry. The views from the two self-catering units, each with private deck, are fantastic; try to book these rather than the downstairs rooms. *Note:* Land's End also owns a two-bedroom garden suite, "Lodge 743," at Fancourt (see above).

P.O. Box 9429, George 6530. ✆ **044/889-0123.** Fax 044/889-0141. www.vicbay.com. 4 units. High season: R840–R960 ($105–$120), depending on room. Low season: R672–R768 ($84–$96). Half-price for children under age 12. AE, DC, MC, V. At the end of Beach Rd., Victoria Bay. **Amenities:** Dining room/bar; water-sport equipment rental; laundry. *In room:* TV, minibar, tea- and coffee-making facilities, hair dryer.

In Wilderness

The Dune Guest House ★★ *Finds*   You know you're on holiday when you wake up and hear, smell, and see the ocean from your bed, then slide open your doors, step out onto your private patio, and pad down a short boardwalk onto an almost solitary beach that stretches as far as the eye can see. One of the few B&Bs on the entire coast that is literally right on the beach, The Dune comprises four comfortable en-suite bedrooms, each with semi-private decks furnished with teak deck chairs. Top choices are White (literally, entirely white) and Africa, the only semi-sea-facing option, but a very stylish room nonetheless. A self-catering apartment is ideal for groups or families. Architecturally the building is rather charmless, so if you're not set on a seaview or are traveling here in winter, you'd be better of at Moontide.

31 Die Duin, Wilderness 6560. ©/fax 044/877-0298. www.thedune.co.za. 5 units. R1,000–R1,150 ($125–$142) double; R1,250 ($156) apt. Low season R840–R950 ($105–$119). Rates include breakfast. AE, MC, V. Children by prior arrangement only. **Amenities:** Pool. *In room:* TV, minibar.

Moontide Guest Lodge ★★ *Value*   Situated on the banks of the Touw River, in gardens that flow into its tidal waters, this B&B (the only one right on the river) offers one of the best value-for-money options on the Garden Route. The thatched homestead, with separate suites, is set among 400-year-old milkwood trees and an abundance of ferns and flowering potplants. Guests can choose from the Stone Cottage, the Milkwood Suite, the Rondawel, the Boat House, or the River Suite. The last two are personal favorites: River Suite is the most luxurious and enjoys great garden views from the king-size bed; Boat House is the most private, with an entrance (and views) right on the lagoon. Milkwood, a separate duplex cottage with an upstairs bedroom, is ideal for younger couples; the quaint Stone Cottage is also separate from the main house and has the largest bathroom (shower only); and Rondawel has both a bathtub and shower in a bathroom that is private, but not en-suite. Guests have exclusive use of the lounge with a large log fireplace and sliding doors leading to the terrace overlooking the tranquil lagoon—shallow but great for swimming, especially when the lagoon is tidal.

Southside Rd. (at the end of the cul-de-sac), Wilderness 6560. © **044/877-0361**. Fax 044/877-0124. www. moontide.co.za. 4 units. R400–R850 ($50–$105), depending on season and room. Rates include breakfast. AE, MC, V. Children by prior arrangement only. **Amenities:** Lounge; boat. *In room:* TV, minibar.

Palms ★★   One of the main reasons to book into the Palms is the restaurant—one of the best in Wilderness, it's often full, and guests obviously enjoy preferential booking. Rooms, each with a private entrance from the garden, are spacious and stylishly furnished in crisp whites, deep blues, and black. Green is the other dominant color, supplied by the lush gardens, and the red and pink hibiscus flowers make a stark statement against the black marbled pool. Palms is Swiss-owned and -managed, and things do run rather like clockwork, with four hosts to attend to guests' needs, complemented by an enthusiastic staff. The only drawback is the lack of views.

Owen Grant St. (opposite the Wilderness Hotel), Wilderness 6560. © **044/877-1420**. Fax 044/877-1422. www.palms-wilderness.com. 12 units. R900 ($112) double. Ask about winter discounts. Rates include buffet breakfast. AE, DC, MC, V. **Amenities:** Restaurant; pool; room service; laundry. *In room:* TV, hair dryer.

Wilderness National Park *Value*   Accommodations in the Wilderness National Park (called **Ebb & Flow** rest camp) offer exceptional value, though some of the rondawels in Ebb & Flow North are very rudimentary and share washing facilities. Your best options are in Ebb & Flow South, particularly the timber "forest huts" numbered 24 to 33. These are slightly raised and built right on the Touw River—you can almost cast for fish from your front door. Bear in mind that not all units are en-suite showers, so remember to specify your requirements. All forest huts have kitchenettes and braai areas. Of the four-bed log cabins (better equipped if you prefer to self-cater) units 7 to 13 enjoy the best location, on the Serpentine River. All units are serviced daily. There is a rudimentary shop, so you'll have to bring in your own supplies (there is a large well-stocked Pick 'n Pay grocery store on the outskirts of George) or dine out.

Off N2, 2km (just more than 1mile) east of Wilderness; follow signs. Bookings: P.O. Box 787, Pretoria 0001. Bookings: (℗ **012/428-9111.** Fax 021/343-0905. Direct: (℗ **044/877-1197.** www.parks-sa.co.za. 45 units comprising 4-bed cottages and forest huts and 2-bed rondavels, not all with bathrooms. R500 ($62) en-suite cottage; R275 ($34) en-suite forest hut with kitchenette; R170–R190 ($21–$24) huts with communal ablutions and kitchens. Camping from R90 ($11) double. AE, DC, MC, V.

WHERE TO DINE

If the restaurant scene is indicative of a city's cultural pulse, then the opening of **The Conservatory at Mead House** (℗ **044/874-1938;** 91 Meade St.; 7:30am– 5pm) means that George has finally outgrown its backwater status. A large airy space, attached to a rather nice gift shop and tiny bookshop, with an array of seating options (couches, armchairs, barstools, dining chairs), the conservatory offers shaded tables spilling out onto the paved lavender garden. It's open all day for confectionary and coffee, but the small lunch menu is extremely tempting: a variety of garden fresh salads and tarts, generous sandwiches, and slightly larger mains like bangers and mash, or sesame-crusted Norwegian salmon with lime dressing, served on citrus mash and a warm tomato salad. But for real home-cooked fare in a laid-back publike venue (an extension of a potters' workshop), head for **Leila's Arms** (℗ **044/873-2378;** 42 York St.). Here Leila personally presides over large steaming platters you choose from—tandoori chicken, roasted vegetables, or her speciality, sweet potato with creamy cottage cheese layered with spinach (first fried in olive oil and garlic), chicken tikka, and dates, and finished with a squeeze of lemon.... This is also one of the best-value deals on the Garden Route, with the most expensive item costing R35 ($4.50). Both of these venues close at nights (though Leila sometimes opens for dinner Fri at her farm), so dinner is best taken at one of the recommended Wilderness options (a 10-min. drive from George), reviewed below.

The Palms ★★ FRENCH/INTERNATIONAL Vying with Serendipity as the most romantic dining experience in Wilderness, but a lot less formal, the Palms offers attentive service yet laid-back atmosphere (Serendipity probably offers better value in terms of creativity, however). Weather permitting, book a table on the candlelit veranda to enjoy the gardens. The four-course set menu is prepared daily (so guests never get bored) but always includes a choice of starters (marinated blue rock cheese on watercress salad, for example, or summer salad with seafood), a soup or small pasta (langoustines on lemon grass risotto), followed by a palate-clearing sorbet and a choice of mains (baked leg of lamb on mint sauce or grilled Cape sole on fruit chutney butter) and a choice of desserts. Portions are smartly sized so that you don't feel overly full, but if you don't like the choices, you can always opt to replace items from the small a la carte menu.

George Rd., opposite the Wilderness Hotel. (℗ **044/877-1420.** Set menu R160 ($20). AE, DC, MC, V. Mon–Sat 7–11pm.

Riverside Kitchen ★★ (Value) SOUTH AFRICAN/ECLECTIC Located on the banks of the Touw River, in a large double-volume thatch building with tables outside overlooking the river, the Riverside Kitchen is charming, unpretentious, and good value, catering to a wide-ranging clientele, from local farmers and B&B owners to globetrotters. Recommended starters include black mushrooms topped with slices of fresh pear and melted Roquefort cheese, or the avocado and mandarin salad—lettuce topped with slices of avocado, mandarin orange, smoked salmon, roasted almonds, and a creamy horseradish dressing. If you haven't yet tried ostrich, this is the place to do so; chef-patron Roxanne does it to a turn. Either order the Espetada—tender chunks of ostrich meat (do specify ostrich, it's more tender than the beef), sizzling with herbed butter dripping down its vertical skewer—or coated with a Moroccan rub and served with an onion and red wine jus on couscous. Linefish is also recommended—if you're lucky it's *kabeljou,* rolled in herbs and crushed pepper and topped with rose geranium jelly and toasted macadamias.

Pirates Creek (signposted off N2). ✆ **044/877-0900**. Main courses R24–R60 ($3–$7.50). AE, DC, MC, V. Tues–Sun 7–10pm (open daily mid Dec to mid-Jan); Sun 12.30–2.30pm.

Serendipity ★★ INTERNATIONAL/MODERN CAPE   The only Wilderness restaurant to make it in *Wine* magazine's 2003 top 100 selection, this is the village's fine-dining option—great if you're in a celebratory mood or like your food Cordon Bleu, but a little uptight if your idea of a holiday is hanging barefoot and fancy-free. Despite it's haute credentials, it's very much a family affair: Lizelle is the young ex–Prue Leith chef; husband, Rudolf, is front-of-house; and the venue—a house on the banks of the lagoon—is Lizelle's parents' retirement home. Lizelle changes the four-course set menu every week, but expect fresh locally procured ingredients, combined with creativity and skill: caramelized onion and feta tartlet is served with biltong shavings; spring rolls are stuffed with ostrich *bobotie* and served on a banana, coriander, and peanut sambal; kudu (antelope) is wrapped in bacon and served with traditional samp and bean stew, green beans, and fruit jus; and sweet-corn fritters are stacked with roasted tomatoes, baby spinach, and mushroom duxelles. Even the crème brûlée has a twist— it's made with Amarula (a local version of Baileys Irish Cream).

Freesia Ave. (off Waterside Rd.), Wilderness ✆ **044/877-0433**. Set menu R159 ($20). MC, V. Mon–Sat 7–10pm (closed winter months).

SEDGEFIELD & GOUKAMMA RESERVE

The drive from Wilderness to Sedgefield on the N2 is very pleasant, with a series of lakes on the left and occasional glimpses of the ocean on your right. Sedgefield looks very unattractive from the road—a motley collection of shops, estate agents, and service stations—but it's worth turning off and heading for the beach, which is one of the most attractive along this stretch (mostly because the houses are set back behind the sand dunes). One of the best Garden Route beach walks starts here: During low tide, walk westward to **Gericke's Point,** a low hillock of sandstone where locals come to pick fresh mussels.

Next stop is the 2,230-hectare (5,500-acre) **Goukamma Nature Reserve,** which encompasses forests, an estuary, beaches, reputedly the highest vegetated dune in southern Africa, and Groenvlei, or "Lake Pleasant," a freshwater lake. There are a few rudimentary accommodations options and several hiking trails that cover various habitats in the reserve, including a 4-hour beach walk and a short circular walk through a milkwood forest. Admission to the Goukamma Reserve is R15 ($1.95), and its gate hours, accessed via the Buffalo Bay turnoff, are daily 8am to 6pm. For more information, contact ✆/fax **044/383-0042.**

WHERE TO STAY & DINE

If you're looking for the tranquillity that comes with isolation, and you want a chance to truly appreciate why this region is known as the Garden Route, book one of the three self-catering timber chalets at **Buffalo Valley Lodge** ★★ (© **044/384-1235;** R400–R500/$50–$62 double), in a private conservancy bordering the Goukamma Nature Reserve. Choose between River Lodge, perched high up on a vegetated dune with beautiful views of the river; Vlei Lodge, situated on a wetland and ideal for birders; or Forest Lodge, built on the riverbank with its own private jetty. The beach is a short paddle away (each lodge has access to a two-person canoe) and you'll wake to the moving sound of the fish eagle, with bustling Knysna a mere 20-minute drive away. Note that Sedgefield finally has a hip dining option: **Satsung Durbar** (26 Main Rd.; © **044/343-2109;** open daily for breakfast, lunch and tea; dinner Tues–Sat) serves organic vegetarian fare (with a nod to carnivores in the form of seafood and wild fowl) in a Balinese-themed restaurant-cum-lounge that attracts hippies from as far afield as Knysna and Wilderness. The owner has opened an adjacent bookshop stuffed to the gunnels with books to awaken and cleanse your spirit; order a cappuccino and take a browse, but note that you may only enter after washing your hands.

Lake Pleasant Hotel ★★ Arguably the most luxurious hotel this side of Plettenberg Bay (though not when you include guesthouses like Parkes Manor), this is situated on the south bank of Groenvlei, making it one of the few hotels on the Garden Route located in a nature reserve and bird sanctuary. Don't let this mislead you, however; the N2 hum is hardly ever out of earshot. Despite this, the atmosphere is immensely peaceful, and the views across the lake are lovely. The hotel had a substantial upgrade in 2001, and now enjoys all the amenities of a five-star SATOUR–graded hotel—unfortunately, none of the old country inn atmosphere has been retained, and though decor in rooms and public spaces is perfectly comfortable and tasteful, it all feels a little mass produced. Aside from its proximity to Knysna (a 10-min. drive), the hotel has canoes, horses, and numerous nature trails, and the beach is 2.5km (1½ miles) away.

Off N2, 16km (10 miles) west of Knysna. P.O. Box 2, Sedgefield 6573. © **044/349-2400.** Fax 044/349-2401. www.lakepleasanthotel.com. 36 units. R1,800–R2,400 ($225–$300) double. Rates include breakfast. AE, DC, MC, V. **Amenities:** Restaurant; bar; pool; tennis; spa; room service; laundry; horseback riding; canoes; a bird hide. *In room:* TV, A/C, minibar, tea- and coffee-making facilities, hair dryer, underfloor heating.

KNYSNA

The founder of Knysna (pronounced *nize*-na) was one George Rex. In 1802, at the age of 39, he—having shocked the Cape community by shacking up with a woman "of colour"—purchased the farm, which included the whole basin containing the Knysna lagoon. By the time of his death in 1839, he had engaged in a number of enterprises, the most profitable of which was timber, and had persuaded the Cape authorities to develop Knysna as a port. Knysna's development and the decimation of its forests were well under way. That there are any areas of forests to have escaped the devastation of the 19th century is thanks to farsighted conservation policies introduced in the 1880s, and today Knysna has the largest areas of indigenous forests left in South Africa. The Knysna elephants have fared less well—attempts to augment their numbers by relocating three young cows from Kruger National Park failed miserably when it was discovered that the last remaining Knysna elephant was also a female. The surviving cows have subsequently been relocated to the Shamwari game reserve in the Eastern

Cape. Detractors believed the forest pachyderms to be extinct, and that the only free-roaming elephants left in Knysna were those painted on road markers warning drivers to "beware." Then in October 2000, a 20-year-old elephant bull was spotted—and photographed—deep in the forest, making headlines throughout the Western Cape, and in 2003 author and environmentalist Gareth Patterson set about collecting dung for Lori Eggbert, a scientist from the Smithsonian Institute, to perform DNA tests and hopefully prove his theory that at least nine or ten elephants remain at large. Actual sightings have yet to be repeated, however, and you're more likely to spot one if you overindulge in the delicious local beer.

Knysna used to be a sleepy village inhabited only by a handful of hippies and wealthy retirees, but the last decade has seen a tourist boom that has augmented numbers substantially—nowhere is this more evident than on the congested main road that runs through town. Still, Knysna has retained a great deal more of its original charm than either George or Plettenberg Bay, and remains the emotional heart of the region. Its raison d'être is the large tidal lagoon, around which the town has grown, and the towering sandstone cliffs (called the heads) that guard the lagoon's narrow access to the sea. The eastern buttress has unfortunately been developed, but this means you can drive to the top of the cliff for good sea views, or to the bottom and walk to the churning mouth. Better still, head for the unspoiled western side—a visit to the Featherbed Nature Reserve should be high on your list of priorities.

ESSENTIALS

VISITOR INFORMATION   The **Tourism Information Bureau** (© **044/ 382-1610;** www.visitknysna.com; open Mon–Friday 8am–5pm, Sat 8:30am– 1pm; hours are extended Dec–Jan), on 40 Main St. Adjacent is the booking service; contact **Knysna Reservations** (© **044/382-6960;** booking@mweb. co.za) for accommodations and other bookings. You can also visit the independent **Central Reservations** (© **044/382-5878** or 082-558-1661; open daily 9am–6pm) for advice and bookings.

GETTING THERE   The closest airports are at **George** (See "Getting There: George & Wilderness," earlier in this chapter) and **Plettenberg Bay;** both are about an hour's drive away. **SA Airlink** (© **044/533-9041**) flies from Johannesburg to the small Plett airport daily where you can arrange to have a rental car waiting. Contact **Budget** (© **044/533-2198**) or **Economic Car Hire** (© **082-800-4258**).

GETTING AROUND   For a fun way to get around (not to mention avoid Knysna's seasonal traffic congestion), rent a mountain bike from **Knysna Cycle Works** (© **044/382-5153**) (see "Staying Active," earlier in this chapter). For a taxi, call **Benwill Shuttle** (© **083/728-5181**) or **Glory's** (© **083-226-4720**). To explore the lagoon in a small cabin boat, rubber duck, or speedboat, contact **Tait Marine Boat Hire** (© **044/382-4460**); Tait also arranges water-skiing charters.

GUIDED TOURS   **Rogue Eco Safaris** (© **044/382-4545**) is highly recommended, offering a range of informative drives or walks through the forest or along the coast with qualified field guides (the sunset ramble, which ends with a fireside meal on the beach, is wonderful). **Forest Explorer** (© **083-702-5103**) runs more standard 90-minute (minimum) orientation tours of Knysna, as well as tours of the forests, Belvidere, Noezie, the goldfields, Tstisikamma, Oudtshoorn, and various tailor-made options. For a range of **sailing or ferry tours**

of the lagoon, see "Staying Active" at the beginning of the chapter. For a **"Township Trail"** tour that includes a visit to a *sangoma* (healer), a *shebeen* (drinking house), a local rasta community, a "temporary" timber home, and a community project, call the **Heads Adventure Centre** (© **044/384-0831** or 083-232-8898).

BOAT TOURS With comfortable seating and a restaurant/bar on board, the floating double-decker **John Benn Ferry** (© **044/382-1693**) offers a 90-minute trip on the lagoon that costs R50 ($6.50) for adults, meals and drinks extra. R40 ($5) buys you a ticket on their River Catcher Ferry—the only ferry licensed to go through the Heads. **Waterfront Ferries** (© **044/382-5520**) runs a number of 90-minute as well as a 2½-hour sunset lagoon trip daily; all ferries depart from the Knysna Quays Waterfront. For sailing trips, contact **Waterfront Sailing Charters** (© **044/874-5928**)—aside from regular 90-minute cruises, it offers a sunset cruise through the Heads (weather permitting) with platters of oysters, bubbly, and seafood and vegetarian snacks (R250/$30). Or contact **Spring Tide Charters** to charter the luxury yacht *Outeniqua* for an exclusive, very romantic breakfast, all-day, sunset, or dinner cruise (© **082-470-6022**), prices on application.

ACTIVITIES The **Heads Adventure Centre** can organize a number of outdoor experiences, from sea kayaking and scuba diving to canoeing and abseiling. Contact © **044/384-0831** or 083-232-8898.

SPECIAL EVENTS Knysna gets very busy during the **Knysna Oyster Festival** held every July. For information, contact the Tourism Bureau.

WHAT TO SEE & DO IN KNYSNA

Besides the top attractions listed below, one of the first things first-time visitors are encouraged to do is take a drive to the **Knysna Heads** ★★, where you can walk right up to the lagoon mouth and watch skippers gingerly navigate the treacherous surf. Stop for tea at the East Head Cafe, or lunch at Paquitas, then view the rare Knysna seahorse at the small NSRI aquarium, currently endangered by the ongoing development happening in and around the lagoon.

   Exploring the forests is another major drawing card (see below), as are **lagoon-based activities;** several companies run boat trips on the lagoon, home to 200 species of fish and a major supplier of oysters—expect to see this on almost every Knysna menu. (For ferry and sailing options, see "Boat Tours," above.)

   Another local product definitely worth trying is the beer. **Mitchell's Brewery** (Arend St.; © **044/382-4685**) produces four types of unpasteurized "live" ales, the best of which are Bosun's Bitter and Forrester's Draught. You can either take a 15-minute tour and tasting (Mon–Fri 10:30am; R25/$3) or sample them with your meal at any of the Knysna eateries. Ask for directions or a list of outlets from the Tourism Bureau, or combine an oyster- and beer-tasting with a lagoon trip by boarding the **John Benn Ferry** (© **044/382-1693**) and heading for the bar. Alternatively, pack a picnic hamper of oysters (purchased from Knysna Oyster Tavern; see "Where to Dine," below) and head for the beach. To reach the closest sandy shore, you'll need to head west to **Brenton-on-Sea,** an endless stretch of sand 16km (10 miles) from Knysna, or east for **Noetzie Beach** ★★, some 11km (7 miles) from town. Unless you overnight (see "Phantom Forest," below), it's a steep walk down to this beautiful little beach, but a small, very swimmable estuary spilling out into the ocean and five over-the-top crenellated castles overlooking the beach make it more than worthwhile. Knysna lagoon's **Bollard Bay,** accessed from Leisure Isle, is an excellent family beach, with safe swimming in the shallow waters of the lagoon.

Last but not least, Knysna offers some of the best shopping this side of Cape Town, much of it very hippie-inspired and craftsy. For the most sophisticated take on African crafts, take a look at the small selection on display at **Am-Wa** (© **044/382-0561;** 13 Main Rd., Knysna). The buyer has an exceptionally good eye for what is described here as "original functional art."

THE TOP ATTRACTIONS

Featherbed Nature Reserve ★★   This privately owned nature reserve on the western head of Knysna is a National Heritage Site and home to the endangered blue duiker antelope. Guests are ferried over and then ascend the head in a large open-topped vehicle to enjoy the magnificent views of the lagoon, town, and ocean. Qualified guides then lead the visitors down through milkwood forests and coastal flora onto the cliffs and coastal caves on the 2km (just more than 1-mile) **Bushbuck Trail** (you can also choose to drive down). Meals are served at the **Tavern;** main courses range between R22 and R125 ($3 and $15), and focus on seafood. You don't have to eat here, but you will have to wait for the others before being ferried back. *Note:* The reserve's peace is seriously compromised during Knysna's busiest season, when additional trips are made.

Ferry leaves from Municipal Jetty, Remembrance Ave., off Waterfront Dr. © **044/382-1693.** Admission R80 ($10) adult, R30 ($3.75) children 3–12. Lunch extra. Depart daily at 10am (more scheduled, depending on demand; phone ahead). Duration approximately 4 hr.

Knysna Forests ★★★   These, the last pockets of indigenous forest, are located some distance from the town: **Goudveld State Forest** is 30km (19 miles) northwest of Knysna, while **Diepwalle** is some 20km (12 miles) northeast of town. Goudveld is a mixture of plantation and indigenous forest, making Diepwalle, with its ancient yellowwoods, the better option for the purist. Look out for the emerald Knysna Loerie and the brightly hued Narina Trogon in the branches. Diepwalle has three excellent circular trails color-coded with red, black, and white elephant markers. The routes are all 7km to 9km (4–5 miles) long, and the red route is recommended, because it features the most water.

Diepwalle: Take the N2 east, after 7km (4 miles) turn left onto the R339 for 16km (10 miles) before taking turnoff to Diepwalle. Goudveld: Take the N2 west, turn right into Rheenendal Road. © **044/382-9762.** Admission R6 (80¢). Open daily 8.30am–4pm.

Outeniqua Choo-Tjoe ★★★ *Kids*   One of the top attractions on the entire Garden Route, the **Choo-Tjoe train** provides some of the best views of the coastline and hidden valleys inaccessible by car. First opened in 1928, the 68km (42-mile) Choo-Tjoe is the last fully operational steam train in South Africa and chugs across the Knysna lagoon into the verdant valleys and lakeside settings that lead to Wilderness, where it traverses the Kaaimans River gorge, past Victoria Bay to George. Most locomotives date back to 1948 (though some are over a century old) with timber-and-leather–fitted carriages dating from 1903 to 1950. Grab a window seat—the views really are spectacular—and settle in for a truly enjoyable excursion. *Tip:* To avoid traveling back the way you came (which will take up the whole day), book through **Kontours** (© **082569-8997**). For R120 ($15) per adult (R80/$10 children), Kontours provides a map showing the places and points of interest as seen from the train, picks you up from George station, and returns you to Knysna station. (The reverse trip by arrangement only.)

The Station, Remembrance Ave. © **044/382-1361.** R60 ($7.50) adult one-way or round-trip; R40 ($5) ages 3–16. Train departs Mon–Sat 9:45am and 2:15pm. Duration one-way is 3 hr.

Other Attractions

Knysna Elephant Park *(Overrated)*   This "exclusive safari," undertaken in four-wheel-drive vehicles that depart from reception every half-hour, is little better than viewing elephants in a zoo, though here you are guaranteed an opportunity to touch the three elephants that roam the 75-hectare (185-acre) "reserve." There are now seven elephants, most of whom were born in Kruger, and have now—according to the park's promoters—been returned to "the home of their ancestors." For a hefty R675 ($84), you can walk with them through the forests—"an experience described by many as a lifetime high." One can only wonder what these "many" must have been smoking—possibly their "Friends of the Elephant" certificate, included in the price and made from elephant dung. If you're traveling with kids, the 45- to 60-minute tour is probably sufficient.

Off N2, 22km (13½ miles) east of Knysna. © 044/532-7732. 45–60-min. tour R85 ($11) adults, R45 ($5.25) kids. You'll need to book the sunrise and sunset elephant safari in advance (R675/$84, including light snacks/breakfast, drinks, and membership certificate).Tours daily 8:30am–5:30pm.

WHERE TO STAY

Prices vary considerably depending on season, with most specifying low, mid-, and peak seasons. Low season is usually from May 1 to August 31 with peak or high season usually from mid-December to mid-January.

If you want to stay right on the beach, book a room at one of the Noetzie castles; call **Knysna Castles** ★★ (© 044/384-0963; www.knysnacastles.com; from R1,400–R1,800/$175–$225 double, including breakfast, closed Dec 15–Jan 15) or **Phantom Castle** ★★★ (see below).

If you'd prefer to have the lagoon at your doorstep, look into renting an apartment, home, or loft in the attractive new **Thesen Island** development (© 044/302-5735; www.theisland.co.za) or at the **Knysna Quays** marina: Parkes (see below) has a delightful three-bedroom apartment for R1,000 to R1,500 ($125–$188) double, depending on season; alternatively, there is the two-bedroom "Quay Nine" apartment, costing from R1,400 ($175) (© 044/384-0134; www.sahols.co.za). Golfers may consider staying at one of the golf villas on the **Sparrebosch** golf course (© 044/384-0925; from R900/$112 double).

For more options, contact **Knysna Booking Services** (© 044/382-6960; booking@mweb.co.za).

Expensive

Belvidere Manor ★   Belvidere's detached cottages, situated on lawns that sweep down to the water's edge, are the most upscale places to stay on the actual lagoon. (But nowhere near as nice as Phantom Forest or Parkes!) The best units remain the original "lagoon" suites, which cost about R300 ($37) more than the so-called "garden" suites—unfortunately, the addition of these suites in the manor's back garden turned what used to be a very exclusive retreat into a more run-of-the-mill hotel experience. Even so, the suites, which are in effect small cottages, are spacious, tastefully decorated, and fully equipped should you wish to self-cater. Meals are served either on the veranda of the historic Belvidere House, a national monument, or in the charming pub. The manor is located in the exclusive suburb of Belvidere.

Duthie Dr., Belvidere Estate, Knysna 6570. © 044/387-1055. Fax 044/387-1059. www.belvidere.co.za. 30 units. Low-season R960–R1,260 ($120–$158) double; high-season R1,440–R1,880 ($180–$235) double. Rates include breakfast. AE, DC, MC, V. Children age 10 plus. **Amenities:** Restaurant; bar; pool; room service; laundry. *In room:* TV, fans, tea- and coffee-making facilities, hair dryer.

Parkes Manor ★★   The owners of this national monument have done a great job of transforming it into a gracious English-style country guesthouse, with established trees, green hedges, and manicured lawns (edged with a profusion of colorful beds), creating a delightful foreground to the equally inspiring lagoon views. It will probably be a better option for the older traveler than Phantom Forest; certainly the accommodation is the best in this "country house" class (superior to Belvidere or Falcon's)—all rooms are situated upstairs; huge, comfortable, and elegantly understated, each has access to an outdoor seating area. It is a little close to the N2, so do try to book a garden-facing suite (which are generally bigger and offer much better value); nos. 5 and 7 are particularly recommended. Of the lagoon-facing rooms, no. 3 is recommended. The small size of the guesthouse ensures attentive, personalized service, but it has many hotel-like aspects, such as light luncheons (served in the garden or at the pool), and a range of treatments at the attached health and beauty center.

1 Azalia St., Knysna 6570. ⒸⒸ 044/382-5100. Fax 044/382-5124. www.parkesmanor.co.za. 7 units. Low-season R794–R1,024 ($100–$126) double; high-season R1,312–R1,576 ($165–$195) double. Premier suite R1,136–R1,634 ($140–$204). Rates include breakfast. AE, DC, MC, V. Children by arrangement only. **Amenities:** Dining room (breakfast and dinner only); bar; pool; room service; laundry. *In room:* TV, minibar, fans, tea- and coffee-making facilities, hair dryer.

The Phantom Forest Eco-Reserve ★★★   This is without a doubt the best accommodation in Knysna, particularly if you're looking for a lodging option with strong safari overtones. Located on a 137-hectare (338-acre) nature reserve on a hill overlooking the Knysna River, it offers visitors the chance to explore indigenous forest and estuarine wetland. Meandering boardwalks connect the public spaces to the privately located suites, which are more like luxurious tree-houses tucked into the forest canopy. Each comprises a large double-volume bedroom with sitting area leading out to a small elevated deck, and a large bathroom (with or without bathtub). One entire wall of each lagoon treehouse is a sheer sheet of glass, affording a stupendous view of the forest and Knysna lagoon shimmering in the distance. The newer tree suites have a Moroccan theme. Service is not always up to par (you have to leave your car at the foot of the hill and wait for a vehicle to traverse the steep road; this can take longer than is comfortable), and there's a lack of attention to detail, but the incredible setting, charming architecture, and fabulous views more than make up for this. ***Note:*** **Phantom Beach,** located in a castle right on secluded Noetzie beach, has got to be one of the most romantic destinations in the world: only four en-suite rooms, each with private terrace and lagoon and beach views . . . this is the ideal place to celebrate a relationship (or rekindle one!).

Off Phantom Pass, 7km (4⅓ miles) from Knysna. Mailing address: P.O. Box 3051, Knysna 6570. Ⓒ 044/386-0046. Fax 044/387-1944. www.phantomforest.com. 12 units. Forest R2,250 ($275) double; Beach R2,320 ($290) double; ask about specials. Rates include breakfast; dinner R225 ($28). AE, DC, MC, V. Children age 12 plus. **Amenities:** Restaurant; bar; pool (with incredible view); sauna; massage treatments; laundry; walking trails; canoes; boat; mountain bikes. *In room:* Minibar, tea- and coffee-making facilities, fans, hair dryer.

Moderate

Falcon's View Manor ★   Set high up on the hills overlooking the lagoon and surrounded by peaceful gardens, this guesthouse offers a gracious retreat from the hustle and bustle of town. The manor house (ca. 1899), features a wrap-around veranda and elegant sitting room, as well as garden- or lagoon-view rooms on the upper level—these are a little fuddy-duddy and small; opt instead for one of the luxurious garden suites ★★, where the generously sized en-suite bedrooms, each comfortably furnished in muted modern colors, lead out onto private terraces overlooking the gardens and pool. A rather self-satisfied and snooty attitude permeates and ruins an otherwise soothing atmosphere.

P.O. Box 3083, Knysna 6570. © **044/382-6767.** Fax 044/382-6430. www.falconsview.com. 10 units. Standard rooms from R1,200 ($150) double; garden suites from R1,650 ($205). AE, DC, MC, V. **Amenities:** Dining room; bar; pool; room service; laundry. *In room:* A/C, TV, tea- and coffee-making facilities in garden suites, hair dryer, heated towel rails.

Headlands House ⭐ Although it is unfortunate that Knysna's eastern head has been developed, there is at least a good guesthouse from which you can enjoy the stunning ocean and lagoon views. Perched high above the town and overlooking the ocean, all four rooms enjoy breathtaking views, as does the pool. The "honeymoon suite" has sliding doors opening onto one of the most dramatic sea views on the Garden Route and is worth the extra rands.

50 Coney Glen Dr., The Heads, Knysna 6570. © **044/384-0949.** Fax 044/384-1375. www.headlandshouse. co.za. 4 units. High season: R1,240–R1,960 ($155–$245)) double. Low season: R860–R1,300 ($106–$162)) double. Rates include continental breakfast. AE, DC, MC, V. Children under age 10 not permitted. **Amenities:** Lounge/bar; small pool. *In room:* TV, tea- and coffee-making facilities, hair dryer, heated towel rails.

Lightley's Holiday Houseboats ⭐ *(Kids)* The best way to escape the seasonally congested streets of Knysna is to hire a houseboat and cruise the lagoon. You need no experience to skipper—just switch on and "drive" (navigational video, charts, maps, and instructions are supplied by Lightley's). You can fish for dinner from your boat (fishing rods are hired) or simply chug along to Crab's Creek or Belvidere Manor for a meal. Houseboats come equipped with everything: stove, fridge, hot and cold water, chemical toilet, radio/tape decks, CB radio, electric lights, crockery, and cutlery, and barbecues—just remember to pack towels and detergent, and don't run out of fuel. Parents should request a boat with a water slide. Rates quoted are for **Leisure Liners,** which sleep four; **Aqua Chalets** sleep six, are more luxurious, look better, and cost R265 to R380 ($32–$48) more, depending on the season. *Note:* If you'd prefer a more luxurious boat, complete with your own skipper and chef, charter the *Outiniqua* (© **082-470-6022;** www.springtide.co.za), a 50-foot luxury yacht comprising three double bedrooms and a large saloon.

P.O. Box 863, Knysna 6570. © **044/386-0007.** Fax 044/386-0013. www.houseboats.co.za. 12 houseboats. Low season: R620–R875 ($78–$110) per day. High season: R895–R1,275 ($110–$158) per day. MC, V.

Under Milkwood ⭐⭐ *(Kids)* This timber village, set under centuries-old milkwood trees, with cobbled streets running past quaint higgledy-piggledy bungalows

---

(Tips The Best Room in Knysna

The aptly named "Paradise Room" at **Kanonkop** (© **044/382-2374;** www. kanonkoptours.com), a new guesthouse on the outskirts of Knysna, will have you wishing your entire holiday could be spent here. Owner Chris Conyers has spared no expense—from maximizing the superb views (including the elevated tub surrounded by elegant travertine) to the rich, sumptuous decor and wonderful personal touches (complimentary biscotti, divine smelling toiletries, vegetable crisps, with everything sourced from small local producers). He has succeeded in making you feel on top of the world—literally. The room is an incredible value in winter (R1,090/$135 double), and (compared with places like Phantom), not bad in summer (R1,590/$195 double). Rates include breakfast.

to a sandy beach and the lagoon, is charming. It's also convenient, with the Knysna Heads, Paquitas, and East Head Café within walking distance. Each two-bedroom chalet (double bed in main bedroom and two single beds in second bedroom) has a fully-equipped kitchen and an open-plan lounge, a sun deck, and barbecue facilities. If you want to be right on the beach, ask for a "front" chalet: Sailor's Arms, Sinbad, Manchester, or Bottom. Skylark, Bayview, Curlew, and Schooner, all "hillside" chalets, offer the best value for money but require climbing stairs. Note that the "middle" chalets have the least privacy, and chalets Captain Cat and Schooner have parking places some ways away. Unless you're traveling with kids, peak season prices do not represent good value.

P.O. Box 179, The Heads, Knysna 6570. © **044/384-0745**. Fax 044/384-0156. www.milkwood.co.za. 16 units. Low season: R520–R770 ($64–$96) double, depending on location. High season: R1,375–R2,225 ($170–$275) double or 4 persons. DC, MC, V. **Amenities:** Babysitting; canoes; paddle-skis; sailboard. *In room:* TV, fan, tea- and coffee-making facilities, hair dryer.

Inexpensive

Inyathi Guest Village *(Value* Located in the heart of Knysna, Inyathi attracts a younger visitor with a great combination of value and taste. Despite its location just off the busy main road, with tourist information and a number of dining options within close walking distance, the village affords a great sense of privacy. Innovatively laid out around a courtyard, many of the double-bedded timber cabins feature beautiful stained-glass windows, and each has a luxurious slipper bathtub. While the rooms are charming, and decorated with charm and creativity, they are relatively small—not the sort to lounge around in all day.

52 Main St., Knysna 6570. ©/fax **044/382-7768**. www.inyathi-sa.com. 11 units. R370–R530 ($45–$65) double, depending on season. Rates include breakfast. AE, DC, MC, V. **Amenities:** Bar, babysitting, laundry. *In room:* TV, tea- and coffee-making facilities, hair dryer.

Knysna River Club *(Kids* This resort, a cheaper alternative to Under Milkwood, is very popular with South Africans, so book months in advance, particularly if you want to bag a lagoon chalet (which you do!). All the cabins are equipped for self-catering, spacious and simply but comfortably furnished. Choose between one-, two-, and three-bedroom configurations, all with outdoor decks. The **River Club Café** (© **044/382-1751**) serves "creative country cuisine"—anything from Thai-style curries to pasta.

P.O. Box 2986, Knysna 6570. © **044/382-6483**. Fax 044/382-6484. www.knysnariverclub.co.za. 35 units. Low season: R300–R800 ($37–$100) double. High season: R700–R1,300 ($88–$162) double or more. AE, DC, MC, V. **Amenities:** Restaurant/bar; pool; canoes; game room (in season); babysitting; laundry. *In room:* TV, hair dryer on request.

WHERE TO DINE

Crab's Creek *(Kids* *(Value* PUB People come here in droves, despite the fact that the fare is really average pub grub—a great location and a casual holiday atmosphere seem to outweigh the needs of the palate. Certainly Crab's Creek is a great place for kids—they tend to gather around the lagoon edge to look for the restaurant's namesake. In December, when up to 700 people a day descend on the Creek, you'd be well advised to arrive as early as 11am for lunch and 6pm for dinner to bag one of the rustic timber tables arranged along the edge of the lagoon. Popular dishes are burgers, chicken, and seafood "buckets," mussels, and ostrich steak (much like beef, only more tender; ask for it medium-rare unless you usually order well-done). During peak season, service can be slow—order a Mitchell's beer and soak up the sun. Under new ownership, a cigar bar, a wine cellar, and a fine-dining option are in the pipeline.

On the road to Brenton-on-Sea (6km/about 4 miles from town), Belvidere. © **044/386-0011**. Reservations for 10 or more only. Main courses R35–R57 ($4.25–$7). DC, MC, V.Daily 11–late.

Knysna Oyster Tavern ★★ SEAFOOD   This no-frills tavern is part of the cultivated oyster farm, operating since 1948, that put Knysna oysters on the map. You can buy takeaway oysters (a standard dozen, opened, will run you between R48–R60/$6–$7.50), or sit down at one of the waterside tables—with great views of the Knysna Heads—to sample the difference between the wild and the cultivated (you can order single units). Other light dishes include garlic mussels, a choice of two fish patés, and the seafood salad: prawns, mussels, calamari, shrimp, and crabsticks served on a French salad. Linefish, prawns, and mussels are the most popular main courses. The tavern is right next to the oyster processing facility; you can watch from your table or opt for guided tours—R20 ($2.60) includes a glass of sparkling wine and an oyster tasting *Note:* **The Oystercatcher** (© **044/382-9995**), located in the small-craft harbor at Knysna Quays, is offering some stiff competition—it's less authentic than the working oyster farm, but it's a great venue, this time with views of the marina, and attracts a younger crowd.

Bottom end of Long St., Thesens Island, Knysna 6570. © **044/382-6941**. Reservations evenings only. Main courses R30–R99 ($3.75–$12). AE, DC, MC, V. Take-away oysters from 8am. Daily 10am–6pm, closed Sun 5pm. (Hours extended to 9pm Dec–Apr and Oyster Festival in June).

Mackintosh's ★★ *(Value)* FUSION/DELI   If you're self-catering or about to go on a picnic, head for this "fine food emporium" (we're talking truffle oil) and fill a basket with farm-fresh vegetables and fruit, an array of delectable cheeses (many produced locally), pickles, meats, freshly baked breads and pastries . . . or give in to the aroma from the kitchen and sit down at one of the mismatched tables and order the homemade spring rolls (shrimp, crab, pickled ginger, lime, and coriander, served with marinated bean sprouts and wakame seaweed), lamb *tikka* (marinated in fresh papaya yogurt, and served with egg noodles, wilted greens, deep-fried vermicelli, mango *achar* [relish], and coriander yogurt), or Spanish squid (pan-fried and served with tomato cilantro, onion, chile, and lime salsa). They also do a mean eggs Benedict. The only drawback is the lack of view (for that, go to sister outfit **34° South;** see below).

Thesen House, 6 lower Long St. © **044/382-6607**. Meals R26–R49 ($3.25–$6.25). DC, MC, V. Daily 7–5.30pm (kitchen 8am–4pm).

The Phantom Forest ★★★ PAN-AFRICAN   It's worth dining here just to soak up the atmosphere and views in this stunning ecoreserve (see "Where to Stay," above), but with only 10 nonguests accepted, reserve early. Get here early enough to order a predinner drink at the Eyrie bar, and grab a chair next to the pool to watch as the enormous sky changes into its sunset hues, reflected in the lagoon waters below. The table d'hôte dinner, served in a large treehouse, changes daily but always features a soup, a choice of four starters (the fresh green asparagus with Hollandaise sauce was devoured in seconds), sorbet, followed by a (difficult) choice of four main courses (the Moroccan springbok *tagine,* served with couscous, was thoroughly delicious). A cheese is followed by a choice of four desserts before an African blend coffee is served outside around the large bonfire, where dinner guests can mingle or simply lose themselves in the flames. A truly romantic experience, and worth the irritation of having to wait to be transported from the base of the hill in the reserve's four-wheel-drive.

Off Phantom Pass Rd. © **044/386-0046**. Reservations essential in high season. Set dinner R260 ($32). AE, DC, MC, V. Daily 6:30–8:30pm.

Pink Umbrella ⭐ *Value* VEGETARIAN/SEAFOOD   Proprietor June Davis has been pulling the crowds to her candy-pink umbrellas and flower-filled garden for 20 years. Her dal terrine, made with nuts and lentils and served with an aromatic sauce, is delicious, as are the tuna and spinach roulade with creamy cheese sauce, and corn and herb pie. The Pink Umbrella is also famous for its wickedly delicious desserts: If "Death by Chocolate" doesn't slay you, the "Great American Disaster" surely will. June has a very small wine list, so you're welcome to bring your own. *Note:* It can get very hot in summer, when you're probably better off in an air-conditioned restaurant, and service can be slow when June's busy.

14 Kingsway, Leisure Island. © 044/384-0135. Reservations essential in high season. Main courses R30–R96 ($3.75–$12). MC, V. Daily mid-Dec to mid-Jan 9am–5pm ; otherwise, closed Mon.

34° South ⭐⭐ SEAFOOD/DELI   This is the best of the many dining options available in the Knysna Quays waterfront development, and offers better fare than either Paquita's or Crabs Creek. Overlooking the marina's waterways, the restaurant serves food that is super-fresh and delicious: The linefish and calamari is always good, but top rating goes to the kingklip *espetada* (R64.50/$8)—a firm white fish, cubed and served, sizzling with lemon butter, on a long skewer. Alternatively, put together a picnic from the superb deli, bakery, and the upstairs winery; the latter stocks a truly excellent selection of South African wines, culled from the annual Nederberg Auction. (Pick one out even if you're dining here; a R10/$1.30 corkage fee will be charged).

Knysna Quays. © 044/382-7268. Main courses R28–R275 ($3.50–$35). AE, DC, MC, V. Daily 9am– 9:30pm. Closed Sun during winter.

Upstairs Restaurant ⭐⭐ *Finds* THAI & SINGAPOREAN   When owner-chef Moc opened his doors in 2000, Knysna's more cosmopolitan and vegetarian residents breathed a collective sigh of relief. Here finally is an authentic alternative to the plethora of seafood, grill, and pizza-pasta joints. Don't come for views or a fine dining atmosphere—it's strictly about the food. Moc offers a small but excellent menu (regulars don't even bother looking at the menu; for them Moc will toss together old favorites from previous menus like Saigon lamb or tofu and vegetable curry). Current recommendations are crispy beef with plum sauce, ginger fried chicken, and prawns steamed with lemon grass and ginger.

Pledge Sq., Knysna. © 044/382-4052. Reservations recommended. Main courses R45–R85 ($5.50–$11). Tues–Sun 6:30–10pm. AE, DC, MC, V. Open for lunch during peak season.

PLETTENBERG BAY & SURROUNDS

Several miles of white sands, backed by the blue-gray outline of the Tsitsikamma Mountains and lapped by an endless succession of gentle waves, curve languidly to create **Bahia Formosa**—the "Beautiful Bay"—as the Portuguese sailors who first set eyes on it named it. Over the years its beauty has inevitably drawn an ever-increasing string of admirers, with some 50,000 of Jo'burg's wealthiest individuals descending on the seaside town of **Plettenberg Bay** every December. But in the off season, when the vast majority of holiday homes stand empty, a far more laid-back atmosphere prevails.

There's not much to do in town itself but laze on the beach; try **Lookout** ⭐⭐⭐ on the eastern side (one of the few beaches in the world to be awarded blue flag status), or **Robberg** on the west. The much smaller **Central Beach,** dominated by the timeshare hotel Beacon Isle, is the area from which most of the boats launch. Sadly, money and taste seem to have enjoyed an inverse relationship in Plettenberg Bay; huge monstrosities line most of the beachfront, particularly Robberg Beach, with the exception being the less developed far-western edge, bordering the reserve. **Robberg Nature Reserve** ✦✦✦ (© **044/533-2125**), the rocky peninsula on the western side of the bay, offers fantastic whale-watching opportunities during the course of a 9km (5-mile) trail. The going gets very rocky, so be sure to wear sun protection and good shoes, and try not to time your visit with high tide.

For the less energetic, there are shorter 2½-hour versions; pick up a map from the reserve gate when you pay your R15 ($1.95) to get in; to find it, follow signs off airport road; the gate is 8km (5 miles) southeast of town. The reserve is open from 7am to 5pm daily; in high season from 6:30am to 7:30pm.

Plettenberg Bay (or "Plett," as the locals call it) is blessed with two estuaries, with the Keurbooms River in the east by far the larger and least spoiled. You can only access the **Keurbooms River Nature Reserve** ✦✦ (© **044/535-9648; open daily 6am–7:30pm/7:30am–5:30pm winter; R5/65¢**) by water—it's definitely worth paddling upstream to view the lush vegetated banks and bird life, however; keep an eye out for Knysna loeries, kingfishers, and fish eagles. A canoe and permit will run you R40/$5 (R80/$10 for a double canoe); both are available at the gate kiosk at the slipway, or from **Aventura Eco.** There is also a highly recommended overnight canoe trail in the reserve—see "Staying Active," at the beginning of the chapter. For R70 ($8.75) per adult (R30/$3.75 children under age 12), you can head upstream without lifting a finger by boarding the **Keurbooms River Ferry** (© **044/532-7876**; departs from slipway). Daily scheduled trips, which last approximately 2½ hours, take place at 11am, 2pm, and sundown, and include an optional 30-minute walk or picnic (bring your own food and pack a costume). Beach lovers who find Plett's urbanization depressing should consider spending a day on the relatively unspoiled **Keurbooms Beach** (follow signs off N2). This wide beach shares the same bay and has rock arches and pools to explore, but the swimming is not quite as safe, so take care.

The inland area from Keurbooms River to the Bloukrans River is known as **the Crags**—if you don't mind not being on the beach, it has a few lovely accommodations options, as well as **Monkeyland** ✦ (signposted off N2, 16km/10 miles east of Plett; © **044/534-8906;** open 8am–6pm), a primate sanctuary situated in indigenous forest that houses 13 different species. Saved from laboratories or the illegal pet trade, the majority of these free-roaming primates are either endangered or critically vulnerable. Admission is free, while foot safaris, guided by knowledgeable rangers, cost R60 ($7.50) adult, R30/$3.75 children. A little farther east lies **Nature's Valley,** a tiny hamlet on a wide, deserted sweep of beach, and beyond this **Storms River Mouth,** both in the **Tsitsikamma National Park** ✦✦✦—a must on any Garden Route itinerary (see later in this chapter).

For more information, you could visit the local **Tourism Bureau,** located in Melville's Corner Shopping Centre (© **044/533-4065;** open Mon–Fri

---

Moments 3, 2, 1, Aaaaaaa!

If Plett's views aren't enough to take your breath away, remember that the world's highest bungee jump is only a 15-minute drive east on the N2. For R550 ($69), you can have the rare privilege of free-falling for 216m (708 ft.) off the Bloukrans Bridge, then watch yourself doing it all over again on video (see "Staying Active," at the beginning of the chapter). Booking for this and all other adventure activities in the region can be made through © **083/231-3528** or 042/281-1458.

Sea and Air Safaris

Top on your list of things to do in Plettenberg Bay is a **marine safari** ✫✫✫ in the mammal-rich bay; you'll be provided with plenty of excellent photo ops as well as new insights into the various species' behavior and characteristics. Apart from the Bryde whale, the Indo-Pacific humpback, and the bottlenose and common dolphins who feed in the bay year-round, Plett also enjoys seasonal visits from the Southern Right, humpback, and killer whales during their annual migration (July–Oct)—it's worth booking a "close encounter" trip with a boat licensed to approach the whales up to 50m (164 ft.). Coastal and pelagic bird life and the historical and geological makeup of the bay are also discussed. Tours last approximately 2½ hours and cost R300/$37 (R475/$58 for a "close encounter"); proceeds benefit whale and dolphin research and conservation. The longest running operators are **Ocean Blue Adventures** (✆ **044/533-5083;** www.ocean adventures.co.za) and **Ocean Safaris** (✆ **044/533-4963**). A noisier way to view Plett's marine mammals—at least for those on the water and ground—is by air. **African Ramble Air Safaris** (✆ **044/533-9006**) offers 30-minute low-level flights over the bay and up the coast, entering the Knysna estuary through the Knysna Heads, then returning via the forested inland. These require a minimum of two passengers and cost R300 ($37) per person.

8:30am–5pm, Sat 9am–1pm); however, staff are well-meaning but not very switched on.

WHERE TO STAY

Like Knysna, Plett prices vary considerably depending on the summer or winter season, with December and January considered by most to be peak.

In Plettenberg Bay

The Lodge on the Bay ✫✫✫   From a decor and design point of view, this thoroughly modern guesthouse competes with the world's most sophisticated boutique hotels. Pick of the rooms is the **Zen suite,** a large, beautifully furnished and finished room (maple wood, quartz, and limestone) with its own patio and plunge pool. If you're looking for wonderful sea views, you may prefer the **Mercer suite,** featuring dark wood, slate-gray-and-white silk bedding, and rich Donghia fabrics. Despite its small size, the lodge has a spa room where you can indulge in a range of therapies, as well as an extensive (1000+) library, many of them design books and magazines (the latest issues of *Wallpaper,* of course), as well as a great video and CD collection. Oh, for a rainy day.

77 Beachy Head Dr., Plettenberg Bay 6600. ✆ 044/501-2800. Fax 044/501-2850. www.thelodge.co.za. 6 units. High season: R3,600–R5,950 ($450–$735). Low season: R2,650–R4,200 ($325–$525). Rates include breakfast. AE, DC, MC, V. Children age 12 plus. **Amenities:** Dining room; pool; spa; laundry; CD and video library; wine cellar. *In room:* A/C, TV, minibar, hair dryer, video, CD player, underfloor heating.

Periwinkle Guest Lodge ✫ *Value*   This guesthouse (next to the Lodge on the Bay) is one of a handful that provides guests with excellent access and views of the beach and ocean, which is just across the narrow coastal road that traverses Robberg's beachfront. All rooms are relatively spacious and comfortably outfitted with wrought-iron beds and marine blues, whites, and/or sand colors; each has a small patio or balcony with a varying degree of privacy and views. Room nos. 1, 4, and 5 (particularly no. 4) are luxury rooms that enjoy the best views of the beach and ocean; all of these rooms have fireplaces. Of the standard rooms, no. 6 is the best option, while no. 3 is the proverbial "last chicken in the shop." The open-plan lounge, dining room, and deck is airy, comfortable and—with wonderful views of the ocean and Robberg peninsula—filled with light. Dinners and lunches by prior arrangement; hosts are happy to make suggestions and arrangements for dining out.

75 Beachy Head Dr., Plettenberg Bay 6600. ℂ/fax **044/533-1345**. www.periwinkle.co.za. 7 units. Low season: R550–R750 ($69–$95) double. High season: R800–R1,500 ($100–$188) double. Rates include breakfast. AE, DC, MC, V. Children age 12 plus. **Amenities:** Lounge; laundry. *In room:* TV, fridges, tea- and coffee-making facilities, hair dryer, heated towel racks.

The Plettenberg ★★★   Situated on a hill overlooking Lookout Beach, with views all the way to Keurbooms and the blue-gray mountains beyond, this hotel has one of the best vantage points in the country. (Make sure you've booked a room that makes the most of this, as the standard double rooms with views of the parking lot are still pretty pricey, and definitely not worth it.) Rooms are individually decorated, and differ somewhat in size—the luxury double rooms with sea view are worth the extra R400 ($50). The "Blue Wing" comprises only suites and has beautiful views of the Beacon Isle Beach, but it's situated across the road, and guests occasionally complain of feeling cut off; personally I would specify a Lookout Beach view. The Plettenberg is a Relais & Chateaux hotel, and as such you can expect excellent food in the formal dining room. The emphasis is on seafood, but Karoo lamb is also a specialty. Service is attentive, but this is not a place to let your hair down.

40 Church St., Lookout Rocks. Mailing address: Box 719, Plettenberg Bay 6600. ℂ **044/533-2030**. Fax 044/533-2074. www.plettenberg.com. 38 units. High season: R2,500 ($310) double (no sea view); R3,300 ($410) luxury double no view; R3,300 ($410) luxury sea-facing double; R3,750 ($475) suite; R4,350–R5,050 ($525–$605) suite with sea view. Low season: R1,950–R4,200 ($244–$510). AE, DC, MC, V. Children age 12 plus. **Amenities:** Restaurant; bar; 2 pools (1 heated); business services on request; salon; room service; laundry. *In room:* TV, A/C, minibar (suites only), hair dryer.

Plettenberg Park ★★★ *(Finds*   Situated a few minutes from town, perched on the cliffs overlooking the Indian Ocean and surrounded by a private nature reserve, this is without a doubt the most exclusive retreat in Plettenberg Bay, offering unparalleled luxury, privacy, and service. Guests are accommodated in what used to be the owner's holiday house; its northern aspect overlooks a tranquil inland lake and a wild duck sanctuary, and the southern views are of the pounding ocean. A path winds from the elevated timber decks down the cliff face to a tidal pool and private beach, but it's a stiff walk back! A new wing has been built with five new rooms, Jacuzzi, gym, and sauna, but this wing has all the bland aspects of a hotel, so request one of the rooms in the original house and specify the view you'd prefer (sea or lake) when making reservations. There are four choices here: a good value (small) sea-facing room or three huge sea- or lake-facing rooms, each with its own fireplace and decorated in what has come to be known as the Afro-colonial style (natural materials in neutral, earthy tones; crisp whites; bleached animal skulls . . .). Service is attentive and personal; the chef will even create the daily menu around each person's preferences. If you're looking for a romantic retreat with very little disturbance from the outside world, Plettenberg Park is perfect—the only drawback is that you have to share it at all.

Off the Plett Airport road. P.O. Box 167, Plettenberg Bay 6600. ℂ **044/533-9067**. Fax 044/533-9092. www.plettenbergpark.co.za. 9 units. High season: R3,600–R4,680 ($450–$580) double. Low season: R2,040–R2,540

($255–$310) double. Rates include all meals, (local) drinks, and laundry. AE, DC, MC, V. Children age 12 plus. **Amenities:** Dining room; bar; pool; room service; laundry. *In room:* TV, minibar, hair dryer, video, stereo, fireplaces.

Southern Cross Guest House ⭐ *Value*   This pale-pink-and-white timber beach house is one of the most beautiful homes in Plettenberg—an American-Colonial seaboard-style home that wouldn't look out of place on Long Island. It's also Plett's only guesthouse built right on the beach; a timber boardwalk leads through the vegetated dunes to the sand. Located on the western side of Robberg Beach, close to the reserve, the beach is pretty deserted and provides an excellent sense of getting away from it all. Rooms are extremely tasteful—like the rest of the house, they are decorated predominantly in cool whites with an occasional touch of black or natural wood; bathrooms are spacious, with expensive finishes. The owners (who live upstairs) have definitely bagged the best views, however—all the guest rooms are built around a central grassy courtyard, so none of them enjoys a sea view; and unless you close your doors and curtains, they also lack privacy. Breakfasts are served in the sunny lounge and dining area or on the patio overlooking the beach and sea—bliss on a beautiful day.

2 Capricorn Lane, Plettenberg Bay 6600. ©/fax **044/533-3868**. www.southerncrossbeach.co.za. 5 units. High season: R1,100 ($138) double. Low season: R750 ($95) double. Rates include breakfast. AE, DC, MC, V. **Amenities:** Lounge; laundry. *In room:* TV, tea- and coffee-making facilities.

Around Plettenberg Bay

Some of Plett's best accommodations are found outside of town, surrounded by indigenous bush and forests, beautiful gardens, or riverside settings. The only drawback is that you'll have to drive to the beach.

Hog Hollow Country Lodge ⭐ *Value*   Overlooking the dense indigenous forests that drop away below the lodge and carpet the Tsitsikamma Mountains beyond, Hog Hollow offers charm, comfort, and privacy. Both duplexes and simplexes (recently upgraded to suite status—all now have private lounges and extended decks) are recommended: French doors lead out onto private balconies or decks with hammocks and chairs to soak in the views of the verdant gorge. The "forest" luxury suites are huge, but with no minibar or telephone, it's a long walk to the main house to place a drink or tea order. One of the most charming suites is the "round house"; the en-suite master bedroom with wooden balcony is upstairs, and the lounge with fireplace is downstairs. Hog Hollow is renowned for its food—dinner is a set affair that will run you R175 ($21). Meals are served around the large dining-room table, turning the event into an informal dinner party. The service is excellent.

Askop Rd., The Crags, Plettenberg Bay 6600. ©/fax **044/534-8879**. www.hog-hollow.com. 12 units. High season: R1,560 ($190) double. Low season: R1,380 ($172) double. Rates include breakfast. AE, DC, MC, V. Closed June. 16km (10 miles) east of Plett signposted off the N2. Children by prior arrangement only. **Amenities:** Dining room; bar; pool; laundry. *In room:* Hair dryer, fireplace.

Hunter's Country House/Tsala Treetops Lodge ⭐⭐⭐   Hunter's comprises charming cottages set in beautifully manicured gardens, each individually furnished with antiques, and each with its own fireplace and private patio. This is not a place for modern design enthusiasts (for this, you'd be better of at the Lodge on the Bay)—the frills and florals in some of the rooms are almost cloying. Orchard Suites offer rather good value when compared with any of the top-end options in this area; premier suites are larger than garden suites but not necessarily better; classic suites have private pools and outdoor showers. Meals are excellent (both Hunter's and Tsala are Relais & Chateaux members), and the personal, warm, discreet service has earned this luxurious family-run hotel its many accolades. The biggest drawback is that Hunter's offers no views, which is just one reason to bypass the Hunter's turnoff and head straight for Tsala Treetops. Located on the same property (just 500m/1,600 ft. from Hunter's) but with totally separate amenities, Tsala offers a sublime combination of privacy, luxury, and the sense of space that should come packaged with every holiday. Very much in the style of the luxurious safari camps up north, Tsala features a large double-volume open-plan public space surrounded by generous decking, off which the elevated boardwalks connect to 10 privately situated glass and timber "treehouses." These are literally mini-houses, with fabulous views of the forested surrounds from every vantage, including the comfortable lounge (each with fireplace and chess set) and deck with private plunge pool. Unless you desire a sea view, this is the best option on the Garden Route, offering more space, greater luxury, and better service than that found at Phantom Forest.

10km (6 miles) west of Plett, off the N2. P.O. Box 454, Plettenberg Bay 6600. ℂ **044/532-7818**. Fax 044/532-7878. www.hunterhotels.com. Tsala: 10 units; Hunter's: 24 units. Tsala: R4,380 ($545). Hunter's Orchard suites: R1,980 ($245); Garden suites: R2,380 ($274). Premier suites: R2,700 ($339). Classic suites (including Forest suite): R3,980–R4,900 ($498–$620). All rates include breakfast; call for winter discounts. AE, DC, MC, V. **Amenities:** Dining rooms; lounges; bar; pool; concierge; business services; room service; massage; laundry; library. *In room:* TV, minibar, hair dryer, pool (Classic and Forest suites only; all Tsala suites), fireplaces.

Kurland ★★★ *Kids*   Surrounded by paddocks and polo fields, the Kurland vies with Hunter's as the most gracious country hotel on the Garden Route. It's more intimate (only 12 rooms), a little less frilly, and more relaxed (kids are expressly welcome)—which definitely gives it the edge for parents. Rooms are huge (each with a living area, some with private plunge pools), and are comfortably decorated in English-country–manor style, with antiques and original oil paintings. Superior rooms have their own swimming pools. Ten suites have loft rooms, with mini-furnishings for children—even an extra pool just for the kids. As with all of these out-of-town options, you have to drive to the beach, but there's plenty to do on the premises—like lying flat on your back on a massage table, lounging around the library, or mounting one of the polo ponies to explore the estate—and meals are of a high standard; just some of the reasons it was placed as a runner-up in *Tatler*'s 2002 "Hotel of the Year" award.

19km (12 miles) east of Plett off N2. P.O. Box 209, The Crags 6602. ℂ **044/534-8082**. Fax 044/534-8699. www.kurland.co.za. High season: R6,000 ($750) double. Low season: R4,400 ($559) double. Rates include dinner and breakfast. **Amenities:** Dining room; bar; 2 pools; tennis; spa; room service; babysitting; laundry; horseback riding; library (with Internet facilities). *In room:* TV, minibar, hair dryer, fireplace.

WHERE TO DINE

Sundown at Lookout Deck (see below) is a hard act to follow, but if you tire of the beautiful views (and the semi-attired *Baywatch*-type babes and bums tossing back Mermaid's Orgasms and Beach Affairs), take a look at the following. For sparkling wine and designer pizzas, the stylish Plett set head for **Cornutti Al Mare** (ℂ **044/533-1277**)—you can't miss it; it's located to the left of the hill you have to drive down to get to Central/Robberg beach, with the facade and balcony covered in hand-painted tiles and mosaics, and great views across the bay from the outdoor tables. Attracting a more hippie crowd, but also offering exceptional views, this time from high above Plett, the bar at **Weldon Kaya** (ℂ **044/533-2437**) is another good place to enjoy a sundowner. If you're after a more romantic, fine-dining experience, look no further than the dining rooms at Plett's best hotels: **Sand at The Plettenberg** ★★ (ℂ **044/533-2030**) offers magnificent views and is another excellent venue to kick off the evening with sundowners, or the more cozy candlelit atmosphere at **Tsala Treetops Lodge** (✆ **044/532-7818**), where the excellent fusion/pan-African table d'hôte menu will run you a mere R175 ($21).

Brothers ✰ *Value* INTERNATIONAL   The restaurant was started by—you guessed it—two brothers, one of whom was fortunate enough to be engaged to the excellent chef who helped build both the Plettenberg and Hog Hollow's reputation for fine food. She has since left their kitchen (though they're still married!), but her legacy lives on in the popular dinner dishes she created (like the lamb curry, grilled tuna with vegetables, homemade herbed tagliatelle with smoked salmon trout). During the day, a lighter lunch menu of salads, pitas, and bagels is served. Brothers has a view of the distant ocean, particularly from the open-air terrace; try to reserve a table here if the weather's pleasant. *Note:* A good alternative is the smaller bistro-style **Blue Bay Café,** another popular Plett stalwart with distant ocean views from a small balcony. Blue Bay is located a little farther down the main road in the Lookout Centre (✆ **044533-1390**).

Shop 4, Melville Corner, Main Rd. (on main circle), Plettenberg Bay 6600. ✆ 044/533-5056. Reservations essential in high season. Lunch main courses R20–R50 ($2.60–$6.50); dinner main courses R45–R85 ($5.50–$11). AE, DC, MC, V. Open daily 8:30am–3pm and 6:30–10pm; off season closed Mon.

The Islander ✰✰ *Value* SEAFOOD   This family-run restaurant in simple wood-and-thatch buildings has been going strong for almost 20 years, providing diners with an incredible array of seafood dishes. Drawing on island cuisine (Indonesia, Polynesia, Seychelles), as well as Portuguese, Creole, and South African traditions, the chefs have created the impossible—a buffet where almost every dish is exceptional. *A few tips:* Make sure this is your main meal of the day; don't fill up on the delicious bouillabaisse soup; don't miss the roasted tuna, herbed calamari, sailfish parcels, and smoked butterfish; and don't show up without reservations in high season.

Off N2 between Knysna and Plett (8km/5 miles west of Plett). P.O. Box 663, Plettenberg 6600. ✆ 044/532-7776. Reservations essential. Buffet R135 ($17) per person. AE, DC, MC, V. High season: Mon–Sat 7–9pm; off season Tues–Sat 7–9pm, subject to minimum bookings. Closed Aug.

Lookout Deck ✰ *Kids* SEAFOOD/AMERICAN   It's the location that draws the people rather than the food, but what a location! Right on the beach, with awesome views across the ocean to the Tsitsikamma Mountains stretching beyond, this is probably the best-placed restaurant on the Garden Route. Owner Chris has developed an upstairs and a downstairs component. Enjoy a "sunrise" breakfast on the upstairs deck, or get here for sundown and try the Lookout's famous wild oysters, picked off the Plett coast. The upstairs deck generally offers a more casual dining experience, with a vast array of meals ranging from hamburgers to prawns, steaks to pastas, Thai-style stir-fries to salads. The menu is very similar downstairs, though it's a more formal atmosphere and is glassed-in for inclement weather.

Lookout Beach. ✆ 044/533-1379. Reservations for downstairs only; essential in season. Main courses R39–R89 ($5–$11) (crayfish R350/$44). AE, DC, MC, V. Upstairs daily 9:30am–11pm; downstairs Wed–Mon 7–11pm.

The Mermaid Slipper ✰✰ *Finds* MODERN FUSION   Situated a few kilometers north of Plett, on the Bitou River, this has fast become one of the area's most popular restaurants, with everyone from fellow restaurateurs to locals traveling from as far afield as Knysna to sample the Slipper's celebrated fish and chips (innovatively plated) and tender filet béarnaise. Other popular dishes include prawns marinated in garlic, black pepper, and lime and then flash-fried and served with chile and lime noodles; and the pork ribs, marinated in Indonesian soy, sesame oil, sweet chile sauce, and honey, then grilled and served with Chinese noodles, red onion, red pepper, and baby corn. If it's a lovely day, call ahead and book a table on the outside deck; watching the river with its attendant bird life is a delightful way to keep your eye off the time . . . yes, service can at times be slow.

Signposted off the N2, north of Plettenberg Bay. (©) 044/533-0754. Reservations recommended in high season. Main courses R35–R150 ($4.50–$19). AE, DC, MC, V. Daily 9am–10pm.

TSITSIKAMMA NATIONAL PARK & STORMS RIVER MOUTH

Starting from just beyond Keurboomstrand in the west, this narrow coastal belt extends 80km (50 miles) along one of the most beautiful sections of the southern Cape coastline, and includes a marine reserve that stretches 5.5km (3½ miles) out to sea. The craggy, lichen-flecked coastline is cut through with spectacular river gorges, and the cliff surrounds are carpeted in fynbos (a beautiful and diverse floral kingdom) and dense forest—the fact that the Otter Trail, which takes in the full length of the coastline, is South Africa's most popular trail gives some indication of its beauty (see "Staying Active," earlier in this chapter for more information).

Tsitsikamma is roughly divided into two sections: De Vasselot (which incorporates **Nature's Valley**) in the west, and Storms River Mouth in the east. There is no direct road linking them; but it's well worth taking the detour off the N2 and visiting both, though Storms River Mouth is the more awesome sight of the two. To reach Nature's Valley, the only settlement in the park, take the scenic R102 or Groot River Pass. Call in on the ever-helpful Beefy and Tish, who run a local information center from the **Nature's Valley Restaurant, Pub and Trading Store** (© 044/531-6835); contact them for anything from a weather report to local B&B or self-catering accommodation options.

To visit **Storms River Mouth,** take the marked turnoff, some 60km (37 miles) from Plettenberg Bay, and travel 10km (6 miles) toward the coast. (*Note:* Do not confuse Storms River Mouth with Storms River Village, which is just off the N2, and has nothing much to recommend it.) The gate is open 24 hours, and the entry fee is R20 ($2.60), ages 2 to 16 R10 ($1.30). You can eat at **Jabulani** (© 042/281-1190). Located at the beginning of the walk to the Storms River mouth, it has one of the best locations on the entire Garden Route, right on the sea, but features pretty standard fare—a variety of linefish, steak, spareribs, and the like.

EXPLORING ON FOOT

With no roads connecting sites of interest, this is, for most, the only way to explore the park (there is also a snorkeling and scuba-diving trail, however; for equipment and a guide, contact **Stormsriver Adventures** (© 042/281-1836), the outfit that offers a host of activities in and around the park, including abseiling into the gorge and blackwater tubing down the river. The easiest and most popular trail is the 1km (just more than a half-mile) boardwalk, which starts at the visitors' office and Jabulani and winds its way along the mountainside, providing beautiful glimpses of the sea and forest, and finally descending to the narrow mouth where the dark waters of the Storms River surge into the foaming sea. This walk also takes you past the appropriately named **Mooi** ("pretty") **Beach,** a tiny cove where the swimming is safe, though the water can be very cold. Once at the mouth, don't miss the excavated cave with its displays relating to the Khoi *strandlopers* (beachcombers) who frequented the area more than 2,000 years ago.

You can cross the suspension bridge that fords the mouth and climb the cliff for excellent ocean views, though it's steep going. To explore the otherwise inaccessible gorge, catch the *Spirit of the Tsitsikamma* 𝄞, a boat that departs from the old jetty below the suspension bridge from 9.30am to 4pm every 45 minutes for a half-hour journey upstream. The trip costs R35 ($4.50) per person. To find out more about the various trails, pick up a map from the visitors' office (© 042/ 281-1607) at the rest camp. Hours are from 7am to 6pm daily.

WHERE TO STAY & DINE

Storms River Mouth Restcamp 𝄞 *Value*   The S.A. Parks Board is not about to win any architectural awards, but Storms River is their best attempt by far. Almost all the units enjoy good sea views, particularly the "oceanettes." Try to book a ground-floor apartment; in front is a narrow strip of lawn with your own barbecue, and beyond lie the rocks and the pounding surf. You can head off into the forest or walk the rocks; at low tide the rock pools reveal a treasure trove of shapes and colors. The only drawback to staying in the oceanettes is that they are the farthest units from the restaurant, though the short drive, which snakes along the coast, is hardly unpleasant. If you're going to have all your meals at the restaurant, consider staying in the forest huts, particularly 1 and 2, which overlook a burbling stream; keep in mind that the cabins are sweltering hot in peak summer and you share ablutions. Better still is to book one of the following log chalets: 8 (one bedroom) and 9 (family) are right on the ocean, as are the three honeymoon suites.

Reserve through National Parks Board, P.O. Box 787, Pretoria 0001 © 012/428-9111. Direct inquiries © 042/281-1607. www.parks-sa.co.za. 46 units, consisting of 8-bed, 7-bed, 4-bed, and 2-bed log chalets; 3- and 4-bed oceanettes; and 2-bed forest huts with no kitchen or ablution facilities. Rates start at R200 ($25) for forest huts; R430–R530 ($54–$65) double for log cabin; R650 ($82) for family cottage; R350–R650 ($44–$82) for oceanette. 10% discount May–Aug. AE, DC, MC, V. **Amenities:** Restaurant; pool; relatively well-stocked shop; self-service laundry facilities.

5 The West Coast

For many the West Coast is an acquired taste—kilometers of empty, often windswept beaches and hardy coastal scrub, low horizons and big skies, lonely tree-lined dirt roads and distant mountains behind which lie lush pockets carpeted in vineyards make this a truly off-the-beaten track experience. The main reason most visitors venture up here is to catch the spring flower displays that occur in the West Coast National Park anytime from the end of July to early September; but this aside, there are a few more gems to uncover—like eating fresh crayfish with your feet in the sand or living like the landed gentry at the Melck homestead at Kersefontein.

ESSENTIALS

VISITOR INFORMATION   The very helpful **West Coast Peninsula Tourism** (© 022/714-2088) is in **Saldanha,** on Van Riebeeck Street. There's very little reason to visit this industrialized town, however; **Langebaan,** the closest town to the West Coast National Park, may be more convenient. The **Tourist Information** (© 022/772-1515) is at the corner of Oostewal (the road in from R27) and Bree streets. For up-to-date information on the best places to view flowers at any given time, contact the **Flowerline** at © 083-910-1028 or 021/ 418-3705; Monday through Friday August through October.

GETTING THERE   From Cape Town, take the N1, then turn north onto the R27. If you intend to travel farther north, say, to Cederberg, and want to get

---

(*Tips*   **Flower Viewing Tips**

It is impossible to predict when each annual flower season will occur, but rainfall is obviously key. Another determinant is temperature, which is why flowers rarely open before 10am and hardly at all on overcast days. Remember that flowers turn toward the sun, so make sure you have the sun behind you when traveling. For the same reason, the flowers are at their best during the hottest part of the day, from 11am to 4pm. The floral carpets are spectacular from the car, but you'll need to stop and walk to marvel at the myriad species—at last count some 4,000. To find out where the best displays are, call the **Flower Line** (*C* **083-910-1028**).

---

there quickly, take the N7 off the N1; this is the main road north to Namaqualand (the flower region) and Namibia.

GETTING AROUND   The only way to explore the area is by car or with a tour operator. **Cape Eco Trails** (*C* **021/785-5511;** ecotrail@mweb.co.za) offers four-wheel-drive tours up the West Coast, including trips into the Kalahari Desert to view game and rafting on the Orange River.

DARLING

A small town a mere 50-minute drive from Cape Town, Darling attracts its fair share of visitors, particularly in September when its **annual wild flower and orchid show** is on—usually held during the third weekend in September—as well as the **Hello Darling Arts Festival** at Pieter Dirk Uys's informal theater and restaurant, **Evita se Perron** (*C* **022/492-2831**) on Arcadia Street. Famous for creating the marvelous character of Evita—the tannie (auntie) who held sway over the imaginary homeland of Bapetikosweti, and now the First Lady of Darling—Uys is one of South Africa's most accomplished satirists. He has managed to make even the most conservative South Africans laugh at the country's tragic ironies (not an easy task for a man who dresses in women's clothing).

If you're not here in September, no matter, Evita se Perron has cabaret shows every weekend. Evita presides over many of these, but during her September Arts Festival, she steps aside and showcases the best local talents. You can also sample some of Tannie Evita's traditional fare (try the Madiba lamb curry) at her Station Café after the show. "Evita se Dagkombuis" (literally "day kitchen") serves breakfasts and light meals throughout the day: gay muffins, affirmative tarts, and the self-proclaimed "best toasted sandwiches in the world." To view pure Afrikaans kitsch, take a wander through her **Boerassic Park,** where garden gnomes preside over plastic flowers and political figurines.

To get to Darling, take the R27, or West Coast Road as it's known, and turn off toward Mamre and Atlantis. From Mamre, the road to Darling cuts through fields of wheat and vineyards, and before you know it, you've arrived in town. In Darling, the local **Tourism Information** office (*C* **022/492-3361;** open daily 9am–1pm and 2–4pm) staff will happily dispense various maps, details of nearby flower reserves (don't miss the **Tienie Versveld Wild Flower Reserve**), and any other information needed.

WEST COAST NATIONAL PARK 🖈🖈

The West Coast National Park encompasses almost 30,000 hectares (74,100 acres) of wilderness as well as a 16km-by–4.5km (10-mile–by–3-mile) marine

The West Coast & Side Trips to Northern Cape

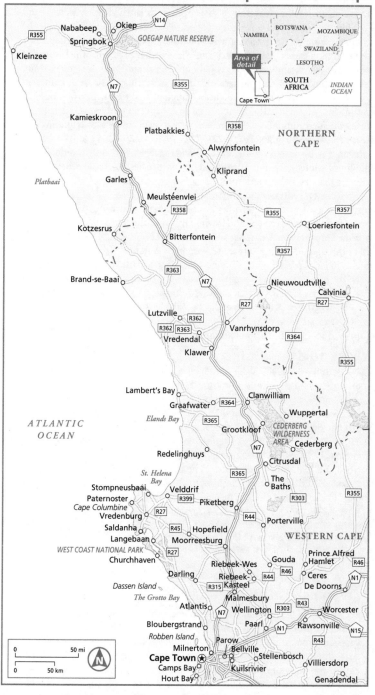

lagoon on which the coastal town of Langebaan is situated. Pack a picnic and head for one of the picture-perfect coves near Preekstoel and Kraalbaai where the strikingly azure waters gently lap white sands and brilliant green succulents. Be sure to pack a camera and bathing suit. The **Postberg** section, which contains zebra, wildebeest, and gemsbok, is only open in August and September, from 9am to 5pm, when the flowers are most spectacular. The community at **Churchhaven** (marked by the Anglican church of St Peter), which was founded in 1863 by George Lloyd, a deserter from an American merchant vessel, has now closed the road running past it; the only way to gain access is to rent one of its basic self-catering cottages (© **022/7722799** or 022/7722489). The hamlet enjoys a unique setting on one of the world's greatest wetlands. Overlooking a blindingly white beach and surrounded by salt marshes, the settlement is visited by more than 140 bird species (including the greater flamingo).

There are two entrances to the park: one off the R27, some 100km (62 miles) north of Cape Town, and the other just south of Langebaan. You can see a good deal of it by entering the one and leaving by way of the other, but make sure you visit the **Information Center** at **Geelbek** (© **022/772-2799**), on the southern tip of the lagoon. Light meals are served, and a number of short trails take you to bird hides overlooking the lagoon—this is particularly rewarding in summer, when the hides provide views of thousands of migrant waders and flocks of pelican, flamingo, curlew, and sandpipers. Admission to the park is R15 to R20 ($1.95–$2.60) per person, depending on the season. The park is open daily from October 1 to March 31 from 6am to 8pm; from April 1 to September 30 from 7am to 7:30pm. For more information, contact © **022/772-2144.**

WHERE TO STAY & DINE

The Farmhouse ★★ With the West Coast National Park right at your doorstep, tasteful decor and the azure Langebaan lagoon visible from almost every room, this is by far the best place to stay in Langebaan. The comfortable guest suites, of which 10 have their own fireplace, are very spacious, and it's worth booking a luxury with a sweeping view of the lagoon—ask for room no. 9, 10, or 18. In the cheaper category, room nos. 2 and 4 have the best views. Room no. 12 (R920/$115) is spacious and ideal for families—large with a king-size bed and two three-quarter beds. The restaurant, pub, and terrace all enjoy the same beautiful view of the lagoon. A la carte meals include traditional choices like oxtail and chicken pie and, of course, seafood.

5 Egret St., Langebaan 7357. © **022/772-2062.** Fax 022/772-1980. www.thefarmhouselangebaan.co.za. 18 units. R750–R920 ($95–$115) double, includes breakfast. Low season: R560 ($70). AE, DC, MC, V. **Amenities:** Restaurant; bar; pool; access to Langebaan's Country Club facilities including golf, tennis, and bowls; babysitting; laundry. *In room:* TV, minibar, tea- and coffee-making facilities, hair dryer on request.

Fun Fact **Out of Africa**

In one of two leading paleoanthropoligical theories regarding the origin of man, it is believed that Homo sapiens evolved in Africa about 200,000 years ago, migrating north in successive waves during the Pleistocene ice ages, displacing Homo erectus and Neanderthal man in Europe and Asia. Part of the body of evidence supporting this theory resides in the Langebaan lagoon: The world's oldest fossilized tracks of Homo sapiens—dating back 117,000 years—were discovered here in 1997.

Kersefontein ★★ (Value) (Finds)   This is one of the most authentic, unusual experiences to be had in the country—to be hosted by what is effectively a South
African aristocrat in his beautiful Cape Dutch farmstead, a national monument
(dating back to 1744) on the banks of the Berg River. A 7,000-hectare (17,290-
acre) working wheat and cattle farm in the rugged Sandveld, Kersefontein has
been owned by the Melck family since 1770, and the sense of history is almost
palpable—on the way to the grand dining room you will pass, for instance, the
skull of the last Berg River hippo, shot by Martin Melck in 1876 after it bit his
servant. Julian, the eighth-generation Melck, is a bit of a Renaissance man and an
eccentric and charming host; it's worth taking the drive up here just to spend an
evening in his company (the authentic farm-style food is also delicious). Accommodation is separate from the main house: either in one of the two "African"
rooms (top choice, with doors opening onto a small private veranda and sweeping lawns), the Victorian suites (with a communal lounge and a kitchen should
you wish to self-cater), or the self-catering cottage (a personal favorite), situated
a short drive away and blissfully tranquil. All have been masterfully decorated by
Graham Viney (the man responsible for refurbishing the Orient Express hotels),
utilizing family antiques found in what must be a massive attic! Even if you opt
for a self-catering unit, breakfast will be prepared and served at your own dining-
room table. It's a 90-minute drive from Cape Town; if you can tear yourself away,
the West Coast National Park lies under an hour away

Box 15, Hopefield 7355. ©/fax **022/783-0850**. www.kersefontein.co.za. 4 units. R680–R820 ($85–$100)
double, including breakfast. Dinner R130 ($16) including drinks. AE, DC, MC, V. Follow signs off R45 between
Velddrif and Hopefield. Children welcome. **Amenities:** Dining room; pub (located in what used to be the old
Kersefontein farm bakery; laundry); mountain bikes; boats; ranch riding; private air trips (Julian is also a pilot).

PATERNOSTER & COLUMBINE NATURE RESERVE ★★★

To reach these West Coast gems, stay on the R27 past the West Coast National
Park and Langebaan, then take the R45 west to Vredenburg. Drive straight
through this ugly town and take the 16km (10-mile) dirt road to **Paternoster,** a
tiny fishing village that—due to strict development guidelines—retains a classic
West Coast feel with almost all of the 2,000-odd residents living in picturesque
whitewashed fisherman-style cottages. If you're just here on a day trip, time your
visit to stop for lunch at **Voorstrand** ★★★ (© **022/752-2038;** open daily
10am–10pm). This rustic shack of a restaurant is right on the beach, and you
can sit with your feet in the sand while your waitress brings you an ice cold bottle of wine—when the sun sparkles off the crescent-shaped beach and ocean, the
sense of contentment is almost surreal. The small simple menu is in Afrikaans,
but if you're here during November to April there's only one thing to order: succulent crayfish tails (R80–R140/$10–$18, depending on size), served with garlic or lemon butter. Other popular dishes include the Malaysian seafood curry
(R55/$7) and the "three fish dish"—good way to sample the linefish caught off
this coast. If you can't bear to leave (and believe me, it's hard), book a self-catering cottage on the beach through **Lyndré** (© **082-405-8656;** R250–R1,250/
$30–$155 night) or the **Paternoster Hotel** (© **022/752-2703**). Or take a look
at the **Blue Dolphin** (© **022/752-2001;** www.bluedolphin.co.za; R400/$50
double including breakfast); it too enjoys a sublime location on the beach, with
lots of nooks to curl up with a book, but the decor can be a tad fussy and frilly.

The 263-hectare (650-acre) **Cape Columbine Nature Reserve** (© **022/752-
2718;** open 8am–5pm) is home to a wide variety of flowers; the best time to
visit is obviously in spring, but the reserve's superb location is a welcome relief

Moments   The West Coast Beach Barbecue

For dining, a meal at one of the West Coast alfresco restaurants is an unforgettable experience: Sitting on the beach breathing in the aroma of seafood on hot coals and the fresh sea breeze, you drink in the sun and the sound of seagulls, sink deeper in the sand as course after course keeps flowing, and lick your fingers clean (scrubbed mussel shells are often the only cutlery provided). Your only worry will be how you're ever going to manage to save enough space for the crayfish still to come. These eateries are so informal they're hardly restaurants, but if you like casual dining and don't mind sharing your space with strangers, they're well worth trying out. The food, prepared in the manner of one huge beach barbecue, is excellent and usually consists of several kinds of fish cooked in various ways (sometimes with jam, a West Coast specialty), *bokkoms* (salted, dried harders, or small fish) with grapes, mussels, calamari, paella, *waterblommetjie bredie* (waterlily stew), and crayfish. There's also piping-hot white bread baked on the beach and served with fresh farm butter and a number of fruit preserves—this is the killer; you'll want to devour an entire loaf, much to the detriment of the remaining courses. The (on average) 10-course self-service meal will cost in the region of R130 ($16) per person.

Of the West Coast alfresco "restaurants," **Muisbosskerm** ★★★ (© **027/432-1017**) is still the best. Located on the beach 5km (3 miles) south of Lambert's Bay on the Eland's Bay Road (3 hr. from Cape Town), this is where the open-air West Coast restaurant concept was born—for years Edward and Elmien Turner had simply shared their favorite food with friends on the beach, and in 1985 they decided to broaden their guest list. The food is delicious, and you can usually count on a selection of fresh linefish, fresh green mealies, local potatoes and sweet potatoes, seafood *potjies* (pots of stew), curried tripe, *waterblommetjie bredie*, roast lamb, crayfish, mussels, and the legendary West Coast breads and preserves. It's a long drive home after a meal like this, so head for Paternoster, or ask the Turner family to recommend a few accommodations options when you phone for reservations. Booking ahead is essential.

from the coastline's ongoing degradation by developers. The campsites (R60/$7.50) are situated right on the sea, and the hikes are beautiful. Try to avoid visiting during school holidays and weekends.

LAMBERT'S BAY

This fishing port, the last bastion of "civilization" on the coast, lies 75km (47 miles) north of Velddrif and 65km (40 miles) west of Clanwilliam. There are two main reasons to visit: to view the colony of birds on Bird Island, and feast at one of the coast's best outdoor restaurants.

Bird Island is accessed via a stone breakwater in the Lambert's Bay Harbour. This island houses a colony of Cape gannets, jackass penguins, and cormorants—to be amid the cacophony of a 14,000-strong community all jostling for position on the island is a rare privilege. Alternatively, book a sunset cruise that takes you out to see the marine life of the bay from **Eco Boat Trips** (℃ **082-922-4334**).

6 Cederberg

Around 200km (124 miles) north of Cape Town lies the Cederberg Wilderness Area. This hikers' paradise features majestic jagged sandstone mountains that glow an unearthly deep red at sunset; strange-shaped rock formations that dominate the horizon; ancient San (bushman) rock painting sites; burbling streams in which to cool off; a variety of animals such as baboon, small antelope, leopard, lynx; and rare mountain fynbos such as the delicate snow protea and gnarled Clanwilliam cedar. You can drive to a number of designated spots, but the best way to explore this area is on foot.

In keeping with its "wilderness" designation, there are no laid-out trails, though maps indicating how to reach the main rock features—the huge Wolfberg Arch, and the 30m (98-ft.) high Maltese Cross, as well as to the two main Cederberg peaks—are available. Covering 710 sq. km (440 sq. miles), the Cederberg Wilderness Area is reached via a dirt road that lies halfway between the towns of Citrusdal and Clanwilliam. Of the two, the pretty town of Clanwilliam is the more attractive base, with a few attractions of its own, including the country's main Rooibos tea-processing factory (see "Sampling the 'Erb," below), the Ramskop Wildflower Reserve, and a spectacular drive to the nearby Moravian mission station of **Wuppertal** ✦✦. Citrusdal's main attraction is **The Baths** (℃ **022/921-3609**), a mineral spa resort (day visitors R35/$4.50 per person), and the ideal place to soothe aching muscles after a strenuous hike. You can camp in the Cederberg, or book a self-catering chalet through Cape Nature Conservation; but if you don't want to rough it and are particularly interested in rock art, look no further than the ultra-luxurious Bushmans Kloof, northeast of Clanwilliam (see below).

ESSENTIALS

VISITOR INFORMATION The Clanwilliam Information Centre (℃ **027/482-2024;** www.capewestcoast.org; Mon–Fri 8:30am–5pm, Sat 8:30am–12:30pm) is opposite the old jail on Main Street. To camp or walk in the Cederberg Wilderness Area, you will need a permit from **Cape Nature Conservation** in Algeria (℃ **022/931-2088**).

GETTING THERE   By Car   Clanwilliam lies just over 2 hours' drive from Cape Town. Head north up the N7; after approximately 160km (100 miles), you'll pass the town of Citrusdal to your left. About 28km (17 miles) farther north on the N7 is the turnoff for Cederberg Wilderness Area; 26km (16 miles) farther is the Clanwilliam, also on your left.

By Bus   Intercape (see chapter 2 for local numbers) travels the N7 to Namibia. Note, however, that unless you have someone to pick you up, you'll be left stranded on the highway.

WUPPERTAL ✦✦✦

It's worth visiting this isolated rural community just to travel the 90-minute dirt-road trip from Clanwilliam, with its breathtaking views of the twisted shapes and isolated tranquillity of the northern Cedarberg. Once here, you'll feel lost in time: **Wuppertal** looks pretty much the way it did when it was established as a Moravian mission station in the 1830s. In fact, Wuppertal farmers still use sickles to reap, donkeys to thresh, and the wind to sift their grain.

> ## (Fun Fact Sampling the 'Erb
>
> **Rooibos** (literally, "red bush," pronounced roy-boss) is a type of fynbos that only occurs in Clanwilliam and the surrounding area. Its leaves have been used to brew a refreshing, healthy drink for centuries but were first exported during World War II, when the Ceylon variety was scarce. Since then it has become popular in the Japanese, German, and Dutch markets, and research shows some amazing health properties. Rooibos is caffeine-free, is rich in vitamin C, and contains antioxidants, iron, potassium, copper, fluoride, zinc, magnesium, and alpha-hydroxy acid. Drinking it "neat" is an acquired taste; try it with honey, ginger and/or lemon; or with milk and sugar. You can sample it at the **Rooibos Ltd factory** (Rooibos Ave.; ℰ 027/482-2155), or order it just about anywhere in South Africa. Also recommended is the aptly named Honeybush Tea.

You can't miss the **Tourism Bureau** (ℰ 027/492-3410) on the Church Square next to Leipoldt House. This oldest building in the village also houses the **Lekkerbekkie** ("little sweet mouth"), which serves refreshments. To get to Wuppertal, drive east of Clanwilliam via the Pakhuis Pass on the road to Soetwater. Take the road south some 40km (25 miles) off the Pakhuis Pass Road at the appropriate sign to the Biedouw Valley. From here you have to travel some 30km (19 miles) via the Uitkyk and Kouberg passes.

EXPLORING THE CEDERBERG'S OPEN-AIR GALLERY ✸✸✸
Archaeological graduate and environmental expert **Catherine Price** (ℰ 083-2677350; kukummi@yahoo.com) offers personal "rock art" tours of the Cederberg, where archaeologists date some of the artworks, created by the now-extinct Southern San or Xam (pronounced Tsum), back 10,000 years—8,000 years before the rapacious pastoralists arrived to displace these gentle artists. Visitors stay in self-catering cottages at the basic Traveller's Rest; if you're looking for a great deal more comfort, service, and meat (Catherine only cooks vegetarian), book into Bushmans Kloof (see below). If you want to view only one rock-art example, look out for the sign on the R364 north of Clanwilliam, 2km (1¼ mile) before the Wuppertal turnoff.

WHERE TO STAY & DINE
If you want to get away from it all, **Tree Tops** (ℰ 022/921-3626; R220/$27 double)—four self-catering treehouses on the banks of the Olifants River, close to Citrusdale—is worth looking into. The most luxurious option in Clanwilliam itself is **Saint Du Barry's Country Lodge,** a B&B with five units, each with a television and fridge (R400–R580/$50–$72; ℰ/fax 027/482-1537). **Rietdak** (ℰ 022/931-2088; www.capenature.org.za; R470/$58 for four), a thatched cottage 400m (437 yd.) from the river, is one of Cape Nature Conservation's best self-catering units in the Cederberg.

Bushmans Kloof Wilderness Reserve ✸✸✸   This Relais & Chateaux lodge is by far the most luxurious option in the Cederberg surrounds, with accommodation that's on a par with the best game lodges near Kruger. Located on 8,000 hectares (19,760 acres) stocked with game and filled with flowers in spring, the reserve has more than 125 rock-art sites, and a resident rock-art specialist to explain anything from the mythology to technique behind this ancient art. Declared a South African Heritage Site, Bushmanskloof—"the world's largest open-air gallery"—is dedicated to preserving the unique biodiversity of the region as well as the history of the San. Early-morning rock-art tours provide visitors with insights into this fascinating community, followed by botanical walks, mountain biking, or simply lazing about in the crystal-clear rock pools. Sunset brings game drives in open Land Rovers. The ultra-luxurious bedrooms overlook the rolling lawns and river—ask for rooms in River Reeds or Water's Edge. Swimming pools, set above the river, offset the harsh, magical surrounds of the Cederberg beautifully. The lodge is easiest accessed by charter flight; it's a 35-minute flight from Cape Town.

Past Clanwilliam turn due east for 34km (21 miles) on Pakhuis Pass; entrance is on right. P.O. Box 53405, Kenilworth 7945. Lodge ⓒ **027/482-2627**; Reservations ⓒ 021/797-0990. Fax 021/761-5551. www. bushmanskloof.co.za. 16 units. R3,010 ($375) double, includes all meals, guided rock art walks, and game drives. AE, DC, MC, V. No children under age 12. **Amenities:** 2 dining areas; bar; 4 swimming pools; beauty spa; room service; laundry. *In room:* A/C, minibar.

7 Side Trips to the Northern Cape

A DRIVING TOUR OF NAMAQUALAND

Most of the year the sandveld region north of the Olifants River, a vast semi-arid area known as Namaqualand, sees very little visitors. But come the rains in August or September, the seeds that lie dormant under these dusky plains explode into magnificent multicolored carpets, as 4,000 species burst into vivid bloom. Because of the huge distances to cover to get to Namaqualand (Springbok is some 544km [337 miles] from Cape Town), you might want to make sure that the season has begun before you set off on a self-drive tour (though you'll struggle to find accommodation if you don't book well in advance)—note that the season starts on the coast and moves inland. Getting there is pretty straightforward: The area is reached via the N7 highway, which connects Cape Town with Namibia. If you find the distances daunting, note that **National Airlines** (ⓒ **021/934-0350**) flies regularly from Cape Town to **Springbok Airport** (ⓒ **027/712-2380**), where you can rent a car from **Tempest** (ⓒ **027/718-1600**).

The seasonal flower displays start quite close to Cape Town (see "Darling" and West Coast National Park," earlier in this chapter), but you enter the more remote and more spectacular flower region soon after the N7 bypasses Vanrhynsdorp, 283km (175 miles) north of Cape Town. This marks the halfway point between Cape Town and Namaqualand's "capital," Springbok, and while it's strictly still part of the Western Cape, it's well worth planning an overnight stop in the region. To do this, ascend the African plateau by taking the R27 via Van Rhyn's Pass to charming **Nieuwoudtville** ✦✦, touted as "the bulb capital of the world," and famed for its white sandstone architecture; or travel farther east to **Calvinia.** If you're traveling in late August, note that the biggest *braai* (barbecue) in the country—the annual **Hantam Meat Festival**—is held in Calvinia at this time, offering rare tastings of such native delicacies as *kaiings* (salted crackling) and *skilpadjies* (liver in caul fat). To overnight in Nieuwoudtville during flower season, you'll have to reserve long in advance: try booking **Ystervark Cottage** (ⓒ **027/218-1522**), a converted stone barn that sleeps two, or **Waenhuis,** with two single beds in two bedrooms (ⓒ **027/218-1535;** nieuvz@intekom.co.za). Contact the **Nieuwoudtville Publicity Association** (ⓒ **027/218-1336**) for more accommodations options.

For the best tours in this region, provided in a sawn-off bus, contact **Neil MacGregor** ✸✸✸ (✆ **027/218-1200**), a third-generation farmer who has hosted the likes of David Attenborough and his BBC team when they were filming "The Private World of Plants" at his farm, Glenlyon. Having traversed the **Knersvlakte** (literally, "plains of grinding teeth"), the first important stop north of Vanrhynsdorp is **Kamieskroon** (174km/108 miles farther on the N7), the last town before Springbok, which lies some 67km (42 miles) farther north on the N7. Kamieskroon is literally a one-horse town, but its claim to fame is the nearby **Skilpad** ("tortoise") **Wildflower Reserve** ✸✸✸ (✆ **027/672-1948;** ask to speak to conservationist Matthew Norval; open 8am–4pm in-season only). Created by the World Wildlife Fund, and part of the Namaqua National Park, the reserve (18km/11 miles west of town on the Wolwepoort Road) catches what little rain blows in off the sea, and is always magnificent during the flower season. The other reason to stop here is the **Kamieskroon Hotel** (✆ **027/672-1614;** kamieshotel@kingsley.co.za). The hotel charges R320 ($40) per person, and offers 7-day photographic workshops that could transform the way you look at things. The workshops, co-founded by local photographer Colla Swart and the internationally renowned Canadian photographer Freeman Patterson, cost R3,500 to R6,000 ($438–$750) per person. *Note:* Try to get your hands on a copy of *Freeman Patterson's Garden of the Gods* (Human & Rousseau), which features the beauty of Namaqualand in full bloom, to whet your appetite for a trip north.

The best place to stay (and eat) in Springbok is the **Springbok Lodge & Restaurant,** on the corner of Voortrekker and Keerom roads (✆ **027/712-1321;** fax 027/712-2718; R200/$25 double). The lodge is clean, but it's far from luxurious. Owner Jopie Kotze is a mine of information, and his restaurant walls are lined with photographs and artifacts relating to the area. You can also overnight in self-catering chalets at the top attraction, the **Goegap Nature Reserve** ✸✸ (✆ **027/712-1880**), 15km (9¼ miles) southeast of Springbok. The reserve is open daily from 8am to 6pm, though the office closes at 4pm. Admission is R10 ($1.30) adults, R5 (65¢) children.

5

Settler & Xhosa Country: The Eastern Cape

Situated between the Western Cape and KwaZulu-Natal, and bordered by the Orange River and Drakensberg Mountains in the north, the Eastern Cape's unspoiled coastline and vast hinterland offer a rare combination of beauty and solitude. It's rarely at the top of the list of holiday destinations, largely because so many of its attractions are off the beaten track, but for many this is the province's chief drawcard. It remains primarily a rural area, particularly with the post-apartheid incorporation of two large former Xhosa *"bantustans,"* Ciskei and Transkei, and traditional ways of life still hold sway here. It is also one of the poorest provinces in South Africa: farming and the manufacture of automobiles provide the region's main source of income, but are unable to generate the sizeable growth needed to absorb the province's large numbers of unemployed.

That said, the Eastern Cape is an interesting place to visit. Some of the country's most powerful political figures, like Steve Biko and Nelson Mandela, were born here; and capital city Port Elizabeth was a crucial center of the anti-apartheid movement, with a notoriously deadly security police in close attendance. Today a number of good operators offer excellent township tours that provide an insight into Port Elizabeth's role in South African history, as well as an authentic introduction into traditional Xhosa rites and ceremonies.

Within easy striking distance of Port Elizabeth—often the entry or end point of a Garden Route tour—is the Addo Elephant National Park, the country's third-largest reserve. If this isn't wild enough (and with no major predators, Addo is rather tame), the nearby Shamwari and Kwandwe private game reserves offer a chance to stay in luxury and see the Big 5.

The Eastern Cape is also steeped in English-settler history (as opposed to the Dutch influence in the Western Cape), with Grahamstown offering some of the finest examples of English-settler architecture; today this university town is an important cultural and educational center, hosting the largest arts festival in the Southern Hemisphere.

Moving north into the thirstlands of the Karoo, you will find vast, uninhabited plains with such atmospheric names as the Valley of Desolation, near Graaff-Reinet, the Eastern Cape's oldest settlement. If you like unpopulated spaces and picturesque architecture, this is a recommended detour, possibly on a self-drive tour between the Garden Route and Gauteng. But most visitors tend to stick to the coastal attractions, from surfing the perfect wave in Jeffrey's Bay to exploring the aptly named Wild Coast, where you'll find some of the coast's most unspoilt beaches.

Eastern Cape

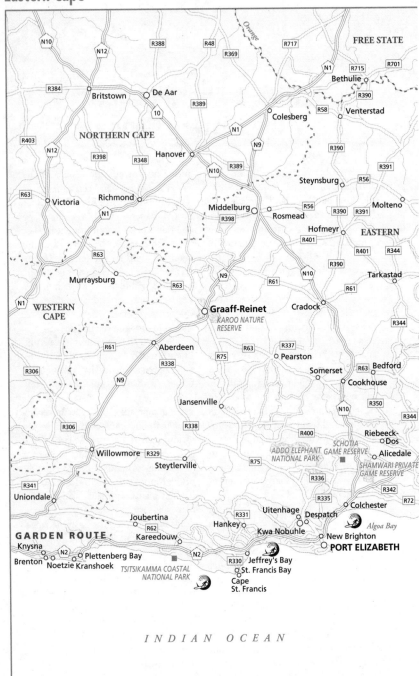

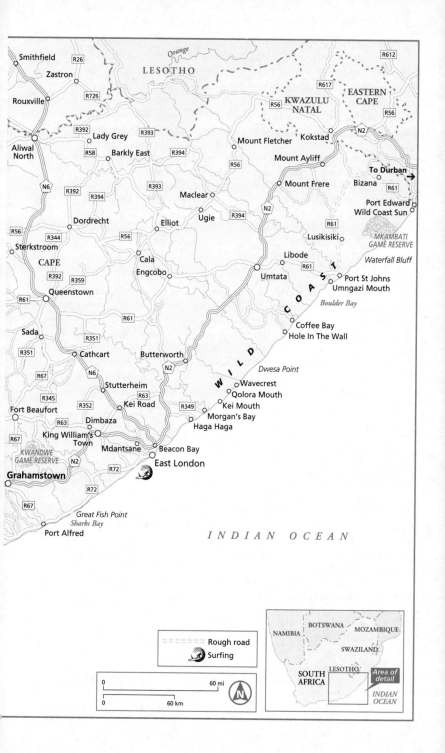

Smithfield

Zastron

Rouxville

Aliwal
North

LESOTHO

Orange

KWAZULU
NATAL

EASTERN
CAPE

To Durban

R26

R726

R392

R58

Lady Grey

Barkly East

R393

R394

R617

R612

R56

R56

Mount Fletcher

Kokstad

Mount Ayliff

N2

Bizana

R61

N6

R56

R344

Sterkstroom

CAPE

R392

R359

Queenstown

Sada

R351

R351

R67

Cathcart

N6

R345

R352

Fort Beaufort

R63

King William's
Town

R67

KWANDWE
GAME RESERVE

N2

Grahamstown

R67

R61

R392

R394

R393

Dordrecht

R56

Maclear

Ugie

Elliot

R394

Cala

Engcobo

R61

N2

Mount Frere

Lusikisiki

Libode

R61

Umtata

Stutterheim

R63

Kei Road

R349

Butterworth

N2

Dimbaza

Mdantsane

R72

Beacon Bay

East London

R72

Great Fish Point
Sharks Bay

Port Alfred

Port Edward
Wild Coast Sun

MKAMBATI
GAME RESERVE

Waterfall Bluff

Port St Johns
Umngazi Mouth

Boulder Bay

Coffee Bay
Hole In The Wall

Dwesa Point

Wavecrest
Qolora Mouth
Kei Mouth
Morgan's Bay
Haga Haga

W I L D   C O A S T

I N D I A N   O C E A N

Rough road

Surfing

0   60 mi

0   60 km

NAMIBIA

BOTSWANA

MOZAMBIQUE

SWAZILAND

SOUTH
AFRICA

LESOTHO

Area of
detail

*INDIAN
OCEAN*

1 Port Elizabeth

763km (473 miles) E of Cape Town; 1,050km (651 miles) SW of Johannesburg

The approach to Port Elizabeth, referred to by locals as "P.E." and by a slightly desperate marketing team as "The Friendly City," is somewhat depressing. Factories alternate with brown brick houses on the freeway into town, the ocean breeze is colored by the stench of smokestacks, and a network of elevated highways has effectively cut the center of the city off from the sea.

There is enough here to keep visitors entertained for a couple of days, but for most, Port Elizabeth is simply an entry or departure point—usually for a trip up or down the Garden Route. If you have a day to kill, take a township tour that covers some of the capital's political history, or amble along the Donkin Heritage Trail and take in P.E.'s settler history. If you don't have the time to visit another reserve in southern Africa, spend the day driving around the Addo Elephant National Park, where you'll find the world's densest elephant population, or Shamwari, a Big 5 reserve that's a mere 50-minute drive away.

ESSENTIALS

VISITOR INFORMATION   Port Elizabeth tourism has been renamed **Nelson Mandela Bay Tourism** (© **041/585-8884;** open Mon–Fri 8am–4:30pm, Sat and Sun 9:30am–3:30pm), but it's still located in the Donkin Lighthouse Building, Donkin Reserve, central P.E. Possibly more convenient is the **Eas'-capism Tourist Information Centre** (© **041/5077912;** www.eascapism.com), operating daily from 8am to 7pm from the beachfront entrance to the new Boardwalk Casino and Entertainment World.

GETTING THERE   By Car   P.E. is on the N2, which runs between Cape Town (7 hr. away; through the Garden Route) and Durban.

The 1820 Settlers: Deceit, Despair & Courage

The Industrial Revolution and the end of the Napoleonic wars created a massive unemployment problem in Britain. With their underpopulated colony in southern Africa under threat by the indigenous tribes, the British authorities came up with the perfect solution: Lured by the promise of free land and a new life, 4,000 men, women, and children landed at Algoa Bay in 1820, more than doubling the colony's English-speaking population. Many were tradesmen and teachers with no knowledge of farming, and they were given no prior warning of their real function: to create a human barrier along the Fish River, marking the eastern border of the Cape Colony. On the other side of the river were the Xhosa (pronounced *ko*-sa). The settlers were provided with tents, seeds, and a few bits of equipment, and given pockets of land too small for livestock and too poor for crops. Pestilence, flash floods, and constant attacks by the Xhosa laid waste their attempts to settle the land, and most of them slowly trickled into the towns to establish themselves in more secure trades. Thanks in no small measure to their stoic determination, Port Elizabeth is today the biggest coastal city between Cape Town and Durban, and the industrial hub of the Eastern Cape, with road, rail, and air links to every other major city in South Africa.

By Air   Port Elizabeth Airport (© 041/507-7319) is 4km (about 2½ miles) from the city center. **SAA** (© 041/507-1111) and **Nationwide** (© 041/507-7290) fly between P.E. and Johannesburg, Cape Town, and Durban. **British Airways Comair** (© 041/581-6055) flies between P.E. and Johannesburg. Call **Supercab Shuttle** (© 041/52-3720) for airport transfers.

By Bus   **Greyhound, Baz Bus,** and **Translux** all connect P.E. with Johannesburg, Cape Town, and Durban. **Intercape** runs between P.E., Johannesburg, and Cape Town. (See chapter 2 for regional numbers.)

By Train   For the ultimate in luxury (with a R20,000+/$2,500 price tag!), take the 2-day train trip that runs from Cape Town to P.E. from December to March on the legendary **Blue Train** (© 021/449-2672; www.bluetrain.co.za); see chapter 2 for more details on the train. The national mainline train runs between Johannesburg and Port Elizabeth; for details, call Shosholoza Mail © 086-000-8888.

GETTING AROUND   **By Car**   The best way to explore the Eastern Cape is with your own wheels. **Avis** (© 041/581-1306), **Budget** (© 041/581-4242), **Hertz** (© 041/508-6600), **Imperial** (© 041/581-4391), and **Tempest** (© 041/581-1256) all have desks at the airport.

By Taxi   **Hurters Taxi Cabs** (© 041/585-7344) has a 24-hour taxi service. **Molo Tours** (© 082-970-4037) offers direct safari transfers to the game reserves.

By Air   Contact **John Huddlestone** (© 041/582-2597 or 083-653-4294) for a helicopter trip to Addo Elephant National Park, Shamwari, or Kwandwe, or an aerial tour of P.E.

GUIDED TOURS OF PORT ELIZABETH & BEYOND   Besides the highly recommended township tours (see "What to See & Do," below), you can **sail Algoa Bay** on *Spirit of the Millenium,* a gaff-rigged schooner (© 041/583-2141); orient yourself with a 90-minute **Friendly City Tour** (© 041/585-1801); or book a full-day "big-game" excursion with **Pembury Tours** (© 041/581-2581). Pembury also offers 3-day Karoo or 3- to 10-day Garden Route tours. For guided hikes along the best of the coastline, contact **Tanaqua Tours** (© 083-270-9924).

FAST FACTS: **Port Elizabeth**

Area Code Port Elizabeth's area code is **041**.

Auto Repair Call **AA Breakdown** (© 0800/010101).

Emergencies For an ambulance, call © **10177; National Sea Rescue Institute (NSRI),** call © **041/507-3911; Police Flying Squad,** call © **10111; Police,** call © **041/394-6313.** The best private hospital is **Greenacres** (© 041/390-7000).

WHAT TO SEE & DO

TAKING A TOWNSHIP TOUR ★★★   To gain real insight into the city, the following tours are highly recommended: If you're prepared to make a night of it, **Mzolifi Quza,** of **Molo Tours** (© 082-970-4037), offers one of the best township tours in the country. After visiting an initiation camp (see "Rights of Passage," below), he will take you on a tour through the Walmer township,

> **Fun Fact Rites of Passage**
>
> It is not unusual to pass young men covered in white clay on the road—in rural as well as urban areas of the Eastern and Western Cape. These are Xhosa initiates, boys who are about to learn the customs of their clan, culminating in the removal of the foreskin (without anesthetic) to mark their transition to manhood.

visiting a youth center along the way, before taking you home to enjoy dinner with a Xhosa family. This is followed by a trip to a community choir rehearsal, and ends after a visit to a local *shebeen* (informal drinking house). **Calabash Tours** (© 041/585-6162) offers an excellent morning tour: the 4- to 5-hour "Real City Tour" starts in the center and looks at Port Elizabeth's history and the forced removal of residents out of the city to coloured and black townships. Xhanpi of **Fundani Tours** (© 082-964-6563) will tailor to your requirements, and also offers a 3-day tour that follows the "Footprints of Mandela's Youth." Fundani offers accommodation at a number of Xhosa family homes, and—if the timing is right—can arrange for you to witness a traditional Xhosa ceremony.

A WALK THROUGH SETTLER HISTORY   If you're interested in P.E.'s early history, take the 5km (3-mile) **Donkin Heritage Trail,** a self-guided walk marked with a blue staggered line that takes you past 47 places of historical interest in the old Hill area of central P.E.

You can pick up a map from the tourism office in the Donkin Lighthouse Building, which is in the **Donkin Reserve,** located below Belmont Terrace and Donkin Street—a quaint row of Victorian houses collectively declared a National Monument. The reserve was proclaimed an open space in perpetuity by Sir Rufane Donkin, the Cape's acting governor in 1820. Take a stroll to the large stone pyramid monument the governor erected to his late wife, Elizabeth, after whom he also named the city—look for the touching inscription. From here you might want to visit the **No. 7 Castle Hill Museum** ⚑ (© 041/582-2515; open Mon–Sat 10am–1pm, Mon–Fri 2–4:45pm; free admission), one of the oldest settler cottages in the city, dating back to 1827.

At the bottom of the hill you can either turn right to browse the **Wezandla Craft Centre** (© 041/585-1185), or left to view the pretty **City Hall** and the **City Library,** both on Govan Mbeki Avenue (recently renamed after the father of the current president); it's worth entering the library, a Gothic-Revival building dating back to 1902, to take a look at the stained-glass dome on the second floor.

EXPLORING THE BEACHFRONT   Enjoying an average of 7½ hours of sunshine a day, Port Elizabeth beaches see a lot of action. The waters of Algoa Bay are safe and relatively warm, and there are more than a dozen beaches in and around P.E. to choose from, some only 2km (just more than a mile) south of the city center. The first crescent is **King's Beach;** a safe swimming beach, it has good family facilities, including the **McArthur Baths Swimming Pool Complex** (© 041/582-2282), which stretches south to **Humewood Beach,** another good swimming beach. Additional attractions at Humewood include taking a scenic day trip on the **Apple Express** (© 041/507-2333), a restored narrow-gauge steam train.

Port Elizabeth's major beachfront attraction is its **Museum Complex** (© 041/584-0650; open daily 9am–4:30pm; admission R27/$3.50), just opposite Humewood Beach. The highlight is the **Oceanarium,** which features dolphin and seal acrobatics at 11am and 3pm daily. The complex also houses a small aquarium, a snake park, and a museum, which features fossils, scale reconstructions of shipwrecks, and a display on the Xhosa. A little farther along is the beachfront entrance to the new **Boardwalk Casino and Entertainment World,** where you'll find a number of restaurants and a cinema.

To escape the crowds, keep traveling the beachfront road until it becomes Marine Drive, then take the Sardinia Bay Road to visit the big dunes of Sardinia Bay. This is the start of the **Sacramento Trail** ⋆ (© **041/585-9711**), a great 8km (5-mile) coastal walk.

IN SEARCH OF BIG GAME ⋆⋆

By the turn of the 20th century, the prolific wildlife that occurred here naturally had been all but eradicated by settlers, the land subdued and sublimated into farmland. The terrain and climate are not suited to traditional farming, however, and thankfully there's an ongoing drive to rehabilitate fallow land and restock it with game. If you have time, it's definitely worth exploring one of the Eastern Cape reserves, but bear in mind that the terrain—most of which is prickly low-lying scrubland—is not the classic picture-postcard landscape of Africa. For that you will need to head for a reserve in Mpumalanga or the Northern Province, the North-West, or Botswana. A major bonus is that the Eastern Cape reserves are malaria-free (as are some of the reserves in the North-West; see chapter 6). If the price of a day trip to Shamwari is too high, but you really want to see lion, note that **Schotia** (© **042/235-1436**), a small (1,700-hectare/4,199-acre) reserve east of Addo, offers 3- to 4-hour night drives in which you track one of the reserve's six lions on the prowl. This costs R450/$56 (including transfers from P.E./Addo and supper around the fire), R750/$95 if you want to include a game drive through Addo.

Addo Elephant National Park ⋆   A 45-minute drive from Port Elizabeth, the Addo provides an excellent opportunity to view elephants in their natural habitat. Proclaimed a park in 1931, when only 11 elephants remained in the area, Addo is now home to over 300, and the reserve encompasses some 90,000 hectares (222,300 acres). Although elephants are in evidence year-round, the most attractive time of the year to visit is in spring, when the harsh Eastern Cape bushveld is softened with flowers, and the gray behemoths can be seen standing in carpets of yellow daisies. Other animals to look for are black rhino, buffalo, zebra, red hartebeest, eland, kudu, bushbuck, warthog, and a few endemic species such as the flightless dung beetle, found almost exclusively in Addo. To ensure best sightings, head for the watering holes (pick up a map at the entrance). Alternatively, take a guided game drive in an open-topped Land Rover: The resident

---

The Crushing of Black Consciousness

Take a detour from the Heritage Trail and visit the sixth floor of the otherwise charmless building located on 44 Strand St.: This is where Steve Biko—the charismatic black-consciousness leader of the 1970s—died while being interrogated by the security police. This, combined with the Soweto uprising, led to the imposition of the arms embargo by the U.N. Security Council. Until the recent Truth and Reconciliation Commission hearings, the official version of events was that Biko slipped and fell, and no one was ever arrested. You can visit the room in which Biko was interrogated; it houses items relating to the man and his past.

Bukani Travel & Tours (② 042/233-0091; R140–R220/$18–$28) conduct morning, afternoon, sundown, and night drives—the only way to view the nocturnal activities of such carnivores as the black-backed jackal and bat-eared fox. If you do the latter, look into overnighting (see "Where to Stay," below).

Off R335, 72km (45 miles) northeast of Port Elizabeth. ② 042/233-0556. www.addoelephantpark.com. Admission R20 ($2.60). Daily 7am–7pm. Take the N2 east for 17km (10½ miles), looking out for the Addo sign/R335.

Shamwari Private Game Reserve ⊛⊛ Thanks largely to the efforts of visionary Adrian Gardiner, the Big 5 once again roam the Eastern Cape plains at Shamwari, only 50 minutes from the P.E. airport. Gardiner's 20,000-hectare (49,000-acre) reserve has garnered numerous international awards for conserving a vanishing way of life—not only for reintroducing game, but also for the reserve's respectful focus on settler and African culture. After a buffet-style lunch, day-trippers are taken to **Kaya Lendaba,** an African art and culture village created by controversial *sangoma* (traditional healer) Credo Mutwa. The Kaya gives visitors the opportunity to understand much of Xhosa culture and ceremonies. This is followed by a visit to the **Born Free centre,** a sanctuary for abused animals, and a 3- to 4-hour game drive in which you explore the five ecosystems of the reserve in an open-topped Land Rover, driven by a knowledgeable ranger. Besides the Big 5, you will spot antelope (the reserve has 18 species), giraffe, wildebeest, hippos, and, if you're lucky, cheetah.

Off R342. Follow the N2 east for 65km (40 miles), turn left at the Shamwari sign on to gravel (R342). Shamwari's entrance is 7km (4½ miles) away. ② 042/203-1111. Day visit: R1,000–R1,400 ($125–$175), depending on season. 11am–7pm daily.

WHERE TO STAY & DINE

Note that the city is a 5-minute drive from the airport. Lodges and camps in the options listed under Addo & Surrounds provide a tranquil alternative to staying in the city, yet are only 50 minutes (Shamwari and Addo) to 90 minutes (Kwandwe) from check-in. The P.E. accommodation options listed below house some of the city's best restaurants (particularly the romantic **Hacklewood Hill,** which—much to the delight of P.E. locals—recently started welcoming nonguests into its candlelit dining room). If you don't feel like dining in, you might want to try **& Plate,** Bay Berry Fountain, Lutman Street, Central (② 041/585-1558), where the city's trendsetters and foodies sit down to chef Alan Fryer's creative fusion cooking. Alternatively, there's **34° South,** (② 041/583-1085), sibling to the hugely popular Knysna restaurant-cum-deli (see Knysna Oyster Tavern in chapter 4), located at the new Boardwalk Casino & Entertainment Complex, and the best place to stock up on a picnic.

IN PORT ELIZABETH

Beach Hotel ⊛ Opposite Hobie Beach, this is P.E.'s best beachfront option, with a well-respected restaurant, **The Bell,** serving classic French cuisine in an old-fashioned atmosphere. It's also adjacent to the Boardwalk Casino and Entertainment World (which has a number of restaurant choices) and within walking

---

⎛ *Tips* **No Oranges, Please . . .**

Be aware that no citrus fruit can be taken into the park. Addo elephants regard them as a delicacy, and when they pick up the scent they can become quite aggressive.

distance of Humewood Beach's museum complex. Service is relatively good; but the decor is of the bland-hotel type—you could be anywhere in the world, probably on a conference. If you like traveling in style, the Hacklewood is where you should be.

Marine Dr., Humewood 6001. ©/fax 041/583-2161. www.pehotels.co.za. 58 units. Seaview R840 ($105) double; non-seaview R670 ($84). Children stay free in parent's room. AE, DC, MC, V. **Amenities:** 3 restaurants; 3 bars; pool; room service; babysitting; laundry. *In room:* A/C, TV, minibar, tea- and coffee-making facilities, hair dryer.

The Chapman Manor House *Value*   The Chapman offers arguably the best deal in town. Situated on Brookes Hill, overlooking Algoa Bay, it's within walking distance of attractions like the museum complex and the main swimming beaches. A manor house it ain't, but all rooms have fabulous sea views, as does the pool. Best of all, it houses an excellent seafood restaurant, also with great views: **Blackbeards** (© 041/584-0623; 6pm–late; R45–R75/$5.50–$9) serves up a number of beef, pizza, and pasta choices, but the emphasis is firmly on seafood: Try the highly recommended "brodino" dishes—your choice of fish, combined with mussels and calamari, cooked in a tomato, white-wine, and garlic sauce (herbs are secret), and served in a cast-iron pot.

No. 1 Lady Bea Crescent, Brookes Hill, Humewood. © 041/584-0678. Fax 041/585-0305. www.chapman. co.za. 24 units. R480 ($56) double. AE, DC, MC, V. **Amenities:** Restaurant; pool; room service; laundry. *In room:* A/C (top floor only), TV, minibar (by prior arrangement), hair dryer.

Hacklewood Hill Country House ★★★   It's almost worth making a special detour to P.E. to stay at what is rather presumptuously called a "country house"— 4 minutes from the airport, Hacklewood is *very* much in the heart of the city. Built in 1898, the Victorian manor house has been artfully converted, with none of the generous spaces of the original home compromised. If you have a thing for bathrooms, these are world-class. Each is bigger than most hotel rooms and is furnished with the same class and care as the bedrooms: Victorian bathtubs are set in the center of the room, with comfortable seating provided in deep armchairs should you wish to converse in comfort. The entire house is furnished with beautiful period pieces, with colors and fabrics evincing exquisite taste, and a staff that's eager to please. The four- and five-course dinners (R185/$23), presided over by Cordon Bleu–trained chef Petro van Rooyen, are the city's best fine dining option—well worth it even if you aren't overnighting.

152 Prospect Rd., Walmer 6065. © 041/581-1300. Fax 041/581-4155. www.pehotels.co.za. 8 units. R2,320 ($290) double, including breakfast. AE, DC, MC, V. Children age 16 and over. **Amenities:** Dining room/bar; pool; tennis; room service; laundry; award-winning wine cellar. *In room:* A/C, TV, tea- and coffee-making facilities, hair dryer, heated towel rails.

ADDO AND SURROUNDS

Addo Elephant National Park (see review, above) has continued to expand both its borders and its options, and there are now two luxury alternatives to the park's rest camp (see below): In September 2003 **River Bend Country Lodge** ★★ (© 042/233-0161; www.riverbend.za.com; R6,400/$800 double, all inclusive) was incorporated in the park. This eight-bed lodge offers elegant colonial-style accommodations, a tranquil atmosphere, and excellent service—it's pricey, yes, but game walks, game drives, and spa treatments are all included in the rate, and the accommodation really is in a class all its own.

Addo Park Rest Camp *Value*   Many of these self-catering cottages have bush views—often with elephants. All units (bar some of the forest huts) are en-suite, though you need to specify if you want a semi- or fully equipped kitchen, or shared cooking facilities. Units 1 to 6 (two-bed with communal kitchens) have views of the water hole, as do units 7 and 8 (six-bed with kitchens); units 17 to 24 and 29 to 32 (four-bed) have good views of the park. A restaurant serves basic, filling meals—chicken, fish, steaks (including kudu and ostrich), and a few traditional dishes like *umcabosi,* a mix of spinach and pap (maize porridge).

Bookings: SA Parks Board, Box 787, Pretoria 0001. ✆ 012/428-9111. Direct ✆ 042/233-0556. www. parks-sa.co.za. 42 units, comprising 6-bed cottages, 4-bed cottages, 4-bed forest huts, and 2-bed rondavels. From R395 ($50) double. **Amenities:** Restaurant; swimming pool; tennis; store. *In room:* A/C in some units.

Kwandwe Private Game Reserve ★★★ Operated by the hugely successful CCAfrica (Londolozi, Phinda, to mention but two), Kwandwe is set to give Shamwari a run for its money. Covering 16,000 hectares (39,000 acres), the reserve accommodates a maximum of 18 guests at its main lodge (a family or group of six can be accommodated at **Uplands,** a gracious 1905 farmhouse), is a member of Relais & Chateau, and has the added benefit of 30km (19 miles) of Great Fish River frontage—a big contrast to the slightly arid Eastern Cape environment. In one of the biggest success stories of 2001, more than 7,000 animals were relocated to the reserve, including lion, rhino, elephant, buffalo, and cheetah (leopards were already resident). Located on the banks of the river, the lodge looks like it's been furnished for Karen Blixen: Persian rugs, antique chests and wardrobes, handstitched damask linen and cut-glass decanters, African spears and old-style hunting prints—it's all very *Out of Africa.* The nine luxury suites, each privately situated, feature fabulous views (even from your Victorian tub), indoor and outdoor showers, thatched viewing decks, and private plunge pools. Besides the de rigeur morning and evening game drives and/or walks, evenings are further augmented by a local historian's fascinating tales about the region—from the period of the Bushmen to the great frontier wars, it makes for fascinating tales. Staff will also arrange excursions to view rock paintings or to the nearby university town of Grahamstown. Kwandwe is a 90-minute drive from the P.E. airport.

Bookings through CCAfrica: Private Bag X27, Benmore 2010. ✆ 011/809-4300. Fax 011/809-4315. www. ccafrica.com. 9 units. High season: R10,450 ($1,306). Low season: R6,600 ($825). Prices include all meals, local beverages, game activities, and laundry. Ask about Uplands rates. AE, DC, MC, V. **Amenities:** Boma; dining area/bar/lounge; room service; laundry; game drives; bush walks. *In room:* A/C, minibar, hair dryer, plunge pool.

Shamwari Private Game Reserve ★★ This award-winning reserve (see review, above) now has a choice of six accommodation options. Aimed at the top-end market are **Eagles Cragg,** comprising nine junior suites, and **Lobengula Lodge,** with six suites. Eagles Cragg suites all have private viewing decks with plunge pools (as do two of Lobengula's junior suites—make sure you bag one of these). These thatched lodges offer in many ways the most authentic African-safari experience, with huge suites luxuriously furnished in ethnic-chic decor. However, with only four rooms, **Bushmans River Lodge** (an original 1860 settler farmstead), is the most intimate lodge; as a result it's extremely popular, so book ahead. Personally, I think **Bayethe,** the new luxury tented camp with nine en-suite tents, offers better value—at least in the hot summer, when you can lounge around your private deck, periodically dipping into your very own plunge pool. If the idea of a tent doesn't appeal, you'll have to settle for **Riverdene,** comprising nine twin rooms (and no private pools!). The least successful (but popular with older clientele, and the only option for parents) is **Long Lee Manor,** a pink Edwardian manor built in 1910, accommodating 36 guests in a more overtly colonial style. It too is beautifully furnished and well-staffed, but is the most like a hotel and commands the same price as Bayethe, Riverdene, and Bushmans.

Bookings: P.O. Box 32017, Summerstrand, Port Elizabeth 6019. © **042/203-1111.** Fax 042/235-1224. www. shamwari.com. High season (Sept–Apr): Lobengula and Eagles Cragg R10,500 ($1,312); Long Lee Manor from R8,650 ($1,080) double; Bushmans River, Riverdene, and Bayethe R8,650 ($1,080). Low season: From R4,450–R10,300 ($552–$1,162); Some lodges close; check when booking. Rates include all meals, drinks, game drives, and bush walks. AE, DC, MC, V. **Amenities:** Dining room/bar; pool; airport transfers; laundry; cultural village; game drives; bush walks; binocular rentals. *In room:* A/C, TV (Long Lee and Bushmans only), hair dryer.

2 Jeffrey's Bay

75km (46½ miles) W of Port Elizabeth

Situated on the 186km (115-mile) stretch between Storms River and Port Elizabeth, this is an easy detour on the way to or back from the Garden Route, particularly if you feel like stopping for lunch at the beach (see "Where to Dine," below). If you're a surfer, however, this coastal town will be a top priority on your itinerary. Considered one of the top three surfing spots in the world, "J-Bay" (as it's affectionately known to locals) shot to international fame in the 1960s cult movie *Endless Summer,* which featured the break at Supertubes—the fastest and best-formed break on the South African coast, as well as "Bruce's Beauties," a rare right-point break you'll find a little farther west, at the quiet coastal hamlet of Cape St Francis.

ESSENTIALS

VISITOR INFORMATION   The **J-Bay Tourism Office** (© **042/293-2588;** www.jeffreysbaytourism.com; open Mon–Fri 8:30am–5pm, and Sat 9am–12pm) is on the corner of Da Gama and Drommedaris roads. To find out where the surf is, or for lessons, call **Brenton** at the **South Coast Surf School** (© **083-549-6795;** R150/$19 for 2 hr., includes all equipment)—it's never too late to start; some of Brenton's students are in their 50s and 60s.

GETTING THERE   Jeffrey's Bay can only be reached by car or bus; take the turnoff south off the N2. The **J-Bay Sunshine Express** (© **042/293-2221**) shuttles between Jeffrey's Bay and Port Elizabeth. **The Baz Bus** (© **021/439-2323**) calls in every day on its run between Cape Town, P.E., and Durban.

GETTING AROUND   Once here, you can get around on foot or by car. **Derek** from **Aloe Africa** (© **042/296-2974** or 082/576-4259) offers tours of the area, including various adventure activities like surfing, sandboarding, mountain biking, and kloofing (in which you follow a river through a mountain gorge, swimming and clambering your way out).

WHERE TO STAY

The most upmarket option on the final stretch of coast between the eastern end of the Garden Route and Port Elizabeth is the **Beach House** ★★ (© **042/294-1225;** www.stfrancisbay.co.za), in St Francis Bay, a small coastal town 20-minutes' drive west of J-Bay. The small thatched lodge (only four rooms) offers 180-degree ocean views, beach access, and luxurious accommodation, at a price: R2,590 ($324) double, including breakfast.

Diaz 15 ★   This is the best guesthouse in Jeffrey's Bay, and one of the few along the coast located right on the beach. A well-cropped lawn abruptly dissolves into Main Beach, and the ocean is literally a stone's throw from your sliding windows. Self-catering apartments, tiled in white throughout, are very spacious: Choose between two- and three-bedroom apartments; each bedroom has its own balcony and bathroom, kitchens are open-plan and modern, and living rooms are comfortably furnished with sliding doors opening onto a veranda or balcony. The penthouse has wraparound sea views; alternatively, numbers 3, 5, and 10 have good sea views. Note that the P.E. airport is a mere 75km (46½ miles) away. Given notice, proprietor Coenie Nel will stock your fridge or serve breakfast, and Breakers restaurant is a few minutes' walk away.

15 Diaz Rd., Jeffrey's Bay 6330. ⓒ/fax **042/293-1779**. www.diaz15.co.za. 8 units. High season: (Oct–Apr) R1,250–R1,600 ($156–$200)) double. Low season: From R1,000 ($125) double. AE, DC, MC, V. **Amenities:** Laundry. *In room:* TV, hair dryer.

WHERE TO DINE

Walskipper ⭐⭐ *Kids* TRADITIONAL/SEAFOOD If you haven't had a chance to sample the open-air West Coast restaurants, Walskipper, run by Grace and Phillip Koornhof, offers a fairly similar experience. Situated right on the ocean, it's a casual affair housed in a simple open-air structure—even the waiters are barefoot. Most dishes are cooked over hot coals, including the ever-popular Walskipper special—a plate of prawns, calamari, mussels, scallops, and crab sticks. Traditional S.A. dishes include oxtail and tomato *bredie*. Guests are seated on rough benches, wine is served in tin mugs and meals come on enamel plates, and chunks of freshly baked bread and jam accompany every meal.

Jeffrey's Bay. Take the road to Aston Bay (next to J-Bay), follow sign to Marina Martinique. ⓒ **042/292-0005** or 082-800-9478. Reservations essential. Main courses R48–R65 ($6–$8). Open daily in season; out of season Tues–Sat 12–9:30pm.

3 Grahamstown

125km (77½ miles) NE of Port Elizabeth

Grahamstown was named after Colonel John Graham, who established a garrison here in 1815 with orders to drive the Xhosa eastward over the Fish River—a ruthless expulsion that was to spark the 100-year Frontier War. Reminders of its English colonial past can be seen everywhere: streets lined with charming Georgian and Victorian buildings, the only Victorian camera obscura in the Southern Hemisphere, one of South Africa's oldest English-speaking universities, and a number of highly regarded English-style private boarding schools dating back to 1885. But with the old Fish River frontier a mere 60km (36 miles) east, signs of the impoverished Xhosa community are equally visible, both on the streets and on the hills surrounding the valley.

As something of a microcosm of South Africa's social and economic problems, Grahamstown is certainly worth visiting, and never more so than in July, when the town hosts its 24-year-old arts festival, said to be the biggest in the Southern Hemisphere, and second in size only to Edinburgh's.

ESSENTIALS

VISITOR INFORMATION The helpful Grahamstown tourism is now known as **Makana Tourism** (ⓒ **046/622-3241;** www.grahamstown.co.za; open Mon–Fri 8:30am–5pm, Sat 8:30am–12pm) and is located at 63 High St.

GETTING THERE By Car Take the N2 out of Port Elizabeth; some 125km (77½ miles) northeast is the turnoff for Grahamstown.

By Bus Greyhound and **Intercape** operate daily between Grahamstown and Port Elizabeth. Call ⓒ **046/622-2235**. For **Translux** queries call ⓒ **046/622-3241.**

GETTING AROUND   Contact **Beeline** (© **082-651-6646** or 082-652-0798) for a taxi.

By Car   You can rent a car from **Avis** (© **046/622-8233** or 0800/021-111).

GUIDED TOURS   Cocks Tours (© **046/636-1287**) offers city walking tours as well as trips to Addo Elephant National Park, the Sunshine Coast via the settler town of Bathurst, and the Frontier Forts and Great Fish River Reserve (rates dependent on numbers). Fiona Masterson's **Lynx thru Africa** (© **082-784-1458**) provides 3-hour city tours (includes township; see below), 5-hour Settler Country tours, and a 4-hour night drive in the nearby Double Drift Game Reserve. Contact **David** to view Khoisan rock art (© **082-254-5489**).

TOWNSHIP TOURS   Despite Grahamstown's patent lack of industry, people continue to pour in from the former *bantustan* (homeland) of Ciskei. A township tour provides insights into the stark contrasts of this growing community, as well as much-needed income

> **Fun Fact   Bag Ladies**
>
> The **Masithandane Association** owes much of its success to rubbish. Plastic bags—referred to as the new S.A. national flower because of the way they flourish on fences and trees surrounding the townships—are collected by township women, who in return receive a meal. The bags are then skillfully woven by Masithandane members into colorful hats and bags.

and purpose. An **Umthati Township Tour** ★★ (© **082-784-1458**; R130/$16) takes you from Grahamstown into the heart of the Rini township, where eight out of every ten people are unemployed. At Umthati's kitchen gardens and education center, you will be served a traditional Xhosa meal, learn something about the culture and customs, visit a member's house and local shop, and be taken to the **Masithandane Association** (see below) to purchase local crafts. Stimulating heritage craft and the visual arts (printmaking) is the focus of the **Egazini Outreach Project;** to view these, contact Zandisile at © **083-545-0842.**

SPECIAL EVENTS   Grahamstown's **National Arts Festival** (© **046/622-4341;** www.nafest.co.za) held every July, is Africa's biggest arts event: Some 1,500 events are staged over 11 days.

EXPLORING GRAHAMSTOWN

Start your tour by driving or walking to the top of Gunfire Hill, where the **1820s Settlers National Monument** overlooks Grahamstown, which is situated in a small valley flanked by hills. To your right you will see Makanaskop, where the Xhosa took their last stand against the British. Enter to view the Cecil Skotnes artworks, then head back down the hill to the **Albany Museum** on Somerset Street (© **046/622-2312**) or the interesting **International Library for African Music** ★ on Prince Alfred Street (off Somerset). The library houses more than 200 traditional instruments and has hundreds of recordings of traditional African music from southern and central Africa, much of it on sale. For an introduction and tour by internationally renowned ethnomusicologist **Andrew Tracey** (the director), phone ahead and make an appointment (© **046/603-8557;** open Mon–Fri 8:30am–12:45pm and 2:15–5pm; free admission). Farther on Somerset Road is the **SA Institute for Aquatic Biodiversity** (© **046/636-1002;** open Mon–Fri 8.30am–1pm and 2–5pm), where you can view two stuffed specimens of the coelacanth (see "Fishing for Dinosaurs," below).

> *Fun Fact* **Fishing for Dinosaurs**
>
> In 1938, J. L. B. Smith identified a strange fish species—caught off the East
> London coast, and sporting six limblike fins—as a coelacanth, a 200-mil-
> lion-year-old species thought to have died out 50 million years ago. The
> latest catch, made in 2000, was off the coast near St Lucia Wetland Park
> (see chapter 8 for more on the coelacanth).

Moving to the center of town, at the junction of High and Hill streets, you
will find the town's most prominent landmark (also the tallest spire in South
Africa): the **Cathedral of St Michael and St George** (✆ 046/622-2445).
Nearby, at the top of Bathurst Street, is the **Gothic-Revival Methodist Com-
memoration Church** (✆ 046/622-7210), which dates back to 1850. Diagonally opposite is a winged statue of peace, dedicated to the men who died in the
Anglo-Boer War. Note the inscription; Rudyard Kipling wrote it especially for
the memorial.

Next door to the Methodist church are the premises of **T. Birch & Co**
(✆ 046/622-7010)—an old-style family store—and the **City Hall,** dating back
to the 1870s. It's definitely worth purchasing something from Birch's just to
watch your money fly across the room—they still use the Lamson trolley system,
an overhead cash delivery system dating back to the 1950s.

Stroll down Bathurst Street to the **Observatory Museum** ✰✰, where you can
see a 360-degree view of Grahamstown reflected in the restored Victorian camera obscura. The camera, constructed in the mid-1850s, is housed in a custom-
designed cupola above the home and shop of the eccentric H. C. Galpin. A
watchmaker by trade, Galpin also built a turret housing a clock above his home,
the pendulum of which swings in the rooms two stories below. The museum
holds interesting exhibits relating to Galpin and his hobbies, as well as early-set-
tler artifacts (✆ 046/622-2312; open Mon–Fri 9am–1pm and 2–5pm, and Sat
10am–2pm; admission R8/$1). The cupola holds a maximum of eight people.

WHERE TO STAY & DINE

The dining room at the atmospheric **The Cock House** ✰ (see below) is where
Grahamstown diners go to celebrate a special occasion. Chef-patron Belinda
changes her menu regularly to ensure that her regular diners are never bored, but
you can expect country-style cooking, utilizing local ingredients like Karoo lamb,
ostrich, and venison. Lunch is served daily; dinner Monday through Saturday
(R10/$13 for three courses). Alternatively, head for **La Galleria** ✰✰ (13 New St.;
✆ 046/622-2345; lunch and dinner Mon–Fri). Part of this little gem's charm is
the fact that the kitchen is visible from the street—in the afternoon you can look
through the window and see pasta drying for the evening meal. Meals start with
the antipasto trolley, followed by a typically Italian selection of main courses; try
the *barese* (creamed spinach and ricotta with mushroom and bacon). The *pollo
cremonese* (chicken breasts prepared with herbs and lemon) is also recommended.

The Cock House ✰✰　Built in 1826, this charming two-story settler house
(once the home of author Andre Brink) was bought and renovated by owner-
managers Belinda and Peter Tudge in 1991. Very much a country-style inn, this
is considered the best accommodation in Grahamstown (though the Hermitage
is a personal favorite) and has hosted a number of illustrious guests; Nelson
Mandela has stayed here twice. Rooms are tasteful and spacious, though the

bathrooms above the public spaces are looking a little tired. Among the rooms in the converted stables, the honeymoon suite is the best.

10 Market St., Grahamstown 6140. © **046/636-1287.** Fax 046/636-1295. www.cockhouse.co.za. 10 units. R600 ($75) double, including breakfast. (Prices are subject to increase during festival week in July). AE, DC, MC, V. **Amenities:** Restaurant; bar; laundry. *In room:* TV, tea- and coffee-making facilities, fans.

The Hermitage ★★ *Value*   If you don't mind being in a B&B (and note that the location of the rooms and size of the house are large enough for a sense of total privacy), this is the best place to stay in Grahamstown. Situated in a beautiful historic home and decorated with immense flair and impeccable taste by artist Beau Jeffray, the Hermitage has only two rooms, but one is supremely grateful that the Jeffrays are prepared to share their home at all. Of the two rooms, the one overlooking the back garden is far larger, with a small sitting room leading out to the tranquil garden. Every detail is pleasing (even the breakfast table is laid with antiques and cut glass), and the Jeffrays are the most charming of hosts.

14 Henry St., Grahamstown 6140. ©/fax **046/636-1503.** 2 units. R350 ($44) double, including breakfast. No credit cards. *In room:* TV, tea- and coffee-making facilities, fridge, hair dryer.

4 Graaff-Reinet

254km (157½ miles) N/NW of Port Elizabeth

Graaff-Reinet, South Africa's fourth-oldest town, is 837km (519 miles) south of Johannesburg—a good stopover if you're driving down to the Garden Route. Should you have time, try to prolong your stay for a full day. Spend a morning admiring some of the 220 national monuments, then take one of the worthwhile side trips. This is one of the few towns surrounded by a nature reserve, and you'll find one of the world's best examples of outsider art in the nearby hamlet of Nieu Bethesda.

ESSENTIALS
VISITOR INFORMATION   The helpful **Graaff-Reinet Publicity Association** (© **049/892-4248;** www.graaffreinet.co.za; open Mon–Fri 8am–12:30pm and 2–5pm, Sat–Sun 9am–12pm) is housed in 13A Church Street.

GETTING THERE   By Car   From Johannesburg you travel south on the N1, then take the N9 south at Colesberg to Graaff-Reinet. From Port Elizabeth you take the R75 north, a 3-hour drive.

By Bus   Translux and **Intercape** buses pull in daily from Cape Town, the Garden Route, and Port Elizabeth. See chapter 2 for phone numbers.

GETTING AROUND   The easiest and best way to explore the town is on foot or on a bicycle. For guided tours of the town and surrounds, and bicycle rentals, contact **Karoo Connections Adventure Tours** ★ (© **049/892-3978;** karooconnections@intekom.co.za). They will provide the following trips: town and township tours; trips to the Valley of Desolation, Bushman Rock Art, the Owl House, and Karoo Farms; game-viewing drives in the Karoo Nature Reserve; and a number of horseback riding and hiking tours.

WHAT TO SEE & DO
With more national monuments than any other South African town, the streets of Graaff-Reinet are a pleasure to simply stroll along. Incorporate an informal walking tour with a visit to at least one of the four buildings that comprise the **Graaff-Reinet Museum** (© **049/892-3801;** open Mon–Fri 8am–12:30pm and

2–5pm, Sat 9am–3pm, Sun 9am–12pm and 2–4pm; admission R15/$2). Of these, **Reinet House,** a stately Cape Dutch home facing Parsonage Street, is by far the most interesting. Built in 1812 as the Dutch Reformed Church parsonage, its large, airy rooms display period furniture, a collection of antique dolls, and various household objects. Within walking distance, the **Old Library Museum,** on the corner of Church and Somerset streets, houses a collection of fossilized Karoo reptiles that inhabited the area more than 200 million years ago (see "Fishing for Dinosaurs," above). Other buildings worth noting are the stately **Dutch Reformed Church,** one block up from the Old Library Museum, which dates back to 1886, and the delightful **Graaff-Reinet pharmacy,** a typical Victorian chemist that still operates at 24 Caledon St.

GREAT SIDE TRIPS

Graaff-Reinet lies in the center of the 15,000-hectare (37,050-acre) **Karoo Nature Reserve** (open daily dawn to dusk; free admission), the highlight of which is the **Valley of Desolation** ☆☆☆, 14km (8½ miles) from Graaff-Reinet. Sunset is the best time to visit, when the dolomite towers that rise some 800m (2,600 ft.) from the valley below turn a deep red, and the pink light softens the Camdeboo plains. On your return, keep an eye out for the endangered mountain zebra—the Karoo Nature Reserve is one of its last remaining habitats.

Another highly recommended excursion is to **Nieu Bethesda;** 50km (31 miles) northeast of Graaff-Reinet. This typical Karoo *dorp* (small rural town) is charming; modern-day luxuries like electricity are a relatively recent phenomena, and donkey carts still a main source of transport, but the main attraction is the **Owl House and Camel Yard** ☆☆☆ on New Street (✆ 049/841-1603). In her late 40s, after the deaths of her parents, Helen Martins became obsessed with transforming her house into a world of her own making, a project that was to absorb her for the next 30 years. She was obsessed with light: The interior features large reflecting mirrors to maximize this, and every conceivable surface is covered with finely crushed glass, with colors creating large patterns, including a favored sunbeam motif. In the candlelight, the interior glitters like a jewel. Helen Martins' inner vision spread into her backyard, enveloping her in a mystical world of glittering peacocks, camels, mermaids, stars, shepherds, sphinxes, towers, and serpents. Immortalized in the award-winning play and movie *Road to Mecca* (starring Kathy Bates), the house is one of the world's most inspiring examples of Outsider Art. Tours are held from 8am to 6pm daily (9am–5pm June–Sept); admission is R12 ($1.50).

Tea and light meals are available daily at the **Village Inn** (✆ 049/841-1635), on the corner diagonally opposite the Owl House. There is no official Tourism Bureau, but owner Egbert can assist with just about anything . . .

WHERE TO STAY & DINE

Andries Stöckenstrom Guest House ☆   The main reason to stay in this listed house built in 1819 is the **food** ☆☆☆—the only way to guarantee a table is to overnight. Beatrice is a self-taught chef, but her passion for the medium has rendered her a true artist. Representative of her creative spirit is the appetizer of smoked loin kudu salad or baked fig with Gorgonzola; lightly curried sweet-potato soup with crumbled roasted almonds; or Karoo lamb or deboned quail for a main course. Beatrice constantly darts from the kitchen to ensure that her imaginative meals are to her guests' satisfaction, while Andre describes them seductively and discreetly keeps topping off wine glasses. A truly marvelous experience—book early and for no. 5, the largest and most comfortable room.

100 Cradock St., Graaff-Reinet 6280. ©/fax **049/892-4575**. 5 units. R1,260–R1,440 ($158–$180) double. Rates include breakfast and dinner. AE, DC, MC, V. **Amenities:** Dining room/bar; limited room service; laundry. *In room:* A/C, hair dryer.

Drostdy Hotel ★ *Value*   The original home and offices of Graaff-Reinet's first magistrate, this elegant Cape Dutch building is in the heart of the historical center. The gracious public spaces are tastefully furnished with antiques and period artworks, and the bedrooms are all situated in the adjacent Stretch's Court—a row of cottages formerly occupied by freed slaves and dating back to 1855. Most of the standard rooms are cramped, and a few have damp walls, making a luxury suite well worth the extra R200 ($25). All the rooms in Ferreira House are charming, particularly F3, which has a fireplace and private garden, and F5, which is furnished with beautiful antiques. Light meals are served in the garden from 9am to 5pm (the Drostdy's chunky whole-wheat bread is unbeatable); a la carte meals are served in De Camdeboo restaurant, and the seven-course meals (R105/$13) are served in the Old Courtroom; these feature traditional South African dishes such as *boontjiesop* (bean soup), *kerrievis* (curried fish), and Karoo lamb.

30 Church St., Graaff-Reinet 6280. © **049/892-2161.** Fax 049/892-4582. www. drostdy.co.za. R580–R780 ($72–$98) double. AE, DC, MC, V. **Amenities:** Restaurant; bar; pool; room service; babysitting; laundry. *In room:* A/C, TV, minibar, tea- and coffee-making facilities, hair dryer.

5 The Wild Coast ★★

The northernmost section of the Eastern Cape stretches 280km (174 miles) from the Kei River in the south to the mouth of the Mtamvuna River, bordering KwaZulu-Natal. The coast is lush and largely uninhabited, with innumerable rivers spilling into large estuaries, waterfalls plunging directly into the ocean, coastal, dune, and mangrove forests, long sandy beaches, rocky coves, and a number of shipwrecks, all of which have earned it the name "Wild Coast." This region was part of the former *bantustan* (homeland) Transkei, where any Xhosa that weren't of economic use to the Republic were dumped, and as such it has suffered from overgrazing and underdevelopment and is one of the poorest areas in South Africa. Despite this, the people are incredibly hospitable, and exploring this region will provide you with one of the most unaffected cultural experiences available to visitors in South Africa. Note, however, that much of the coastline is difficult to access—dirt roads are pitted with deep potholes, there is virtually no public transportation, and accommodations options are limited. The exceptions to this are the coast south of Qora Mouth, and the coastal towns of **Coffee Bay** and **Port St Johns** ★.

The only way to reach these coastal towns is via the N2, which cuts through the middle of the hinterland, passing through unfenced green valleys dotted with traditional Xhosa huts and the old Transkei capital of Umtata. The top attraction here is the **Nelson Mandela Museum** ★★★ (© **047/532-5110;** www.mandela-museum.org.za; open Mon–Fri 9am–4pm, Sat 9am–12pm; admission free). Madiba, the clan name by which Mandela is affectionately known, was born near Qunu, where he still returns for holidays (this is also where he and Oprah Winfrey distributed thousands of Christmas gifts to an overexcited crowd in 2002). The museum is situated in the Bhunga Building, a gracious colonial structure that once housed municipal offices, and comprises several rooms that have been filled with Mandela memorabilia, among them gifts from respectful statesmen, adoring children, and various other admirers. Excellent displays, including posters, videos, and photographs, record the life and works of the greatest statesman Africa has ever known.

ESSENTIALS

VISITOR INFORMATION   There is no central tourism bureau. Contact **Wild Coast Holiday Reservations** (✆ **043/743-6181;** meross@iafrica.com) in East London, or Ukhenketho **Tourism Port St Johns** (✆/fax **047/564-1187**). For information on Wild Coast nature reserves (of which Mkambati is recommended), contact central bookings at ✆ **040/635-2115.**

GETTING THERE & AROUND   By Car   The N2 traverses the length of what used to be called the Transkei, with roads to the coast leading southeast off it. Most roads to the coast are untarred, some are badly marked, and all are time-consuming. Look out for livestock on the road, and don't travel at night. You can also charter a flight from Durban to **Umngazi River Bungalows,** the Wild Coast's best lodging.

By Bus   The **Baz Bus** (see chapter 2 for regional numbers) travels from Port Elizabeth to Durban, with stops at Coffee Bay and Port St Johns.

On Foot   Wild Coast Meander ☆ (✆ **043/743-6181;** meross@iafrica.com) offers a 5-day hike that covers 55km (34 miles), from Qora Mouth to Morgan Bay, accompanied by a member of the local community. Hikers ford rivers and traverse isolated beaches, but each night is spent in a hotel. Five days, including accommodation, meals, and transfers from East London airport, costs from R2,400 ($300) for 4 people.

On Horseback   The 3- to 6-day **Amadiba Trails** (✆ **031/791-0178**) is a camping trip completed on horseback and canoe. You will be accompanied by a local guide, and meals may be enjoyed with members of the local community. Trails (R1,100/$140 for 4 days) start at the Wild Coast Casino, on the border between the Eastern Cape and KwaZulu-Natal.

WHERE TO STAY & DINE

One of the most comfortable ways to experience the rugged splendor of the Wild Coast is on a 5-day Wild Coast Meander (see above).

Umngazi River Bungalows ★★ (Kids)   If you want to sample the subtropical pleasures of the Wild Coast without roughing it too much, this is the coast's finest and best value-for-money resort—you'll want to stay here for the duration of your holiday. Located just south of Port St Johns, Umngazi is situated in its own private nature reserve, overlooking a large estuary and deserted beach, and flanked by dense coastal vegetation. With a safe lagoon, boats and gillies for hire, river trips, skiing, snooker, a saltwater swimming pool, a host of babysitters, and a separate toddlers' dining room, it offers the perfect family holiday, yet the honeymoon bungalows are private enough for lovers to remain blissfully unaware of the pitter-patter of little feet. (This is, incidentally, where Nelson Mandela chose to spend his first Christmas with wife Graca.) The en-suite bungalows are very basic, with outdoor showers from which you can watch the dolphins surfing—it's definitely worth requesting a sea-facing bungalow (Brazen Head and units 41–43 are choice). Meals are large buffets and/or table d'hote featuring fresh salads, fish, meat, and chicken, homemade breads, and cheese, all served in the large thatched dining room. The service is generally good, though with English very much a second language, patience is, as always, a virtue.

P.O. Box 75, Port St Johns 5120. ✆/fax **047/564-1115.** www.umngazi.co.za. 48 units. High season: R710–R840 ($90–$104) double. Low season: R640–R770 ($80–$97) double. Honeymoon suites R880 ($110). Rates include all meals. AE, DC, MC, V. **Amenities:** Tennis; boating; guided walks; mountain biking; bird-watching. *In room:* En-suite bathtubs, coffee- and tea-making facilities.

6

Place of Gold: Gauteng & North-West Province

The landlocked provinces of Gauteng and North-West lie on the highveld plains of South Africa and share a common border, but there the similarity ends. While the North-West is characterized by the wide open spaces of great bushveld plains and endless maize fields, Gauteng, the country's smallest and most densely populated province, is an ever-growing concrete sprawl.

Gauteng was built both literally and figuratively on gold—its name, translated from the Sotho language, means "place of gold." It comprises the Pretoria-Witwatersrand-Vaal triangle, a heavily industrialized region in which three major cities are situated and where a population of 7 million produces almost 40 percent of the country's GDP. In the north is Pretoria, currently the administrative capital of the country and a quieter, more laid-back alternative to neighboring city Johannesburg, some 50km (31 miles) south. Granted, Pretoria is pretty dull when compared with Johannesburg, but it does contain a good number of historical and cultural sights. If it's sassy big-city action you crave, however, head to Johannesburg, known as the "gold capital of the world" and the hub of Witwatersrand, a metropolis that stretches some 120km (74½ miles) across the province. Among its top attractions are the new Apartheid Museum, which provides poignant insight into what it was like to live under one of the world's most iniquitous systems of discrimination; a descent down a working mine shaft to

tour the richest bowels of the earth; a visit to the Cradle of Humankind, a World Heritage Site where paleoanthropologists are still unearthing clues to mankind's origins; and a trip to Soweto, a geographically separate city inhabited by an estimated 2 to 4 million people, almost all of whom are black, and most of whom are poor—an enduring legacy of the country's racist and separatist history.

Most leisure travelers use Gauteng as a gateway to the attractions in neighboring provinces and countries. Of these, the North-West, which borders Botswana in the north, contains some of the country's most easily accessed game reserves and is also malaria-free. Pilanesberg National Park, referred to as the "Jewel of the North-West," is the closest option (a 1½- to 2-hour drive from Johannesburg). It's located next to Sun City and the opulent Palace of the Lost City, which rates as one of the world's most over-the-top theme parks. Pilanesberg's proximity to Sun City means that it can become relatively crowded—if you're looking for a real sense of safari you'd be better off traveling north to the larger Madikwe Reserve, where the varied terrain (including Kalahari sandveld) is home to the "Magnificent Seven": In addition to sightings of the Big 5, you stand an excellent chance of seeing cheetah and wild dog, Africa's most endangered predator.

Time allowing, those with a penchant for solitude should venture even farther northwest, into the vast expanses of the Kgalagadi Transfrontier National Park, where the red dunes of the Kalahari Desert support a surprisingly varied, rich—and highly visible—game population. (*Note:* To compare these reserves with others, go to "Planning Your Safari" in chapter 2.)

1 Johannesburg

1,402km (869 miles) NE of Cape Town, 58km (36 miles) S of Pretoria

The bushveld plains that remained unchanged for millions of years were irrevocably transformed when a prospector named George Harrison stumbled onto the richest gold reef in the world in 1886. Within 3 years, a nondescript part of the bleak highveld plains had grown into the third-biggest city in South Africa, and soon Johannesburg, or "eGoli" as it came to be known, would become the largest city south of Cairo. The speed at which it grew was due in part to the power and greed of men like Cecil Rhodes—whose diamond mines in Kimberley provided the capital to exploit the rich gold-bearing reefs of the Witwatersrand—and to the availability of cheap labor. Along with other "randlords," as the most powerful consortium of mining magnates were known, Rhodes founded the Chamber of Mines in 1889, which created policies regarding recruitment, wages, and working conditions. In 1893 it institutionalized the "colour bar," which ensured that black men could aspire to no more than manual labor.

By 1895, the ever-expanding mining settlement far outnumbered the original Boer settlers, who had fled here from what they felt to be the oppressive policies of the British in the Cape. Disgruntled by this secondary "invasion," Botha, president of the then South African Republic (ZAR), denied these *uitlanders* (foreigners) the vote, and refused to develop an infrastructure to support mining activities. Four years later, the ZAR and Britain went to war, and in 1902 Britain annexed the republic. The British Empire relinquished its hold in 1910 when the Union of South Africa was proclaimed, but for the millions of black migrant laborers who toiled below the earth, working conditions remained relentlessly harsh. By 1946 more than 400,000 black people were residing in and around Jo'burg; in August that year, 70,000 African Mineworkers Union members went on strike over living and working conditions—to no avail, despite the death of 12 men and injuries to over a thousand.

During the 1950s Johannesburg's uniquely black urban culture was given a name. "Kwela" had its own jazzy sounds, heard in the *shebeens* (drinking houses) of Sophiatown, and a slick, sophisticated style, as evidenced in the pages of *Drum* magazine. But this was also the decade of forced removals, when thousands were dumped into the new suburbs of Soweto, and consequently a growth phase for the African National Congress (ANC), which in 1955 proclaimed its Freedom Charter—the basis of the current constitution—in what is now known as Freedom Square.

But it would be another two decades before the black majority revolted. On June 16, 1976, police opened fire on a peaceful student demonstration in Soweto and sparked a nationwide riot—South Africa's black youth had declared war on apartheid. Student activism escalated during the 1980s and came to a head during the early 1990s, when political parties jostled for power after Nelson Mandela's release from prison. Some townships were reduced to utter chaos, with a mysterious "third force" (later proven to be state-funded) pouring fuel on the flames. Political peace finally came with the 1994 elections, and Jo'burgers returned to their primary pursuit: making money.

For many, however, this remains an elusive goal. South Africa has the most productive mines in the world, but the size of its gold-mining force has fallen by half since 1990. Industries like manufacturing, banking, IT, and media service sectors have shown more consistent growth since the fall of apartheid, but not at a rate that can absorb the sprawling city's burgeoning population. Unemployment has spawned crime that in turn has bred a culture of fear, and walled neighborhoods, burglar bars, security guards, and guard dogs are common sights, particularly in the northern suburbs. But Jo'burg's 113-year history is nothing if not unpredictable. Initiatives like iGoli 2002, the general upswing in development, and the emergence of a sophisticated, wealthy black middle class, has resulted in a sexy new-found confidence, and the city continues to attract entrepreneurs from all over the continent. Jozi, as she is affectionately known, remains the original cultural melting pot, and for every person living in fear, there are a dozen more enjoying the most racially integrated city in Africa, finding it more diverse, vibrant, and exhilarating than ever.

ESSENTIALS
ARRIVING
BY PLANE   Most international flights to South Africa arrive in the relatively small but sophisticated **Johannesburg International Airport** (© **011/921-6262**). If you've arrived early or are waiting for a connection, consider relaxing in one of the Rennies Travel "Premier Club" lounges which offers the same facilities as a First Class lounge, for a mere R80/$10 (international terminal) or R42/$5 (domestic terminal) entry fee. The **Gauteng Tourism Authority** has a branch in the airport's International Arrivals hall (© **011/390-3614**), and is open daily from 6am to 10pm. Foreign exchange is available 24 hours, and the easiest is to use the ABSA Bank ATM.

The airport is 25km (15½ miles) from the city and a 30- to 40-minute drive from the northern suburbs. Lines queue up directly outside the exit; make sure you discuss the price upfront (it should cost you about R250/$30) to get to a Sandton/northern suburbs hotel). A cheaper, more convenient option, particularly if you're traveling alone, is the **Magic Bus Shuttle** (in the Multistory Parkade; © **011/394-6902/3** or 082-234-1800; or e-mail them before you leave at info@magicbus.co.za and ask them to meet you with a nameboard). Transfers to the Sandton center take place every 30 minutes and cost R95 ($12) per person; a door-to-door transfer (to your hotel, for example) will cost a little extra.

BY TRAIN   Given time, there's nothing better than trundling through the country by train, particularly on the legendary **Blue Train** (© **011/773-7522; bookings 012/334-8459**) or the equally luxurious **Rovos Rail** (© **012/ 323-6052**). Both roll in to Pretoria via Johannesburg from Cape Town (taking around 28 hr.); Rovos also operates other luxury trips throughout the country and as far afield as Dar es Salaam; see chapter 2 for more details on both. If you like the romance of rail, but can't face the steep fares, a good option is to book the new Premier Class coupe from Cape Town on **Shozolozo,** South Africa's main line passenger services (© **086-000-8888**). The train arrives from Cape Town every Wednesday (and departs for Cape Town from Pretoria/Jhb every Thurs), and costs R1,485/$185 per person one-way (all inclusive).

Warning: Because **Park Station** (corner of Rissik and Wolmarans sts., Braamfontein) is a major center for people arriving from all over Africa, the consequent rich pickings for criminals has made this a dangerous area, so arrange for a hotel transfer from the platform in Pretoria, or enquire about disembarking at Kempton and arranging a transfer from here.

Tips **Staying Safe**

Inevitably, with the promised redistribution of wealth taking longer than many expected, the city is a hothouse for those who have realized that the easiest way to make it is to take it. Carjackings are common; when driving in the city, be on the lookout for suspicious-looking vehicles or persons, and keep your car doors locked and windows up. Don't leave valuables in plain sight in the car, even when you're in it. Though you can be carjacked anywhere, it is more likely to happen in quiet suburbs where there are few eyewitnesses—which means locals rather than tourists are targeted. Make sure your car is never closed in from the front and back; if your car is bumped from behind and you feel uncomfortable with the situation, don't stop; drive straight to your hotel or call the police on your cellphone. If you feel the situation is a potentially threatening one, keep in mind that crossing against a red light—carefully, of course—is allowed.

Generally speaking, inconspicuous consumption is the order of the day: People who have nothing worth stealing will not be bothered. Don't carry or wear anything of obvious value when you're exploring the central business district, including Braamfontein and Newtown (though some say it's worth carrying a small sum of cash to satisfy a demand), and don't look lost. Hillbrow, Berea, and Yeoville are best avoided unless you're accompanied by a guide who is totally familiar with the area. If you need to look at a map, go into a store to do it. If you are ever mugged, don't protest—just hand over the goods or money and walk away.

If this sort of talk makes you nervous, it may be wise to tour in a group with a guide (see "Guided Tours," below). Alternatively, you can book one of the lodging options recommended below—which are situated in safe areas—and spend your time sampling the city's many fine restaurants.

BY CAR   The N1 connects Johannesburg with Cape Town (see box on p. 248 for route tips), the N4 with Nelspruit, the N3 with Durban. Another popular route is to travel north from the Garden Route (via Graaff-Reinet) to Johannesburg.

BY BUS   The intercity buses   **Greyhound, Intercape,** and **Translux** (see chapter 2 for numbers), all arrive at Park Station.

VISITOR INFORMATION

Besides the office in the airport you will find a **Gauteng Tourism Authority** office located in Sandton Square (Entrance 6, Shop L31G, near Postnet, © 011/784-9596/7/8; www.gauteng.net). Hours are from 8.30am to 6pm daily. It's worth picking up a copy of *What's On in Gauteng,* which details most of the city's current attractions. It has a map of the city and surrounding suburbs, but if you intend driving yourself you'd be well advised to pick up *Mapstudio's Rosebank Sandton Guide.* Both are free. There's also a Gauteng Tourism Authority **satellite office** in Rosebank Mall (© 011/340-9000), open between 8 and 9am and 5 and 6pm daily (depending on season) on the Upper Roof (where the Craft Market is held).

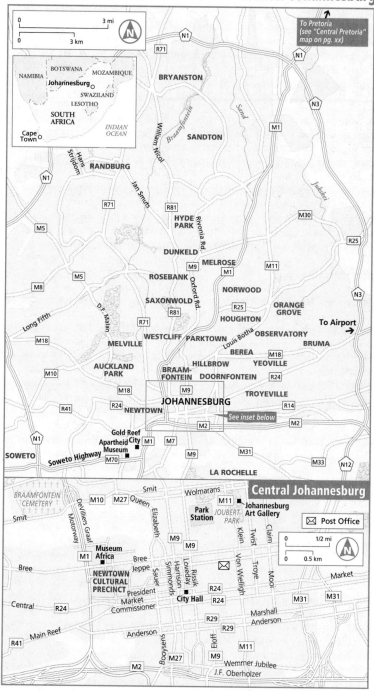

Greater Johannesburg

To Pretoria
(see "Central Pretoria"
map on pg. xx)

0   3 mi
0   3 km

NAMIBIA
BOTSWANA   MOZAMBIQUE
Johannesburg
SWAZILAND
LESOTHO
SOUTH
AFRICA
Cape Town   INDIAN OCEAN

N1

R71

BRYANSTON

N1

N3

M1

Braamfontein   *Sand*   *Jukskei*

SANDTON

William Nicol

Harts Stridom   RANDBURG

N1

Jan Smuts

R71

R81

HYDE PARK

Rivonia Rd.

M30

M5

R25

DUNKELD

M9   MELROSE   M11

M8   M5   ROSEBANK   M1

Oxford Rd.

NORWOOD

SAXONWOLD   R81   R25   ORANGE GROVE

D.F. Malan   R71   HOUGHTON

Long Fifth   To Airport

M18   WESTCLIFF   PARKTOWN   OBSERVATORY

Louis Botha   BRUMA

MELVILLE   BEREA   M18

M10   AUCKLAND PARK   HILLBROW   YEOVILLE

BRAAM-FONTEIN   DOORNFONTEIN   R24

M18   M9   TROYEVILLE

R41   R24   JOHANNESBURG   R14

NEWTOWN   M2   M2

N1   Gold Reef City   M1   M7

Apartheid Museum   M9   M31   M33   N12

SOWETO   Soweto Highway   M70

LA ROCHELLE

Central Johannesburg

BRAAMFONTEIN CEMETERY   Smit   Wolmarans

M10   M27   Queen

Smit   M11

Park Station   JOUBERT PARK   Johannesburg Art Gallery

DeVilliers Graaf Motorway   Elizabeth   M9   Klein   Twist   Claim

Museum Africa   M9   ⊠ Post Office

M1   Bree   Jeppe   Troye   Mooi

Bree   NEWTOWN CULTURAL PRECINCT   Sauer   Loveday   Russik   ⊠   Von Wielligh   Market

President   Harrison   Simmonds   R24   M31   M31

Central   R24   Market   City Hall   R24

Commissioner   R29   Marshall

Main Reef   R29   Anderson

R41   Anderson   Eloff   M11

M2   Booysens   M27   M9   Wemmer Jubilee

J.F. Oberholzer

0   1/2 mi
0   0.5 km

217

If you plan to travel farther afield in Africa and haven't consulted a doctor, visit the **SAA-Netcare Travel Clinic** in Sandton (© **011/301-0287**) for up-to-date advice and/or vaccinations. This is also one of the few places in South African where you can purchase a course of Malarone, the best precaution against malaria and one you need start only a day prior to traveling to a high-risk area.

NEIGHBORHOODS IN BRIEF

CITY CENTER   The streets of the town center (which includes the newly revamped **Newtown** on the northwestern outskirts) and the surrounding inner-city suburbs (**Joubert Park, Hillbrow,** and **Berea**) are lined with skyscrapers at the foot of which hurrying commuters and shoppers jostle for space with pavement traders. Although the lily-white north has a preponderance of shopping malls, many Sowetans are geographically still forced to shop in the city center, and many have given up living in shacks to join the African immigrants who've thronged to the inner city, taking over abandoned office blocks and decaying warehouses. The streets are a great deal more lively than those elsewhere in the city, but they are also more dangerous—at least on foot. Unless you're accompanied by a guide (see "Guided Tours," below), the safest way to get a feel for Jo'burg's center is by driving through it (see map), stopping only at the sights highlighted.

The city center's most interesting sights (see "Top Attractions" and "More Attractions," later in this chapter) are reasonably safe to visit on your own—the **Carlton Centre** and **Johannesburg Art Gallery** both offer secure parking, and the installation of security cameras at the **Newtown Cultural Precinct** (where many of the top attractions are located) has seen crime there reduced by 70%; however, it's still worth being on your guard and not carrying any obviously valuable items with you. It's certainly inadvisable to explore the inner-city suburbs of **Hillbrow** and **Berea**—both full to the brim with rundown high-rise tenements. This is where the vast majority of African immigrants arriving in the City of Gold settle down—at least initially, or so they hope. On the northern edge lies **Braamfontein,** a business district where the Witwatersrand University's **Gertrude Posel Gallery** and the city's central train station, **Park Station,** are located. East of the city lie the residential suburbs of **Yeoville** and **Observatory,** where some backpacker establishments offer cheap accommodations, albeit in an increasingly dangerous area, as well as **Bez Valley** and **Troyville,** less-than-salubrious suburbs that attract an interesting local mix.

THE EASTERN SUBURBS   Sadly, **Yeoville,** east of Berea, has become increasingly violent. A trip to the bars, clubs, and cafes of Rockey Street (around which Yeoville nightlife is centered) may offer an exhilarating insight into cosmopolitan Africa, but it's definitely no longer considered a safe thing to do. Gunshots are a regular sound effect (no, it's not part of the soundtrack), and you're likely to feel highly visible. A little farther east is **Observatory,** a quiet area with large houses, a few with views (a real luxury in Johannesburg) and one of the best-value accommodations options in Jo'burg (see "Where to Stay," later in this chapter). But the money you save on lodging will likely be offset by taxi or rental-car expenses—Sandton's shopping malls and Melville's bars are 18 to 20 minutes away.

Directly east of the city center are **Troyville** and **Bez Valley,** patches of which are slowly being gentrified by the more creative Jo'burgers bored by the seamless high-walled northern suburbs and unable to afford Melville. With no highlighted attractions, tourists seldom find a reason to explore this area.

THE NORTHERN SUBURBS   As the city center gradually slipped into decay (a process, incidentally, that predates the inauguration of the New South Africa), the financial center effectively relocated to the northern suburbs, and it is here that you'll find the greatest concentration of hotels, restaurants, and shopping malls.

The northern suburb closest to the city is **Parktown,** where the randlords built their Edwardian mansions. Just west of Parktown is **Westcliff,** which, if you can afford it, has the best accommodations option in the city, an elevated cliff-side "village" overlooking the urban forests of Johannesburg—said to be the largest in the world. It's in striking distance of the northwestern suburbs of Melville, Greenside, and Rosebank.

Directly north of Parktown are the well-established, "old-money" suburbs of **Saxonwold** and **Houghton**—the latter is often included in city tours because the house where Mandela and his new wife, Graca, stay when they're in town is located here. Next up is **Rosebank,** then **Hyde Park, Sandton,** and **Morningside,** all predominantly white and very wealthy enclaves. Of these, Rosebank offers the best shopping environment but it is Sandton that holds the highest concentration of business and retail outlets; with the move here in 2000 of the Johannesburg Stock Exchange, it has officially become the new financial center of the city. Most of the accommodations options offered below are centered around the shopping malls of Rosebank and Sandton. Fortresslike homes and hotels and gated communities means it's relatively safe but dull, particularly at nights, when what little street life there is retreats behind high walls and city malls.

THE NORTHWESTERN SUBURBS   For a more lively option, head for **Melville** ★★, northwest of Parktown, and no more than a 15- to 20-minute drive south from Sandton. Adjoining Auckland Park, which is where the SABC (South African Broadcasting Corporation) and RAU (Rand Afrikaans University) are located, Melville has a bohemian mix of residents, including actors, artists, producers, lecturers, architects, and film crew, and is considered one of the city's most textured suburbs. Come here to drink coffee, dine at one of the many restaurants, or catch the latest jazz act at Bassline (see "Johannesburg After Dark," later in this chapter). Aside from a vibrant street life centered around 7th Street and 4th Avenue, Melville also has the Melville Koppies Nature Reserve

---

Gone, But Not Forgotten

Sophiatown was once one of the most vibrant black suburbs in the city (within walking distance from Melville), where journalists, gangsters, and leaders like Mandela and Sisulu jived to legendary musicians like Hugh Masekela and Miriam Makeba. Considered a criminal and political hotbed, the entire suburb was razed to the ground in the 1950s, rebuilt for poor whites, and crassly renamed Triomf ("triumph") by the apartheid government. The only remaining Sophiatown building is the Church of Christ the King—in a nod to some moral sensibility, apartheid's bulldozers were not allowed to flatten religious buildings—but you can get some sense of what was lost through Museum Africa's displays, which include a re-created *shebeen* (see "Top Attractions," later in this chapter). For a specialized tour of Sophiatown, run at certain times of the year, contact the **Parktown and Westcliff Heritage Trust** (© **011/482-3349;** Mon–Fri 9am–1pm).

(see later in this chapter) close by. The nearby suburb of **Greenside** (a short drive west of Westcliff) has enjoyed a resurgence in property value and investment, with Green Way, the main thoroughfare, a great street for restaurant-hopping; another great area for restaurant browsing is nearby **Parkhurst.** Farther north is **Randburg,** but the only reason you'd venture this far northwest is to curio hunt the man-made Waterfront (see "Shopping," later in this chapter).

GETTING AROUND

Public transport can be unreliable, inflexible, and, after hours, nonexistent. Unless you plan on using a tour operator, Johannesburg is best explored by car, but be warned: Jo'burg drivers are aggressive, as the myriad skidmarks on the roads will attest, and you will need a map. If you intend to stay for a while, it's worth investing in a good one (see "Fast Facts: Johannesburg," below).

By Car   You can rent a car from **Avis** (© **0861-02-1111** or 011/394-5433; www.avis.com), **Hertz** (© **011/390-9700;** www.hertz.com), **Budget** (© **011/ 394-2905;** www.budget.com), or **Imperial** (© **011/397-5695;** www.imperial. ih.co.za), all of which have desks in the airport. Of the above, Budget tends to offer the better rates. **Res Q** (© **011/867-6552;** www.resqrentacar.co.za) will deliver and collect at the airport, and offers secondhand budget options that have the added advantage of being less desirable to carjackers. **Britz Africa** (© **011/396-1860;** www.britz.co.za) specializes in fully equipped four-wheel-drives and camper vans, and will pick you up at the airport.

Parking   Parking on the street can be unsafe in town (park in the Carlton Garage—entrances from Marshall, Main, and Kruis sts.) but shouldn't be a problem in the suburbs recommended below—provided that you never leave anything in the car in open view. Most hotels offer valet parking.

By Taxi   Taxis don't cruise the streets, so you'll have to call for one. **Roses Taxi** (© **011/403-9625;** R5.50/70¢/km), **Maxi Taxi** (© **011/648-1212;** R6/80¢km), and **Good Hope Taxis** (© **011/725-6431;** R4.50/60¢/km) are all recommended. Don't be tempted to travel by minibus taxi, the mode of transport for most South Africans. At best, it's a hair-raising experience.

GUIDED TOURS

The following recommended operators all travel in comfortable minibus vehicles, and cover the city's top attractions, like the Carlton Centre and Museum Africa, with minor variations. Do bear in mind, however, that all are very flexible, so discuss the itinerary upfront and make sure your interests are covered— art lovers may want to ensure that a stop at the Johannesburg art gallery is included, and a visit to the Apartheid Museum is well worth the extra hour or two (and additional charge) if you are interested in South Africa's turbulent history. Call **Max Maximum** (© **011/938-8703**), **Moratiwa** (© **011/869-6629**), or **Jimmy's** (© **011/331-6109;** www.face2face.co.za). Recommended national operators for day or evening trips to Pretoria, Lesedi, Pilanesberg, or Sun City are **Welcome Tours** (© **011/328-8050;** www.welcome.co.za) and **Springbok Atlas** (© **011/396-1053;** www.springbokatlas.com). Alternatively, check out the following specialized tours:

CRADLE OF HUMANKIND TOURS 🟠🟠🟠   Palaeo-Tours (© **082-804- 2899** or 011/837-6660; www.palaeotours.com) offers fascinating trips to some of the key sites in what has become known as the Cradle of Humankind, declared a World Heritage Site in 1999 for the significant paleoanthropological and archaeological discoveries made in the area since 1966. The Cradle again made headlines in 2003, when a new dating technique (called "burial cosmogenic dating") revealed that the Little Foot Skeleton, found in 1997, is 4.17 million years old—the oldest in South Africa, and one of the oldest in the world. Guides are paleoanthropology scientists or Ph.D. students who explain the history of evolution while taking you to working excavation sites. The area is some 20 minutes from the city and tours, comprising two site visits, and usually last 5 hours; it may be a good idea to ask for the tour to be extended to include lunch at Cornuti at the Cradle (see "Where to Dine," later in this chapter), possibly followed by a game drive in the Cradle Game Reserve, where you may spot giraffes, rhinos, leopards, and a variety of antelope. Note that all Palaeo-Tours are by arrangement only, so it's worth booking one before you leave home.

TOWNSHIP TOURS ✿✿✿   A growing trend in South Africa, "township tourism," which originated in Soweto (see later in this chapter) takes visitors on community-based tours of the segregated black neighborhoods constructed during the apartheid years. (Incidentally, the word township—used to denote poor black suburbs—dates back to 1912, and while commonly used should ideally be phased out; it's something you may want to discuss with your guide.) These tours offer a fascinating insight into the ubiquitous economic contrasts found in the city of gold, particularly if you choose to visit Alexandra, where an estimated 600,000 people live in abject poverty in a 7.6-square-mile (4,864-acre) enclave, just 10 minutes from glitzy Sandton, one of the city's wealthiest suburbs. Among the sights on Alex's "Heritage Trail" tour is the house Mandela lived in when he first came to Johannesburg and the headquarters of the Msomi gang, who terrorized the community in the late 1950s. To arrange a tour, contact the **Alexander Tourism Association** at ✆ **011/882-0673.**

MINE & MONEY TOURS ✿✿✿   If you want to get under Jo'burg's skin—literally—book an **Operational Mine Visit.** Betty Elliot (✆ **011/498-7100** or 083-263-7776) negotiates a roster of mine visits with the Chamber of Mines every 6 months. Preference is given to groups with a direct interest in mining, but given enough warning Betty will try to include individuals in these visits. The tours are physically strenuous and can be psychologically stressful as well; under no circumstances should you attempt one if you are under 16, over 60, or at all claustrophobic. After being given a brief operational and geological overview of the mine in question, visitors are supplied with full underground gear. Keep in mind that conditions 2km (just over a mile) below the surface of the earth are humid and hot, and rock temperatures in working mines can reach 131°F (55°C). Even though refrigerated air is pumped through, air temperatures can exceed 90°F (32°C). After a 1- to 2-hour tour, visitors return to the shaft and shower (towels are supplied). The tour often ends with drinks and snacks, hosted by the mine's management, and costs R475 to R500 ($59–$63) per person. Betty also offers tours of the **SA Mint,** where you can visit the factory where money is made—literally; South Africa produces coins for 12 countries, including the new euro coin.

If Betty cannot assist, every fourth Friday of the month a group is taken 790m (2,592 ft.) below the surface of the earth at **Cullinan's Premier Mine,** site of the world's most famous diamond finds and still a productive mine. Tours cost R90 ($11) but need to be booked well in advance; for details, see "Pretoria: The Top Attractions," later in this chapter.

Note: If an Operational Mine Visit sounds too daunting, you can descend the historic No. 14 shaft at **Gold Reef City** (see "The Top Attractions," later in this chapter).

SPECIALIST WALKING TOURS   Beryl Porter loves Jozi with a passion, and has set about making its strange beauty more accessible to visitors with a wide selection of walking tours—even glitzy Sandton fascinates her as she enthuses how (while walking to its key sites), within a mere three decades, it has been transformed from a sleepy suburb of cow-grazed tracts of land to the new financial center of the city. Personally, I'd opt for a tour of the city center and/or the nearby Newtown Cultural Precinct. Another recommended tour is viewing the derelict attractions of semi-seedy Kensington and Troyville and its predominantly Portuguese community (don't miss lunch at the Troyville Hotel, the best and most authentic Portuguese restaurant/bar in the city). Beryl also offers a unique "downtown dinner-hop" evening, where you kick off on Constitution Court, travel to the Turbine Hall via the Bag Factory (see "Shopping," later in this chapter) for your first course, then sit down for your main at the Rand Club before ending off at Top of the Carlton. Call Beryl at ✆ **011/444-1639** or take a look at www.walktours.co.za.

ARCHITECTURE & HISTORY TOURS   In addition to seeing the city center, where century-old relics rub shoulders with sheets of towering glass, make time to view the Edwardian mansions and gardens of Parktown and Westcliff—the very first garden suburbs created by the wealthy randlords, featuring some of celebrated architect Sir Herbert Baker's finest domestic architecture, dating from 1897 to 1905. Though many of the original buildings have been replaced with bland office blocks, it is still well worth exploring. (*Note:* If you want to drive around on your own, you should seek out Ridge Road, particularly **The View** at no. 18, built in 1897; its 1902 neighbor **Hazeldene**—which also houses **The Herbert Baker** restaurant (✆ **011/484-6197**); **Jubilee Road;** and **Rock Ridge Road**—no. 5 was Baker's own residence.) Contact the **Parktown & Westcliff Heritage Trust** ★★★ (✆ **011/482-3349;** http://home.intekom.com/parktown/co.za; office hours Mon–Fri 9am–1pm) to find out if it plans to offer this tour while you are in the city. The trust also arranges walking or bus tours that cover many other interesting aspects of the city, from "Art Deco and Edwardian Elegance" to "Ghandi's Johannesburg" and "The Jewish Tour." Tours cost R50 to R80 ($6.50–$10) per person.

SPECIAL EVENTS

The city's biggest festival for the performing arts, **Arts Alive** (✆ **011/838-1383;** www.joburg.org.za/artsalive), takes place in September, with program details available from late June. The highlight of the festival is "Jazz on the Lake," which takes place on Zoo Lake (opposite the Zoo). Featuring some of Africa's richest talent, the concert draws a huge cosmopolitan and friendly audience. Another event worth attending is the annual **Dance Umbrella** (www.jazzart.co.za), which takes place in March (various venues) and showcases South Africa's considerable dance and choreographic talents.

FAST FACTS: **Johannesburg**

Airport See "Arriving," earlier in this chapter.

American Express The head office is in Rosebank at Shop GF03, The Zone, opposite Rosebank Mall (✆ **011/880-8382**). Hours are Monday to Friday 8:30am to 5pm, and Saturday 9am to 12pm. There is also an office in

Sandton City shopping center, upper level (✆ 011/883-1316). For lost or stolen cards, call ✆ 011/359-0111 and ask for the card division.

Area Code Johannesburg's area code is 011.

Climate Days are usually sunny with averages of 70°F (20°C). The area has a very mild winter temperature (May–Aug), though frost may occur at night. See "When to Go," in chapter 2.

Drugstores Drugstores are known as chemists or pharmacies in South Africa. Contact **Daylight Pharmacy** (in Sandton City shopping center; ✆ 011/883-7520; open 8:30am–8pm daily) or **Morningside Dispensary** (corner Rivonia and Allen roads; ✆ 011/883-6588; open 8.30am–9pm).

Embassies & Consulates Note that all embassies are in Pretoria (see later in this chapter). Australia, 292 Orient St., Arcadia (✆ 012/342-3740); Canada, 1103 Arcadia St., Hatfield (✆ 012/422-3000); Ireland, Tulbagh Park 1234 Church St., Colbyn (✆ 012/342-5062); United Kingdom, 256 Glynn St., Hatfield (✆ 012/483-1400); United States, 877 Pretorius St., Arcadia (✆ 012/343-1048); Zambia, 353 Sanlam Blvd., Hatfield (✆ 012/342-1541); Zimbabwe, 798 Merton St., Arcadia (✆ 012/342-5125).

Emergencies Dial ✆ 10111 for flying-squad police, or ✆ 999 for an ambulance or ✆ 082-911 for emergency medical assistance. In case of fire, call ✆ 011/624-2800. For northern suburbs ambulance or fire emergencies call ✆ 011/286-6000. For car breakdowns, call the Automobile Association toll-free at ✆ 0800-01-0101.

Hospitals Hospitals with 24-hour emergency rooms include **Johannesburg Hospital** (✆ 011/488-4911) in Parktown, and **J.G. Strijdom** (✆ 011/489-1011) in Auckland Park. To avoid a long wait you'd be better off at a private hospital like **Morningside Clinic** (✆ 011/783-8901), off Rivonia Road, or **Millpark Hospital** (✆ 011/480-5600), off Guild Street, Parktown.

Maps You'll find an array of options at CNA/PNA newsagents. The Witwatersrand Street Guide is the most comprehensive.

Newspapers/Magazines Good dailies include *The Star* and *The Sowetan*. The weekly *Mail & Guardian* is published every Friday and offers an excellent overview of national events (albeit heavily political) and "what's on" listings. The monthly *SA City Life* magazine covers events in Johannesburg, Pretoria, and Cape Town, as well as interesting urban issues. You can purchase these at local newsagents. **Exclusive Books** is a good national chain of bookstores; branches can be found in the malls of Sandton (✆ 011/883-1010), Rosebank Mall (✆ 011/447-3028), and Hyde Park (✆ 011/325-4298).

Post Office Your hotel or guesthouse should be able to assist, or use Amex.

WHERE TO STAY

The following options are in areas where you'll be perfectly safe and, with the exception of the Westcliff, Fairlawns, and the Cottages, within walking distance of some of the city's best restaurants and shops. All can arrange or offer a shuttle service to and from the airport, 25km to 35km (15–22 miles) away—about a 30- to 40-minute drive. Johannesburg is not a popular leisure destination, and hotels generally cater to businessmen, with the Westcliff being the notable exception. If you're looking for a more intimate boutique-style hotel experience, with personalized service, Fairlawns is your best bet, but you may also want to take a look at the **Saxon** in Sandhurst (© **011/292-6000;** www.thesaxon.com; 26 units). An imposing edifice (once the private home of one of South Africa's most successful insurance agents, and where Nelson Mandela wrote *The Long Walk To Freedom* after he split with wife Winnie), the fortresslike house rises from a huge pool floating amid vast green lawns. It's arguably the city's most exclusive hotel (certainly it's most expensive)—this is after all where the likes of Oprah and Charlize Theron prefer to stay, but unless you're a big name, service does not always match the rate (R4,150–R15,900/$515–$1,980), hefty for Johannesburg.

On the other end of the spectrum is the small-town bohemian feel of Melville, with excellent bars and restaurants within walking distance; here you'll get a real sense of outdoor nightlife (as opposed to the predominantly mall culture of the city). It has no luxury accommodations options, however, so it may suit you to just dine here one night.

Casino lovers with limited time should consider booking into the Tuscan-inspired **Palazzo Intercontinental Montecasino** (© **011/510-3000;** from R1,350/$168 double), part of a leisure, entertainment, and retail complex and 15 minutes from the airport, or **Caesars Gauteng Hotel Casino** (© **011/928-1000;** from R735/$90 double), the latest offering from the Caesars World group and only 2 minutes from the airport.

NORTHERN SUBURBS
Very Expensive
The Grace ✸✸✸   Devised as a more intimate alternative to the large city hotel, the family-owned Grace, within walking distance of Rosebank's boutiques, galleries, and art cinemas, is a gracious residence that feels more like a London gentleman's club than a 75-room hotel. In stark contrast to the brutal Hyatt (also in Rosebank) or the over-the-top opulence of the Michelangelo, the Grace is designed to human scale and furnished and finished in tasteful, traditional English style. Wood paneling, floral brocades, generous sofas, gold-framed paintings, and well-thumbed books create a serene, comfortable, and warm atmosphere. The Grace is also generous, with no hidden extra costs—you get complimentary in-room continental breakfasts and a selection of complimentary teas, coffee, and cakes (a slice of the *"melktert,"* a traditional Afrikaans dessert, is a must) served in the library where comfortable sofas invite you to peruse the dailies or books from the ample collection. Small touches like fresh milk and home-baked biscuits, supplied with in-room tea- and coffee-making facilities, as well as the generous size of the comfortable rooms and bathrooms, simply add to this. The service is gracious and personal yet unobtrusive, and the staff do their utmost to ensure your complete comfort. The dining room at the Grace enjoys an excellent reputation (the breakfast buffet is particularly ample and features smoked salmon, ham, and every fresh juice and fruit imaginable), and is regularly included in critics' selections of Johannesburg's top restaurants. The Grace is a great choice, but it's worth bearing in mind that for more or less the same money you could book a luxury room at the Westcliff and enjoy the best view of the city.

54 Bath Ave., Rosebank 2196. © **011/280-7200** or 011/280-7300. Fax 011/280-7474. www.grace.co.za. 75 units. R2,360 ($290) double; R2,860–R3,620 ($355–$450) suite. Children stay free in parent's suite. AE, DC, MC, V. **Amenities:** Restaurant; lap pool; access to Health & Racquet Club; small gym; activity desk; car rental;

VIP limousine; salon; room service; babysitting; laundry; croquet lawn; library; valet parking. *In room:* A/C, TV, minibar, tea- and coffee-making facilities, hair dryer, Internet access.

The Westcliff ★★★   Clinging to the steep incline of Westcliff ridge, this fully walled hillside "village" is, like the Michelangelo, a member of *Leading Hotels of the World*. But while the Michelangelo's focus remains on the business traveler, this is the number-one hotel destination for the well-heeled leisure traveler. Understated elegance is the order of the day, particularly in the "tobacco" rooms, and the palatial marble bathrooms are a real treat. Each room is uniquely positioned and sized, so accommodations options vary considerably. Do insist on a room with a view, preferably with a balcony (units in Villa 4, appropriately named "Cliffside," are recommended, particularly no. 401, 405, 406, 423, or 424; alternatively, try for no. 105, 201, 503, or 605). Hanging on the lip of the large infinity pool, you have Johannesburg spread out before you, and you could easily spend the day gazing at the endless forested canopy of the northern suburbs. Dining areas enjoy the same spectacular views, as does the poolside terrace. Ironically, the hotel's biggest drawback arises from its excellent cliff-side location; in a rather unwieldy arrangement, cars are left at reception and guests are shuttled around by vehicles that regularly traverse the cobbled streets. A complimentary shuttle will take you to the shopping districts of Sandton, Hyde Park, and Rosebank, some 15 minutes away; Melville is a 10-minute drive away.

67 Jan Smuts Ave., Westcliff 2193. © **800/237-1236** in the U.S., or 011/646-2400. Fax 011/646-2666. www. westcliff.orient-express.com. 120 units. R2,470–R3,070 ($300–$380) double; R3,650–R7,310 ($450–$910) suite; R9,480–R11,950 ($1,185–$1,490) penthouse suites. Children 12–18 pay 50%. AE, DC, MC, V. **Amenities:** 2 restaurants; lounge bar; 2 heated swimming pools; 2 plunge pools; golf (enjoy full membership facilities of a nearby club); tennis court; gym; VIP limousine service; business center; salon; 24-hr. room service; babysitting; laundry; film collection and delivery; the *New York Times* by fax; 24-hour on-call doctor. *In room:* A/C, TV/VCR, fax machine, minibar, hair dryer.

Expensive

Fairlawns Luxury Hotel ★★   Located in a peaceful suburb a few minutes' drive from Sandton, Fairlawns, like the Grace, provides generous touches: complimentary tea trays are delivered to your room on request, rooms have complimentary sherry, cars are cleaned overnight, and shoes left outside the door are shined. But the real reason to stay here are the palatial-size (and -styled) rooms. Decorated by owner Anna Thacker, a master at paint techniques and interior detailing, each room has its own individual theme and personality. Personal favorites include the Swedish (pale blue and gold—beautiful!), the French Provincial, the Bismarck, and Louis—truly fit for a king. The Africa suite, one wall of which teems with wildlife, is so big you can barely see the TV from the bed. Fairlawns offers a tranquil respite from the city, with a comfortably furnished terrace (where most meals are served; dinner on request) overlooking the lawn and pool, but some people may find it a little too cut off from the action. *Note:* If Fairlawns is full, they will refer you to **10 Bompas** (© **011/325-2442**), another boutique-style hotel with an excellent reputation—check it out at www. tenbompas.co.za.

Alma Road, Morningside Manor, Sandton 2052. © **011/804-2540/1/2/3.** Fax 011/802-7261. www.fairlawns. co.za. 19 units. R1,850 ($230) double; R2,100–R2,800 ($260–$350) suite. Rates include breakfast. AE, DC, MC, V. Children over age 15 only. **Amenities:** Dining room; lounge; bar; pool; golf, tennis, and squash by arrangement; health spa/gym; secretarial services; laundry; terrace. *In room:* TV, minibar, tea- and coffee-making facilities, hair dryer.

Melrose Arch ★★   The latest addition to the Melrose Arch lineup, this is Jozi's self-proclaimed Hip Hotel, and celebrates the city's newfound confidence and optimism. It's ideal for the young (or young at heart) traveler looking for some action—you're a stroll from some of the city's hippest restaurants and bars—and has a quirky edge that clearly differentiates it from the more established hotels in the city. The concept is clearly based on the Philippe Starck–Ian Schrager look, and though it's not in the same league (and quite derivative), it has plenty of eye-catching elements, like the entrance lobby floor that constantly changes color, the long drapes that hang from oversized chrome coat hangers, and different "mood" elevators for day and night. Guest rooms feature the latest in stylish technology (like flat-screen TVs) and playful decor: wooden parquet flooring vies with block-print carpets, glass-top work stations with exposed brick walls, and chintz drapes with Roman blinds—a mishmash of elements sure to disturb the purist but delight the postmodernist. Separated from the bedroom only by a large curtain, the bathrooms feature deep oval tubs and superb walk-in "rain" showers. Service is patchy; walk the walk or you'll be eyed up and down at the front door by a bouncer-type doorman more concerned with keeping the riff-raff out than helping you with your bags.

1 Melrose Sq., Melrose Arch, Johannesburg 2196. © 011/214-6666. Fax: 011/214-6600. www.proteahotels. com/melrosearchhotel. 118 units. R1,650–R2,100 ($205–$260). AE, DC, MC, V. **Amenities:** Restaurant; 3 bars; pool ; golf and tennis privileges; access to nearby health club; 24-hr. room service; laundry; sound room. *In room:* A/C, TV, DVD-player/hi-fi, dataport, minibar, tea- and coffee-making facility, hair dryer.

Moderate

Villa Via (Value) Considering its location (opposite the Village Walk—one of Sandton's smaller shopping centers, and a few minutes' walk/drive from the Sandton City shopping center) and spacious accommodation (each suite has two or three bedrooms with a separate lounge and well-equipped kitchen), Villa Via offers very good value for money, particularly for families or friends traveling together—a two-bedroom suite with one bathroom can be had for R820 ($100). Fittings and furnishings are all new, and choices are relatively tasteful albeit lacking personality. *Tip:* Each suite has a small basic kitchen—provide a shopping list, and you will have your fridge and cupboard stocked upon arrival.

Corner Rivonia and Linden roads, Sandown, Sandton 2196. © 011/883-0646. Fax 011/883-0772. 20 units. R820–R920 ($100–$112) 2-bedroom units. Rates include continental breakfast, delivered to your room. Children under age 15 stay free. AE, DC, MC, V. **Amenities:** Pool; 24-hr. reception; laundry on request. *In room:* 2 TVs, equipped kitchen, hair dryer.

NORTHWESTERN SUBURBS (MELVILLE)

A good-value option in Melville, within easy walking distance of its many restaurants and bars, is the lovely **Thulani Lodge** (85 3rd Ave.; © 011/482-1106; www.thulanilodge.co.za; from R500/$60 double). It has seven rooms (each with TV, fridge, four-poster beds) to choose from; opt for one in the garden.

Moderate

A Room with a View ☆ This Tuscan-inspired B&B is arguably the best option in Melville, and no doubt the reason that it has expanded from 7 to 12 rooms in 2 years. It's not as ideally placed as Die Agterplaas (see below), but it's still within walking distance of Melville's 50-odd restaurants and bars, including those on 7th Street, a 12-minute stroll away. Your hostess, Lise, is enthusiastic about her neighborhood and happy to make (good) recommendations; she will also arrange to have you dropped off and picked up. The lounges and dining-room areas are a bit overdressed, with eclectic objects and furnishings, but somehow it all works, and most of the bedrooms are fabulously comfortable. Try to book a room on the upper floor—these all have lovely views, mostly of the Melville Koppies Nature Reserve. One of the largest, no. 1, has a big conservatory that leads out onto the balcony, shared with room nos. 3 and 4 (note that no. 4 has a separate bathroom), but a personal favorite remains room no. 2, which offers excellent value at R600 ($75) for two, and has a sweet Juliet balcony.

1 Tolip St., corner 4th Ave., Melville. (©) **011/482-5435** or 011/726-8589. roomview@pixie.co.za. 12 units. R500–R1,000 ($60–$125) double. Rates include breakfast. AE, DC, MC, V. **Amenities:** Lounge/dining areas; pool; laundry; day room. *In room:* TV, minibar, tea- and coffee-making facilities, hair dryer; some with gas fireplaces.

EASTERN SUBURBS (OBSERVATORY)
Inexpensive

The Cottages *★★* *(Kids)* Set at the end of a gravel drive, in luxuriant well-established gardens that cling to Observatory Ridge, these 13 stone-and-thatch cottages are the perfect antidote to anonymous hotel rooms and ideal for long stays. Each cottage is totally unique, featuring either a fireplace (Hideaway), self-catering facilities (Poolview), great garden views (Fisherman's View), or sweeping views of the suburbs (Treetops and Rooftops) or of the ridge (Mountain View). All have private garden areas, with Owl View enjoying the largest—making it popular with parents. Breakfast is served in the garden or in the main house, which dates back to the early 19th century; dinners are offered by prior arrangement (from R65/$8). It's easy to forget that you're in the largest city south of Cairo while walking in the 1-hectare (2½-acre) English garden, which attracts great birdlife, or tackling the adjoining hiking trail to the top of Observatory Ridge. Its only drawback is that it's not within walking distance to restaurants and shops; Sandton, Melville, Greenside, and Parkhurst are a 15- to 20-minute drive away.

30 Gill St., Observatory 2198. (©) **011/487-2829** or 011/648-4279. Fax 011/487-2404. http://users.iafrica. com/m/mc/mckenna. 13 units. R400–R450 ($50–$56) double, including breakfast. Children staying in parents' room R100 ($12). AE, DC, MC, V. **Amenities:** Dining room; rock pool; laundry. *In room:* TV, tea- and coffee-making facilities, hair dryer on request.

NEAR THE AIRPORT

Bear in mind that Johannesburg and Pretoria are only a 30- to 40-minute drive away. Still, if you have a tight transfer or need that extra half-hour of shut-eye, book into the new **Southern Sun Intercontinental** (© **011/961-5400;** www. southernsun.com; R1,750/$215 double), which is within walking distance of both the domestic and international terminals. A cheaper (in every sense) alternative is the **Johannesburg International Airport City Lodge** (© **011/392-1750;** www.bid2stay.co.za; R540/$65 double).

A MOUNTAIN RETREAT

Mount Grace *★★★* It may be a tad off the beaten track, but this romantic retreat is well worth the 1-hour drive from Jo'burg or Pretoria to luxuriate in clear mountain air, relax in the tiptop spa, and savor exquisitely prepared food on a lantern-lit lawn. Besides, the Sterkfontein Caves (part of the Cradle of Humankind, one of Johannesburg's top attractions) are only 15 minutes away, and the De Wildt Cheetah Centre and Lesedi Cultural Village are nearby attractions; Mount Grace also makes the ideal stopover if you're traveling to Sun City or Madikwe Game Reserve. All the typical Grace touches are here—spacious, comfortable rooms; friendly, smart staff; understated luxury; and a thorough understanding of how to make guests feel really pampered. Even the thatched-roof Spa at Mount Grace brings a refreshing "healthy hedonism" ethos to spa culture: After unwinding in the Hydrotherapy Spa Garden—steam bath, cold plunge, Jacuzzi, waterfall, reflexology pool, and flotation pool with African music piped in underwater—you'll be served a glass of good South African wine on the spa veranda. Accommodations are stellar: Thatchstone Village rooms overlook garden pathways, Grace Village rooms have patios with garden views, and Treetops Village, set apart from the rest of the hotel in a forested ravine, offers huge luxury suites with balconies or patios. But it's worth asking for one of the 10 rooms in the recently upgraded Mountain Village that have private heated plunge pools on balconies overlooking the glittering valley below. From there you can walk down steps carved into the hillside to one of two warmly lit restaurants, with both indoor and outdoor seating.

Mount Grace Country House Hotel, Private Bag 5004, Magaliesburg 1791 (take Rte. 24 northwest from Johannesburg). ② 0145/771-350. Fax 0145/771-202. www.grace.co.za. 84 units. R480–R1,100 ($58–$138) per person double. Rates include full breakfast. AE, DC, MC, V. Transportation to and from hotel available. Ask about spa packages. Children 10 and over only. **Amenities:** 2 restaurants; spa cafe; bar and billiard room; 3 swimming pools; tennis; spa; gift shop; mountain biking; croquet lawn; fly-fishing; bird-watching and bird walks; horseback riding, squash, and hot-air ballooning by arrangement; library. In room: TV, minibar, tea- and coffee-making facilities, hair dryer, heated towel racks.

WHERE TO DINE

At last count there were more than 2,000 restaurants in Gauteng, most of them in Johannesburg. Just about every national cuisine is represented; so if you have a particular craving, simply ask your concierge or host to point you in the right direction. Alternatively, take your pick from the listings below, located within reasonable distance from the above accommodations.

If you like cafe society and browsing through menus and venues before deciding on where to hand over your credit card, head for one of the following neighborhoods.

MELVILLE   This is where you'll find some of the city's most established restaurants (with Sam's Cafe, Pomegranates, and Soi the pick of the village), and conveniently placed accommodations options within walking distance. Its popularity means that it can suffer at times from congestion, and its vibrant and varied nightlife options are aimed at attracting the city's trend-setters rather than serious foodies.

GREENSIDE   It's blander than Melville but offers a host of excellent eateries, of which the pick of the bunch is **Yum** (see below). Others worth considering are **Ma Passion** (36 Gleneagles Rd.; ② **011/646-3438**) for West African–inspired flavors like chicken with palm nut sauce; **Icon** (51 Greenfields Rd.; ② **011/646-4162**) for superb, simple contemporary Greek food; and **Karma** (2 Gleneagles Rd.; ② **011/646-8555**) serving Indo-Pakistani fare with a twist (ever tried avocado *korma*?). Greenside's other restaurant strip is Greenway—aside from Bite (see below) recommended options are the appropriately named **Addictions** (137 Greenway; ② **011/646-8981**), an intimate restaurant serving delicious, great-value fusion fare (try the filet with peppercorn and plum sauce with wilted spinach and root vegetables); or an outside table at **Café Flo** or **Ove Flo** (116 Greenway; ② **011/486-4576**), popular for its interesting chalked-up specials (salmon on wasabi mash with watercress sauce) and fabulously innovative pizza combinations (like aubergine and roast lamb).

PARKHURST   This is the city's most relaxed restaurant nexus, and the newest. Locals flock here (particularly to 4th Avenue), not only for its sidewalk restaurants but also for its quaint specialty stores—selling anything from Belgian chocolate to African art or English antiques. Recommended restaurants are **Ruby Grapefruit** (24 4th Ave.; ② **011/880-3673**) for good sushi; **Cilantro** (24 4th Ave.; ② **011/327-4558**) for sublime calamari; or the more fine-dining

Anno Domini (4th Ave. & 13th St.; © **011/447-7634**), where ex-Savoy chef Aristotle Ravagales serves up contemporary European fare in a romantic atmosphere.

NORTHERN SUBURBS (PARKTOWN TO SANDTON)
Expensive

The Butcher Shop & Grill *★★★* GRILLHOUSE "The only vegetarians you'll find in my shop are in the fridge," jokes owner Alan Pick. Pick, who grew up in his parents' butcher shop, specializes in—you guessed it—South African meat, generally considered some of the best in the world. Only "super aged" meat is used (that is, carcasses are hung for 3 days, after which time the rump, filet, and sirloin are "wet aged" for periods varying from 10 days to 2 weeks, and T-bones are "dry aged"). Also available are ostrich and a daily game dish, usually kudu or springbok. *Note:* If the Butcher Shop is full, or you're with kids or based in Rosebank, the wet-aged steaks at **The Grillhouse** (The Firs Shopping Centre; © **011-880-3945**) have been pulling in committed carnivores since 1994; in some ways the restaurant offers a more relaxing atmosphere than that found at the Butcher Shop.

Sandton Sq. (under the Michelangelo Hotel). © **011/784-8676**. www.thebutchershop.co.za. Reservations essential. Main courses from R60 ($7.50). AE, DC, MC, V. Noon–10:30pm daily. No children under age 14.

Linger Longer *★★★* INTERNATIONAL In 1976 Walter Ulz opened his restaurant in a Braamfontein prewar rooming house to much acclaim. Twenty-five years later, having followed big business to the safety of Sandton's suburbs, Ulz is still creating a fine dining ambience that patrons (who include Nelson Mandela) find hard to leave. His legendary fare is truly international, but doesn't attempt to combine different traditions in the same dish (Ulz says fusion food is con-fusion . . .). There are a number of solid French classics, but if you want to globetrot some good options are the fresh oysters served with seafood ceviche (lime and lemon-marinated) on rocket, a rich foie gras terrine with artichoke and green peppercorn, and the veal medallions (stacked with chives, cream cheese, garlic, and fresh basil).

58 Wierda Rd. W, Wierda Valley, Sandton. © **011/884-0465**. Reservations recommended. Main courses from R95 ($12). AE, DC, MC, V. Mon–Fri 12.30–3pm; Mon–Sat 7–10pm.

Moderate

Deluxe *★★* CONTEMPORARY/INTERNATIONAL In a city that has fallen in love with its street life, this is regarded as "the pavement cafe of the moment." Andrea Burgener changes her menu regularly, knowing that fresh, organic ingredients are the key to great food. The decor is delightfully quirky (you can't miss the restaurant—simply look out for the huge plastic yellow duck on the pavement), and her combinations really work—Ethiopian-style kudu

---

(Moments Waiter, There's an Elephant in My Soup . . .

Book a table at the Westcliff (© **011/646-2400**)—either at the Loggia for breakfast or the three-course luncheon, or the poolside terrace for afternoon tea or sundowners—and try to spot an elephant. If it isn't pink, you're looking at the Johannesburg zoo's elephant and rhino enclosure, clearly visible from the hotel's elevated position on the cliff. And if the animals are in hiding, never mind—the view of the urban forest, said to be the largest in the world, is astounding.

(a South African antelope) tartare is legendary; mussels, flown in from the west coast, are served in a Thai-style coconut and saffron sauce, while truffle and pistachio sausages are served on mash with a black-bean brandy sauce. She also serves a mean sake martini, and is famed for her sweet tooth—"deluxe" desserts are just that, the best in town.

Corner of 7th and 3rd aves.; Parktown North. ℂ **011/880-8696**. Reservations essential over weekend. Main courses R42–R65 ($5–$8) (R100/$12 prawns). AE, DC, MC, V. Tues–Sat 12–3pm; Mon–Sat 6.30pm–late. Sun (all-day brunch) 9.30am–4pm.

La Cucina di Ciro ★★★ ITALIAN   Ciro Molinaro's three-star Michelin experience in France's Loire region simply honed his talent for home-cooked Italian fare that locals rate the best in Jo'burg, if not the country (La Cucina was voted one of the country's top 10 in 2002, the only Italian restaurant to make it). It's a totally unpretentious venue (and small, so book) where the focus is firmly on the food: The menu changes weekly, depending on what's in season, but if it's featured do try the roast aubergine and lentil soup, followed by cannelloni with butternut, sun-dried tomato, and ricotta. The menu usually features at least one fish or meat dish to satisfy the carnivores—and if you're lucky, the salmon and spinach lasagna will be it. In summer, be sure to book a table on the pavement and enjoy the balmy highveld temperatures.

17 4th Ave., Parktown North. ℂ **011/442-5346**. Reservations essential. No credit cards. Main courses R50–R80 ($6.50–$10). Mon–Fri 8am–late; Sat 8am–3.30pm.

Moyo World Music Restaurant and Bar ★★★ MODERN PAN-AFRICAN   Generally considered the best African restaurant in the country, the new Moyo sprawls across a multi-storied venue and is frequented by locals and tourists alike; this is a great place to people-watch—even if you don't eat here, come for the mango daiquiris and lounge around in the bar or on the alfresco couches, warmed by wood-burning braziers and blankets in winter. This is Africa, but not as anyone else does it—from the waitron's bright cerise-pink headdresses to the huge Bushman paintings on the adobe-like walls, this is pastiche with a tongue-in-cheek twist. Popular dishes include fragrant North African stews, slow-cooked with ginger, cinnamon, coriander, cumin, and saffron, and served with couscous; the South African venison *bobotie* (a mild, sweetish curry); or the grilled ostrich, prepared with aromatic Ethiopian spices. If you'd prefer something light, the ostrich burger, served on sweet-potato and pumpkin bread, is a good option. More than a restaurant, Moyo's is an experience, particularly on weekends when the best world-music DJs spin tunes from 10pm to 12am.

No 5 Melrose Sq., Melrose Arch. ℂ **011/648-1477/8**. Reservations essential. Main courses R28–R121 ($3.50–$15). AE, MC, V. Daily noon–3pm and 7pm–late.

NORTHWESTERN SUBURBS (MELVILLE & GREENSIDE)
Expensive
Sam's Cafe ★★ MEDITERRANEAN   Simplicity is the key to this elegantly understated restaurant on Melville's trendiest high street. Big glass windows provide ample opportunity to watch the passing parade as you taste a sampling of chef Theresa Beukes' dishes—all conveniently available only in starter portions. The choice is difficult, made more so by the delectable specials, but recommended options include the chilled avocado, red pepper, spring onion, and cucumber gazpacho; the warm prawn and zucchini salad, garnished with basil and sun-dried tomato; and the grilled calamari, served with *peri-peri* (hot chili pepper) jelly. Grilled meats, particularly chicken, can be a little on the dry side.

Tips **Got a Yen for Sushi or a Thing for Thai?**

If you're in the mood for topnotch Japanese or Thai food, head for Sandton. You'll find what is generally considered to be the city's best Japanese restaurant, **Daruma** (🕐 **011/780-5157**), in the Sandton Sun hotel. **Wangthai** (🕐 **011/784-8484**), on the first floor of Sandton Square, is considered one of the best Thai restaurants in the city.

Try the caramelized camembert with fig preserve—a great South African combination—and drink it down with a Vin de Constance, arguably South Africa's best dessert wine. The biggest drawback is the smug maître d', but thankfully, the table waiters are charming.

11 7th St., Melville. 🕐 **011/726-8142**. Reservations essential for window seating. Portions R15–R48 ($1.95–$6.25) (you'll need to order about 3 each). AE, DC, MC, V. Mon–Fri 12:30–2.30pm; Mon–Sat 7–10:30pm.

Yum 🟆🟆🟆 CONTEMPORARY SOUTH AFRICAN You have to book weeks in advance to get a table at this unpretentious and thoroughly charming restaurant—for two years running voted one of the top 10 in the annual "Eat Out" awards, and together with La Cucina considered the best in the city. Owner-chef Dario D'Angeli dazzles with provocative experimentation, producing dishes for the sophisticated palate; his charming mum, Del, greets guests and takes particular pride in running through the specials, her gesticulating fingers capturing the essence of wonderful tastes to come . . . tender oyster filets, marinated in mustard, herbs and red wine, and infused with honey and spices, is a winner, as is the carpaccio of pink salmon, served with a delicate champagne dressing. When it comes to mains, there's no beating the roasted tender duck: deboned, cooked three times to remove excess fat, and served with an apricot glaze and a reduction of molasses and ginger. For a real South African classic with a twist, order the oxtail—braised off the bone with a hint of paprika and served with polenta. It's quite brilliant. Yum also has one of the best wine lists you're likely to find anywhere, and each bottle is affectionately described and matched with suitable dishes. *Note:* At the time of writing, plans were underway for Yum to relocate to a new, nearby venue, so use the online address to plan ahead—you can also use the Web to peruse the latest menu and book in advance.

12 Gleneagles Rd., Greenside. 🕐 **011/486-1645**. www.yum.co.za. Reservations essential. Main courses: R70–R90 ($8.75–$11). AC, DC, MC, V. Tues–Sat 12.30–2pm and 7–10.30pm.

Moderate

Bite 🟆🟆🟆 *Value* ASIAN Bite's minimalist clean-lined interiors—strictly executed in red, white, and black—don't allow for a relaxed long luncheon or romantic dinner, but if you want the proverbial quick bite, this is the place to be (and if the menu doesn't suit, you're in the heart of Greenside's restaurant strip). The menu fuses Japanese, Chinese, and Indonesian cuisines, and there's something here for everyone. Start with tempura prawns and a seared tuna salad in a wasabi sauce, or a combination of salmon sashimi and California rolls, then move on to flat ramen noodles with sweet chili chicken and cashew nuts, or thin ramen noodles with pumpkin, coconut milk, and chili. It's a winning combination of super-fresh ingredients, simple but deft preparations, and excellent value.

137 Greenway, Greenside. 🕐 **011/486-0449**. Main courses R18–R90 ($2.35–$11). DC, DC, MC, V. Mon–Thurs 12-3pm; Mon–Sun 6–10.30pm.

CITY CENTER
Moderate

Gramadoelas SOUTH AFRICAN   For 30 years Eduan Naude and Brian Shalkoff have entertained royals, rock stars, presidents, and audiences from all over Africa in this marvelously cluttered restaurant in Newtown's Cultural Precinct. Not everyone enjoys the food, and the menu sometimes sacrifices excellence in favor of authenticity, but Senator Hillary Clinton apparently loved the mopani worms, and the *mogodu*, a black tripe and wild African spinach stew, is one of Mandela's favorites. For the more timid, there are prawns, and the mild Cape-Malay vegetarian and meat curries. *Note:* If you're keen to try typically South African cuisine (as opposed to fusion), **Baccarat,** in Admiral's Court, Rosebank (© **011/880-1835**), does not have the illustrious history (or guest list) of Gramadoelas, but it's currently considered the better option, and may be more conveniently located.

Market Theatre Complex, Bree St., Newtown. © **011/838-6960** or 011/838-6729. Main courses R50–R150 ($6.50–$19). AE, DC, MC, V. Tues–Sat 12–3pm; Mon–Sat 6.30–11pm.

Inexpensive

Kapitan's ⭐ INDIAN   This is Jozi's oldest restaurant—75-year-old Kapitan remembers Mandela sampling his first Campari here—and it's still going strong, despite the mass exodus of so many businesses from the center to the northern suburbs. Popular with tourists and businessmen from the nearby Anglo-American and De Beers headquarters (they also love the large selection of Cuban cigars), Kapitan's is where you come for a sense of authentic history (the decor has remained pretty much the same since the '50s), and a fiery curry (the chicken or mutton *vindaloo* is a popular choice) washed down with Amstel beer.

11A Kort St., Johannesburg. © **011/834-8048**. Reservations recommended. Main courses R35 ($4.50); prawns R120 $15). AE, DC, MC, V. Mon–Sat 12–3pm.

CITY OUTSKIRTS
Expensive

Cornuti—The Cradle ⭐⭐ FRENCH/ITALIAN   Located on the vast nature reserve The Cradle, part of the Cradle of Human kind World Heritage Site (see "The Cradle: Where Do We Come From?", below), Cornuti has been masterfully designed to blend into the surrounding countryside. The food is good, but it's views of the reserve that are outstanding—as you tuck into chilled vodka-infused melon soup or tear into tiger prawns or venison filet medallions (saturated with a gooseberry and plum flavor), you can watch for passing giraffe, white rhino, zebra, or wildebeest. For a table on the viewing deck outside, however, you'll need to book well in advance. If the views don't suffice, reserve a Cradle game drive or a bush walk with a ranger (R530/$65 and R200/$25, respectively) to explore the grassland plains; or request a visit to one of the Cradle's paleoanthropological digs where excavations are taking place.

Kromdraai Rd. Take R512 to Kromdraai, turn off, then follow signs. © **011/659-1622**. Reservations recommended, particularly for Sun lunch. Main courses R64–R90 ($8–$11). Sun lunch fixed-price menu R150 ($19). AE, DC, MC, V. Tues–Sat noon–3pm and 6:30–10pm; Sun noon–4pm.

THE TOP ATTRACTIONS

Apartheid Museum ⭐⭐⭐   Opposite the Gold Reef City casino is the architecturally inspired Apartheid Museum, built, ironically, with money amassed by the Kroc brothers (owners of the casino) by selling skin-lightening products. That fact shouldn't detract from the experience of interacting with South Africa's recent (and often shameful) history by way of thoughtful multimedia displays and spaces that evoke both oppression (like the 121 hangman's nooses symbolizing the number of political prisoners "accidentally" executed during apartheid rule) and freedom (there is a peaceful park and lake). Give yourself at least an hour to absorb the impressive displays in this world-class museum. It's a harrowing history and thus not advised for children under 10.

6km (4 miles) south of city center. Use directions to Gold Reef City (below), or take Boysens Dr. turnoff (off M1), and follow signs. © 011/309-4700. www.apartheidmuseum.org. Admission R25 ($3); R12 ($1.50) children. Tues–Sun 10am–5pm.

Gold Reef City ★ *Kids*   Six kilometers (4 miles) south of the city center, Gold Reef City is built around the No. 14 Crown mine shaft that began operating in 1887 and by the time of its closure in 1975 had produced over 1,400 tons of gold. A re-creation of the Victorian town of the gold-rush era, the "city" houses a variety of gold-related exhibits and museums of which the most interesting is the 200m (655-ft.) descent into the old mine shaft, after which you can watch demonstrations of gold being poured and minted. Make sure you time your visit to coincide with a performance by the **gumboot and traditional dancers** ★★★—by far the best entertainment on offer (at least for adults). These take place two to three times a day; call for times.

Gold Reef City has benefited enormously from a million-dollar investment project, and during the school holidays its target audience becomes apparent as teenagers jostle for space on rides like the Anaconda roller coaster and Tower of Terror, and toddlers screech as they trundle past on the Prospector Train. A choice of 30 rides means there's something to suit all ages, and adults can take an emotional roller-coaster ride in the adjacent casino, reached via a skybridge, or enjoy a great fine-dining experience in the Three Ships restaurant. The "city"

(*Fun Fact* The Cradle: Where Do We Come From?

"There is more evidence for the origin of humankind in this valley than in any other site in the world," says Dr. Lee Berger, the director of the Wits' (Witwatersrand University) Unit for Research and Exploration in Paleoanthropology. "Who knows what secrets it will still unlock about our common ancestry?" It's incredible to think that 3 million years ago, while cities like New York and London were under permanent ice caps, this very valley was populated with man's ancestors. The **Cradle of Humankind,** as the valley is now known, first leapt to fame in 1947 when Dr. Robert Broom discovered "Mrs. Ples," the first known adult cranium of an "ape man," dating back 2.5 million years, in the **Sterkfontein Caves.** Recently named a World Heritage Site because of its status as one of the most productive paleontological sites in the world, the valley has continued to produce record-breaking finds, including "Little Foot," a complete skull and skeleton found in 1997, in an area still under excavation. In 2003, a team of South African and U.S. scientists, using a revolutionary new dating method, placed the age of "Little Foot" at 4.17 million years old, a million years older than first thought—fueling one of the most strident debates raging in South African science. These are the most easily accessed hominid digs in the world—ironic, really, considering the fact that prior to 1994, evolution was a banned topic in South African schools. To visit, see Sterkfontein Caves, below, or "Cradle of Humankind Tours," under "Guided Tours," earlier in this chapter.

itself is plenty of fun, but it's very much a theme park; for a more authentic experience, visit a real mine (see "Mine & Money Tours," earlier in this chapter).

Tip: It's not really necessary to take one of the well-advertised guided tours to Gold Reef City, as it's a one-stop visit and easy to find if you're in your own car; but if you feel the need, call **Gold Reef Guides** at ✆ **011/496-1400.**

Off Xavier Road (off M1), Ormonde. ✆ **011/248-6800.** www.goldreefcity.co.za. Admission R65 ($8); includes all rides, shows, and entertainment except mine tour, which costs R40 ($8). Free for children under 1.2m (4 ft.). Tues–Sun 9:30am–5pm.

Hector Pieterson Memorial ★★   Erected in memory of the 1976 student protest, when police opened fire on hundreds of Sowetan schoolchildren who were peacefully demonstrating against the use of Afrikaans as a medium of instruction in their schools. Inside are video footage of the event and many moving photographs taken by brave and talented photographers like Peter Mangubane and Sam Nzima, including the infamous shot of Hector Pieterson—one of the young boys who died in a hail of police bullets—being carried by a young man whose face is contorted in disbelief and pain. Hector's sister runs alongside, her mouth a silent wail of grief. The police reported 59 dead; the actual toll was thought to be closer to 500. Children turned on their parents, something hitherto unheard of in traditional society, and destroyed everything they could belonging to municipal authority—schools, post offices, and the ubiquitous beer halls. The police retaliated with brutal assaults, arrests, and killings. These photographs offer a window on the anger, the fear, the aggression, and the grief of these times, after which Soweto and South Africa were never to be the same.

Hector Pieterson Square, Soweto. ✆ **011/536-0611.** R10 ($1.30) entry. Daily 9.30am–5pm.

The Johannesburg Art Gallery ★★   Predictably, the city's first gallery was financed with the sale of a diamond. In 1904 Lady Phillips, wife of the first chairman of the Rand Mines Company, sold her 21-carat ring to purchase three paintings by Wilson Steer. Over the next 5 years she wrangled money from her wealthy connections to purchase more artwork, and commissioned Sir Edwin Lutyens to design the elegant building that now houses her collection. It is unfortunate that the gallery lies in the rather seedy center of town, as it has arguably the best international collection in South Africa, including works by El Greco, Picasso, Rodin, Dalí, and Lichtenstein. But you should have no problem if you drive in, and secure parking is available. Happily, despite ignoring black talent during the apartheid years, the gallery also has a good selection of South Africa's best, including sculptures by Venda artist Jackson Hlungwani and paintings by Helen Sebidi, Alfred Toba, and Gerard Sekoto. The rather boring Flemish and Dutch collections are more than made up for by the Brenthurst Collection of African Art, comprising curios plundered by European explorers in the 19th century, and later collections of traditional southern African artworks.

Joubert Park. ✆ **011/725-3130.** Free admission. Tues–Sun 10am–5pm. To reach the secure parking: From the M1 take the Wolmarans turnoff and turn left, then right onto Wanderers, and second left onto Bok, which runs into Klein; entrance off Klein.

Lesedi Cultural Village ★★   The Lesedi Cultural Village comprises four totally separate homesteads, inhabited respectively by a Zulu, Xhosa, Pedi, and Basotho family, all of whom live here permanently looking after the cows, chickens, and tourists that wander through the veld. The 3-hour tour commences at 11:30am and 4:30pm daily. I recommend choosing the evening experience; it's a great deal more atmospheric at night. On arrival you are given a welcome drink and a 30-minute presentation on these tribes (as well as a short talk on the Ndebele), followed by a guided walk through the four homesteads, which allows for interesting cross-cultural analysis regarding the architectural and social organization and customs of these groups at the turn of the century. The tour does not really cover current lifestyles and customs, so you'll have to ask questions to find out what changes the 20th century has wrought. After this, a traditional singing and dancing session is held in the *boma* (a circular open-air enclosure), and a pan-African buffet meal—representing East, West, North, and South African traditional cuisine—is served. Lesedi is a commercial venture, but if you're yearning to do the cultural village thing, this is a convenient 45-minute trip from Johannesburg. The easiest way to visit is with a tour operator (see "Guided Tours" at the beginning of the chapter); expect to pay about R680 ($85) for the full experience and transfer.

Off the R512; phone for directions. © 012/205-1394. R260 ($32) for tours that take place daily at 11.30am and 4.30pm.

Museum Africa ✿✿✿   Housed in the old Market Building, and part of the cosmopolitan hub that is the Newtown Cultural Precinct, Museum Africa was opened in 1994 as the first national museum to offer a truly modern take on the complex history of South Africa. The best permanent exhibit is "Tried for Treason," an evocative display using video interviews, old radio broadcasts, newspaper headlines, and photographs to tell the tale of the Treason Trial (1956–61), which put, among others, Nelson Mandela behind bars on Robben Island. "Johannesburg Transformations" includes walk-through re-creations of shacks, a miners' dorm, and a *shebeen* (illegal drinking house). As you explore these makeshift rooms, you are accompanied by some well-selected soundtracks from the musical giants that Sophiatown and Soweto spawned, like Miriam Makeba and Hugh Masekela. Museum Africa also houses the **Museum of South African Rock Art,** and the **Bensusan Museum of Photography and Geological Museum.**

121 Bree St. © 011/833-5624. Admission R7 (90¢) adults, R2 (25¢) age 18 and under. Tues–Sun 9am–5pm.

Sterkfontein Caves ✿   Part of the Cradle of Humankind, this treasure trove contains more than 500 perfectly preserved hominid fossils—some of the oldest surviving in the world—that have provided vital evidence on man's evolution. A 45-minute guided tour of the caves takes place every half-hour. Visitors are not taken to the working sites, tour guides are not specialists, and the experience is more about the history of the caves than the history of man. The adjacent **Robert Broom Museum** of fossils is a little rundown, although there are plans to refurbish. A more interesting way to experience the Cradle of Humankind is with a scientist; book a **Palaeo-Tour** (© **082-804-289;** see "Guided Tours," earlier in this chapter).

Sterkfontein Cave Rd. (a 40–60-min. drive from Sandton; call for directions). © 011/956-6342. R15 ($1.90) adults, R6 (75¢) ages 6–14. Tues–Sun 9am–4pm.

MORE ATTRACTIONS: FROM AFRICAN ART TO JO'BURG ZOO

Most city tours kick off from the **"Top of Africa"** ✿✿ (© **011/308-2876;** daily 8am–7pm; R7.50/$1), and with good reason. The top floor of the 50-story Carlton Centre provides great views of the city, and it has a bar should you time your visit at sunset (from 5.30pm in winter) and wish to toast the city of gold as it turns pink. Access is relatively easy: From the M1 follow the M2 East/City signs, take the Rissik Street turnoff, continue along Rissik, and turn left into Marshall, where you'll see the parking sign for the Carlton Towers.

Soweto: South Africa's Original Township

Dispossessed of their land during the 1800s and further reduced to virtual slavery by taxation, thousands of black men were forced to find work in the minefields of eGoli. As more and more settled in inner-city slums, the segregationist government's concerns about the proximity of blacks to white suburbs grew until, in 1930, a solution was found. A farm, 11 miles to the southwest of Johannesburg, was designated as the new township, and blacks living in and around the city were served with eviction papers. It would now take 3 hours to get to work. There were as yet no roads, no shops, no parks, no electricity, no running water. Public transport and policing were hopelessly inadequate. Not surprisingly, most people refused to move; but in 1933 the government declared the Slums Clearance Act and forcibly evicted blacks from the inner cities. Defeated, these new homeless moved in, and Soweto, acronym for the South Western Township, was born, just 18km (11 miles) from Johannesburg. In 1944 James Mpanza led a mass occupation of open land near Orlando, the original heart of Soweto, and within 2 years this, the country's first unofficial squatter camp, housed 40,000 people. Rural poverty meant that Soweto remained a magnet for millions searching for a better standard of living, and today Soweto is arguably South Africa's largest city and home to soccer heroes and politicos, record producers and *shebeen* queens, multimillionaires and the unemployed, murderers and Nobel Peace–Prize winners. Population estimates range from 2 to 4 million; with people mistrusting the reasons for compiling a national census, a proper headcount is virtually impossible.

Very few white South Africans venture here for pleasure, despite the warm welcome Sowetans are famous for and the fact that the few *umlungu* ("whitey") inhabitants of Soweto say they feel safer here than in the suburbs. For most, however, the crime statistics are frightening: Murders are common, and it is estimated that a rape occurs every 30 minutes. For safety and real insight, Soweto is best visited accompanied by a knowledgeable guide. Most operators cover similar ground: the **Mandelas' old home;** a stop at the **Hector Pieterson Memorial** (see above); a drive down **Vilakazi Street** (the only street in the world to have housed two Nobel Prize winners); **Freedom Square,** where the ANC's Freedom Charter was proclaimed to thousands in 1956; and the **Regina Mundi Church,** the "Parliament of Soweto," where the bullet-marked walls are witness to ex-security-police brutality. Recommended operators are **Jimmy's Face to Face Tours** (© **011/ 331-6109;** 3-hr. day tours R240/$30), the more personalized **Imbiza Tours** (© **011/838-2667;** R280/$35, plus R70/$8.50 for lunch), or long-standing Sowetan resident Stella Dubazana (© **011/82-488-1660**), who offers private tours on arrangement. The downside of driving around in a bus armed with a camera is the sense that you are treating people like animals in a reserve. For this reason you are encouraged to get out of the vehicle and talk to the people on the street. It is, after all, a sense of community that distinguishes life in Soweto from that in Johannesburg or Pretoria.

ARCHITECTURE   Buildings worth noting on a short driving tour are the **Rand Club** (Loveday St.; ℂ **011/834-8311;** Mon–Sat 8–4pm, Sun 8–1pm; free admission), where the city's mining magnates, or "randlords," used to congregate and compare (bank) notes, as well as the **Magistrate's Court** (West St.), **Gauteng Legislature** (Harrison St.), **Public Library** (corner Market and Sauer sts.), the **Post Office** (corner Market and Rissik sts.), and the **Rand Supreme Court** (Pritchard St.). Besides the Rand Club, the only place worth stopping is the **Standard Bank Art Gallery** ⚑ (corner of Simmonds and Frederick sts.; ℂ **011/636-4231**), which displays some of the work of the best contemporary South African artists as well as the World Press photography awards. Call ahead to arrange off-street parking.

Diagonal Street ⚑⚑, where you'll find the old beacon marking the southwest corner of the original farm from which Johannesburg grew, is one of the city's most fascinating. In the shadows of striking skyscrapers—the most impressive of which is **De Beers** or **"Diamond House"** (11 Diagonal St.), which was designed to mimic the

> **Fun Fact City Limits**
>
> Note how the skyscrapers suddenly fall away a few blocks south of Commissioner Street? This is because gold-mine tunnels run beneath this part of the city, making the ground highly unstable for high-rise construction.

facets of the gem upon which the company's fortune was built—are myriad street hawkers and tiny shops selling anything from Sotho blankets to traditional medicine *(muti).* The most famous of these is **Museum of Man and Science** (14 Diagonal St.; ℂ **011/836-4470**)—it's worth stopping here to stoop under the herbs, bark, and pungent animal bits that hang like a stalactite forest from the ceiling. The Johannesburg Stock Exchange was located at 17 Diagonal St. until 2000, when it followed the trend started by big business in the late 1980s and relocated to the northern suburbs.

MUSEUMS   Moving west to the **Newtown Cultural Precinct** to view **Museum Africa** (see "Top Attractions," above) you may wish to tour the **SAB World of Beer** (15 President St., Newtown; ℂ **011/836-4900;** Tues–Sat 10am–6pm; 90-min. tour R10/$1.25), which showcases the hops' heritage, from ancient Mesopotamia to a traditional Soweto *shebeen,* and concludes with two complimentary beers. The nearby **Worker's Library Museum** ⚑ (52 Jeppe St.; ℂ **011/834-1609;** daily 8:30am–4.30pm; free admission), housed in a national monument that housed approximately 400 municipal workers from 1910, shows the iniquitous living conditions of migrant labor, including a punitive "lock-up" room.

ART GALLERY   For art aficionados and anthropologists, it's worth arranging a stop at the **Gertrude Posel Gallery** ⚑ on the Wits (Witwatersrand University) campus (Senate House, Jorissen St.; ℂ **011/717-1365**) in Braamfontein (on the outskirts of the city center). The gallery has an extensive collection of tribal art and clothing, exploring how the latter relates to identity, as well as a fascinating display on South African soccer.

After this, take a look at the nearby **Old Fort** (no number), the infamous apartheid prison built in 1899, and site of the newly built **Constitutional Court and Square,** for more fine views of the city.

OUTDOOR PLEASURES   If the concrete jungle (and sad history) starts to get to you, the **Melville Koppies Nature Reserve** ⚑ has a nature trail that ends

Up, Up, and Away

Discover the most picturesque part of Gauteng, the **Magalies River Valley,** with **Bill Harrop's Original Balloon Safaris** (✆ **011/705-3201**), also located northwest of Johannesburg. Flights cost R1,730 ($215) per person, last about an hour, and include sparkling wine (served onboard) and a hot breakfast on landing, as well as transfers from the northern suburbs (an hour away).

at an Iron Age settlement. It's open the first three Sundays of each month (call ✆ **011/788-7571** for times). A guided tour is recommended; call Wendy Carstens (✆ **011/482-4797**). On the northeast corner of the reserve is the city's **Botanical Garden,** which reputedly has the largest rose garden in Africa. The roses are at their best in late September. The garden lies on the banks of the Emmerentia Dam; enter off Thomas Bolwer Street. Guided tours are offered by Jackson Maeta; call ✆ **011/782-7064** for more information. Alternatively, take a stroll or row around **Zoo Lake,** the city's finest park and a great place to take kids. Across the road is the **Johannesburg Zoo** (Jan Smuts Avenue; ✆ **011/ 646-2000;** daily 8:30am–5:30pm; R20/$2.50 adults, R13/$1.60 children), through which you can access the surprisingly popular **Museum of Military History** (✆ **011/646-5513;** daily 9am–4:30pm; R5/75¢). Along with examples of tanks and aircraft (a Messerschmitt Me-262 jet is one of only two to have survived), a submarine, swords, guns, uniforms, and medals from both world wars, it houses mementos from every civil war South Africa has fought.

If you've always dreamed of cuddling with a lion cub, the 494-acre **Lion Park** (✆ **011/460-1814;** 8.30-5; R120/$15 per car) is a 35- to 40-minute drive northwest of Sandton. If you'd like to see more than just lions, the 3,700-acre **Rhino & Lion Nature Reserve** (✆ **011/957-0109;** 8am–5pm; R40/$5), 45 to 50 minutes northwest of Sandton, boasts 30 species. While the buffalo, zebra, wildebeest, and antelope roam free, predators are kept in large enclosures, and it's little more than a comfortable zoo. Be warned, however, that the animals are not as tame as they look: Stepping out of his minibus for a better photo once cost a visitor an arm and a leg—really. If you're there on a Sunday, coincide your visit with the nearby **Heia Safari Ranch** ✦ (✆ **011/659-0605;** R145/$18 per person including barbecue), where Mzumba tribal dances take place from 2 to 4:30pm. Unless you're obsessed with spotting lion, the best option of all the above is lunch and a game drive, bush walk, or horse trail at the **Cradle Reserve.**

SHOPPING—FLEA MARKETS TO HIGH-END CRAFTS

Johannesburg attracts people from all over the continent with one sole purpose: to shop till they drop. To that end the city has more than 20 malls to choose from, but the best atmosphere by far is found in **Rosebank,** which has plenty of outdoor areas to break the monotony of mall shopping as well as a good selection of essentials such as travel agents, music, book, fashion, and crafts shops (see below). The rooftop at **Rosebank Mall,** which is open every Sunday and public holidays from 9:30am to 5pm, hosts the city's best market. The largest flea market, and a great deal closer than tacky Bruma Lake (it's 3 min. west of Sandton), is located at the **Randburg Waterfront** ✦ (✆ **011/789-5052;** www.rwaterfront.co.za). The flea market has a selection of 350 stalls, and the Waterfront has plenty to entertain kids, but if you have a critical eye, you're likely to return to your hotel room exhausted and empty-handed.

CITY CENTER & SURROUNDS The **Newtown Cultural Precinct** has a small market that operates daily, but the best shop in Newtown is the **Bus Factory** (1 President St.; ☎ **011/834-9569;** Tues–Fri 11am–6pm; Sat 10am–4pm), located in an old transport depot that was revamped as part of the regeneration of Newtown. Administered by the Craft Council, under the excellent curatorship of Susan Sellschop, the Bus Factory showcases the finest crafts pieces available in the country. Other places of interest in the city include **Diagonal Street**—look for Sotho blankets—and the **Mai Mai Bazaar** under the M1. The latter sells mostly to the Zulu community, and you're best off visiting here with a guide.

Less than 1km (just over a half-mile) from Newtown (follow Jeppe St. into Fordsburg) is the **Oriental Plaza shopping center** ✦, where Johannesburg's shrewd Indian traders barter and cajole. Look for fabrics, cotton clothing, brasswares, and, of course, spices. This is also a great place to sample *samoosas,* fried meat- or vegetable-filled pastry triangles. A stone's throw from the Plaza is the **Bag Factory** (10 Minaar St.; ☎ **011/834-9181;** www.bagfactoryart.org.za), an art gallery where standards vary but prices are more than reasonable. Also known as the Fordsburg Artists' Studios (FAS), it was a dilapidated ex-bag-factory building until being converted to a multicultural studio facility for professional artists.

NORTHERN & NORTHWESTERN SUBURBS Rural Craft ✦✦ (☎ **011/788-5821**), in Rosebank's Mutual Gardens, Shop 42E (next to the House of Coffee), markets goods on behalf of the Crafts Association of South Africa, and all profits are returned to the communities. Also in Mutual Gardens is **Afrika Dijalo** (☎ **011/447-9304**), where you can find a good selection of arts and crafts from all over Africa. In nearby Mutual Square is **CD Warehouse,** where staff will assist with a selection of African music. Fashionistas looking for distinctive "where-did-you-get-that?" designer items need to head for The Zone@Rosebank to **The Space** (Lower Level; ☎ **011/327-3640**) or to **Stoned Cherrie** (Upper Level; ☎ **011/447-9629**) for the best Afro-chic threads in town. For a more serious selection of South African art, visit the **Everard Read Gallery** ✦ (6 Jellicoe Ave., Rosebank; ☎ **011/788-4805**), considered the best commercial art gallery in the country, but make sure your wallet is bulging. More world-class collectors' pieces by South African artists are available at the **Kim Sacks Gallery** (153 Jan Smuts Ave., Parkwood; ☎ **011/447-5804**), and the nearby **Goodman Gallery** (163 Jan Smuts Ave.; ☎ **011/788-1113**). Back in Sandton, take a look at **Gallery on the Square** (in Sandton City Mall; ☎ **011/784-2847**)—particularly the beautifully crafted Nesta Nala beer vessels, which will run you anywhere between R1,850 ($230) and R2,100 ($260). Then head for the **African Feelings Artworks,** a gallery 100% owned and operated by black South African women who have created a vital link between rural artists and crafters and commercial buyers (154 Linden St., Sandown; ☎ **011/884-1148.**

JOHANNESBURG AFTER DARK
THE PERFORMING ARTS
The city has two main theaters to choose from. The **African Bank Market Theatre,** Bree Street, Newtown Cultural Precinct (☎ **011/832-1641**), is famous for having spawned a generation of protest theater, and is likely to have a good selection of local talent. The **Civic Theatre,** Loveday Street, Braamfontein (☎ **011/403-3408;** www.showbusiness.co.za), is one of the largest and most technologically advanced theaters in the country; this is where large-scale musicals, operas, dance, and orchestral music are performed.

Smaller theaters that mostly focus on cabaret shows and music revivals include the **Barnyard Theatre,** Broadacres shopping center, Cedar Avenue, Fourways (② **011/467-9333**) and **Off-Broadway,** Grant Avenue, Norwood (② **011/403-1563**). Another option is the **Liberty Theatre on the Square** (Sandton Square; ② **011/883-8606**; www.at.artslink.co.za/~tots).

Big shows can also be found in the lavish casinos springing up all over Johannesburg, including **Pieter Toerien's Montecasino Theatre,** William Nicol Drive, Fourways (② **011/511-1818**), set in a Tuscan-themed casino village; and the **Globe Theatre,** Gold Reef City (② **011/248-5168**).

For current listings for all these venues and more, check out the daily "Tonight" section in *The Star,* and the weekly *Mail & Guardian* (www.mg.co.za). Tickets for most shows can be booked and paid for by phone; call **Computicket** (② **011/340-8000;** www.computicket.com).

THE CLUB, PUB & MUSIC SCENE

If you like to club- or bar-hop, there are several areas where you will find a concentration of them. The most recent is **Melrose Arch,** a newly developed playground for Johannesburg's rich and famous and their friends, with stylish restaurants and bars lined up along one street, well-lit with plenty of parking. **Melville,** close to central Johannesburg, features a bewildering variety of restaurants and bars within walking distance of each other, both classy and down-to-earth, in old Melville (7th St.) or new Melville (Main Ave.). **Newtown,** home of the Market Theatre, the Horror Café, and Carfax (see below), are all within a block or two of each other. In the northern suburbs you can opt for **Rosebank.** Catch an art movie in the Mall before heading for the Zone across the road, a bright, modern center with more movie theaters, bars, and restaurants.

If you're a jazz aficionado, some names to watch for are Gloria Bosman, African Jazz pioneers, McCoy Mrubata, Zim Ngqawana, Louis Mhlanga, Moses Khumalo, and Pops Mohamed. Kwaito acts to look for are Brothers of Peace (BO), Mandoza, Mafikizolo, Zola, and Bongo Maffin.

Clubs generally start up at around 11pm and close between 4am and 7am; most offer secure parking for a small donation to the freelance guards who watch over cars while their owners dance the night away.

Live Music Bars

The Bassline ★★★   A popular live-music venue dedicated to local talent, this bar gives space to blues and rock bands, jazz stars, and world music. Open through the week with an ever-changing lineup catering to diverse audiences, this is a regular hangout for Jo'burg's multiracial intelligentsia. 7 7th St., Melville. ② 011/482-6915, www.basslinejazzclub.co.za. Cover R30–R50 ($3.75–$6.50).

The Blues Room ★★★   In the heart of Sandton, this upmarket nightclub serves up blues, jazz, fusion, comedy, and even rock 'n' roll on most nights for an older and mostly white crowd. Village Walk Mall, corner Rivonia and Maude sts., Sandton. ② 011/784-5527, www.bluesroom.co.za. Cover R50 ($6.50).

Kilimanjaro ★★★   The trendiest, classiest spot for Africa's hip and well-heeled crowd. It has a restaurant, bars on two levels, and a stage where jazz, kwaito, and other local acts perform over weekends. Melrose Arch, Melrose. ② 011/834-9187. Cover depends on events.

Kippies ★★   This small, laid-back downtown venue in the Market Theatre complex—the city's oldest jazz club—gets crowded when big names in South African jazz play to passionate crowds on Fridays and Saturdays and sometimes during the week. Market Theatre, Bree St., Newtown. © 011/833-3316, www.kippies.co.za. Cover around R40 ($5).

Clubs

115 Anderson Street ★★   Located in the center of town, this small but lively venue throbs with drum 'n' bass and deep house on Fridays. On Sundays it is Remedy from 7pm to 2am, a gay club night with funky, uplifting, vocal and tribal house. 115 Anderson St., Johannesburg Central. © 011/331-2878. Cover from R40 ($5).

Bitch ★   The city's biggest gay club, open on Saturdays, with commercial music on the main floor and cutting-edge beats in the basement. Corner of Hendrik Verwoerd Drive and Jan Smuts Ave., Randburg. © 082/775-9715, www.clubbitch.co.za. Cover from R20–R40 ($2.60–$5).

Café Vogue ★★★   A trendy crowd flocks here on Thursdays (R&B and hip-hop), Fridays (fusion), and Saturdays (disco and French house). The music is fine and the cocktails are cool. Corner of 9th St. and Wessels Rd., Rivonia. © 011/728-3448. Cover from R30–R60 ($3.75–$7.50).

Carfax ★★★   Set in an old warehouse, this super-cool venue caters to discerning clubbers with a range of off-the-beaten-track events taking place almost every weekend, from performance art to French-house parties and hip-hop and jungle nights. 39 Pim St., Newtown. © 011/834-9187. Cover depends on events.

Horror Café ★★   With brilliant decor consisting of horror and science-fiction movie memorabilia, this vibrant nightspot features reggae, ragga, and dancehall on Thursdays and usually jazz, world music, and African rhythms over weekends. 15 President St., Newtown. © 011/838-6735. Cover from R30 ($3.75).

Insanity ★★   Downtown Jo'burg comes alive on Fridays with a multiracial crowd grooving to deep house, drum 'n' bass and hip-hop, as well as graffiti, breakdancing, and skating displays. 248 Jeppe St., Johannesburg Central. © 011/336-1026, www.insanity.co.za. Cover from R30 ($3.75).

2 Pretoria

50km (31 miles) N of Johannesburg

An almost uninterrupted ribbon of development connects Johannesburg and Pretoria, yet Pretoria's atmosphere is much more laid-back, and, some would say, comparatively dull. But the administrative capital of South Africa, once an Afrikaner stronghold, has become home to a much more cosmopolitan population since Nelson Mandela was inaugurated the first democratically elected president at its Union Buildings, and a number of good restaurants in particular cater to the burgeoning diplomatic community.

Pretoria has some fine lodging options, but frankly, by staying here you miss out on Jo'burg's excitement and energy, not to mention its better choice of accommodations. Still, the city and its outlying areas have enough in the way of cultural and historical sights to fill a full day trip, particularly in October and November, when its 70,000 jacarandas are in full bloom, and the streets are carpeted in purple blossoms.

ESSENTIALS

VISITOR INFORMATION   The **Pretoria/Tshwane Information Centre** (© 012/337-4337), on Church Square, is open from 8am to 4pm Monday and Friday. The staff can supply brochures and maps, as well as a free dining magazine *Be My Guest.*

GETTING THERE   By Plane   Pretoria is some 50km (31 miles) from Johannesburg International Airport. A **Pretoria-Airport bus shuttle** (© 012/ 343-1179; bookings **084-556-2048**) connects the airport to the tourist office in Church Square every hour, from 6am to 7pm, and costs R120 ($15) per person. A taxi to the center should cost about R250 ($30).

By Car   From Johannesburg take the M1 north; this becomes the N1 to Pretoria.

By Train & Bus   Intercity buses and **trains** arrive at the Pretoria Station (© 012/315-2757), another Herbert Baker design, located on Railway Street. Trains arrive from Johannesburg, Cape Town, Nelspruit (near Kruger Park), Durban, and Port Elizabeth. Beware of pickpockets and muggers.

GETTING AROUND   The center of town is easily walked, but renting a car or using a tour operator is the best way to see sights like the Voortrekker Monument and Cullinan Mine. Municipal buses pass nearby sights like the Botanic Gardens, Art Museum, and Union Buildings. The **bus terminal** and information is on Church Square (© **012/308-0839**). You'll usually find a few **taxis** waiting on the Square; alternatively call **Rixi Mini Cabs** at © 012/325-8072 or **SA Taxi** at © 012/320-2075. For **rental-car** options from the airport, see "Johannesburg: Getting Around," earlier in this chapter. In Pretoria, contact **Avis** (© 012/301-0700) or **Budget** (© 012/341-1143).

GUIDED TOURS   Ulysses Tours & Safaris (© 012/344-4377) conducts excellent tours of the city, as well as excursions to Cullinan Diamond Mine, De Wildt Cheetah and Wildlife Centre, Soweto, Gold Reef City, Lesedi Cultural Village, Sun City, and Pilanesberg National Park. They will also arrange overland packages, luxurious rail safaris, and tours to Mpumulanga and KwaZulu-Natal. For more options, see "Johannesburg: Guided Tours," earlier in this chapter. Specialist **Leone Jackson** offers **Baker's Dozen** ⭐ (© 012/344-3197), a lecture-type tour that focuses on the mythology and symbols in the work of Sir Herbert Baker (known, together with Lutyens, as the great imperial architect and one of South Africa's most prolific), particularly his Union Buildings, which Leone is passionate about. She also offers in-depth tours of Melrose House. Tours of the Pretoria townships (black suburbs) are not as commercialized as those that visit Soweto townships, but they can also be a little disorganized— pick up the "Moatwana" brochure from the tourist office to find out more about these tours and operators.

CITY LAYOUT   Sights in Pretoria's **city center** can all be explored on foot, including the zoo, just north of the center. The area from the Transvaal Museum in **Paul Kruger Street** is now a Museum Mall, with paved walkways and signs to direct you to attractions. You can catch a bus northeast from Church Square to the Union Buildings, located in **Arcadia**, the suburb in which most of the embassies and consulates are situated, as well as the Pretoria Art Museum. East of the city are the suburbs of **Sunnyside** and **Hatfield**, where most of the city's nightlife options and restaurants are. Southeast of the center lies the upmarket suburb of **Brooklyn**. Together these suburbs form the nucleus of the "Ambassadorial Belt," named for the many embassies and diplomats housed here. South of the city is the Voortrekker Monument, built on a hill, and visible for miles around.

Tip: The center of the city is not as safe as it used to be. Be on the lookout, don't carry obvious valuables, and don't explore on foot after office hours.

EXPLORING THE CITY ON FOOT

Pretoria grew around the diminutive **Church Square** ⭐⭐⭐, which is surrounded by an array of impressive buildings that were funded by the discovery

Central Pretoria

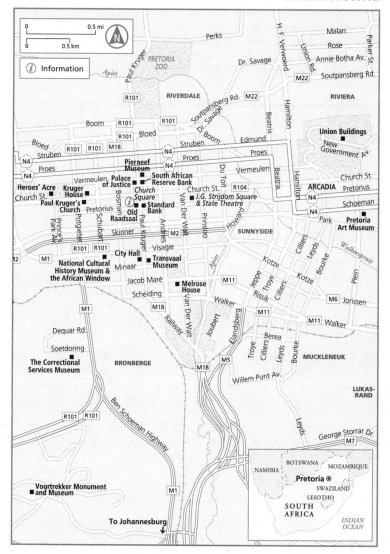

of gold in 1886; it makes sense that a walking tour start here. In the center of Church Square is Anton van Wouw's **statue** of a dour Paul Kruger, facing north (no doubt away from the British). Kruger was proclaimed head of the ZAR (Zuid Afrikaanse Republiek) in the Square no less than four times. The house museum of the sculptor—who between 1890 and 1930 was responsible for most of the state-funded sculptures of cheerless Afrikaner leaders—is at 299 Clark St., Brooklyn (© 012/460-7422; Mon–Fri 10am–4pm; free admission).

After visiting the tourism office, located in the 1896 **Netherlands Bank Building,** pop in at neighboring **Café Riche** (© 012/328-3173; 2 Church Sq.), Pretoria's oldest cafe.

On the southwest corner is the **Old Raadsaal,** completed in 1891; directly opposite are the **Palace of Justice,** on the northwest corner, and the original **South African Reserve Bank** (like the Union Buildings, designed by Herbert Baker). East of this are a number of banks; **Cuthberts Corner,** dating back to 1904 when George Heys (of **Melrose House**) used to run his coaching operation from here; and the neoclassical **Standard Bank,** built in 1935.

West of the Square, on Church Street, is **Kruger House** (see below) and **Heroes Acre,** the burial place for a number of historical figures. Moving east down Church Street you'll come across **Strijdom Square,** where the ugly bust of even uglier former prime minister J. G. Strijdom, a staunch supporter of white rule in the 1950s, came tumbling down on May 31, 2001, exactly 40 years after South Africa was declared a republic. (This name has come to have a more sinister connotation since 1993, when namesake Barend Strijdom opened fire here on random black targets. Despite showing no remorse, he was subsequently released under political amnesty.)

Five blocks north of Church Square, along Paul Kruger Street, is Boom Street; turn right here for the **zoo** or left to reach **Marabastad,** where Pretoria's Indian community trades. Alternatively, move south down Paul Kruger to the **Transvaal Museum,** opposite City Hall—the two statues outside, incidentally, are of Marthinus and Andries Pretorius, the Trekker after whom Pretoria was named. Two blocks west of here, on Schubart Street, is **African Window,** Pretoria's modern cultural history museum. Or go south for 2 blocks from the Transvaal, turn left onto Jacob Mare, to find **Melrose House,** opposite Burgers Park. For more on the sights mentioned in this tour, see below.

THE TOP ATTRACTIONS

The African Window ★★   This relatively new exhibition center of the National Cultural History Museum attempts to celebrate the diverse cultures that make up the South African community. One such successful display is **"People's Choice,"** in which selected South African groups (from schoolchildren to church groups to old-age pensioners) were given the opportunity to choose items (from a range of 3,000 museum-owned objects) to display in selected themes. The objects all have the same function but different form; themes are simple, such as "cooking implements" or "toys," and provide tactile proof of the heterogeneous nature of the Rainbow Nation.

Enter from 149 Visagie St. ✆ 012/324-6082. Admission R8 ($1). Open daily 8am–4pm.

Kruger House ★★   Kruger House (1884) is on every tour group's itinerary, but because most of the furnishings are simply of the period, rather than the very things Paul and his wife lived with, the house does little to conjure up the spirit of the man (for this a guided tour, available for R15/$1.95, is well-advised). A boy during the arduous Great Trek north, and present at the Battle of Blood River, this first president of the ZAR (Zuid Afrikaanse Republiek) was known as a pious, stern Calvinist. He was also oddly approachable, and would hold court on his veranda, chatting to anyone passing by—provided they were white, of course. Here are personal pieces, including his pipes, spittoons, and the knife he used to amputate his thumb after a hunting accident; but the best exhibit is a photograph of the cantankerous old codger sitting next to the stone lions that still guard the entrance to the house. Opposite is the church in which he preached.

Church St. W. ✆ 012/326-9172. Admission R12 ($1.50) adults, R5 (65¢) children. Tour R15 ($1.95). Mon–Fri 8:30am–4:30pm; Sat–Sun 9am–4:30pm.

Melrose House ★★★   This neo-baroque mansion—a cross between English Victorian and Cape Dutch styles—was built in 1886 for George Heys, who made his fortune in stagecoach transportation. Melrose House has been carefully restored to ensure its authenticity and, unlike that of many other South African house museums, the furnishings have not changed much since the Heys family lived here. During the Anglo-Boer War (1899–1902), the house was requisitioned by the British, and the Treaty of Vereeniging, which marked the defeat of the Boers for the second time at the hands of the English, was signed at this dining-room table on May 31, 1902. The house often hosts exhibitions, and you can take tea and scones in the Outdoor Room.

275 Jacob Mare St. ℂ 012/322-2805. Admission R5 (65¢) adults, free for children under 6. Tues–Sun 10am–5pm.

The Pretoria Art Museum ★★   If you're an art lover, this showcase of South Africa's rich and varied talent, in refreshingly bland spaces that allow the art to dominate, is not to be missed. The first museum to focus on South African art, this now houses the best collection of work by white South African artists—it has an even better collection of Pierneefs than the Pierneef Museum on Vermeulen Street. Curators, who are to be commended for their taste, have in the past decade made great strides in collecting black artists as well, including the celebrated Sekoto and Ephraim Ngatane. Currently the museum has more than 3,000 artworks, which are regularly circulated by creating themed exhibitions. The prebooked guided tour (R5.20/65¢) is recommended.

Arcadia Park, corner of Wessels and Schoeman sts. ℂ 012/344-1807. Admission R3 (40¢) adults, R2 (25¢) children. Tues and Thurs–Sat 10am–5pm; Wed 10am–8pm; Sun 12–5pm.

The Union Buildings ★★   This is another attraction that is on every tour group's agenda. With the best views of the city, the Union Buildings are a great place to orient yourself, even though access has become much more restricted since the inauguration of Thabo Mbeki. Probably the best-known creation of prolific "British Imperial" architect Sir Herbert Baker, the buildings—the administrative headquarters of the South African government and the office of the president since 1913—are generally considered his finest achievement. The office-block wings are said to represent the British and Afrikaner people, linked in reconciliation by the curved amphitheater. African natives were, of course, not represented; nor were they allowed to enter the buildings except to clean. In 1994 the buildings and gardens were the scene of huge emotional jubilation as everyone from Castro to then vice-president Gore witnessed the inauguration of Mandela, South Africa's first black president, and African praise-singers in traditional garb exorcised the ghosts of the past. Visitors are allowed to walk along Government Avenue, the road that traverses the facade, but entrance is only gained by those on official business. Anyone interested in a truly in-depth interpretation of the symbols and mythology of the building and its maker should contact tour guide Leone Jackson (ℂ **012/344-3197**).

Meintjieskop Ridge. ℂ 012/325-2000. Accessed 24 hr.; no entry free.

Voortrekker Monument and Museum ★★   In 1938 the secret Afrikaner *Broederbond* (brotherhood) organized a symbolic reenactment of the Great Trek, and sent a team of ox-wagons from Cape Town to Pretoria to celebrate its centenary. By the time the wagons reached Pretoria, more than 200,000 Afrikaners had joined, all of whom camped at Monument Hill, where the foundation stones for a monument were laid. Ten years later, the monument was completed,

and the Afrikaner Nationalist Party swept to power. This massive granite structure, sometimes compared irreverently to a large Art Deco toaster, dominates the
skyline at the southern entrance to the city. Commemorating the Great Trek, in
particular the Battle of Blood River, fought on December 16, 1838, the monument remains hallowed ground for many Afrikaners. Every year on that date,
exactly at noon, a ray of sunlight lights up a central plaque that reads WE FOR
YOU SOUTH AFRICA." The "we" refers of course to Afrikaners—in the marble
frieze surrounding the lower hall depicting the Trek and Battle, you will find no
carvings of the many black slaves who aided the Boers in their victory.

The museum below has memorabilia relating to the Great Trek; most interesting is the "female" version of the monument frieze—huge tapestries depicting a romanticized version of the Great Trek's social events. Even more
interesting than this sanitized take on the pioneer days are the photographs of
the "tannies" (literally "aunties," an Afrikaans term of respect) who created these
tapestries. They are the perfect foil to the Afrikaner men: ladies plaiting threads
while the men wrest with stone in the monument.

6km (4 miles) south of city. © 012/326-6770. Monument admission R6 (80¢) per car, R20 ($2.60) per adult,
R5 (60¢) per child. Daily May–Aug 8am–5pm; Sept–April 8am–6pm.

OTHER ATTRACTIONS

The Correctional Services Museum ⚡   This museum can be easily taken
in on the way to the Voortrekker Monument. A frightening array of hand-fash-
ioned weapons (even a toilet seat, sharpened, can be life-threatening!), as well as
artworks made by prisoners are displayed—make sure the resident guide shows
you the ingeniously hidden *dagga* (marijuana) pipe in the model train. There is
also a replica of Mandela's cell on Robben Island.

Prison Reserve, Potgieter St. © 012/314-1766. Free admission. Mon–Fri 9am–3pm.

The Pretoria Zoo *(Kids*   The 3,500 animals residing here may be living in one
of the largest zoos in the world (75 hectares/185 acres), but considering the relative proximity of vast game reserves, a sad air of imprisonment still pervades. It
is, however, touted as one of the best in the world—you can catch a cableway
across the length of the zoo, letting you view the animals from the air (a big hit
with kids), or whiz around in a hired golf cart (R60/$7.50/hour), and the zoo is
home to a number of rare mammals you're unlikely to see elsewhere (including a
few endangered South American species like the maned wolf). The night tours,
where you can watch the zoo's nocturnal creatures at play, are recommended.

Off Boom St. © 012/328-3265. R27 ($3.25) adults, R17 ($2) children. Open daily 8am–6pm. Night tours
(book in advance) take place at 6.30pm on Wed, Fri, and Sat.

Transvaal Museum ⚡   The whale skeleton erected outside this natural science
museum—Pretoria's oldest—is one of its most impressive exhibits. An uninspir-
ing selection of stuffed animals follows, and many displays resemble high-school
projects. However, it's worth seeking out **"The Genesis of Life"** ⚡⚡ on the second floor, an exhibition that relates to the development of early man, much of it
based on fossil finds at the Sterkfontein and Kromdraai caves; it's awe-inspiring
to realize you are looking at remains that are more than a million years old. The
Geoscience Museum is worth a quick look just to marvel at the earth's myriad
colors and textures. **Robert's Bird Hall** is billed as a haven for bird-lovers, but I
suspect most birders would find this collection of very dead birds depressing.

Paul Kruger St. © 012/322-7632. Admission R8 ($1) adults, R5 (65¢) children. Mon–Sat 9–5; Sun 11–5.

FARTHER AFIELD

Cullinan Diamond Mine Tours ⭐   Yielding an average 2 million carats a year since 1902, the town's Premier Mines is one of the richest diamond mines in the world, and is still producing finds. The 2-hour surface-mine tours include a video of the mining process, a look at the Cullinan Big Hole (40 hectares/100 acres in area, and 500m/1,640 ft. deep), and displays of uncut diamonds, as well as replicas of the world's most famous diamonds—the Cullinan, Centenary, and Premier Rose were all unearthed here. The Cullinan, at 3,106 carats the world's largest diamond, was presented to Edward VII by the Transvaal government. It was divided into nine jewels, and the 530-carat Great Star of Africa (the largest cut diamond in the world) and the 317-carat Lesser Star of Africa are now on display in the Tower of London, in the Royal Scepter and Imperial State Crown. You'll find a number of places to eat here (the Sir Thomas Cullinan is currently your best bet), some of which are housed in original century-old buildings.

Note: A truly authentic introduction (though it can be daunting) is the **Cullinan mine descent** ⭐⭐⭐, where you actually descend the working mine shaft to see what it's like in tunnels some 2,500 feet below the surface of the earth. This tour is only offered on the fourth Friday of every month (8am–12.30pm; R90/$11). Only 15 persons are allowed, so you'll need to book well in advance. See "Guided Tours: Mine & Money Tours" at the beginning of the chapter for more details.

95 Oak Ave., Cullinan (50km/31 miles east of Pretoria). © 012/734-0081. Booking essential. Admission R38 ($4.75). Tours at 10:30am daily; Mon–Fri at 2pm. Please note: Children under age 10 are not admitted.

De Wildt Cheetah and Wildlife Centre ⭐   This facility is internationally renowned for successfully breeding and researching endangered species, including cheetah, king cheetah, brown hyena, and the African wild dog—with between 3,000 and 5,000 left in the world, the latter is Africa's most endangered predator. The 3-hour guided tours are by arrangement only; call ahead.

Off Pretoria N. Rd. [R513], Farm #22 (about 45 min. north of Pretoria city center). © 012/504-1921/2. R130 ($16). Tues, Thurs, and Sat–Sun at 8:30am and 1:30pm. Children under age 6 not admitted.

Doornkloof/Jan Smuts House Museum ⭐   Jan Smuts, one of South Africa's most enlightened leaders and a man who was often accused of focusing too much on affairs outside of the country (much like the current president Mbeki), lived in this humble wood-and-galvanized-iron home from 1909 to 1950. Rooms are furnished pretty much as they were during his life, and the guided tours (R10/$1.30) offered by Elizabeth Eltze provide anecdotal insight into one of the world's most visionary statesmen.

Take Irene Rd. off the M1, follow signs to Doornkloof (16km/10 miles south of Pretoria city center). © 012/667-1176. R5 (65¢) adults, R3 (40¢) children. Mon–Fri 9:30am–4:30pm; Sat–Sun 9:30am–5pm.

WHERE TO STAY

With Johannesburg becoming an increasingly safer option than it was, say, 4 years ago, as well as being a truly vibrant and energetic city, it seems unnecessary to stay in Pretoria anymore, although it does have some great sights (see above) and restaurants (see below) that make it perfect for a day trip. That said, accommodations are geared very much toward the diplomatic market, so if you're here on business, you have a number of options besides standard hotels, such as comfortable apartments with hotel-type facilities or guesthouses run like small hotels; prices for these are also very reasonable. Most are located in the "Ambassadorial Belt" (Arcadia, Hatfield, Sunnyside, and the up-market suburb of Brooklyn), which are at most a 10-minute drive from the city center.

Driving from Johannesburg to Cape Town

You have two choices should you decide to drive from Jo'burg to Cape Town. You can drive directly south on the N1 to Cape Town, overnighting at Bloemfontein or at the Karoo National Park (2km/1¼ miles south of Beaufort West); this will take approximately 13 to 14 hours. Another alternative, time allowing, is to travel southwest via the N12, overnighting at Kimberley, where you can take in some diamond history before heading south, where the N12 meets up with the N1 at Three Sisters, some 70km (43 miles) north of Beaufort West. With no sightseeing on the agenda, this should take 15 hours. But if you decide to take your time and see the sights, consider the following places to stay and visit:

VIA KIMBERLEY   Kimberley is approximately 5 hours from Johannesburg, and 10 hours from Cape Town. If you choose to overnight here, book a room at **Edgerton House** (5 Edgerton Rd., Belgravia, 1km/just over a half mile southeast of the center, along Du Toitspan Road; ℭ **053/831-1150**), where most of Kimberley's wealthiest families lived at the turn of the 20th century. The Edgerton House is now an elegantly restored national monument (distinguished guests include Mandela); from R590 double ($73). Opposite is the **McGregor Museum** (ℭ **053/842-0099**), once a sanitarium; within walking distance is the **Duggan-Cronin Gallery,** where you can view a fascinating collection of century-old photographs. You can take a walking tour of Belgravia suburb; get maps at the Edgerton or the Kimberley Tourism Office. If you decide to spend another night—and you may, because there's plenty to see here—check out the excellent **Kimberley Mine Museum,** site of the largest

Top among the recommended lodgings in Pretoria is the **Illyria House** ✦✦✦ (327 Bourke St., Muckleneuk 0002; ℭ **012/344-4641; R2,450/$305**), a grand colonial manor house and a favorite of CEOs and state dignitaries from around the world. A less-expensive option is the **Courtyard at Arcadia** ✦ (corner of Hill and Park sts., Arcadia 0001; ℭ **012/342-4940;** www.citylodge.co.za; R620–R1,100/$75–$135), built around a lovely turn-of-the-20th-century manor house; its spacious suites make it a good choice for families. For good value and a great location, Pretoria's oldest hotel, the **Victoria Hotel** (corner of Scheiding and Paul Kruger sts., Pretoria 0001; ℭ **012/323-6054;** R450–R610/$55–$75 double), is a charming choice opposite the train station.

WHERE TO DINE

Pretoria's three top restaurants are **La Perla, La Madeleine,** and **Brasserie de Paris.** Because the latter two specialize in classic French cuisine, I've only listed La Madeleine below, which is generally considered the better, but should it be full, diners should try Christophe Dubois' **Brasserie de Paris** (525 Duncan St., Hatfield; ℭ **012/362-2247**). If you prefer Italian, head to **Ristorante Ritrovo** (ℭ **012/460-4367**), run by a father-and-son team and still the best Italian restaurant in Pretoria.

man-made excavation in the world. Contact **Kimberley Tourism** (✆ **053/ 832-7298**) next to the Civic Complex on Bulfontein Road.

VIA BLOEMFONTEIN Bloemfontein is a leisurely 4 hours from Johannesburg, and approximately 8 to 9 hours to Cape Town. There's no reason to stop in town, so head 35km (21½ miles) south on the N1 until you reach the Riversford exit, off of which you'll find **De Oude Kraal** (✆ **051/564-0636**; fax 564-0635), a working merino sheep farm. Guests stay in the restored farmhouse and enjoy a five-course farm-style dinner (expect lamb and large portions). Rates are R590 to R790 ($73–$99) double, including breakfast, dinner R115 ($14).

FROM BEAUFORT WEST Beaufort West is approximately 9 hours from Johannesburg and some 4 hours from Cape Town. If you're too tired to make it to Cape Town, the ⚑ **Karoo National Park** (✆ **023/415-2828**) is a wonderful place to overnight—you drive only a few kilometers off the N1; but once there, you are in the tranquil nature reserve, surrounded by empty plains and a low ridge of mountains, and a world away from the rumbling highway. Gate hours are from 5am to 10pm daily; accommodation is in large self-catering chalets costing from R330 ($40) a night. For reservations, which are essential, contact the **Parks Board** in Pretoria (✆ **012/428-9111**). Alternatively, try the 25,000-acre **Lemoenfontein Game Reserve** ⚑⚑ (✆ **023/4152847**; fax 023/4151044; www. lemoenfontein.co.za; R520/$55 double including breakfast; look for the signs 4km (2½ miles), north of Beaufort West; the accommodations and dining are a great deal more luxurious, and you can take an early-morning game drive before setting off for the final leg to Cape Town.

Generally speaking, Pretoria diners are committed carnivores—hence the number of tip-top steakhouses; of these **Pachas** (✆ **012/460-5063**) in Club Two Shopping Centre, **The Famous Butcher's Grill** (✆ **012/347-9970**) in Waterkloof Ridge Lifestyle Centre, and **The Grill Club** (✆ **012/368-1460**) in the Menlyn Park Shopping Centre, are all recommended. Vegetarians are advised to dine at the city's best Indian restaurant, **Pride of India** (✆ **012/346-3684**), located in Groenkloof.

If you prefer exploring for dining options on foot, head for Esselen Street in Sunnyside, or wander down Burnett and Duncan streets in the "restaurant suburb" of Hatfield, where most of the city's informal restaurants and bars are centered—you'll find Pretoria's trendoids sipping cocktails, picking at ostrich carpaccio, or puffing on cigars at Hatfield's **Cuban Cafe** (129 Duxbury Rd.; ✆ **012/362-2504**), while budget-hunters in quest of an interesting cross-cultural crowd should head straight for **Cool Runnings** (1071 Burnett St., Hatfield; ✆ **012/362-0100**).

EXPENSIVE

Gerard Moerdyk ⚑ SOUTH AFRICAN If you haven't yet done the traditional thing, or if you have and love it, Gerard Moerdyk prepares real *boerekos* (literally "farmer's food," meaning sweetened vegetables and slow-cooked meat stews) in a fine dining atmosphere. The Cape Country Sample is an excellent first-time choice: a sample helping of *bobotie* (spicy meatloaf) and beef casserole (this is likely to be replaced by a *waterblommetjie bredie* May–Aug when this Cape waterlily is harvested). Or try the mutton curry, flavored with mild, almost sweet Malay spices; ostrich filet with wild mushrooms; or oxtail stew. End the meal with the Moerdyk Cape Brandy Pudding.

Corner of Park St. and Beckett, Arcadia. ℂ **012/344-4856.** Reservations recommended. Main courses R79–95 ($10–$12). AE, DC, MC, V. Mon–Fri noon–2pm; Mon–Sat 6–9pm.

La Madeleine ✮✮✮ FRENCH   La Madeleine is on every food critic's top picks list, and international credits include a mention in the *Courvoisier Book of the Best*. Relocated from Esselen Street to a guesthouse in Lynnwood, the menu now includes slightly lighter French cuisine, with charming owner-chef Daniel Leusch personally presenting the dishes of the day in a seductively heavy French accent. His superb food is a blend of classical methods, creative inspiration, and seasonally fresh products; favorites are the legendary rack of Karoo lamb, foie gras spring rolls, and the langoustine and scallop salad dressed with an orange vinaigrette and topped with calamari chips. Daniel's wife, Karine, is responsible for desserts, including the sinful "death by chocolate" pudding.

122 Priory Rd., Lynnwood Ridge. ℂ **012/361-3667.** Reservations essential. Main courses R80–R90 ($10–$11). AE, DC, MC, V. Tues–Sat 7–9pm.

MODERATE

La Perla ✮✮ SWISS-ITALIAN   For almost two decades brothers Marco and Franco Balmelli have been producing the best beef carpaccio in town; a fine kudu (South African antelope) filet pan-fried in red wine and mushroom sauce; deboned quails pan-fried with herbs; and poached salmon with hollandaise sauce. The decor may be bland at this long-time favorite with the diplomats, businessmen, and politicians working the city, but the emphasis remains solidly on producing consistently good classic dishes and serving the cosmopolitan clientele with old-fashioned courtesy.

Brooklyn Lodge, corner Tram and Bronkhorst sts. ℂ **012/460-1267.** Reservations recommended. Main courses R60–R80 ($7.50–$10). AE, DC, MC, V. Mon–Fri noon–2:30pm; Mon–Sat 6:30–9pm.

3 Sun City & the Palace of the Lost City

187km (116 miles) NW of Johannesburg

Set within the southern border of the Pilanesberg National Park, this glitzy Vegas-style resort is made up of casinos, cinemas, theaters, restaurants, two world-class golf courses, man-made jungles, lakes, and the Palace of the Lost City, the most over-the-top five-star hotel in Africa. Developer Sol Kerzner, the boxer-turned-businessman known locally as the "Sun King," capitalized on apartheid South Africa's stern anti-gambling laws by situating Sun City in the then-homeland of Bophuthatswana, the hodgepodge of inferior land into which the Tswana were forced. As an "independent" state, headed by the corrupt Lucas Mangope, Bophuthatswana was literally a law unto itself, and millions began to swarm to "Sin City," not only to gamble but to see international acts like Sinatra, George Benson, and Elton John, who ignored the cultural boycott at the time.

EXPLORING THE RESORT

The resort is relatively easy to get around, and shuttle buses are constantly moving from one end to the next. A **"sky train"** takes visitors without cars from the entrance to the entertainment center. Closest to the entrance are the **Kwena**

Crocodile Sanctuary, Waterworld, and the **Cabanas,** followed by the tacky **Sun City Hotel, Casino,** and world-famous **Gary Player Golf Club.** Adjoining this club to the north is the more up-market **Cascades Hotel and Entertainment Centre,** from where you enter the grounds of the **Palace of the Lost City**—for most visitors, the star attraction.

The Palace was built 12 years after Sun City opened, and the sheer magnitude of its opulence is proof of the amount of money taken from those frequenting Sun City's slot machines and tables. Separated from the rest of the resort by **"The Bridge of Time"**—a large stone structure that shudders and rumbles at pre-appointed times from a mythical earthquake, and is lined with a "guard of honor" of carved elephants—the Palace is entered through the massive Mighty Kong Gates. Looking down on the rivers and jungle vegetation, you truly feel as if you are entering another world; it's hard to imagine that just a decade ago this was nothing but a dusty, rocky plain. From the bridge, you can clearly see the **"Valley of Waves,"** where landlocked Gautengers learn to surf on simulated waves, tan on manmade beaches, and hurtle down steep waterslides, reaching speeds of up to 35km (22 miles) an hour (note that the Valley is closed in winter). In the distance, overlooking a lake filled with live flamingos, is the majestic Palace, with what seems like an entire jungle of carved animals in attendance. Surrounding the Palace is what must be the most artfully landscaped garden in Africa, featuring 5 trails through 22 different sections of forest. The theme (that of a "lost city" that has been rediscovered and restored) is sometimes carried to ridiculous extremes, but the craftsmanship is world-class; the fantasy landscape is quite overwhelming. With Michael Jackson a regular visitor and now the majority shareholder, things can only get weirder.

SUN CITY ESSENTIALS

A number of tour operators offer day trips to Sun City (see "Guided Tours" in Johannesburg and Pretoria, earlier in this chapter). Alternatively, you can fly to Sun City on **SA Airlink** (© 011/978-1111), take a **bus** from Johannesburg airport or the Sandton Sun Hotel (R200/$25 one-way; © 011/780-8300), or hire a car and drive: it's a 90-minute-to-2-hour drive northwest of Jo'burg. You take the N1 to Pretoria, then head west via the N4 before turning right on the R556. Note that you will need an accommodations reservation number to enter for free; nonresidents pay R55 ($7) to enter (of which R30/$3.75 are "Sunbucks," the "local" currency) and, more important, will not be allowed to enter the Palace. Overnighters pay no entry anywhere. Day-trippers can play golf at the **Gary Player Country Club** ✪, host of the Nedbank Million Dollar Tournament, or the Lost City Country Club which Player has stated is one of his top courses.

To organize 2½-hour safari trips in elevated open-topped vehicles into neighboring **Pilanesberg** from Sun City (R200/$25), contact **Gametrackers** (© 014/552-1561) or book at their safari desk at the Sun City Hotel (note that if you have your own transport to the reserve gates the rate is R150/$19, but you should then book through Gametrackers in the reserve at © 014/555-5469). The September 2002 arrival in Pilanesberg of Chikwenya, Sharu, Sapi, Mana, and Michael—5 elephants orphaned some 18 years ago in Zimbabwe and subsequently hand-reared—has meant that Gametrackers can now also offer 3-hour elephant-back safaris, costing R1,400 ($175) per person; an elephant "interaction safari" costs R330 ($40) and lasts 90 minutes. To book, call © 014/552-5020 or visit www.gametrac.co.za.

For more information on Sun City facilities, call © 014/557-1544 or 014/557-1000 and ask for the Welcome Centre.

WHERE TO STAY & DINE

There are four accommodations options: the over-the-top Palace, the good-value Cascades, the overrated Sun City hotel, and the family-orientated Cabanas. The Sun City hotel, situated in the same building as the main casino and nightclub, is only marginally cheaper than Cascades yet is by far the tackiest choice and not reviewed here; it's best avoided unless you're solely here to gamble and want to be as close as possible to the jangling slot machines. All lodgings have a number of restaurant options, from grill rooms and pizza dens to fine-dining rooms.

The Cabanas *Value* *Kids*   Closest to the resort entrance and overlooking "Waterworld" (the resort's largest artificial lake, where a variety of watersports and cruises are offered), these terraced cabanas are designed to appeal to families; ask for a lake-facing unit. The Cabanas is not only the most relaxed and casual of the hotels, but a fully supervised program of kid activities and facilities is available at Kamp Kwena, on the Cabanas' lawns. And at 10am and 4pm kids can witness the free flying display of birds from Animal World. It's the most downmarket option but guests enjoy access to all the Sun City and Palace facilities, which are immense.

P.O. Box 3, Sun City 0316. (C) 014/557-1000. Fax 014/557-1902 or 014/557-1131. 380 units. R1,350–R1,555 ($168–$190) double; R1,715–1,925 ($214–$240) family rooms. Children under 18 stay free in parent's room. AE, DC, MC, V. **Amenities:** 2 restaurants; 2 bars; massive pool; Gary Player Country Club (includes golf, gym, and spa/salon); mini-golf; children's programs; babysitting; laundry. *In room:* A/C, TV, minibar (on request), hair dryers.

The Cascades ★★ *Value*   A comfortable, better value-for-money option than either the Sun City Hotel or the Palace, this is a classic example of early '80s opulence—J.R. Ewing wouldn't look amiss here. All rooms are spacious (many with sunken Jacuzzis in the bedroom) and overlook huge tropical gardens with waterfalls, weirs, lagoons, and shaded walks. If you ask for a room on one of the top floors, you'll have a view of the Gary Player–designed golf course, and beyond, the bushveld plains. The restaurant locations are lovely—the Peninsula is set next to a lake, while the Fishmonger is tucked under a waterfall—but consider dining at the Palace; the walk is short and spectacular.

P.O. Box 7, Sun City 0316. (C) 014/557-1000. Fax 014/557-1902 or 014/557-1131. 243 units. R2,280–R2,850 ($285–$355) double; R5,120–R13,940 ($640–$1,742) suite. Children under 18 stay free in parent's room. AE, DC, MC, V. **Amenities:** 2 restaurants; 2 bars; 2 pools; Gary Player Country Club (includes golf, gym, and spa/salon); tennis; concierge; business center; 24-hr. room service; babysitting; laundry. *In room:* A/C, TV, minibar, hair dryer.

Palace of the Lost City ★★★   From the beautiful life-size carvings of animals arching out of fountains and hand-painted domed ceilings to the tusklike pens in every room, the decor of this fantastical hotel is totally over the top, and a must for anyone even remotely interested in design. Standard rooms are a little disappointing given the opulence of the public spaces (even the lifts feature exquisite carvings), so make sure you book a lake-facing room, where the view will make up for it. If money is no option, however, you can't beat a suite on the top floor of the Palace—just ask Michael Jackson.

For the best fine-dining experience in Sun City, book a table here at the **Villa Del Palazzo,** which serves northern Italian cuisine in a romance-soaked double-volume room overlooking the water, or the **Crystal Court,** where 7m (23-ft.) high doors open onto rolling views of the Valley of Waves.

P.O. Box 308, Sun City 0316. (C) 014/557-1000. Fax 014/557-1902 or 014/557-1131. 338 units. R3,745–R4,685 ($488–$585) double; R5,455–R37,980 ($680–$4,747) suite. Children under 18 stay free in parent's room. AE, DC, MC, V. **Amenities:** 3 restaurants; bar; (massive) pool; golf; spa/salon; concierge; Internet and business services; 24-hr. room service; babysitting; laundry. *In room:* A/C, TV, minibar, hair dryer.

4 Game Reserves in North-West

PILANESBERG NATIONAL PARK ★★

Some 1.4 billion years ago, the Pilanesberg plains were bubbling away in the second-largest alkaline volcano in the world. Today the rim of this ancient crater, eroded by time, forms the natural boundary of undulating Pilanesberg National Park. Typified by concentric rings of rocky hills, and centered on a large hippo- and crocodile-filled lake, Pilanesberg is one of Africa's most picturesque parks, and—as it's a mere 90-minute to 2-hour drive—an ideal place to visit if you're stuck in Jo'burg with limited time to go elsewhere.

In 1979, the once overgrazed farmland of Pilanesberg was transformed by Operation Genesis, which saw the translocation of over 7,000 animals into the 58,000-hectare (143,000-acre) reserve. Today it is home to 364 different species, and among its 35 large mammals are the Big 5, as well as leopard, cheetah, and brown hyena. The park's natural beauty, abundance of wild animals, and lack of malaria have made it one of the area's strongest drawing cards, though most visitors here are based at Sun City. Pilanesberg's proximity to Sun City and Gauteng means that its well-maintained network of roads can get very busy, and first-time visitors to the bush should note that this is not the kind of untamed wilderness you'd encounter at, say, Welgevonden (see chapter 7) or Madikwe (see below)—and both these reserves are also malaria-free and also relatively accessible—2½ and 3½ hours from Gauteng, respectively.

PILANESBERG PARK ESSENTIALS

The main entrance and reception (© 014/555-6135) are at the Manyane Gate on the park's eastern side. From Sun City, the nearest entrance is Bakubung Gate, west off the resort on the R565. Gates open from 5:30am to 7pm November through January, from 6am to 6:30pm September through October and from 6:30am to 6pm for the rest of the year. The park can be easily explored in your own car. Entry costs R20 ($2.60) per adult (R15/$1.95 children), you can purchase a map (R10/$1.30) as you enter, and the roads are in good condition. If you have your own transport you can arrange a 2½-hour game drive in an open-topped Land Rover with **Gametrackers** (© 014/555-5469; R150/$19 per person); the pickup point is the Manyane restaurant. Gametrackers also offers 4-hour **walking safaris** accompanied by armed rangers (R220/$28 per person; four-person minimum); 3-hour **elephant-back safaris** (R1,400/$175); and **balloon safaris** (© 014/552-1552; R2,300/$290 per person) for a bird's-eye view of the park.

WHERE TO STAY & DINE

It's worth overnighting in Pilanesberg just to have the run of the reserve at dawn, before the day-trippers from Sun City descend. Reservations for one of the park's budget camps (usually in a permanent tent) must be made through **Golden Leopard Resorts** (© 014/555-6135; reservations © 011/406-3443; www. goldenleopard.co.za). Bakubung and Kwa Maritane lodges pitch themselves as the park's up-market alternatives, but frankly, they're not recommended. If you're looking for a certain level of luxury but still want to feel as if you're living in the untamed bush, there is only one place in Pilanesberg worth considering.

Tshukudu Lodge ★★★   Climbing the 134 steep steps to the lodge (the luggage is carried for you), you may be forgiven for cursing Tshukudu, or "place of the rhino." Get to the top, however, and the panoramic view alone is likely to replenish your reserves. The setting, atop a *koppie* (hill) overlooking a large open plain and waterhole, provides great views of a variety of game from the dining area/bar platform. The luxury cottages are designed to make the most of the view, with the spacious interior divided into two distinct areas. The bedroom overlooks a small lounge (with fireplace) that opens onto a private balcony overlooking the plain. The sunken bathtub also has a view of the plain, so that you won't miss the action just because you happen to be taking a bath. The two standard cabins are basic by comparison and don't have views. Game walks and drives are scheduled daily, and because Tshukudu is located in a private part of Pilanesberg that's inaccessible for Sun City day-trippers, this is a tranquil experience.

P.O. Box 6805, Rustenburg 0300. Guests are transferred from Bakubung Lodge, located just west of Sun City on the southern edge of the reserve. (© **014/552-6255.** Fax 014/552-6266. 7 units. Luxury rooms: R4,360 ($545) double; weekend: R4,200 ($523). Standard cabins R2,500 ($311). Rates include all meals, drinks, game drives, and bush walks. AE, DC, MC, V. Children age 12 and over only. **Amenities:** Dining room; bar; rock pool. *In room:* Minibar.

MADIKWE ✦✦✦

In 1991, a 75,000-hectare (185,250-acre) area on the South Africa/Botswana border was proclaimed the Madikwe Game Reserve, transforming a previously overgrazed farming area into South Africa's fourth-largest reserve. Within 6 years, 10,000 animals were once again roaming the Madikwe plains in what was dubbed Operation Phoenix, the largest game translocation exercise in the world. The decision to do this here was based on the area's highly diverse ecozones— bordered by the Dwarsberg Mountains in the south and the Marico River in the east, the reserve's rocky hills, perennial rivers, seasonal wetlands, acacia bushveld, savannah grassland, and Kalahari's desertlike sandveld allow it to support an unusual range of animal species. Ecologically, Madikwe is better suited to support wildlife than livestock, and today it has the second-largest elephant population in the country, and visitors are assured of sighting what they term "the Magnificent Seven" on a 2-night stay. This includes the Big 5 as well as cheetah (rare in the reserves around Kruger) and wild dogs, Africa's most endangered predator. With only three commercial lodges (and a handful of corporate lodges) within the entire 185,000-acre area, Madikwe is also large enough to satisfy visitors starved for solitude, something the more popular Mpumulanga reserves can't always deliver.

MADIKWE ESSENTIALS

Madikwe is some 280km (174 miles) northwest of Johannesburg. Lodges will arrange air transfers (it's a 45-min. flight); or, you can travel by car. The trip on well-maintained dirt roads takes about 3½ hours from Pretoria; ask the lodge to fax you a map. The latter is definitely the recommended route—with no one else on the road, and surrounded by bush and classic big African skies, the journey alone is a holiday.

WHERE TO STAY & DINE

Madikwe River Lodge ✦✦ *(Kids* *(Value* Madikwe comprises a compact central public area—with bird-viewing deck, rock pool with open-plan lounge and dining area—and free-standing thatched chalets, following the curve of the narrow Marico River. Each chalet is attractively furnished with indigenous woods and white linen and features a split-level bedroom and a lounge that opens onto a small deck area overlooking the river. Madikwe offers separate "children's game drives" that take into account both kids' curiosity and limited attention spans. This, combined with the variety of game and the fact that the lodge lies in a malaria-free area, makes Madikwe one of the best young-family destinations in the country.

P.O. Box 17, Derdepoort 2876. Reservations. © 014/778-0891. Fax 014/778-0893. www.threecities.co.za. 16 units. R3,300–R3960 ($400–$496) double, depending on season. Includes all meals and game activities. AE, DC, MC, V. **Amenities:** Dining area/lounge/bar; pool; babysitting; game drives (including separate children's game drives); bush walks. *In room:* Minibar, hair dryer.

Tau Lodge (© **011/315-5272;** R3,000–R4,600/$375–$575 double, depending on season; includes all meals and game activities) is the oldest lodge in Madikwe, and has a lovely location overlooking a productive water hole, but accommodation is not of the high standard you'll find at the small, exclusive, but child-friendly **Jaci's Safari Lodge** ★★ (© **0883-447-7929;** www.madikwe. com; R4,760–R6,590/$595–$824; includes all meals and game activities). Its sister lodge, **Jaci's Tree Lodge,** opened in 2002 and comprises 8 treehouses built around giant Tambotie and Leadwood trees; it offers similar amenities and prices, so you'd be hard-pressed to choose between the two. This is generally considered the most upmarket option in Madikwe, but when it comes to good value, it simply cannot compete with Madikwe River Lodge.

5 Game Reserves in the Northern Cape

KGALAGADI TRANSFRONTIER PARK ★★★

It's a 904km (560-mile) hot and dusty drive northwest of Johannesburg, but it's well worth taking time out to include this breathtakingly beautiful desert reserve on your itinerary. The sandveld environment alone is stunning—rust-red Kalahari sand dunes and wispy blonde grasses contrast starkly with huge cobalt-blue skies—yet this harsh and arid landscape supports a surprisingly varied and rich amount of game. Besides the big-maned "Kalahari" lion, you will find cheetah, hyena, elephant, jackal, and, of course, the gemsbok, or oryx.

First proclaimed in 1931, the Kalahari Gemsbok National Park and adjoining Botswana's Gemsbok Park were renamed Kgalagadi Transfrontier Park in 1999, formalizing a decade-long joint management arrangement that has ensured that game are free to wander long, ancient migratory routes in search of water. While the Kgalagadi (literally "place without water") is one of Africa's biggest reserves—covering an area of more than 38,000 sq. km (9.4 million acres)—most of the established accommodation options are still in the South African region.

These comprise three rest camps and three brand-new tented camps. Of the rest camps Twee Rivieren is the most developed, and Nossob, on the dry river bed that creates a natural unfenced boundary between South Africa and Botswana, the most isolated, but it is the tented camps that should be your final destination.

For the best game-viewing opportunities, make sure you rise early (see box in "Kruger National Park," in chapter 7 for more game-viewing tips), take plenty of extra water, and be prepared to travel long distances—the shortest circular drive is 100km (62 miles) long. Inquire at Twee Rivieren about evening game drives with experienced rangers—these are recommended.

ESSENTIALS

GETTING THERE   By Car   From Jo'burg, it's a 904km (560-mile) drive: Take the N14 to Kuruman, then the R31 to Hotazel (it really is), across vast empty plains to join the R360 for the final leg to the park. You can drive here from

Cape Town, taking the N7 north to Springbok or taking the R27 north from Vanrhynsdorp and Calvinia to Upington. The R360 takes you north to the park.

By Plane SA Airlink (© 054/332-2161) flies from Johannesburg and Cape Town to **Upington Airport** (© 054/337-7900). From here you can charter a flight with **Walkers Fly-in Safaris** (© 082-820-5394) into the park's Twee Rivieren camp (to hire the four-seater craft costs R2,500/$310) and pick up a prearranged car (see below).

GETTING AROUND Avis has a desk (© 054/332-4746) at the Upington Airport, and will also drop a car off at the park should you charter a flight directly there. Unless you intend to enter Botswana, you won't need a four-wheel-drive to travel to and around in the park, despite the fact that most of the roads are dirt.

GUIDED TOURS Jaco ✦ (aka Jacels Tours; www.jacelstours.com), an honorary ranger for S.A. National Parks and a rich source of information on the Kgalagadi, offers fully-catered specialist tours in the park as well as other places of interest in the Northern Cape. Contact Jaco at © 082-572-0065 or info@jacelstours.com.

VISITOR INFORMATION Direct all booking inquiries to the **National Parks Board,** 643 Leyds St., Muckleneuk, Pretoria (© 012/428-9111; fax 012/343-0905; reservations@parks-sa.co.za; www.parks-sa.co.za). The park is quite popular, particularly the new tented camps, so book well in advance. The **Visitor's Centre** (© 054/561-2000) is at Twee Rivieren, the park's headquarters. Admission is R30 ($3.75) per person. Note that you can enter the Botswana side from Twee Rivieren, but you'll need to have a passport, and any information on campsites comes from the **Department of Wildlife and National Parks** in Maun, Botswana (© 267/686-0376).

WHEN TO GO Rain falls mainly between January and April. The best time to visit is between March and May (autumn), when it's neither too hot nor too dry. In summer, temperatures may exceed 104°F (40°C). In winter, temperatures at night are often below zero. Note that the park's gate hours vary considerably depending on the season and are strictly adhered to—if you aren't going to arrive between 7:30am and 6pm, call ahead to find out exactly what time the gates close.

WHERE TO STAY & DINE

At 100,000 hectares (247,000 acres), **Tswalu Kalahari Reserve** ✦✦✦ is the largest privately owned reserve in South Africa, with accommodations in thatched stone minihouses on a par with the luxurious lodges in the reserves abutting Kruger. This is where people who find the Parks Board accommodations too primitive come to experience the stark beauty of the Kalahari; rooms are expansive and beautifully finished (the property was originally developed in conjunction with CCAfrica, owners of Londolozi and Phinda) but pricey: R8,800/$1,100 double, all inclusive. Among the 9,000 head of game that the late Steven Boler imported to his $6-million enterprise are lion, black rhino, cheetah, leopard, and buffalo—and sightings are excellent as there's no thick vegetation to conceal animals. You can either stay here en route to the Park from Johannesburg, or charter a flight in from Johannesburg (R2,900/$363 per person return). Call © 011-883-7918 or direct 053/781-9311 for information, or visit www.tswalu.com.

Fun Fact Lost and Found

The park recently made headlines when the ANC government handed over a large tract of land to the last remaining San tribe still living in the area, thereby bringing to a close centuries of destitution and persecution. For years, the migratory San, not understanding the concept of land ownership, continued to hunt on their ancestral lands long after they had been "annexed" by black and white immigrants to southern Africa. As a result, they were seen as vermin and ruthlessly hunted down. The final settlements moved to the inhospitable Kalahari Desert, where a few small communities still survive; you will no doubt meet a few San people on the side of the road, trading ostrich-shell and horn jewelry. For a greater insight into the fascinating world of these gentle people, read Laurence van der Post's *Lost World of the Kalahari* (Harcourt Brace; 1977).

In the Park

Unless you've flown in, it's a good idea to book your first night at **Twee Rivieren** ✸, just beyond the entrance to the park, since you've more than likely covered vast distances to get here and will need to cover at least another 2½ hours to get to another camp. This is also the only camp with a restaurant, a pool, and air-conditioned units. Each of the self-catering 2-, 3-, 4-, and 6-bed chalets, all en-suite, has a fully equipped kitchen and a *braai* (barbecue) area. Each chalet costs a minimum of R330 ($40) a night for two people—best bet is to book the family cottage for R360 ($45) (book early!). Besides the basic restaurant there is a take-out shop, fuel station, and grocery shop; you can buy basic supplies like milk, bread, wood, frozen meat, eggs, and tinned food here, but it's best to stock up on a few extras in Upington.

From here the shortest game drive is to follow the course of the dry Auob River—which offers excellent game-viewing opportunities—to Mata Mata, but if you don't leave before noon you'll have to spend the night at **Mata Mata,** which lies 120km (74 miles; 2½ hours) away, or preferably at one of the two new tented camps. Mata Mata is a great deal more rustic than Twee Rivieren, and the best accommodations—none of which have air-conditioning—are limited to eight chalets (R300/$38 double); again the best one here is the family chalet, which is available for R500 ($63). If you need to, fill up here (there is a shop stocked with basic supplies and a fuel station) and press on to the relatively swish **Kalahari Tented Camp** ✸✸, which lies about 3km (1.8 miles) farther. Here you overnight at one of 10 en-suite desert "tents" (sandbag and canvas constructions with amenities like kitchenettes, bathrooms, and ceiling fans), or, pick of them all, the honeymoon unit, costing R550 ($69) or R650 ($82) for two, respectively. There are also 4 family tents, sleeping four. Alternatively, head farther north to the en-suite desert cabins at **Grootkolk Tented Camp** ✸. With only 4 units (R500/$63 double), each with its own barbecue unit (worth utilizing, otherwise you have to share the communal kitchen), this is the real deal—gloriously remote and silent. If you like the sound of this, you should consider hiring a 4WD just to make the journey to the four en-suite reed cabins at **Bitterpan** ✸ (R450/$56 for two), the most rustic and remote camp in the park, located between Mata Mata and Nossob, and for many the highlight of their visit.

7

Big-Game Country: Mpumalanga & Limpopo Province

The Limpopo Province and its southern neighbor, Mpumalanga, form the northeastern corner of South Africa, and with the neighboring countries of Swaziland, Mozambique, Zimbabwe, and Botswana, make up southern Africa's big-game plateau. Most people come to this region seeking out the romance of precolonial Africa, a place where vast plains of bush savanna teem with game, rivers are swollen with lumbering hippos and lurking crocodiles, dense indigenous jungles shroud twittering birds, horizons shimmer with heat, and the nights are lit only by stars and crackling campfires. This you will find—and more. Here lies the Escarpment, carpeted in the world's largest man-made forests and offering some of the country's most breathtaking drives and views; the Blyde River Canyon, third-largest canyon in the world; the lush subtropical gardens of the legendary Rain Queen; and Stone Age sites and perfectly preserved boomtowns that tell of Mpumalanga's short but turbulent gold-rush–era history.

But the primary destination remains Kruger National Park, one of Africa's greatest game parks, and the private game reserves that surround it. Kruger's budget facilities and well-maintained roads make an African safari experience tremendously accessible, but for those who can afford them the private game reserves that flank the Kruger's western unfenced borders offer a truly close-up encounter with the Big 5, and a few days here are highly recommended.

Predictably, even in this scenic environment you cannot escape the ironies and contrasts that are South Africa: Neighboring the ultra-luxurious private game reserves are the economically deprived communities of Lebowa, Gazankulu, and Kangwane. Many in these communities resent what they see as a white man's playground; others are grateful for the increased employment opportunities, particularly in the park. As the region enters a new century, the challenge will be to find a balance between the needs of industry and those of the communities, pulling them into a general economic interdependence and prosperity for the region, with Kruger National Park at the hub. To a large extent, the growth of tourism is doing just that.

1 Staying Active

If you're looking for a one-stop advice and booking shop, contact **Golden Monkey** (© 013/737-8191; www.big5country.co.za), an agent for the largest selection of adventure operators in the Sabie, Graskop, and Hazyview areas, as well as a booking and information agent.

Mpumalanga & the Limpopo Province

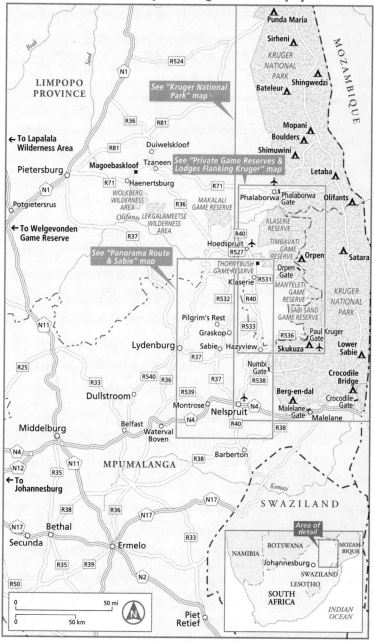

ABSEILING Choose between an abseil (rappel) down the Sabie waterfall (R80/$10) or leap off a granite outcrop (R180/$22) before heading into Kruger; bookings are through Golden Monkey (see above).

BALLOONING Take off at sunrise and float over the foothills of the Escarpment, possibly sighting some game, then alight for champagne breakfast at a nearby lodge. Based 10km (6 miles) from Hazyview and White River, **Balloons Over Africa** ✦ ((℃ **013/741-1247**; R1,530/$190 per person) prides itself on its expertise—the company's chief pilot, Kevin Roberson, won the South Africa Hot Air Balloon Championship for 6 years running.

BIRD-WATCHING Along with KwaZulu-Natal, this is the prime bird-watching destination in South Africa, providing enormously varied habitats. For expert advice and tailor-made tours to these areas, as well as to other top birding destinations in southern Africa, contact **Lawson's Birdwatching Tours** ✦✦✦ ((℃ **013/741-2458**; www.lawsons.co.za).

ELEPHANT SAFARI **Kapama** has introduced **elephant-back safaris** ✦✦✦ in its Big 5 reserve located near Hoedspruit; either overnight at its new luxury tented flagship, Camp Jabulani, or book a 90-minute ride for R1,500 ($185) ((℃ **015/793-1633**; www.kapama.co.za).

FLY-FISHING **Trout fishing** ✦✦✦ on the highland Escarpment is well established, with an infrastructure of self-catering cottages, guesthouses, and lodges situated on well-stocked lakes and streams. **Dullstroom** is the unofficial capital of the trout-fishing areas, and rod rental, fees, and accommodations can be arranged through its helpful **Tourist Information Centre** (℃ **013/254-0254**). For information on trout fishing in the Limpopo Province's Letaba area, contact **Magoebaskloof-Byadladi Tourist Association** (℃ **015/276-4972** or 276-5047; www.magoebaskloof.com).

GOLFING The nine-hole course at **Skukuza** (℃ **013/735-5543**) is quite possibly the most dangerous course in the world—it is unfenced, and wild animals wander the greens at will. More wild golfing experiences await at the exclusive 18-hole course at **Leopards Creek** ✦✦✦ (℃ **013/791-2000**), co-owned by Jack Nicklaus and Gary Player. Besides the resident leopard, crocs and hippos lurk in the aptly named water hazards. To play here, you'll have to book into the **Malelane Sun Intercontinental** (℃ **013/790-3304**). Or you can book into luxurious **Makalali** (see "Where to Stay & Dine," in "Private Game Reserves," later in this chapter), a private game lodge that lies just under an hour away from the 18-hole **Hans Merensky Country Club** ✦✦ (℃ **015/781-3931**), which borders Kruger and is often visited by its residents.

HIKING The region's myriad **hiking trails** ✦✦✦ offer excellent scenic opportunities. For hiking and tracking animals in game reserves, see "Kruger National Park: Wilderness Trails," later in this chapter. Ngala, a luxury lodge in the Timbavati reserve, offers walking safaris for the well-heeled; see "Private Game Reserves: Where To Stay & Dine," later in this chapter. If you're traveling here via the Panorama Route, note that the region has a number of excellent day trails, most of which are near the Escarpment towns of Sabie and Graskop—the 14km (9-mile) **Loerie Trail** (R5/60¢) per person) takes you through some of the region's most attractive surrounds. If you're not that active, stroll the pretty 3km (1.8-mile) **Forest Falls Walk.** If you're traveling through the Letaba area, the 11km (7-mile) circular **Rooikat Trail** ✦ (reservations: ℃ **015/307-4310**; R5/60¢), which follows a stream through the forests of Agatha, is highly recommended.

The top overnight hike in the Mpumalanga area is the 5-day **Blyde River Canyon Trail** (R30/$3.70 per person per night), a 65km (40-mile) walk that traverses the full length of the Blyde River Canyon Nature Reserve, descending from the panoramic heights of God's Window to the tranquil waters of the

---

> **Tips** **Golfing in the Wild**
>
> Golfing in big-game country is not to be taken lightly—a golfer at Hans Merensky was trampled to death by an elephant that had broken through the fence from neighboring Kruger. Golfers at these clubs should heed the warning signs posted at water hazards and elsewhere. Should you encounter a large mammal or predator, you are advised to remain still, then back away quietly—under no circumstances should you run. If the thought of meeting a large pachyderm or leopard in the rough puts you right off course, you can choose a safer scenic route: the nine-hole **Pilgrim's Rest course** (⌀ **013/768-1434**) or the more challenging 18-hole championship course at **White River Country Club** (⌀ **013/751-3781**) are both popular.

Blyderiviespoort Dam (tempting in summer, but hikers should be wary of crocodiles and hippos). Hikers' huts are basic: bunk beds, flush toilets, braai sites, pots, and firewood are provided; all else must be carried in (don't forget toilet paper!). The views and vegetation make this one of the most popular trails in South Africa, so book in advance (⌀ **013/759-5341**).

South African Forestry (SAFCOL) (now marketed in the region as Komatiland Ecotourism) created hiking trails with overnight facilities through some incredibly scenic areas in the Limpopo Province, including the relatively tough 2-, 3-, and 5-day **Magoebaskloof Trails** (highly recommended) and the 2-, 3-, and 5-day **Fanie Botha Trails** (both R47/$6 per person per night). For details and bookings, contact ⌀ **012/481-3615** or ecotour@safcol.co.za).

HORSEBACK RIDING   **Equus Horse Safaris** ⭐⭐ (⌀ **011/788-3923**) offers riding safaris that take place in the Waterberg, Limpopo Province, where you will track game, including black rhino, and learn about the local ecology. See "The Waterberg Mountains," later in this chapter, for more information. **Filly's Way Mountain Horse Trails** operates in the Tzaneen area (⌀ **082-808-0866**).

HUNTING   Hunting season usually runs from April to September, though some farms enjoy year-round concessions. For more information on procedures and bookings, contact Rian de Lange at the **Mpumalanga Parks Board** (⌀ **013/759-5336**); for information on professional hunters and outfitters, contact the **Lowveld Hunting Association** (⌀ **013/752-3575**) between 8am and 12pm.

MOUNTAIN BIKING   Sabie is a fabulous area to explore by bike; rent a bike and an experienced guide (R100/$13) per person for 2 hr.) from **Bike Doc** (⌀ **013/764-1034**), who will plot out your journey; ask about the Ceylon Trails. If you're traveling in the Letaba area, the exhilarating 19km (12-mile) **Debengeni Downhill** ⭐, a forestry road that starts at the top of the Magoebaskloof Pass and plummets down to the Debengeni Falls, is highly recommended for adrenaline junkies. Bikes here are rented by the hotels listed.

QUAD BIKING   **BacTrac Adventure Trails** (⌀ **082-808-0866**) offers excursions on "quad bikes" (four-wheel motorcycles) through the Magoebaskloof forests; unless you really want the T-shirt and a visit to a crocodile farm, the best value option is the R420 ($52) per half-day trip.

RIVER RAFTING   River rafting ⭐⭐⭐ takes place on three rivers during the summer months (usually Sept–May). The **Blyde River** ⭐ (a few grade IVs, overall grade III) offers the most exciting rafting in this area. This 8.5km (5-mile) trip is completed in one (tiring!) day; expect to pay R650 ($80) for a day trip, R950 ($118) to overnight. A day trip down the **Olifants Gorge** ☆ (overall grade II, some IV) will run you R385 ($48). But the 2-day trip is recommended—approximately 60km (37 miles) long, it passes through spectacular scenery, and the night is spent on a sandy beach flanked by steep mountainside and baobab trees. Expect to pay R950 ($118) per person for a 2-day trip and R1,150 ($143) for a 3-day trip. The minimum age is 10, but minors must be accompanied by parents. The tranquil **Sabie River,** ideal for families (ages 6 and up only), offers a 3- to 4-hour trip on flat water (R190/$23), covering some 12km (7 miles). **Hardy Ventures** (✆ 013/751-1693, www.hardyventure.com) runs all three rivers, while Wynand from **Otter's Den** (✆ 083-279-5565) concentrates on the Blyde River and Olifants Gorge.

2 Organized Tours

If you don't want to follow the suggestions below for exploring this region in your own car, you may want to consider going with one of these recommended tour operators.

Thompson's Indaba tours (✆ 013/737-7115; www.indaba.co.za) offers open-vehicle safaris with an experienced game ranger to Kruger—expect to pay R585 ($72) per person for a full day (5/6am–7/5:30pm) or R470 ($58) for a morning; prices exclude meals. Walking safaris in Kruger (weather dependent) will run you R830 ($103). Thompson's also offers night safaris; these take place either in Kapama, which can include an afternoon visit to the Hoedspruit Research & Breeding Centre (R755/$94; dinner included), or in the Sabi Sands (R830/$103), arguably the most game-dense private reserve in South Africa. The Panorama Route tour, with a stop for lunch at Pilgrim's Rest or Graskop, costs R595/$74 per person. (Other tours include Mohololo Centre and Shangana Cultural Village, but if you have your own vehicle, you're better off visiting these places on your own.) **Safaris Direct** (✆ 013/737-7945; cellphone 082-804-5026; www.safarisdirect.co.za) offers similar tours at similar rates—a full-day safari in an open-vehicle costs R560 ($70). Safaris Direct also offer a night drive for R580 ($72), including a sundowner. Both of these tour companies offer longer itineraries, covering the entire country.

SPECIALIST TOURS

John Williams at **Monsoon's African Travel and Adventures** (✆ 015/795-5114 or 083/700-8921; www.monsoongallery.com) will help plan a self-drive itinerary that takes in the less-publicized cultural and archaeological sights in the big-game regions of the lowveld, offering the opportunity to meet many of the artists and craftspeople whose works stock Williams' gallery. He will also assist visitors in visiting the far reaches of the Limpopo Province, an area that is not yet well geared for tourism. For accompaniment by a specialist guide, be sure to make arrangements well in advance.

Science on Safari ☆ (✆ 013/751-2446; www.scienceonsafari.com) provides special-interest safaris for those who seek more detailed information on everything from fossils to prehistoric art to African wildlife. An upcoming tour includes participation in a lion capture program.

Peter Lawson offers superb tailor-made tours for budding birders and mega-tickers–see "Staying Active: Birdwatching," above.

3 En Route to Big-Game Country

The journey between Gauteng and Kruger—a comfortable 5-hour drive with no major detours—includes some of South Africa's most dramatically beautiful drives, and the surrounds become scenic within 2 hours of leaving Johannesburg. The three routes described below take you from the highveld plateau before dropping, usually quite spectacularly, to the lowveld, much of which is taken up by Kruger National Park and the surrounding private game reserves. The best way to savor the journey is to overnight at one of the many places that lie between 2 and 4 hours away from Gauteng and make the most of the Escarpment's dramatic scenery before setting off for big-game country.

The first, most popular route takes you via the Escarpment towns of Sabie and Graskop (**Pilgrim's Rest** ✿ is an optional but recommended side trip), before traversing the Escarpment rim along what is called the **Panorama Route** ✿✿✿—a spectacular half-day drive. This journey will definitely warrant an overnight stay, preferably two, and you are then ideally positioned to enter one of Kruger's southern or central gates.

The second approach is via Machadodorp on the N4, the main artery connecting Gauteng with Nelspruit, the capital of Mpumalanga—this is ideal if you need to enter one of Kruger's southern gates and don't have time to do much sightseeing or overnight along the way.

A lesser-known way to get to central Kruger, but in parts even more scenic, particularly from June to August, is to follow in the footsteps of the Voortrekkers on the Great North Road (N1) as far as Pietersburg, then branch off eastward via the **Letaba/Magoebaskloof area** ✿, also known as "land of the silver mist" and "garden of the Rain Queen." This route will also necessitate an overnight stay, and the following are recommended. The **Coach House** ✿ (P.O. Box 544, Tzaneen 0850; ✆ **015/306-8000;** fax 015/307-1466; www.coachhouse.co.za) lies on a 560-hectare (1,383-acre) working fruit and nut farm and offers excellent amenities and a great location. Rates are R1,300 to R1,750 ($162–$218) double; R1,850 ($230) suites. The **Magoebaskloof Hotel** (off the R71, Magoebaskloof Pass; ✆ **015/276-4776;** fax 015/276-4780) is an old-fashioned, generous, and friendly hotel—from the zealous porter to the well-priced wine list, there are no hard edges or nasty surprises. Best of all, they love children, and in an area not renowned for this sentiment, this open embrace will come as a relief to beleaguered parents. Rates are R550 to R790 ($69–$99) double, including breakfast. Both hotels have solid inhouse restaurants.

⌒Tips Need to Save Time?

The quickest way to get to the Kruger is to fly directly from Cape Town direct to the Kruger-Mpumalanga International or the Hoedspruit/Eastgate airports, or from Johannesburg direct to the Kruger-Mpumalanga International, Hoedspruit/Eastgate, or Phalaborwa airports.

If you plan to drive to Kruger and will be arriving in the afternoon, plot your route so that you enter the park via the gate closest to the camp where you will be overnighting. Gate times are strict, as are the park's rules regarding speed limits—at 50kmph (30 mph) this can make for slow going. It may cause you to arrive at your camp later than you'd planned and find yourself unable to check in—camp admission times are also inflexible. See "Kruger National Park," later in this chapter, for details.

4 The Escarpment & Panorama Route

This is the most popular route to big-game country, with roads taking you past endless pine and gum forests, pockets of tangled indigenous jungle, plunging waterfalls, and breathtaking views of the subtropical plains. A 4-hour drive from Gauteng, it's an easy escape for Johannesburg's ever-harassed city dwellers, desperate to breathe fresh air and drive around with unlocked doors. Unfortunately, the air is not always that fresh; Mpumalanga's industrial activities are responsible for one of the highest acid rainfalls in the world. This is compounded during the dry winter months, when veld fires are rife, coloring the air with a hazy smog that obscures the views. While this is one reason to consider traveling via the Letaba/Magoebaskloof area (see later in this chapter), which is generally a great deal greener in the winter, nothing matches the magnificent view of the lowveld plains from the aptly named God's Window, or watching the Blyde River snake through Blyde River Canyon, thousands of meters below. In addition, the region's popularity makes for a plethora of great accommodations options; it's worth noting that, with the exception of Pilgrim's Rest, overnighting in any of the Escarpment towns (as opposed to the outlying areas) would be a mistake—the surroundings offer a lot more in the way of views and setting.

In short, the route is as follows: After driving through **Dullstroom,** the highest town on the Escarpment, you drop down the eastern slopes via the scenic **Long Tom Pass** to the forestry towns of **Sabie** and **Graskop.** (Pilgrim's Rest, a restored gold-mining village, lies another mountain pass away, and warrants a separate visit of at least a half day, excluding travel time.) Graskop is the gateway to the **Panorama Route,** a drive that curls along the rim of the Escarpment, with lookout points along the way that provide relatively easy access to some of the most panoramic views in Africa (see "Driving the Panorama Route," below). Once past the canyon lookouts, the final descent to the lowveld follows the Abel Erasmus Pass to **Hoedspruit,** which offers easy access to Kruger via the centrally located Orpen Gate, or the private game reserves of Timbavati, Thornybush, and Manyeleti. Or head south to **Hazyview** for access to the Paul Kruger Gate or Sabi Sands Reserve, or complete the loop to return to Sabie or Graskop. *Note:* If you fly directly to Hoedspruit's Eastgate airport, you can still tour the Panorama Route as a day trip—just exclude Dullstroom and Long Tom Pass from the itinerary.

ESSENTIALS

GETTING THERE   By Car   If you're traveling from Johannesburg, take the N12, which joins up with the N4, the main artery between Pretoria and Nelspruit, capital of Mpumalanga. When you reach Belfast, turn north onto the R540 to Dullstroom and Lydenburg, then take the R37 east to Sabie. From here the R532 runs north through Graskop along the Panorama route.

By Plane   From **Cape Town: SA Express** flies daily to Hoedspruit's Eastgate Airport—this is the best airport to fly to if you want to do the Panorama Route as a day trip. From **Johannesburg: SA Express** flies daily to Hoedspruit's Eastgate Airport. Note that you can also fly from Cape Town, Johannesburg, and Durban to the relatively nearby Kruger-Mpumalanga International Airport.

VISITOR INFORMATION   Golden Monkey (✆ **013/737-8191**) is one of the few centralized sources of information on the Sabie, Graskop, and Hazyview areas. The **tourism bureau** in **Dullstroom** (✆ **013/254-0254;** Shop 9, Hugenote St.; www.dullstroomreservations.co.za; open Mon–Fri 8am–5pm,

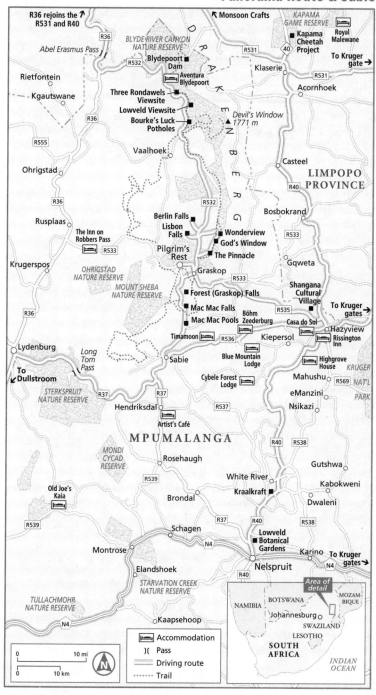

R36 rejoins the R531 and R40

Abel Erasmus Pass

R36

R532

Monsoon Crafts

KAPAMA GAME RESERVE

Kapama Cheetah Project

Royal Malewane

BLYDE RIVER CANYON NATURE RESERVE

Blydepoort Dam

Aventura Blydepoort

Three Rondawels Viewsite

Lowveld Viewsite

Bourke's Luck Potholes

R531

40

Klaserie

To Kruger gate →

Rietfontein

Kgautswane

R36

R555

Ohrigstad

Rusplaas

The Inn on Robbers Pass

Krugerspos

R36

Lydenburg

To Dullstroom

OHRIGSTAD NATURE RESERVE

MOUNT SHEBA NATURE RESERVE

Long Tom Pass

STERKSPRUIT NATURE RESERVE

MONDI CYCAD RESERVE

Old Joe's Kaia

R539

R531

Acornhoek

Vaalhoek

Devil's Window 1771 m

Casteel

LIMPOPO PROVINCE

R40

R532

Berlin Falls

Lisbon Falls

Pilgrim's Rest

Graskop

Forest (Graskop) Falls

Mac Mac Falls

Mac Mac Pools

Timamoon

Sabie

Hendriksdal

Artist's Café

MPUMALANGA

Rosehaugh

R539

Brondal

R37

Schagen

Montrose

Elandshoek

STARVATION CREEK NATURE RESERVE

TULLACHMOHR NATURE RESERVE

Kaapsehoop

Wonderview

God's Window

The Pinnacle

R533

Bosbokrand

Gqweta

Shangana Cultural Village

To Kruger gates →

R535

Böhm Zeederburg

Casa do Sol

Kiepersol

Blue Mountain Lodge

Cybele Forest Lodge

R536

Hazyview

Rissington Inn

Highgrove House

Mahushu

R569

eManzini

Nsikazi

KRUGER NAT'L PARK

R537

R40

R538

White River

Kraalkraft

Gutshwa

Kabokweni

Dwaleni

R37

R40

R538

Lowveld Botanical Gardens

N4

Nelspruit

Karino

To Kruger gates →

N4

R40

0   10 mi
0   10 km

N

Accommodation

)(Pass

Driving route

Trail

Area of detail

NAMIBIA   BOTSWANA

Johannesburg

SWAZILAND

LESOTHO

SOUTH AFRICA

MOZAMBIQUE

INDIAN OCEAN

265

Sat 9am–5pm, Sun 9am–2pm) is one of the best but focuses only on the immediate area. In **Sabie:** Contact **Panorama Information,** at Sabie Market Square (© **013/764-1125;** www.panoramainfo.co.za; open Mon–Fri 8am–5pm, Sat–Sun 9am–1pm). A better service, **Graskop Information,** is offered at Graskop, located in the Spar Centre, Pilgrim's Way (© **013/767-1833;** open Mon–Sat 8:30am–5pm; www.wildadventures.co.za). In **Pilgrim's Rest:** See "Pilgrim's Rest: Visitor Information," later in this chapter.

GETTING AROUND Most lodges supply transfers from the airport; otherwise, contact **Eastgate Lodge Transfers** (© **015/793-3678**). **Avis** and **Budget** have desks at all three airports in the Kruger region; see chapter 2 for contact details.

DULLSTROOM

At 2,012m (6,600 ft.) above sea level, Dullstroom is the highest town on the Escarpment—expect bitterly cold evenings in the winter, and don't be surprised to find fires lit even in midsummer. The town, some 230km (142½ miles) northeast of Johannesburg, dates back to the 1880s, when a committee under the chairmanship of Wolterus Dull collected money in Holland to assist Boers who had suffered losses in the First Anglo-Boer War. The town was razed to the ground again by the British in the Second Anglo-Boer War, but despite perennial mist and low temperatures, the townsfolk simply rebuilt it. Today it is the center of the highveld's trout-fishing industry, and regularly reports 6- to 7-pounders caught in its well-stocked dams and streams.

WHERE TO STAY

For more options focusing on fly-fishing needs, call or e-mail Dullstroom reservations (© **013/254-0254;** reservations@dullstroom.net).

Dullstroom Inn *Value* This small-town inn is one of the few fully-catered family-friendly establishments in the Dullstroom area. It offers an excellent value-for-money stopover on the way to the Escarpment. Established almost a century ago, the building retains much of its original design, with comfortable beds taking up most of the space in the small bedrooms. A busy Laura Ashley decor—florals and stripes abound—doesn't help. Specify whether you prefer a shower or a bathtub. There are fireplaces everywhere downstairs, but heaters, carpets, duvets, blankets, and hot-water bottles help ward off the Dullstroom chill in the rooms. Equally warming is the pub fare, served in the cozy, convivial atmosphere of the inn's pub, recently voted one of the best in the country. Bank on solid comfort food: bangers and mash, steak and kidney pie, hunter's pot, curries, and, of course, fresh trout.

39 Orange St., opposite the village green. © **013/254-0071.** Fax 013/254-0278. 11 units. R420 ($53) double; R510–R535 ($63–$67) family rooms. AE, DC, MC, V. **Amenities:** Restaurant; pub; babysitting by prior arrangement. *In room:* Coffee- and tea-making facilities, hair dryer by arrangement, no telephone.

Walkersons *Set* in green, misty surrounds with trout-filled dams and weirs winding their way through the 600-hectare (1,500-acre) estate, Walkersons' grounds are pure Scottish highlands. Inside, the decor only adds to the illusion. From issues of *Majesty* to framed photographs of the Duke and Duchess of Windsor, the Walkersons have striven to create a home reminiscent of English aristocracy. Walls are covered in tapestries and Victorian oil paintings (purchased at Sotheby's, of course), windows are draped in heavy fabrics, floors are carpeted with sisal upon which Persian rugs add color, and all of the rooms have individual antique pieces. Each bedroom is huge, with a king-size bed, a writing desk, and two comfortable chairs facing the fire (lit before you arrive). The lodge offers a full selection of fly-fishing tackle (R40/$5 a day).

10km (6 miles) north of Dullstroom off R540. © **013/254-0145.** Fax 013/254-0262. 21 units. R1,670 ($208) double; stable room (no fireplace or telephone) R1,270 ($160) double. Rates include breakfast. AE, DC, MC, V. Children age 12 and older welcome. **Amenities:** Restaurant; pub; room service (6:30am–9:30pm); helipad; runway; jogging/hiking trails; horseback riding; fly-fishing. *In room:* A/C, TV, minibar, coffee- and tea-making facilities, hair dryer, fireplace.

WHERE TO DINE

The **Tonteldoos Bistro** (© **013/254-0115**), on the main road in Hugenote, is still one of the most popular restaurants in town. Try the grilled trout topped with almonds and lemon-and-herb butter; beef filet topped with Camembert and red wine; or pork chops flamed with *mampoer,* a locally distilled liquor. Or settle for a simple sandwich made with home-baked bread. Tonteldoos is open for breakfast and lunch daily and for dinner on Fridays and Saturdays. Also on the main road is the legendary **Harrie's Pancakes** (© **013/254-0801**), open daily. See "Where to Dine: Sabie & Surrounds," later in this chapter, for a write-up on the original Harrie's, located in Graskop. But the honors for the best restaurant in Dullstroom go to newcomer **Fibs** (© **013/254-0059;** closed Mon), located on Voortrekker Street in an old general dealer's store, which serves creative delicacies like roasted quail with a grape and tarragon stuffing. Fibs (which incidentally has nothing to do with what the chef has to say and everything to do with the tall tales of the fly-fishermen patrons) is open for lunch Tuesday to Sunday, and dinner Tuesday to Saturday. For great pub fare, head for **Dullstroom Inn;** for a romantic fine dining experience, book a table at **Walkersons** (see above for details on both).

Note: It's worth reserving a table at these establishments on weekends, when Jo'burg's desperados make the 2-hour drive to soak up Dullstroom's country living over lunch before setting off for the traffic jam back home.

LYDENBURG & LONG TOM PASS

Lydenburg, or "place of suffering," was founded by a party of depressed Voortrekkers who, having lost a number of loved ones to a malaria epidemic in nearby Ohrigstad, retreated to its mosquito-free heights in 1849. Happily, "lydenburg" proved to be a misnomer, and today the town has a substantial center, though there's little to see beyond some interesting examples of pioneer architecture. The town is also known for a famed archaeological find: the **Lydenburg Heads,** seven ceramic masks that date back to the fifth century and were discovered in the late 1950s. You can see replicas of the heads (the originals now reside in the South African Museum in Cape Town) at the **Lydenburg Museum** (© **013/235-2121,** ext. 278), situated in the **Gustav Klingbiel Nature Reserve,** 3km (2 miles) out of town on the R37. For guided tours (by appointment only), call ahead. Hours are Monday through Friday from 8am to 3:30pm, Saturday and Sunday from 8am to 5pm; admission R4 (50¢).

From Lydenburg, the R37 east takes you down the **Long Tom Pass** ★★—at 2,150m (7,052 ft.) the second-highest mountain pass in South Africa. It was named after the Creusot siege guns that the Boers lugged up the pass to try and repel the British forces during the Second Anglo-Boer War (1899–1902). These guns, or cannons, were known as Long Toms because of their extended necks, which could spit a shell 9.5km (6 miles). Near the summit of the pass, at the **Devil's Knuckles,** a Long Tom replica commemorates the 4-day battle that was fought on this mountainside in 1900—the original cannons were destroyed by the Boers to prevent them from falling into British hands. You can still see the holes blasted by the cannons as the Boers retreated down the **Staircase,** a series of hairpin bends that zigzag down the pass.

Continuing east along the R37, passing the turnoff south for Hendriksdal, you come to the small forestry town of Sabie.

SABIE & SURROUNDS

The origins of Sabie (pronounced *sah*-bee) date back to 1871 when a few friends, picnicking at the Lower Sabie Falls, were showing off their marksmanship skills. Bullets chipped the rocks behind the mock targets, revealing a glint of gold, and prospectors promptly followed. The initial boom was short-lived, though the mining industry was still to transform Sabie. The first commercial trees, intended for mine props, were planted in 1876 and today form the heart of what are claimed to be the largest man-made forests in the world. To date, more than a million acres have been planted with pine and eucalyptus, and many of these are destined to prop up shafts in the mines that run deep below Gauteng's surface. Find out more at the **Forestry Museum,** which takes up an entire block on 10th Avenue (✆ **013/764-1058;** open Mon–Fri 8am–4:30pm, Sat 8am–12pm, R10/$1.30 admission).

From here you can head east on the R536 to Hazyview (the closest town to the Kruger, a mere 10 minutes drive) or travel north on the R532 to complete the Panorama Drive.

The area surrounding Sabie and Graskop is renowned for its waterfalls. If your idea of a waterfall worth detouring is Victoria Falls, however, give these a miss and head straight for Pilgrim's Rest and/or the Panorama Route. If you visit only one waterfall, consider **Lone Creek Falls,** reached by traveling 10km (6 miles) on the Old Lydenburg Road northwest from Sabie. You will pass turnoffs for both the **Bridal Veil** (R5/65¢ per person) and **Horseshoe Falls** (R5/65¢ per person) before reaching the **Lone Creek** gate (R5/65¢ per person). Besides being a short walk from the car, this pretty waterfall is also one of the few lookouts in the area that is wheelchair friendly, though the recent addition of toilets and barbecue facilities has detracted from its natural beauty. The single cascade plunges 68m (223 ft.) into an attractive pool and is framed by the lush green foliage of a small damp rain forest.

A little farther along the R532, you will see the sign for the **Forest Falls** (R10/$1.30 per person for permit, obtainable from Forestry Museum), an easy 3km (2-mile) trail that was badly damaged during the floods in 2000. It's a very pretty walk, and well worth tackling, time allowing. To view the Lisbon and Berlin waterfalls, take the Panorama Route following the rim of the Escarpment.

WHERE TO STAY

The following establishments are located amid lush plantations, subtropical farms, or indigenous bush, and most feature superb views and luxurious suites—all of which come at a price. For a good budget alternative, check out the **Graskop Hotel** (✆ **013/767-1244;** www.graskophotel.co.za; R440/$55 double, including breakfast) in the town of Graskop, which offers decent decor and good service at a reasonable rate, or **Bohm's Zeederberg Country House** (✆ **013/737-8101;** www.bohms.co.za; R640/$80 double, including breakfast), which offers 10 chalets in lush subtropical gardens with great views—ask for no. 5, 6, 10, 11, 12, or 14.

Near Sabie

Blue Mountain Lodge ★★★ Do not book into this 494-acre estate if your taste runs to spartan minimalism—from the dark timber and mustard yellow walls of the "Bismarck Room" to the floral and leopard-print "Fassler," each Victorian Suite has its own unique personality, yet all share a Versace-like opulence. Located in eight separate cottages set below ponds, palms, a pool, dining terrace, and a grand staircase that sweeps down to more immaculately manicured lawns, Blue Mountain is the most luxurious (and expensive) accommodations option on the Escarpment, but don't expect the consistency of service you find for a comparable price in the cities, though the new owners may change this. Over and above the Victorian Suites are the Manor Houses and the Quadrant Rooms—while the latter are not as pricey, they're very average, and you'd be better off at one of Timamoon's private lodges or Cybele. Food is yet another reason why Blue Mountain enjoys such an excellent reputation—head chef Elvis Mnisi prepares a new menu every day, a copy of which is delivered to your room in the late afternoon along with canapés and an invitation to predinner drinks.

P.O. Box 101, Kiepersol 1241. (Take the Kiepersol turnoff, 28km [17 miles] east of Sabie on the R536, follow for 4km [2½ miles] before turnoff.) ℂ 013/737-8446. Fax 013/737-8446. www.blu-mountain.com. 13 units; 2 manor houses. Presidential Suite R3,520 ($440) double; Victorian Suites R2,508 ($312) double; Quadrant Rooms R1,760 ($220) double. Rates include dinner and breakfast; AE, DC, MC, V. No children under age 12. **Amenities:** Restaurant; bar; large pool; room service (6:30am–11pm); same-day laundry. *In room:* A/C, minibar, hair dryer.

Timamoon ★★ If you're self-driving, it's hard to beat the total peace offered by these four secluded thatched two-bedroom suites, located a few minutes' drive from each other. Kruger lies but 40 minutes away, but you'll be hard-pressed to leave your well-appointed and spacious "lodge," furnished with artifacts that the owners have collected from years of travel throughout Africa. Each lodge features two en-suite bedrooms with four-poster beds draped in mosquito netting, private plunge pools, and decks overlooking a forested gorge through which the Sabie River cascades. River Moon, the latest, is built on the lip of the gorge in the style of a Moroccan castle, as is New Moon, which offers better value. Luxurious bathrooms and outdoor showers enjoy similar views. All this privacy comes at a price, and with no phone there's no chance of room service and you have to drive to get to the dining room, a candlelit restaurant built on stilts. Dinner menus are set three-course meals, followed by a selection of cheeses (any dietary preferences need to be cleared in advance). A good budget alternative are the two fully serviced self-catering cottages; although they don't have pools, they are furnished with flair and are extremely spacious. Each features two bedrooms, two bathrooms, a lounge, a private balcony (with wonderful forest views), and a fireplace. Dinner (R120/$15) may be booked at the restaurant a day in advance, or opt for one of the many choices in the area.

Postnet Suite 1, Private Bag X2640, Hazyview 1242. (24km/15miles east of Sabie turn off from R536, follow signs for 3km/2miles). ℂ 013/767-1740 or 082-445-3788. Fax 013/767-1889. www.timamoonlodge.co.za. 5 units. 4 lodges: R1,700–R2,600 ($212–$325) double (from R700/$88pp for four people sharing). Rates include breakfast and dinner. Self-catering cottages: R750 ($95) double; R1,200 ($150) four people; rate includes breakfast. No children under age 12 in lodges. **Amenities:** Restaurant; private plunge pool (lodges). *In room:* TV (cottages only), minibar (lodges only; cottages on request), hair dryer on request.

Near Hazyview

Casa do Sol ★ *Kids* A charming Mediterranean-style village, complete with cobbled streets, white stucco walls, and terra-cotta roof tiles, set in award-winning tropical gardens behind which stretch 500 hectares (1,250 acres) of indigenous bush, Casa do Sol was established in 1968, and still retains a vaguely 1970s feel, despite regular decor updates. The C and D suites are ideal for families—the D suites are upstairs and feature views of the valley and estate from the private patio. Dinners offer a choice of three starters, three main courses, and

Driving the Panorama Route

This drive takes you past the Blyde River Canyon, the third largest canyon in the world, and the sheer 1,600m (5,200-ft.) drop from the Escarpment to the warm lowveld plains shimmering below. Hot air rising over this wall generates the heavy mists and high rainfall that in turn create the unique montane grasslands and riverine forests of the Blyde River Canyon Nature Reserve, which start just north of Graskop before broadening out to include the Blydepoort Dam, 60km (37 miles) north. To complete the Panorama Route as a circular trip (approximately 160km/100 miles), stopping for most of the viewpoints and returning to either Sabie or Graskop, set aside a day.

As you follow the tour below, refer to the "Panorama Route & Sabie" map in this chapter for more information.

To drive this route, take the R532 north out of Graskop, before turning right on the R534. The first stop is the **Pinnacle**—a thin, 30m (100-ft.) tall quartzite rock topped with trees that juts below the viewpoint—but **God's Window** 🎯🎯, 4km (2½ miles) farther, which offers the first view of the open lowveld plains, is more impressive. (Wonderview is a variation of this and can be skipped if you're pressed for time.) The looping R534 now rejoins the R532. Turn left and look for the sign if you want to visit **Lisbon Falls**, which drop 37m (120 ft.). To continue on to Blyde River Canyon, turn right onto the R532, taking in the 48m (159-ft.) **Berlin Falls** on the way. If you're ready for refreshments, the **Berlin Peacock Tavern** 🎯 (© 013/767-1085) lies on the way to the Berlin Falls—aside from some spectacularly over-the-top baroque decor, the food is delicious, and according to the visitors' book, even rival lodge-owners visit regularly.

Back on the R532, head north for **Bourke's Luck Potholes** (© 013/761-6019). Here gold-digger Bourke predicted that he would strike it lucky, but he found nothing in these large scooped formations, carved by the movement of pebbles and water in the swirling whirlpools created by the confluence of the Blyde and Treur rivers. Bourke was not the last person to be disappointed by the Potholes—it's a long walk to look at them, and they reveal very little. Nor does the visitor center, which, in addition to some dry displays on the geology of the area, features a few dusty stuffed animals that look close to decomposing. The lichen trail is very easy, and good for children. Gates open from 7am to 5pm; admission is R20 (¢).

Some 20km (12 miles) north is the lookout for the **Three Rondawels** 🎯🎯🎯, by far the most impressive stop of the entire trip. The name—which refers to the three circular hut-shaped outcrops that are more or less opposite the lookout—does nothing to describe the humbling size of what beckons. A sheer drop threatens to pull you off the precipice; thousands of feet below, the Blyde River snakes its way through the canyon to the tranquil Blyde Dam, embraced by green mountains. Beyond, the great lowveld plains shimmer in the distance.

Tip: If you're feeling thirsty, drop into the **Aventura Blydepoort Resort** (the turnoff is a couple of miles north past the Three Rondawels and clearly signposted; ℂ 013/769-8005), which offers another angle on the Three Rondawels from its terrace; however, much beyond a toasted sandwich is not recommended. (To take a look at its budget self-catering lodging, go to www.aventura.co.za—and ask for a cottage with a view.)

From here you will descend the **Abel Erasmus Pass,** before passing through the J.G. Strijdom Tunnel—approximately 20km (12 miles) from here is the turnoff for **Monsoon Gallery** (ℂ 015/795-5114), off the R527. Monsoon is renowned for its fine selection of African crafts, but recent visits have found stocks much depleted. You can enjoy a light meal at the adjacent **Mad Dogz Café** (ℂ 015/795-5425) or make an appointment to meet with John Williams (see "Specialist Tours," earlier in this chapter) about archaeological and ecotours.

At this point, you can stay on the R527, heading east for Hoedspruit, if you wish to enter the Timbavati private game reserve, or head for the airport. If not, take the R531 southeast to Klaserie—look for the turnoff to **Aventura Swadini** (ℂ 015/795-5141). From here you can take a 90-minute boat trip on the Blyde Dam to see the mouth of the canyon and look up at the Escarpment towering above (R60/$7.50 per adult; R30/$3.75 children ages 5–15). The R531 takes you to Kruger to enter via Orpen Gate (the closest to the Satara Rest Camp), or to travel to the Manyeleti or northern Sabi Sand reserves via Gowry Gate. Turn north on the R40 to Kapama, a fenced private reserve, and site of the popular **Hoedspruit Research and Breeding Centre for Endangered Species** (ℂ 015/793-1633), also known as the "Cheetah Project." This is also the pick-up point for Kapama's exciting new elephant-back safaris. The latter is well worth considering: For R1,500 ($188) you get to be transported through big-game country on the back of one of the these lumbering giants and learn more about this most intelligent of species; for times and bookings, call Rika at ℂ 015/793-1633. The Cheetah Project is equally educational but far less exhilarating. Guided tours (every hour, 8am–3pm, daily) kick off with a video presentation, after which you are driven through the center by a ranger, sighting cheetahs, wild dog, rhino, and various bird species. At 90 minutes the tour is a tad long, and although one of the cheetahs has been successfully released into the wilds, it still feels a little like a large, comfortable zoo. The tour that takes in the rare Barbary lion—identified by his extended black mane—is more like a traditional game drive (the lions are kept in a 17-acre area) but will take 3 hours out of your day.

To return to Graskop, take the R40 south from Klaserie, then follow the R533 from Bosbokrand, climbing Kowyn's Pass to Graskop. (Note that the R40 between Hazyview and Acorn Hoek is unsafe to travel at night when animals wander at will, and a few travelers have been ambushed. During daylight you're more likely to be pulled over for speeding, so take it easy.)

a dessert and cheese board; diners are welcome to indulge in all nine courses. This is an all-round excellent hotel, though it doesn't offer the well-bred intimacy of lodges like Blue Mountain, Highgrove, or Cybele.

P.O. Box 57, Hazyview 1242, off the R536, 39km (24 miles) east of Sabie and 5km (3 miles) west of Hazyview. ✆ 013/737-8111. Fax 013/737-8166. www.casadosol.co.za. 54 units. Casa R880–990 ($110–$124) double depending on season; Villa R1,080–1,180 ($135–$148); C and D suites R1,300–1,610 ($162–$202). All rates include breakfast and dinner. Children under age 12 R145 ($18); age 12 and over R275 ($34). AE, DC, MC, V. **Amenities:** Restaurant; bar; 2 large swimming pools; 4 golf courses within 20 minutes' drive; all-weather tennis court; 24-hr. room service; babysitting; same-day laundry; horseback riding; bass fishing; trails to view antelope; tours and safaris arranged with recommended operators. *In room:* A/C, TV, minibar (villas and suites), hair dryer.

Cybele Forest Lodge ★★★

Long before crime encouraged Jo'burgers to take regular long weekend getaways, the rooms at Cybele were booked months in advance, and the way you pronounced the name said a lot about how happening you were (it's pronounced "sigh-*bee*-lee"). Even Capetonians traveled north to sample the legendary cuisine (the lodge is a member of Relais & Chateaux) and to relax in the subtropical surrounds. Over the years, owners Rupert and Barbara Jeffries have added a number of freestanding suites, and a pool has replaced the farm dam, but the standard of the food and the beauty of the 120-hectare (300-acre) grounds remain unchanged. The original farmhouse, where the lounge and dining room are situated, is wonderful: Rooms are painted in rich, warm colors and are cluttered with an eclectic mix of antiques, English country–style fabrics, kilim rugs, and a few African crafts. The original bedrooms have recently been revamped, the spa recently opened, and the entire lodge has been upgraded by Relais & Chateaux to Yellow Shield status, defined as "the refined comfort of a magnificent residence." And it rather is.

P.O. Box 346, White River 1240. (Take the Kiepersol turnoff, 28km [17 miles] east of Sabie on the R536; follow for 10km [6 miles] before taking a road to the left marked "whitewaters" and following Cybele signs. Alternatively, follow signs off the R40 between Hazyview and White River.) ✆ 013/764-1823. Fax 013/764-1810. www.cybele.co.za. 12 units. R1,770–R2,190 ($220–$272) double; R2,790–R3,380 ($348–$422) suites; R3,980–R4,530 ($498–$566) Paddock suites. Rates include breakfast and dinner. Inquire about winter rates. AE, DC, MC, V. No children under age 10. **Amenities:** Restaurant; bar; pool; spa; horseback riding (the surrounds are truly beautiful); hiking trails; trout fishing (tackle is provided). *In room:* TV, fans (A/C suite 14), minibar, stereo, hair dryer, fireplaces, private pool (suites).

Highgrove House ★★

It's no wonder Highgrove House won the category for Best Retreat/Small Luxury Hotel in the customer-determined AA Awards for 3 years running—the grand tree-lined driveway provides some clue as to what lies at the end of the cul-de-sac: an elegant old-fashioned country retreat where guests are treated like royalty.

"English-country" style is a constant theme in South African decor, but here it is particularly well done; the eight garden suites (of which Orchard 1 is a personal favorite, and well worth the extra R500/$62) are decorated in pale, earthy colors and feature separate sitting rooms with log fireplaces and double doors that lead onto verandas with marvelous views over the forest or valley. Beautifully presented dinners, prepared by the talented Anna Mahlele under the watchful eye of proprietor Mary Terry, are—together with the meals served at Blue Mountain—considered by many to be the best in Mpumalanga (see "Where to Dine," below). The candlelit atmosphere is romantic but may be a bit formal for some vacationers—no jeans or sneakers allowed.

P.O. Box 46, Kiepersol 1241. (Off R40, 17km [10½ miles] south of Hazyview.) ✆ 013/764-1844. Fax 013/764-1855. www.highgrove.co.za. 8 units. R2,300 ($288) double; Orchard Suites R2,800 ($350); rates include dinner and breakfast. AE, DC, MC, V. Children age 14 and over welcome. **Amenities:** Restaurant; bar;

1 large pool and 2 private pools (each Orchard Suite has a private pool and sauna); limited room service. *In room:* Minibar in Orchard Suites, hair dryer.

Rissington Inn ⋆ *Value* *Kids* Rissington offers unbeatable value, and with Kruger's Phabeni Gate just 10 minutes away, it makes an extremely comfortable base from which to explore Kruger and the Escarpment surrounds. What it lacks in style (the honeymoon suite has a false thatch roof jutting over the bed), the inn makes up for in charm, comfort, and great food. With the addition of three new garden suites (Rissington is understandably popular), seating in the dining room for non-residents is now limited—all the more reason to book ahead to ensure a seat. The food is excellent value as well, with most main dinner courses costing about R45 ($5.50). Of the 10 rooms, Euphorbia (sunset-facing, with a sitting room and a super-king-size bed) and Ivory (a garden view, a deep veranda with built-in day bed, and super-king-size bed) are highly recommended. Camelfoot and Sycamore, both spacious and furnished with two queen-size beds, are good choices for families. Proprietor Chris Harvie is known throughout the region for his great sense of hospitality, dry humor, and sensible approach to pricing.

P.O. Box 650, Hazyview 1242. (1km [½ mile] south of Hazyview, follow signposts off R40.) © 013/737-7700. Fax 013/737-7112. www.rissington.co.za. 7 units. R470–R780 ($60–$98) double, includes breakfast. Children sharing R80 ($10). AE, DC, MC, V. **Amenities:** Restaurant; bar; pool; room service; laundry; library. *In room:* Hair dryer on request.

WHERE TO DINE

Sabie is the town with the most restaurants, but only one is worth stopping for. **Country Kitchen** (78 Main St.; © **013/764-1901**) is by far the best restaurant option in town. The venue may lack atmosphere, but the food, prepared by Hilton-trained Edmund Idzik, is excellent (try the crocodile strips served with papaya, followed by guinea-fowl galantine, filled with figs, bacon, sweet onion and served with port-wine sauce). For ambience, the **Artists Café** (see below) is well worth the detour. Note also that many of the places listed in "Where to Stay" section, above, are renowned for their fine cuisine and romantic atmosphere. Besides **Blue Mountain Lodge** (reviewed below), **Highgrove** is definitely worth considering. Superb five-course dinners (R120/$15 per person) are served in a candlelit fine-dining atmosphere (note that you are required to dress up) and recent fare included a goat's cheese and tomato soufflé served with hazelnut and Parmesan sauce, followed by East Coast sole baked with bay leaves and oregano—really worth writing home about! The **Cybele Forest Lodge** (see above) is another romantic fine-dining dinner experience; you can also opt for a light lunch in their gardens (R25–R85/$2.60–$5.75)—the vegetables are home-grown, the house salad is picked fresh daily, and the pasta is homemade.

If you're looking for great-value home-cooked fare, served in a truly laid-back atmosphere, **Rissington Inn**'s convivial vibe is unbeatable—order the smoked-trout cheesecake or the beef stroganoff—Chris also serves up the most delicious filet this side of Hazyview. Last but not least, if you're interested in sampling traditional African fare accompanied by some superb singing and dancing by local Shangaan people, book an "Evening Festival" at the nearby **Shangana Cultural Village.**

Near Sabie

Artists Café ⋆⋆ *Value* RURAL ITALIAN This delightful trattoria in the middle of nowhere has recently been purchased by Leon and his wife, Jane, but thankfully, chef Jane Mabaling, trained by the original owner, is still here, preparing delicious trademark dishes like Agnello di la Arrosto (lamb shank slow-braised in wine and herbs). In keeping with the simple food, the atmosphere in the restaurant is casual—chairs are mismatched, dishcloths serve as napkins, and walls are covered with local artworks as well as crafts from across Africa, most of which are for sale. The wine list features an excellent selection of South African wines, and the food is well-priced and delicious—try the slow-roasted free-range duck served with a piquant orange sauce. (*Note:* You needn't tear yourself away after sampling the superb selection of South African dessert wines; four en-suite bedrooms are available for R490/$62 double, including breakfast.)

Hendriksdal siding, 17km (10½ miles) south of Sabie. Take the Hendriksdal turn off the R37. ✆ 013/764-2309. Reservations recommended. Main courses R36–R47 ($4.50–$5.90). AE, DC, MC, V. Daily 8am–11pm.

Blue Mountain Lodge ★★ FRENCH PROVENÇAL   This is alfresco dining at its most romantic, so make sure to get here before dark to enjoy a drink on the deep verandas overlooking the lush, manicured gardens of this 200-hectare (494-acre) estate. The cuisine is as over-the-top and sumptuous as the decor (anyone for strawberry champagne soup served with gin cream and Madagascar green peppers?), and although executive chef Elvis Mnisi uses many of the ingredients grown on the farm—among them, avocados, macadamia nuts, and litchis—his imagination (and budget) is in no way limited to local produce. The small a la carte lunch menu offers a choice of hot or cold starters, two soups, and a meat, fish, or vegetarian main, as well as a choice of delicious sandwiches (crumbed smoked salmon, lemon pepper, chunky cottage cheese, and marinated julienned cucumber) and desserts. (see "Where to Stay," above, for more information).

Take the Kiepersol turnoff 28km (17 miles) east of Sabie on the R536, then follow signs. ✆ 013/737-8446. Breakfast R45 ($5.50); lunch main courses R27–R68 ($3.25–$8.50); dinner R180 ($15). AE, DC, MC, V. Daily 7am–5pm and 7pm till late.

In Graskop

Harrie's Pancakes ★ *Value* PANCAKES   You'll come across a number of pancake restaurants in the Escarpment towns, all spawned by the success of the legendary Harrie. Harrie Sietsema opened his doors 14 years ago, and today you can find his restaurant by simply looking for the congregation of tour buses. Tasting one of his thick crepes should definitely be high on your priority list—some of the most popular savory fillings include trout mousse and horseradish, and butternut with cumin and blue cheese sauce. If you're in time for tea, the black cherries and liqueur sauce or green fig preserves and pecan nuts—both with either cream or ice cream—are knockouts. Note that Harrie's is unlicensed.

Corner Kerk and Louis Trichardt sts., Graskop (23km/14 miles north of Sabie). ✆ 013/767-1273. R18–R31 ($2.35–$3.80). MC, V. 8am–6pm daily.

Thistle's Country Kitchen ★ *Finds* COUNTRY FARE   If you can't face the tourist hordes but don't mind sharing a table, Thistle's is a very intimate affair: only three tables, each seating 4 to 8, and personally attended to by Bevvie Myberg, Graskop's one-woman wonder, who cooks, waits, and washes in her home-style restaurant. The small menu, written up on a blackboard, is prepared daily and changes regularly, but meals are renowned for their fresh taste combinations and beautiful presentation.

11B Main St., Graskop (in courtyard behind the forest shop). ✆ 082-467-5276. Advanced bookings only; hours vary, so it's best to call ahead and check.

PILGRIM'S REST

The village of Pilgrim's Rest was established in 1873 after "Wheelbarrow" Patterson discovered gold in the stream that flows past what was to become the first gold-rush town in South Africa. Having struck out on his own to escape the crush at Mac Mac, he must have been horrified when within the year he was joined by 1,500 diggers, all frantically panning to make their fortunes. A fair number did, with the largest nugget weighing in at 24 pounds; but by 1881 the best of the pickings had been found, and the diggings were bought by the Transvaal Gold Mining Estates (TGME). A century later, the village still looked much the same, and the entire settlement was declared a national monument, with the Works Department and Museum Services put in charge of restoring and preserving this living museum.

If you're looking for historical accuracy, then you'll find Pilgrim's Rest over-commercialized; the town's streets are probably a great deal prettier than they were at the turn of the 20th century, and the overall effect, from the gleaming vintage fuel pumps to the flower baskets, is a sanitized, glamorized picture of life in a gold-rush town. As theme parks go, however, Pilgrim's Rest is a pleasant experience. Most of the buildings line a single main street, and the architecture is of the quaint Victorian variety prevalent in so many of colonial Africa's rural towns—walls are corrugated iron with deep sash windows, and corrugated-iron roofs extend over large shaded *stoeps* (verandas).

ESSENTIALS

GETTING THERE   Travel north from Sabie on R532. The R532 meets with the R533 in a T-junction; head northwest on R533 for 15km (just over 9 miles). Pilgrim's Rest is 35km (22 miles) north of Sabie and about 360km (223 miles) northeast of Johannesburg.

VISITOR INFORMATION   Contact the **Tourist Information Centre** (© **013/768-1060**) and if possible ask for the information officer. The center is clearly marked on the main street. Hours are daily from 8:30am to 12:45pm and 1:15 to 4:30pm; the staff will supply free town maps as well as tickets to the museums, and will book tours for you.

GETTING AROUND   Pilgrim's Rest has no street numbers; it's literally a one-horse town, with buildings stretched along a main road. Uptown, or Top Town, is literally the higher (and older) part of the main road, while Downtown stretches below the turnoff into town. Most of the tourist sights are situated in Uptown, as is the tourist office. For guided tours, contact John Pringle (ex–Information Officer for the town) on © **083-522-6441.**

WHAT TO SEE & DO

St. Mary's Anglican Church, seen overlooking the main street as you enter town, is where sinners' souls were salvaged. Higher up the hill, the evocative **Pilgrim's Rest Cemetery** ★★ is definitely worth a visit. Besides the tombstone simply inscribed ROBBERS GRAVE—easily identified because it is the only grave that lies in a north-south direction—the many children's graves are moving testimony to how hard times really were, and the many nationalities reflect the cosmopolitan character of the original gold-rush village.

The three museums in town, the **Dredzen Shop and House Museum,** the **News Printing Museum,** and the **House Museum,** can all be visited with the ticket sold at the Tourist Information Centre (R10/$1.30 adult; R5/65¢ 12 and under). They open and close for the day at the same time as the information center, and close for half an hour at 1pm (because Pilgrim's Rest is effectively owned by the government, it is plagued with a civil-service mentality). Neither of the house museums feels particularly authentic; furnishings and objects are often propped haphazardly and look much the worse for wear.

The **Alanglade Museum** 𝕬𝕬 (no phone; R20/$2.60), which used to house the TGME's mine manager and his family, is more interesting. Although the furnishings, which date from 1900 to 1930, are not original, they have been selected to represent the era and are maintained with more care than those in the house museums. It is set in a forested grove 1.5km (about 1 mile) north of town. Tours, which cost R20 ($2.60), are offered at 11am and 2pm, Monday through Saturday, and must be booked half an hour in advance from the Pilgrim's Rest Tourist Information Centre.

Don't leave town without popping in to the Royal Hotel's **Church Bar** 𝕬 (the tiny building used to be a church in Mozambique before it was relocated here, thereby answering the prayers of the thirsty Pilgrims of Mpumalanga).

WHERE TO STAY

District Six Miners' Cottages 𝘝𝘢𝘭𝘶𝘦   The District Six cottages date back to the early 1920s. Set high up on the hill overlooking the town, these spartan accommodations have lovely views from their verandas, and are serviced daily. Each has two bedrooms, a living room, a bathroom, and a fully equipped kitchen. Not surprisingly, these cheap, charming cottages are popular during school holidays—so make sure to book ahead. Keys are collected at the Royal Hotel.

Public Works Private X516, Pilgrim's Rest 1290. Book in advance; there is no on-site office. ℂ **013/768-1261.** Fax 013/768-1113. 6 units. R170 ($21) for 4-bed and R210 ($26) for 6-bed cottage. No credit cards.

The Royal Hotel 𝕬   The Royal first opened its doors in 1873, and more than a century later it's still going strong—this is one of the most charming places to overnight on the Escarpment. Besides the 11 original hotel rooms, which are arranged around a small courtyard behind the reception area, the hotel has grown to include 39 rooms located in buildings adjacent to the hotel, all dating back to the turn of the 20th century and impeccably restored and furnished in the Victorian style. The relatively small bedrooms feature brass beds, many of them four-poster, wooden ceiling fans, marble-and-oak washstands and ball-and-claw bathtubs. This is not a luxurious experience, however—the mattresses are a little monastic, and corrugated-iron houses can become bitterly cold in winter. The honeymoon suite, situated in the Bank House, is the only room with a fireplace, and during June and July, when temperatures drop close to freezing, it's worth booking well in advance. The buffet breakfasts are lavish and served in the classy Peach Tree Creek. The Digger's Den, which also has a period feel, is where lunch and dinner are served.

Main Road, Uptown, Pilgrim's Rest 1290. ℂ **013/768-1100.** Fax 013/768-1188. www.royal-hotel.co.za. 50 units. R850 ($106) double, including breakfast. Ask about winter specials. AE, DC, MC, V. **Amenities:** 2 restaurants; bar; golf, tennis, horseback riding, and trout fishing can be arranged; babysitting; laundry. *In room:* Hair dryer.

WHERE TO DINE

You'll find a number of places to eat and drink, all ranged along the main road. Besides the reputable **Vine** (ℂ **013/768-1080**), downtown's **Jubilee's** (ℂ **013/768-1151**) boasts the best burgers in town. **Scott's Cafe** (ℂ **013/768-1061**) specializes in salads, pancakes, and good but pricey African art. For quality home-style country cooking, and lovely views, your best bet is **Inn on Robber's Pass** ✪ (off the R533, 15km/9.3miles from Pilgrim's Rest; ℂ **013/768-1491**), but you'll have to drive to get there.

5 Kruger National Park ✪✪✪

Southern (Malelane) gate: 428km (265 miles) NE of Johannesburg
Northern (Punda Maria) gate: 581km (360 miles) NE of Johannesburg

Proclaimed by South African president Paul Kruger in 1898, this jewel in the National Parks Board crown stretches 381km (236 miles) from the banks of the Crocodile River in the south to the Limpopo River in the north and covers almost 2½ million hectares (6.2 million acres).

Even more impressive than its size, however, is the diversity of life the Kruger sustains: 16 ecozones (each with its own geology, rainfall, altitude, and landscape) are home to more than 500 bird species and 147 mammal species, including some 2,000 lions, 1,000 leopards, 1,800 rhinos, 8,000 elephants, and 15,000 buffaloes. Cheetahs, wild dogs, hyenas, zebras, giraffes, hippos, crocodiles, warthogs, and a large number of antelope also roam Kruger's open plains and waterways. The rich plant life varies from tropical to subtropical; almost 2,000 species have been identified, including some 450 tree and shrub species and 235 grasses. The opportunity to see wildlife is superb—many people report seeing four of the Big 5 (the most elusive being leopard) in one day.

Kruger also has a number of archaeological sites, the most interesting being Thulamela, a 12th-century stone-walled village overlooking the Luvuvhu River in the north. Others include the Stone Age village at Masorini and San engravings and paintings found at the Crocodile Bridge hippo pool or on the Bushman and Wolhuter trails. Historical sites relating to early European explorers and Kruger's beginnings are also dotted throughout the park.

Finally, in what is arguably the continent's most exciting development in ecotourism, fences between the Kruger and Zimbabwe's Gonarezhou National Park and Mozambique's Gaza Reserve were removed in 2002. At 37.5 million hectares (92.5 million acres), the **Great Limpopo Transfrontier Park,** or, simply, **Limpopo Park,** as the park is currently referred to, is the biggest conservation area in the world. For more on the park, go to **www.gkgpark.com**.

ESSENTIALS
ARRIVING
BY PLANE   There are three airports in the Kruger vicinity: Kruger-Mpumalanga International Airport (near White River and Hazyview, southern Kruger), Eastgate Airport (Hoedspruit, southern/central Kruger), and the Kruger Park Gateway Airport (Phalaborwa, central Kruger). **From Cape Town: SA Express** (www.saexpress.co.za) flies daily to Hoedspruit's Eastgate Airport. **SA Airlink** (www.saairlink.co.za) flies daily to the relatively nearby Kruger-Mpumalanga International—as does **Nationwide** (www.flynationwide.co.za), but you'll have to stop in Johannesburg for at least 20 minutes to pick up

---

⟨ *Fun Fact* **Going to the Dogs**

While most tourists love chasing after lion, it takes a small scruffy dog with rather powerful jaws to excite a ranger: The wild dog is Africa's rarest and most endangered predator.

> **Tips   Saving You Time & Money**
>
> **Expressions of Africa** (© 011/978-3552; www.saexpress.co.za), a division of SA Express, caters to travel agents and individuals wanting to fly in to safari destinations throughout southern Africa. Work out a rough itinerary and contact them directly for the best deals on flights and possible savings on accommodations.

passengers. **From Johannesburg:** SA Express flies daily to Hoedspruit's Eastgate Airport; SA Airlink and Nationwide fly daily to Kruger-Mpumalanga International. SA Airlink also flies daily from Johannesburg into Kruger Park Gateway Airport. **From Durban:** SA Airlink flies Sunday through Friday to Kruger-Mpumalanga airport.

BY CAR   There are nine entrance gates, most a comfortable 5- to 6-hour drive from Johannesburg or Pretoria. The closest gate, Malelane, is 428km (265 miles) from Johannesburg, while Punda Maria (the farthest) lies 581km (360 miles) northeast. The southern gates: **Malelane, Crocodile Bridge, Numbi, Phabeni,** and **Paul Kruger.** The central gates: **Orpen** and **Phalaborwa.** The northern gates: **Punda Maria** and **Parfuri.** Allow sufficient traveling time to the park; entrance-gate hours (see "Fast Facts," below) are strictly adhered to. Note that officials recommend using the new Phabeni Gate from safety and ease of access point of view.

VISITOR INFORMATION   All inquiries and applications should be made to the **National Parks Board** (643 Leyds St., Muckleneuk, Pretoria; © 012/428-9111; www.parks-sa.co.za; Mon–Fri 8am–3:30pm, Sat 8am–1pm). Or you can e-mail them at reservations@parks-sa.co.za or traveltrade@parks-sa.co.za. For short-notice bookings (3 days or less in advance), you can also phone the park directly at © 013/735-4000 or © 013/735-4246. The park's headquarters is situated at Skukuza Rest Camp, located in the southern section, on the banks of the Sabie River (see later in this chapter).

GETTING AROUND   By Car   Avis has a desk at the Eastgate Airport (© 015/793-2014); at the Kruger-Mpumalanga airport (© 013/741-1087); and at Phalaborwa's Kruger airport (© 015/781-3169). **Budget** operates from the Kruger-Mpumalanga airport (© 013/741-3871) and Phalaborwa's Kruger airport (© 015/781-5404). It's exciting to explore the park at your own pace in a rental car, but at least one guided game drive in an open-topped vehicle is recommended (see "Organized Tours," at the beginning of the chapter). Also see "Guided Game Drives," below—these take place in a variety of vehicles and are organized by Kruger officials.

WHEN TO GO

Each season has advantages. Between October and March, when summer rains (often in the form of dramatic thunderstorms) have transformed the dry landscape into a flowering paradise, the park is alive with baby buck and migratory birds, but at the same time temperatures can soar above 105°F (40°C), dropping to 68°F (20°C) in the balmy evenings. The dense junglelike foliage hides game, and the malaria risk is at its highest. In the winter, when water is scarce and the plant life dies back, animals are easier to spot, especially at water holes and riverbeds. Because this is the most popular season, however, be prepared to share your sightings with other motorists. The days are warm, but temperatures can drop close to freezing at night, and units are not heated. Try to avoid going during the school holidays, particularly in winter, when the park is packed to capacity.

FAST FACTS: Kruger National Park

Admission Hours **For the Park**   Entrance gates open from January to February from 5:30am to 6:30pm; March from 5:30am to 6pm; April from 6am to 6pm; May to July 6am to 5:30pm; August to September 6am to 6pm; October from 5:30am to 6pm; and November to December from 5:30am to 6:30pm.

For the Rest Camps   The gates follow the same hours except in the summer months (Nov–Jan) when they open an hour earlier (that is, 4:30am). Camps are fenced off to protect residents from predators. If you're changing rest camps, try not to travel more than 200km (124 miles) to ensure that you get to your new camp before its gates close. Operating hours for camp receptions are from 8am to 5:30pm; for shops from 8am to ½ hour after camp gates close; for restaurants from 7 to 9am, 12 to 2pm, and 6 to 9pm.

Bank & ATM Networks   There is a bank and ATM at Skukuza, and an ATM at Letaba.

Driving Rules   Unlike private game reserves where rangers are free to drive off road, everyone at Kruger drives on roads; the public drives on approved roads only. The speed limit is 50kmph on paved roads; 40kmph on gravel roads; 20kmph in rest camps (30, 25, and 15 mph, respectively). If photographs of fatally maimed animals don't help ensure that these speeds are adhered to, speed traps do. Stay in your vehicle unless you're at a designated picnic site.

Fees   Admission is R30 ($4.75) per person and R24 ($3) per vehicle; children ages 2 to 15 R15 ($2).

Fuel   There is a fuel/petrol station in every rest camp. You must pay in cash.

Malaria   The highest risk is between October and May, during which time a course of prescription anti-malaria drugs is advised (for more information, see chapter 2).

Medical Emergencies   There is a doctor in Skukuza (© **013/735-5638**). If you need help during the night, drive to the camp gate and beep your horn. The closest hospitals are in Nelspruit, Hoedspruit, and Phalaborwa.

Money   South African rand, traveler's checks, Visa, MasterCard, Diners Club, and American Express are accepted. Foreign currency can be exchanged at all rest camps.

Reservations   Preference for choice units is given to written applications (this includes fax and e-mail) received 13 months in advance. Pay your deposit as soon as possible to ensure the booking—this can be done over the telephone with a credit card.

Safety   Don't let the tarred road fool you—once you've left the safety of your fenced-off rest camp, you really are in the wilds. *Under no circumstances* should you leave your vehicle unless at a designated site (see "Designated Pit Stops & Picnic Sites," below, or get a map from a rest camp shop); one ranger who left his game drive to "relieve" himself didn't survive to do up his zipper, so make sure to take care of any bathroom business before leaving camp. When in camp, try not to be frightened by spiders and other small insects you may encounter; unlike mosquitoes, they can do you no harm. Snakes are a rare occurrence in camps; if you do spot one, alert reception. (See chapter 2 for more safety tips on safaris.)

EXPLORING THE PARK

Parks Board officials make no bones about the fact that their main concern is wildlife; Homo sapiens are a necessary nuisance. Although an effort is made to service visitors' needs, such as providing escorted night and day drives (highly recommended unless you're going on to a private game reserve), the rules (like gate opening times) are inflexible, the staff can be bureaucratic, and, because services are geared toward the South African self-catering market, you're pretty much expected to toe the line. Here's how.

THE LAY OF THE LAND

Despite its many defined ecozones, to the untrained eye much of the park looks the same, with a major portion covered with a large shrublike tree called mopane. You'll find the most variation in the south and far north of the park—old bush hands in fact divide the park into three distinct regions: The south they call the "circus"; the central area, the "zoo"; and the north, the "wilderness." These are apt descriptions, particularly in the winter months, when the human and animal population soars in the water-rich south, while the less-accessible north remains a calm oasis.

Southern Kruger supports some of the richest game concentrations in Africa, which in turn attracts the most people. The busiest—and often very rewarding—road linking Skukuza to Lower Sabie Rest Camp is often referred to as **Piccadilly Highway,** and motorists have been known to jostle each other to get a better view of lions and even create traffic jams around great sightings.

The **central area** still features a wide variety of species, particularly around Satara Rest Camp. A little more laid-back, with fewer camps, but with a reputation for the highest concentration of lions, this area continues to attract its fair share of tourists.

Most of the 7,500-odd resident elephants are found north of Olifants rest camp, but mile after mile of dense mopane scrubland makes even these huge animals difficult to see. The **northern part** of the park is probably not the best destination for a first-time visitor, unless it's combined with a sojourn in the south; but this wilderness area has definite advantages for real bush lovers, not least because there are fewer people. As you travel farther north, the mopane is broken by the lush riverine vegetation of the Shingwedzi, the baobab-dotted sandveld, and finally, the tropical floodplains that lie between the Luvuvhu and Limpopo rivers. This northernmost part of the park is in fact at the crossroads of nine of Africa's major ecosystems, and the countryside is full of contrasts. Spend at least 5 days in the Kruger if you include the north in your itinerary.

DESIGNATED PIT STOPS & PICNIC SITES

The designated sites dotted throughout the park are *the only places visitors are allowed to get out of their vehicles.* Maps, available at all rest camp shops, will indicate where these are located, as well as the types of facilities each has. (These may include restrooms, boiling water, barbecues, seating, shade, telephones, educational displays, and shops manned by attendants who sell wood, hot refreshments, and cold drinks.) The two best-equipped and most popular sites are **Nkulu,** on the Sabie River between Skukuza and Lower Sabie (that is, off Piccadilly Highway), and **Tshokwane,** named after an elephant bull that frequents the area. The shop here sells everything from scones to brandy. Less busy, and with good game- and bird-viewing opportunities, are **Orpen Dam,** an elevated picnic spot overlooking the water, east of Tshokwane, and **Parfuri,** considered the best picnic site in the park, but located in the far north.

GUIDED GAME DRIVES & WALKS

Even if you're self-driving, a guided game drive is a good way to get oriented; it also allows you to travel park roads that are usually inaccessible to tourists and have the animals around you identified by experienced rangers without having to look it up in a book. Sadly, the major rest camps provide these in large 23- to 46-seat vehicles; the only way to avoid the potential noise and obstructed views is to book into one of the recommended bush camps, where game drives take place in 10-seaters (See "Where to Stay: Bush Camps," below).

The best option, offered almost everywhere, is an **early-morning drive** ★★★ (R95/$12 per person, R130/$16 bush camps), which departs any time from 4 to 6am (30 minutes before gates open). There is also now a 2-hour **mid-morning drive** that departs at 9am (R70/$8.75 per person, R110/$14 bush camps), but the early morning usually sees more activity. The 3-hour **sunset drives** (R95/$12; bush camps R130/$16), departing 2 hours before the gates close, are popular, but the 2-hour **night drive** ★★★ (R95/$12), departing 2 hours after the gates close, is the one to make sure you're on. Outside the concession areas, this is the only way to see the Kruger at night, giving visitors an opportunity to view the nocturnal activities of such animals as bushbabies, porcupines, civets, hyenas, honey badgers, and aardvarks. Be warned, however, that nocturnal animals are shy, and on a bad night sightings can be frustratingly rare. Night drives cost R80/$10 (R120/$15 in bush camps) and are currently only available from the following rest camps: Letaba, Mopani, Olifants, Pretoriuskop, Skukuza, and Shingwedzi, and from bush camps Shimuwini and Sirheni—all subject to change, so check when booking. You can book any of these drives when making your accommodations booking—particularly advisable for early-morning and night drives and during school holidays.

In another attempt to become more visitor-friendly, a few rest and bushveld camps in Kruger now also offer **Bush braais,** late-afternoon game drives that conclude with a barbecue under the stars, and **Bush "breakfasts,"** where you break for a sandwich-type meal in the bush; cost for either is R175 ($22) per person. **Guided morning walks** ★★★ (R175/$22 per person), usually lasting 3 to 4 hours, with a maximum of 8 people, are also now offered at selected rest camps and bushveld camps—these too are recommended.

For private tour operators offering full-day and half-day game drives in the park (the advantage of these trips being that they cater to fewer people), see "Organized Tours," at the beginning of this chapter.

WILDERNESS TRAILS ★★★

These 3- or 4-day trails (R1,690/$211 per person for the duration), catering to a maximum of eight people, offer the only opportunity to experience the real essence of the African bush in Kruger. Although you are unlikely to see quite as

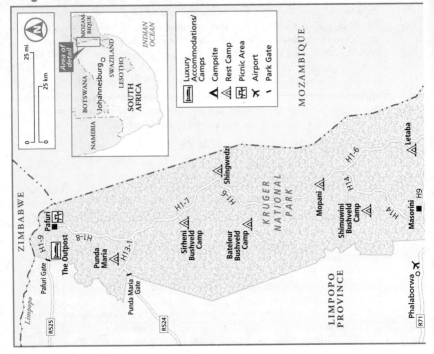

much big game on foot (and you may spend a lot of time hoping you don't), and you won't get as close to most animals as you can in a vehicle (animals don't associate the smell of gasoline with humans), you will be introduced to the trees, insects, and animals that make up the surrounding bush under the protection of an armed and experienced ranger. The emphasis is on reconnecting with the wilderness in some elemental way rather than ticking off species, but rangers are armed for a reason.

As yet, there has never been a human fatality on any of the Kruger trails, and considering the caliber of the rangers on hand, it is unlikely to ever occur, but do follow their instructions—given at the start of each trail—closely.

The locations of the base camps—comprising thatched A-framed two-bed huts with reed-walled, solar-heated showers and a shared flushing toilet—have been selected for their natural beauty. Note that, unlike the trails offered in KwaZulu-Natal's Hluhluwe-Umfolozi reserve, you'll return to the same base camp every night. Besides bedding, towels, cutlery, and food, the park supplies rucksacks and water bottles. Drinks (which you must supply) are kept cold in gas fridges. Age limits are 12 to 60 years, and a reasonable degree of fitness is required—you will be covering from 8km to 15km (5–9 miles) a day.

You have seven trails to choose from: The **Napi, Bushman,** and **Wolhuter** are all situated in the southwestern section, known for white rhino, granite hills, and Bushman rock paintings. The **Metsi-Metsi,** which overlooks a small waterhole, and the **Sweni,** which overlooks the marula and knobthorn savanna, are in the central area, known for its lions. **Olifants Trail** ✹, which overlooks the perennial Olifants River, west of its confluence with the Letaba, is particularly scenic and one of the most popular. **Nyalaland,** situated in the pristine northern

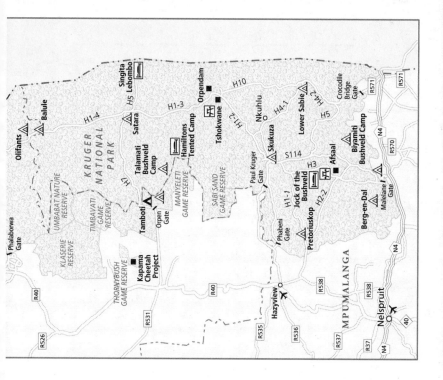

wilderness among the sandveld's fever tree and baobab forests, is a favorite of birders. But even if you're not a birder, the vegetation and views more than make up for the relative lack of game.

Reservations often need to be made a year in advance, but cancellations do occur. For bookings, call ☏ **012/426-5111;** for more information, check the park's website or request a brochure—see "Essentials," above, for contact details.

WHERE TO STAY & DINE

The Parks Board runs its camps like large hostels, and many South Africans share a certain nostalgia in coming back year after year to find the same impala-lily and bird fabric on every curtain, cushion, and bed, *Custos Naturae* stamped on every sheet, and the kudu crest embossed on every soap—but it's not everyone's idea of a holiday. If, however, you are prepared to rough it a little, the en-suite accommodations—situated throughout the park—are scrupulously clean, relatively comfortable, and, for the most part, unbelievably cheap. They are also remarkably varied, with 12 rest camps, four satellite camps, five bushveld camps, and one bush lodge (the latter is only suitable for large groups). Of these, the bushveld camps are highly recommended—with only 7 to 15 units, they offer a great deal more privacy than the large rest camps (Skukuza, the largest, has more than 200 chalets), and the game drives offered by the park are in smaller vehicles. You will, however, have to do your own cooking when the camp gates are locked at night—only the rest camps have restaurants.

The good news is that the park—realizing that its prowess lies in conservation, not accommodating discriminating guests—has awarded concessions to private operators, who have over the past year built superluxurious lodges; the

---

Tips **Better Wildlife Viewing for the Self-Guide Safari**

1. **Purchase a detailed map** that indicates all rivers, dams, dirt roads, lookout, and picnic points. These are available at all rest camp shops. Though the tone is a little schoolmarmish, the illustrated *Make the Most of the Kruger* will tell you what ecozone you're in, which species you should look out for, and point out the geology and historical sites. The *Find It* booklet is a shorter version.

2. Between picnic spots there are no restrooms, fuel stops, or shops, so **plan your journey along the way** and make sure you have something to drink and eat in the car should you wish to stay with a sighting for some time.

3. **Be there at the right time.** The best times to view wildlife are in the early morning and late afternoon; animals don't move much in the heat of the day. So try and set off as soon as the camp gates open (4:30–6:30am, depending on the season). Hopefully, camp gate hours will be extended in the near future.

4. You're bound to bump into something if you **follow a river.** Traffic allowing, always stop on bridges when crossing and look for crocodiles, herons, leguaans (large amphibious lizards that can grow up to 10 ft.), hippos, and so on. In winter you are almost always assured of seeing animals at a water hole or dam; just park your car and wait.

5. **Spot a spotter.** A stationary car with binoculars pointed in a certain direction is an obvious clue. It is not considered bad form to ask what they have spotted (but you're unlikely to get a polite answer if you obscure their view).

6. **Appreciate the rare.** Most first-time visitors want to tick off the Big 5, but it's worth finding out more about other species. Sighting a

---

bad news is that staying there won't come cheap. If you're not prepared to shell out for these yet want a certain level of luxury (we're talking double beds, bathtubs, TV), you will (aside from Skukuza's new riverside bungalows) have to stay in one of the hotels or guesthouses situated on Kruger's periphery and enter the park daily. Rissington Inn is a recommended option and only 10 minutes from the new Phabeni Gate (see "The Panorama Route: Where to Stay & Dine," earlier in this chapter). Ten minutes from the Malelane Gate, with excellent views overlooking the banks of the Crocodile river, **Buhala Country House** is another option worth considering. With only eight bedrooms, and no children under age 10 allowed, this is a truly tranquil option; rooms are elegant and cool (iron beds, white linen, thatched ceilings), and dining is superior to anything you'll find in the rest camps. Buhala will also organize tours of the Escarpment as well as safaris into the park (ⓒ **013/792-4372;** www.buhala.co.za; R1,700/$212 double, including breakfast). The **Malelane Sun Intercontinental** is even closer to the gate and offers all the comforts and anonymity of a hotel chain at a relatively reasonable price; with access to the exclusive 18-hole Leopard's Creek course, this is a good choice for golfers (ⓒ **013/790-3304;** www.suninternational.com; R1,500/$188 double, including breakfast).

wild dog becomes that much more exciting when you know there are fewer than 400 left in the park.

7. **Bring a good pair of binoculars** and drum up some enthusiasm for the vegetation—that tree you stop to admire may reveal a leopard.

8. **Drive slowly**—sharing the shadow of the tree you just whizzed past could be a pride of lions. (The recommended speed for viewing is 25kmph/15 mph.)

9. Dirt roads give a great sense of adventure, but **don't shun the tar roads:** Besides being quieter, less dust makes for tastier grass verges.

10. **Consult the animal-sightings book** at your rest camp reception area—many animals are territorial and don't cover huge distances. Some experts advise that you concentrate on a smallish area, getting to know the movements of the animals, rather than driving all over the park.

11. Animals have the right of way on the roads. If a group of elephants is crossing, **keep a respectful distance,** switch the car off, and wait. If you're lucky enough to spot a black rhino (which has a hooked lip rather than the wide, square lip of the white rhino), be *very* wary.

12. **Never feed the baboons and monkeys** that hang out at picnic sites; this is tantamount to signing their death warrant as they then become increasingly aggressive and have to be shot.

13. Most important, **be patient.** The only way you'll ever witness a kill, or any interesting animal interaction, is by watching a situation unfurl.

Note: If you're traveling during the summer, especially with kids, make sure to book into a camp with a swimming pool: Berg-en-Dal, Lower Sabie, Pretoriuskop, Mopani, Skukuza, and Shingwedzi.

PRIVATE CONCESSIONS

Using the model so successfully initiated by the Botswana government, the new Kruger concessions—effectively an area on which operators enjoy sole traversing rights—are awarded for a 20-year period on the condition that camps should in no way disturb the environment (hence the fact that most camps are raised off the ground). In keeping with the kind of service offered in the unfenced private reserves that flank the Kruger, rangers within these concessions can drive off-road to track or view animals from a close-up perspective, but it's worth noting that animals found off-road in Kruger are not as acclimated to vehicles as those in the unfenced private reserves that neighbor Kruger (see "Private Game Reserves," later in this chapter). Competition for these tenders was understandably stiff, and the operators chosen all come with experience, utilizing the best in the business to establish these camps. The following are the top concessions open at press time.

Hamiltons Tented Camp ★★ *Value*   A far cry from the tents in the days of Hemingway and Blixen, modern tented camps provide every comfort needed (bedside lamps, king-size beds, crisp white linen, flushing toilets, showers or slipper baths (clawfoot tubs) with hot and cold running water . . .) yet still offer a sense of authenticity, of close communion with the bush. Proof of their ongoing popularity is the runaway success of Hamiltons, the most recent tented camp to be opened (Sept 2002) by Three Cities, a large South African–based hotel group. The best camp in the Imbali concession (the two other components—Imbali Main Camp and smaller Hoyo Hoyo—are not in the same class), this small tented camp comprises a mere six luxury en-suite East African–safari tents, each with a private viewing deck with outside shower overlooking the Ngwenyeni dam. Tents are privately situated and linked via raised timber walkways to the open tented lounge and dining room and pool. Hamiltons' size makes this an ideal camp for anyone wanting to escape the rat race. It's also one of the best-value safari camps to come on the market—its R5,700 ($712) rates puts it in the same category as Tanda Tula's tented camp (R4,400–R6,000/$550–$750) but is half the price of Ngala (R10,450/$1,300). Book soon—it's very popular.

Booking office in U.S.: ✆ 305/792-0172. In S.A.: ✆ 086-1000-333 or 27/31-3103333. www.threecities.co.za. 6 units. R5,700 ($712) double. AE, DC, MC, V. Children ages 8 and older only. **Amenities:** Boma; dining/bar area; pool; butler/room service; laundry; game drives; bush walks. *In room:* A/C, fans.

Jock of the Bushveld ★★ *Value*   Named after the book written by Percy Fitz-patrick about the legendary Jock (a dog whose adventures took place during South Africa's first gold rush in the Kruger area), it was only fitting that Duncan MacNeillie, who produced and directed the movie *Jock of the Bushveld,* should win the tender for what used to be the most popular bushveld camp in Kruger. After an extensive upgrade, the first private lodge in Kruger opened in December 2001. Jock has already carved a name for itself as a warm, convivial camp, elegant and tasteful yet without pretensions of grandeur. The large thatched suites, situated for maximum privacy, each feature great bushveld views, tasteful furnishings, and large bathrooms with tubs and indoor as well as outdoor showers. Situated in the south, at the confluence of the Mitomeni and Biyamiti rivers, where herds of antelope and elephant gather to cool off or quench their thirst, it's known for enjoying one of the highest concentrations of game in the Kruger. It's also easily accessed from the Malelane and Skukuza gates (a 30-min. drive from the Kruger-Mpumalanga airport to the gate, then a 90-min drive through the park). The only possible drawback is its size (at 6,000 hectares/14,820 acres, this is Kruger's smallest concession), but given the density of game, you don't need to travel far to start ticking of species—begin by asking for lunch to be served on your private sala (a shaded outdoor lounge), which overlooks the river. Winter rates are the best in southern Africa. *Note:* Also in the pipeline is an ox-wagon camp, due to be open in May, where you can experience life as a pioneer (or rather as the pioneers could only dream life could be!)

19 7th Ave., Parktown North 2193 ✆ 011/537-4620. Fax 011/447-0993. www.jocksafarilodge.com. 12 units. Summer: R5,500 ($688) double; winter: R2,920 ($363) per person double. Rates all inclusive except for drinks. AE, DC, MC, V. Children under age 12 pay 50%. **Amenities:** Boma; dining area; bar; pool; room service; babysittimg; laundry; game drives; bush walks. *In room:* A/C, minibar, hair dryer.

The Outpost ★★   Cantilevered out of the mountainside, these 12 en-suite units, designed by Italian-born architect Enrico Daffonchio, are open to the elements except for the rockface they "grow" out of, and like Singita each offers unparalleled views, this time of the surrounding floodplains of the Limpopo and

---

Tips **Camps for Travelers with Disabilities**

Facilities for travelers with disabilities are available at Crocodile Bridge, Berg-en-Dal, Lower Sabie, Skukuza, Satara, Olifants, Letaba, Mopani, Shingwedzi, Pretoriuskop, and Tamboti.

Luvuvhu rivers—a richly textured terrain of ancient baobabs, thorny acacias, and lush palms. Located in the far north, this 11,000-hectare (28,000-acre) concession (awarded to the owners of Honeyguide and Ten Bompas, a boutique hotel in Johannesburg) encompasses the northeastern border of South Africa (shared with Mozambique and Zimbabwe), making it relatively inaccessible (it's a minimum 7-hour drive from Jo'burg, so a fly-in is advisable)—but this inconvenience only serves to heighten the sense of remoteness. With the imminent opening of the Great Limpopo Transfrontier Park (the transfrontier park comprising the Kruger, Mozambique's Gaza Reserve, and Zimbabwe's Gonarezhou National Park), it is expected that by 2004 visitors will be able to visit the Mozambican and Zimbabwean parts without requiring visas. With the Outpost, it's clear that the owners of Honeyguide, known for its good value, are ready to enter the more competitive top end of the market. Book number 12 for the most stupendous views.

Lodges of Manyaleti (Pty.) Ltd., 10 Bompas Rd., Dunkeld West, Johannesburg. ✆ 27/11-341-0282. www. theoutpost.co.za. 12 units. R7,000 ($875) double, all-inclusive. **Amenities:** Dining room; bar; laundry; pool; game drives; bush walks; river safaris; library; wine cellar. *In room:* Safe-deposit box, 180-degree views of the Limpopo River Valley.

Singita Lebombo ★★★ Singita's new Kruger camp opened on March 7, 2003, to huge acclaim. Designed by the same team responsible for Singita (see "Private Game Reserves," later in this chapter), the interiors will no doubt be featured in every leading design magazine, and the location is simply unbeatable. The most modern camp in Africa, it features fabulous home-grown furniture—a combination of local craftspeople working with funky young designers—contrasted with retro-modernity (think early *Wallpaper* magazine). The whole effect is more Afro-Euro chic boutique hotel than game lodge. Yet game lodge it is: Situated in a 15,000-hectare (37,000 acres) concession in a remote eastern section of Kruger National Park bordered by Mozambique, the camp is elevated on a sheer cliff, with stunning views of the ancient ryolite ridges of the Lebombo Mountains and the surrounding bushveld plains. Constructed from bleached wood and floor-to-ceiling glass walls in an open-plan, contemporary style, each of the 21 suites (complete with outside bed and shower) makes the most of these views—ask for a suite close to the river for maximum privacy. Guests can choose to fly in or drive, entering via either the Orpen or Paul Kruger gates (both equidistant to the edge of the concession). This is the name that the hip and the trendy will be dropping as the best game-viewing experience in Africa.

P.O. Box 23367, Claremont 7735. ✆ 021/683-3424. Fax 021/683-3502. www.singita.co.za. 21 units. R13,600 ($1,700) double, all inclusive (bar French champagne). No seasonal discounts. AE, DC, MC, V. Children over age 10 only. **Amenities:** Dining room; lounge; room service; laundry; game drives; bush walks. *In room:* A/C, minibar, coffee- and tea-making facilities.

REST CAMPS

The most popular accommodations in Kruger are the main rest camps, which offer a variety of cottages, bungalows, huts, and safari tents. All units are sparsely furnished and semi-serviced (that is, beds are made and floors are swept, but you'll have to do your own washing up). Water is scarce, so "en-suite" usually means flushing toilet, sink (often in the bedroom), and shower. The bigger camps are like small suburbs and are designed to encourage interaction among guests (units are close together and often emulate the old Voortrekker *laager,* a circle, facing inward), so there is little privacy and—unless you're here to photograph another kind of wildlife—the South African *braaier* is not the best of views. Try to book a river-facing unit (assuming there is one) or check to see whether you can book a perimeter unit; these face into the bush, albeit through a fence.

The three- to six-bedroom guest cottages represent the top accommodations option in each rest camp. It's well worth investigating these if you're traveling with friends, as they offer the most privacy and small luxuries (like a bathtub).

The restaurant food (usually a three-course set menu, with minimum choice, or buffet) varies between edible and filling. A soup starter may be followed by goulash, baked fish, chicken casserole, lamb chops, overdone roast beef, and the like, and desserts are of the "ice cream with chocolate sauce" ilk. Breakfast will run you R45 ($5.50), lunch R65 ($8), dinner R85 ($11). The service varies from well-meaning to indifferent, and the (usually over-lit) atmosphere is non-existent—far better to barbecue, which is what most visitors do. Most basics such as milk, bread, butter, wood, dishwashing liquid, tea, tinned products, cereal, cold drinks, firelighters, and wood can be purchased from the camp shop, but don't expect anything fresh, or "delicacies" like olive oil, balsamic vinegar, or fresh fruit. Meat is frozen, and potatoes, tomatoes, and onions are usually the only vegetables available. Vegetarians and epicurians are advised to shop at a supermarket in one of the Escarpment towns before entering Kruger. The wine selection in the camp shops can be surprisingly good, however—if you don't know what you're looking at, choose one of the Nederburgs, an old standby.

The Top Rest Camps

Berg-en-Dal ⭐⭐ This is one of Kruger's newer rest camps, and as such is rather different from its predecessors: Gone are the characteristic round rondawels, and walls are finished in ugly brick face. Perhaps this is supposed to reflect the granite surrounds—besides being the ideal habitat for leopard and rhino, Berg-en-Dal's hilly terrain comes as some relief to the reserve's mostly flat bushveld. The two-room, six-bed family chalets are a great deal more spacious (try to book no. 26), and each unit has an enclosed patio and braai area, offering a sense of privacy that is lacking in so many of the other camps. In true puritan Parks Board style, however, any attempt at romance is foiled by the beds, which are not only single, but built-in. The indigenous gardens are also very attractive. Where the trail leaves the river and follows a narrow path through dense bush, Braille signs are set out to guide the visually impaired past plants and animal skulls on display. The dam sees much wildlife activity, although you may have to sit on one of the benches and wait for it: Crocodiles lurk—and hunt—in its waters. This is one of the few camps to offer bush *braais* (barbecues).

Enter through Malelane Gate, southern Kruger. ⓒ **013/735-6106.** Fax 013/735-6104. 94 units, consisting of 3-bed bungalows, 6-bed family cottages, and guesthouses (all en-suite). Rates start at R360 ($45) double. **Amenities:** Restaurant; pool; game drives and walks; laundromat; shop; information center; fuel.

Letaba ⭐ This rest camp is set in elephant country, just where the mopane terrain starts to become monotonous. The location, along a large bend of the Letaba River, sees plenty of activity, particularly in the winter. The nearby

Engelhardt and Mingerhout dams are also excellent game sites, and the gravel road that follows the Letaba River is worth exploring. Letaba is also one of the few camps in Kruger to offer **night drives** and **bush braais.** Unfortunately, very few of the units have views, but the restaurant has one of the best; eat lunch while watching various plains animals wandering down for a drink. Accommodation is in thatched units set in the gardens that are shaded by well-established apple leaf trees, acacias, mopane, and lala palms—ask for a unit on the perimeter fence as game often venture quite close. Furnished safari tents are a budget alternative, but you'll have to share bathrooms and kitchen facilities. A pool is planned.

Enter through Phalaborwa Gate, central Kruger. ℂ 013/735-6636. Fax 013/735-6662. 112 units, consisting of 2- and 3-bed bungalows with or without kitchenettes; 3-bed huts with communal bathrooms; 6-bed guest cottages and guesthouses. All but huts en-suite. Rates start at R200 ($25) double. **Amenities:** Restaurant; bar; game drives and walks; laundromat; shop; information center; fuel; bush braais and breakfasts.

Lower Sabie ★★★   Overlooking the banks of the Sabie River, with large lawns and mature trees, this is one of Kruger's most pleasant camps, particularly if you manage to bag one of the units with a waterfront view (11–24 or 73–96; 3–10 also have river views, but they are a little too close to the camping and caravan area, which can be noisy during school vacations). In the camping area officials have now erected 20 new East African–safari tents; all feature twin beds, en-suite shower and toilet, and an outdoor "kitchen" (hotplate, fridge, barbecue)—make sure you bag one with a riverside view. Just about every animal has been spotted drinking along the riverbanks, and at night (if you switch your fridge off) you'll fall asleep to the grunting of hippos. Elephants are often found just west of the camp, and with two dams in the immediate vicinity, Lower Sabie provides an excellent base for observing wetland birds. Every unit has a braai, but most have no cutlery or crockery, though the basics can be rented for a small fee (R20/$2.50) from reception; alternatively, check to see if they have introduced the bush braai game drive here. Once again, there is no privacy, as most units share walls, but the 9pm curfew keeps things quiet. Stroll along the paved walkway that overlooks the Sabie River at night with a torch: The red eyes you light up probably belong to hyenas, tempted by the smell of braaiing meat.

Enter through Crocodile Bridge Gate, southern Kruger. ℂ 013/735-6056 or 013/735-6057. 97 units, consisting of 2-bed en-suite bungalows with or without kitchenettes; 2-, 3-, and 5-bed huts with communal bathrooms; 5-bed family cottages; and a guesthouse. All but the huts en-suite. Rates start at R190 ($17) double. Recommended riverview bungalows are R400 ($50) double; riverview tents R350 ($44) double; bushview tents R325 ($40). **Amenities:** Restaurant; pool; game drives and walks; laundromat; shop; fuel; bush braais.

⟨ Fun Fact   Chewing Up the Scenery

An elephant consumes up to 200 kilograms (480 lb.) of vegetation daily; a herd thus has a huge, potentially destructive impact on the landscape. This is why elephant numbers need to be controlled, either by culling or translocation. Elephants are extremely sensitive animals, however, and actively mourn the death of a family member, performing intricate burial ceremonies. When clans reunite, they make a great show of affection, "kissing" (probing each other's mouths with their trunks) and trumpeting their joy. To find out more about this amazing species, book a 90-minute **elephant safari** (ℂ 015/793-1633) or stay at **Camp Jabulani** (located at Kapama, a Big 5 fenced private reserve near Hoedspruit; www.kapama. co.za).

Olifants ★★★ Situated on a hilltop 100m (328 ft.) above the banks of the Olifants River, with views of the vast African plains that stretch beyond to the hazy Escarpment, this smallish camp is a favorite, and you'd be well advised to book as soon as you read this. Units 1 to 24, which are situated along the camp's southwest perimeter, not only have the most spectacular views of the river and the animals that are constantly in attendance, but are also the most private—it's almost worth rearranging your trip until one is available! One feels less caged in here than at Kruger's other camps; while all camps are surrounded by wire fencing to keep predators out, the sudden drop below Olifants' bungalows means that the expansive views are totally uninterrupted. Like many of the Kruger units, the veranda incorporates both kitchen and dining area, and it's the place where you drink it all in. Throughout the day, animals drink from the pools, watched by basking crocodiles. Birds, in particular eagles, wheel below, searching for prey, and it feels as if you're quite literally on cloud nine.

Enter through Phalaborwa Gate, central Kruger. © **013/735-6606.** Fax 013/735-6609. 114 units, consisting of 2- and 3-bed rondawels; a 4-bed family cottage; 4-bed guest cottage; and guesthouses. All en-suite. Rates start at R350 ($44) double. **Amenities:** Restaurant; game drives; laundromat; shop; fuel.

Punda Maria ★★ *Finds* Very few people have the time to travel this far north, just one of the reasons why Punda Maria—which is close to the Zimbabwean border—is the number-one choice for wilderness lovers. Built in the 1930s, this small thatched and whitewashed camp retains a real sense of what it must have been like to visit Kruger half a century ago. All units have fridges, but you must specify one with kitchen facilities if you don't want to live on restaurant food. The area does not support large concentrations of game, but it lies in the sandveld where several springs occur, and borders the lush alluvial plains, making it a real must for birders. A nature trail winds through the camp, and the area surrounding the camp is scenically splendid. Head north to the Luvuvhu River, the only real tropical region of the park, to spot a variety of birds, including the colorful Narina trogon. Overlooking the river is one of Kruger's most interesting archaeological sites, **Thulamela.** A little farther east along the river is the most beautiful picnic site in Kruger, **Parfuri,** which lies under massive thorn, leadwood, and jackalberry trees, with water constantly on the boil for tea.

Enter through Punda Maria Gate, northern Kruger. © **013/735-6873.** Fax 013/735-6873. 24 units, consisting of 2-bed bungalows with or without kitchenettes; and 4-bed cottages. All en-suite. Rates start at R350 ($44) double. **Amenities:** Restaurant; game drive to Thulamela Hill; laundromat; fuel; shop; bush braais.

Satara ★ The second-biggest and one of the three most popular camps in Kruger (the others being Skukuza and Lower Sabie), Satara is located in one of the finest game-viewing areas in the park. The rich basaltic soils support sweet grasses that attract some of the largest numbers of grazers (such as buffalo, wildebeest, zebra, kudu, impala, and elephant), which in turn accounts for what is considered to be the largest lion population in the park. Just as well, for the setting and housing are rather disappointing: 5 massive *laagers,* each 25-rondavel strong, with verandas all facing inward. The best options are the units in semi-circles that face the veld (numbers 161–179); though you have to look at it through an electrified fence. The road just south of Satara toward Gudzani Dam is famously beautiful, with wonderful river views in summer, and the area around Tshokwane is said to have the highest concentrations of lions in the world.

Enter through Orpen Gate, central Kruger. © **013/735-6306.** Fax 013/735-6304. 165 units, consisting of 2- and 3-bed bungalows with or without kitchenettes; 5- and 6-bed cottages; and guesthouses. All en-suite. Rates start at R380 ($48) double. **Amenities:** Restaurant; game drives and walks; laundromat; fuel; shop; bush braais.

Tracker Tips

Of course, you can't expect to know in a few days what professional trackers have gleaned in many years of tracking animals or growing up in the bush, but nature does provide a myriad of clues for the amateur tracker.

1. **Look for "hippo highways":** Hippos don't pick up their feet when they move, they drag them, so if you see a trail of trampled grass leading to a water hole, it's likely a hippo has been there, going to and from the water (where it stays during the heat of the day) to the grass it feeds on. Don't tarry on a hippo highway; once they set off down their well-trodden paths, very little will stop them.

2. **Use your nose.** Elephant urine has a very strong scent; waterbuck have a distinctive musky smell.

3. **Train your vision.** Vultures wheeling above may indicate the presence of predators, as may fixed stares from a herd of zebra or giraffe. A cloud of dust usually hovers over a large herd of moving buffalo. And of course, paw prints provide vital information, not only to what has passed by (you should purchase a wildlife guidebook to recognize the differing imprints), but how recently it was there—the latter a skill, frankly, that takes years of experience to hone.

4. **Examine trees.** For instance, bark and branches sheared off trees or trees rubbed raw are evidence that elephants have passed by—they eat the bark and use trees as scratching posts. And certain trees attract specific species—giraffe, for example, love to browse the mopane.

5. **Listen to the sounds of the bush.** The lead lioness makes a guttural grunt to alert her pride. Baboons, monkeys, squirrels, and birds give raucous alarm calls in the presence of predators. Kudus bark when frightened.

6. **Look for droppings and dung:** Elephant dung is hard to miss—extra-large clumps full of grass and bark, while a trail full of fresh black pancakelike dung marks the passing of a herd of buffalo. A good wildlife guidebook will have illustrations of many species' dung.

7. **Watch bird behavior:** Follow the flight of oxpeckers and you're likely to locate a herd of Cape buffalo; oxpeckers survive off the ticks and other insects that cling to the buffalo hide. Cattle egret dine on the insects and earthworms kicked up by grazing herbivores.

Skukuza ★★   Just east of the Paul Kruger Gate, you will find Skukuza, so-called capital of Kruger. Skukuza (or "he who sweeps clean") refers to Kruger's first warden, Stevenson-Hamilton, who set up his base camp here. Today Skukuza accommodates some 1,000 people in prime game-viewing turf. This is an ideal spot for first-time visitors, though it would be a pity if this were your only experience of the park, because it really is like a small town. Besides the people and cars, there is the noise of the occasional charter planes landing, though this doesn't seem to distract the many visitors strolling along the wide walkway that follows the course of the Sabie River. Accommodation is in a range of thatched en-suite units, the best of which are the luxury riverside bungalows. These bungalows (book one from 88–96) offer the best riverfront views and were rebuilt after the 2000 floods, now furnished with luxuries such as a double bed, fully-fitted kitchen and satellite TV. However there is still no overture to privacy, with bungalows approximately 10m (11 yd.) apart. All other units have fridges on their small verandas, some with hotplates and cooking equipment. For the budget-conscious, there are furnished East African–style tents; but you have to share bathrooms and kitchen facilities with the hordes of campers and RV-drivers who descend on the camp, particularly in June/July and December/ January. A pool has finally been built.

Enter through Paul Kruger Gate, southern Kruger. © 013/735-4152. Fax 013/735-4054. 218 units, consisting of 2- and 3-bed rondavels with or without kitchenettes; 4-bed cottages; and guesthouses. All en-suite. Rates start at R380 ($48) double; tent R190 ($24). Riverside bungalows R700 ($88) double. **Amenities:** Restaurant; bar; pool, game drives and walks; car rental; laundromat; shop; library; information center; airport; bank post office; doctor; fuel.

Other Camps

Among the other camps to choose from, tiny **Balule** (© 013/735-6606; rates start at R130/$16) is ideal for the hard-core bush enthusiast; it has no shops, restaurants, or electricity—and the six huts have no real windows, let alone fans or air-conditioning, making them unsuitable for high summer no matter how much you want to get back to basics. **Crocodile Bridge** (© 013/735-6012; rates start at R380/$48 double) is much too close to civilization, across the river from the farms that neighbor Kruger, and you might just as well be there, ensconced in a comfortable guesthouse. **Mopani** ⭐ (© 013/735-6536; rates start at R350/$44 double) is the most modern camp in Kruger and one of the few camps with a swimming pool. Book one of the popular units with dam views (nos. 9–12, 43, 45, 47–54, and 101–102). **Orpen** (© 013/735-6355; rates start at R180/$23 double) is one of the Kruger's smallest camps, and enjoys a reputation for fine sightings—lions, leopards, and wild dogs are regularly seen in the area. **Pretoriuskop** (© 013/735-5128; rates start at R350/$44 double) is Kruger's oldest camp and can house nearly 350 guests. It's popular, but consider stopping only one night here—it is only 8km (5 miles) from the Numbi Gate and most people prefer to go deeper into the bush. **Shingwedzi** (© 013/ 735-6806; rates start at R350/$44 double) is a medium-size rest camp on prime elephant territory with old-style accommodations and a pool. **Tamboti** (© 013/ 735-6355; rates start at R190/$24 double) is Kruger's answer to the East African safari, and comprises 30 tents located among apple leaf, jackalberry, and

---

(*Fun Fact* **Yech!**

When an acacia or mopane tree is heavily browsed upon, its damaged leaves release a chemical into the air, which alerts the remaining leaves to imminent danger. These leaves quickly manufacture a foul-tasting substance to reduce their palatability. Leaves begin to taste so bad that the browser moves away, giving the tree time to recover.

Fun Fact **The Mightiest Bite**

- The term **"Big 5"** originated in the days when Africa's big game was hunted by gun rather than camera, and referred to the 5 animals that were most dangerous when wounded: lions, leopards, elephants, black rhinos, and buffaloes.
- The docile-looking **hippo** is responsible for more human deaths than any other mammal in Africa (which kind of blows the theory that vegetarians are less aggressive!).
- The most dangerous wildlife in Africa is not much bigger than an eyelash—check under "Fast Facts: Kruger National Park," earlier in this chapter, for tips on protecting yourself from malaria-carrying **mosquitoes** (who just happen to be female).

---

sycamore fig trees. The camp is one of Kruger's most popular, however, mostly because of its location on the banks of the Timbavati River—animals, particularly elephants, are attracted by the promise of water.

Bushveld Camps

The five bushveld camps are much smaller than the major rest camps and provide a greater sense of being in the bush. They have no restaurants or shops, however, so you must do your own cooking, and any last-minute shopping will have to be done at the nearest rest camp. On the plus side, most of the en-suite units are more spacious than rest-camp options and feature well-equipped kitchens with braai (barbecue) spots. Only residents are allowed to travel the access road, which makes these an excellent get-away-from-it-all option. Best of all, the game drives are in vehicles that accommodate 8 to 10 people. You pay a little more for the seclusion—rates range from R600 to R700 ($73–$87.50) for two to four persons—but it's still a bargain.

The centrally located **Talamati** ☆☆☆ (close to the Orpen Gate; ✆ 013/735-6343) and southern **Biyamiti** ☆☆☆ (close to the Malelane Gate; ✆ 013/735-6171) are the most popular, located as they are in Kruger's game-rich areas. Shimuwini, Bateleur, and Sirheni are all located in the northern section of the park. **Shimuwini** ☆☆ (✆ 013/735-6683), which is reached via the Phalaborwa Gate, and **Sirheni** ☆☆ (✆ 013/735-6860), halfway between Shingwedzi and Punda Maria, both have scenic waterside settings that attract a variety of game and birds, and offer night drives. **Bateleur** ☆☆ (✆ 031/735-6843) is the oldest bushveld camp and—with only 7 thatched units rather than the usual 15—the most intimate. The closest gate to Bateleur is Phalaborwa. For more information, contact Kruger reservations (see "Visitor Information," earlier in this chapter).

CAMPING

Campsites (from R85–R90/$10–$11) are available at **Balule, Berg-en-Dal, Crocodile Bridge, Letaba, Malelane, Maroela, Lower Sabie, Pretoriuskop, Punda Maria, Satara, Shingwedzi,** and **Skukuza.** Every site has a braai (barbecue) and many also have electricity; you will need to bring in all your own equipment, however, including a tent (see Skukuza, Letaba, or Tamboti for furnished tents). Campers enjoy shared bathrooms (shower/toilet blocks) and kitchens, and have access to all rest-camp facilities.

6 Private Game Reserves

Flanking the western section of Kruger Park and covering over 150,000 hectares (370,500 acres) are South Africa's most famous private game reserves, owned by groups of freehold landowners and concession-holders with traversing rights. Because most of the fences that separated the private reserves from Kruger have been taken down, animals are to some extent able to follow natural migratory routes, and you will find as many species in these reserves as you will in Kruger. That, however, is where the similarity ends.

The difference between a visit to a Kruger camp and a private lodge is so big as to be almost incomparable. Not only do the luxurious accommodation options offer supreme privacy and make the most of the bushveld surrounds, but visitors are taken in open-topped and elevated Land Rovers to within spitting distance of animals by Shangaan trackers and armed rangers, who give a running commentary on anything from the mating habits of giraffe to the family history of a particular lion. Animals in these reserves, particularly Sabi Sand, are so used to being approached by vehicles that they almost totally ignore them—you can trail a leopard at a few feet without it so much as glancing backward. Two-way radios between rangers, many of whom are allowed to traverse on each other's land, ensure good sightings, although these can be somewhat marred when three or sometimes four vehicles (the maximum lodges allow) converge on the same spot.

The 2- to 4-hour game drives take place in the morning and again in the late afternoon and evening, with stops in the bush for a hot drink and muffins in the morning (particularly in winter) and cocktails in the evening. It can be bitterly cold in the winter, and you may want to opt instead for an escorted walk after breakfast—another service included in the rate.

In addition to pursuing animals off-road through the African bush, these private reserves offer unfenced accommodations of luxuriously high standards. Equally high end is the cuisine—as all meals are included in the rate, this is certainly not the time to go on a diet. Breakfasts feature a selection of cereals and fresh fruit, yogurt, and freshly baked bread and muffins. Hot breakfasts are cooked to order, and usually comprise eggs, sausage, bacon, and tomato, or omelets. A few lodges offer variations like eggs Benedict or eggs Florentine. Lunch is the lightest meal, usually a buffet with interesting salads and cold meats. Breakfasts are served late (after the morning game drive, which usually ends at about 10am), so some lodges prefer to skip lunch altogether and serve a high tea at 3pm, with quiches, sandwiches, and cakes. From there you depart on

---

Moments Wish You Were Here

It's 5am. The phone rings. It's the lodge manager. He politely asks how you slept, then requests that you do not leave your room as planned. There has been a leopard kill meters from your chalet. He apologizes for the inconvenience and informs you that an armed ranger will be along shortly to escort you to the dining room for coffee before you depart on your early morning game drive. This seldom happens, but every so often it does. Lodges in private reserves are not fenced off from predators, so you are advised to exercise extreme caution—under no circumstances are guests, whatever their age, to walk about unaccompanied after dark.

Private Game Reserves & Lodges

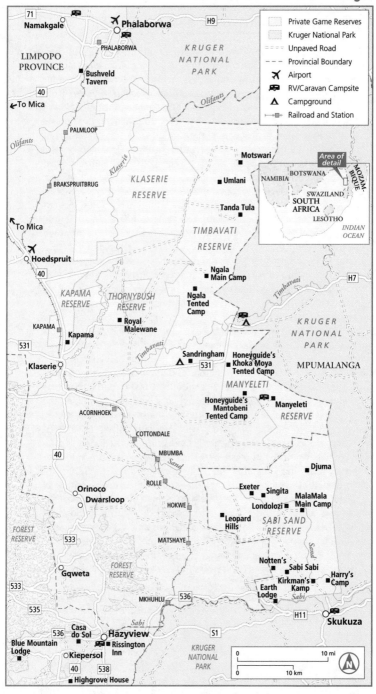

Legend:
- Private Game Reserves
- Kruger National Park
- Unpaved Road
- Provincial Boundary
- ✈ Airport
- RV/Caravan Campsite
- ▲ Campground
- Railroad and Station

71
Namakgale

H9

✈ Phalaborwa
PHALABORWA

KRUGER
NATIONAL
PARK

LIMPOPO
PROVINCE

■ Bushveld
Tavern

40
←To Mica

Olifants

PALMLOOP

Olifants

KLASERIĒ
RESERVE

BRAKSPRUITBRUG

Klaserië

Motswari

Umlani

Tanda Tula

Area of
detail

NAMIBIA   BOTSWANA

MOZAM-BIQUE

SWAZILAND
SOUTH
AFRICA

LESOTHO

INDIAN
OCEAN

TIMBAVATI
RESERVE

←To Mica

✈ Hoedspruit

40

KAPAMA
RESERVE

THORNYBUSH
RESERVE

Ngala
Main Camp

Ngala
Tented
Camp

H7

KRUGER
NATIONAL
PARK

KAPAMA

■ Royal
Malewane

Kapama

Timbavati

MPUMALANGA

531

Klaserie

Sandringham ▲

531

Honeyguide's
Khoka Moya
Tented Camp

MANYELETI

Honeyguide's
Mantobeni
Tented Camp

Manyeleti

ACORNHOEK

RESERVE

COTTONDALE

40

MBUMBA

Sand

Djuma

ROLLE

Orinoco
Dwarsloop

HOKWE

Exeter   Singita

Londolozi

MalaMala
Main Camp

Leopard
Hills

SABI SAND
RESERVE

FOREST
RESERVE

533

MATSHAYE

FOREST
RESERVE

Gqweta

Notten's

Sabi Sabi

Harry's
Camp

533

535

MKHUHLU

Earth
Lodge

Kirkman's
Kamp

Sabi

536

Sand

H11

Skukuza

536

Casa
do Sol

Hazyview

S1

Blue Mountain
Lodge

Rissington
Inn

Kiepersol

40   538

Highgrove House

KRUGER
NATIONAL
PARK

0   10 mi

0   10 km

N

Tips Choosing Your Private Reserve

Besides looking at the new concessions within the Kruger (see "The Kruger National Park: Where to Stay & Dine," earlier in this chapter), you'll need to consider the three major private reserves that border one another and Kruger's southern and central section. They are, from south to north, **Sabi Sand, Manyeleti,** and **Timbavati.** None of these reserves are fenced off from each other or Kruger, allowing a seamless migration of animals through an area roughly the size of Massachusetts. Each of these three reserves feature the Big 5 (lion, leopard, elephant, rhino, and buffalo), as does **Thornybush,** a relatively small reserve almost surrounded by Timbavati, but currently still fenced. Other private reserves in the region worth considering are: **Makalali,** a large buffalo-free reserve that lies within striking distance of Kruger's central Phalaborwa Gate, and **Welgevonden,** a malaria-free Big 5 reserve 2½ hours from Johannesburg. To make a truly informed decision, read the brief summaries on each of the reserves below, and refer to "Planning Your Safari," in chapter 2.

Each private reserve usually has a number of luxury lodges or camps that share traversing rights on land, thereby increasing the range of their vehicles. Many also report major sightings to the other reserves. In fact, with a cumulative 6 hours of every day spent tracking game, you will almost certainly see four of the Big 5 during a 3-night stay (the most elusive being leopard). Bear in mind that you will enjoy yourself a great deal more (and irritate your ranger less) if you spread your focus to include an interest in the myriad species that make up life in the bush.

Sabi Sand ★★★, a 66,000-hectare (163,000-acre) reserve that encompasses the southern lowveld, enjoys a reputation for being the most game-rich area in the country, and most guests leave having sighted all of the Big 5—indeed, after 3 decades of intensive safari action, animals here have practically been born to the clicking of cameras, making them the easiest to track and approach in Africa. It's hardly surprising, then, that this has become known as the continent's most exclusive reserve, with the largest number of luxury camps, of which established names like **MalaMala, Sabi Sabi,** and **Londolozi** are bandied about in the most well-traveled circles. However, **Singita** is the name to drop in informed company; not only does it offer game viewing on a par with MalaMala, but the standards of service and luxuriousness of the accommodation are incomparable, hence its nomination by the readers of *Condé Nast Traveler* as Best Destination in the World for 2 years running.

During the apartheid era, when blacks were not allowed to vacation in Kruger, **Manyeleti** ★—the region just north of Sabi Sand—was considered "their" reserve, and a visit to the original Manyeleti Rest Camp makes the most basic Kruger camp look like a luxury option. Officially, it's actually still a public reserve, within which private companies operate a few key concessions. At press time, only the good-value **Honeyguide**—which has taken over the Khoka Moya concession—was operating commercially, which means that at any given moment, a maximum of eight vehicles traverse the entire 23,000 hectares (56,800 acres).

Timbavati 🐾🐾, the 65,000-hectare (160,500-acre) reserve located alongside Kruger's central section, first became famous for the white lions who resided here (unfortunately, no more—all were captured and taken to the Johannesburg zoo to "protect" them; you *will* see plenty of the tawny types, however). Although it offers a comparable game experience to the much-vaunted Sabi Sand, the vegetation is less arresting, and rhino are scarce. Animals are almost as habituated to vehicles here as at Sabi Sand, and you can get within a few feet of large predators. The main reason to choose Timbavati over Sabi Sand is the fact that it has far fewer camps, and, like Manyeleti, the rates are generally friendlier.

Bordered in the north and west by Timbavati, the 14,000-hectare (34,580-acre) **Thornybush** 🐾🐾 game reserve is currently still a fenced reserve, thereby curtailing animal migration. It boasts a high percentage of lion, but the thicket-type vegetation is not as conducive to sightings of varied species. The best reason to choose this reserve is **Royal Malewane,** a lodge that offers unbelievably luxurious accommodation and style that's on a par with Singita but at a slightly reduced price.

If you're not hung up on ticking off the Big 5, the **Makalali** 🐾 conservancy, which lies farther north and is cut off from Kruger, extends over 10,000 hectares (24,700 acres) and has lions, leopards, rhinos, and elephants.

For visitors with limited time, the 40,000-hectare (98,800-acre) **Welgevonden** 🐾🐾 and 35,382-hectare (87,393-acre) **Lapalala** reserves lie only a 2½-hour drive north of the Johannesburg airport. The Welgevonden reserve is extremely well-run, with strict rules—vehicles are not allowed off-road, for example, which can be a major drawback if you spot a lion lying 100m (328 ft.) away, and which makes leopard sightings extremely rare. Aside from its proximity to Johannesburg, what makes this reserve appealing is its malaria-free status, and the mountainous landscape, which is very different from Kruger. The high density of animals still ensures good sightings, and the intimacy of the small lodges is most conducive to relaxing. Lapala has no lion but is a good budget alternative to those wanting a remote bush experience.

Note: If you are planning a second visit to South Africa, or are keen to combine a visit to one of the above reserves with one that has a totally contrasting biome, the other Big 5 private reserves worth considering are **Madikwe** 🐾🐾, which covers more biomes than Kruger, thereby offering a greater variety of species, and **Tswalu Kalahari Reserve** 🐾🐾, a desert reserve and the largest private reserve in southern Africa; both are malaria-free (see chapter 6). Kwazulu-Natal's **Phinda** 🐾, **Mkuze Falls** 🐾, and **Ndumo** 🐾 offer subtropical vegetation and birdlife. (See chapter 8 for more information.) Whatever you do, don't miss an opportunity to visit the reserves on Botswana's **Okavango** 🐾🐾🐾—the "original Eden" (see chapter 10).

a 3- to 4-hour evening game drive, traveling with a spotlight in the dark, tracking nocturnal creatures on the move. You will more than likely be expected to dine with your game-drive companions (if this is a problem, alert the staff in advance, and alternative arrangements will be made). Dinners feature grilled or roasted meat, giving visitors an opportunity to taste at least one species spotted earlier that day—kudu, springbok, impala, and warthog are particularly popular. Lodges cater to dietary requirements but require advance warning, as supplies take time to arrive in the bush. If you're a vegetarian or keep kosher, notify the lodges prior to your arrival. Almost every lodge rotates dinners from their dining room to the ever-popular open-air *boma* (an open-air enclosure lit with a large fire), and some even offer surprise bush dinners, with a game drive concluding at a serene spot where tables have been set up under trees or in a riverbed.

The drawback to all this? A hefty price tag. If you've come to South Africa to see big game, however, it's definitely worth delving a little deeper into your savings and spending at least 2 nights in a private game reserve, preferably 3. Prices (which are often quoted in U.S. dollars and include all meals, game drives, bush walks, and occasionally your bar bill) do vary considerably (from season to season, for example), and it is possible to find affordable options, the best of which are described below (see Umlani and Honeyguide in particular).

Note: An admission fee is charged at the entrance gates of some of these reserves, so make sure you have R40 to R80 ($5–$10) on hand if you're traveling by road. A conservation levy is paid for at the lodge.

GETTING THERE

The closest international airport is Johannesburg, from where it's a 5- to 7-hour drive to this region, depending on which route you choose (see the Panorama, Lowveld, and Letaba routes, earlier in this chapter). Alternatively, you can fly directly from Johannesburg, Cape Town, or Durban—see "Kruger National Park: Essentials," earlier in this chapter. At an additional cost, all camps and lodges will organize pickups from any of these airports, as well as arrange transfers by air or land to or from competitors. If you are driving, the camp will fax you directions when you make your reservation. You can fly to any of the three airports in the region, but the following provides the closest alternatives.

To reach the Sabi Sand: Fly to Hoedspruit's Eastgate airport or Kruger-Mpumalanga airport.

Tips Kidding Around

Bear in mind that many camps and lodges do not welcome children; over and above a concern for other guests' peace is the belief that the bush holds too many inherent dangers, not least of which is the ever-present threat of malaria (see "Fast Facts: Kruger," earlier in this chapter). Even if they are allowed, young children may not go on game drives or dine in the outdoor boma, and you will have to sign an additional indemnity form. The exception to this is **Madikwe River Lodge,** in the malaria-free North-West, which has special game drives for kids. **Kudu Lodge,** in Welgevonden, is another lodge in a malaria-free area that accepts children. Lodges adjoining Kruger that accept children include: **Londolozi, MalaMala, Ulusaba, Sabi Sabi, Koka Moya, Ngala,** and **Umlani** (see reviews below).

To reach the Manyeleti: Fly to Hoedspruit's Eastgate Airport.

To reach the Timbavati or Makalali: Fly to either Hoedspruit's Eastgate Airport or Phalaborwa's Kruger Park Gateway Airport.

To reach Welgevonden or Lapalala: See the "The Waterberg Mountains," below.

WHERE TO STAY & DINE

Because lodges and camps need adequate warning to stock up on fresh produce (remember, all meals are included in the rates below), transfers need to be pre-arranged, and many are extremely popular, booking ahead is essential, and any dietary requirements need to be sorted well in advance. Although winter is the best time to view game, many lodges experience a seasonal drop-off and reduce prices from May to August—some by as much as 50%. Note that the camps in the new concessions inside Kruger (See "Kruger National Park: Where to Stay & Dine," earlier) are run in much the same way as the following camps.

IN SABI SAND

Djuma (Value) Comprising three separate camps—**Galago,** a self-catering single unit lodge, **Bush Lodge,** and **Vuyatela** ⭐⭐, the flagship—Djuma has access to more than 9,000 hectares (22,230 acres), of which it owns 7,000, making it one of the largest landowners in the Sabi Sand Reserve. Bush Lodge has benefited from an upgrade and, like Galago, offers good value for money. But it is the pricier Vuyatela, completed at the turn of the millennium, that is definitely Djuma's most exciting option. A celebration and fusion of southern African culture, the lodge is fashioned from architectural materials similar to those used in villages and townships—adobe mud-pack walls are offset by corrugated iron, for instance—and the crafts and artworks reflect African-style pop art, of which the Coca-Cola bottle chandelier is a particularly fine example.

Accommodations comprise eight thatched chalets, each with a generous bedroom, dressing room and bathroom, separate lounge, and large private deck with small plunge pool and shower. The cuisine reflects the lodge's pan-African theme. Djuma is very much owner-managed, which means that service is excellent, and the game viewing is pure Sabi Sand. Djuma is accessed via Gowrie Gate on 55km (34 miles) of dirt road that has recently been upgraded—but you might consider flying in on the Djuma Shuttle, a fly-in package that can be arranged through the lodge.

P.O. Box 338, Hluvukani 1363. ℂ 013/735-5118. Fax 013/735-5070. www.djuma.co.za. Vuyatela: 8 units; Bush lodge: 7 units; Galago: 5 units. High season: Vuyatela R7,900 ($988) double; Bush lodge R5,500 ($688) double; Galago R600 ($75) per person, minimum of 6. Low season (winter): Vuyatela R5,300 ($662) double; Bush lodge R3,960 ($495) double. Rates include all meals, drinks (at Vuyatela), game drives, and bush walks. Children under age 12 pay 50%. AE, DC, MC, V. **Amenities:** Boma; dining room; lounge/bar area; pool; game drives; bush walks; cultural village visit. Vuyatela offers: Room service; massage; laundry; Internet library; gymnasium; small aquarium. *In room:* A/C, minibar (Vuyatela only), hair dryer, Internet connection (Vuyatela only).

Exeter ⭐ Exeter's new owner has totally refurbished the lodge—gone are the stuffed animals and lurid animal-print fabrics, replaced by shades of ochre and clay, taupe and teak. The double-volume lounges and dining areas are huge, magnificent open-sided rooms with views of the nearby Sand River—and this is where you'll want to spend your day, because the rooms, though now extremely tasteful, with large beds and huge indoor-outdoor bathrooms, are very much on top of each other. The suites offer much more privacy, with private plunge pools, but for this money you might as well stay at Djuma's Vuyatela.

Sadly, Exeter's excellent-value **Leadwood Lodge** has been closed and is being upgraded to fully catered status, and will no doubt reflect this in the price.

P.O. Box 2060, Nelspruit 1200. ℂ **013/741-3180** or 013/741-3181. Fax 013/741-3183. exeter@cis.co.za. Exeter Lodge: 10 units. High season: R6,600 ($825) double; R8,600 ($1,075) suite. Low season (winter): R4,600 ($575) double. R6,600 ($825) suites. Rates include all meals, game drives, and bush walks. AE, DC, MC, V. Children age 12 and over only, except at Leadwood. **Amenities:** Boma; dining room; bar; pool; game drives; bush walks. *In room:* A/C, minibar, coffee- and tea-making facilities, hair dryer.

Leopard Hills ★★ If you're traveling in winter, this small lodge, which traverses the same land that Exeter and Ulusaba do, offers excellent accommodations. Situated in the western sector of the Sabi Sand, Leopard Hills is—like Ulusuba's Rock Lodge—built on a hilltop, and the views of the African bush savanna go on forever. You can enjoy these views from the public areas as well as from five of the huge suites (specify savanna views), which are a great deal more tasteful and generous than those at Ulusaba, though not in the same class as Londolozi's Bateleur chalets, which are marginally cheaper. Wraparound glass frontage opens onto private sun decks, each with its own plunge pool (specify a savanna view). The muted cream, white, tan, and brown African-themed decor is executed with a mixture of rough untreated timber, bamboo, concrete, sisal, and leopard-print fabric, used sparingly. A fully stocked wine cellar, fine cuisine, and a library with a cozy fireplace and more fabulous views complete the picture. Specially designed Land Rovers provide absolute comfort as you traverse the 10,000 hectares (24,700 acres) to which Leopard Hills has access; and although this sector sees a fair amount of traffic, sightings are limited to a maximum of three vehicles.

P.O. Box 612, Hazyview 1242. ℂ **013/737-6626.** Fax 013/737-6628. www.leopardhills.com. 8 units. R10,800 ($1,350) double. Winter R8,400 ($1,050). AE, DC, MC, V. Children stay on request. **Amenities:** Boma; dining area; lounge; bar; pool; room service; laundry; game drives; bush walks; library. *In room:* A/C, minibar, tea- and coffee-making facilities, hair dryer.

Londolozi ★★★ In 1969 the Varty brothers inherited a large tract of land from their father, built four simple huts, and offered basic safaris with the emphasis on conservation. Today Londolozi has four separate luxury camps— **Pioneer, Founder, Bateleur** ★★★, and **Tree** ★★★—and offers such a high standard in accommodations, cuisine, and game viewing that it has become the model upon which all the subsequent luxury lodges were based.

The vegetation surrounding the camps (which are built on the banks of the Sand River and within walking distance, but out of sight of one another) is the closest to jungle you'll find in the predominantly bushveld savanna. Choose the Bateleur chalets, which are slightly less expensive than the suites but have large granite en-suite bathrooms and beautifully appointed bedrooms—mood lighting is controlled from a bank of switches and dimmers—and your king-size bed overlooks a totally private timber deck with your own plunge pool. By comparison, the chalets at the Pioneer and Founder camps are overpriced. If money is no object, the Tree Camp's suites are the most intimate choice (the camp is half the size of the others), but Bateleur's Granite Suites deserve a special mention— book no. 1 and you'll find yourself swimming in a private pool that drops onto the boulders that form the Sand River banks, close enough to hear the river running from your bath. Londolozi is a Relais & Chateaux lodge, which sets high standards for both accommodation and cuisine, but it's worth noting that there are conflicting reviews regarding the quality of the dining. Service is intelligent, and with more than 15,000 hectares (37,050 acres) to traverse, there are excellent game-viewing opportunities, not least of which is finding the famed Londolozi leopards, aided by some of the best trackers in the business.

Having set the standard, Londolozi remains one of the top (and most expensive) lodges in southern Africa. Bear in mind, however, that Londolozi's ever-increasing size has compromised the sense of exclusivity that the even more luxurious Singita offers.

Private Bag X27, Benmore 2010. ⓒ **011/809-4300.** Fax 011/809-4315. www.ccafrica.com. Pioneer Camp: 6 units; Founder's Camp: 6 units; Bateleur Camp: 12 units; Tree Camp: 6 units. Chalets: R10,450 ($1,305) double; Suites: R12,100 ($1,510). No seasonal discounts. AE, DC, MC, V. Children under age 11 pay 50%. **Amenities:** Each camp offers its own boma, dining area, bar; pool; room service; babysitting (no children at Tree); laundry; game drives; bush walks. *In room:* A/C, minibar, hair dryer, plunge pool (at Bateleur and Tree camps only), fireplace (only suites at Pioneer Camp).

MalaMala 🔆 MalaMala is probably the best-known game lodge in Africa. Alas, this is more a result of the quality of the game-viewing than anything else. As the largest of the privately owned reserves in the Sabi Sand, MalaMala shares an unfenced border of 30km (19 miles) with Kruger, and the Sand River flows through most of its length. Not only are you most likely to see the Big 5 in one day (it's not uncommon for rangers to record Big 5 sightings 332 days of the year), you'll get a certificate to prove it. The rangers, most of whom are graduates in the natural sciences, act as personal hosts, serving drinks and taking their meals with you—although this level of obsequious service pleases some, it can be seriously claustrophobic to others. Rooms are spacious and comfortable, with his-and-her bathrooms and aluminum windows and doors sliding open to reveal manicured lawns leading down to the Sand River, but stylistically they're very old-fashioned, and there's no outdoor privacy. Food is nothing to write home about either—sometimes bordering on the truly awful—but the evening dinners in the huge boma, lit by flames, are atmospheric.

Situated farther south, **Kirkman's Kamp** 🔆🔆, the most tasteful of the three camps, with colonial-style decor that pays homage to nostalgic hunting days of yore, is the recommended option, offering relative value. The recently relocated **Harry's Camp** is the reserve's budget option, but once again the decor, featuring an ill-guided attempt to incorporate Ndebele-inspired motifs, disappoints. Both offer a more intimate, relaxed experience than the hotel-like **Main Camp,** and the same high-quality game-tracking, for almost half the price.

Private Bag X284, Hillcrest 3650. ⓒ **031/765-2900.** Fax 031/765-3365. www.malamala.com. Main Camp: 25 units. Kirkman's Kamp: 18 units. Harry's Camp: 12 units. Main Camp: R8,000 ($1,000) double; R9,000 ($1,125) suite. Kirkman's Kamp: R5,600 ($700) double. Harry's Camp: R4,400 ($550). No seasonal discounts. Children under age 12 (only at Main Camp) pay 50%. AE, DC, MC, V. **Amenities:** Boma; dining areas; bar; pool (in each camp); tennis (Kirkman's); gym (Main Camp); room service (Main Camp); game drives; bush walks. *In room:* A/C, minibar, hair dryer on request.

Notten's Bush Camp 🔆 *Value* Wedged between MalaMala and Sabi Sabi, this small camp—the cheapest fully catered option in the Sabi Sand reserve—is an oasis of calm. Gilly and Bambi Notten have created a home-away-from-home atmosphere (lions are framed next to family photos); and if the number of repeat

---

But It's Still a Tasty Sundowner

Even today, otherwise intelligent folks swear that drinking gin and tonics can actually help keep malaria at bay. That the miniscule amount of quinine found in tonic works as a serious precaution against malaria is simply an old chestnut from the decadent old colonial days. And there's nothing in the gin itself but a lovely sense of caring less about catching malaria in the first place!

visits is anything to go by, it's a winning formula. The raised open veranda, where the substantial tea and breakfast are served, provides a wonderful view of the water hole and surrounding grass plain where just about every mammal under the African sun has been spotted.

Most of the rooms are tiled with attractive slate and warmed with sisal carpets. Rooms 2, 4, and 5 enjoy the best views. Comfortable furnishings are offset by the fact that rooms have no electricity; showers are heated by an old donkey boiler. Note that if luxuries like air-conditioning leave you cold, Umlani's huts (see below)— which go for a similar price—give an even greater sense of being in the bush. Notten's food is better than both of the above, however: home-cooked cuisine that's refreshingly unfussy and totally delicious. In place of lunch, there's usually a high tea, and dinner features one dish (rump steak, say, with mushroom sauce and oven-roasted potatoes) rather than a buffet. The major drawback here is that because of the camp's size (some 3,500 hectares/8,645 acres), you may not spot as much game as on neighboring territories.

P.O. Box 622, Hazyview 1242. ⓒ 013/735-5105 or 013/735-5750. Fax 013/735-5970. 6 units. R4,550 ($569) double. Winter R3,600 ($450) double. Rate includes all meals, game drives, and bush walks. AE, DC, MC, V. Children over age 8 only. **Amenities:** Boma; dining area; lounge; bar; pool; game drives; bush walks.

Sabi Sabi ★★   After 21 years in the business Sabi Sabi has just completed a radical upgrade and refurbishment program, investing R60 million ($7.5 million) to rebuild **Bush Lodge,** refurbish **Selati** ★★, and create its brand-new **Earth Lodge.** The largest of the three, Bush Lodge offers generous dark-gray, ochre, and cream suites set amid the camp gardens and furnished with a mixture of plush colonial-style and Balinese pieces, with African artifacts and kilim rugs adding warmth. This has made it a great deal more tasteful than MalaMala's Main Camp (same rates)—but, like Main Camp, you still feel as if you're in a hotel, with units too close together for privacy. For this you'd be better off booking into Selati, which offers the best value for money of the three. Previously a hunting lodge and named after the famed turn-of-the-20th-century railway line that ran through the area and into Kruger Park, this elegant lodge is filled with vintage railway memorabilia, antiques, and old sepia photographs depicting those early days. The thatched free-standing chalets (now air-conditioned) are spacious and beautifully furnished, with dark stinkwood beds offset by swathes of white mosquito netting—try to book the ultra-luxe honeymoon suite. The newest addition to the Sabi Sabi stable is Earth Lodge, where the architects— perhaps in an attempt to emulate Singita's success—have clearly been briefed to build a thoroughly modern lodge for the new millennium. The entire lodge looks as if it has been built into the earth, with one of the most spectacular open-air entrance foyers in Africa. Rooms are less impressive (certainly when compared with those at Singita or Royal Malewane), with dark interiors, tiny plunge pools, and hard modern edges.

P.O. Box 52665, Saxonwold 2132. ⓒ 011/483-3939. Fax 011/483-3799. www.sabisabi.com. Bush Lodge: 25 units. Selati Lodge: 8 units. Earth Lodge: 13 units. Bush Lodge: R8,000 ($1,000) double. Selati: R9,000 ($1,125); Selati's presidential suite (own Land Rover and ranger): R10,800 ($1,350). Earth Lodge: R10,000 ($1,250); Earth Lodge's presidential suite (own butler, Land Rover, and ranger): R20,000 ($2,500). Rates include all meals, local beverages (for Selati and Earth), game drives, and bushwalks. AE, DC, MC, V. Children pay 50 percent. **Amenities:** Boma; dining area; bar; pool;; laundry; room service game drives; bush walks; IT centre (Bush and Earth). Earth Lodge also offers: Fully-equipped gymnasium; state-of-the art spa; 8,000-bottle cellar. *In room:* A/C, minibar, hair dryer.

Singita ★★★   For the second year running, Singita has been awarded top honors as the Best Destination in the World by *Condé Nast Traveler,* which comes as no surprise—Frommer's has rated this lodge as the best in the country since 1998. While you might find it difficult to leave your room at Londolozi, here it is virtually impossible. Why bother when you can take a dip in your own personal plunge pool or enjoy a massage or pedicure on your private deck, watching the wildlife on the open plains beyond the river? Still, with traversing rights to more than 18,000 hectares (44,500 acres), Singita offers game-viewing on a par with MalaMala, and you'll want to sign on for at least one game drive.

Singita is separated into two lodges, **Boulders** and **Ebony,** each with its own large, open main lounge. The lodge buildings are low-impact, with separate suites built into a raised section overlooking the Sand River, which both subtly hides the suites from one another, yet affords excellent views (insist on a river view). Each of the suites in the newly renovated Boulders Lodge is the size of a small house and features a massive Balu teak deck and private pool, sliding floor-to-ceiling glass walls, a stone fireplace, en-suite bathroom with Victorian-style bath with uninterrupted views, a beautifully furnished lounge, and a king-size bed dressed in embossed linen. Colors are earth tones and textures are organic, combining stone, polished concrete, timber, granite, and ceramics with soft fabrics in muted browns offset by crisp white. Ebony Lodge features the same standard of luxury, service, privacy, and space, but the decor has an African colonial theme, right down to the giant Cape buffalo mounted head in the main lodge.

A Relais & Chateaux lodge, Singita offers superb three-course lunches using the freshest of ingredients to fashion creative takes on traditional Cape dishes like *bobotie* (meat pie), and dinners always feature a vegetarian option. Wine tastings (largely South African wines) in Boulders' handsome wine cellar are popular ongoing events. The Singita staff is one of the friendliest around, and the vibe is a happy one, without the imperiosity of luxe resorts elsewhere in the world.

P.O. Box 23367, Claremont 7735. © **021/683-3424.** Fax 021/683-3502. www.singita.co.za. Ebony Lodge: 9 units. Boulders Lodge: 9 units. R13,600 ($1,700) double. Rates include everything (bar French champagne). No seasonal discounts. AE, DC, MC, V. Children over age 10 only. **Amenities:** Dining room; lounge; bar; spa and salon; home and curio shop;; room service; laundry game drives; bush walks; 12,000-bottle wine cellar; IT room. *In room:* A/C, minibar, coffee- and tea-making facilities, private pool, fireplace.

IN MANYELETI

Honeyguide ★★ *Value* A member of the upscale Classic Safari Camps of Africa, Honeyguide's tented camps offer some of the best value-for-money game experiences in the country, and tend to attract a young, occasionally raucous crowd. The original safari camp, now referred to as **Mantobeni Tented Camp,** has been moved to Honeyguide's trails camp location, but very little else has changed, with leather couches, cotton sheets, old-style lanterns, and damask linen retaining its *Out of Africa* styling. Guests are accommodated in en-suite (showers only) East African–style tents. Set in a riverine forest, the 12 tents overlook a riverbed (usually dry) or the water hole. The central thatched lounge/living area is relatively sparsely furnished, and tents can become quite hot in summer—thankfully, a pool is being built. Early-morning drums alert you to the dawning game drive, and tea is brought to your tent—a luxury even the most upmarket camps don't always offer. The 12 en-suite tents at the new **Khoka Moya Tented Camp,** opened in April 2003, offer almost exactly the same experience, but the cream tents are more spacious and are furnished with contemporary furniture. It remains to be seen which will be the more popular—my money is on Mantobeni.

P.O. Box 786064, Sandton 2146. © **011/341-0282.** Fax 011/341-0281. www.honeyguidecamp.com. Mantobeni: 12 units. Khoka Moya: 12 units. R3,960 ($495) double. AE, DC, MC, V. **Amenities:** Boma; dining room; lounge; bar; small pool; game drives; bush walks.

IN TIMBAVATI

Ngala *Kids*   Conservation Corporation (CCAfrica), one of southern Africa's premier safari operators (owners of Londolozi), has done its utmost to turn this old Kruger bush camp into a luxury lodge, but it's had to live with a number of inherited flaws. The thatched cottages, all connected by narrow paved walkways leading through lawns, were not designed with any privacy in mind, and the lodge accommodates a lot more people than is usual in a private game lodge, turning it into a small hotel rather than a safari camp. A much better option is its **tented camp** *★★★*, comprising six deluxe en-suite tents on the banks of the Timbavati River—it's a more authentic bush experience by far. Ngala offers excellent service, good food (CCAfrica chefs are all carefully handpicked and provide huge buffets to satisfy all tastes), and—with exclusive operating rights within 14,000 hectares (34,580 acres) of land—one of the best game-viewing experiences outside of Sabi Sand. The lodge is also one of the few child-friendly options, with enough noise from other people's kids to enable guilt-ridden parents to relax. Note that Ngala has introduced a 3-day walking safari; the most luxurious walking safari in the Kruger area will run you R16,500 ($2,060).

Private Bag X27, Benmore 2010. *(C)* **011/809-4300.** Fax 011/809-4315. www.ccafrica.com. Main Camp 21 units. Tented Camp 6 units. Main Camp: R8,250 ($1,030) double (R6,600/$825 winter). Tented Camp R10,450 ($1,305) (no seasonal discounts). All rates include meals, game drives, and bush walks. Children under age 11 pay 50%. AE, DC, MC, V. **Amenities:** Boma/restaurant; lounge; bar; pool; game activities; room service; babysitting; laundry; 24-hour doctor on call. *In room:* A/C, minibar (stocked in advance), hair dryer on request.

Tanda Tula *★★*   One of the very first luxury tented camps in the Kruger area, Tanda Tula gives a real sense of being in the heart of the bush. The en-suite East African–safari-style tents, erected on timber deck floors, offer all the comforts of a well-furnished room, while the tent walls do nothing to filter out the sounds of the wilds. The eight tents are all privately situated, each with its own furnished *stoep* (veranda). Because the surrounding bush is quite dense, however, you're more likely to spend time in the elegant and comfortably furnished open-sided lounge and dining area, which leads out onto the lawns and pool (a resident warthog family keeps these lawns well-clipped). This is where drinks are served, as well as lunch, and at night a huge fire is lit, even if dinner is served in the adjacent boma. Tanda Tula means "to love the quiet," and the team does everything possible to ensure that you can do just that. Game drives cover a potential 20,000 hectares (59,400 acres), providing Tanda Tula with access to the largest area in Timbavati, and you'll likely spot at least 3 of the Big 5 in one day.

P.O. Box 32, Constantia 7848. *(C)* **021/794-6500.** Fax 021/794-7605. www.tandatula.co.za. 9 units. R6,000 ($750) double. Off-season R2,920 ($365). Rates include all meals, game drives, and bush walks. AE, DC, MC, V. Children age 12 and over only. **Amenities:** Boma; lounge; bar; pool; laundry; game drives and walks. *In room:* A/C, minibar, hair dryer.

Umlani Bushcamp *★* *Value* *Kids*   One of the most authentic bush experiences, Umlani ("place of rest") is a personal favorite. Not only does it offer a relatively affordable alternative to the luxury lodge, but it's a really relaxed camp, the kind of place you sit with your toes in the sand listening to the sounds of the bush (rather than the hum of the pool filter)—it has no formal gardens and very few staff, the en-suite huts are relatively basic, and at night the camp is lit only by firelight and paraffin lamps. There are also no official camp guards to escort you in the evenings as you follow the flame-lit sandy walkway to your bed; suddenly the huts, which in the light of day seem a little too on top of each other, are reassuringly close. During the day, as you swing in the hammock waiting for a predator to come padding down the dry Nshlaralumi riverbed, the tranquil camp is far too laid-back to promote paranoid feelings. Marco and Marie-Louise Schiess are the owner-managers who have created this rustic haven, and every effort has been made to retain a sense of what it's like to camp in the middle of the bush; there's even a stilted treehouse overlooking a water hole where you can spend the night with only the sounds of nocturnal animals for company. Children are also expressly welcome, with three family huts that sleep four. The limited set menu (advise of dietary preferences ahead of time) is of the home-cooked variety. Umlani is small, but with traversing rights to parts of Tanda Tula, it effectively covers 10,000 hectares (24,700 acres) and regularly has good sightings.

P.O. Box 26350, Arcadia, Pretoria 0007. ℭ **012/346-4028.** Fax 012/346-4023. www.umlani.com. 8 units. R3,400 ($425) double; 3-night special R8,700 ($1,088) double. Winter (May–June) rates R2,400 ($300). Rates include all meals, drinks, game drives, and bush walks. Children under age 12 pay 50%. AE, DC, MC, V. **Amenities:** Boma/dining room; bar; pool; game drives; bush walks.

IN THORNYBUSH

Royal Malewane ★★★ Like Singita, this award-winning lodge offers such sumptuous accommodations that you will be hard-pressed to leave your suite, even for game drives. Elevated walkways are the only link between the six private thatched suites set on stilts among the bush, each with a huge open-plan bedroom/sitting room with fireplace and equally enormous bathroom and terrace. Whether you're lying draped in Ralph Lauren linen in the antique canopied king-size bed, or luxuriating in the elegant claw-foot bathtub or huge open shower, floor-to-ceiling windows provide wonderfully unobscured views of your private outdoor terrace with pool, outside shower and gazebo, and beyond, the bush. The lounge and dining areas are similarly decorated in "modern colonial" style, and the boma, which unlike most is open, affording a view of the bush, is one of the best-dressed in Kruger. Even surprise meals served in the bush are silver-and-crystal affairs. The palatial Presidential Suite accommodates four guests in absolute luxury, with services including a 24-hour private butler, private chef, and masseur—at R38,500 ($4,812) it's the ultimate honeymoon destination. With traversing rights on 11,500 hectares (28,400 acres) and one of only two master trackers in South Africa, the lodge also offers excellent game-viewing opportunities—elephant and lion are seen within the hour. For all its superlative luxury, it's a remarkably unpretentious lodge, and a great place to unwind.

P.O. Box 1542, Hoedspruit 1380. ℭ **015/793-0150.** Fax 015/793-2879. www.royalmalewane.com. R10,900 ($1,363) double. Rates include all meals, local beverages, game drives, and bush walks. AE, DC, MC, V. **Amenities:** Boma; dining room; lounge/bar; room service; laundry; game drives; bush walks; library. *In room:* A/C, minibar, coffee- and tea-making facilities, hair dryer, fireplace, plunge pool.

IN MAKALALI

Garonga ★ Garonga's approach to the bush experience is more "soul safari" than big game. Although boundary fences between it and Makalali have been down for some time, providing access to four of the Big 5, the emphasis is on "re-earthing" the senses rather than tracking down large mammals. But they're there: A herd of elephants hanging out on the access road made us very late for lunch. This is the perfect place to end a frenetic vacation, with no scheduled game drives imposed on you—an easel, pencils, and small Zen garden are placed in your room, and an aromatherapist is on standby to further help de-stress you.

Accommodations are sublime. Situated on raised platforms along the seasonal Dhlulamiti River, the six units have low adobe walls, colored a warm pink by mixing local river sand into cement, and are topped by a vast tent of cream canvas. King-size beds are swaddled in acres of white muslin, and a large hammock swings above every deck. Because of water restrictions, the en-suite bathrooms have no bathtubs; but, as is the case in most lodges, you have a choice of indoor or outdoor shower. For those who love to soak, the staff will set up a private bush bath with candles and bath salts. Guests are pampered with meals served by the fire, next to the pool, on your deck, in the bush, or in the hide.

P.O. Box 2058, Parklands 2121. ℂ **011/537-4620.** Fax 011/447-0993. www.garonga.com. 7 units. R5,200 ($650) double; winter: R2,750 ($344). Hambledon suite: R6,100 ($763). Rates include all meals, drinks, game drives, and bush walks. AE, DC, MC, V. Children over age 12 only. **Amenities:** Boma; dining area; bar; pool; laundry; game drives; bush walks; aromatherapy; reflexology. *In room:* Hair dryer. Hambledon suite: A/C, minibar.

Makalali Private Lodge ★★ (Value) The year Makalali opened, *Tatler* magazine voted it the "Most Innovatively Designed Hotel in the World." Architect Silvio Rech has combined architectural styles from all over Africa—shaggy East African roof thatching adorns mud and stone walls, while rugged North African–inspired turrets create a mythical village palace sensibility. There is not a right angle to be seen; hardly surprising, since everything is handcrafted, from the tap handles to the built-in clay chairs and the large metal screens that divide the large rooms into bed- and bathroom. Bleached skulls are displayed like totems, and the sense of drama is heightened at night, when the dark rooms flicker with patterns and shadowed images loom large on walls. Makalali consists of four camps—each with its own swimming pool, boma, and enclosed lounge and dining area—situated on various points of the Makhutswi River, which flows for approximately 8 months of the year. Rooms are huge and totally private; each features a fireplace as well as a *sala,* joined to your hut via a boardwalk, where you can arrange to have a massage, or enjoy a romantic dinner. Try and book a room in camp 4, where the rooms are most dispersed and you reach your public areas via a swingbridge—*very* romantic. Camp 2 is ideal for birders, while 3 has a lovely pool. Whatever you do, don't get stuck with room no. 4 in Camp 1; it's too close to the kitchen—which, incidentally, produces wonderful food. Game drives are not always as productive as those in the reserves that abut Kruger (hence the two- rather than three-star rating), but for those who enjoy a more holistic view of nature, the interesting and varied terrain more than makes up for it.

P.O. Box 809, Hoedspruit 1380. ℂ **015/793-1720.** Or book through Three Cities in U.S. ℂ 305/792-0172. www.threecities.co.za. 4 camps each with 6 units. R5,400 ($675) double. Winter rates: R3,400 ($425). Children under age 12 pay 50%. AE, DC, MC, V. **Amenities:** Boma; dining/lounge area; bar; pool; under-6 children's activities; room service; babysitting; game drives; bush walks. *In room:* A/C (Camp 4), fans, hair dryer.

7 The Waterberg Mountains

Approximately 350km (217 miles) north of Johannesburg

The Waterberg, a 150km (93-mile) long mountain ridge that rises quite dramatically from the bushveld plains to 2,085m (6,839 ft.) above sea level, is substantially less populated than the big-game country that lies to the east of the Escarpment. With no major roads and only one town (Vaalwater) within a 15,000-sq.-km (9,300-sq.-mile) area, the region is almost totally devoid of humans—and, with no forestry or industry contributing to pollution, it's one of

Moments Close Encounter on Horseback

Your horse stops, its ears pricked. It is staring at a large shadow in the trees. The shadow stares back. Although leopard sightings are not common here, they do occur, which is one reason **Equus Horse Safaris** ★★★ (© 011/788-3923; 36 12th Ave., Parktown North, Johannesburg 2193; www.equus.co.za) expects you to be both fit and an experienced rider. It's a wonderful way to explore the unspoiled beauty of the Waterberg. Base camp comprises three fully furnished en-suite tents; cost is R700 ($88) per person per day, all inclusive.

the most pristine wilderness areas in the country. It also offers a more varied terrain than most of Kruger, with majestic mountainscapes and rocky ravines, grassed valleys and lush riverines. For many, however, the major reason to go on safari here is that it is malaria-free, year-round.

Waterberg has three major players. At the southwestern end of the mountain range is the National Parks Board's **Marakele Park,** and the adjacent **Welgevonden Reserve**—both feature the Big 5, as well as 16 species of antelope and some 250 species of birds, but Marakele is only accessible by four-wheeldrive vehicles and offers basic accommodation in furnished tents (contact the National Parks Board: © 012/428-9111; www.parks-sa.co.za). By contrast, Welgevonden, a magnificent 40,000-hectare (98,800-acre) wilderness, has been managed and restocked by a consortium of wealthy concession holders, all of whom have had to develop their camps along very strict guidelines. On the down side, ranger vehicles are not permitted to leave the dirt roads in search of game.

Separated from these two reserves by a large area of game and hunting farms is the 35,382-hectare (87,394-acre) **Lapalala Wilderness,** the second-biggest privately owned game reserve in Africa (Tswalu in the Northern Cape is the largest), and internationally renowned for its black rhino conservation and environmental education efforts—more than 45,000 pupils from all over the world have been hosted by the Lapalala Wilderness School.

ESSENTIALS

GETTING THERE   By Plane   There are four landing strips on Welgevonden Reserve—your lodge will arrange the 1-hour charter from Johannesburg airport, the closest international airport to the Waterberg.

By Car   To make the 2½-hour journey, take the N1 north from Johannesburg or Pretoria; take the turnoff for Nylstroom after the toll gates, then head 72km (44½ miles) northwest on the R33 for Vaalwater. The main entrance to Waterberg (from where your lodge will arrange a transfer) lies 26km (16 miles) west of Vaalwater, and the entrance to Lapalala is 70km (43½ miles) north.

VISITOR INFORMATION   For information on **Waterberg Tourism** you will have to contact the municipality (© 014/717-1344/5). Geraldine at the **Waterberg Centre** (© 014/755-4189) has information on the Lapalala area.

GETTING AROUND   At Welgevonden: You leave your car at Main Gate and are transferred by your lodge. **At Lapalala:** You can drive to your camp, but once there you have to explore on foot or horseback—except for guests at Rhino Camp, who can arrange for ranger-led game drives (R90/$11 per person).

WHERE TO STAY & DINE

Clearwater Lodges ⭐ (P.O. Box 365, Stellenbosch 7599; ✆ **082-556-8244;** www.clearwaterlodges.co.za; R7,150/$694) double; winter R4,750/$594), a member of Relais & Chateaux, comprises two totally separate camps: **Tsheshepi Lodge,** built next to a stream at the foot of a wall of mountain, is great if you've always wanted to be serenaded by baboons, but it feels cocooned when compared with **Kudu Lodge** ⭐⭐, set in the middle of an open sweet-grass savanna, surrounded by grazing antelope, zebra, and rhino. Here each generously sized chalet has a deck from which you can enjoy the passing parade at the nearby watering hole. Both lodges accept children—a bonus in a malaria-free reserve.

For solitude at an unbelievably low price, **Lapalala** (central reservations: P.O. Box 348, Vaalwater, Waterberg 0530; ✆ **014/755-4395;** Wilderness Bush Camps: R390–R430/$49–$54 double, minimum 2/3 nights; Rhino Camp: R180–R190/$23–$24 per person, minimum 6 persons) is unbeatable. Lapala has 10 **wilderness bush camps**—rustic self-catering fully equipped camps located in the bush or next to the river, all with flush toilets. Once settled, you're on your own (not even cleaning staff intrude), and because driving in the reserve is not allowed, you won't come across another human until you leave. The presence of crocodiles and hippos means the river should be approached only with extreme caution.

The stone-and-thatch **Makweti Safari Lodge** ⭐⭐ (P.O. Box 310, Vaalwater, Waterberg 0530; ✆ **011/837-6776;** www.makweti.com; R5,700/$715 double; winter R3,500/$438; rate includes all meals, game drives, and bush walks), architecturally the most attractive option in Welgevonden, offers fantastic views of the bush from the rocky ravine on which it is perched. The generous chalets, each with king-size beds and verandas on stilts, offer privacy and peace. The beautifully presented meals are accompanied by fine South African wines.

8

Kingdom of the Zulu: KwaZulu-Natal

Demarcated in the west by the soaring Drakensberg Mountains, its southern tip and eastern borders lapped by the warm Indian Ocean, the densely vegetated KwaZulu-Natal is often described as the country's most "African" province. Its subtropical latitude translates into long, hot summers—at times oppressively humid—and balmy winters, while the warm Mozambique current ensures that the ocean is never more than 2 to 3 degrees cooler than the air. These sultry conditions have not gone unnoticed by its landlocked neighbors, resulting in an almost unbroken ribbon of development along the coastal belt south of the Tugela River, a region dubbed "the Holiday Coast." In its center is Durban, the busiest port in Africa, and the region's industrial and tourism hub.

The region north of the Tugela River is known as Zululand, where the amaZulu rose to power during the early 19th century under the legendary ruler Shaka. Besides the rich selection of local crafts (the Zulus are arguably South Africa's most prolific artists), traditional ways still play a major role in contemporary life here, and visitors are welcome to attend special events such as initiation ceremonies and annual reed dances. Zululand is also home to the majority of KwaZulu-Natal game reserves, some of Africa's oldest wildlife sanctuaries, and a recommended addition to

a safari in Mpumalanga or Botswana. A mere 3 hours' drive north of Durban, you can see the Big 5 at Hluhluwe-Umfolozi Game Reserve or Phinda Private Reserve—also one of the few places in the world where you can track a pride of lions in the morning, then spend the afternoon cruising the lush waterways of the Greater St Lucia Wetland (a World Heritage Site) for hippo and croc, or diving the rich coral reefs off Sodwana Bay. If you have time, join the privileged few who have explored the 60km (37 miles) of pristine coastline at Rocktail Bay, north of Sodwana. The more intrepid nature lover should head even farther, to the Kosi Bay Nature Reserve, located in the far northern corner of the province. Inland are Mkuze and Ndumo, the country's premier birdwatching reserves, while to the west lie the famous battle sites of the many wars fought among the Zulu, British, and Boers in the 19th century.

Pride of place for those in search of real tranquillity and breathtaking beauty must however go to the soaring Drakensberg, or "Barrier of Spears," as the amaZulu called them. Site of more than 35,000 ancient San rock paintings, thought to be the mostly densely concentrated area on the African continent, the Drakensberg was declared a World Heritage Site by UNESCO in December 2000, bringing a much deserved focus to southern Africa's most majestic mountainscape.

1 Staying Active

Adrenaline junkies might want to contact **180 Adventures** (© 082-588-2426) or **Wild Sky Adventures** (© 039/832-0224,** based in the Drakensberg) for one-stop adventure shopping, including hiking, fly-fishing, rafting, horseback riding, mountain biking, tubing, paragliding, and abseiling (rappelling). **Little Berg** (© 082-455-9390; www.littleberg.net) puts together tailor-made active trips in the Drakensberg—a combination of guided walks, swimming, mountain biking, and horseback riding through the beautiful Champagne Valley.

BIRD-WATCHING   Two of South Africa's best bird-watching destinations—the Mkhuze and Ndumo reserves—are located here. Contact Peter at **Lawson's Birdwatching Tours** ★★★ (© 013/741-2458), which operates throughout southern Africa and invariably includes both reserves in its fully catered bird-watching safaris. A 4-hour drive from Durban, Mkhuze has very basic facilities (it has no restaurant, for example), but the park is magnificent (see "Zululand: The Greater St Lucia Wetland Park," later in this chapter). Or head for the laid-on luxuries of **Ndumo Wilderness Camp,** on the border between KwaZulu-Natal and Mozambique. Located in the exquisite Ndumo Game Reserve, this area is often compared with the Okavango Delta (in Botswana), with pans and jungle teeming with more than 400 bird species—60% of South Africa's birdlife. The camp offers eight well-appointed en-suite safari tents, each situated on a raised wooden deck and linked by a boardwalk under a canopy of giant fig trees. For more information, contact **Wilderness Safaris** (© 011/883-0747; fax 011/883-0911; www.wilderness-safaris.com).

HIKING   The wilderness trails in **Umfolozi Game Reserve** ★★★, in which you track game on foot, are considered the best in the country, superior even to those in Kruger. You can choose the type of hike you prefer, based on your fitness level and personal comfort, but the **Traditional Trail,** in which all your gear is carried by donkeys, is recommended, although a fair degree of fitness is required. The **Summer Bushveld** trails, in which you have a chance to relax between the morning and afternoon walks, are worth asking about if you're not such a keen walker (contact © 035/573-9004; for bookings (© 033/845-1067; www.kznwildlife.com). See also "Zululand: Hluhluwe-Umfolozi Game Reserve," later in this chapter. The **Mziki Trail** ★★ (located in the Mfabeni area) in the Greater St Lucia Wetland Park comprises three 1-day loops of 10km to 18km (6–11 miles). Accompanied by an armed field ranger you explore the park's estuary shore, dune forests, and coastline, with the chance to see elephant, buffalo, hippo, and crocodile. The 3km (2-mile) circular guided **Mkhuze Fig Forest Trail,** through one of the area's rarest and most attractive woodlands, is also recommended; to arrange this call © 035/573-9004. Kosi Bay's 4-day **Amanzamnyama Trail** ★ takes in all four lakes, coral reefs, pristine beaches, and the country's largest mangrove forest; to arrange this, call Eric Dickson at © 035/592-0236. Of the many trails traversing the Drakensberg, the **Giant's Cup Hiking Trail** ★★ (located in the Cobham area), a 3- to 5-day self-guided clearly marked hike that takes you past caves with San paintings, crystal-clear rivers, pools, and deep grass valleys, is recommended for relatively inexperienced hikers. For detailed information about the Drakensberg trails, call John Carsen (© 033/702-0831); for bookings, contact KZN Wildlife (© 033/845-1067; www.kznwildlife.com).

SURFING   To rent a surfboard and arrange lessons, contact **Surf Zone** (© 031/368-5818) in the Ocean Sports Complex, on Marine Parade in

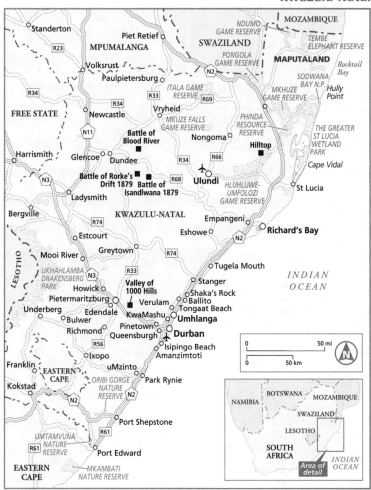

Durban. Good surf spots around the city are North Beach and the adjacent "Bay of Plenty." Check out Green Point, Scottburgh, the Spot, Warner Beach, and Cave Rock; the latter has an excellent right reef break.

SWIMMING **Dolphin Encounters** (✆ 011/462-4551) offers 4-day swimming-with-dolphin packages just north of the KwaZulu-Natal border—visitors must arrange to travel to the Kosi Bay border post (4 hours' drive from Durban) With warm water year-round, the entire coast is popular with swimmers, and shark nets protect the main swimming beaches from Port Edward to the Tugela; note, however, that many beaches shelve suddenly into deep surf, with strong undertows—swim only where boards indicate safety, or where there are lifeguards. (Keep an eye out for Portuguese man-of-war jellyfish as well.) **North Beach** is the most popular beach for Durbanites; also good is **Umhlanga,** a 20- to 30-minute drive north of town. If you prefer your water without waves, head for the **Rachel Finlayson Baths** (✆ 031/337-2721), a saltwater pool on Marine Parade.

(*Moments* **Sangomas at Dawn**

Walk along a Durban beach at dawn, and you may see a group of Zulu *sangomas* (traditional healers), their beads and buckskin adornments covered in brightly colored cloth, wading into the ocean to collect seawater, to be used in *muti* (traditional medicines) to protect crops. An estimated two-thirds of South Africans regularly consult sangomas, and recently even large pharmaceutical companies have been tapping into their knowledge of the medicinal properties of plants.

WHITE-WATER RAFTING   **Umko** offers a full day (R395/$49) on the Umkomaas River, considered one of the best commercial-run rivers in South Africa (up to grade-5 rapids). These can be extended into 2 days; call Dave at ℂ **083-270-0403.** For trips on the Buffalo River (grade-2 to -4 rapids), Zululand, call **Isibindi Reservations** (ℂ **011/463-3376**).

2 Durban

1,753km (1,087 miles) NE of Cape Town, 588km (365 miles) SE of Johannesburg

The Union Jack was first planted in Durban's fertile soil in 1824, a year after George Farewell fortuitously happened upon its harbor. It was only after the fledgling settlement was formally annexed in 1844, however, that the dense coastal vegetation was gradually consumed by buildings with broad verandas, and civilized with English traditions such as morning papers, afternoon tea, and weekend horse racing.

Sugar was this region's "white gold," with large fortunes made by the so-called sugar barons. The most famous of these was Sir Marshall Campbell; today his home, housing the Campbell Collection, is one of Durban's star attractions, and one can still travel along the beachfront in the two-wheeled "rickshaws" he introduced to the city in 1893. The world's voracious appetite for sugar was also responsible for the strong Indian influence on Durban's architecture, cuisine, and customs—during the 19th century, thousands of indentured laborers were shipped in from India to work the sugar plantations, and today Durban houses the largest Indian population outside of India.

South Africa's third-largest city, Durban attracts the lion's share of South Africa's domestic tourists, and offers a completely unique atmosphere. It's certainly worth scheduling 2 or 3 days here before heading west to the Drakensberg or north for the game parks and marine reserves of Zululand. To experience the essence of South Africa's most multicultural city, a walking tour of the Indian District, where Indian shops and markets are interspersed with Zulu hawkers touting traditional wares, is recommended—though be aware that it's a rather seedy part of town. The Kwa Muhle Museum provides an excellent insight into the iniquitous system of apartheid. Anyone who is interested in the region's arts and crafts should make it a priority to visit the Durban Art Museum and NSA, with a possible side trip to a nearby cultural village, such as Phezulu, located in the Valley of a Thousand Hills.

ESSENTIALS

VISITOR INFORMATION   You can make all your travel arrangements at the Tourist Junction, where **Durban Africa** (ℂ **031/304-4934;** www.durban experience.co.za; open Mon–Fri 8am–4:30pm, Sat–Sun 9am–2pm) is located,

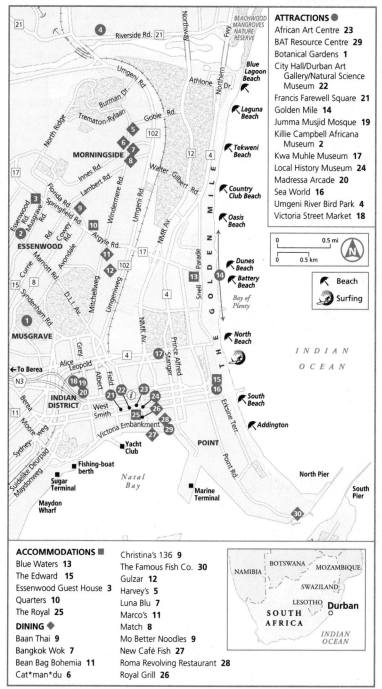

as is a branch of **KwaZulu-Natal Wildlife (KZN Wildlife)** and Tourism KwaZulu-Natal. The Tourist Junction is in the Old Station Building (160 Pine St.). For details on local events, pick up a free copy of *What's On in Durban and KwaZulu-Natal.* *Note:* if you plan to travel north to the Zululand reserves and beyond, **Camera Africa** are recommended agents who specialize in the Zululand and Maputaland area (© **031/266-4172;** www.camera-africa.com).

GETTING THERE By Plane **Durban International Airport** is 15km (9 miles) south of the city center, but plans are afoot to relocate to La Mercy (about 35 min. north) and rename it King Shaka International Airport. Until then, most flights remain domestic. For arrival and departure information, call © **031/451-6666;** for reservations, call **SAA** © **031/250-1111.** Taxis are always lined up outside, or you can use the **airport bus service** (© **031/465-5573**) that travels between the domestic terminal and the SAA building on Aliwal Street every hour from 6am to 9pm. For 24-hour service, call **Super Shuttle** (© **0860-333-444**). A bank at the International terminal is open for arrivals.

By Train The **Trans-Natal** from Johannesburg pulls into Durban Station (© **031/361-7621** or 031/361-7609), on NMR Avenue.

By Bus Country-wide operators **Greyhound, Intercape,** and **Translux** (see chapter 2 for contact information) all arrive and depart at the station complex. The **Baz Bus** has an office at Tourist Junction and does dropoffs at hostels.

By Car The N2 from Cape Town runs parallel to the coast as far as Zululand; the N3 to Johannesburg meets the N2 at Durban.

WHEN TO GO The best time to visit is from February to mid-May, when it's not too humid. Temperatures range from 61°F to 73°F (16°C–25°C) winter and 73°F to 91°F (23°C–33°C) summer (Sept–Apr).

GETTING AROUND By Car The city center is relatively small, but to explore farther afield you're best off renting a car. A number of companies have desks at the airport—contact **Avis** (© **031/408-1282** or 031/304-1741) or **Budget** (© **031/408-1809** or 031/304-9023) (the latter usually offers a slightly better rate). For a cheaper deal, call **Windermere Car Hire** (© **031/312-0339** or 082-454-1625) or **Maharani** (© **031/368-6563**).

By Bus The city center, beachfront, and Berea are serviced by **Mynah** buses (© **031/309-5942**); trips cost from R1.20 (US15¢). Alternatively, contact **Durban Transport** (© **031/309-5942** or 031/309-4126). You can catch the **Umhlanga Express** (© **082-268-0651**) to Umhlanga Rocks. For coaches to the South Coast, contact **Margate Mini Coach** (© **039/312-1406**) or **U Tour** (© **031/368-2848**).

By Taxi The three-wheeled Asian-style *tuk tuks* queue 24 hours a day on Marine Parade (opposite the aquarium) and will take you anywhere between the beach and central Durban, as will **"mozziecabs"** (© **031/263-0467**). **Aussies** (© **031/309-7888**) is one of the largest and most reputable cab companies. **Super Shuttle** (© **0860-333-444**) offers personalized transfer service to any destination in KwaZulu-Natal.

GUIDED TOURS On Foot Historical Walkabout and **Oriental Walkabout** 🏃🏃 walking tours (both R40/$5) can be arranged through **Durban Africa** (© **031/304-4934**).

By Bus The **Durban Ricksha Bus** (© **083-289-0509**) is an open-topped double-decker bus that offers a 2½-hour guided city tour every Tuesday, Thursday, and Sunday afternoon (R40/$5). The most authentic city tour is offered by **Tekweni Ecotours** ★★★ (𝄐 **031/303-1199**). The full-day tour takes in the multicultural sights of the city and the harbor before moving on to the township of Cato Manor, where a local guide takes you on a short walking tour that ends at a *shebeen* (informal bar) where you enjoy a meal with members of the community; the cost is R275 ($34), including transport, drinks, and dinner. Best of all, a percentage of the tour price is reinvested in the community. **Strelitzia Tours** (𝄐 **031/266-9480**) offers 3-hour Durban City tours (R210/$26), as well as a number of tours farther afield—the Midlands Meander (R695/$85) and Sani Pass (R995/$124) are both highly recommended. Strelitzia Tours can also arrange special-interest tours for golfers, divers, and deep-sea fishermen. **Stud Farm Tours** (𝄐 **031/314-1500**) is a day trip to the top stud farms, located in the scenic Midlands, and includes a lunch at a top country hotel.

By Boat   Board the luxury charter yacht *African Queen* (𝄐 **082-961-4313**) for a cruise, and set sail for the north coast. Trips last 3 hours and cost R120 ($15) per person. Less romantic is the engine-powered **Sarie Marais Pleasure Cruisers** (𝄐 **031/305-4022**), a ferryboat that does 30-minute harbor cruises and 90-minute "deep-sea" cruises (R30/$3.70), or minibay cruises (R15/$1.85) every 30 minutes. **Adventure Ocean Safaris** (𝄐 **082-960-7682**) is the only licensed boat-based whale-watcher in the Durban area—Wayne is incredibly knowledgeable and tours are very informative. For more boating options, contact the **Durban Charter Boat Association** (𝄐 **031/301-1115**).

By Air   Nac Helicopters (𝄐 **031/564-0176**) offers a variety of trips, from a 20-minute flight around greater Durban and a 1-hour trip along the coast and the Valley of a Thousand Hills to golf trips, Drakensberg tours, and game tours.

CITY LAYOUT   Sightseeing in the city can be divided into roughly four areas: the **city center,** which encompasses the buildings and memorials surrounding Francis Farewell Square, as well as the Indian District; the tacky **"Golden Mile,"** which runs east of the city, following the beachfront; the **Victoria Embankment** (or **Esplanade**), which runs at more or less 90 degrees to the Golden Mile, along the harbor's edge, creating the city's southern border; and the western outskirts of the city, particularly **Berea,** where you'll find some top attractions and many of the city's best restaurants. Ironically, this upmarket residential suburb borders **Cato Manor**—an African township where temporary shacks contrast with Hindu temples and subtropical vegetation. It's an excellent place to view Durban's unique cultural melting pot, preferably with a guide.

FAST FACTS: Durban

American Express Located in 'The Vibe' East Coast Radio House, Umhlanga Rocks Drive (𝄐 **031/566-8650;**open Mon–Fri 8am–5pm, and Sat 8:30–11am).

Area Code Durban's area code is **031**.

Emergencies For an **ambulance,** call 𝄐 **10177** and ask to be taken to the casualty unit at **Entabeni Private Hospital** (𝄐 **031/204-1300**). Staff will also treat nonemergencies. **Police:** 𝄐 **300-3333; Flying Squad:** 𝄐 **10111; SAP Tourist Protection Unit:** 𝄐 **031/368-4453. Fire brigade:** 𝄐 **031/309-4341; NSRI** (sea rescue): 𝄐 **031/361-8567; Rape Crisis:** 𝄐 **031/312-2323.**

Pharmacy Late-night chemists include **Medicine Chest** (℃ **031/305-6151**), 155 Berea Rd., and **Day-Night Pharmacy** (℃ **031/368-3666**), 9A Nedbank Circle, corner of Point and West (the latter has free delivery).

Safety Malaria was pushed north to Zululand by development and pesticides, with no reported incidences in Durban in more than 50 years. If you plan to travel into northern Zululand, a course of antimalarial drugs is necessary (see chapter 2). Like any large city where a large percentage of the population is poor, Durban is troubled by street crime. The display of wealth is unwise anywhere in the city or beachfront, and visitors are advised to do their explorations of these areas during the day.

Weather For a weather report, call ℃ **082-231-1603**.

EXPLORING THE CITY & INDIAN DISTRICT

Start your tour by visiting the Tourist Junction and African Art Centre (see "Shopping for Arts & Crafts," below), housed in the Old Station Building at 160 Pine St., then head south to the Francis Farewell Square. It was here that Henry Francis Flynn and some 20 hard-living traders and ivory hunters first set up shop in 1823. A decade later, the tiny settlement was named "Durban" in an attempt to curry favor with the then governor of the Cape, Sir Benjamin Durban, and to gain protection from the amaZulu. It would take another 20 years, however, for Natal to be proclaimed a British colony, annexed to the Cape.

On the south side of the square is the **City Hall** (1910), a stone-for-stone replica of the City Hall in Belfast, Ireland. Time your visit for Wednesday at 1pm, and catch the weekly concert hosted on the steps by Durban Arts; it could be anything from Zulu dancing to a community choir. To find out who's performing, contact **Big Boy Zungu** (℃ **031/312-1236**).

The City Hall's first floor houses the **Natural Science Museum** ★ (℃ **031/ 311-2256;** open Mon–Sat 8:30am–4pm, and Sun 11am–4pm; free admission). Visiting schoolchildren help make it the busiest museum in the country. The usual array of very dead-looking animals is useful as a crash course in wildlife identification if you're traveling north. Kids will also appreciate the gross-out qualities of the "Kwanunu" section, where the insect displays include some large, truly revolting roaches. One floor up is the excellent **Durban Art Gallery** ★★ (see "Top Attractions," below).

East of the City Hall, facing Aliwal Road, is the **Old Court House,** home of Durban's local-history museum (℃ **031/311-2229;** open Mon–Sat 8:30am– 4pm, and Sun 11am–4pm). The first public building erected in Durban (1866), this is a lovely example of the Natal Verandah style, and today houses a rather dry collection of exhibits, focusing on 19th-century history. Wander past the costumes worn by the disparate groups that made up Durban society for over 200 years (look for the beadwork items). A few of Gandhi's artifacts are also housed here (see "The Making of Mahatma: Gandhi's Turning Point," later in this chapter). A great deal more stimulating is the **Kwa Muhle Museum** ★★★, an annex of the Local History Museum (see "Top Attractions," below), a 10-minute walk north up Aliwal Road to where it intersects with Ordnance Road— but because this does not ideally position you to tackle the Indian District, it should possibly be seen as a separate trip.

From the Old Court House, it's a 15-minute walk east to the **Golden Mile** (you can also take a Mynah bus from the depot diagonally opposite the museum, on West St.), and a 15-minute walk west to what is known as Durban's central **Indian District** ★★★. The latter is by far the more interesting option, so head down West Street, then north up Grey Street. In Durban's most fascinating streetscape, the Indian dealers trade in everything from spices and sari fabrics to fresh fish and meat, while Zulu street hawkers ply passersby with anything from haircuts to *muti,* traditional medicine—baboon skulls, bits of bark, bone, and dried herbs—used to heal wounds, improve spirits, ward off evil, or cast spells.

While on Grey Street, look out for the **Patel Vegetarian Refreshment Room** (Rama House, 202 Grey St., next to SK Naidoos Sari Boutique; ✆ **031/306-1774**). If you're ravenous, try the *bunnychow* takeaway—this half-loaf of bread, with the dough scooped out and stuffed with curry, is unique to Durban. West off Grey Street is the **Madressa Arcade,** a bazaar where you will be exhorted to spend your rand on cheap rubbish, mostly from China. Either walk through to Cathedral Street, or follow Grey for another block and admire the gilt-domed minarets of **Juma Musjid Mosque** (corner of Queen and Grey), the largest mosque in the Southern Hemisphere. Visitors are welcome to enter provided they remove their shoes and are modestly dressed; for a guided tour, call the **Islamic Propagation Centre** (✆ **031/306-0026**).

To get into the sway of traditional Indian music, head down Queen Street and take your pick from the selection at **Bombay House** (36 Lockhart Arcade; ✆ **031/306-0466**). West lie the purple minarets of the **Victoria "Street" Market** ★ (✆ **031/306-4021;** open Mon–Fri 8am–5pm, Sat 8am–2pm, and Sun 10am–2pm), on the corner of Queen and Russell streets. This garish building was built after a fire destroyed much of the original Indian market, and has become increasingly touristy; but you can still purchase incense, patterned stencils to henna hands and feet, stick-on dots for foreheads, and bags of spices whose names (Atomic Bomb and Mother-in-Law Exterminator, for example) provide some guide to chili content. If the meat market doesn't kill your appetite (the offal shops are pretty, well, awful), pick up a couple of *samoosas* (vegetable- or meat-filled pastries) upstairs at **Khan's Take-Away** (✆ **031/301-0065**).

TOP ATTRACTIONS

Blue Lagoon *Finds* The locals love this spot for romantic early evenings. It's a soulful place, where you can take in the salty sea air and meditate on the incoming tide of the Umgeni River mouth and the distant misty afternoon view of Durban's beachfront skyline. It's a great bird-watching spot, too—look for the majestic African fish-eagle and the wading giant goliath herons—as well as a fisherman's paradise.

Continue along Snell Parade as if going to North Coast. No phone. Free admission.

The Campbell Collections ★★★ Housed in Muckleneuk, the neo–Cape Dutch home that sugar baron Sir Marshall Campbell built for his family in 1914, this museum is arguably Durban's top attraction. Tours are conducted by the knowledgeable Jenny Harkness and take in the gracious gardens and the Cape Dutch furniture and artwork collected by Campbell's son (whose private hunting farm became what is today the private game reserve MalaMala), as well as the extensive Africana library and ethnological artifacts collected by his daughter, "Killie" Campbell. The latter collection, known as the **Mashu Museum of Ethnology,** is considered one of the country's finest groupings of African artifacts and is the highlight of the tour. Killie collected traditional utensils, ornaments, art, musical instruments, sticks, beadwork, and various items of beaded clothing— don't miss the necklace of redcoat (British) buttons worn by Zulu warriors as a sign of bravery. Killie commissioned more than 250 illustrations from Barbara Tyrrell, who in the early 1940s set off into relatively uncharted areas in a battered old 1934 Chevy to record people in tribal dress. Hairstyles and the colors and patterns of clothing were unspoken indications of, among other things, marital and tribal status. Tyrrell's costume studies provide invaluable insights into this subtle and largely vanished code of communication. Note that tours are by appointment only.

Corner of Marriott and Essenwood roads (off Musgrave Road), Berea. R20 ($2.60). By appointment; for guided tours, contact Jenny at ⓒ 031/207-3432 or harkness@nu.ac.za.

Durban Art Gallery ⭐⭐ Back in the 1970s, this was the first national gallery to recognize African crafts as art, and today it has arguably the most representative and exciting collection of traditional and contemporary South "Africana" art in the country (see "Zululand: Vukani Collection Museum," later in this chapter, for more). There is a great deal more than is possible to display; to view specific crafts, artworks, or artists (like the famous Zulu potter, Nesta Nala), call Gill (number below) to arrange a viewing of these in the Conservation Centre. Don't miss the happening "red eye @rt" temporary exhibits, held on the first Friday of every month (see "Durban After Dark," later in this chapter).

City Hall, Smith St. ⓒ 031/311-2264. Free admission. Open Mon–Sat 8:30am–4pm; Sun 11am–4pm.

Kwa Muhle Museum ⭐⭐⭐ Also known as the "apartheid museum," Kwa Muhle contains aural and visual exhibits that graphically illuminate how the segregationist policies of the city affected the majority of the city's population. Certainly anyone interested in South Africa's history of race relations should not miss an opportunity to view the exhibition titled the "Durban System." It provides a graphic explanation of how the System, a municipal race policy that evolved in Durban in the early 1900s, granted itself sole monopoly on the brewing and distribution of beer (provided traditionally by women), which it sold through "African-only" beer halls. Proceeds were in turn used to finance the administration and control of black labor in this very building—these were the offices of the Bantu Administration Board, where the city's black inhabitants were "processed." The "Durban System" is a highly evocative exhibit, and an accompanying audiotape ensures that the information is accessible. The "Pass System" exhibition, located toward the back of the museum, is comparatively text-heavy but provides some insight into the humiliation and hatred evoked by the hated "pass books" that controlled the influx and movement of black people throughout the country from 1948 to 1986.

130 Ordnance Rd. ⓒ 031/311-2233. Free admission. Open Mon–Sat 8:30am–4pm; Sun 11am–4pm.

Umgeni River Bird Park ⭐⭐ *Kids* Rated as one of the top three of its kind in the world, this bird park is situated near the banks of the Umgeni River. More than 300 species from around the world are housed in large aviaries, three of which are walk-through, and each is planted with palms, cycads, and other tropical plants. The variety of colors and sounds is astounding, and somehow the lush environment makes up for the fact that most of these hapless creatures are caged. The educational "Free Flight" bird show, in which handlers introduce a variety of birds (including a parrot, blue crane, and Cape vulture) and demonstrate their flight patterns, is definitely worth catching.

490 Riverside Rd., Durban North. From the M4 take Riverside/Umgeni off-ramp. © **031/579-4600**. R25 ($3).
Free Flight bird shows held Tues–Sun at 11am and 2pm. Open daily 9am–5pm.

SHOPPING FOR ARTS & CRAFTS

The **African Art Centre** ★★★ (© **031/304-7915;** open Mon–Fri 8:30am–
5pm, and Sat 9am–1pm), conveniently located on the first floor of the Tourist
Junction, is one of the best places in the country to examine the woodcarvings,
ceramics, beadwork, baskets, tapestries, rugs, fine art, and fabrics created by predominantly Zulu craftsmen and artists. Staff here are extremely knowledgeable
and helpful (ask for development director Anthea Martin), and it's worth buying at least one item—proceeds are reinvested in the development of local talent. If this whets your appetite, a visit to the **KwaZulu-Natal Society of the
Arts (NSA) Gallery** ★★★, at 166 Bulwer Rd., Glenwood (© **031/202-3686;**
open Tues–Fri 9am–5pm, Sat 9am–4pm, Sun 10am–3pm), is a must. The excellent exhibitions feature artists from different cultural and ethnic backgrounds
and may include paintings, mosaics, beadwork, lithograph, and embroidery.
The adjacent shop has a wide variety of visual arts, including works by master
craftspeople.

It can't compete in terms of variety, but the **BAT shop** ★ © **031/332-9951;**
open daily 9am–4:30pm) in the **BAT Resource Centre** (Small Craft Harbour,
45 Maritime Place; © **031/332-0451;** www.batcentre.co.za) offers good prices
and a harborside setting. Established in 1995, this innovative community arts
center is a pleasant place to shop, with several art studios where you can watch
artists at work, a few excellent shops, a restaurant, and an evening music venue.
Plan your visit for a Friday afternoon, hang around until the harbor lights come
on, then soak up some good local jazz (see "Durban After Dark," later in this
chapter). Another BAT Centre shop worth seeing is the **Bayside Gallery**
(© **031/368-5547;** open Tues–Sun 10am–4pm), which has a very good selection
of South African talent—if they're in stock, look out for the Nesta Nala pots,
Carol Boys' pewterware, and the artful creations from Ardmore Studio in the
Drakensberg. Located in The Workshop, a shopping center on Aliwal Street,
Springbok Art and Jewelers (© **031/304-8451**) claims to offer the largest selection of African masks in the country. Finally, if you're looking for quirky, funky
clothing and accessories, visit the **Durban Designer's Emporium** at 77A Musgrave Rd., Musgrave, where you'll find a great selection of top local labels—Durban is considered to be the spawning ground for South Africa's most creative
clothing designers (a claim that's hotly contested by Capetonians, of course).

For an informal shopping experience, check out the **street hawkers** who line
the entire Marine Parade beachfront, or head for the **Amphitheater Flea Market** (north of Marine Parade, between Snell Parade and the Bay of Plenty), held
every Sunday. **Essenwood Flea Market** in Berea Park is held every Saturday
morning. The brave should also consider visiting the **Dalton Road Market:** a
truly African market not aimed at tourists, this is where craftsmen sell traditional
items such as the *amabheshu* (apron), *izimboko* (staff), and shields to Zulu men
wishing to participate in ritual dances.

SIDE TRIPS FROM DURBAN

With limited time, a visit to **Phezulu,** the Zulu cultural village overlooking the
Valley of a Thousand Hills (a 30-min. drive) is recommended; alternatively, take
a leisurely drive up the **North Coast,** swimming at Umhlanga and enjoying a
barefoot lunch at Razzmatazz, or drinking in the view from the pool deck at
Zimbali Lodge, a 30- to 40-minute drive from the city.

PIETERMARITZBURG

Pietermaritzburg lies 80km (49½ miles) northwest of Durban, and visitors should try to take in the **Valley of a Thousand Hills** along the way. But neither the "heritage" capital or the evocative-sounding valley (which in reality could be described as Valley of a Thousand Hovel-Covered Hills) merit more than a brief detour on your way to the battlefields or the Drakensberg. The chief draw of the valley, aside from shopping for African curios, is **Phezulu Safari Park,** one of the most accessible Zulu cultural villages, where you are guided through a re-created traditional village, have the various traditions and rituals of the Zulu explained, and are treated to ceremonial dancing.

To reach the valley, head for Pietermaritzburg northwest from Durban along the M3, following the Pinetown Road signs. Take the Hillcrest/Old Main Road turnoff to the right, and follow the Old Main Road or R103 along the valley, which finally rejoins the M3 to Pietermaritzburg. You will also find the **1000 Hills Tourism Information Centre** (© **031/777-1874;** www.1000hills.kzn. org.za) on the Old Main Road.

Most consider Pietermaritzburg's highlight to be the **Tatham Art Gallery** ★★★ (Commercial St.; © **033/342-1804;** open Tues–Sun 10am–6pm; free admission), situated in the old Supreme Court (built in 1871) diagonally opposite the City Hall. The Tatham features a predominantly European collection including minor works by Degas, Renoir, Picasso, Matisse, and Hockney, with a much smaller but equally interesting collection of South African artworks.

THE HOLIDAY COAST

Durban's coastline is a 5-hour drive from dry, dusty Jo'burg, and even less from the Free State. With every middle-class family demanding their place in the sun, this subtropical belt south of the Tugela River has been swallowed up by condominiums, timeshares, brick-face homes, and tatty caravan parks, ruining, at least for nature lovers, almost the entire "Holiday Coast." Thankfully, there are a few areas where the lush coastal vegetation hides all signs of human habitation—from the beach at least. The fecund vegetation is, in fact, the saving grace of this coastline; wild banana trees and masses of flowering shrubs and trees, often alive with monkeys, do much to soften concrete lines. Unless you're traveling to or from the Eastern Cape, wish to dive the Aliwal Shoal, or are here on

---

Fun Fact **The Making of Mahatma: Gandhi's Turning Point**

On June 7, 1893, a young lawyer named Mohandas Gandhi, recently arrived in Durban, found himself stranded at the Pietermaritzburg Station after being ejected from a whites-only first-class carriage. He spent the night mulling the incident over in the waiting room, and, according to the great man himself, "[his] active non-violence started from that day." Mohandas (later to become Mahatma) was to spend the next 21 years peacefully fighting the South African laws that discriminated against Indians before leaving to liberate India from English rule. You can visit the platform where Gandhi was unceremoniously tossed (at the seedy end of Church St.), the **Gandhi statue** (near the City Hall end of Church St.), or the **Natal Museum** (237 Loop St.; www.nmsa.org.za/info.htm), which has a few exhibits relating to the man.

a golfing vacation, the 160km (99-mile) South Coast stretch, incorporating the "Hibiscus Coast" and the "Strelitzia Coast," is best avoided in favor of the slightly less-developed North Coast.

The most popular seaside suburb on the North Coast (comprising the "Sugar Coast" and "Dolphin Coast") is Umhlanga Rocks (pronounced *um*-shlung-ga), a 20-minute drive north of Durban. Originally part of Marshall Campbell's sugar estate, it is now simply an extension of Durban, with well-developed facilities, safe bathing areas, and plenty of accommodations options. The region's **Sugar Coast Tourism Association** (© 031/561-4257; open Mon–Fri 8am–5pm, Sat 8am–1pm) is also situated here, on Chartwell Drive. Come here first if you intend on venturing inland to the rolling sugar cane fields.

If you're tired of sunbathing and swimming, the one noteworthy place worth visiting in Umhlanga are the offices of the **Natal Sharks Board** (see below).

If you're looking for uncrowded beaches, you'll have to head farther north. In and beyond Ballito, development starts to taper off, with **Zimbali Lodge** (see below) the Holiday Coast's premier resort. At **Blythedale,** roughly 25km (15½ miles) north of Ballito and 70km (43 miles) north of Durban, a total ban on high-rise construction has created the best preserved beach on the Holiday Coast, while 13km (8 miles) farther the tiny hamlet of **Zinkwasi** is the least developed beach resort on the North Coast, and marks the end of the Holiday Coast. If you intend to spend some time in this area, contact the **Dolphin Coast Tourist Information** (© 032/946-1997; fax 032/946-2434) in Ballito.

Natal Sharks Board ⊛ (Kids) One of the most prestigious centers for shark research in the world, the board offers informative audiovisual presentations about these awesome predators—up to 14 species swim off this coast. Get there for the first showing at 9am, or at 2pm, and you can watch one of the sharks—who are regularly caught in the shark nets—being dissected. Currently the most viable protection for swimmers, these controversial nets are responsible for the deaths of hundreds of sharks as well as numerous rays, dolphins, and endangered turtles. If the thought of these innocent creatures' plight makes you feel uncomfortable, take a look at the informative display about the history of shark attacks along the coast. You can also catch a ride on a **Sharks Board** skiboat to observe first-hand how the meshing crews go about servicing the shark nets; trips are 2 hours and need to be prebooked (© 082-403-9206).

1a Herrwood Dr. © 031/566-0400. www.shark.co.za. Presentation hours: Tues–Thurs at 9am and 2pm, with additional showings on Sun. R15 ($1.95) adults, R10 ($1.30) children.

WHERE TO STAY

Unlike the lodgings in Cape Town and along the Garden Route, most hotels here have a year-round rate, though there's no harm in asking for a discount during the winter months. The center of town is only 17km (10½ miles) from the airport, so it's not necessary to book into a nasty airport hotel to catch a late-night or early flight—all the establishments listed will arrange airport transfers. If none of the options below suit, consider **La Bordello** (© 031/309-6091; R500/$60 double, including breakfast). Located in the heart of the restaurant strip (right next door to Bean Bag Bohemia), this earthy, artsy 7-room B&B is ideal for the younger traveler. Note that if you're keen on a beach-based stay, you should book into a hotel in Umhlanga Rocks, a popular coastal town that is 15 to 20 minutes from the city center, or even farther north. Bear in mind that, with the exception of Zimbali, which is about 40 minutes north of the city center, the city listings offer much better value (and are generally classier).

IN DURBAN

Blue Waters   You don't book into the Blue Waters for a luxury experience—the price precludes it—but for anyone interested in 20th-century design, and unafraid of kitsch, this hotel is a gem. Commissioned by present owner and architect Robin Jiran after a trip to Miami, the original hotel (now the south wing) was completed in 1957, and the east and north wings were added in the early 1970s. It has a number of classic, albeit run-down, features: the glass wall in the indoor pool, which looks into the Cascades function room; the Coimbra bar (incidentally currently very much the place to be seen according to local movers), which has original Hille bucket chairs and Michael Leu prints; and the Art Deco–inspired spiral staircase in the lobby, designed by Antonio Avelini. The hotel sits on the northernmost tip of the Golden Mile beachfront (a 20-min. stroll from the city center)—request a sea-facing room. *Tip:* Dine out.

175 Snell Parade, Durban 4000. ℂ **031/332-4272.** Fax 031/337-5817. www.bluewatershotel.co.za. 260 units. R460 ($56) double; R600 ($75) suite. Children age 2–12 R50 ($6.50). Rates include breakfast. AE, DC, MC, V. **Amenities:** Restaurant; 2 bars; pool; sauna; room service; babysitting; laundry; squash court. *In room:* A/C, TV, tea- and coffee-making facilities, hair dryer.

The Edward ★★ *Kids*   The grand dame of Durban's beachfront, The Edward has played host to princes and presidents, field marshals and millionaires, and movie stars and holy men since the 1920s, though its current incarnation as part of the Protea chain is a little less glam. Its proximity to both the city sights (it's a 10-min. stroll to the center) and the Golden Mile beachfront (across the road) is ideal, however. This is also a good family hotel, particularly considering that children sharing the spacious sea-facing double, with a bay window overlooking the beachfront, and two double beds, stay free. If you like your space, the deluxe suite has a separate lounge with a dining room table, a writing desk in the bay window, and a separate balcony—ask for room no. 211 and you'll have the pleasure of knowing how the Dalai Lama enjoyed his stay in Durban. Meals are served in the **Brasserie,** which isn't going to win any culinary awards.

149 Marine Parade, Durban 4000. ℂ **031/337-3681.** Fax 031/332-1692. www.proteahotels.com. 101 units. R850 ($106) non-sea-facing double; R1,050 ($130) sea-facing double; R1,550 ($190) suite. AE, DC, MC, V. **Amenities:** Restaurant; bar; pool; room service; business services; babysitting; laundry. *In room:* A/C, TV, minibar stocked on request, tea- and coffee-making facilities, hair dryer.

Essenwood Guest House ★★ *Value*   If you don't enjoy the anonymity of a hotel and would like to experience firsthand what it's like to live in the most sought-after residential area in Durban, then Essenwood Guest House is ideal. A rose-tinted colonial homestead built in 1924 in a large tropical garden with a pool, this was originally the family home of one of Durban's sugar barons. Paddy and John, themselves former sugar cane farmers, have restored the house, furnished it with tasteful antiques and artworks, and—thankfully—opened it to guests. The six spacious suites have views of the city and distant ocean; request one of the three that have private, broad verandas. The city center and Morningside's restaurants are a mere 5-minute drive away. Dinners can be served by prior arrangement.

630 Essenwood Rd., Berea 4001. ℂ/fax **031/207-4547.** www.essenwoodhouse.co.za. 6 units. R640 ($80) double, includes breakfast. AE, DC, MC, V. Children age 12 and over only. **Amenities:** Pool; laundry. *In room:* A/C, TV, minibar, tea- and coffee-making facilities, hair dryer on request.

Quarters ★★   Comprising four Victorian houses set on fashionable Florida Road (see "Where to Dine," below), Quarters is a classy, boutique-style hotel—the best-dressed joint in town. Walls feature striking black-and-white photographs of South African life by Angela Shaw. All rooms are relatively spacious and have queen-size sleigh beds, and are double-glazed to eliminate neighborhood noise, though this is scant protection from the sound of the person above flushing his/her toilet—ask for a room on one of the top floors. Bathrooms are big and well designed; specify shower or bathtub. The **Brasserie** has a small but good menu that attracts the city's trendiest diners. Alternatively, some 30 restaurants lie within a 5km (3-mile) radius, many within walking distance.

101 Florida Rd., Durban 4001. © 031/303-5246. Fax 031/303-5269. www.quarters.co.za. 24 units. R930 ($115) double, including breakfast. AE, DC, MC, V. Children by prior arrangement only. **Amenities:** Restaurant; bar; business services; room service; laundry. *In room:* A/C, TV, tea- and coffee-making facilities, hair dryer.

The Royal ★★★ *Value*   A member of *The Leading Hotels of the World*, The Royal is generally considered the best hotel in the city, although it caters primarily to businessmen and visiting politicians and doesn't have the grace of the Edward. That said, it's certainly the best value top-end city hotel in South Africa, and is within walking distance of almost all of Durban's top attractions (as well as the Tourist Junction and Backstage, the city's best theater). It also offers terrific views of the busy port and city and features extraordinarily high levels of service, with every staff member primed to make you feel special. Rooms and bathrooms have all benefited from a much-needed refurbishment, with creams, reds, and dark woods predominating; all are supremely comfortable. Breakfast is served at the **Top of the Royal,** which offers spectacular bay views. You can dine at **Ulundi,** which has good Indian fare, or at the hotel's 70-year-old flagship restaurant, the **Royal Grill,** renowned for its fine dining atmosphere (see "Where to Dine," below).

267 Smith St., Durban 4000. © 031/333-6000. Fax 031/333-6002. www.theroyal.co.za. 271 units. From R550 ($68) double; rates include breakfast. AE, DC, MC, V. **Amenities:** 3 restaurants; 2 bars; coffee shop; rooftop pool; gym; squash courts; concierge; business services; salon; room service; babysitting; laundry. *In room:* A/C, TV, minibar, tea- and coffee-making facilities, hair dryer.

THE NORTH COAST

For a more beach-oriented holiday, you can't beat the north coast. Chichi newcomer **Ballito Manor,** a 12-roomed Three Cities hotel (owners of The Royal in the city centre), is another North Coast option worth considering. A 30-minute drive from the city center (15 min. from Umhlanga), the coastal town of Ballito is unremarkable (parts of it are downright ugly), but the "Manor" is situated right on the beach, and with a health and beauty center to pamper you, there's no real reason to leave. Rooms start at R1,900 ($238) double, including breakfast. Take a look at www.ballitomanor.com, or call © 032/946-3290.

Zimbali Lodge ★★★   Opened in 1998 to much acclaim, Zimbali (a 35-min. drive north of Durban) has brought some much needed class to the Holiday Coast. Totally surrounded by secluded indigenous coastal forest, with a private beach (no shark nets, though), the lodge is inspired by the architecture of tropical climates, with local influences including the nearby sugar baron estates and Indian temples. The opulent interior (decorated by the same team responsible for the Palace of the Lost City) is arguably the country's finest example of Afrocolonial chic style. From staircases to trusses, beds to deck chairs, each item is beautifully crafted and custom-made—down to the organic ashtrays, made from seedpods. Set on a bluff, the buildings (including bedrooms, which are situated in the gardens surrounding the lodge) overlook a natural lake, surrounded by forested hillsides and beyond, the ocean. A large number of activities are on offer, including the Tom Weiskopf–designed 18-hole championship golf course.

P.O. Box 404, Umhlali 4390 (off M4 just before Ballito). ⓒ **032/538-1007.** Fax 032/538-1019. www.sun international.com. 76 units. R2,420 ($300) double; R4,775 ($595) suite. Ask about winter specials; children's rates by arrangement. AE, DC, MC, V. **Amenities:** Restaurant; bar; pool; golf; tennis; spa; room service; laundry; private beach; horseback riding; bicycles. *In room:* A/C, TV, minibar, tea- and coffee-making facilities, hair dryer.

WHERE TO DINE

A combination of creative cooking, gracious venues, and balmy weather makes the Durban restaurant scene the country's most exciting, after Cape Town. Windermere and Florida Roads, both in Morningside, a suburb on the western outskirts of town, are where you'll find the largest concentration of restaurants.

WINDERMERE ROAD   Starting at the town end of Windermere is **Bean Bag Bohemia** ⓚ (#18; ⓒ **031/309-6019**), a swinging bar and fusion restaurant that is hugely popular with the arty set (see "Durban After Dark," below); upstairs the vibe is more fine dining. At the bottom end of Florida and Windermere roads, **Marco's** (#45; ⓒ **031/303-3078**), is where Luciana Conte cooks pasta just like mama wanted to make in a casual but welcoming trattoria. For Middle Eastern–inspired food, keep going to #411 and 413, where you'll find the popular **Cat*man*du** (ⓒ **031/312-7893**). **Luna Blu** (#427; ⓒ **031/312-4665**), popular for its interesting thin-based pizzas (marinated chicken breast, green curry paste, coconut, and coriander) and pasta combinations, is a short stroll away. End the evening at **Match,** the adjacent late-night coffee bar.

FLORIDA ROAD   Book a table on the veranda overlooking Florida Road at **Baan Thai** (#138; ⓒ **031/303-4270**), vying with Bangkok Wok (see below) as the city's best Thai restaurant; or check out what's up at neighbor **Christina's** ⓚⓚ (#134; ⓒ **031/303 2111**), a convivial training restaurant run by Christina's pupils (her private chef's course was incidentally recently voted third in the world) with an interesting good-value menu that changes fortnightly, or at **Bistro 136** (#136; ⓒ **031/303-3440**), where Swiss-trained chef/patron Willi serves up classic continental fare. If you're in the mood for light Asian, head straight for **Mo Better Noodles** ⓚⓚ (Shop 5, Florida Centre, 275 Florida Rd.; ⓒ **031/312-4193**), a London-inspired noodle bar. Further along the ridge, in the mainly residential enclave of the Berea, you'll find real Thai food, prepared by real Thai chefs, at **Bangkok Wok** ⓚ (#440; ⓒ **031/201-8557**), incidentally one of the best value-for-money dinners you'll have in Durban.

The following is a selection of the city's fine-dining venues, but because all have fusion-inspired chefs at the helm, be sure to also sample the local Indian fare (see "King of Curry," below).

Harvey's ⓚⓚⓚ INTERNATIONAL   Consistently crowned Durban's best since 1997, this stylish restaurant is known for its innovative flavor combinations, excellent presentation, and efficient service. The menu changes every two months, but may feature porcini cappuccino infused with fennel seeds and topped with roasted almonds, kudu filet on rosti with red onion marmalade and mascarpone, and seaweed parcels filled with salmon and prawns. Despite the deserved accolades, visitors may find that the experience is not that memorable; the menu makes no attempt to incorporate cuisine local to the area, and the venue, a converted house styled in a postmodern fashion, could be anywhere.

77 Goble Rd., Morningside. ⓒ **031/312-9064.** Reservations recommended. R59–R75 ($7–$9). AE, DC, MC, V. Tues–Fri noon–2pm; Mon–Sat 7–9:30pm.

Royal Grill ⓚⓚ INTERNATIONAL   This grand venue—the only part that remains of the original Royal Hotel—is one of the most romantic in Durban, and the perfect place for a candle-lit dinner. Plush velvet banquette seating, high ceilings with chandeliers, antique dressers, and stained-glass skylights create a luxurious ambience, with old-style service in a class of its own. The menu is more contemporary than the setting, including the likes of a wild mushroom ravioli topped with poached egg and hollandaise sauce, or pot roast lamb shank on a Parmesan and poppy-seed risotto.

Royal Hotel, Smith St., Durban. ✆ 031/333-6000. Main courses R45–R85 ($5.25–$11). AE, DC, MC, V. Tues–Fri noon–2:30pm; Mon–Sat 6–10.30pm.

KING OF CURRY

Durban is the next-best place to India for sampling Indian food. The city's Indian District is a great starting point for a cheap lunch (see "Exploring the City & Indian District," earlier in this chapter), but a meal at one of the many Indian restaurants in the city is a must. If you have time, make a booking at both Gulzar and Jaipur Palace, Durban's two top Indian restaurants. The more down-home **Gulzar** ★★★ (71 Stamford Hill Rd., Greyville; ✆ 031/309-6379) is where proud proprietor Rajen Frank specializes in authentic North and South Indian cuisine. Food is cooked to order, which lets diners control the spiciness of the curry, and the ambience is ideal for a romantic night out. *Tip:* Order the prawn curry with tomato base. Providing fierce competition, and certainly winning the prize for the best venue, is **Jaipur Palace** ★★★ (3 Riverside Complex, North Way, Durban North; ✆ 031/563-0287). Here diners enter through large carved entrance doors (imported from Delhi) and marble-inlaid floors to be seated under a central chandelier and frieze copied from Jaipur's Rambagh Palace. The food is excellent, and the buffet (R90/$11) allows you to sample flavors characteristic of a number of Indian regions.

TABLE WITH SEA VIEW, PLEASE

If you've ever thought the world revolved around you, **Roma Revolving Restaurant** ★★ (John Ross House, Victoria Embankment; ✆ 031/337-6707) is the place to prove it. Enter John Ross House from a slightly seedy side alley off the Victoria Embankment, whoosh up 32 floors in the small lift, and you'll step directly into a plush 1970s haven. The Roma revolves completely every 60 minutes, providing great views of the city, harbor, and beachfront from every table. Best of all, the classic Italian fare is good—the gnocchi is legendary. For a more one-dimensional, but no less spectacular take on Durban, head south down Point Road to the **Famous Fish Co.** (Kings Battery North Pier; ✆ 031/368-1060). Seated right at the harbor entrance, diners on the deck are often meters away from the towering tankers, luxury liners, and sailboats that enter and depart Africa's busiest harbor. The rather pricey menu is seafood-dominated and good. Alternatively, head for the new Wilson's Wharf development, also at the southern end of Durban's bay, where you can choose between six restaurants, all with decks overlooking the harbor. Of these, **Charlie's Crofts** is recommended for innovative game dishes and fresh fish, but the view is the really hot item. Another good harbor option is **The New Café Fish** (Yacht Mole, Victoria Embankment; ✆ 031/305-5062), this time situated in the middle of the yacht marina with big windows overlooking the jetty. The nearby **Transafrica Express** at the BAT Centre (✆ 031/332-0804), also overlooking the harbor (and a good place to browse for crafts), is one of the few places in the city where you can sample African stews served with *pap* (maize porridge), samp, and beans.

THE NORTH COAST

The North Coast dining scene has improved remarkably in the last 2 years, not least because the Mauvis family decided to move their premises to Umhlanga after their popular restaurant on Florida Road burned down. **Ile Maurice** ✦✦ (© 031/561-7609; closed Mon), considered by foodies to be the best in Umhlanga (and one of the top five in the Durban area), offers the same mix of Mauritian and French cuisine, with old favorites like the *vindaye de poisson*—flavored with mustard seeds and turmeric—and the tender filet *en croute* pulling the punters back into Madame Mauvis's lap. Over the road, in the Beverly Hills Hotel, the **Cabin** (© 031/561-2211) specializes in seafood, but it is the nostalgic, romantic atmosphere (warm wood-paneling, intimate lighting, and subdued live music) that keeps diners coming back for more.

Razzmatazz ✦✦ *Value* SEAFOOD/GAME   People come here as much for the view—with most tables situated on a deck overlooking the beach, you can't get closer to the ocean—as for the food. The house specialties are recommended: Calamari is pan-fried with butter, garlic, a touch of chili, and fresh cream; linefish is prepared with cream, wine, mushrooms, and shrimp and served in phyllo baskets; and langoustines are steamed with lemon grass and fresh herbs and served in a bamboo basket. Game dishes are also excellent: ostrich filet is prepared in a Cape gooseberry sauce; and guinea fowl is deboned (heavenly!) and roasted with apple and Calvados. Service is super-quick and the ambience laidback, with plenty of bikinis and bare feet as befits a place this close to the sea.

Umhlanga Rocks. © 031/561-5847. R30–R110 ($3.70–$14). Daily noon–2:30pm and 6:30–9:30pm.

DURBAN AFTER DARK

For an evening of top local dance acts (look out for the Fantastic Flying Fish Dance Company and top Durban theater director Jerry Pooe and his Eager Artists Dance/Theatre Company) or interesting theater, head for **The Playhouse** (29 Acutt St.; © 031/369-9444), a mock-Tudor venue that stages three separate theaters with particularly the Playhouse Drama and Cellar stages showcasing productions reflecting the rich African and Indian cultural heritage of Durban. Call ahead or pick up a free copy of *Playhouse News* from the Tourist Junction. Also find out what's happening at the **Kwasuka Theatre** (Stamford Hill Rd.; © 031/309-2236), an alternative theater house where you can see original local plays, many of them internationally acclaimed. At the **University of Natal's Elizabeth Sneddon Theatre** (© 031/260-2296 or 031/260-2506); look out for shows by Flatfoot Dance Company, the university's resident dance project, and the annual Jomba Dance Festival held in August. The **KwaZulu-Natal Philharmonic Orchestra (KZNPO)** performs regularly at the City Hall.

In the last several years Durban has witnessed an explosion in popularity of the supper-theater genre, with a number of establishments offering quality stage revues combined with gourmet dining. Easily the biggest hit among these is the **Barnyard Theatre,** the enormous and quaintly rustic establishment located inside Durban shopping colossus Gateway (© 031/566-3045 or 031/566-3046). In Durban's only 5-star hotel, the Royal, is the suitably ritzy **Backstage** (© 031/333-6000), while the brand-new Wilson's Wharf, right on the edge of the harbor, offers the **Catalina Theatre** (© 031/305-6889).

CLUBS & PUBS

330 ✦✦✦   Situated in the heart of the dockside red-light district, this club has hosted the leading lights of the dance world since 1988 (Carl Cox, Dave Seagram,

---

> ## ⌒Tips All that Jazz . . .
>
> The depth of jazz talent in Durban is renowned, and swish Durban jazz
> venue **Rivets** ★★★ (© **031/336-8204**), located at the Hilton Hotel, con-
> tinues to enjoy a reputation as Durban's top live jazz haven; catch a local
> legend in action every Tuesday and Thursday night from 7pm. On Friday
> evenings, the "African journey through music and food" takes off in
> Durban harbor with top-drawer live music at the **TransAfrica Express
> Café** ★★★ (© **031/332-0804**). Located at Durban's pulsating cultural
> melting pot, the BAT Centre, this exciting new venture right on the har-
> bor's edge offers breezy balcony vibes, sumptuous pan-African fare, and
> some of the finest live jazz in town. If your appetite is still not sated,
> spend the following afternoon, from 2:30 to 6:30pm, at the new **Zack's**
> (© **031/201-4768**), located at Wilson's Wharf. Then head for **Upstage Jazz
> Café** (© **083-630-8981**), in the historic Playhouse Complex in Smith Street,
> where a quality resident band, Whole Tone, performs every Saturday
> night from 9pm, free admission.

Tony de Vit, and Josh Wink have all shredded the decks here) and continues to
play the hardest, fastest house on the biggest rigs in town. Consistently rated as
one of the top 10 in the world, with a sister establishment in London, this is a
must for the most unrepentant members of the dance fraternity. 330 Point Rd. www.
330.co.za.

Axis ★★★   Head here for a wild night out with gay flavor, great atmosphere,
and the most uplifting tunes in town. An oasis of decadent class in the rotting
tooth of Durban's Addington Beach, here gay hedonists join pleasure-seekers of
all persuasions every Friday and Saturday to grind to the pulse of the club's top
resident DJs until way past sunrise. Gillespie St. (next to Addington Hospital), Beachfront.
© **031/332-2604.**

Bean Bag Bohemia ★★   This perennially popular cocktail bar/restaurant
with atmospheric interiors and exteriors (recently overhauled) has withstood the
onslaught of the cocktail crowd's fickle tastes to establish itself as the timeless
taste-beacon of the city's decadenzia. Join the madding crowd on Salon Wednesdays (all cocktails are R12/$1.50 from 5:30–6:30pm) for live jazz piano and DJs
who play a soulful selection of old-school cool; other good nights are Friday and
Saturday. 18 Windermere Rd. © **031/309-6019.**

Home ★★★   A genuine fusion of the creative spirits of artists, DJs, culinary
maestros, and cocktail inventors, Home is currently the hottest place in town. It
provides not only a feast for the eyes but for the ears as well, with some of Durban's top DJs laying on the best in breaks, lounge, trip-hop, funk, and hip-hop
as you sip a cocktail and watch the city's beauties at play. Corner of Innes & Windermere Rd. © **031/303-7950.**

Rainbow Restaurant & Jazz Club ★★   This local legend has been rocking
the suburbs since the early '80s when it defied apartheid legislation to bring people of all color together to celebrate the transcendent pleasures of Afro-Jazz. Some
of the country's biggest names play at the weekly concerts held on Sunday—a lazy
lunch, followed by some evening jazz, is just the ticket to some genuine Rainbow
Nation atmosphere. 23 Stanfield Lane, Pinetown. © **031/702-9161** or 083-463-8044.

3 Zululand

Cross the Tugela River (88km/54½ miles north of Durban), traditionally the southern frontier of Zululand, and it soon feels as if you've entered an entirely new province. Passing a largely poor, rural population through KwaZulu-Natal's Big 5 reserves and coastal wetlands, you are now traveling the ancestral lands of the Zulu, and the designated Zulu "homeland" prior to 1994.

Most visitors to Zululand spend at least 2 days in or near Hluhluwe-Umfolozi, the province's best game reserve. Run by KwaZulu-Natal Wildlife, it is home to the Big 5, and has the most sought-after wilderness trail in the country. In addition, its proximity to Durban (less than a 3-hr. drive) makes it one of South Africa's most accessible Big 5 game reserves, and its varied vegetation and top accommodations give Kruger stiff competition.

If, however, your idea of the "wild life" is pausing in your pursuit of lion with a drink poured by your personal ranger, look no further than Phinda. Northeast of Hluhluwe, and part of the Greater St Lucia Wetland, this luxurious private game reserve is close enough to the coast to add diving with dolphins, sharks, and tropical fish to your Big 5 experience—the combination of big game, lagoon, and beach is in fact one of the major benefits of choosing a safari in KwaZulu-Natal. Thankfully, a number of luxurious lodges are now offering stiff competition to Phinda, at a fraction of the price.

The first area in South Africa to be declared a World Heritage Site, the Greater St Lucia Wetland Park is a top destination for South Africa's divers, fishermen, and birders, as well as the rare loggerhead and leatherback turtles that return to the beaches to breed every summer. Encompassing the foothills of the Lebombo Mountains, wetlands, forests, lakes, and the coastal coral reefs, the park is a paradise, though purists will find the shoreline ruined by four-wheel-drivers who use the beach as a quick and easy alternative to the highway. To find the highlight of the coast, you'll have to travel farther north, to Rocktail Bay, where no more than 22 guests at any given time find themselves alone on a 60km (37-mile) stretch of pristine beach.

For those with more time, a sojourn in the far northeastern corner, where a chain of lakes empty into the beautiful Kosi Mouth, is definitely recommended. You will need to rent a four-wheel-drive (or set off on foot) to explore this as yet untouched coastline, one of the three richest floristic areas in Africa.

ESSENTIALS

VISITOR INFORMATION   The **Thungulu Regional Council** (Thungulu House, Kruger Rand St., Richard's Bay; © **035/789-1404;** open Mon–Fri 7:30am–12:30pm and 1–4pm) is the central bureau for the Zululand area, but because this large industrial port (173km/107 miles north of Durban) has nothing to recommend it beyond its air links, the best regional office to visit en route from Durban is **Eshowe Publicity** (© **035/474-1141;** open Mon–Thurs 7:30am–4pm; Fri till 3pm) on Hutchinson Street, or the **St Lucia Publicity Association** (© **035/590-1075;** open Mon–Fri 8am–5pm, Sat 8am–2pm) on Mackenzie Street. For information on the provincial game reserves, almost all of which are located in Zululand, contact **KwaZulu-Natal Wildlife** (© **033/845-1002;** www.kznwildlife.com).

GETTING THERE   **By Air**   The quickest way to get to Zululand is to fly to Richard's Bay Airport with **SA Express** (© **035/786-0301**) from Johannesburg and rent a car here, or fly to Durban and drive.

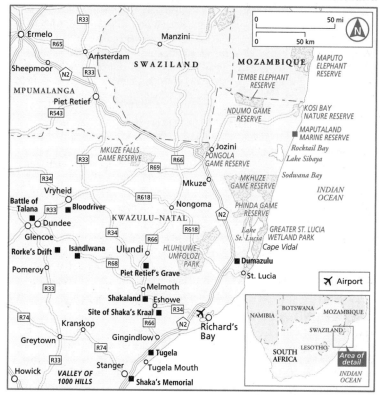

By Car The N2 leading north out of Durban traverses the Zululand hinterland; east lie the Greater St Lucia Wetland Park, Phinda private game reserve, and the birding reserves (Ndumo and Mkuzi); west lie Hluhluwe and most of the Zulu museums and cultural villages. From Gauteng, take the R29 through Piet Retief to Pongola; this becomes the N2 south.

By Bus Contact **Greyhound** or **Translux** (see chapter 2 for regional numbers) to travel to Richard's Bay from Durban or Johannesburg, respectively.

SAFETY Northern Zululand (Ndumo, Kosi Bay, Rocktail Bay) is a high-risk malarial area, and there is a medium-to-low risk in the Greater St Lucia Wetland Park, depending on the time of the year. For the most up-to-date advice, contact your doctor (also see chapter 2).

GETTING AROUND **By Car** There is virtually no public transport in Zululand, so once here you'll have to contact a tour operator or rent a car (Rocktail Bay supplies transfers from Richard's Bay). To explore Kosi Bay on your own, you'll need to rent a four-wheel-drive. Car rental can be arranged through **Avis** (© **035/789-6555;** four-wheel-drives © **035/789-3097**) or **Imperial** (© **035/786-0309**). Both have desks at the airport.

GUIDED TOURS Ex-mayor of Eshowe and proprietor of local Eshowe hangout the George Hotel, **Graham Chennells** ✿✿✿ offers the most authentic and exhilarating opportunities to see contemporary Zulu life in Africa

(*National Geographic* commissioned no less than three film shoots of his tours in 2002!). Guests are provided with a Zulu guide (Walter Cele or Victor Mdluli), who will then introduce them to friends in the broader community. On most weekends, Graham can arrange attendance at Zulu weddings, coming-of-age celebrations, sangomas' healing rituals, and traditional church services, where guests are treated as part of the extended family. For more information, go to www.eshowe.com, or call the George Hotel (36 Main St., Eshowe; *©* **035/474-4919** or 082-492-6918). For guided tours of the Zululand reserves, contact **Umhluhluwe Safaris** (*©* **035/562-0414**); choose between night, half-, and full-day game drives in Hluhluwe-Umfolozi, Mkuzi, and the St Lucia Wetlands. **Brett Adventure Tours** (*©* **032/456-3513** or 083-744-8288) specializes in a variety of Zululand experiences, from golfing to visiting Maputaland and Zulu villages. (For tour operators departing direct from Durban, see "Durban Essentials," earlier in this chapter.)

SPECIAL EVENTS   On February 23, Sangoma Khekheke's **Annual Snake Dance,** attended by 6,000 to 8,000 people, is held. September also sees King Shaka Day Celebrations and the Zulu Kings Reed Dance—here some 15,000 maidens congregate to dance for Prince Gideon. Most of October is taken up with the prophet Shembe's celebrations, with Sundays seeing some 30,000 people participating in prayer dancing. To arrange attendance at any of these, contact Graham Chennells (see "Guided Tours," above).

DISCOVERING ZULU HISTORY

The proud amaZulu have fascinated westerners ever since the first party of British settlers gained permission to trade from the great Zulu king Shaka, known as "Africa's Napoleon" for his military genius. As king, he was to unite the amaZulu into the mightiest army in the Southern Hemisphere and develop better fighting implements and tactics, including the highly successful "horns of the bull" maneuver to outflank the enemy. In 1828, Shaka was murdered by his half-brothers Mhlangana and Dingaan, and Dingaan was crowned king.

Distrustful of the large number of "white wizards" settling in the region, Dingaan ordered the massacre of the Trekker party led by Piet Retief, whom he had invited—unarmed—to a celebratory banquet at his royal *kraal* uMgungundlovu. (A *kraal* is a series of thatched beehive-shaped huts encircling a central, smaller *kraal,* or cattle enclosure.) Dingaan paid heavily for this treachery at the **Battle of Blood River** (see "A Brief History of the Battlefields," later in this chapter), where the Zulu nation suffered such heavy casualties that it was to split the state for a generation. In 1840, Dingaan was killed by his brother Mpande, who succeeded him as king.

The amaZulu were reunited again under Mpande's eldest, Cetshwayo, who, having in turn murdered a number of his siblings, became king in 1873, and built a new royal kraal at Ulundi. Though by all accounts a reasonable man, Cetshwayo could not negotiate with the uncompromising English, who now wanted total control of southern Africa, with no pesky savages to destroy their imperialist advance on the gold fields. In 1878 the British ordered Cetshwayo to disband his army within 30 days, give up Zululand's independence, and place himself under the supervision of an English commissioner. This totally unreasonable ultimatum, designed to ignite a war, resulted in the **Battle of Islandwana,** and England's most crushing defeat (see the "A Brief History of the Battlefields" box, later in this chapter). Nine months later, on July 4, 1879, 5,000 British redcoats under a vengeful Lord Chelmsford advanced on Ulundi and razed it to the ground. A captured King Cetshwayo was exiled to Cape Town and later England; he was reinstated as a puppet in 1883. This was to be the last Anglo-Zulu battle; the might of the Zulu empire had finally been broken.

The area known today as Emakhosini, "Valley of the Kings," applied in July 2003 for status as a World Heritage Site; in the meantime you can visit Dingane's homestead at **uMgungundlovu** (or "secret place of the great elephant"), part of which has been reconstructed and features 200-year-old artifacts; there is also a memorial to Piet Retief and his 100-strong delegation (© **035/450-2254;** open daily 9am–4pm; R10/$1). You can also visit a reconstruction of the royal kraal at **Ondini,** near Ulundi. To get here, take the R68 off the N2 to Eshowe, stopping to visit the **Zululand Historical Museum** and the **Vukani Collection** first (see reviews below), or to meet Graham Chennells at the George Hotel for his highly recommended tours of the region (see "Guided Tours," above). To reach uMgungundlovu, take the R34 to Vryheid and look for the turnoff on your left.

The Vukani Collection Museum 🐘🐘🐘 *Finds*   While Westerners head for cultural villages, many urban Zulu parents bring their children here to gain insights into the rituals, codes, and crafts of the past. This is the finest collection of Zulu traditional arts and crafts in the world, and a visit to the unassuming Vukani Museum is essential for anyone interested in collecting or understanding Zulu art, particularly traditional basketware.

Another highlight is the collection of pots made by master potter Nesta Nala (her work is sold in international galleries throughout the world). Nesta walks for miles to find just the right clay before grinding and mixing, then sunbaking her paper-thin shapes and firing them in a hole in the ground. Pots are finally rubbed with fat and ashes, applied with a river stone. Keep an eye out for another award-winner, Allina Ndebele, whose tapestries are inspired by Zulu myths and legends as told to her by her grandmother. This is one of the best museums in the province. Donate generously.

Nongqai Rd. © 035/474-5274. R10 ($1.30). Daily 9am–4pm. Special tours on request.

Zululand Historical Museum 🐘   Housed in Fort Nongqayi (1883), where the Natal "Native" Police were garrisoned, the Zululand Historical Museum traces the history of the fort and the "enslavement" of the Zulu as a result of a poll tax. The beadwork collection, dating back to the 1920s, is worth seeking out. There is also a collection of John Dunn's furniture—the son of settlers, Dunn became King Cetshwayo's political advisor, and was the only white man to become a true Zulu chief. Embracing Zulu polygamy by taking 49 wives, he almost single-handedly spawned Eshowe's "coloured" community.

Nongqayi Rd. (marked off the R68). © 035/474-2419, ext. 247. R20/$2.50 adults, R4/50¢ children. 9am–4pm daily.

ON SAFARI IN ZULULAND

If you're looking to tick off the Big 5, your KwaZulu-Natal options are limited to the **Hluhluwe-Umfolozi,** and the privately owned **Phinda** and adjoining **Mkuze Falls reserves.** With the introduction of two lions, **Tembe** is now classified a Big 5 reserve, but accommodation options this far north are currently still limited to the relatively rudimentary Tembe Elephant Safari Camp (www.tembe.co.za). Note that if bagging a tiger fish is your idea of a big game rush, the best place to do so is at Lake Jozini, and the gorgeous **White Elephant Lodge** (© **082-922-4997;** www.whiteelephantlodge.co.za) is the place to stay.

Run by the KwaZulu-Natal Nature Conservation Services, Hluhluwe-Umfolozi, by far the province's largest reserve (96,453 hectares/238,239 acres),

---

Fun Fact **The Great White Rhino Recovery**

The recovery of the world's white rhino population—from fewer than 100 individuals in the 1920s to more than 7,000 worldwide today—is largely due to the efforts of the **KwaZulu-Natal Wildlife** (formerly the KwaZulu-Natal Nature Conservation Services). Early conservation efforts ensured a steady increase in numbers at Hluhluwe-Umfolozi, giving rise to Operation Rhino in 1961, whereby surplus numbers of white rhino were relocated to other protected areas and to private land. By 1997 this worldwide distribution had reached a total of 3,912, and white rhino numbers had increased to such an extent that it was the first species to be removed from the World Conservation Union's Endangered List in 1994. There are hopes of the same success with the extremely rare black rhino (the same color, incidentally, but slightly smaller and with a distinctive hooked lip). There are currently only 2,640 black rhinos in the world, of which almost half are in South Africa; most are in KwaZulu-Natal, which has the world's second-largest population (after Namibia).

---

offers the best value, and is open to day-trippers as well as overnight visitors. For exclusivity and laid-on luxuries (we're talking room service and private plunge pools), Mkuze Falls—a private reserve that comprises more than 17,000 hectares (42,000 acres)—is one of the best-value Big 5 reserves in the country. Phinda's camps—particularly Vlei Camp—offers the most stylish bush accommodation in the province, but note that for this kind of money you could be staying in a topnotch lodge in the lauded Sabi Sand reserve flanking Kruger.

HLUHLUWE-UMFOLOZI GAME RESERVE ✦✦

Established in 1895, Hluhluwe-Umfolozi (pronounced shloe-shloe-whee), once separate reserves, is one of the oldest wildlife sanctuaries in Africa. United in 1989, when the land between them was proclaimed the "Corridor Game Reserve," the reserve today covers 96,453 hectares (238,239 acres), and is the provinces' premier wildlife destination, and the second most popular park after Kruger. Though only a twentieth of the size of its Mpumalanga competitor, the reserve is home to a large variety of wildlife, including the Big 5, cheetah, hyena, wild dog, wildebeest, giraffe, hippo, zebra, and a large variety of antelope. Certainly this is the best place in the world to spot rhino, particularly white (or square-lipped) rhino, which KwaZulu-Natal Wildlife single-handedly brought back from the brink of extinction. Many consider its unique combination of forest, woodland, savanna, and grasslands, and its hot, humid, wet summers, the "real" Africa—well worth visiting in addition to Kruger.

Treks along the **wilderness trails** ✦✦✦ are conducted by rangers from March to November in the 25,000-hectare (61,750-acre) Umfolozi wilderness, once the royal hunting grounds of King Shaka. Access to this area is permitted only on foot or horseback, helping to make this some of the most pristine bush territory in the world. Unlike in Kruger, where walkers return to the same bush camp every night, provisions and luggage are carried by donkeys to new sites, providing hikers with a sense of heading deeper into the jungle. Book trails well in advance through KZN Wildlife (see "Staying Active: Hiking," earlier); cost is R1,950 ($244) per person (4 nights all inclusive), and R1,100 ($138) per person (2 nights).

VISITOR INFORMATION   Open daily March through October from 6am to 6pm, and November through February from 5am to 7pm. Admission is R35 ($4.50) per vehicle and R30 ($3.75) per person. Guided 2-hour walks (R80/$10) take place in the early morning and afternoon, as do the 3-hour game drives, early morning or evening (R80/$10). For more information, see Hilltop Camp, below.

GETTING THERE   The reserve lies approximately 280km (173½ miles) north of Durban, with two entrances leading off the N2. The quickest way to get to Hilltop Camp is via Memorial Gate, 50km (31 miles) north of Mtubatuba (Hilltop is approximately 30 min. from here), but if you want to enter the park sooner enter via Nyalazi Gate (turn off on the R618 at Mtubatuba). Adhering to the 40kmph (25 mph) speed limit, it's about a 50-minute drive to the camp. The third entrance, Cengeni Gate, is approached from the west, 30km (18½ miles) from Ulundi. To drive from Cengeni to Hilltop, allow 3 hours.

Where to Stay & Dine

Of the two public rest camps in Hluhluwe-Umfolozi, **Mpila,** an unfenced camp located in Umfolozi, offers for the most part basic accommodation (shared kitchen facilities and ablutions), but if you're prepared to self-cater you may want to ask about one of the two-bedroom cottages or (en-suite and electrified, but shared kitchen) tents. The Mpila camp shop provides basic provisions, but a restaurant and a pool were planned by late 2003, as well as an additional five en-suite tents and 12 twin-bed thatched huts. **Hilltop,** in the Hluhluwe section, is rated as one of the best public camps in the country; it's a good base, not just for the reserve, but also for day forays to Mkuzi or Lake St Lucia (2 hr. from Hilltop).

Note: There are also a number of **lodges** situated in secluded areas, run by KZN Wildlife, at locations picked for their natural beauty. These are unfenced, necessitating the protection of an armed ranger for bush walks; most also have a resident cook (though you may have to provide ingredients; check beforehand), or you may choose self-catering. These lodges (sleeping six to eight) are only available for single bookings, making this option suitable for a group or family, or a couple prepared to pay a little extra for total privacy. For more information on these, take a look at www.kznwildlife.com, or write to bookings@kzn wildlife.com and ask for the brochure "Red Ivory Collection" to be sent to you.

Hilltop Camp ⭐ *Value*   Appropriately named, this KZN Wildlife camp commands lovely views of the surrounding hills and valleys, and offers a variety of accommodation options. Pick of the bunch are the two-bed en-suite chalets (all feature bar fridges and tea- and coffee-making facilities; Zone has an equipped kitchenette) and the four-bed chalets (all with equipped kitchens). For some of the best locations, request numbers 10 to 14, 28 to 33, or 44 to 49. The shop sells basic provisions (frozen meat, fire lighters, liquor, camera film), but it's worth stocking up in Durban or dining at the restaurant. If *nyala* steak is on the menu, order it; the meat of this shy, pretty antelope is delicious, and you're unlikely to find it elsewhere.

KN NCS, P.O. Box 13053, Cascades 3202. Reservations ☎ **033/845-1000.** Fax 035/562-1001. www.kzn wildlife.com. (Direct inquiries, but no bookings, ☎ **035/562-0255**). 70 units, consisting of 2-bed huts (no bathroom), 2-bed rondawels, 2- and 4-bed chalets, and one 9-bed lodge. From R380 ($48) double; R770 ($96) for 2- or 4-bed fully equipped chalet. AE, DC, M, V. **Amenities:** Restaurant; bar/lounge; pool; babysitting; limited laundry; fax; fuel station.

THE GREATER ST LUCIA WETLAND PARK ☆☆☆

From the Mfolozi swamps in the south, this park—declared a World Heritage Site in December 1999—stretches 220km (136 miles) northward to Mozambique, incorporating the **St Lucia Game and Marine Reserves, False Bay Park, Cape Vidal, Sodwana Bay,** and **Mkhuze Game Reserve.** Covering 254,500 hectares (628,615 acres), it encompasses five distinct ecosystems, including one of the three most important wetlands in Africa, mangrove forests, the dry savanna and thornveld of the western shores and the vegetated sand dunes of the eastern shores, the Mkuze swamps (home to the rare Pel's fishing owl), and the great estuary and offshore coral reefs.

The most easily accessed aspect is Lake St Lucia. A 38,882-hectare (96,038-acre) expanse of water dotted with islands, it supports an abundance of wildlife, including Nile crocodile, hippo, rhino, elephant, buffalo, and giraffe, as well as numerous waterbirds, including pelican, flamingos, herons, fish eagles, kingfishers, geese, and storks. The lake is flanked on the west by typical bushveld terrain and on the east by the highest forested dunes in the world. These, incidentally, contain large deposits of titanium and zirconium, and conservationists waged a long-running war with mining consortia over their fate, a battle they thankfully won.

The easiest way to explore the lake is to catch a ride on the 85-seater *Santa Lucia* ☆☆☆ (bookings advisable; ✆ **035/590-1340**). The 90-minute guided tours depart daily at 8:30am, 10:30am, and 2:30pm, and cost R70 ($8.75). If you're there on a Friday or Saturday, take the 4pm sundowner cruise; there's a fully licensed bar on board. The launch point is clearly marked off the R618 east, which leads to St Lucia Village, located at the mouth of the St Lucia Estuary. Top attraction here is the informative **Crocodile Centre** ☆☆ (McKenzie St.; ✆ **035/590-1387**; open daily 7:30am–4:30pm; R17–R22/$2.20–$2.80, depending on time). There are literally hundreds of crocodile parks throughout the country, but this is by far the best—the only recognized crocodile research facility in South Africa. Get there at 2pm on a Saturday for a snake presentation followed by feeding time for the crocs at 3pm. The center houses all of the African species of crocodile—though you'll certainly spot at least one of the estimated 2,000 Nile crocs that lurk in the lake if you take a cruise on the *Santa Lucia*—swimming in the lake, understandably, is strictly prohibited. The center also has a good restaurant that specializes in—you guessed it—crocodile.

The only other reason to find yourself in St Lucia Village is because you're on your way to **Cape Vidal** ☆, a 2-hour trip north to the coast. Besides the Umvubu Forest and Imboma trails, which take you over the tallest vegetated dunes in the world, the offshore reef at Cape Vidal makes the sea safe for swimming and ideal for snorkeling, and a whale-watching tower provides an excellent view of passing marine mammals (including 59-ft.-long whale sharks). The

---

⎛Tips How to Avoid Becoming Dinner

Always keep a distance of about 3m (10 ft.) from the water's edge—remember that crocodiles can remain underwater for up to 2 hours, in only a foot of water, so don't assume you're safe just because there's no sign of 'em. If you see a V-shape on the surface of the water moving toward shore, get away fast; if the critter actually gets ahold of you, try to locate its eyes and stick your thumbs in as deep as they'll go.

beaches are also now off-limits to four-wheel-drives, making for a relatively untouched paradise. Day-visitor numbers to Cape Vidal are restricted to 100 vehicles, so it's worth considering an overnight at the camp. Comprising 18 five-bed and 11 eight-bed log cabins (R368/$46 double), all well equipped for self-catering and relatively privately situated, this is one of the best value-for-money options in the area. The log cabins are all a stone's throw from the beach and warm ocean, but the large dune precludes any sea views, and the dune forest makes for a slightly gloomy atmosphere. Stop for provisions in St Lucia Village.

Birders should include a visit to **Mkhuze Game Reserve** ✦ (⟨℘⟩ **035/573-9004;** 5am–7pm; R35/$4.50 per vehicle, R30/$3.75 per person), which is connected to the coastal plain via the Mkuze River. Reached via the N2 (take the Mkuze Village turnoff; the Emshopi Gate entrance is 28km/17 miles farther), this reserve has 430 species of bird on record, which is indicative of the varied vegetation and landscape. Maps are issued at the reception office; don't miss the two bird hides at Nsumo Pan, where you can picnic and watch the changing spectacle on the waterway. This is also the start of the 3km (2-mile) circular guided (R60/$7.50) **Mkhuze Fig Forest Trail,** one of the area's rarest and most attractive woodlands.

Last, but certainly not least of the Greater St Lucia Wetland Park attractions, is **Sodwana Bay** ✦, South Africa's diving mecca (see "Staying Active," earlier in this chapter). Here, the warm Agulhus current is responsible for some 1,200 varieties of fish, second in number only to Australia's Great Barrier Reef. This is the best place in the country to become a qualified diver; but if you just want to snorkel, head for Jesser Point. For the best value accommodation (R360/$45), book one of KZN Wildlife's fully-equipped self-catering five-bed log cabins in Sodwana Bay Park, the closest you can get to the bay itself. Buy provisions in town, 8km (5 miles) west of the camp. If you don't want to self-cater, book into **Sodwana Bay Lodge** (⟨℘⟩ **031/310-3333;** from R1,100/$138).

Where to Stay & Dine

The only dining options are in St Lucia Village, but don't expect miracles—you're a long way from civilization. Proof of this is the menu at **The Zulu & I** (⟨℘⟩ **035/590-1386**), the restaurant at the Crocodile Centre, where you can order anything from crocodile pizza to crocodile curry. **Quarterdeck** (⟨℘⟩ **035/590-1116**), on McKenzie Street, is known for its seafood. If you're cooking, buy fresh fish from the Fishing Den next door; they also sell tackle and bait.

There are a few B&B and hotel options in St Lucia Village, but the village itself holds few attractions; much better to stay in one of the privately owned lodges on the western shore. The exclusive **Makakatana Bay Lodge** (⟨℘⟩ **035/550-4189;** www.makakatana.co.za) is situated in the St Lucia Wetland Reserve and comprises six privately located suites overlooking the lake, with a variety of activities on offer—from *mokoro* safaris through the wetlands and snorkeling the coastline to full-day safaris in nearby Hluhluwe-Umfolozi and Zulu dancing at Dumazulu. The all-inclusive rate (all meals and game activities), is R3,590 to R4,400 ($438–$550) double. If this strikes you as steep, check out the slightly larger **Hluhluwe River Lodge** (⟨℘⟩ **035/562-0246;** www.hluhluwe. co.za). With 12 thatched chalets, it offers much the same by way of activities, for slightly less money (R2,390/$295 double inclusive of all meals and activities; R1,730/$215 double, including breakfast and dinner only). Also worth considering is newcomer **Falaza Game Park,** with gorgeously outfitted en-suite tents, located on the western dunes of False Bay (⟨℘⟩ **035/562-2319;**

Fun Fact   Curse of the Coelacanth?

Thought to be extinct until 1938, when one was caught off the Eastern Cape coast, the coelacanth are closely related to the first fish that came ashore to live on land 360 million years ago. Sightings are still incredibly rare, and when three of these 400-million-year-old dinosaurs of the deep were discovered off the coast of St Lucia in November 2000, several diving expeditions were arranged in an attempt to film a living specimen. Since then, three members of the coelacanth expedition have died while diving. Admittedly, deep dives are dangerous (coelacanths swim at depths of 500 ft.–1,950 ft.), but these events have begged the question: Is this the curse of the coelacanth?

---

www.falaza.co.za; R1,120–R1,300/$140–$160, including breakfast and dinner; R1,780–R2,600/$220–$325 all inclusive).

Another option is to hire a **self-catering unit** within the reserve from **KwaZulu-Natal Wildlife**—the best camps are at Cape Vidal, Charters Creek, and Sodwana Bay (see above). To find out more about these, or to check out the other options within the reserve, contact **KZN Wildlife,** P.O. Box 13053, Cascades 3202 (www.kznwildlife.com; for reservations ✆ **033/845-1000**/fax 033/ 845-1001; for inquiries ✆ 033/845-1002).

If you're still stumped for accommodations, call **St Lucia Tourism,** an informal bureau run by volunteers ✆ **035/590-1247.**

PHINDA PRIVATE GAME RESERVE
Adjoining Mkhuze Game Reserve in the south, the 17,000-hectare (41,990-acre) Phinda covers seven ecosystems, including sand forests, mountains, wetlands, and river valleys, and is home to the Big 5. Wildlife numbers are not as abundant as in Mpumalanga, but most visitors (who have to overnight to gain access) are here for the exceptional range of experiences available—referred to as **Phinda Adventures,** these include diving expeditions to the coral reefs at nearby Mbibi and Sodwana, flights over the surrounding Maputaland wilderness (including to Lake Sibaya, the largest freshwater lake in Africa), deep-sea fishing, black rhino trailing in Mkuzi, turtle-tracking, and canoeing and cruising the Mzinene River. Phinda also offers the most stylish bush accommodation in KwaZulu-Natal.

Phinda Lodges ★★   Each of the four camps, which operate totally separately from one another, is a member of *Small Luxury Hotels of the World;* **Forest** and **Mountain** are the two larger camps, while **Vlei** and **Rock** are the more exclusive (and expensive) options. When CCAfrica launched Forest Camp in 1993, the Zen-like glass boxes—each privately located within a torchwood tree forest, and constructed with minimum impact on the environment—were lauded as the most stylish bedrooms in Africa. Some might find the forest a bit gloomy, however. Mountain Camp is the oldest and least modern of the four camps but is the most family friendly, and has excellent views of the distant Lebombo Mountains and surrounding plains. The pick of the bunch are the modern glass boxes at Vlei Camp (pronounced *flay*): six glass-fronted timber dwellings on stilts located a discreet distance from one another, each with a private plunge pool overlooking marsh and woodland. Equally exclusive, but a bit more hippie,

Rock consists of six adobe-like chalets, built into the mountainside, also with private plunge pools, and overlooking a watering hole.

Private Bag X27, Benmore 2010. ✆ **011/809-4300.** Fax 011/809-4315. www.ccafrica.com. Rock and Vlei, 6 units each; Forest 16 units; Mountain 20 units. Rock and Vlei R10,450 ($1,300). Forest and Mountain R6,600–R8,250 ($825–$1,030), depending on season. Rates include all meals and activities within the reserve. AE, DC, MC, V. **Amenities:** Dining room; bar; pool; room service; babysitting (Mountain & Forest only); laundry; airport transfers from Richard's Bay; game drives; guided bush walks and the Phinda Adventures (see above). *In room:* A/C, minibar.

MKUZE FALLS GAME RESERVE

Mkuze Falls (not to be confused with the KZN Wildlife–owned Mhkuze reserve) is a 10,000-hectare (24,700-acre) private game reserve with all the luxuries and exclusivity associated with the upmarket reserves flanking Kruger, and home to the Big 5. As such, it is providing stiff competition to the much pricier Phinda (located some 90 min. south, in the Greater St Lucia Wetland Park), but Phinda's camps still have the edge when it comes to accommodations.

Mkuze Falls Lodge ★★ *Value* Some may find the fake elephant tusks surrounding the headboard a little over-the-top, but no one complains about the generous size of the chalets, the private plunge pools, or the views—each of the nine stilted and thatched units, connected via boardwalk, enjoys lovely views of the Mkuze River and the surrounding plains, which support a variety of game. Accommodations options have now been extended with the creation of a tented lodge, accommodating a maximum of 10 guests in luxury East African–style safari tents. As is the case in most private reserves and lodges throughout southern Africa, the daily highlights are the early-morning and evening game drives in open-topped vehicles with experienced rangers at the wheel. The bonus here is that, like Phinda, the staff can arrange additional diving, fishing, or turtle-viewing trips along the KwaZulu-Natal Coast.

Off R66. PO Box 238, Pongola, Zululand 3170. ✆ **034/414-1018.** Fax 034/414-1021. www.mkuzefalls.com. High season Aug–April: Chalets R5,000 ($625) double; Tents R2,200 ($265). Low season Chalet R2,800 ($350) double; Tents R2,000 ($250) double. Rates include all meals, game drives, and bush walks. AE, DC, MC, V. Mkuze Falls is close to the southern border of Swaziland, and a 4½-hr. drive from Durban. **Amenities:** Private deck and plunge pool; outside showers; en-suite facilities.

MAPUTALAND RESERVE & KOSI BAY

Home of the Tonga and Mabudu peoples, the northeastern corner of KwaZulu-Natal is the most remote part of the province, with large tracts accessible only by four-wheel-drive vehicles. Combined with the total ban on vehicles on the beach and outboard motors at sea, this inaccessibility has protected it from development, and the coastline is absolutely pristine—though the new Lebombo Road may change all of this. A minimum stay of 3 days is needed to really validate the effort it takes to get here—but you'll find plenty to do, like sunbathing, snorkeling, fishing, bird-watching (60% of the birds occurring in South Africa have been recorded here), canoeing the lakes (avoiding hippo and croc!), sampling the local *ilala* palm wine, and just getting to know the flora; almost 7,000 species grow in this region alone.

South Africa's largest freshwater lake, Lake Sibaya, lies only 10km (6 miles) north of Sodwana; but if you're headed for Rocktail or Kosi Bay, this is a major detour by road, and there's nothing much to do here but bird-watch or canoe. This in itself may be a major benefit—if you'd like to overnight here, **Sibaya Lake Lodge** offers all the comforts and total peace (✆ **011/616-9950;** www.lake-sibaya.co.za; R1,860/$230 double all inclusive). On the west side of Sibaya is **Mabibi,** one of the most remote and beautiful campsites in Africa. To book one of the 10 campsites, contact **KwaZulu-Natal Wildlife** (see above).

The **Kosi Reserve** is about 15km (9 miles) northeast of Kwangwanase via a dirt road. You will, however, need a four-wheel-drive (and guide) to get to the mouth (some 5km/3 miles from the camp), where one of the most impressive views in the country overlooks Kosi Bay (in reality an estuary), laced with intricate Tonga fish traps and unchanged for centuries. Turning back, you can see each of Kosi's four lakes, linked by narrow channels, extending inland for some 20km (12 miles). **Lake Amanzamnyama** ("dark waters") is the most southerly lake, fringed by large subtropical swamp and raffia palm forests, and accessible only by canoe or guided hike—the best way to explore the area. Hikers should ask about the 1-day guided hike through the forest and lagoon to the beach (R40/$5) or the 4-day guided **Amanzamnyama Trail,** which takes in the four lakes as well as coastal dunes, raffia forests, coral reefs, and beaches (R250/$28). Contact the **reserve office** 🕿 **035/592-0236** or the **KN NCS central office** 🕿 **033/845-1002.**

Note: Northern Maputaland is a malarial area, and you're advised to start taking medication beforehand (see chapter 2 for more information on malaria).

Where to Stay & Dine

If you wish to stay near the river mouth that empties into Kosi Bay, your best bet is in one of the **KZN Wildlife huts** (🕿 **033/845-1002/1;** www.kznwildlife. com) but you will need a four-wheel-drive vehicle to get here.

Rocktail Bay ★★★   This is a castaway fantasy come true: 10 thatched en-suite chalets (small but adequate, and very simply decorated) raised on stilts into the forest canopy, each with its own wooden deck and within close walking distance of the beach. There are no telephones, TVs, or radios to disturb, and—with the exception of guests—no one to bump into on the 60km (37-mile) shoreline. A charming lounge/pub area has a small plunge pool, and all meals are served around a communal table in the dining area. The food is simple, but well cooked. Lunches are light and feature salads and quiches, and dinners are a sit-down three-course affair with limited choice (anything from roast lamb to pan-fried fish). With advance notice, any dietary needs will be taken into consideration. A boardwalk winds from the lodge through the dune forest to the beach and ocean, which appear totally deserted.

Armed with flippers and snorkel, you discover a world of color beneath the water's surface. Nature walks, four-wheel-drive treks, and picnics to Black Rock (another excellent snorkeling spot) are arranged, and, in summer, there are sea turtle expeditions. This is a highly recommended experience for stressed city dwellers. Note that you do not need a four-wheel-drive vehicle to get here—transfers are arranged from nearby spots or even from Richard's Bay airport.

Wilderness Safaris, P.O. Box 78573, Sandton 2146. 🕿 011/883-0747. Fax 011/883-0911. www.wilderness-safaris.com. 10 units. R3,900 ($495), includes all meals and activities. AE, MC, DC, V. **Amenities:** Lounge/pub; private decks; en-suite facilities.

4 The Battlefields

Ladysmith: 251km (155½ miles) NW of Durban
Dundee: 320km (198 miles) N of Durban

Most of the battles fought on South African soil took place in the northwestern corner of KwaZulu-Natal, where the rolling grasslands were regularly soaked with blood as battles for territorial supremacy would in turn pit Zulu against

Boer, Brit against Zulu, and Afrikaner against Brit. The official Battlefields Route covers 4 wars, 15 towns, and more than 50 battlefields, and includes numerous museums and memorials to the dead and victorious; but few would argue that the heroic Anglo-Zulu battles that took place on January 22, 1879, at Isandlwana and Rorke's Drift—immortalized in the movie *Zulu,* starring Michael Caine—are the most compelling, and best for those with limited time.

Another site worth investigating is that of the Battle of Blood River, which took place 41 years earlier, this time between the Trekkers and the Zulus. This victory was to validate Afrikaner arrogance and religious self-righteousness. Visitors should also visit Ladysmith to immerse themselves in the siege that jump-started the Second Anglo-Boer War—it would take the world's mightiest nation 3 years and thousands of pounds to defeat one of the world's smallest, and embroil some of the century's giants, like Winston Churchill and Gandhi.

This is one area where a guide is almost essential, and top of the line is David Rattray (see below), who offers an award-winning performance that regularly reduces onlookers to tears. If, however, you are eager to tackle a self-guided tour, but are unfamiliar with the historical background of the wars, a brief chronological account is supplied below.

ESSENTIALS

VISITOR INFORMATION   Contact Karin van Tonder, the **Battlefields Route Secretary** (© 082-802-1643), and she'll direct you to the information officer in charge of each of the 15 Battlefields towns. The main centers are **Dundee** (Rorke's Drift and Isandlwana), **Ladysmith** (Second Anglo-Boer War), and **Vryheid** (Battle of Blood River). The **Ladysmith tourism information bureau** (© 036/637-2992) is very helpful.

GETTING THERE   By Car   It takes around 3½ hours by car from Durban to get to the battlefields; 4½ hours from Jo'burg. You have a choice of a number of routes. If you're interested in Zulu culture, travel to or from Durban via Eshowe.

By Bus   Greyhound and **Translux** (see chapter 2 for regional phone numbers) both travel through Ladysmith daily.

GUIDED TOUR   Exploring with a guide is definitely recommended. The best, David Rattray, is based at his lodge at **Fugitives' Drift** (© 034/642-1834; see also "Where to Stay," below). A consummate storyteller, Rattray may err a tad on the historical side, but his detailed research on the individuals who fought on both sides of the Anglo-Zulu War humanizes the battles, and even those who hate history are enthralled. If he is not available his hand-picked staff are well-versed and also recommended. Space allowing, nonresidents may join these tours at a cost of R495 ($60).

Other guides worth mentioning are **Prince Sibusiso Shibe,** the resident historian at Isibindi (see "Where to Stay," below); **Rob Gerrard,** resident historian at Isandlwana Lodge (see "Where to Stay," below); **Pat Rundgren** (© 082-690-7812), an avid researcher and collector based in Dundee; **Maureen Richards** (© 033/342-8252), an expert on the Anglo-Boer War; and natural scientist **John Turner** (© 035/835-0160), who combines battlefield tours with trips to nearby reserves such as Hluhluwe-Umfolozi, where he puts his degree in animal behavior to excellent use.

THE TOP ATTRACTIONS

Isandlwana Battlefield ★★   Other than the rather beautiful "Zulu-necklace" monument and the many white painted rocks, there is not much here to

A Brief History of the Battlefields

The first major battle in this area took place some 48km (30 miles) east of Dundee, at what came to be known as **Blood River.** Following the treacherous murder of Retief and his men (see "Discovering Zulu Culture," earlier in this chapter), and Dingaan's ruthless persecution of white settlers, Trekker leader Andries Pretorius moved an Afrikaner commando of 464 men to a strategic spot on the banks of the ironically named Ncome ("peace") River, where he created an impenetrable *laager* (a circular encampment of wagons, with oxen in the center) with 64 ox-wagons, and prayed for victory. On behalf of the Afrikaner nation, Pretorius made a solemn vow to God that should they survive, Afrikaners would hold the day sacred in perpetuity. On December 16, 1838, the Zulus attacked. Three times they were driven off by fire before Pretorius led a mounted charge. Eventually, the Zulus fled, leaving 3,000 dead and the river dark with blood. Not one Boer died, giving rise to the nationalistic Afrikaner myth that their Old Testament God had protected them against invincible odds, proving that they were indeed the chosen race. Today December 16 remains a national holiday (though renamed "Day of Reconciliation"), and visitors can view the eerie spectacle of a replica laager, 64 life-size ox-wagons cast in bronze, at the original site of **Blood River Battlefield.** The site is off the R33, and is open daily 8am to 5pm.

Zulu might rose again under Cetshwayo. This clearly did not fit in with British imperialist plans, and, having delivered a totally unreasonable ultimatum, three British columns under an overconfident Chelmsford marched into Zululand in January 1879. On January 21, Chelmsford set up temporary camp at **Isandlwana Hill** and, believing that the Zulu army was elsewhere, took a large detachment to support a reconnaissance force, leaving the camp defenseless. Six kilometers (4 miles) away, 24,000 Zulu soldiers sat in the long grass, waiting silently for a signal. At about 11:30am the following day, a British patrol inadvertently stumbled upon them, and the Zulu warriors quickly surrounded the patrol, chanting their famed rallying cry, *"uSuthu"* (oo-*soo*-too).

Two hours later, 1,329 of the 1,700 British soldiers were dead. Survivors fled across **Fugitive's Drift,** where more died, but two men made

evoke the 1879 battle of Isandlwana, but with a good guide you may be able to hear the sound of 20,000 Zulu warriors chanting *"zee, zee, zee"* like angry bees amassing, before attacking with the Zulu war cry *"uSuthu, uSuthu, uSuthu,"* ultimately delivering the most crushing defeat the mighty British Empire was to suffer in Africa—at the hands of "savages armed with sticks." The white cairns mark the places where British soldiers fell and were buried. The British were horrified to find their men disemboweled—proof, they thought, of the savagery of the Zulu. In fact, the Zulus were honoring the men by setting their spirits free.

Off the R68 between Nqutu and Babanango. ✆ **034/271-8165.** Admission R10 ($1.30) adult. Mon–Fri 8am–4pm; Sat–Sun 9am–4pm.

it to the nearby mission station called **Rorke's Drift,** where a contingent of 139 men, of which 35 were seriously ill, were waiting with provisions for Chelmsford's return. With seconds to spare, the men barricaded themselves behind a makeshift wall of army biscuit boxes, tinned meat, and bags of maize meal, and warded off the 4,000-strong Zulu onslaught. The battle raged until dawn, when the Zulus finally withdrew. Despite incredible odds, only 17 British soldiers died at Rorke's Drift, and 11 Victoria Crosses were awarded—more than at any other battle in British history. Six months later, on July 4, 1879, the Zulus suffered their final defeat at Ondini.

A year later the British would begin a new brawl, this time with the Afrikaners, and although a peace treaty was signed in March 1881, it sowed the seeds for the Second Anglo-Boer War, a 3-year battle that captured the world's attention and introduced the concept of guerrilla warfare. On October 20, 1899, the first battle was pitched on **Talana Hill,** when 14,000 Afrikaners attacked 4,000 British troops. The Brits managed to repel the attackers, and on November 2, the little town of Ladysmith was besieged by the Afrikaners for 118 days. Thousands died of disease, trapped without access to clean water, and more fell as the British tried to break through the Afrikaner defenses. (Winston Churchill, covering the war for the *London Morning Post,* narrowly escaped death when the train he was traveling on was blown up by Boer forces some 40km [25 miles] south of Ladysmith.)

The most ignominious battle during this time took place on **Spioenkop** (literally, "spies hill") when Boers and Brits battled for this strategic position until both sides believed they had lost. The British were the first to withdraw, leaving the astonished but triumphant Boer in force on this strategic hill (off the R600). Two years later, following the scorched-earth policy of the British—when hundreds of acres of farmland were burnt, and Afrikaner women and children were placed in concentration camps where they perished from malnourishment and disease—the Boers acceded defeat.

Ladysmith Siege Museum 𝄢𝄢 If your interest lies in the battle between the Boers and the British, this is an essential stop. Displays and photographs vividly depict the wars that so greatly affected 20th-century South Africa as well as the appalling conditions at the end of the siege, when 28 to 30 people died daily. On Keate Street is the **Cultural Centre and Museum** (✆ 036/637-4922; Mon–Fri 9am–4pm; R2/25¢ adults), where you can listen to the sweet a cappella sounds of **Ladysmith Black Mambazo,** the best-selling group that shot to fame with the record *Homeless.*

Murchison St. (the main road running through Ladysmith), next to the Town Hall. ✆ **036/637-2992.** R2 (25¢). Mon–Fri 9am–4pm; Sat 9am–1pm.

Rorke's Drift ✿✿   Located in the reconstructed hospital where 100 men holed up for 12 hours, and successfully warded off 4,000 Zulus led by Cetshwayo's brother Dabulamanzi, this is the most evocative interpretation center on the route. Realistic scenes are augmented by battle sounds and electronic diagrams. An added bonus is the adjoining **ELC Craft Centre** ✿ (© **034/642-1627**), where you can browse for textiles, carpets, tapestries, and pottery.

Off the R68, 42km (26 miles) from Dundee on the road to Nqutu. © **034/642-1687**. Admission R10 ($1.30) adult. Mon–Fri 8am–4pm; Sat–Sun 9am–4pm.

WHERE TO STAY & DINE

There are no real restaurants in the area. Your best option in Dundee is the **Miner's Rest Restaurant** (in the Talana Museum, off the R33; © **034/212-2654**), which serves light lunches like chicken pie and salads. In Ladysmith your best bet is the **Royal Hotel** (© **036/637-2176**). Most guides will include picnic lunches on request.

Fugitive's Drift Lodge ✿ (© **034/642-1843**; www.fugitives-drift-lodge. com; R1,900–R2,700/$238–$330 double, depending on season; includes all meals) is situated within a 2,500-hectare (6,175-acre) nature reserve in the heart of battlefield country; it is owned by David Rattray—generally considered the finest battlefields guide in South Africa. All rooms are spacious, but try to book the one designed by top British designers in collaboration with rural Zulu craftworkers. If you like stylish accommodations at a more reasonable rate, you're better off at neighboring **Isibindi Lodge** ✿✿ (reserve through P.O. Box 1593, Eshowe 3815; © **035/474-1504**; direct © **034/642-1620**; www.zulunet.co.za; high season [Oct–April] R1,780/$220 double, includes all meals and a game drive); or **Isandlwana Lodge** ✿✿ (P.O. Box 30, Isandlwana 3005; © **034/271-8301**; www.isandlwana.co.za; R1,100–R2,100/$138–$260 double, depending on season; includes all meals). The rooms at Isibindi take a traditional Zulu beehive hut as their departure point, and must rate as the most successful blend of Western and African architecture in Zululand. Islandlwana, situated overlooking the historic battlefield, is very much an elegant Afro-colonial lodge, and the closest to a hotel experience in the area.

5 The Drakensberg Mountains

The Drakensberg extends from just north of Hoedspruit in the Northern Province 1,000km (620 miles) south to the mountain kingdom of Lesotho, where a series of spectacular peaks some 240km (149 miles) long creates the western border of KwaZulu-Natal—it is this border that most refer to when they speak of the Drakensberg. Known as *uKhahlamba* (or "barrier of spears") to the Zulus, they were renamed "Dragon Mountains" by the Trekkers seeking to cross them. Both are apt descriptions of South Africa's premier mountain wilderness—the second largest range in Africa and, thanks to the haven it provided for the ancient San people, the largest open-air gallery in the world, with more than 35,000 images painted at 600 sites.

The main range falls within the uKhahlamba-Drakensberg Park, a 243,000-hectare (600,210-acre) semicircle that forms the western boundary of the province. Of this, the northern and central sections are most spectacular, with majestic peaks surrounding grassed valleys fed by crystal-clear streams and pools—a hiker's paradise. But you don't have to be a keen and fit walker to appreciate the San rock paintings, or spot rare raptors, or simply enjoy the

chance to breathe the air in the aptly named Champagne Valley or Cathedral Peak. To enjoy the benefits of this World Heritage Site, all you need is a couple of days, a car, and the following information.

ESSENTIALS

VISITOR INFORMATION   Northern Berg: The Drakensberg Tourism Association (©036/448-1557; open Mon–Fri 9am–4pm) is based on Tatham Road in Bergville, which you have to pass to access the Royal Natal National Park. **Central Berg:** If you're traveling to Cathedral Peak, take time to visit the informal bureau at **Thokozisa Centre** (off the R600, 13km/8 miles from Winterton; © 036/488-1207), where you can grab a bite to eat and browse for local crafts. Much of the Berg falls under the protection of **KwaZulu-Natal Wildlife,** so inquiries may also be directed to its head office by visiting www.kznwildlife. com or writing to P.O. Box 13053, Cascades, 3202, Kwazulu-Natal, or calling © 033/845-1002 (bookings © 033/845-1000).

GETTING THERE   By Car   Roads to the Berg all branch off west from the N3 between Maritzburg and Ladysmith. Take the R75 west to Winterton (for Cathedral Peak or Giant's Castle); farther north is Bergville for the turnoff to the Royal Natal National Park.

By Bus   Most hotels offer transfers from the **Greyhound** or **Translux** terminals in Estcourt and Ladysmith (see chapter 2 for regional phone numbers). There is, however, no transport to any of the **KwaZulu-Natal Wildlife** properties, and you won't be able to explore the area in full.

GETTING AROUND   There are no connecting road systems, making long, circuitous routes necessary to move from one part of the Berg to the next. It's best to base yourself in one or two areas: stay at Royal Natal or Cathedral Peak, followed by a night at Giant's Castle.

On Foot   Walks range from a few hours to several days. Detailed maps are available at Parks Board camps, the departure point for all of the best hikes. The most popular book is still David Bristow's *Drakensberg Walks: 120 Graded Hikes and Trails in the Berg* (Struik), which is light enough to carry, and is available from the Parks Board shops. Because winter snows and summer rainfalls can put a damper on hiking expeditions, the best times to explore the Berg, as locals call it, are spring and autumn. (For more information, see "Staying Active: Hiking," earlier in this chapter.)

By Plane   Nac Helicopters (© 082-572-3949) operates from Champagne Sports Resort, and has champagne sunset cocktails in the mountains. Guests staying at the Cathedral Peak Hotel have access to the hotel's helicopter.

GUIDED TOURS   Stef Steyn (© 033/330-4293) specializes in guided hikes in the Drakensberg.

EXPLORING THE DRAKENSBERG

The **Northern Drakensberg** is dominated by the **Amphitheatre,** a dramatic wall of rock that is some 8km (5 miles) long, flanked by the Sentinel (3,165m/ 10,381 ft.) and Eastern Buttress (3,047m/9,994 ft.). Falling within the 8,000-hectare (19,760-acre) **Royal Natal National Park,** it's the most awesome rock formation in the Drakensberg, and the most photographed. This is where you'll find **Mont-aux-Sources,** at 3,282m (10,765 ft.) the country's highest peak, and source of five of South Africa's major rivers, including the Tugela. The 6-hour

Tugela Gorge Walk will take you past the base of the **Tugela Falls,** where the Tugela River plunges 948m (3,109 ft.) from the plateau, its combined drop making it the third highest falls in the world, and affords marvelous views of the Amphitheatre. Entrance to the Royal Natal costs R25 ($3), and it opens at 6am and closes at 6pm (10pm if you are staying at Thendele).

If you don't feel like walking the 6-hour round-trip, you can take a look at it from the top by traveling north on the R74 and taking the Oliviershoek Pass past the Sterkfontein Dam until you get to a T-junction where you turn left onto the R712, following the signs to Witsieshoek Mountain Resort. Just before the resort, take the road marked SENTINEL CAR PARK, the departure point for the steep 2-hour hike to the summit of Mont-aux-Sources via chain ladder. Anyone with a reasonable degree of fitness can complete this, a fact attested to by the unfortunate litter along the way. The views, litter notwithstanding, are stunning.

Central Drakensberg comprises four distinct areas: the beautiful **Cathedral Peak** in the north; followed by relatively populated **Champagne Valley,** where most of the Berg resorts are based; **Injisuthi,** an isolated wilderness ideal for hikers, and at 3,459m (11,345 ft.), the Berg's highest peak; and **Giant's Castle,** famous for its San Rock paintings. The easiest mountain to climb (a 9-hr. round-trip) is Cathedral Peak (3,004m/9,853 ft.), which, conveniently, has the best hotel in the Drakensberg at its feet. The more hard-core hiker in search of solitude should opt for **Giant's Castle Game Reserve,** where the Injisuthi and (relatively luxurious) Giant's Castle camps serve as the departure point for numerous trails, serviced by overnight huts and caves. The reserve is open daily April through September from 6am to 6pm, and October through March from 5am to 7pm; admission to Giant's Castle is R20 ($2.60) per person, to Injisuthi R15/$1.95 per person. Initially established to protect the eland, Africa's largest antelope, the Giant's Castle reserve is today one of the few places where you'll see the rare **lammergeier,** or "bearded vulture" (occurring only here and in the Himalayan foothills). Visitors keen to spot the lammergeier—thought to be an evolutionary link between the vulture and the eagle—should visit the **Lammergeier Hide** ✦ (✆ **036/353-3616;** R115/$14 per person; minimum four persons or R400/$50; maximum six persons; May–September only; advance reservations are essential). Visitors are driven in a four-wheel-drive to the hide at 7:30pm (you'll have to walk down), and meat and bones are laid out to attract the birds.

WHERE TO STAY & DINE

Hikers wanting to overnight in the mountains must book their huts and caves through the KwaZulu-Natal Wildlife office closest to the trail; the camps below are the best bases for walking—hikes start literally from your front door. *Note:* There is an entry fee (R15–R25/$1.95–$3) into all the parks.

If you don't like hotels, **Cathedral Peak** is a comfortable good-value alternative; using the Drakensberg caves as their departure point, KZN Wildlife developed **Didima Camp** ✦ in 2002, with each of the 63 comfortably outfitted two-bed chalets shaped to resemble a cave (R520/$65 double). Should you wish to self-cater there are also two four-bed chalets and a three-bedroom lodge; all units are equipped with satellite TV and fireplaces. There is also a restaurant, bar, and lounge, as well as a San Art Interpretive Centre.

If you decide to visit the Ardmore Studio (on the R600, which leads to Champagne Castle), stop at **Thokozisa Mountain Café** ✫ (13km/8 miles from Winterton; ✆ **036/488-1273**) for a light meal made with organic produce; a little farther is the **Nest** (✆ **036/468-1068**), where filling food (roasts, cottage pie) is served in a rather fusty atmosphere. Should you wish to overnight in Champagne Valley, the old-fashioned **Champagne Castle Hotel** (✆ **036/468-1063;** fax 036/468-1306; www.champagnecastle.com, also off the R600) is closest to the mountains and enjoys the best views, though it's nowhere as remote or charming as Cathedral Peak.

Giant's Castle (see below) is one of KZN Wildlife's flagship rest camps, but if you'd prefer to stay in the lap of luxury and visit the San paintings at Main Caves as a day visitor, **Hartford House** (✆ **033/263-2713;** www.hartford.co.za; from R1,140/$142 double) in nearby Mooi River is one of the top country lodges in South Africa. The historic homestead and luxuriously appointed cottages are absolutely beautiful, and the cuisine, prepared by Richard Carstens, is superb.

Cathedral Peak ✫✫✫ *Kids* This is without a doubt the best option in the Drakensberg. The only hotel situated in its own valley, at the base of the mountains within the Natal Parks' protected area, it offers great views, comfortable rooms, a super-friendly staff, and a relaxed atmosphere. Even getting here is a good experience, on a road that provides charming vignettes of rural bliss. Book a luxury room; they cost very little more and are the most modern, with French doors opening onto the gardens, and some with excellent views of the mountains. The varied facilities also make this one of the best family resorts in the country. Trails start from the hotel, and maps are provided. The 11km (7-mile) Rainbow Gorge round-trip is recommended. Meals are huge buffets with a large variety of dishes. Some are exceptionally tasty; others suffer from standing around. But there is at least something for everyone, including finicky kids.

P.O. Winterton, KwaZulu-Natal 3340. ✆/fax **036/488-1888.** www.cathedralpeak.co.za. 90 units. R900–R1,110 ($112–$140) double; R1,370–R2,330 ($170–$290) suite. All rates include dinner and breakfast. Children under age 10 sharing from R42 ($5.25). AE, DC, MC, V. All routes clearly signposted from Winterton. **Amenities:** Dining room; bar; pool; (9-hole) golf; tennis; babysitting; hiking; bowling; squash; volleyball; horseback riding; helicopter trips. *In room:* TV.

Giant's Castle ✫ The camp's proximity to the Lammergeier Hide assures its popularity, but the camp itself is one of the best in the KZN Wildlife stable. Comprising 37 comfortable two-bed self-catering cottages (equipped with cutlery, crockery, bedding, and fireplaces), four larger two-bedroom chalets, and four three-bedroom chalets, as well as the three-bedroom Rock Lodge, which has a truly exceptional and private setting, Giant's Castle is definitely worth including on your Drakensberg itinerary. All units are well equipped for self-catering, but a fully licensed restaurant and bar with viewing deck make it unnecessary. A shop offers basic provisions, but visitors planning to self-cater should stock up before arriving.

Bookings through KZN Wildlife (see "Visitor Information," above). Direct ✆ **036/353-3718.** 44 units, consisting of 2- and 4-bed chalets, 6-bed cottages, and a 7-bed lodge. From R520 ($65) double. **Amenities:** Restaurant; bar; shop; San paintings; lammergeier hide; filling station.

Thendele Hutted Camp ✫✫ Situated deep within the Royal Natal National Park, with awesome views of the Amphitheatre, these units enjoy the best location of all the KwaZulu-Natal Wildlife camps, but the fact that it has no restaurant could be a drawback. There's a shop with basic provisions, but for fresh supplies stock up in Bergville. Another option will be the restaurant at the Orion Mount-au-Sources hotel, which is about 15 minutes away, but note that you must get back to camp before 10pm, when the gates close. Upper camp has slightly more modern units, but for totally unobstructed views of the Amphitheatre, book cottage 1 or 2, or the wonderfully situated 3-bed lodge—they're more expensive (more bedrooms), but worth the extra money.

Reservations through KZN Wildlife (see "Visitor Information," above). Direct © **036/438-6411.** 29 units, consisting of 2- and 4-bed bungalows, 2- and 4-bed cottages, and a 6-bed lodge. From R480–R692 ($60–$88) double.

9

World Wonder: Victoria Falls & Vicinity

Straddling the western border between Zimbabwe and Zambia, at the point where the Zambezi River drops into the Batoka Gorge, Victoria Falls is justifiably called one of the Wonders of the Natural World. Famously described in 1855 by the explorer David Livingstone as exuding such power that they must have been "gazed upon by angels in their flight," and named by him for his Queen, the falls are the world's largest, spanning almost 2km (just more than 1 mile) and dropping some 100m (328 ft.; twice the height of Niagara). The sight of more than 9 million liters of water crashing down into the Batoka Gorge is one not easily forgotten; on a clear day the veil of roaring spray can even be seen from up to 80km (50 miles) away. It is this phenomenon that gave the falls its local name: *Mosi-Oa-Tunya*—literally, "the smoke that thunders." Protected by the Victoria Falls National Park, the rain forest on the cliff opposite the falls is nourished

by this perennial spray and is one of the few places on the Zimbabwean side in which you will find no commercial distractions. Unlike its namesake, the Victoria Falls Village has little to commend it, and in recent years more and more visitors have in fact chosen to base themselves in lodges that offer bush surrounds, awesome views of the gorge, or the more tranquil stretch of the Upper Zambezi. Most of the latter are on the Zambian side, where visitors can utilize the facilities at Livingstone, a far less touristy destination—at least for now.

To experience the falls and view some wildlife, 2 to 3 days should suffice (one if all you want to do is see the falls), unless, of course, you're an adventure-sports junkie. People come here not only to immerse themselves in the spectacle of the falls, but also to partake in the varied adventure activities, from surfing the most commercially challenging rapids in the world to tracking game on elephant-back—not

---

Tips Country Codes

This chapter contains phone numbers for three countries. So that you'll know which country each is in, all phone numbers in this chapter start with the country code, as well as the local code. Phone numbers starting with **263** are in Zimbabwe; those starting with **260** are in Zambia; those beginning with **27** are in South Africa. The Zimbabwean telephone exchange is temperamental (make that hair-tearingly frustrating), and you will find that at certain times of the day it is impossible to get through to any number you dial. E-mail, strangely, almost always works. For more information, see "Telephone Tips" in chapter 2.

for nothing has this area been dubbed the adrenaline capital of southern Africa.

If, however, your idea of the ideal holiday in Africa is kicking back with a gin and tonic, admiring tropical gardens or bushveld savanna, or watching elephant ambling over to a water hole or crocodiles patrolling the great Zambezi, rest easy: A trip to the falls will provide this—and more.

1 Orientation

VISITOR INFORMATION

In Zimbabwe   You'll find the **Victoria Falls Publicity Association** at 412 Park Way (© **263/13/44202;** Mon–Fri 8am–5pm [may close for lunch], Sat 8am–4pm, Sun 8am–12.30pm). The staff, unfortunately, is not really on the ball; for excellent service, head for the **Backpacker's Bazaar,** across the road at Shop 5, Victoria Falls Centre (© **263/13/45828** or 263/13/42208 or mobile 263/11/404960; backpack@africaonline.co.zw; Mon–Fri 8am–5pm, public holidays and Sat–Sun 8am–4pm). This independent service will direct you to the widest variety of tours and activities available, as well as advise on budget lodgings, transfers, and the most cost-effective way to travel the region.

For more essential information on Vic Falls, including getting there, travel documents, health, and more, see chapter 2.

In Zambia   Head for **Makoro Quest** (© **260/3/324-253;** guest@zamnet. zm) on 216 Mosi-Oa-Tunya Rd., or **Safari Par Excellence** (© **260/3/32-0606;** waterfront@zamnet.zm) at Zambezi Waterfront Lodge, located off Mosi-Oa-Tunya Road, halfway between Livingstone and the Vic Falls bridge.

GETTING THERE
BY PLANE

SAA and Comair fly directly from Johannesburg to Victoria Falls daily. Air Zimbabwe was due to resume this flight in April 2003. Nationwide Air flies daily directly from Johannesburg to Livingstone (the closest town on the Zambian side of the falls). See "Getting There," in chapter 2, for contact details. If you have to make a visa payment at the airport in Zimbabwe, make sure you have the correct amount or you will be given change in Z$ (see "Money Matters," below). Please note that you will have to pay a US$30 departure tax when you leave Zimbabwe; make sure that this is included in your ticket or have the cash on you.

Victoria Falls Airport (© 263/13/44250 or 263/13/44552) is about 20km (12 miles) south of Victoria Falls Village (which is within walking distance of the falls). Most hotels offer a complimentary shuttle from the airport; arrange this in advance. Alternatively, arrange a ride through Backpacker's Bazaar—the maximum charge is US$12 to take you into town. (A taxi will sting you a minimum US$20 for the same trip.)

You can fly from Maun (Okavango, Botswana) to **Harare International Airport** (© **263/4/575-528**), Zimbabwe's capital; then catch a connecting flight to Victoria Falls with Zimbabwe Air. Easier still is to charter a flight to Kasane (gateway to Chobe), which is no more than a 40-minute drive from the Zambian side of the falls.

BY TRAIN

Both the super-luxurious **Blue Train** and its competitor **Rovos Rail** no longer chug into Victoria Falls, citing the current volatile political situation and the

⌒**Tips** **Money Matters**

Because nearly every rate is quoted in US$ and most operators don't accept credit cards, it is imperative that you carry foreign currency on your trip to Zimbabwe. Visitors are advised not to change foreign currency into Z$, not only because foreign currency (US$, pounds, rands) or traveler's checks is the preferred method of payment, but the official exchange rate does not reflect the full devaluation of the Z$; for the same reason, you should only use your credit card in Zimbabwe if you're being charged in US$ or you may be charged at the bank rate of US$1:Z$55 (the rate is estimated to be closer to US$1,200). Don't let the bank rate tempt you into changing money in black-market dealings, however—at best you'll wind up with a fistful of newspaper; at worst you'll end up in jail. Note also that if you intend to fly into Victoria Falls Village, only to transfer by road to a lodge on the Zambian side of the falls (less than an hour's drive), these lodges can usually obtain a visa waiver (a saving of US$35 for U.S. citizens; US$65 for UK citizens). Passport details must be given to the lodge at least a week prior to arrival. To enter and leave Victoria Falls, you will still need a multiple entry visa for Zimbabwe (at present: US$45; US$70 for U.K. citizens). Single entry is US$30 to US$55, depending on your nationality. If you want to do a day trip to Livingstone, you can purchase a day visa to Zambia for US$10.

tripling of haulage costs. The only alternative worth considering is the 16-day **Shongololo Express** train tour from Johannesburg to Vic Falls, with days spent touring sites in Swaziland, Mozambique, Kruger, Zimbabwe, Livingstone, and Botswana (© **27/11/486-2824;** www.shongololo.com; US$2,550–US$3,920 per person).

BY CAR
If you're driving from South Africa, you'll pass through the border at Beit Bridge (about 5 hr. from Jo'burg). From here, follow the A6 to Bulawayo (about 7 hr.), then the A8 to Victoria Falls via Hwange (about 4 hr.). From Harare, take the A5 to Bulawayo, then the A8 to Vic Falls (about 9 hr.).

BY BUS
Because of chronic fuel shortages, most South African bus operators have canceled their Vic Falls route. However, you can still catch a Greyhound bus from Johannesburg/Pretoria to Harare; **Blue Arrow** (© **263/4/72-9514**) runs from Harare to Vic Falls.

GETTING AROUND
Victoria Falls Village is a very small town, with most attractions (including the falls) within walking distance, or, at worst, a short taxi ride away. Taxis are relatively cheap (make sure you negotiate the price upfront), but almost all of the hotels and lodges offer a shuttle service to the falls and town. **Safari Par Excellence** (see "Visitor Information," above) offers a shuttle from both airports and Victoria Falls Village to the Waterfront Lodge in Zambia, where many adventure activities take place. To get to Livingstone, catch a taxi or rent a bike—it's less than an hour's cycle away.

BY CAR

Budget (*C* 263/13/42243) usually offers the best rates; compare it with **Hertz** (Bata Building, Park Way Dr.; *C* **263/13/44297** or 263/13/44772) or **Avis** (corner Livingstone Way and Mallett Dr.; *C* **263/13/44532**). It's not necessary to rent a car unless you're intent on traveling farther afield, and with the fluctuating fuel prices (increases of 100% are not uncommon) and ongoing fuel shortages, this could be risky. Far better to take advantage of the numerous outfits offering overnight safaris in appropriate vehicles within Zimbabwe, as well as to Zambia, Botswana, and Namibia. If you're determined to go it alone, book a four-wheel-drive in advance. For rentals, as well as information on out-of-town transfers and repair and maintenance services, contact **United Touring Company** (7 Park Way; *C* **263/13/44267**, 263/13/44772, or 263/13/44297).

BY BICYCLE

Biking is a great way to get around; you'll find some to rent in Park Way Drive. Expect to pay about US$2 for an hour or US$10 for the day.

BY BOAT

Breakfast, lunch, bird-watching, and sunset river cruises are operated by a number of companies. All cruises take place on the calmer, game-rich waters above the falls, and are usually in large, twin-deck boats—a wonderful way to enjoy the water wildlife, such as hippos, elephants, and aquatic birds, though you'll probably also see plenty of other tourists. Some of the oldest operators are **Dabula** (*C* 263/13/44453) and **Kalambeza Safaris** (*C* 263/13/44480). Sunset cruises cost on average US$25 to US$30; shop around for the best prices. If you're averse to crowds, it's worth inquiring about cruises offered on smaller (maximum eight people), shallower, propeller-free "jet boats"; they're a bit more expensive (US$35) but quieter, and can explore places larger boats can't get to. (Also see "Canoe Safaris," later in this chapter.)

BY TRAIN

A 1922 Class Ten steam locomotive, operated by **Victoria Falls Safari Express** (Customs House, Railway Station, Victoria Falls; *C* 263/13/44682), crosses the mighty Zambezi via the Victoria Falls Bridge—do the bridge run for US$55, or head for Livingstone for US$110, including lunch or dinner. Booking is advisable—trips are only confirmed with 10 clients.

FAST FACTS: Zimbabwe

Banks Almost everyone prefers foreign currency, and the bank rate (US$1:Z$55) is appalling (see "Money Matters," above). If you really do need local currency, there are a few local banks along Livingstone Way. Try **Zimbank, Barclays,** or **Standard Chartered.** Bank hours are usually Monday to Tuesday and Thursday to Friday from 8am to 3pm (Zimbank stays open till 4pm), Wednesday from 8am to 1pm, and Saturday from 8 to 11:30am.

Business Hours Shops are generally open Monday through Saturday from 8am to 5pm (some close Sat evening), and Sunday mornings. Activity centers and markets are open daily; many only close when the last traveler leaves.

Climate The most comfortable temperatures are between April and September, but this is not necessarily the best time to view the falls. See "The Best Times to Come," above.

Currency See "Money," in chapter 2.

Doctor Contact Dr. Nyoni at the **Victoria Falls Surgery** (West Dr., off Park Way; ✆ **263/13/43356**; Mon–Fri 9:15am–4:30pm, Sat 9:15am–12:30pm, Sun 10–11am; after hours: ✆ **263/13/43380** or 263/11/404949). If you're based on the Zambian side, contact Dr. Tigdi at the **Healthcare Clinic** (20 A.S. Sananga Rd. in Livingstone; ✆ **260/3/322-038**) or Dr. Shafik (49 Akapelwa St.; ✆ **260/3/32-1130**).

Drugstore Drugstores are called chemists or pharmacies. **Victoria Falls Pharmacy** is located in Phumula Centre, Park Way (✆ **263/13/44403**; Mon–Fri 9am–6pm, Sat–Sun 9am–1pm). There is also a drugstore in the Kingdom Hotel, open daily. After hours, call mobile ✆ **011-221-730** or 011-212-014.

Electricity Electricity in southern Africa runs on 220/230V,50Hz AC, and sockets take round- or flat-pinned plugs. Bring an adapter/voltage converter; be aware that some bush camps do not have electricity.

Embassies & Consulates All offices are located in Harare.

Emergencies For medical emergencies, contact **Medical Air Rescue Service,** a 24-hour emergency evacuation service, at 162 Courtney Selous Crescent (✆ **263/13/44764**). For an **ambulance,** call ✆ **994;** for the **police,** call ✆ **995;** to report a **fire,** call ✆ **993;** for **general emergencies,** call ✆ **999.**

Language English is the official language, but the most widely spoken languages are Shona and Ndebele.

Safety **Malaria** Consult your physician before leaving about starting a course of anti-malarial prophylactics. If you suspect you have malaria, get to a doctor immediately for a test (about US$3). For more information, see "Health, Safety & Insurance," in chapter 2.

Crime Despite the land-grab crisis elsewhere, the falls remain largely unaffected, though the fatal stabbing of a visitor in January 2003 has highlighted the importance of avoiding deserted areas; sadly, this includes the banks of the Zambezi. Avoid petty crime by not flashing valuables, and stay in groups, particularly at night.

Taxes Sales tax is 10%; make sure that this is included in the price upfront.

Telephone This chapter contains codes for three countries. See "Country Codes," above. For tips on how to make international and local calls, see chapter 2.

Time Zone Zimbabwe is 5 hours ahead of GMT, or 7 hours ahead of Eastern Standard Time.

Tipping For a meal, leave 10%; for small services such as hotel porters carrying your bags, tip US$1–$3 or the equivalent.

Water Tap water is generally considered safe, but it's worth asking first.

Wildlife Keep your eye out for elephant and hippo when you're out walking, cycling, or canoeing—do not block their routes; it's best not to turn around, but back away slowly. When driving on highways that are part of national parkland, never speed, and keep a watchful eye out for animals emerging from the bush to cross the road.

Tips **The Best Times to Come**

The falls are most impressive from January to April after the summer rains, when up to 700,000 million cubic liters (182,000 million gal.) per minute rush over the 100m (328-ft.) high lip into the gorge below. The spray can become so thick during this time, however, that it obscures the view. From May, nights can be cold, but it starts to warm up by the end of August. By September and October, at the end of the dry season, the flow is down to about 3%, but the view is clearest.

2 What to See & Do

Victoria Falls Village still retains some of its old-world "jungle junction" charm, but as all its available energy is given over to the pursuit of the tourist buck, it's not a town you'll want to tarry in long.

The area is famous for its myriad adventure activities, and offers an excellent opportunity to view wildlife, but when all is said and done, it's the falls that are the star of the show.

Baboons are a nuisance on both sides of the falls. Keep food out of sight and remember that—like all wild animals—they are unpredictable and potentially dangerous.

SOAKING UP THE FALLS

There are three great vantage points, each offering a different angle, and it's worth trying to cover them all. Do this by walking through the rain forest directly opposite the falls in the Vic Falls National Park, then continuing along Livingstone Way to cross the Victoria Falls Bridge, and finally viewing them from the Zambian side, in the Mosi-Oa-Tunya Park. This will take at least half a day. Break your return journey by stopping for a sumptuous high tea at the Victoria Falls Hotel—a real highlight.

The Victoria Falls National Park ★★★   The Victoria Falls National Park—which affords the best vantage point of the falls—is a 2,340-hectare (5,780-acre) narrow strip that runs along the southern bank of the Zambezi River and protects the sensitive rain forest around the falls. You will almost certainly get drenched by the permanent spray, so rent a raincoat or umbrella at the entrance or at **Raincoat & Camping Equipment Hire Services** (307 Park Way Rd.; © 260/13/44528), and remember to put your camera in a waterproof bag. A clearly marked trail runs through the lush and fecund rain forest (look out for the aptly named flame lilies), with side trails leading to good viewing points of the falls. Head down the steep stairs to **Cataract View** for views of **Devil's Cataract** ★★; this is also where you'll find the unremarkable statue of David Livingstone. The final viewpoint, nearest the falls bridge, is called **Danger Point**—here you can perch right on the edge of a cliff and peer down into the abyss. When the moon is full, the park stays open later so that visitors can witness the lunar rainbow formed by the spray. Not only is it a beautiful sight, but the experience is untarnished by the sounds of helicopters and microlights, which are something of a noise nuisance during much of the day.

You don't need a guide to visit the falls. Many unofficial guides stand near the entrances, but unless you want to learn more about the rain forests (in which case hire a guide from a reputable company), the chances are that they won't be able to show you anything other than the direction of the path. Livingstone Way leads from the Victoria Falls Village directly to the entrance.

No phone. Admission US$20. Open daily 6am–6pm, later during full-moon nights when entry is US$40.

Mosi-Oa-Tunya 👣👣 (Value   The Zambian side (you will need to purchase a visa at the bridge) offers a more spectacular vantage point than its Zimbabwean counterpart during high water (Apr–June), when the view is less obscured by spray. Here the focus is on seeing the main gorge and Eastern Cataract; you can also walk (or scramble, rather) across to a vantage called Knife Edge, where you will stand suspended above the churning waters of Boiling Pot—a vicious rapid most rafters get to know a little too intimately. *Warning:* There are no fences on this side of the river—every year, one or two people slip on the wet rocks attempting to get that extra special photograph or experience. The chance of survival is nil.

Entrance off Livingstone Road. No phone. Admission US$10. Open daily year-round 6am–6pm.

VIEWING WILDLIFE

Despite the commercialism of the village, the falls remain surrounded by dense bush, and you can start your African safari right here. You only have to venture a few miles upstream from the river along the Zambezi Drive to take a look at the **Big Tree,** a 1,500-year-old baobab (if you're lucky you'll see elephants, too), or take the **Zambezi river walk** (see "Staying Active: Bush Walks," below) to view species like hippo and crocodile. The Zambezi National Park (see below), a small but well-stocked reserve, is a mere 7km (4 miles) from the falls.

Backpacker's Bazaar (see "Visitor Information," earlier in this chapter) arranges morning, afternoon, and night drives to Zambezi National Park and Hwange (see below), as well as full days in Chobe, Botswana—these should run you US$50 to $55, a full day, US$110 to $130. The best budget option is in Zambia, where a game drive in the small Mosi-Oa-Tunya Park—a sanctuary for white rhino, buffalo, zebra, sable, and giraffe—costs US$30 per person.

The falls are also remarkably close to the borders of four countries, and **Kalahari Holiday Tours** (zambezi@info.bw) offers a whirlwind Four Countries in One Day tour—an action-packed day that kicks off with a minibus transfer through the Matetsi wildlife area in Zimbabwe to the Kazungula border, refreshments on the Chobe River (Botswana), and a cruise through Namibia's Kasai wetlands to Sikoma Island (Zambia), where a short bush walk is undertaken with Zambian guides. After lunch, guests are transferred by boat to Chobe, famous for its huge elephant herds, for a final 3-hour game drive, before returning to Zimbabwe or Zambia. Kalahari Holiday Tours also offers full-day trips in Chobe direct from Livingstone or the Falls Village. Vic Falls Village agents are **Matopo Tours** (© **263/13/42209** or 263/91239311) or contact them direct in Botswana (© **267/625-0821**).

For safaris by canoe, plane, helicopter and horse- or elephant-back, see "Staying Active," below.

LIVINGSTONE, I PRESUME?

If you're interested in African culture, take time out to visit the 700-year-old traditional **Mukuni Village** 👣 (off Mosi-Oa-Tunya Dr., on the way into Livingstone)—where Scottish explorer David Livingstone obtained traversing permission from Chief Mukuni in the mid-1800s. The tree under which Livingstone awaited an audience with the chief still provides shade for those wishing to do the same.

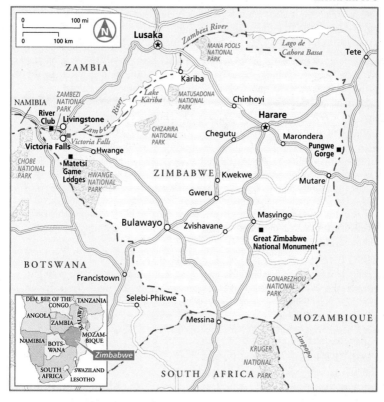

Livingstone Museum ⟨⋆⟩   Livingstone may have been the first white man to view the falls, but archaeological digs show that human occupation of the area dates back 2 million years before. Much of this Stone Age evidence is on-site in the Livingstone Museum—Zambia's oldest and largest. The archaeological exhibits are augmented with historical artifacts, from ancient Tonga drums (the original telephone), to black-and-white photographs from the turn of the 20th century, as well as memorabilia relating to Livingstone, the man who put the falls on the world map.

Mosi-Oa-Tunya Rd., next to the post office. ℭ **260/3/32-4428.** Admission US$3. 9am–4:30pm.

3 Staying Active

Most of the hotels will arrange reservations and give advice on activities. For the widest range of activities, visit the **Backpacker's Bazaar** (see "Visitor Information," earlier in this chapter) or **Safari Par Excellence** (www.safpar.com); Zimbabwe: Phumula Centre, Park Way Dr. (ℭ **263/4/70-0911**); SafPar also operates out of Zambia from the Waterfront (ℭ **260/3/32-1629**) and has offices in South Africa (ℭ **27/11/328-8170**).

ABSEILING ⟨⋆⟩   Rappel down a 50m (164-ft.) drop into the Batoka Gorge with **Abseil Zambia** (ℭ **260/11/21-3838;** abseilzambia@hotmail.com), then tackle the world's highest commercial high wire: spanned 140m (459 ft.) across a 110m (361-ft.) drop. Break for lunch, then try the gorge swing—as often as you like. The cost is US$95 for the full day, inclusive of all meals, refreshments, and transfers (US$100 if you opt for the Zimbabwean side, run by Adrift).

BUNGEE JUMPING ✹✹   The checklists of most adventure-sportsmen aren't complete until they've done the heart-stopping 111m (364-ft.) bungee off the Vic Falls Bridge, stopping about 10m (33 ft.) from the boiling waters in the Batoka Gorge. As you're about to step into the abyss, bear in mind that, statistically, you're about the safest person in Vic Falls—more than 100,000 people have made this jump without a single death. Jumps are done daily (9am–1pm and 2–5pm) at the Victoria Falls Bridge. Because the bridge lies in a "no-man's land," jumpers and spectators are issued a gate pass when they go out onto the bridge, which must be presented to the immigration officials on their return. Allow about an hour before your jump to get from the village and go through all the formalities. The first jump costs US$90 (US$120 for tandem); the second is free if you purchase a video. Fees are nonrefundable, even if you chicken out and don't jump. You can register at the bridge, or book through **Shearwater Adventures** (see above); note that jumps may be delayed during the months of heavy spray (Mar–June).

BUSH WALKS   You can do the **Zambezi River walk** ✹ without a guide, but frankly it's not safe to wander it on your own. You take the river path from just outside the Falls National Park fence upstream to Zambezi River Lodge (4km/2½ miles), then head back along the road to town (6km/3¾ miles). Watch out for hippos entering or leaving the water to graze at dawn and dusk (never block their route); also be on the lookout for crocodile and elephant. If the thought of doing this on your own makes you nervous, choose a guided safari. **Charles Brightman** (✆ 263/13/45821; cat@mweb.co.zw) offers 2- to 4-hour and full-day bush walks accompanied by a knowledgeable—and armed—guide. Numerous companies offer overnight walking safaris, but **Khangela** in particular offers excellent value: US$130/day, and you don't even have to carry your gear; book through Backpacker's Bazaar. Another company offering guided walking trips in Botswana is **Baobab Safaris** (✆ 263/13/44283; untamed@ mweb.co.zw).

CANOE SAFARIS ✹✹   Canoe safaris offer a more sedate option than rafting, with the added bonus of seeing hippos, elephants, and crocodiles while you paddle the broad expanse of the Upper Zambezi. There are no (or very small) rapids on this trip, so you won't get your hair wet, though be aware that hippos do occasionally upend canoes (in which case your guide will whisk you aboard almost immediately). Half-day trips (particularly at **sunset** ✹✹✹) are recommended: For morning trips most operators provide a bush breakfast and a brief break for refreshments and lunch on one of the river's islands; the popular sunset wine tour offers a sampling of regional wines. You can also combine canoeing with game

---

⸤Fun Fact⸥ Courtin' the Zambezi River God

Every year Nyaminyami, the Zambezi River god, claims one or two of the 40,000 lives that hurtle down his course. It is said that by wearing his serpentlike image around your neck, you will escape harm. Hundreds of hawkers in and around the falls make a living selling Nyaminyami necklaces, which forever brand you as a brave warrior who has ridden the mighty Zambezi River.

drives or walks, or choose to overnight on one of the rustic island camps. Half-day trips cost about US$65 to $70, full-day US$75 to $80, and overnight safaris start at US$170 (plus US$15 National Park fee). Contact **Backpacker's Bazaar** (see "Visitor Information," earlier in this chapter) or **Kandahar Canoeing Safaris** (© 263/13/44502 or 263/13/42279; adrift@africaonline.co.zw), which have been operating on the river the longest.

ELEPHANT-BACK SAFARIS ⚜⚜⚜   The **Elephant Company** (© 263/13/44483;** reservations@elephants.co.za) provides a talk on the history of elephant training before introducing you to the elephant who will take you for an hour's ride to the banks of the Zambezi for breakfast or afternoon snacks. Cost is US$90—one of the cheapest elephant rides in Africa. Overnight at **Wild Horizons** (© 263/13/42313; www.wildhorizons.co.zw), a small bush camp 25km (15½ miles) west of the falls, where you'll be assigned your own personal elephant for the duration of your stay (US$170 per person per night).

FLYING ⚜⚜⚜   Take to the skies on a microlight or ultralight flight—both are quieter than helicopter or fixed-wing flights, and you'll be sailing a great deal closer to nature (and, for that matter, the wind). Ultralights, considered marginally safer than microlights, cost US$100 for 30 minutes. **Batoka Sky** (© 260/3/32-0058 or 260/3/32-1513; reservations@batokasky.co.za) operates tricycle-style microlight flights from Zambia, and charges US$75 for 15 minutes. You can't take a camera (if you drop it, it may stop the engine below), so Batoka has a camera attached to the wheels; your pilot will take a photograph of you at the most appropriate moment—flying past the falls.

For helicopter trips, book through an adventure center or direct with the **Zambezi Helicopter Company** (© 263/13/45806; helicopters@shearwater. co.zw; US$75–US$150 for 15–30 min.); for fixed-wing flights, book with **Southern Cross Aviation** (© 263/13/44618 or 263/13/44456; sca@zol.co.zw; US$55 for 25-min. scenic flight).

The most chilled-out way to fly is viewing the sunrise in a tethered balloon; book with Shearwater (see above; US$40).

GOLFING   The 6,205m (6,763-yd.) **Elephant Hills Intercontinental** course is at times just a stroke from the roaring Zambezi River, and the constant presence of the falls—not to mention wildlife—makes this Gary Player–designed course one of the most interesting in Africa. For details, contact Elephant Hills Intercontinental (© 263/13/44793).

HORSEBACK SAFARIS ⚜   **Zambezi Horse Trails** (© 263/13/44611) provides riders with an opportunity to get closer to game than they can on foot or in a car. Rides are led by an experienced guide with an extensive knowledge of the flora and fauna of the Warea, and take place on 30,000 hectares (74,100 acres) of the Matetsi River Ranch, which borders the Zambezi National Park. Experienced riders can choose among half-day, full-day, or multi-day riding safaris. Novices are taken on a 2-hour ride (US$45), and potentially dangerous animals like elephant are avoided; experienced riders ride for 3 hours or a full day (US$65–US$90).

WHITE-WATER RAFTING ⚜⚜⚜   Operators pride themselves on offering the best commercially run rapids in the world. You need to be reasonably fit (not only to deal with the grade 3–5 rapids, but also for the 230m/754-ft. climb down out of the gorge at the end of a tiring day). You should also be a competent swimmer. Don't worry if you haven't done anything like it before—organizers offer dry-ground preparation before launching onto the water, and the safety and guiding standards are excellent. The best time for rafting is when the water is low and the rapids impressive, in September and October. (In Apr–May, when the water is particularly high, some rafting companies close altogether.) You should be aware that there *is* a certain level of danger, and that the rapids claim a few lives every year, though these are usually kayakers. The safest option is to get on a boat that has an oarsman who guides you along the safest path, but the alternative, where everyone in the group has his or her own paddle, is much more fun, despite the fact that—or in large part because of it—you'll definitely end up in the water. Riverboarding is the most hair-raising way to brave the rapids—alone, on a boogie board, you literally surf the waves created by a selection of grade 3–5 rapids. Most river rafting companies offer an optional half-day rafting, half-day boarding experience. The kings of the river are **Raft Extreme** (© **260/3/32-3929;** www.raftextreme.com) and **Safari Par Excellence** (see above). Both offer trips from the Zambian side—though it's a bit of an effort to go across the border, these trips have the added advantage of including a few extra rapids, and they also begin right beneath the falls. Zambian guides are also usually the longest-serving guides and are therefore very familiar with what can be a dangerous river. Expect to pay US$85 for a half or full day. Prices include lunch, drinks, and all equipment.

While you're drifting down the river, keep an eye out for *taita* falcons. These rare swift flying birds nest in the cliffs and can sometimes be spotted from the water swooshing in and out of updrafts.

4 Where to Stay

The Victoria Falls Hotel and Ilala Lodge (see below) are within walking distance of the Falls, as is Zimbabwe Sun's resort **The Kingdom** (© **263/13/44275,** from US$200 double including breakfast), the latest vulgarity Zimbabwe Sun has foisted on the Victoria Falls Village. If Vegas is one of your favorite destinations, take a gander at the company website (www.zimsun.com), but if your taste runs to colonial-style elegance, the top option in town is the Victoria Falls Hotel. If seeing wild animals is high on your priority list, Matetsi Water Lodge, the Victoria Falls Safari Lodge, or the Stanley & Livingstone are your best options (see below for full reviews). Most people opt to stay on the Zimbabwean side of the falls, benefiting from the infrastructure of the commercially oriented village, but with flights from Johannesburg now flying direct into Livingstone, and the opening of two new Sun International resorts on the banks of the Zambezi mere yards before it takes the plunge, Zambia is gearing up for an influx of visitors. Created with all the flash one expects from Sun International, these new resorts have a big selling point in their proximity to the falls, but with a starting B&B rate of US$348 double **(Zambezi Sun)** and US$516 (**Royal Livingstone;** both www.suninternational.com), a more intimate resort like Taita Falcon (see "Gazing into the Abyss," below) offers better value.

IN ZIMBABWE

Elephant Hills Intercontinental ✦ Four kilometers (2½ miles) from the falls, Elephant Hills is more of a business or conference-type hotel, but it offers good service standards and excellent amenities, including the area's only 18-hole golf course, designed by Gary Player—though you don't have to be a resident to play it. Having suffered extensive fire damage, it reopened mid-March 2003

Finds **Gazing into the Abyss**

Three lodges offer stupendous bird's-eye views of the Zambezi River as it carves its way through the gorge some 200m (656 ft.) below. **Taita Falcon Lodge** is 11km (7 miles) from the falls on the Zambian side and overlooks the Batoka Gorge directly above rapids 16 and 17—from here you have literally a falcon's view of rafters the size of ants. Personal service from the enthusiastic owners Faan, Anmarie, and Andre compliments the awesome views, intimate vibe (there are only six suites, privately situated), and good value—US$310 double includes full board (including drinks), airport and Falls transfers, village tour, sunset cruise, and guided bush walks. Contact (C) **260/3/32-1850** or visit **www.taitafalcon.com**.

A little farther downstream, also perched above the Batoka Gorge, **Songwe Village** comprises eight thatched huts laid out according to the traditions of the 700-year-old Thokoleya culture. The emphasis here is on coming to grips with African traditions and history (there's even a human origins museum on-site). Rates are relatively hefty, however (US$610–US$790 double, all inclusive depending on the season). For details, contact Kwando Safaris (C) **267/11/686-1449** (www.kwando.co.za).

Located on the Zimbabwean side, the 10 privately located stone-and-thatch chalets at **Gorges Lodge** offer more superb views. Each unit features wide private verandas that overlook the gorge, and the lodge offers a regular shuttle service to Vic Falls Village, 22km (13½ miles) away. Contact (C) **263/13/43381** or 263/9/72331; gorges@gatorzw.com (rates US$544-US$570 all-inclusive double, depending on season).

after renovating the 135 bedrooms in the River View Wing (the best option, incidentally, not only because all the fittings are brand-spanking new, but the river views at sunset are fabulous) as well as some of the public spaces (including the open-air atrium, which features an ornamental rain forest and fountains). Although the huge hulk of a building—intended, one presumes, to resemble an elephant—is not particularly environmentally sensitive, it is still considered one of the top hotels in Vic Falls and relatively good value (though the Victoria Falls Hotel is more elegant, and the Victoria Falls Safari Lodge is more of a bush experience).

Park Way. Box 300, Victoria Falls. (C) **263/13/44793**. Fax 263/13/44655. Reservations in the U.S. call (C) 800/327-0200. www.suninternational.com. 276 units. From US$328 double. AE, DC, MC, V. **Amenities:** 3 restaurants; 3 bars; 2 pools; tennis; sauna and gym; business services; room service; babysitting; laundry; squash; a bowling green; casino. *In room:* A/C, TV/VCR, tea- and coffee-making facilities, hair dryer, CD player.

Ilala Lodge ⚐ *Value* This small, pleasant thatched lodge offers midrange accommodations an easy 10-minute walk from the falls. It's put together very much along an African theme, with thatched roofs, African-style paintings and fabrics, cane furniture, and views of the lawn and thick bush of the National Park. The hotel is not fenced in, so don't be surprised if you hear the sounds of elephants feeding outdoors at night. Best of all, the food here enjoys a good reputation—even if you don't stay here it's worth taking a table.

411 Livingstone Way. Box 18, Victoria Falls. (C) **263/13/44737/8/9**, or 888/227-8311 from the U.S. Fax 263/13/44417. 16 units. From US$230 double, including breakfast; US$286 high season. DC, MC, V. **Amenities:** 2 restaurants; 2 bars; pool; room service; laundry. *In room:* TV, hair dryer on request.

Matetsi Game Lodges ★★★ Located 40km (25 miles) upstream from the falls, on 73,500 hectares (181,550 acres) with access to the adjacent Zambezi National Park, this really combines a safari experience with a visit to the falls. Previously a hunting-concession area, Matetsi is now home to herds of buffalo, elephant, and sable antelope, as well as predators like lion, hyena, and leopard, all of which range freely throughout the vast, unfenced area. Guests enjoy access to morning and evening game drives, boat cruises, canoeing, fishing, and guided bush walks. Guests have a choice of two locations: the highly recommended **Matetsi Water Lodge** comprises three small, separate camps (each with six suites), built right on the Zambezi River. Each privately located and luxurious suite—teak fittings, canopied king-size beds, enormous bathrooms—has its own plunge pool and deck overlooking the river and its wildlife. Dining takes place on teak decks beside the river, under ancient trees. The slightly less glamorous **Matetsi Safari Camp** offers luxury en-suite tented accommodations overlooking an open grassland that attracts a variety of game.

Reservations through CC Africa, Private Bag x27, Benmore 2010, SA. ✆ **27/11/809-4300.** Fax 27/11/809-4315. www.ccafrica.com. Water Lodge: 3 camps, 6 units each. Safari Camp: 12 units. High season (July–Oct): US$800 double; low season: US$656. Rates include all meals, local brand spirits/beer, all game activities, shuttle, and laundry. No credit cards. **Amenities:** Dining room/bar; room service; babysitting; laundry; morning and evening game drives; boat cruises; canoeing; fishing; guided bush walks. *In room:* A/C, minibar, hair dryer.

Stanley & Livingstone ★★★ Tranquil, luxurious, elegant, the Stanley & Livingstone is the most expensive addition to the upscale and exclusive options in Zimbabwe. Although the hotel only opened in December 1999, it feels as if it's been here since gin and tonics were an accepted prevention for malaria. The decor consists of elegant period furnishings and such colonial-style fittings as ball-and-claw bathtubs. Each of the 10 luxurious, ultra-spacious suites opens onto an elegantly furnished, private veranda; six more are currently being built—an investment that confirms the hotel's popularity. Only 10 minutes from the falls, and 2 minutes from Zambezi National Park, it's located in its own 2,400-hectare (6,000-acre) private reserve (the restaurant and bar overlook a water hole that attracts a variety of species), with a choice of game drives, bush walks, or fishing part of the package. Service is excellent. It's a good option if you prefer colonial styling, but do consider Matetsi's more intimate Water Lodge camp before booking.

Rani Africa, Box 2682, Witkoppen 2068. ✆ **27/11/467-1277.** Fax 27/11/465-6904. www.ipresumeonline.com. 10 suites. High season (July–Dec): US$840 all inclusive. AE, MC, DC, V. **Amenities:** Dining room; bar; pool; complimentary shuttle to village and airport; room service; laundry game drives; bush walks; fishing; canoeing. *In room:* A/C, TV, minibar.

Victoria Falls Hotel ★★ A member of Luxury Hotels of the World, this colonial-style hotel is not only the most genteel accommodation option in the village, but it's located in a prime spot overlooking the Victoria Falls Bridge and within walking distance of the falls. Built in the early-20th-century imperial manner in 1904 for Cecil Rhodes' Cape-to-Cairo railway, the hotel is all columns, arched loggias, chandeliers, and broad verandas. If your budget can handle the extra cost, the deluxe rooms (with views of the spray and bridge) and suites are definitely worth it. Enjoy drinks and high tea served on a generous, sweeping terrace with excellent views—a must even if you're not staying here. A path through the gardens leads to the falls, and a 30-minute trail descends into the gorge to the river. Service is well meaning but can be patchy.

Mallet Dr., Box 10, Victoria Falls. ⓒ **263/13/44751.** Fax 263/13/4586. S.A. central reservations: ⓒ **27/11/886-3430/1.** www.lhw.com. 182 units. High season (July–Oct): from US$386 double, US$414 deluxe, US$725 suite. Rates include breakfast. Low season: from US$372. AE, DC, MC, V. **Amenities:** 3 restaurants; 2 bars; pool; tennis; playground; salon; room service; babysitting; laundry. *In room:* A/C, TV, hair dryer.

Victoria Falls Safari Lodge ⭐⭐   Just 3km (2 miles) from the village, the lodge is set high on a plateau that overlooks the plains of the Zambezi National Park and is surrounded by views of unspoiled bush. Constructed on 11 levels, much like an open-plan thatched treehouse, it overlooks a very productive water hole—the balcony has been described as one of the best places in Africa to breakfast, with everything from elephant to large herds of buffalo quenching their thirst in full view. All the rooms have glass doors that open onto private west-facing balconies, offering spectacular views of the bushveld and sunsets. Guests must be accompanied by guides when walking outside the perimeters of the resort, a reminder of how close to nature you are. The nearby **Lokhutula Lodge** (US$120–US$200 for a 2-bedroom chalet) is the lodge's self-catering option; this is where you'll find the **Boma** (see "Where to Dine," below).

Squire Cummings Rd., Box 29, Victoria Falls. ⓒ **263/13/32014.** Fax 263/13/3205. Bookings through RSA: ⓒ **27/31/310-3333.** www.threecities.co.za. 72 units. High season (July–Dec): US$370–$440 double; Low season: US$308–US$370 double. AE, DC, MC, V. **Amenities:** 2 restaurants; bar; pool; beauty/health spa, games room; room service; babysitting; laundry; library. *In room:* A/C, minibar (suites only), hair dryer.

IN ZAMBIA

Chundukwa ⭐ *Value*   Located 25km (15½ miles) upstream from Vic Falls, the rustic Chundukwa comprises four stilted reed chalets that literally hang over the water. With 4km (2½ miles) of river frontage, the chalets are ideal for birders, and elephant from the Zimbabwe National Park (which lies directly opposite the river) are often seen as they swim to the river islands. Chundukwa is a great place for quiet mediation, with compact, simply furnished units that provide good value. Owner Doug Evans is a retired Zimbabwe conservation officer with a penchant for polo cross (on polo days you can hear the horses thundering over the pitch)—you can hire his horses for guided game-viewing trips along the river.

Bookings through Maplanga, PO Box 2331, Honeydew 2040, South Africa. ⓒ/fax **27/11/7941446.** www.maplanga.co.za. 4 units (plus self-catering bushcamp). From US$170 double; includes full board, airport transfer, and sunset river cruise. MC, V. **Amenities:** Dining room/bar; pool; boat trips; fishing; birding and bush walks; horseback riding.

The River Club ⭐⭐   A neighbor to Tongabezi (see below), this romantic retreat on the banks of the Zambezi, managed by ex–British Army officer Peter Jones, is the most overtly colonial of the Zambian lodges, and was placed in *Tatler* magazine's 101 Best Hotel Destinations in the World Awards 2002. The main house is set back, with gentle lawns rolling down to the pool, which appears to be part of the river. Meals are elegant affairs, particularly dinners, when you're waited on hand and foot by staff in white uniforms and red fez hats, after which you may choose to take a drink in the library or flop into your huge bed, romantically swathed in mosquito nets. The stilted split-level bungalows are built overlooking the river—and the bathrooms, which are almost within touching distance of the river, are a real highlight.

Bookings through SA: ⓒ **27/11/883-0747.** Lodge: 260/97-771032. Fax 27/11/883-0911. www.wilderness-safaris.com. 10 units. High season (July–Oct): US$730 double.Mid season (Apr-June and Nov): US$540. Low season: US$390. Rates are all-inclusive except for premium brand alcohol imports. MC, V. **Amenities:** Dining room; lounge; pool; bush golf; laundry; library; sunset cruises; trips to Zambian side of falls, Mosi-Oa-Tunya National Park, Livingstone and Railway Museum, croc farm, Jewish tour and local African village; croquet; boule; canoeing; fishing. All adventure activities arranged at extra cost.

Tongabezi Lodge ✦✦✦ Situated 20km (12½ miles) upstream from the falls, and overlooking a broad expanse of the Zambezi, Tongabezi Lodge is set in a grove of African ebony trees. Guests can choose to stay in one of the cottages, each with a separate lounge and private veranda overlooking the river, or one of three thatched houses—huge units, open to the elements, and definitely the best choice, particularly **Tree House** and **Honeymoon House.** Like the River Club, taking a bath here is a real highlight, with no walls and tubs low enough to feel as if you're almost part of the Zambezi. For the ultimate in romance ask for a "sampan dinner" (included in the rate), where guests have a private candlelit dinner on a raft, and the waiters bring the courses by canoe. For those who don't mind roughing it a bit (i.e., flushing toilets and running cold water, but hot bucket showers and candles only), a night at the satellite **Sindabezi Island Camp** is a must. Located on an island 3km (1¾ miles) downstream from Tongabezi Lodge, the four thatched chalets have wonderful views of the river and the floodplains of the Zambezi National Park beyond. During the low-water season (July–Mar), Tongabezi also organizes trips to and champagne lunches on Livingstone Island, perched right on the edge of the falls. They can also arrange for you to overnight here—an unbelievable privilege, especially during full moon when there's a lunar rainbow.

Private Bag 31, Livingstone. ℂ 260/97-770-917/18. Fax 263/97-840-920. www.tongabezi.com. Tongabezi 9 units; Sindabezi 4 units. High season: US$620–$790 double; Sindabezi US$400 double. Tongabezi rates include all meals, local beverages, and all amenities listed. Children 7 and up. MC, V. **Amenities:** Dining room/bar; pool; (grass) tennis; laundry; bush/gorge walks; canoeing; fishing; bird walks; game drives; visit to Zambian side of falls; sunrise and sunset boat cruises.

5 Where to Dine

Don't expect miracles from the few restaurants in the village. If the objective is to ward off hunger, you won't be disappointed, but this ain't no Michelin-star experience. During the day a highlight is to take high tea at the Victoria Falls Hotel and drink in the view with your Earl Grey.

For a romantic evening, you can't beat a "Moonlight Dinner" aboard the **Safari Express** (ℂ 263/13/42229; stan@steamtrain.co.zw; see "Getting Around: By Train," earlier in this chapter), though it's only available when a minimum number of people book the trip. A good, albeit rather formal, alternative (jacket and tie, no jeans or sneakers), is the **Livingstone Room** at the Victoria Falls Hotel.

Mama Africa, an old railway house that has been converted into a sort of jazz club with live music, is still the most popular option outside of the hotels, with good food and a great atmosphere. You'll find it next to the railway line, just past the Landela center (ℂ 263/13/41725). The **Cattleman** (Phumula Centre; ℂ 263/13/44767) styles itself as the home of the famous Zimbabwe steak. You'll find the best pizzas at **Pannarotis,** in the Kingdom Hotel.

The **Royal Livingstone** (www.suninternational.com) is by far the best dining option in Livingstone, though the **Tongabezi Lodge** has some fabulous options as well (see "Where to Stay," above).

The Boma ZIMBABWEAN The Boma, situated in the Gusu Forest and partly open to the night sky, promises a unique cultural experience that involves all the senses. On arrival, guests partake in a hand-washing ceremony before sampling traditional beer and snacks. The four-course meal combines a la carte starters with a barbecue buffet that includes such local delicacies as *mopani* worms and game stews (although more standard fare and vegetarian dishes are also available). Entertainment is provided by Shangaan dancers and singers, as well as the restaurant's traditional storyteller, who regales guests with tales of the country's folklore, culture, and heritage.

Lokuthula Lodge (part of Victoria Falls Safari Lodge). ℭ 263/13/43238. Reservations recommended. US$18. AE, DC, MC, V. Open daily year-round from 7pm until late.

6 Shopping

Most shops are off Park Way Drive or off Livingstone Way, with the main shopping centers being the Landela Centre in Elephant's Walk off Livingstone Way (situated behind the Post office, next to Sopers Curios) and those situated in The Kingdom hotel. If you prefer a more memorable shopping experience, and bargain prices, you can find handcrafted items for next to nothing on the streets, as street hawkers selling handsome wood carvings, woven baskets, and Zimbabwean batik fabrics are a dime a dozen. But be warned: This can be an intimidating experience, as desperation (you may represent the only chance of a meal for weeks to come) can result in some pushy behavior and even sometimes fights breaking out between the hawkers. All of course are prepared to bargain, but before you drive those prices down, also keep in mind that cheap curios are putting pressure on the hardwood forests and may mean that these desperately poor people end up chopping down a tree for a couple of bucks. If you're into more serious articles (Zimbabwean sculptors are world-renowned for their soapstone creations), consider visiting **Falls Craft Village** (Stand 206, Soper's Crescent, off Livingstone Way; ℭ **263/13/4309;** daily 8:30am–4:30pm), a complex consisting of the reconstructed huts of five different Zimbabwean tribes from the 19th century, with numerous shops and stalls; or **Soper's Curios** (1911 Adam Stander Rd., Victoria Falls; ℭ **263/13/4361;** daily 8am–6pm), which has been trading in Zimbabwean artifacts since 1911, and where you can still find some of the best wood and soapstone carvings.

10

Original Eden: Botswana

by Tracey Hawthorne & David Rogers

Botswana is known to be southern Africa's premier wilderness destination, largely because of the tranquil Okavango Delta, a 15,000-sq.-km (5,790-sq.-mile) inland flood plain that fans out in the northwestern corner of the country, creating a paradise of palms, papyrus, and crystal-clear channels and backwaters. Set in a massive sea of desert sand, this fragile wonderland of waterways, islands, and forests is an oasis for wildlife, drawn to its life-giving waters from the surrounding thirstlands. Here, the evening air is filled with the sounds of birds calling, frogs trilling, and antelope rustling in the reeds; wildebeest, hartebeest, buffalo, and zebra roam the islands, elephants wade across channels guarded by hippos and crocs, and predators rule the night.

But it is not only animals and birds that are attracted to this huge, verdant oasis. Because the area is so sensitive, the Botswana government operates a policy of low-volume, high-income tourism, making it a pricey holiday destination—but this doesn't stop thousands from flocking to one of the world's most game-rich and unspoiled wilderness areas. To service these visitors, scores of safari companies have been established in and around the delta, particularly in the Moremi Game Reserve, situated in the northeastern sector of the delta. Because it is both expensive and complicated to travel independently in Botswana (huge distances are involved and the road network is poor) and almost

impossible in the delta itself, visitors are advised to contact one of these companies to arrange their trip. Most offer full-package holidays that cover the delta and surrounds, and will organize everything for you, including flights, transfers, accommodations, and game-viewing trips.

Bear in mind that if you do a whistle-stop visit, flying in one night and out the next day, you are likely to be disappointed. The delta has its own unique moods and rhythms, and to experience these you'll need at least 2 full days, preferably 4.

There is more to Botswana than the delta, however. To the northeast lies Chobe National Park, a 12,000-sq.-km (4,630-sq.-mile) home to some 100,000 elephants, while to the southeast are the spectacular Makgadikgadi and Nxai pans, where the space is so vast that, it is said, you can hear the stars sing. Most safari companies include the Chobe and its surrounds on their itineraries, and some venture south into the endless horizons of the Kalahari pans.

Like so many of Africa's wilderness areas, the delta is under threat from human need. A shortage of good grazing on adjacent lands makes the lush grass in the delta a standing temptation to stock farmers, especially in times of drought. The demands of Botswana's diamond-mining industry and the ever-expanding town of Maun (gateway to the delta), both thirsty for water, pose an ongoing threat to the delta's precious liquid reserves, as does

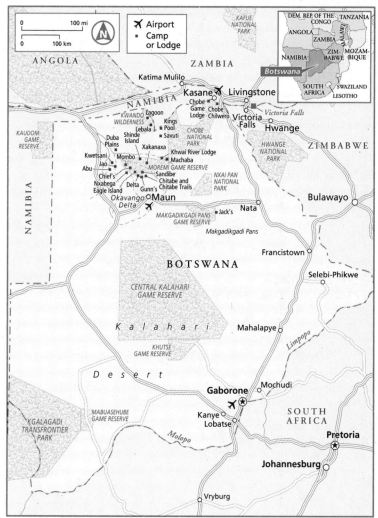

the proposed dam at Popa Falls, Namibia. All of which means that, if you want to experience the untamed Africa of Hemingway, Roosevelt, and Blixen, a trip to Botswana should enjoy the highest priority.

1 Orientation

VISITOR INFORMATION

The **Department of Tourism** has a website (www.gov.bw), but much of the information there (like Maun telephone numbers) is outdated. You can write to the department at Box 131, Gaborone (fax 267/391-2354) or call ℂ **267/397-1405,** but for more relevant and accessible information on the region we suggest you read some of the useful features published in **_Getaway,_** Africa's largest-circulation travel magazine; look them up on **www.getawaytoafrica.com** and click on

Botswana. If you're considering a self-drive safari, you will need to contact **Department of Wildlife and National Parks** (© 267/397-1405; dwnpbots@ global.bw). For essential information on Botswana, including getting there, travel documents, health, and more, see chapter 2.

BOTSWANA TOURISM REPRESENTATIVES

In the U.S.: Kartagener Associates Inc. (631 Commack Rd., Suite 1A, Commack, NY 11726; © **631/585-1270;** fax 631/585-1279; kainyc@att.net).

In the U.K.: Southern Skies Marketing (Barlow Mow Centre, 10 Barlow Mow Passage W4 4PH; © **44/20/8400-6113;** fax 44/20/8987-0488; skiesinfo@aol. com).

GETTING THERE

BY PLANE **SAA, British Airways,** and **Air Botswana** connect the country with the outside world (see chapter 2 for contact details for all of these airlines). To get to the **Okavango Delta,** most (if not all) operators will arrange for you to fly into Maun (or Kasane) and then transfer you to your delta camp by charter flight. To reach **Chobe National Park,** you will need to fly to the Kasane airport, then transfer by air or road.

GETTING AROUND

BY PLANE From Maun, visitors usually join overland safari operators or fly in light aircrafts into their camps. There are many charter companies operating out of Maun; **Sefofane** (© 267/686-0778) is one of the biggest. Each leg of your journey will cost in the region of $180. This is a very exciting way to travel: The plane often has to buzz an airstrip to clear it of herds of grazing animals, and if you're lucky the "departure/arrivals" lounge consists of a bench under a tree.

BY CAR Traveling under your own steam at your own pace could be the adventure of a lifetime and gives you a great deal of freedom, but you won't necessarily save money and it will certainly impact on your time. Your best option is to concentrate on one area—say Chobe—and hire a fully-equipped four-wheel-drive and camping vehicle (fitted out with tables, chairs, cutlery, and bedding). Safer still is to take a guided self-drive trip, which lets you enjoy the experience of driving through Botswana but safely under supervision. Both are offered by **Britz** in South Africa (© 011/396-1860; fax 011/3961937; www.britz.co.za; see "Getting Around," in chapter 2 for rates). In Botswana, try **Avis** (© 267/686-0039), which has a stand opposite the airport (no street address) in Maun. If you

---

Tips Lightening Your Load

Anyone flying in these light charter aircraft should remember that the weight restriction for luggage is usually 10 to 12 kilograms (22 lb.–26 lb.) per person. If you're leaving from and returning to Johannesburg, you can transfer any essentials to a small soft-sided bag and store your heavy bags in the very convenient luggage-storage facility in the Jo'burg airport (Maun and Kasane airports also have luggage-storage facilities, but at this time we don't recommend using them). Or check with your safari operator or ground handler to see what services they provide—a number of them will offer to store your luggage at their offices in Maun or Kasane while you're on safari.

need tents and cooking equipment, make arrangements through **Kalahari Canvas** (✆ **267/686-0568**), which is also near the airport.

To **rent a car,** you must be 25 or older. Your home driving license is good for 6 months (as long as it's in English).

WITH A PACKAGE TOUR   In Botswana it really is worth using an established operator to make your bookings, or at least compare package prices before booking—going it alone can be as expensive as buying a car from spare parts. Packages include, among other things, the flight to Botswana; travel to and accommodations in Maun; transport to the lodge or base camp; accommodation; food and soft drinks (in many cases all alcoholic drinks except for imported liquors); game-viewing, fishing, and photographic expeditions; professional guides; boat hire; and mokoro trips (sometimes you pay extra for park entry fees). See recommended operators under "Specialist Safaris," below.

BOTSWANA BUSH CAMPS: WHAT TO EXPECT

ACCOMMODATIONS   A holiday spent in Botswana, and particularly in the delta area and its surrounds, is not a traditional "hotel" experience (though the Orient Express group comes pretty close!)—operators are awarded a mere 5-year concession by the Botswana government and must leave no permanent mark on the land, so camps are generally raised and built with thatch, timber, and/or canvas. The managers of these camps, many of them husband-and-wife teams, put a high premium on hospitality, however, whether your choice is comfortably rustic or luxuriously colonial. In the tented camps, accommodations are in generously-sized en-suite safari tents and the food is usually prepared in tented bush kitchens. In most camps, laundry can be done on a daily basis.

Visitors to the delta should bear in mind at all times that they are in a wilderness area: Most of the camps and lodges are unfenced, and dangerous animals roam through them. Stay alert and never wander the grounds without a guide or ranger after dark. For more details, see "Safety," in chapter 2.

DINING   Botswana doesn't have an ethnic cuisine to call its own, and food in the camps and lodges is generally designed to appeal to a wide range of cosmopolitan tastes. Although standards vary, most pride themselves on serving wholesome, home-baked fare, and, in the lodges and fixed camps, kitchens can be surprisingly sophisticated. Some, like Orient-Express (formerly Gametrackers), employ chefs who design menus of international standard. Expect the choice of a full English or continental breakfast, including fresh fruit, imported at great expense. Morning and afternoon tea are institutions at most lodges. Game is served in some lodges (although not in those situated in game reserves), so more adventurous diners can experiment with crocodile steaks, gemsbok (oryx) filets, and the like.

South African beers and wines are available in all lodges and camps, and in many camps are included in the rates.

A TYPICAL DAY   You will be woken up early, just before sunrise, with coffee or tea to warm you before the morning game drive. It is often very cold; remember to take a warm jacket, but don't forget a hat and sunscreen—the sun can get downright fierce by the end of the morning, especially in the summer. (In some camps, breakfast is followed by a walk or on a mokoro trip along the channels, with lunch served on an island somewhere far from the camp.) After lunch, guests have the afternoons to rest before regrouping around 4pm for the afternoon game drive, which often includes a stop at a scenic (and open) spot for a sundowner and some snacks as the sun sets. In most camps, afternoon drives turn into early-evening drives where a spotlight is used to help you spy on nocturnal creatures. Once back at the camp, you share cocktails and dinner with your fellow lodge mates (often communally at a big, candlelit table on a raised open-air dining area). After dinner, it is not unusual to be entertained by the camp manager or one of the local guides, who will thrill you with stories of life in the delta. And when it's time for bed, a guide escorts you back to your room or tent.

FAST FACTS: **Botswana**

American Express The office is located in **Manica Travel Services,** Broadhurst Industrial Centre, Unit 4, Gaborone (© **267/391-2677**).

Airport See the "Getting There" sections in this chapter as well as in chapter 2.

Banks **In Maun: Standard Chartered** and **Barclays** are both open Monday through Friday from 8:15am to 12:45pm, and Saturday from 8:15am to 10:45pm.

Business Hours Banks are generally open Monday, Tuesday, Thursday, and Friday from 9am to 2:30pm, Wednesday from 8:15 to noon, and Saturday from 8 to 10:45am. Shop hours are Monday through Friday from 8am to 1 or 2pm, and Saturday from 8:30am to 1pm.

Car Rentals See "Getting Around By Car," earlier in this chapter, and also "Getting Around by Car," in chapter 2.

Currency See "Money," in chapter 2.

Dentist Call the **Delta Dental Clinic in Maun** (© **267/686-4224**); the offices are near the Standard Chartered Bank.

Documents See "Visitor Information & Entry Requirements," in chapter 2.

Directory Inquiries Dial © **192**.

Doctor If you need a doctor in Maun, the **Delta Medical Centre** is on the Tsheko-Tsheko road which runs through the center of town (© **267/686-1411**).

Drugstore Drugstores are called chemists or pharmacies in Botswana. **Okavango Pharmacy** (© **267/686-0043**) is on Maun's main street, in the Lewis Building opposite Riley's garage complex.

Electricity As in the rest of southern Africa, you'll need an adapter/voltage converter. Botswana uses 220/240V 15/13 amp plug sockets. Plugs are 2- and 3-pin, round and flat. Remember that many bush camps do not have electricity, but run on generators.

Embassies & Consulates Note that all offices are in Gaborone. The **U.S. Embassy** is on Embassy Drive, Government Enclave (© **267/395-3982;** fax 267/391-2782); the after-hours emergency telephone number is © **267/357-111.** The **British High Commission** (© **267/395-2841;** fax 267/395-6105) is found at 1079 Queens Rd. The **Canadian Consulate** is located in the Vision Hire Building, Queens Road, Plot 82 (©/fax **267/390-4411**).

Emergencies **Medical Rescue International,** call © **267/391-3231**) or **911;** ambulance, call © **997;** fire, call © **998;** police, call © **999.** If you are on a mobile phone, call © **112.**

Hospitals **Maun General Hospital** (© **267/686-0444**) is 2km (1¼ mile) along the main Ghanzi Road in Maun.

Language English is widely spoken.

Safety Consult your physician (or a travel-health specialist) before leaving about starting a course of anti-malarial prophylactics, and note that children under the age of 12 are generally not allowed in game lodges unless special arrangements have been made with the management. For more information, see "Health, Safety & Insurance," in chapter 2.

Taxes Sales tax is 10% and is included in all prices quoted in this chapter, unless otherwise indicated.

Telephone Phone calls can be made from any post office or business that provides office services. Public call boxes are found in towns. Remember, this chapter lists numbers for Botswana and South Africa, indicated by their country codes. Botswana has no regional or town codes. There are no telephones in the delta. The camps communicate with Maun and each other via radio, and can transmit emergency messages this way. If you do have a satellite phone, you will be asked to keep it switched off.

To call southern Africa from another country: Dial international access code (United States or Canada 011, United Kingdom or New Zealand 00, Australia 0011), plus country code (**27** for **South Africa, 263** for **Zimbabwe, 267** for **Botswana,** and **260** for **Zambia**), plus local number minus the 0 at the beginning of the city/area code.

To make an international call: Dial 00, wait for dial tone, then dial the country code (United States or Canada 1, United Kingdom 44, Australia 61, New Zealand 64), the area code, and the local number.

To make calls within Botswana: Drop the 267 country code; there are no area codes.

To charge international calls: The toll-free international access code for **Sprint** is © **0800-180-280.** At press time, there was no international access code for AT&T and MCI.

Time Zone Botswana is 2 hours ahead of GMT, or 7 hours ahead of Eastern Standard Time.

Tipping Tipping at bush and delta camps is at guests' discretion, but a good rule of thumb is $5–$10 per person per day, to be shared among the staff. The average for guides is $5–$10 per day.

Water Water in all the camps is drinkable, but most camps/lodges do supply plenty of bottled mineral water. There is some disagreement about the safety of water in the smaller towns—to be on the safe side, drink bottled water or bring along a purification system.

When to Go Most operators consider the winter months (July–Oct) as high season; it's cooler, and the delta is usually flooded.

2 Specialist Safaris & Operators

You'll have no trouble finding safari operators or packages, which run the gamut to suit a range of interests and pockets, from fly-in safaris to luxurious lodges to all-hands-on-deck–type trips with nights under canvas.

Contacting Safari Operators

- **Abercrombie & Kent   In the United States:** 1520 Kensington Rd., Oak Brook, IL 60523-214 (℡ **630/954-2944**). **In the United Kingdom:** Sloane Square House, Holbein Place, London SWIW 8NS (℡ **0207/ 730-9600**). **In South Africa:** 31 Harley St., Ferndale, Randburg, or P.O. Box 782607, Sandton 2146 (℡ **27/11/781-1497**; fax 27/11/781-0733; www.abercrombiekent.com).

- **Bush Ways Safari   In Botswana:** Private Bag 342, Maun (℡ **267/ 686-3685**; www.bushways.com).

- **Conservation Corporation Africa (CC Africa)   In South Africa:** Private Bag X27, Benmore 2010 (℡ **011/809-4300**; fax 011/809-4315). **In Botswana:** Kasane Operations Base, P.O. Box 323, Kasane (℡ **267/ 650-119 or 650-617**; www.ccafrica.com).

- **Orient-Express Safaris   In South Africa:** P.O. Box 786432, Sandton 2146 (℡ **27/11/481-6052**; fax 27/11/481-6065; www.orient-express-safaris.com).

- **Game Trail   In Botswana:** Private Bag 62, Maun, Botswana (℡/fax **267/66-2405**; gametrail@info.bw).

- **Hartley's Safaris   In South Africa:** P.O. Box 69859, Bryanston 2021 (℡ **27/11/467-4704**; fax 27/11/467-4758; www.hartleys.co.za).

- **Ker & Downey   In the United States:** 2825 Wilcrest Dr., Suite 600, Houston, TX 77042-6007 (℡ **800/423-4236** or 713/917-0048; fax 713/ 917-0123). **In Botswana:** P.O. Box 27, Maun (℡ **267/686-0375**; fax 267/686-1282; www.kerdowney.com).

- **Kwando Safaris   In Botswana:** P.O. Box 550, Maun (℡ **267/686-1449**; fax 267/686-1457; www.kwando.co.za).

- **Moremi Safaris & Tours   In Botswana:** Private Bag 26, Maun (℡ **267/686-0351**; fax 267-6860571). **In South Africa:** P.O. Box 2757, Cramerview 2060 (℡ **27/11/465-3842**; fax 27/11465-3779; www. moremi.co.za).

- **Okavango Tours & Safaris   In the United Kingdom:** Marlborough House, 298 Regents Park Rd., London N32TJ (℡ **44/020/8343-3283**; fax 44/020/8343-3287). **In Botswana:** P.O. Box 39, Maun (℡ **267/66-0220**; fax 267/66-0589; www.okavango.com).

- **Penduka Safari   In Namibia:** ℡ **264/61/239643**; www.penduka.com.

- **Uncharted Africa Safari Co.   In Botswana:** P.O. Box 173, Francistown, Botswana (℡ **267/241-2277**; fax 267/241-3458; www.unchartedafrica. com).

- **Wilderness Safaris   In South Africa:** P.O. Box 78573, Sandton 2146 (℡ **27/11/883-0747**; fax 27/11/883-0911; www.wilderness-safaris.com).

MOBILE SAFARIS

Most people with limited time opt for fly-in "mobile safaris" (in other words, move between camps). Bear in mind that one of the best ways to appreciate the broad changes of landscape in Botswana is to plan a trip that comprises the

Delta (try to visit both a "wet" and "dry" camp), Chobe, and the Kalahari. Depending on your budget and what you want to get out of your trip, mobile safaris range from basic participation tours, where you will, for instance, be expected to erect your own tent, to the ultra-luxurious where the only time you lift a finger is to summon another cold drink. Participants are transported in a suitably modified open vehicle (or mokoro), and camp or lodge overnight at predetermined destinations, before flying to the next camp. (For contact information for the following operators, see "Contacting Safari Operators," above. For separate reviews on top camps, "owned" by these operators, see "Where to Stay & Dine" later in this chapter.)

   Note: If you're looking to compare prices, contact **Drifters Adventours** *✪* (*✆* **27/11/888-1160;** fax 11/888-1020; www.drifters.com), another good-value operator running extremely low-cost participation camping safaris to Botswana and other parts of southern Africa. Their North American agent is **Premier Tours** (*✆* **800/545-1910** or 215/893-9966; www.premiertours.com).

Abercrombie & Kent *✪✪✪*   This top-end operator needs no introduction—you'll want for nothing. Botswana Hemingway is its most popular luxury option, which incorporates the desert (the Kalahari), the delta, the savanna (Chobe), and Vic Falls. It lasts for 11 days and costs $7,190 per person sharing including all land arrangements.

Bush Ways Safaris *✪ Value*   This operator offers small and custom participation tours, best suited for more adventurous travelers. Guests stay in small dome tents and travel overland in an open Land Rover. Several itineraries are offered, taking in all parts of Botswana including Chobe, Moremi, the delta, Makgadikgadi, and the Kalahari. Cost for the 15-day Lion Trail through northern Botswana is $1,695 per person including food and activities.

Mike Penman's Wild Safaris *✪✪✪*   Voted one of the top 15 safari guides in the world by *Condé Nast Traveler,* Penman—who has produced and facilitated a number of wildlife documentaries—offers private (usually for four guests), custom-made tented safaris for people with an interest in photography or filmmaking. For contact information, see "Photography & Film Safaris," below.

Orient-Express Safaris *✪✪✪*   Voted the "World's Leading Safari Operator" at the 2001 World Travel Awards, Orient-Express (formerly Gametrackers) owns only three camps in Botswana: two in the delta (one "dry" and one "wet" camp) and one in Chobe. In true Orient-Express style, it offers top-of-the-range luxury—at a price. Four nights at any or all of the camps costs a minimum of US$2,224 to US$2,739 per person depending on season, including everything but your ticket to Maun.

Penduka Safari *✪*   Based in Namibia but one of the most established mobile safari companies in Botswana, Penduka offers fully-catered camping trips in national park campsites situated throughout most parts of the country. Its 11-day trip through northern Botswana costs US$2,240 a person; 9 days in central Kalahari costs US$2,100 a person.

Uncharted Africa Safari Co. *✪✪✪*   This is the number-one operator in Botswana's Kalahari and one of the classiest operators in Africa—expect Damask linen, bone-handle cutlery, and outstanding guides. The luxurious "HQ" camp (Jack's Camp; see later in this chapter) is complemented by a funky budget resort option (Planet Baobab; see later in this chapter). Mobile expeditions into the desert, as well as trips north to the delta and Chobe, are also offered.

Fun Fact **What's a Mokoro?**

A *mokoro* is a narrow canoelike boat propelled by a human poler. Traditionally they were made out of hollowed tree trunks, but for environmental reasons many camps now use mokoros made from fiberglass. These are silent craft, enabling you to get close to birds and animals, and are ideally suited to the shallow waters of the delta.

Wilderness Safaris ★★★   This South Africa–based company, which was the world's first recipient of *National Geographic Traveler's* World Legacy Award for sustainable ecotourism in 2002, offers superb all-round service, from silky-smooth transfers to a high standard of guiding. It also owns the most camps in the delta and offers lodges in three categories to suit various budgets: vintage, classic, and premier. The popular 11-day Jacana Safari offers a combination of cross-country drives and light aircraft transfers, providing access to the prime areas of northern Botswana and accommodation in premier and classic camps. The itinerary includes the Okavango Delta, Linyanti, Chobe National Park, and Victoria Falls. From November to June it costs US$3,950 per person sharing; from July to October (high season in the delta) it's US$4,495. The 11-day Mopani Safari follows the same itinerary but includes accommodation in the vintage and classic camps (comfortable, en-suite tents but quite basically outfitted in relation to premier camps); this 11-day safari costs US$1,580 to US$1,870, depending on the season.

MOKORO & CAMPING EXPEDITIONS

The cheapest and one of the most adventurous ways to enjoy the delta is to pack a bag and a tent and join a mokoro trip through the islands, accompanied by a poler with an intimate knowledge of these waters.

Okavango Tours & Safaris ★ *Value*   Best known for its excellent-value tented delta camp, Oddballs, and mokoro camping trips (see "Delta on a Budget," below).

ELEPHANT-BACK SAFARIS

Abu Camp ★★★   Touted by many as the ultimate Okavango experience, this camp—in a fabulous game-rich concession in the western part of the delta—lets you explore the waterways of the region on the back of an elephant. The chief elephant is Abu, star of such motion pictures as *The Power of One, Circles in the Forest,* and Clint Eastwood's *White Hunter Black Heart,* who leads a herd of 12 African elephants, comprising 5 adults and 7 youngsters ranging from 4 months to 40 years of age. Guests are transported in comfortable, custom-made saddles. Elephants not only cope in water and sand with equal ease but also get very close to other game. Accommodation is in six extremely luxurious, custom-designed en-suite tents, beautifully furnished (we're talking kilim carpets and mahogany four-poster beds) and raised on teak decking with a private viewing platform overlooking a lagoon. The only potential drawback for someone with limited time is that you have to stay here for the full 5 nights.

Private Bag 332, Maun. ☎ 267/686-1260. Fax 267/686-1005. www.elephantbacksafaris.com. The 5-night, 6-day, all-inclusive (except for airfare) elephant-themed safari costs about US$7,500 per person. The camp is closed during the wet season between mid-Dec and the end of Feb. There are no seasonal discounts. Accounts must be settled electronically prior to visit. Children under age 12 not permitted. **Amenities:** Main mess tent; swimming pool; well-stocked library.

HORSE SAFARIS

Limpopo Valley Horse Safaris ⭐⭐   These 3- to 10-day horse safaris take place in the Mashatu Game Reserve, where the focus is often on riding with the vast elephant herds. You can either stay in camp every night or opt to explore the area by overnighting in bush camps—the latter is recommended. The first night is spent at **Fort Jameson,** a rustic camp with double safari tents that include en-suite flush toilets and hot-water showers . The next nights are spent in bush camps comprising dome tents, stretchers, and sleeping bags. There are bucket showers and long drops. The horses have been individually selected for temperament and rideability, but again you need to be experienced.

Limpopo Valley Horse Safaris. ✆ **27/31/765-2900l** or 27/12/207-1440. www.lvhsafaris.co.za. Cost: US$200–US$230 per person per night, including the horse, safari, accommodation, and meals. Children under age 16 not permitted.

Okavango Horse Safaris ⭐⭐⭐   These safaris are run in a private concession in the western delta bordering Moremi Game Reserve and take you deep into the wetlands. Expect to spend between 4 and 6 hours a day in the saddle. Minimum riding ability required is a mastery of the basics, including an ability to trot for stretches of 10 minutes at a time and—even more important—the ability to gallop out of trouble! The maximum weight limit is 95 kg (210 lb.). The tack is English style, and each saddle has a seatsaver for comfort. Trail riders move from **Kujwana Camp** (spacious safari tents with shower en-suite and flush toilets) to **Moklowane** (tents have bucket-and-pulley showers and safari toilets) to **Fly Camp** (dome tents with camp beds, long drop toilets, and bucket showers). A maximum of eight riders is taken, and the safaris last between 5 and 10 days.

In Botswana, Private Bag 23, Maun. ✆ **267/686-1671.** Fax 267/686-1672. www.okavangohorse.com. For a 5- or 10-night safari combining 2 or 3 camps the rate is US$432 per person per night June 1–Oct 31. For the rest of the year (except Jan–Feb and Dec, when the camps are closed) the rate is US$378 per person per night. These prices are all-inclusive. Air transfers are US$180 per person return from Maun. There is a 50% single supplement for people unwilling to share. No credit-card facilities. Children are accepted if they are strong, confident riders.

CYCLING SAFARIS

Mashatu ⭐⭐   Radio-linked groups of cyclists set out at dawn and again at dusk on mountain bikes in search of animals; visits to the ruins of 600-year-old settlements on the reserve are included. The program is entirely flexible and can be adapted to the needs and skills of the particular cyclists; game drives can also be included. These safaris are offered in the winter months of April through September, and are conducted from the Mashatu Tent Camp for a minimum of 10 guests and a maximum of 14 guests at no additional charge. For fewer than 10 guests, there is an additional charge of $9 extra per cycle. For more information, call ✆ **27/31/765-2900** (fax 27/31/765-3365; www.mashatu.com).

WALKING SAFARIS

Ker & Downey ⭐⭐   For a pioneer-type safari, take "Footsteps across the Delta"—a 3-day expedition where guests make their way by foot and mokoro from camp to camp. The emphasis is on enjoying the slow pace of the delta—the maximum distance each day is about 6km (3¾ miles) and you can travel light; while you cover the distance, the camp staff transports baggage and camp essentials. Accommodation is in twin-bedded en-suite tents. The cost is between US$370 and US$440 a night depending on the season. Minimum age is 16. For contact details, see "Contacting Safari Operators," earlier in this chapter.

PHOTOGRAPHY & FILM SAFARIS

Mike Penman's Wild Safaris ★★★ These highly adventurous, yet luxuriously tented, safaris focus on learning about wildlife while affording you the best opportunities to capture the experience on film. Penman has been involved in conservation, tracking, photography, and filmmaking in Botswana for 15 years (both producing his own documentaries and helping independent filmmakers and major TV networks), and he personally conducts safaris into Moremi, the delta, Kalahari, Makgadikgadi, Nxai Pans, and Drotsky's Caves. Penman is known for his bold approach to lions and ability to get right into the mix of things, placing you in a great position to capture the moment. Other, tamer photographic and birding safaris with professional guides are offered by Wilderness Safaris (see "Contacting Safari Operators," earlier in this chapter).

P.O. Box 66, Maun, Botswana. © 267/686-3644. Fax 267/686-1045. www.wildlifestyles.com. Luxury mobile safaris cost US$495 per person per day (US$395 in low season). Price excludes additional aspects like national park entry fees; check when booking.

CULTURAL SAFARIS

If you're interested in Bushman (or "San") culture, make sure you spend a few nights with Uncharted Africa Safari Co in the Kalahari (see Jack's & San Camp and Planet Baobab, later in this chapter). Uncharted will also, along with operators like Game Trails and Moremi Safaris & Tours, organize a visit to the **Tsodilo Hills** (in the northwest, near the panhandle), to see the more than 3,000 rock paintings there. These paintings are known for their fine clarity and wide variety, and trips can be made by air or four-wheel-drive. There is also a traditional village in the foothills. For contact details, see "Contacting Safari Operators," earlier in this chapter.

Visitors to the delta can now also immerse themselves in Bushman culture and folklore by spending a night at **Gudigwa,** a 100-percent-Bushman-owned camp that opened in April 2003. The Gudigwa community (a settlement of some 800 "Bukakhwe" Bushman) are indigenous to the Okavango Delta, and though they differ physically somewhat from the Bushman tribes of the Kalahari, their traditional ways of living off the land are very much the same. Guests are accommodated in one of eight large grass huts, all en-suite and comfortably furnished. The camp is situated 5km (3 miles) from the community so as not to disturb its daily life, but visitors are invited to walk with representatives to learn more about the bush, be it medicinal uses of plants, tracking game, or how to discover underground water. In the evenings villagers perform traditional dances and songs, and tell animated stories in their mother tongue—a language of "clicks" and guttural tones. The camp (www.gudigwa.com) is marketed on the Bukakhwe's behalf by **Wilderness Safaris** (see "Contacting Safari Operators," earlier in this chapter); cost during high season (July–Oct) is US$850 per room; Apr–June is $500. Rates are all-inclusive.

3 Maun, the Central Okavango Delta & Moremi Game Reserve

The small but sprawling town of Maun is the regional center of Ngamiland (northwestern Botswana) and the gateway to the Okavango Delta, of which the neighboring Moremi Game Reserve is the most popular destination. Not so long ago, progress (in the form of tarred roads and a couple of garish shopping malls) began creeping into this frontier town, which once resembled the Wild West. As the starting point for most trips into the delta, Maun has an airport, a few shopping areas, banks, a number of hotels and lodges, and a plethora of safari tour operators, most of which are based or represented here.

ESSENTIALS

VISITOR INFORMATION   There is a small **information center** at Maun airport (© 267/686-0222) and an office of the **Department of Wildlife and National Parks** (© 267/686-0368), but this is not the time to start planning your trip or booking transport or accommodation. See "Visitor Information," earlier in the chapter, as well as chapter 2, for resources before you go.

GETTING THERE   The easiest way to get to Maun is to fly **Air Botswana** from Johannesburg; the return flight costs in the region of R2,200 (US$275) per person. At press time, Air Botswana was also offering direct flights from Cape Town to Maun. See "Getting There," earlier in this chapter, as well as chapter 2, for more details on flying into Botswana.

MAUN
WHAT TO SEE & DO

Maun operates principally as a service center for the safari industry and not as a tourist attraction in its own right, so there isn't much to do or see in the town. There is no public transport in Maun, but it's not a big place and most destinations are reachable on foot. Take a stroll to the **Power Station** (near the airport; © 267/686-2037), located in what used to be a derelict coal-fired electricity generation plant where you can order a coffee from the restaurant, a drink from the bar, or wander the **Craft Center** (craftcentre@info.bw), which stocks a wide array of pottery, hand-made paper, wire objects, and other items produced in the region and beyond. Another shop worth browsing through is the **General Trading Company** (© 267/686-0025). The main outlet is located on the main road between Riley's Garage and Shoprite (open Mon–Fri 8am–5:30pm; Sat 8am–1pm). Besides crafts, General Trading Co. stocks a wide range of books, clothing, African music, stationery, and jewelry.

WHERE TO STAY & DINE

Ideally, you'll transfer directly to your wilderness camp without spending a night in Maun.

Riley's Hotel ✸   Although totally rebuilt since its founding in the 1930s, Riley's—conveniently situated on the main road near the town's central shopping areas—harkens back to the old Maun. Its shady gardens are reminiscent of the times when this was a popular watering hole for travelers who had come in on the dusty road from Francistown. Rooms are basic but comfortable, and there's good eating at Riley's Grill, while Harry's Bar is lively.

P.O. Box 1, Maun, Botswana. © 267/686-0204. Fax 267/686-0580. 51 units. US$130 double, includes breakfast. AE, DC, MC, V. **Amenities:** Restaurant; bar; pool; salon; curio shop. *In room:* A/C, TV, tea- and coffeemaking facilities, hair dryer.

THE OKAVANGO DELTA & MOREMI GAME RESERVE ✸✸✸

Located in the northwestern corner of the country, this region is for most the highlight of a trip to Botswana, particularly during the winter months (starting in July) when the "flood" turns it into an aquatic paradise. The northeastern segment of the delta has been set aside as the Moremi Game Reserve, an 1,800-sq.-km (695-sq.-mile) expanse of wilderness extending across both wetland and dry terrain. *Note:* Keep in mind that until new regulations come into force, camps *inside* the Moremi Game Reserve (a national park) are not allowed to have night game drives or drive off designated roads to follow game. Camps that border the reserve aren't bound by those regulations.

The delta originates in Angola, to the northwest, from where the Okavango River flows southward for 1,300km (806 miles) into the Kalahari. Thanks to the same geological activity that caused the Great African Rift Valley, the delta is more or less contained by fault lines between which the crust has sunk and filled up with sediment. It is into this bowl that the Okavango seeps, rather than making its rightful way to the sea. The annual southward flow of water is precipitated by the rainy season in the north, which begins in the Angolan uplands between January and March, and usually arrives at its southernmost point—the delta—around June or July, when the water spreads out to form innumerable pools, channels, and lagoons.

WHERE TO STAY & DINE

Chief's Camp ★★★ This luxury camp, opened by Abercrombie & Kent in 1999, is without a doubt one of the most luxurious in the delta (vying with Mombo and Jao), and situated in the exclusive Mombo Concession of the Moremi Game Reserve, an area that is regarded as the ultimate destination for predators in the delta. (Since the camp opened, more than 52 different lions have been identified in a 9km (5½-mile) radius, and leopard are seen every second or third game drive.) Game drives are conducted in open vehicles in the early morning and late afternoons (night drives are not allowed because it's in a national park). One of the main reasons to book here is that it offers the experience of both a wet and dry camp: from June to October mokoro activities are also offered. Accommodation is typical Abercrombie & Kent, with only 12 luxurious tents, each furnished with large twin beds and comfortable armchairs and featuring spacious well-equipped bathrooms and private viewing decks sheltered by jackalberry and sausage trees.

Book through Abercrombie & Kent (see "Contacting Safari Operators," earlier). Peak season (July–Oct): US$1,190. Green season (Nov and Apr–June): US$790. Low season (Dec–Mar): US$540. MC, V. Children between age 9 and 11 must share with an adult. No children under 9 years of age. **Amenities:** Dining area; bar; swimming pool; craft shop; library. In room: Ceiling fans, hair dryers, emergency telephones.

Chitabe and Chitabe Trails ★★ Situated on an island alongside the Moremi Game Reserve, with classic Okavango scenery of palm trees and open seasonally flooded plains, Chitabe is part of Wilderness Safari's "classic" collection—eight twin-bed en-suite tents that are built on wooden decks under a canopy of trees; with the option of spending a night sleeping under the stars in one of the camp's hides, this will appeal to the nature lover who wants an authentic bush experience. Chitabe Trails is a five-tented camp ideal for smaller parties; tents are similarly outfitted but not raised off the ground.

Book through Wilderness Safaris (see "Contacting Safari Operators," earlier). High season (July–Oct): US$1,050 double. Other (Nov 1–Dec 31; Jan–June 30): US$500–US$740. Rates are all-inclusive. V, MC. Children between age 8 and 12 are permitted but parents must book private game-drive vehicle. **Amenities:** Lounge/dining area; bar; pool.

Delta Camp ★★ *Kids* This is one of the most interesting and tastefully decorated camps in the delta, with stilted cabins cleverly designed so that one side remains completely open to the bush. The most exciting unit is built 20m (65 ft.) up in the topmost branches of a tree! A water-based camp, Delta is situated on the southern shores of Chief's Island and specializes in mokoro trips and walking safaris; this is also one of the few camps to accept children.

Book through Okavango Tours & Safaris (see "Contacting Safari Operators," earlier). 12 units. US$924 double, all-inclusive. MC, V. Children between the ages of 2 and 12 are charged 50% of full price. Children under age 2 are charged 10% of full price. **Amenities:** Dining area; deck; bar.

Duba Plains ★★★ *(Value)*   Located in the farthermost reaches of the delta, Duba is another of Wilderness Safari's "classic" camps, but this is one of that group's best. Situated in a 35,000-hectare (86,450-acre) private reserve, with breathtaking grass plains and gin-clear freshwater pools, it is particularly suited to people who want a comfortable but not stuffy experience. A small camp (only six tents, each with fine linens and a veranda overlooking the floodplains) offers excellent value in terms of game viewing: it is known for its large herds of buffalo (1,500–3,000), which in turn attract lions—the camp is in fact sometimes referred to as the "Lion Capital of Africa"; it's not unusual for guests to see up to 15 lions a day! Guests may choose among game drives (it's a private reserve, so night drives are also on offer), mokoro rides (dependent on flood waters, best is usually May–Oct), and walking safaris. The standard of guiding at all Wilderness Safari Camps is extremely high, and Duba is no exception. It's the friendliest of camps as well, and the evening dinners around a big candlelit table in an open-air dining pavilion with staff and other guests are memorable.

Book through Wilderness Safaris (see "Contacting Safari Operators," earlier). High season (July–Oct): US$1,050 a night. Other (Nov 1–Dec 31; Jan–June): US$500–US$740. Rates all-inclusive. MC, V. Children between age 8 and 12 are permitted only if their parents accompany them in their own private vehicle. **Amenities:** Dining room; bar; pool on a raised terrace overlooking the plains; curio shop.

Eagle Island Camp ★★★   This camp, made up of 15 luxury tents, each with a private deck facing the lagoon, is located at Xaxaba, an island refuge deep in the Okavango. Besides affording you all the luxury you expect from the Orient-Express group, this is the ideal destination for birders. Set among the floodplains (the camp is only navigable by mokoro during the rainy season), Eagle Island enjoys a high concentration of fish eagles and other bird species including kingfishers, herons, cormorants, pelicans, darters, and storks. To augment your water-based game activities, game flights in light aircraft are also available on request, and Orient-Express regularly transfers guests from here to **Khwai,** their "dry" camp in neighboring Moremi, and **Savute Elephant,** their Chobe camp; both are a 25-minute flight away.

Book through Orient-Express Safaris (see "Contacting Safari Operators," earlier in this chapter) US$926–US$1,200 double, depending on the season. Rates are all-inclusive. AE, MC, V. No children under age 12 except by prior arrangement. **Amenities:** Open-air dining area; raised viewing deck with bar; heated swimming pool; shop; laundry service; illuminated walkways; book and video library; airstrip. *In room:* Hair dryer.

Jao Camp ★★★   Named after a Botswana chieftain, Jao Lodge (together with Mombo and the recently renovated King's Pool), is Wilderness Safaris' top camp. Located in one of the finest concessions in the delta, it covers 60,000 hectares (148,200 acres) and borders the Moremi Game Reserve, experiencing huge fluctuations in water levels, with views and game experiences ever-changing, depending on the time of year. But location aside, it is—from a style and luxury point of view—one of the most gorgeous camps in the delta, with Indonesian influences (suites are based on the Balinese long-house) a perfect match for the overall African ethos. The camp was designed by renowned architect Silvio Rech (Makalali, Ngorongoro), and it's one of his most restrained efforts: There's a zenlike simplicity and airy elegance that really soothes—the natural qualities of materials (from rich rosewood floors to white Indian cotton sheets) dominate both in color and texture and neatly offset the great views. The eight suites, all privately situated with viewing decks and connected via raised walkways, are built on stilts alongside a lily-speckled waterway.

Book through Wilderness Safaris (see "Contacting Safari Operators," earlier). High season (July–Oct): US$1,430 double; Other (Dec–Mar; Apr–June): US$600–US$930. Rates are all-inclusive. MC, V. Children between age 8 and 12 are permitted, but special arrangements must be made with management for private vehicles. **Amenities:** Dining area; lounge area; pool; crafts shop.

Khwai River Lodge ★★★

This is one of the oldest lodges in Botswana, opened in 1968 by Harry Selby (who, incidentally, worked for Philip Percival, immortalized by Hemingway as "Pop" in his *Green Hills of Africa*) and adjacent to Moremi. Today it is part of the Orient-Express Group, and arguably the most lavish lodge in the delta, with luxurious facilities that include air-conditioned tents, a heated swimming pool, and a video library. The camp—comprising 15 large twin-bedded tents, each with generous bathroom (his and her vanity units, and so on) and a private deck furnished with hammocks for comfortable eye-balling of the resident hippo and croc—is built in the shade of indigenous lead-wood and fig trees and overlooks the Khwai River floodplain, where you are likely to see large numbers of elephant. Your chances of spotting lion, hyena, wild dog, and leopard are equally high.

Book through Orient-Express Safaris (see "Contacting Safari Operators," earlier). 15 units. US$842–US$1,090 double, depending on the season. Rates all-inclusive. AE, MC, V. No children under age 12 except by prior arrangement. **Amenities:** Dining and lounge areas; bar; heated pool; shop; room service, laundry service; book and video library; VHS video and monitor; airstrip. *In room:* Minibar, hair dryers, fans, intercom.

Kwetsani Camp ★★

Situated in the stunning 60,000-hectare (148,200-acre) Jao Concession area to the west of Mombo and Moremi Game Reserve, this camp features five cute treehouse chalets built under thatched roofs (due to their smallish size the camp is rated "classic" by Wilderness Safaris rather than "premier," making it a relatively good value). Kwetsani is one of the area's small-est camps, allowing for personal service and guest interaction, and offers superb land and water activities, including night drives. Built on a heavily wooded island with mangosteen and fig trees, it is particularly beautiful from May to September when the water levels are at their highest, but the game viewing is best from October to April when the flood plains are dryer.

Book through Wilderness Safaris (see "Contacting Safari Operators," earlier). High season (July–Oct): US$1,050 double. Other (Nov–Dec; Jan–June): US$500–US$740. Rates all-inclusive. MC, V. Children between age 8 and 12 are permitted only if they are in a group with a private vehicle. **Amenities:** Dining area; lounge; bar; pool.

Machaba Camp ★★

Machaba offers great elephant viewing and excellent birding in what is known as the raptor capital of Botswana. It is located on the Khwai River on the northern edge of the Moremi Game Reserve, on the east-ernmost edge of the delta. Activities include game drives in Moremi National Park, night drives, and walks. Accommodation is in eight twin-bed safari-style en-suite tents with sewn-in floors and windows; the lodge has a viewing plat-form overlooking a hippo pool. Visits to a nearby San village are also on offer.

Book through Ker & Downey (see "Contacting Safari Operators," earlier). High season (July–Oct): US$900 double. Low season: US$740. Rates are all-inclusive. Closed Dec 1–Feb 28. DC, MC, V. No children under age 10. **Amenities:** Mess tent; bar; curio shop.

Mombo and Little Mombo ★★★

These two luxury camps are rated the best by seasoned Botswana travelers, not least because they are situated in the best game-viewing area in the delta (it's one of Botswana's top wildlife docu-mentary locations and has hosted *National Geographic* and BBC shoots). The camps are located on an island at the northwestern tip of Chief's Island, deep within the Moremi Game Reserve in an area where dense concentrations of plains game congregate. It is not unheard of to see 12 mammal species—from your veranda! Predators including all the big cats are frequently sighted; the area is especially good for leopard. As one of the new-style Wilderness Safari "premier" camps, Mombo has been completely rebuilt some 800m (2,600 ft.) from the original site and is made up of two camps—comprising three and nine tents respectively—that are connected by a long walkway more than 6 feet off the ground. This allows game to wander freely through the camp but at the same time provides for guest safety. Features include ragged thatch, wooden decks, and elegant furnished tented rooms (all natural materials and white cotton) the size of small houses. Meals are first-rate and plentiful, and you dine in beautiful open-air pavilions. Because it's in a national park, Mombo currently offers no night drives or off-road game viewing, but when new Moremi regulations come into force these too will be on offer.

Book through Wilderness Safaris (see "Contacting Safari Operators," earlier). US$880–US$1,590 double, depending on season. Rates are all-inclusive. MC, V. No children under age 8; July 1–Oct 31 this age limit increases to 12. **Amenities:** Each camp has a dining room; bar; lounging areas; 2 pools; curio shop.

Nxabega Okavango Safari Camp ★★   Like Sandibe, this is part of renowned operator CC Africa's stable (owners of Londolozi and Phinda). Situated deep in the delta, in a private concession in permanent waters on the western border of Moremi Game Reserve, the camp offers year-round wet and dry delta activities including game drives, mokoro trips, boating excursions, and nature walks. Rebuilt after a fire in 2000, it has the feel of a gentlemen's club, with burnished teak, crisp white linen, soft kudu-hide headboards, parchment lampshades, and dressing tables resplendent with leather boxes. Paneled walls are inset with enormous mirrors, bookshelves, and sculptures from around Africa. The ten classic East African safari–style en-suite tents are on raised wooden platforms with private verandas and feature all the comforts—from wardrobes to dressing tables.

Book through Conservation Corporation Africa (see "Contacting Safari Operators," earlier). High season (July–Oct): US$950 double. Low season (Nov–June): US$760. Rates are all-inclusive. There is a single supplement. DC, MC, V. Children welcome. **Amenities:** Dining room; lounge; pool; curio shop; interpretive center.

⟨Value⟩ Delta on a Budget

At a cost of US$198 per person per night, including activities and meals, **Oddball's** is one of the best-value "lodges" in the delta. The emphasis is very much on the young and fun, with a great viewing deck furnished with cushions—ideal for lounging and watching the sun set over Chief's Island. Accommodations are in dome tents set on raised platforms; mattresses, pillows, and a light are provided—you'll have to pack your own sleeping bag and towels. The communal ablution facilities have hot showers and flush toilets. The overnight mokoro camping trips (same price) are highly recommended—set off at dawn with your personal guide/mokoro poler and camp out in privacy in the game reserve; all provisions and equipment (tents, cookery, and such) are provided. It costs US$130 return to fly from Maun into Oddball's (it's accessible only by air); see "Okavango Tours & Safaris," earlier in this chapter.

Sandibe Safari Lodge ★★★   This is CC Africa's most popular Botswana camp (it has better views than Nxabega) with only eight African-style chalets, each with its own large private deck (furnished with hammocks) overlooking game-rich grassy plains, great outdoor showers, and the classy colonial-style fittings and furnishings CC Africa is renowned for. Sandibe is also in an excellent game-viewing area on the southern border of the Moremi Game Reserve (20km/12½ miles from Chief's Island) and adjacent to the Santantadibe river system, offering exclusive access to a vast area that includes permanent water. Sandibe offers land and water activities as well as bush walks and night drives.

Book through Conservation Corporation Africa (see "Contacting Safari Operators," earlier). High season (July–Oct): US$950 double. Low season (Nov–June): US$760. Rates all-inclusive. DC, MC, V. Children welcome. **Amenities:** Lounge/dining area; pool; curio shop. *In room:* hair dryers.

Shinde Island Camp ★★   On a lush palm island in the heart of the northern delta, Shinde is Ker & Downey's most luxurious Botswana camp, surrounded by waterways that teem with birds and game. With only eight twin-bed en-suite safari tents, each furnished with understated elegance, the camp is extremely relaxing, with wooden decks that blend in beautifully with the environment. From the veranda of your tent you can watch game moving across the plains and listen to the sounds of woodpeckers tapping in the trees. Activities include game drives, powerboat excursions, guided walks, fishing, and mokoro safaris.

Book through Ker & Downey (see "Contacting Safari Operators," earlier). Rates US$790–US$990 double depending on the season. High season is July 1–Oct 31. Closed Dec 1–Feb 28. DC, MC, V. No children under age 10. **Amenities:** Split-level dining area with a canvas domed roof; swimming pool; curio shop.

Xakanaxa Camp ★★   Situated within the Moremi Game Reserve, 50km (31 miles) to the west of Khwai in the northern sector of Moremi, Xakanaxa (pronounced ka-*ka*-ni-ka) offers year-round boating trips and extensive nature drives into good game country. The bird-watching is also excellent. The camp has two sections (one has 16 beds; try to book one of the tents in the more intimate eight-bedded camp) comprising East African safari–style tents with en-suite facilities. It may not be the most luxurious option, but it's one of the few camps located in the reserve itself, and offers incredibly good value during the low season.

Book through Moremi Safaris & Tours (see "Contacting Safari Operators," earlier). High season (July–Oct): US$900 double. Shoulder season (Apr–June): US$660. Low season (Nov–Mar): US$460. AE, V (both require prior authorization). **Amenities:** Both camps have open-fronted dining and lounge areas overlooking Xakanaxa Lagoon; pool; laundry; various game activities.

4 Chobe National Park & Surrounds ★★★

The Chobe National Park covers some 11,000 sq. km (4,250 sq. miles) of northern Botswana and offers extreme contrasts and a variety of wildlife experiences. It harbors a large proportion—some 100,000—of Botswana's elephant population (the largest in the world) and more than 460 different species of birds. In the dry season, the Chobe River is the only major source of water north of the Okavango, so game travels here from great distances. The nearby Savuti area, located in the west-central region, was once submerged beneath an enormous inland sea and connected to the Okavango and Zambezi rivers, but that was eons ago and today it's a relatively harsh wilderness landscape. Game viewing is at its peak at the end of the rainy season, when large numbers of zebra and wildebeest move through the area from the Linyanti farther west to the sweeter grasses on offer in the Mababe Depression to the south. Other wildlife to see here are giraffe, buffalo, tsessebe, and large prides of lion and hyena.

ESSENTIALS

VISITOR INFORMATION See "Visitor Information," at the start of the chapter. For information and reservations, go to "Contacting Safari Operators," earlier in the chapter, or one of the camp listings below.

GETTING THERE **By Plane** **Kasane International Airport** (© 267/ 625-0133) is 3km (about 2 miles) from the entrance to Chobe National Park. **Air Botswana** has connections from Gaborone, Maun, and Johannesburg. See "Getting There: By Plane," in chapter 2 for more information on flying into Botswana.

By Car From Victoria Falls, there's a road heading southwest to Kasane to explore the park.

GETTING AROUND For specific guidelines, car-rental information, and warnings, see "Getting Around: By Car," at the beginning of this chapter.

WHERE TO STAY & DINE

Chobe National Park's 35km (22 miles) of river frontage is relatively well developed for tourism: Splendid private lodges fringe the river, and the road network is generally in good condition. Note that Orient-Express also has a lodge here: **Savute Elephant Camp** is a great choice if you want to be cosseted in five-star luxury; rates are the same as Khwai River and Eagle Island (see above).

Chobe Chilwero ⋩⋩ Located near the main gates of the Chobe Reserve, this exquisite lodge offers a wonderful base from which to explore the Chobe National Park; it's also possible to arrange a day trip to Victoria Falls from here. Each large, luxury cottage has a private garden and/or private balcony with wonderful views over the Chobe River islands and flood plains as far as Namibia, huge hand-hewn bathrooms, and indoor and outdoor showers. In addition to game drives, the lodge offers specially adapted safari boats for sunset cruises along the river. Fishing is also available. *Note:* The lodge offers good value from December to March.

Book through Abercrombie & Kent (see "Contacting Safari Operators," earlier). 15 units. Peak season (July and Oct): US$920 double. Green season (Dec–Mar): US$640 double. DC, MC, V. **Amenities:** Dining area; lounge; swimming pool; viewing decks; wine cellar; library and e-communications center. *In room:* A/C.

Chobe Game Lodge ⋩⋩ Overlooking the Chobe River within the Chobe National Park, this is arguably the country's most elegant hotel, famed for having accommodated Liz Taylor and Richard Burton on their honeymoon (after they married for the second time). If the thought of being deep in the bush leaves you cold, Chobe is ideal, but it's very much a hotel experience. If you want to splurge on one of the four private suites, you can enjoy your own swimming pool and outside garden patio.

Reservations through P.O. Box 130555, Bryanston 2021, South Africa. © 27/11/706-0861, fax 27/11/706-0863. P.O. Box 32, Kasane, Botswana. © 267/25-0340. 50 units. US$720–US$840 double; suites US$1,000–US$1,160, depending on season. Rates include meals, game-viewing activities, Chobe National Park fees, and transfers from/to Kasane airport. Children's rates available on request. DC, MC, V. **Amenities:** Restaurant; lounge; bar; gift shop; conference center; wildlife reference library. *In room:* A/C, minibar, fans, hair dryer.

Kings Pool Camp ⋩⋩⋩ Substantially upgraded and reopened in May 2003, this is Wilderness Safari's premier camp in Chobe, and arguably the best in the region. Located in a private reserve in the Linyanti/Savuti Channel area, just outside the western boundary of the Chobe National Park, this is prime elephant country (it's not unusual to see 800 elephant in a single day!). Each of the nine large suites, built on raised teak decks, feature the ultimate in luxury: a private plunge pool and sala (small pavilion) with wonderful views of the Kings Pool Lagoon—this waterway has great birdlife; and hippos, crocodiles, bushbuck, impala, elephant, and sable are all seen from the rooms and private pools on a regular basis. Game-viewing activities include drives in open four-wheel-drive vehicles, night drives, walking with a professional guide, and cruising along the Linyanti River in a double-decker boat (water levels permitting). A cheaper alternative is its **Savuti Camp,** which is also open in summer (see below).

Book through Wilderness Safaris (see "Contacting Safari Operators," earlier). High season (July–Oct): US$1,430 double. Other (Nov–Dec; Apr–June): US$600–US$930 double. Rates are all-inclusive. MC, V. Children ages 8 and 12 are permitted through arrangement with management. **Amenities:** Dining; lounge; bar; pool.

Kwando Lagoon ★★ *Kids*   The Kwando wilderness sprawls over more than 2,300 sq. km (888 sq. miles), making it one of the largest privately-run wildlife areas in Africa. It has some 80km (50 miles) of river frontage on its eastern boundary. The area is noted for its large herds of elephants, especially during the winter months, as well as large numbers of large cats, buffalo, kudu, and tsessebe. If you want to spot Africa's rarest predator, the wild dog, this is the place to come—there has been a resident den on the concession for the past 4 years. With more than 320 species of birds recorded, it's also popular with birders. Kwando Safaris run two luxury tented camps on the river: **Lagoon Camp** and **Lebala Camp**—but the area is so vast that they are nearly 2 hours' drive apart. The former is more intimate, accommodating only 12 guests in stilted luxury safari tents. Lagoon Camp offers morning and night drives as well as boat cruises and fishing expeditions to catch the famed tiger fish. Good news for parents: Specialist guides for children are available.

P.O. Box 550, Maun, Botswana. © **267/686-1449.** Fax 267/686-1457. www.kwando.co.za. US$830–US$1,130 double depending on the season. Rates are all-inclusive. **Amenities:** Dining/lounge; pool; crafts shop.

Savuti Camp ★★ *Value*   If you haven't yet spotted lion, this tented camp, built along the Savuti Channel, lies in a region known for its large number of predators—it's possible to see wild dog, lion, and leopard in one day. Activities include game drives, night drives, and walks. The channel has been dry for some years, but the grasslands here make great game viewing, and the water hole in front of the camp is very productive. Accommodation is in five large walk-in tents; ask for one of the two rooms with dramatic bathrooms that open onto the channel.

Book through Wilderness Safaris (see "Contacting Safari Operators," earlier). High season (July–Oct): US$1,050 double. Apr–June and Nov: US$740 double. Dec–March: US$500 double. Rates are all-inclusive. MC, V. Children ages 8 and 12 are permitted through arrangement with management. **Amenities:** Dining/bar area; plunge pool.

5 The Dry South: Makgadikgadi & Nxai Pans

The Kalahari, one of the longest unbroken stretches of sand in the world, reaches across the center of Botswana, north into Zaire, and south to the Orange River in South Africa. On its northern edge are the enormous complexes of the Makgadikgadi Pans and the relatively small but no less interesting Nxai Pans, characterized by ancient baobabs and large camelthorn trees. Game migrates between the two throughout the year: In the dry season (Apr–Nov), Makgadikgadi is best;

Moments **The Pink Sea**

A spectacular sight greets you on the shores of Makgadikgadi—some 200,000 flamingos, stretched as far as the eye can see, their colors reflected in the mirror-silver waters. The best time to visit here is at the end of the rainy season, when huge flocks of flamingos and pelicans converge on the shallow, nutrient-rich waters that collect in the pans.

during the rains (Nov–Mar), the animals—which include springbok, gemsbok (oryx), red hartebeest, blackbacked jackal, and, occasionally, cheetah and lion—move northward to Nxai.

The Makgadikgadi Pans are a vast (12,000 sq. km/4,630 sq. mile) game-filled expanse of flat, seasonally inundated land. When the pans fill with water after the rains, they host countless migratory birds, most notably huge flocks of flamingos. This is the place to go to experience space at its purest: The horizons seem endless. At night, above the pie-crust surface of the pans, the stars shine with a vibrancy unequalled anywhere else in the world.

ESSENTIALS

VISITOR INFORMATION   For campsite reservations and more information, contact the **Department of Wildlife and National Parks** (P.O. Box 131, Gaborone, Botswana; © **267/397-1405**). The best safari operator here is Uncharted Africa—see "Contacting Safari Operators," earlier in this chapter.

GETTING THERE   By Plane   Your best bet is to fly to Maun and arrange a transfer with a tour company that arranges tours (see "Getting Around," below) in the area or deal directly with Uncharted Africa. Note that rates exclude transfers to camps; this should cost about US$160 one-way.

By Car   It is not a good idea to venture onto the pans without a guide or a four-wheel-drive vehicle. You will find both in the towns of Gweta and Nata. These towns can be reached in 2 days from South Africa in a normal two-wheel-drive vehicle, and can be a useful stopover if you're driving to Maun.

GETTING AROUND   On a Guided Tour   For custom-made tours in the pans, contact Game Trails, Moremi Safaris & Tours, Bushways, Penduka (see "Contacting Safari Operators," earlier in this chapter, for contact details), or one of the other overland operators listed.

WHERE TO STAY & DINE

Deception Valley Lodge 🌟🌟   This small lodge—comprising five thatched units with Victorian-style bathrooms—is situated near the northern border of the massive Central Kalahari Reserve and offers an excellent base from which to explore this vast wilderness. From the deck you can gaze over the vastness of the Kalahari, and on afternoon and night drives guests can expect to see lion, cheetah, leopard, various desert antelope, and the occasional brown hyena. There are also guided walks with traditional Bushmen, providing an opportunity to learn more about their ancient ways.

In South Africa: © **27/12/665-8554**, 27/12/665-8555, or 27/12/665-8556. Fax 27/12/665-8597. www. deceptionvalley.co.za. High season (July–Oct): US$1,130 double. Low season (Nov–June): US$620 double. Rates are all-inclusive. AE, DISC, MC, V. No children under age 12 not. **Amenities:** Lounge/dining area; pool.

Jack's & San Camps ★★★   Voted one of the top-10 honeymoon destinations in the world by the South African editions of *Elle* and *Men's Health,* as well as "Best Safari Camp" by both the *London Sunday Times* and *UK Vogue,* Jack's Camp is the place to go to experience the Kalahari in style. The eight open-air safari tents have recently been upgraded (en-suite bathrooms now have hot and cold running water) but are still Bedoin-meets-Africa, with Persian rugs and teak furniture providing a bizarre counterpoint to the endless desert surrounds (visible from the privacy of your own veranda). If you grow bored of lolling about on antique rugs, you can head out for game drives, walking safaris, or explorations of remote archaeological sites and geological features. During the dry months (Apr–Oct), guests can combine trips to San Camp, a temporary tented camp on the pans and close to the almost surreal rock formation called Kubu Island. This is highly recommended—you set off in four-wheel-drive quad bikes and travel through a stark but beautiful landscape, serenely alone with the elements. After the rains (Dec–Apr), expect to see herds of wildebeest, zebra, and springbok, as well as their predators.

The camp has an outstanding staff, including qualified zoologists and biologists from the U.K., Bushman trackers, and charming and well-trained local guides. All have been thoroughly trained by the very glamorous owner, Ralph Bousfield, whose recent documentaries on the Discovery Channel have made him one of the most famous guides in Botswana. *Note:* The camp has no electricity (lighting is fueled by paraffin), and no pool.

Book through Uncharted Africa Safari Co. (see "Contacting Safari Operators," earlier). US$824 double. Rates are all-inclusive. Children pay full price. AE, MC, V (only Visa is accepted in camp; telegraphic transfer preferred).

Planet Baobab ★ *(Value)*   Imagine a giant anthill with a Planet Hollywood lookalike sign; a bar with a beer-bottle chandelier; a traditional Bakgatla mud hut; and a San grass hut in a grove of ancient baobab trees . . . Owned by Jack's Camp, Planet Baobab provides a fun base for younger budget travelers to explore the fascinating Makgadikgadi Pans. Guided walks with the San to find out more about the plants and trees of this fascinating area are offered, as are trips over the salt pans in four-wheel-drive quad bikes during the dry season. Accommodation is in Bushmen Grass Huts or Bakalanga Mud Huts. *Note:* The camp only offers communal ablution facilities.

Contact ✆ **267/241-2277** or book through Uncharted Africa Safari Co. (see "Contacting Safari Operators," earlier). Double US$28–US$56. Meals, drinks, and activities are extra. Ask about the 3-day, 2-night itinerary. MC, V. **Amenities:** Dining area; expeditions.

Appendix:
South Africa in Depth

South Africa's northeastern border (formed by the Limpopo River) is some 2,000km (1,240 miles) from the Cape's craggy coastline, while the semi-arid West Coast is more than 1,600km (992 miles) from the subtropical East Coast. A vast country with an immensely varied terrain, it supports a rich diversity of animals, birds, and plants, and offers a correspondingly diverse range of experiences. Historically, too, the contrasts are great: Some of the world's oldest hominid remains—dating back some 4 million years—makes this one of the cradles of civilization, yet the country has only recently emerged from the dark shadow of an oppressive policy that made it the pariah of the modern world. Born with the dawning millennium, the "New South Africa," as the post-apartheid South Africa is called, has one of the most progressive constitutions in the world, yet the majority of its people still live in crippling poverty. Fortunately, its unique combination of natural beauty, varied wildlife, sunshine, good value, and comfortable infrastructure has meant that South Africa has emerged as the world's fastest-growing tourism destination, with 6.4 million tourists visiting in 2002 alone. This has translated into a R72.5-billion ($906,250,000) injection into the economy, and the provision of some 1.5-million jobs. So, not least of the many reasons to visit is the very warm welcome you can expect from its citizens.

1 South Africa Today

February 2003. Thabo Mbeki is at the podium, making his fourth State of the Nation address to Parliament. He states, with the confidence of a man at the helm of a country that has risen, phoenix-like, from a bitterly oppressive and divisive past: "The lives of our people are changing for the better. Gradually we are moving away from the entrenched racial, gender, and spatial rigidities of the past. Our people are developing a strong sense of common patriotism. Our economy is demonstrating a resilience and dynamism that is the envy of many across the world. The tide has turned."

It's a far cry from the "two nations" rhetoric (in which he lashed out at the deep economic inequality between black and white in South Africa) that so characterized Mbeki's earlier speeches, and for many who have been visiting South Africa since its first democratic elections in 1994, this newfound confidence is almost palpable.

After a decade of fiscal prudence and self-imposed austerity aimed at breaking the handout culture that cripples much of the continent, the South African economy has, for the first time in 40 years, grown more than the global average, with a budget deficit that stands at 1.6% of GDP (the European average is 3%). South Africa, not long ago the pariah of the world, is now an international hot spot, emerging in 2002 as fastest-growing tourism destination on the globe. And with Mbeki the chief architect of the New Partnership for Africa's Development (NEPAD), a homegrown but Commonwealth- and G8-backed initiative designed to ensure mutual accountability between African nations, South Africa

Moments   Truth + Guilt + Apology . . . = Reconciliation?

Following South Africa's first democratic elections in 1994, the **Truth and Reconciliation Commission (TRC)** was formed to investigate human rights abuses under apartheid rule. The many victims of apartheid were invited to voice their anger and pain before the commission, headed by Archbishop Desmond Tutu, and to confront directly the perpetrators of these abuses in a public forum. In return for full disclosure, aggressors, regardless of their political persuasion, could ask for forgiveness and amnesty from prosecution. Although many white South Africans went into denial, many more for the first time faced the realities of what apartheid meant. Wrenching images of keening relatives listening to killers, some coldly, others in tears, describing exactly how they had tortured and killed those once officially described as "missing persons" or "accidental deaths" were broadcast nationwide. Those whom the commission thought had not made a full disclosure were denied amnesty, as were those who could not prove that they were acting on behalf of a political cause. While some found solace in the process, many more yearned for a more equitable punishment than mere admission of wrongdoing.

Twenty-seven months of painful confessions and $25 million later, the commission concluded its investigation, handing over the report to Nelson Mandela on October 29, 1998. But the 22,000 victims of gross human rights violations had to wait until April 2003 to hear that each would receive a one-time payment of R30,000 ($3,750), a decision that was greeted with dismay by the victims. In contrast, big business (and most whites) were relieved to hear that the government rejected the TRC's proposed tax surcharge on corporations, as well as

is leading the charge for African independence and dignity. Small wonder then that South Africans have found new pride in declaring their place of birth. But there are dissenting voices, and with reason.

Mbeki's most taxing task—that of attracting investment to facilitate economic empowerment for the majority—is somewhat stymied by his failure to implement a strong policy to combat the AIDS pandemic that has infected an estimated 4.7 million people, and to a lesser extent by the totally ineffective "quiet" diplomatic tack taken toward the oppressive regime in neighboring Zimbabwe. But perhaps the most vocal criticism is reserved for the government's failure to provide adequate employment and alleviate the harrowing poverty afflicting so many of its citizens. Until these related specters are tackled, the ANC's economic achievements will remain hollow victories. For while there is no denying that the majority of South African citizens are enjoying an improved standard of living, particularly in regards to housing, electrification, sanitation, and education, this does not mean that the poor are any richer. Quite the contrary.

The economic policies of the ANC have in fact largely benefited the affluent; by allowing white South Africans to keep the assets accumulated during the apartheid years in exchange for surrendering exclusive political power, the government was able to staunch the post-independence white exodus experienced the threatened legal action, driven by New York lawyer Ed Fagan and others in American courts, against companies that had benefited from apartheid, opting instead for "cooperative and voluntary partnerships." Mbeki emphasized that the TRC was not expected to bring about reconciliation but was "an important contributor to the larger process of building a new South Africa."

While it is true that the commission effected a more accurate rendition of recent history, its focus on an individualized rather than a collective approach to human rights abuses under apartheid demanded little by way of white acknowledgement of collective guilt for the suffering their fellow citizens endured. It is against this backdrop that the **Home for All** campaign was begun in 2000. Initiated, ironically enough, primarily by whites involved in the liberation struggle, the campaign was launched to indicate the willingness of white South Africans to accept that they personally benefited from apartheid, with signatories pledging to use their skills and resources to contribute to "empowering disadvantaged people, and promoting a nonracial society whose resources are used to the benefit of all its people."

But apologies come hard in South Africa: According to "Reconciliation Barometer" published by the Institute for Justice and Reconciliation in April 2003, only 22% of whites believe they benefited from apartheid, and only 29% believe that they should apologize. While it is laudable of the government to "build on the future rather than dwell any further on the past," it is feared that as long as this kind of complacency rules the hearts of the privileged minority, South Africa's democracy remains fragile indeed.

in neighboring Zimbabwe (1980) and Mozambique (1975). But critics on the left feel that the government has unfairly prioritized the fears and interests of the privileged at the expense of the majority. As free markets tend to reinforce existing distributions of income and assets, the government's economic strategy (GEAR) has indeed achieved macro-economic stability and fiscal balance, but at a grassroots level it has simply reshaped inequalities: While 43% of the upper-income elite are now black, this represents a mere 10% of the total black population, and intra-black inequality is now greater than that between whites and blacks. Battered by shocking food inflation and the insidious havoc created by the rand's roller-coaster ride (from the world's worst-performing currency in 2001 to its best a year later), many ordinary citizens are no doubt bewildered to hear Mbeki state that their lives are changing for the better, particularly those who—according to official statistics, a whopping 30% to 40% of the population—are unable to find employment.

But South Africans are nothing if not determined. The government has reinvigorated its commitment to majority black empowerment and put in place new policies to stimulate growth in this sector. A recent Growth and Development Summit saw constructive dialogue between big business, labor, and government on job creation. Welfare benefits have been bolstered, which has brought new hope to some of the most disadvantaged sectors of the community. That the present challenges facing the country are daunting is not to be disputed, but compared with the peaceful dismantling of apartheid, the creation and maintenance of the world's most progressive constitution, and the restructuring and resuscitating of a bankrupt economy, they seem ultimately achievable. "The tide has turned," Mbeki said. "Our task is now to take this tide . . . to achieve the goals for which so many of our people have sacrificed." While there is little doubt that April 2004 will again see the ANC voted into power, Mbeki will have to achieve these goals before 2009, when a new post-apartheid generation, with no loyalty to the ANC as liberation movement, has its say at the polls.

2 A Look at the Past

Like all history, South Africa's biography depends very much on who is recounting the tale. Under the apartheid regime, children were taught that in the 19th century, when the first pioneering Voortrekkers made their way north from the Cape Peninsula, and black tribes were making their way south from central Africa, southern Africa was a vast, undiscovered wilderness. Blacks and whites thus conveniently met on land that belonged to no one, and if the natives would not move aside for the trinkets and oxen on offer, everyone simply rolled up their sleeves and had an honest fight—which the whites, who believed they enjoyed the special protection of the Lord, almost always won. Of course, for those who pursued the truth rather than a nationalistic version of it, the past was infinitely more complex—not least because so little of it was recorded.

FROM APES TO ARTISTS Some of the world's oldest hominid remains have been found in South Africa, mostly in the valley dubbed the **Cradle of Humankind** in Gauteng. These suggest that man's earliest relatives were born here more than 3 million years ago.

The country also harbors the oldest fossil evidence of Homo sapiens, this time in the Eastern Cape. The finding proved that man, his brain now much larger, was padding about in South Africa 50,000 to 100,000 years ago. But for many, the most arresting

Dateline

- Circa 8000 B.C. Southern Africa is believed by many paleontologists to be the birthplace of man, with hominid remains dating back some 3.5 million years. Millions of years later the pastoral KhoiKhoi (Hottentots), joined even later by the Bantu-speaking people (blacks), arrive to displace the hunter-gatherer San (Bushmen).
- A.D. 1488 Bartholomieu Dias is the first white settler to round the Cape, landing at Mossel Bay.
- 1497 Vasco da Gama rounds the southern African coast, discovering an alternate sea route to India.
- 1652 Jan van Riebeeck is sent to set up a supply station for the Dutch East India Company. Cape Town is born.
- 1659 The first serious armed conflict against the KhoiKhoi occurs; the first wine is pressed.
- 1667–1700 First Malay slaves arrive, followed by the French Huguenots.
- 1779 The first frontier war between the Xhosa and settlers in the Eastern Cape is fought. Eight more were to follow in what is now known as the "Hundred Years' War."
- 1795 The British occupy the Cape for 7 years, and then hand it back to the Dutch.
- 1806 Britain reoccupies the Cape, this time for 155 years.
- 1815 Shaka becomes the Zulu king.
- 1820 The British settlers arrive in the Eastern Cape. In KwaZulu-Natal, Shaka starts his great expansionary war, decimating numbers of opposing tribes and leaving large areas depopulated in his wake.
- 1824 Port Natal is established by British traders.

evidence of early human activity in southern Africa are the many **rock paintings** that the San hunter-gatherers (or Bushmen, as they were dubbed by Europeans) used to record events dating as far back as 30,000 years. The closest living relative of Stone Age man, a few small family units of San still survive in the Kalahari Desert; but the last San artist must have died over a hundred years ago, as the most recent rock painting dates back to the 19th century.

From these drawings we can deduce that Bantu-speaking Iron Age settlers were living in South Africa long before the arrival of the white colonizers. Dark-skinned and technologically more sophisticated than the San, they started crossing the Limpopo about 2,000 years ago, and over the centuries four main groups of migrants settled in South Africa: the **Nguni**-speaking group, of which the Zulu and Xhosa are part, followed by the **Tsonga, Sotho-Tswana,** and **Venda**-speakers. **Trading centers** were developed, such as those near Phalaborwa, the remains of which can still be seen in Kruger National Park.

By the 13th century most of South Africa's eastern flank was occupied by these African people, while the San remained concentrated in the west. In Botswana, a small number of the latter were introduced to the concept of sheep- and cattle-keeping. These agrarian groups migrated south and called themselves the **KhoiKhoi (men of men),** to differentiate themselves from their San relatives. It was with these indigenous people that the first seafarers came into contact. The KhoiKhoi saw themselves as a superior bunch, and it must have been infuriating to be called Hottentots by the Dutch (a term sometimes used to denigrate the Cape Coloured group, and still considered degrading today).

THE COLONIZATION OF THE CAPE When spice was as precious

1828 Shaka is murdered by his half-brother, Dingaan, who succeeds him as king.

1834 Slavery is abolished in the Cape, sparking off the Great Trek.

1835–45 More than 16,000 bitter Dutch settlers head for the uncharted hinterland in ox-wagons to escape British domination.

1838 A party of Voortrekkers manages to vanquish Zulu forces at the Battle of Blood River.

1843 Natal becomes a British colony.

1852 Several parties of Boers move farther northeast and found the Zuid Afrikaansche Republiek (ZAR).

1854 The Boer Independent Republic of the Orange Free State is founded by another party of Boers.

1858 British defeat the Xhosa after the "Great Cattle Killing" in which the Xhosa destroy their crops and herds in the mistaken belief that with this sacrifice their ancestors will destroy the enemy.

1860 The first indentured Indian workers arrive in Natal.

1867 Diamonds are found near Kimberley in the Orange Free State.

1877 The British annex the ZAR.

1879 Anglo-Zulu War breaks out, orchestrated by the British.

1880–81 First Anglo-Boer War is fought. Boers defeat British.

1883 Paul Kruger becomes the first president of the ZAR.

1886 Gold is discovered on the Witwatersrand.

1899–1902 The Second Anglo-Boer War. British defeat Boers.

1910 The Union of South Africa proclaimed. Louis Botha becomes first premier. Blacks are excluded from the process.

1912 The South African Native National Congress is formed. After 1923 this would be known as the African National Congress (ANC).

1913 The Native Land Act is passed, limiting land ownership for blacks.

1914–18 South Africa declares war on Germany.

1923 Natives (Urban Areas) Act imposes segregation in towns.

continues

as gold, the bravest men in Europe were the Portuguese crew who set off with **Bartholomieu Dias** in 1487 to drop off the edge of the world and find an alternative trade route to the Indies. Dias rounded the Cape, which he named **Tormentoso ("Stormy Cape"),** after his fleet of three tiny ships battled storms for 3 days before he tacked back to what is today known as Mossel Bay. Suffering from acute scurvy, his men forced him to turn back soon after this.

It was 10 years before another group was foolhardy enough to follow in their footsteps. **Vasco da Gama** sailed past what had been renamed the Cape of Good Hope, rounding the East Coast, which he named Natal, and sailed all the way to India.

The Portuguese opened the sea route to the East, but it was the Dutch who took advantage of the strategic port at the tip of Africa. In 1652 (30 years after the first English settled in the United States), **Jan van Riebeeck,** who had been caught cooking the Dutch East India Company books in Malaysia, was sent to open a refreshment station as penance. The idea was not to colonize the Cape, but simply to create a halfway house for trading ships. Van Riebeeck was given strict instructions to trade with the natives and in no way enslave them. Inevitably, relations soured—the climate and beauty of the Cape led members of the crew and soldiers to settle permanently on the land, with little recompense for the KhoiKhoi. To prevent the KhoiKhoi from seeking revenge, Van Riebeeck attempted to create a boundary along the Liesbeeck River by planting a bitter-almond hedge—the remains of this hedge still grow today in the Kirstenbosch Gardens. This, together with the advantage of firepower and the introduction of hard liquor, reduced the KhoiKhoi to no more than a nuisance. Those who didn't toe the line were imprisoned on

1939–45 South Africa joins the Allies in fighting World War II.

1948 D. F. Malan's National Party wins the election, and the era of apartheid is born. Races are classified, the passbook system is created, and interracial sex is made illegal.

1955 ANC adopts Freedom Charter.

1956 Coloureds lose the right to vote.

1958 H. F. Verwoerd, the architect of apartheid, succeeds D. F. Malan and creates the homelands—territories set aside for black tribes.

1959 Robert Sobukwe forms the Pan African National Congress (PAC).

1960 Police open fire on demonstrators at Sharpeville, killing 69 people. ANC and PAC banned. ANC ends its policy of peaceful negotiation.

1961 South Africa leaves the Commonwealth and becomes a republic. Albert Luthuli awarded Nobel Peace Prize.

1963 Nelson Mandela and others sentenced to life imprisonment in the Rivonia sabotage trials.

1970s Worldwide economic and cultural boycotts are initiated in response to South Africa's human rights abuses.

1976 Police open fire on unarmed black students demonstrating against use of Afrikaans as a teaching medium; the Soweto riots follow.

1977 Black-consciousness leader Steve Biko dies in police custody.

1980–84 President P. W. Botha attempts cosmetic reforms. Unrest escalates. Bishop Tutu, who urges worldwide sanctions, is awarded the Nobel Peace Prize.

1985 State of Emergency declared, gagging the press and giving security forces absolute power.

1989 F. W. de Klerk succeeds P. W. Botha.

1990 de Klerk ends the State of Emergency, lifts the ban on the ANC, and frees Mandela.

1993 de Klerk and Mandela are awarded the Nobel Peace Prize.

1994 The first democratic elections are held, and on May 10 Mandela is sworn in as the first black president of South Africa. De Klerk and Thabo Mbeki become joint Deputy Presidents.

Robben Island, and by the beginning of the 18th century the remaining KhoiKhoi were reduced to virtual slavery by disease and drink. Over the years their genes slowly mingled with those of slaves and burghers to create a new underclass, later known as the Cape Coloureds.

In 1666, the foundation stones for the **Castle of Good Hope** were laid, and still more elements were added to the melting pot of Cape culture. Van Riebeeck persuaded the company to allow the import of **slaves** from the Dutch East Indies; this was followed by the arrival of the **French Huguenots** in 1668. Fleeing religious persecution, these Protestants increased the size of the colony by 15%, and brought with them the ability to cultivate **wine.** The glorious results of their input can still be enjoyed in the valley of **Franschhoek (French corner).**

The British enter the picture in 1795, taking control of the Cape when the Dutch East India Company was liquidated. In 1803 they handed it back to the Dutch for 3 years, after which they were to rule the Cape for 155 years.

- **1995** Truth and Reconciliation Commission created under Archbishop Desmond Tutu.
- **1997** South Africa's new constitution, one of the world's most progressive, comes into effect on February 3.
- **1998** Truth and Reconciliation Commission ends. U.S. gives Mandela the Congressional Gold Medal.
- **1999** The second democratic elections are held. The ANC gets 66.03% of the vote; Thabo Mbeki becomes president.
- **2000** UNESCO awards five sites in South Africa with World Heritage status. The Kgalagadi, Africa's first Transfrontier Park, connects vast wildlife tracts between Botswana and S.A., is created. UNAIDS reveals that South Africa has the largest AIDS population in the world. National Conference on Racism is held.
- **2002** Reversal of AIDS policy; government acknowledges the usefulness of anti-retroviral drugs but fails to roll out national treatment program.
- **2003** For the first time in 40 years, S.A. economy grows more than the global average. South Africa emerges as the fastest-growing tourism destination in the world.

One of their first tasks was to silence the "savages" on the Eastern Frontier—these were the **Xhosa,** part of the Nguni-speaking people who migrated south from central Africa. Essential to the plan was the creation of a buffer zone of English settlers. Between 1820 and 1824, thousands of artisans and soldiers were off-loaded in the Eastern Cape, issued with basic implements, tents, and seeds, and sent off to deal with the Xhosa. Four frontier wars followed, but it was the extraordinary **cattle-killing incident** that crippled the Xhosa: In 1856 a young girl, Nongqawuse, prophesied that if the Xhosa killed all their cattle and destroyed their crops, the dead ancestors would rise and help vanquish the settlers. Needless to say, this did not occur, and while four more wars were to follow, the Xhosa's might was effectively broken by this mass sacrifice.

THE RISE OF THE ZULU & AFRIKANER CONFLICTS   At the turn of the century, the **Zulus,** the Nguni group that settled on the east coast in what is now called KwaZulu-Natal, were growing increasingly combative as their survival depended on absorbing neighbors to gain control of pasturage. A young warrior named **Shaka,** who took total despotic control of the Zulus in 1818, raised this to an art form—in addition to arming his new regiments with the short stabbing spear, Shaka was a great military tactician, and devised a strategy known as the **horns of the bull,** whereby the enemy was outflanked by highly disciplined formations that eventually engulfed them. This was used to great effect on tribes in the region, and by the middle of the decade the Zulus had formed a centralized military state with a 40,000-strong army. In a movement known as the **Mfecane,** or forced migrations, huge areas of the country were cleared. People were either killed or absorbed by the Zulus; many fled, creating new kingdoms such as **Swaziland** and **Lesotho.** In 1828 Shaka was murdered by his two brothers, one of whom, Dingaan, succeeded him as king.

On the Cape, British interference in labor relations and oppression of the "kitchen Dutch" language infuriated many of the Dutch settlers, by now referred to as *Afrikaners* (of Africa), and later, *Boers* (farmers). The abolishing of slavery in 1834 was the last straw. Afrikaners objected to "not so much their freedom" as one wrote, "as their being placed on an equal footing with Christians, contrary to the laws of God and the natural distinction of race."

Some 15,000 people (10% of the Afrikaners at the Cape) set off on what is known as the Great Trek, and became known as the *Voortrekkers,* or "first movers." They found large tracts of unoccupied land that, unbeknownst to them, had been cleared by the recent Mfecane, and it wasn't long before they clashed with the mighty Zulu nation, whom they defeated in 1838 at the **Battle of Blood River.** A century later, this "miraculous" victory was to be the greatest inspiration for Afrikaner nationalism, and a monument was built to glorify the battle. Today the **Voortrekker Monument** is still a place of pilgrimage for Afrikaner nationalists and can be seen from most places in Pretoria.

The Boers' victory was, however, short-lived. The British, not satisfied with the Cape's coast, annexed Natal in 1845. Once again, the Voortrekkers headed over the mountains with their ox-wagons, looking for freedom from the British. They founded two republics: the **Orange Free State** (now the Free State) and the **South African Republic** or **Transvaal** (now Gauteng, the North-West, Mpumalanga, and the Northern Province). This time the British left them alone; focusing their attention on places of more interest than a remote outpost with only 250,000 settlers. Needless to say, the 1867 discovery of **diamonds** in the Orange Free State and, 19 years later, **gold** in the Transvaal, was to change this attitude dramatically.

GETTING RICH & STAYING POOR   In both the diamond and the gold fields, a step-by-step amalgamation of individual claims was finally necessitated by the expense of the mining process. In Kimberley, **Cecil John Rhodes**—an ambitious young man who was to become obsessed with the cause of British imperial expansion—masterminded the creation of **De Beers Consolidated,** the mining house that to this day controls the diamond-mining industry in southern Africa. (It is worth noting that the discovery of diamonds was also the start of the labor-discrimination practices that were to set the precedent for the gold mines and the coming apartheid years.) The mining of gold did not result in the same monopoly, and the **Chamber of Mines,** established in 1887, went some way to regulate the competition. **Paul Kruger,** president of the South African Republic, became a spoke in the wheel, however. A Calvinist preacher and survivor of the Great Trek, he did not intend to make things easy for the mostly British entrepreneurs who controlled the gold mines. He created no real infrastructure to aid them, and *uitlanders* (foreigners) were not allowed to vote. Britain in turn wanted to amalgamate the South African colonies to consolidate their power in southern Africa. (British forces had attempted to annex the Transvaal in 1877, just after the discovery of diamonds, but they had underestimated Paul Kruger; and in 1881, after losing the first Anglo-Boer war, they restored the Boer republics' independence.) In 1899, when the British demanded full rights for the *uitlanders,* Kruger responded by invading the coastal colonies.

At first the second **Anglo-Boer War** went well for the Boers, who used hitherto unheard of guerilla warfare tactics, but the British commander **Lord Kitchener** soon found their Achilles' heel. Close to 28,000 Boer women and children died in Kitchener's concentration camps, and his scorched-earth policy, whereby their farms were systematically razed to the ground, broke the Boer spirit. Ultimately, Britain would pit nearly half a million men against 88,000 Boers. In 1902 the Boer republics became part of the Empire—the Afrikaner nationalism that was to sweep the country in the next century was fueled by the resentments of a nation struggling to escape the yoke of British imperialism.

OPPRESSION & RESISTANCE   The years following this defeat were hard on those at the bottom of the ladder. Afrikaners, many of whom had lost their farms, streamed to the cities where they competed with blacks for unskilled jobs on equal terms and were known as "poor whites." Black South Africans had also suffered during the Anglo-Boer War (including the loss of some 14,000 in the concentration camps), but in later years, when Afrikaner fortunes turned, this was neither recognized nor compensated. With the creation of the **Union of South Africa** in 1910, the country joined the British Commonwealth of Nations, and participated in both World Wars. Back home, loyalties were divided, and the Afrikaners were bitter about forging allegiances with a country they had so recently been at war with. In 1934 a new "purified" **National Party (NP)** was established, offering a voice for the "poor white" Afrikaners. Under the leadership of Dr. D. F. Malan, who swore he would liberate the Afrikaners from their economic "oppression," the NP won the 1948 election by a narrow margin—46 years of white minority rule were to follow, before internal and international pressure would finally buckle the NP's resolve.

One of the first laws that created the segregationist policy named **apartheid** (literally, "separateness") was the **Population Registration Act,** in which everyone was slotted into an appropriate race group. This caused the greatest problem for those of mixed descent (see the box "The Coloured Class: A New Race," later in this chapter). One of the most infamous classification tests was the pencil test, whereby a pencil was stuck into the hair of a person of uncertain racial heritage. If the pencil dropped, the person was "white"; if it stuck she/he was classified "coloured." In this way, entire communities, in some cases even families, were torn apart. This new group, dubbed the Coloureds, enjoyed slightly more privileges than their black counterparts—a better standard of housing, schooling, and job opportunities—no doubt an overture to their white ancestors. Interracial sexual relations, previously illicit, were now illegal, and the Group Areas Act ensured that families would never mingle on the streets. The Act also required the destruction and relocation of total suburbs, none of which were white. The **Bantu Education Act** ensured that black South Africans would never challenge the better-educated white South Africans for jobs. During this time, the majority of English speakers condemned the policies of what came to be known as the Afrikaner NP; but because they continued to dominate business in South Africa, the maintenance of a cheap labor pool was in their interests, and life was generally too comfortable for most to do anything. Change came inevitably from the nonwhite quarters.

By the middle of the 20th century, blacks outnumbered whites in the urban areas, but resided "unseen" in **townships** outside of the cities. Their movements were restricted by **pass laws;** they were barred from trade union activities, deprived of any political rights, and prohibited from procuring land outside of their reserves or homelands. **Homelands** were small tracts of land, comprising about 13% of the country, where the so-called ethnically distinct black South African "tribes" (at that time 42% of the population) were forced to live. This effectively divided the black majority into tribal minorities.

The **African Nationalist Congress Party (ANC)** was formed by representatives of the major African organizations in 1912, but it was only in 1934 that it was to find the inspired leadership of **Anton Lembede, Oliver Tambo, Walter Sisulu,** and **Nelson Mandela,** who formed the **ANC Youth League** in this year. The ANC's hitherto passive resistance tactics were met with forceful suppression in 1960 when police fired on unarmed demonstrators in **Sharpeville,** killing 67 and wounding 200. It was a major turning point for South Africa, sparking violent opposition within and ostracism in world affairs.

In 1963 police captured the underground leaders of the ANC—including the "Black Pimpernel," Nelson Mandela, who was by now commander-in-chief of their armed wing, **Umkhonto We Sizwe ("Spear of the Nation").** In what came to be known as the **Rivonia Trial,** Mandela and nine other leaders received life sentences for treason and were incarcerated on **Robben Island.** The imprisonment of key figures effectively silenced the opposition within the country for some time and allowed the NP to further entrench its segregationist policies. But it wasn't all clear sailing: Hendrik Verwoerd, the cabinet minister for Bantu Affairs under Malan and the man who was named "the architect of apartheid," was stabbed to death one morning in the House of Assembly—and strangely, not for political reasons; the murderer insisted that a tapeworm had ordered him to do it. In 1966 B. J. Vorster became the new NP leader. He was to push for the independence of Verwoerd's black homelands, which would effectively deprive all black people of their South African citizenship, as well as enforce the use of Afrikaans as a language medium in all schools. Ironically, the latter triggered the backlash that would finally end Afrikaner dominance.

SOUTH AFRICA GOES INTO LABOR On June 16, 1976, thousands of black schoolchildren in **Soweto** took to the streets to demonstrate against this new law, which for the many non-Afrikaans speakers would render schooling incomprehensible. The police opened fire, killing among others 13-year-old **Hector Pieterson,** and chaos ensued, with unrest spreading throughout the country. The youth, disillusioned by their parents' implicit compliance with apartheid laws, burned schools, libraries, and *shebeens,* the informal liquor outlets that provided an opiate to the dispossessed. Many arrests followed, including that of black-consciousness leader **Steve Biko** in the Eastern Cape, who became the 46th political prisoner to die during police interrogation. Young activists fled the country and joined ANC military training camps. The ANC, led by Oliver Tambo, called for international sanctions—the world responded with economic, cultural, and sports boycotts, and awarded the Nobel Peace Prize to **Archbishop Desmond Tutu,** one of the strongest campaigners for sanctions. The new NP premier, **P. W. Botha,** or, as he came to be known, *"die Groot*

(**Moments** "I am an African . . . "

I am an African . . . I owe my being to the hills and valleys, the mountains and glades . . . to the Khoi and the San. . . . I am formed of the migrants who left Europe . . . of Malay slaves from the east . . . of warrior patriots . . . I am the grandchild who lays fresh flowers on Boer graves . . .
—Thabo Mbeki, President of South Africa

Krokodil" ("the great crocodile"), simply wagged his finger and declared South Africa capable of going it alone despite increasing pressure—in the words of Allen Boesak, addressing the launch of the United Democratic Front, the students of Soweto wanted *all* their rights, they wanted them *here,* and they wanted them *now.* The crocodile's bite proved as bad as his bark, and his response was simply to pour an ever-increasing number of troops into townships. In 1986 he declared a **State of Emergency,** thereby giving his security forces unlimited power to persecute the opposition, and effectively silencing the internal press.

The overwhelming majority of white South Africans enjoyed an excellent standard of living, a state of supreme comfort that made it difficult to challenge the status quo. Many believed the state propaganda that blacks were innately inferior, or remained blissfully ignorant of the extent of the human rights violations; still others found their compassion silenced by fear. Ignorant or numbed, most white South Africans waited for what seemed to be the inevitable civil war, until 1989, when a ministerial rebellion forced the intransigent Botha to resign, and new leader **F. W. de Klerk** stepped in. By now the economy was in serious trouble—the cost of maintaining apartheid had bled the coffers dry, the Chase Manhattan Bank had refused to roll over its loan, and sanctions and trade-union action had brought the country's economy to a virtual standstill. Mindful of these overwhelming odds, de Klerk unbanned the ANC, PAC, the Communist Party, and 33 other organizations in February 1990. Nelson Mandela—imprisoned for 27 years—was released soon thereafter.

BIRTH OF THE "NEW SOUTH AFRICA" The fragile negotiations among the various political parties were to last a nerve-racking 4 years. During this time, right-wingers threatened civil war, while many in the townships lived it. **Zulu nationalists,** of the **Inkatha** party, waged a low-level war against ANC supporters that was to claim the lives of thousands. Eyewitness accounts were given of security force involvement in this black-on-black violence, with training and supplies provided to Inkatha forces by the South African Defence Force. In 1993 **Chris Hani,** the popular ANC youth leader, was assassinated. South Africa held its breath as Mandela pleaded on nationwide television for peace— by this time, there was no doubt as to who was leading the country.

On April 27, 1994, **Nelson Mandela** cast his first vote at the age of 76, and on May 10 he was inaugurated as South Africa's first democratically elected president. Despite 18 opposition parties, the ANC took 63% of the vote and was dominant in all but two provinces—the Western Cape voted NP, and KwaZulu-Natal went to Buthelezi's Zulu-based Inkatha (IFP) Party. Jubilation reigned, but the hangover was bad. The economy was in dire straits, with double-digit inflation, gross foreign exchange down to less than three weeks of imports, and a budget deficit of 6.8% of GDP. Of an estimated 38 million people, at least 6 million were unemployed, and 9 million destitute. Ten million had no access to running water, and 20 million no electricity. The ANC had to launch a program of "nation-building"—attempting to unify what the NP had spent a fortune dividing. Wealth had to be redistributed without hampering the ailing economy, and a government debt of almost R350 billion ($43 billion) repaid.

Still, after 300 years of white domination, South Africa entered the new millennium with what is widely regarded as the world's most progressive constitution, and its murky history was finally held up for close inspection by the Truth and Reconciliation Commission, the first of its kind in the world (see "Truth + Guilt + Apology . . . = Reconciliation?" earlier in this chapter). South African sports heroes, barred from competing internationally for 2 decades, added to the nation's growing pride, winning the Rugby World Cup in 1995 and its first gold Olympic medals in 1996. Augmenting these ideological and sporting achievements were those that have happened on a grassroots level: 1999, when the ANC won the second democratic elections with a landslide victory of 66.03% of the vote, saw a change in ANC leadership style, with new president **Thabo Mbeki** centralizing power and focusing on delivery rather than reconciliation. "Africa," Mbeki promised, "will prosper." By the end of 2000 more than 1 million houses had been completed, 412 new telephone lines installed, 127 clinics built, and 917,220 hectares (2,265,533 acres) of land handed over to new black owners. Some 37,396 households had benefited from land redistribution, and water supply had increased from 62,249 recipients in 1995 to a whopping 6,495,205. Black-owned business grew significantly, and an estimated 4 million blacks comprised half of the top earners in the country. But with unemployment estimated at between 30% and 40%, the concomitant rise in crime was hardly surprising. The specter of AIDS was also stalking South Africa, and by 2000 it would find itself with the highest HIV-positive population in the world. Equally distressing was the continued divide between black and white incomes, reinforcing South Africa's strange mix of first- and third-world elements, and prompting Mbeki's controversial "two nations" speech in which he stated that "the failure to achieve real nation-building was entrenching the existence of two separate nations, one white and affluent and the other black and poor."

But despite these problems, the fiscal discipline that the ANC has pursued has resulted in a robust economic outlook in 2003, with crime either stabilized or reduced, and the delivery of basic services and education extended to the majority of citizens. But the reduction of unemployment levels and concurrent poverty alleviation remain challenges that have not been adequately met. That the New South African nation was born in peace was a miracle, but many feel the ANC will need another to meet its campaign promise of "a better life for all."

3 The Rainbow Nation

South African stereotypes are no simple black-and-white matter. Historically, the nation was made up of a number of widely different cultural groups that under normal circumstances might have amalgamated into a singular hybrid called "the South African." But the deeply divisive policy of apartheid only further entrenched initial differences.

At a popular level, Mandela appeared as the architect of the post-1994 "nation-building," utilizing this rainbow myth to capture the hearts and minds of black and white South Africans alike. Despite the ANC government's stated objective to end racial discrimination and develop a unique South African identity, this "rainbow nation" remains difficult to define, let alone unify. Broadly speaking, approximately 76% of some 38 million people are black, 12.8% are white, 2.6% are Asian, and 8.5% are "coloured" (the apartheid term for those of mixed descent as well as for some 200,000 Cape Malays; see "The Coloured Class: A New Race," below). Beyond these are smaller but no less significant groups, descendents of Lebanese, Italian, Portuguese, Hungarian, and Greek settlers, as well as the 130,000-strong Jewish community. The latter, in particular, has played an enormous role in the economic and political growth of South Africa, as is evidenced at the Jewish Museum in Cape Town.

In an attempt to recognize this cultural diversity, the government has given official recognition to 11 languages: Zulu, Xhosa, Afrikaans, English, Sotho, Venda, Tswana, Tsona, Pedi, Shangaan, and Ndebele. Television news and sports

The Coloured Class: A New Race

Afrikaans-speaking people of mixed descent—grouped together as a new race called "the coloureds" during the Population Registration Act—were perhaps the most affected by the policies of apartheid. They were brought up to respect their white blood and deny their black roots entirely, and the apartheid state's overture to the coloureds' white forefathers was to treat them as second in line to whites, providing them with a better education, greater rights, and more government support than black people. The destruction of their sense of self-worth was made evident when the "New Nationalist Party" (NNP) won the 1994 election race in the Western Cape (where the majority of this group resides). In 1999 the Democratic Party, which had absorbed the NNP, again won the elections in the Western Cape. Voting back into power the selfsame racist party that had created their oppressive new identity was seemingly a direct result of the false sense of hierarchy that apartheid created. Fear of *"die Swart Gevaar"* (an NP propaganda slogan meaning "the Black Danger") is slow to dissipate, and despite calls within the coloured ranks to do away with the label entirely, many still believe that whites are innately superior to blacks, and that the coloureds are in a class of their own.

are broadcast in the four main language groups, English, Nguni (Zulu and Xhosa), Afrikaans, and Sotho. But while languages provide some clue as to the demographics of the population, particularly where a specific language user is likely to live (another apartheid legacy), they give no real idea of the complexity of attitudes within groups—for instance, urban-born Xhosa males still paint their faces white to signal their transition to manhood, but unlike their rural counterparts they may choose to be circumcised by a Western doctor. A group of Sotho women may invest their *stokvel* (an informal savings scheme) in unit trusts, while their mothers will not open a bank account. And an "ethnic" white Afrikaner living in rural Northern Cape will have very little in common with an Afrikaans-speaking coloured living in cosmopolitan Cape Town.

Despite continued poverty, it is the previously disadvantaged who show the most optimism for the future. Proof that life has improved for the majority of the population is not always easy to find, but in the "City of Gold" the black middle class is growing, and it is the "buppies" (black-up-and-coming) who frequent the previously whites-only shopping malls. Even among the new elite, however, there are those who feel that the New South Africa is taking too long to deliver on its promises. "There is no black in the rainbow," an embittered Winnie Madikizela-Mandela said, "Maybe there is no rainbow nation at all." Hardly surprising, really. Years of fragmentation have rendered the nation cautious, suspicious, and critical—a recent survey shows that only 12% of whites have contact with other racial groups outside the workplace, and more than 80% of blacks have never shared a meal with a white person. South Africans are still molded by the social engineering experiment that separated them geographically and psychologically. For a new, shared South African identity to emerge, it will take time, enough at least for the colors to mingle.

Index

Great Trips Like Great Days Begin with a Plan

FranklinCovey and Frommer's Bring You *Frommer's Favorite Places*® Planner

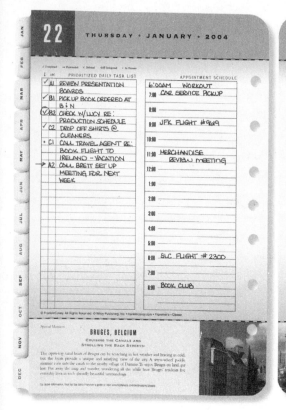

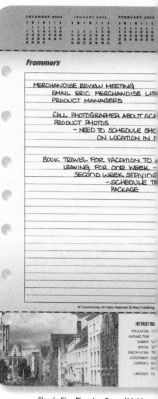

Classic Size Planning Pages $39.95

The planning experts at FranklinCovey have teamed up with the travel experts at Frommer's. The result is a full-year travel-themed planner filled with rich images and travel tips covering fifty-two of Frommer's Favorite Places.

- Each week will make you an expert about an intriguing corner of the world
- New facts and tips every day
- Beautiful, full-color photos of some of the most beautiful places on earth
- Proven planning tools from FranklinCovey for keeping track of tasks, appointments, notes, address/phone numbers, and more

Save 15%

when you purchase Frommer's Favorite Places travel-themed planner and a binder.

Order today before your next big trip.

www.franklincovey.com/frommers
Enter promo code 12252 at checkout for discount. Offer expires June 1, 2005.

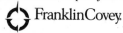

Frommer's is a trademark of Arthur Frommer.